Editorial Services Director
Elizabeth Keaffaber

Managing Editor
Sandy Doell

Director of Marketing
Lynn E. Zingraf

Title Manager
Bryan Gambrel

Acquisitions Editor
Fred Slone

Product Director
Kevin A. Kloss

Production Editor
Jeff Riley

Editors
Kelli M. Brooks
Tom Cirtin
Jeanne Terheide Lemen

Assistant Product Marketing Manager
Kim Margolius

Technical Editor
Ron Schwarz

Technical Specialist
Cari Skaggs

Acquisitions Coordinator
Angela C. Kozlowski

Operations Coordinator
Patty Brooks

Editorial Assistant
Michelle R. Newcomb

Book Designer
Kim Scott

Cover Designer
Dan Armstrong

Production Team
Steve Adams
Angela D. Bannan
Becky Beheler
Brian Buschkill
Jason Carr
Joan Evan
Bryan Flores
Jason Hand
John Hulse
Darren Jackson
Bob LaRoche
Clint Lahnen
Laura Robbins
Bobbi Satterfield
Craig Small
Michael Thomas
Todd Wente

Indexer
Mary Jane Frisby

Dedication

I dedicate my efforts contained within these pages to Patches, a wonderful loving friend and companion who left this world too soon. You will be missed, my friend, and your warmth and gentle nature can never be replaced. You enhanced my life by sharing yours with me. Thank you for all you were. You will be in my heart and memories.

—Russ Jacobs

About the Authors

Russell L. Jacobs is a programmer/analyst for The Prudential and is president of SoftWare Alchemy. He has been programming for 10 years using Pascal, BASIC, C, and C++ in the DOS, Windows, OS/2, and NT environments. Russ has contributed his expertise as technical editor for several Que books, including *Visual Basic 3 By Example, OS/2 2.1 Red Book for Developers*, and *Killer Borland C++*.

Lowell Mauer has been a programmer and instructor for 16 years, including the past six in product support. He has taught programming at Montclair State College and has developed and marketed a Visual Basic application for airplane pilots. As the manager of technical support, he has attended seminars and training sessions in several countries and is an expert in more than six computer languages. He currently is a Senior Software Specialist at Cognos Corporation in Secaucus, N.J., where he installs PC-based software and trains customers how to use it.

Steve Potts received a degree in computer science from Georgia Tech. He has been designing and writing software systems for 12 years. He is a consultant in Windows-based technologies and owns NoBoredom Classes, a computer education firm in Atlanta, Ga.

We'd Like to Hear from You!

As part of our continuing effort to produce books of the highest possible quality, Que would like to hear your comments. To stay competitive, we *really* want you, as a computer book reader and user, to let us know what you like or dislike most about this book or other Que products.

You can mail comments, ideas, or suggestions for improving future editions to the address below, or send us a fax at (317) 581-4663. For the online inclined, Macmillan Computer Publishing has a forum on CompuServe (type **GO QUEBOOKS** at any prompt) through which our staff and authors are available for questions and comments. The address of our Internet site is **http://www.mcp.com** (World Wide Web).

In addition to exploring our forum, please feel free to contact me personally to discuss your opinions of this book: I'm **74201,1064** on CompuServe, and I'm **kkloss@que.mcp.com** on the Internet.

Thanks in advance—your comments will help us to continue publishing the best books available on computer topics in today's market.

Kevin A. Kloss
Product Development Specialist
Que Corporation
201 W. 103rd Street
Indianapolis, Indiana 46290
USA

Contents

Introduction

Visual Basic 4 By Example is a Que book based on the learn-by-doing principle, where learning is best done by actually doing rather than just reading. This principle is sound on the face of it—you wouldn't just read a book about repairing your car's transmission and then expect to install a new transmission. However, through a combined program of reading and "hands-on" application, you probably could change the transmission.

Visual Basic 4 By Example is a "hands-on" book. By the time you finish this book, you'll have read about and worked directly with Visual Basic on many occasions, enough so that you will be comfortable with the program and excited about what you can accomplish with it.

About Visual Basic

Microsoft Visual Basic is an applications development system, and not simply a software package or a language. It is a development tool whose purpose is to empower you to create Microsoft Windows programs. Visual Basic resembles a programming language in that you sometimes write lines of code that include `While` loops, `If` statements, and other traditional programming constructs. It resembles a software package in that you use menu items and tool bars and a graphical user interface to develop your applications. Visual Basic is a pragmatic tool that allows you to create a program with the look and feel that you want, with the least possible effort. Its creators at Microsoft made their design decisions based on keeping development as simple as possible without killing the power of the tool. The result is a great product that can be learned by anyone who likes computers well enough to read this book.

The Microsoft Windows family of operating systems includes Windows 3.1, Windows 95, and Windows NT. These environments offer an amazing ensemble of software equipment for the programmer. With tools like Object Linking and Embedding (OLE) 2.0, multimedia support, sound support, and the Multiple-Document Interface (MDI), you can write programs that will amaze your friends. There is only one problem. Writing Windows programs in C or C++ is not easy. There are a lot of subtle and confusing details that must be handled exactly when writing programs using the Windows Application Programming Interface (Windows API) under C or C++ directly. Even programmers who have years of experience find themselves struggling with the complexity of the Windows API.

So we are faced with a toolset that is irresistible in its richness, but overwhelming in its complexity. That is where Visual Basic comes in. It lets us tap into the majority of the capabilities of Windows, while allowing us to operate in a logical, easy-to-use, and fun environment.

Many computer professionals believe that real applications can only be written in C or C++. While C/C++ compilers allow us to create programs that are truly amazing, there are thousands of very useful Windows applications that do not need that kind of power. Visual Basic was designed to create this kind of application. Visual Basic allows us to use visual tools to see what we are creating while we are creating it. Industrial-strength languages like C++ are less capable in this area. The visual nature of Visual Basic allows us to develop programs incrementally. This incremental development strategy allows the programmer to get one piece of a program working and then show it to the customer. The customer's feedback can then be incorporated immediately, leading to greater satisfaction with the finished product.

Why Learn About Programming?

Maybe you still don't know whether this book is for you. Maybe you're just looking for an answer to the question, "Why learn to program at all?" Following are several reasons to learn more about programming:

- As a possible source of income and employment.
- For fun. Programming is a combination of an artistic, creative process and a never-ending series of puzzles.
- To get something done that you otherwise couldn't do. For example, despite the many commercial computer programs available, you may not be able to buy exactly what you need, or the products you can buy are too expensive or too complicated for the task at hand.
- To satisfy your curiosity. If you're curious about programming and what it entails, this book will help you decide whether or not it is something you want to pursue.

Who Should Use This Book?

This book is written to teach the new programmer the Microsoft Visual Basic application development system. Programmers who are fluent in another programming language (like C or COBOL) will find the book useful in making the transition to visual tools and event-driven programming. If you have extensive programming experience, you will probably want to skim certain parts of the book that bear similarity to your native programming language.

The goal of this book is to maintain a pace and level of detail that makes it possible for the novice to learn to program without the frustration that usually accompanies self-teaching. It is designed in such a way that every chapter is useful to the reader, even if you didn't read the earlier chapters. In this way, you can read the chapters in the order that you find them interesting.

Visual Basic By Example follows a simple format: Each chapter contains several features. With each feature, you first get an explanation of how and possibly why it works, then you get to work directly with the feature. At the end of each chapter is a summary, then review questions and exercises covering each feature.

This approach is designed to serve a broad range of readers from novice to advanced. If you've never programmed before, the learn-by-doing approach will help you move quickly and easily through this book. If you have programming experience, you'll find plenty of material in this book to refine and enhance what you already know, and to give you a solid understanding of how Visual Basic works.

Although definitions are provided for many of the terms used in this book, you should keep close at hand a standard English dictionary and a dictionary of computer terminology such as Que's *Computer Programmer's Dictionary* or Que's *Computer User's Dictionary*. (It's surprising how often computer programmers get into arguments over issues simply because they're both using the same word to mean two different things.)

How Much Should You Know About Windows?

To understand this book, you should be able to identify common objects in the Windows 95 operating environment, including windows, Toolbars, scroll bars, menu bars, title bars, task bars, icons, buttons, and system menus. These objects are explained from a programmer's perspective, but if you've never used them before, understanding how they work will be challenging. Also, you should have a feel for how Windows 95 property sheets work and how to act within them. (If you've used Windows 95 much at all, you probably know this stuff.)

If you're not familiar with Windows 95 and how it works, you should read Que's *Using Windows 95*. Also, if you need to brush up on your basic computer hardware knowledge, read Que's *Computers Illustrated*. *Visual Basic 4 By Example* assumes that you know what the mouse and other common hardware devices are and how to use them; however, if you're not sure which end of a disk to stick in the floppy drive, you should read these two books first.

How To Use This Book

There are several ways to use this book. One obvious method is to begin at the first page and proceed in order until the last. An alternative is to read enough of the book to get you comfortable programming in, and using, Visual Basic. You can then turn to each chapter randomly to learn about features in the order that you want or need to learn them. Either approach will work since this book was written to accommodate both styles. It is critical, however, that any approach employed includes Visual Basic program writing.

Code Listings

Although you can find all of the code listings in this book on our World Wide Web site (**http://www.mcp.com**), many readers prefer to type in most of the examples by hand. This helps them focus on the code one line at a time. Another good approach is to work through an example in a chapter, close the book, and enter it by hand from memory. If you need help, open the book, find the answer, and close the book again. The struggling that you experience will help to deepen your understanding. Remember, getting lost is how you learn.

After each example, experiment a little and see what happens. Change a few properties, add a couple of buttons, and change the code a bit. This will help you enjoy the learning experience more. The most important attribute of a successful learning exercise is fun. If it's fun, you will stay with it longer.

Mouse Operations

In this book, the following phrases tell you how to operate your mouse within Visual Basic:

- *Click.* Move the mouse pointer so that it is in the area of the screen specified and press the left mouse button (If you've reversed these buttons, as many left-handed people like to do, whenever the instructions say to press the left button, press the right button instead.)
- *Double-click.* Press the left mouse button twice rapidly.
- *Drag.* Press and hold down the left mouse button while you're moving the mouse pointer.
- *Drop.* Release the mouse button after a drag operation.

A drag-and-drop operation usually looks as though you actually pick something up, drag it across the screen to a different location, and then drop it.

Conventions

The following conventions are used in this book:

- Code lines, functions, variable names, and any text you see on-screen appear in a special `monospace` typeface.
- Placeholders within code are in *`italic monospace`*.
- User input following a prompt is in **`bold monospace`**.
- File names are in regular text font, usually all uppercase.
- New terms are in *italic*.
- Shortcut keys are underlined. For example, the menu choice "File, Open" can also be accomplished by pressing Alt+F and then pressing O.
- Special-purpose keys are referred to by the text that actually appears on them on a standard 101-key keyboard. For example, press "Esc" or press "F1" or press "Enter."
- The Backspace key, which is labeled with a left arrow, usually is located directly above the Enter key. The Tab key usually is labeled with two arrows pointing to lines, with one arrow pointing right and the other pointing left.
- The cursor keys, labeled on most keyboards with arrows pointing up, down, right, and left, are called the up-arrow key, down-arrow key, right-arrow key, and left-arrow key.
- Key combinations that you must press simultaneously are separated by plus signs. For example, "Press Ctrl+Alt+D" means that you press and hold down the Ctrl key, then press and hold down the Alt key, then press and release the D key. Always press and release, rather than hold, the last key in a key combination.
- Case is not important unless explicitly stated. So "Press A" or "Press a" means the same thing.
- If you're required to type text, the text you must type will appear in **boldface**. For example, "Type **The quick brown fox jumped over the lazy dog**." Usually, however, the line is set off by itself in a monospace typeface, as shown in the following example:

```
This is how text typed outside a paragraph will look
```

Icons Used in This Book

The following icons are used to indicate examples at a certain level of difficulty:

Level 1

Level 2

Level 3

The following additional icons are used to identify material shown in a box:

Tip

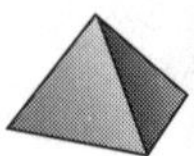

Caution

Note

Pseudocode

Pseudocode is a special way of explaining a section of code with an understandable, English-language description. You often see pseudocode before a code example. The following icon represents pseudocode:

Pseudocode

CHAPTER 1

Visual Basic Overview

In the early 1990s, the conventional wisdom was that procedural languages, such as BASIC and C, were doomed, and that the newer, object-oriented languages such as C++ would soon replace them. But, as normally happens, no one saw the future clearly. While thousands of programmers rushed out and learned C++ terms like "instantiation" and "polymorphism," a smaller group continued to evolve and use the progressively better versions of BASIC Microsoft released. When the shift from DOS to Windows took place, a version of Visual Basic was released for the Windows development environment. The difference between Visual Basic and other Windows development tools is that Visual Basic is easier to learn and more convenient to use. Visual Basic could create a Windows program in less than half the time that it took to write the same program in C or C++.

In the world of computer jargon, terms such as "object" are misused. For example, C++ is referred to as an "object-oriented" language. C++ enthusiasts complain that Visual Basic is not object-oriented because it does not support all of the features assigned to objects by purists. In reality, Visual Basic is very object-oriented, and C++ is very class-oriented. The fact that Visual Basic doesn't readily support the creation of new classes affects its status as a class-oriented language, but not its status as an object-oriented language. (Visual Basic *does* allow you to create class modules, to which you can assign your own properties, and methods.)

In addition, an industry sprang up that sold Visual Basic extensions. These custom controls, or VBXs as they are commonly called, provided functionality that might be of interest to only five percent of the VB developers. This allowed programmers to buy code that was written specifically for their business, without the rigidity that accompanies turnkey solutions in vertical markets. It seemed that the idea of reusable components, written by experts and used by programmers, had finally been realized—not in C++ as had been predicted—but in a derivative of BASIC. In Visual Basic 4, Microsoft generalized the custom controls and gave them a new extension, .OCX, which stands for OLE control extension. Functionally, OCXs work much like VBXs.

The History of BASIC

The programming language part of Visual Basic is a dialect of the Beginners All-purpose Symbolic Instruction Code (BASIC) language developed at Dartmouth College in the early 1960s. Originally, BASIC was developed to make programming easier to learn. The programming languages of the 1950s were designed primarily for solving math problems. Because computers were used mainly by scientists and engineers, language complexity was not a problem. As we rang in the new decade of the 1960s, the academic community began to realize that the computer was useful for much more than number crunching. The desire to expand the computer's use was hampered to some extent by the cumbersome languages of the day. It was in this setting that the original BASIC language was developed at Dartmouth College. BASIC, in its original form, was a very simple and easy-to-use language. Most of the computer scientists who have contributed to the field in the past 25 years first learned to program using BASIC.

By the 1970s, microchip technology had advanced to the point that electronics buffs began to build small computers for fun. The MITS Altair, the first kit computer to be marketed, appeared in 1975. Because the Altair had a whopping 4K of RAM, it could run programs written in assembly language. A couple of hackers, Bill Gates and Paul Allen, decided to write a version of BASIC for the Altair. This made BASIC the official language of PC lovers everywhere.

Through the 1970s, personal computer programs were normally written in BASIC. In 1982, when the IBM/PC was introduced, it was shipped with a version of BASIC (GW-BASIC) included with the DOS operating system. As the technology of programming languages progressed, Microsoft enhanced BASIC and renamed it QuickBasic. QuickBasic was a proprietary product that combined a great debugging environment with support for structures and graphics. The result was a great tool to develop DOS applications. Most of what we used as QuickBasic ships today with DOS under the name QBASIC.

The Advent of Windows

As the decade turned again, Microsoft released Windows 3.0. The DOS programmers of the day weren't much impressed, but the user community was. The smooth graphical look and intuitive interface quickly made Windows 3.0 the platform of choice. Suddenly, the users were not content with even the slickest DOS applications. They wanted fonts, multiple applications open at the same time, dialog boxes, pull-down menus, and all of the "cool" features that were not commonly available in DOS applications.

While the users were applauding the advent of Windows applications, programmers were getting migraine headaches. Under DOS, programmers had a lot of latitude in deciding how things would be done in their programs. Now, under Windows, everything had to be done according to a strict set of rules. This was communism or heresy or something! Actually, it was just plain difficult. Instead of learning to manipulate a dozen or so BASIC language commands, programmers now had to learn a new language, C, and hundreds of function calls. To make it worse, each function call had five or six parameters to be filled in. Whereas the simplest BASIC program could be written in four or five lines of code, the simplest Windows program required pages of commands, all of which had to be exactly right or dire consequences ensued.

The Introduction of Visual Basic

This is where Microsoft Visual Basic makes its grand entrance. Just when it looked like BASIC was dead and buried, it reappeared in a new Windows form. This appearance was not heavily promoted, and no one predicted the phenomenal market success of Visual Basic. At first blush, it didn't seem like anything really important was happening.

This success has occurred because of a number of factors. First, Visual Basic removes the need to do traditional Windows programming in a large number of applications. Second, it replaces C code with simpler BASIC code, which succeeded in getting the amateur programmers into the Windows program development business. Third, Visual Basic could be used by professional programmers to knock out simple parts of applications quickly. Because Visual Basic can call functions stored in Dynamic Link Libraries (DLLs), these programmers can write the hard parts in C/C++, store them in a DLL, and access them from their Visual Basic application. This feature gives Visual Basic the range necessary to satisfy the needs of professional programmers.

The fourth reason for this success is the growth of the third-party controls vendors. Literally hundreds of Visual Basic Extensions (VBXs) are being marketed. These custom controls appear as extra icons in Visual Basic, and behave as if they were a native part of the language. With Visual Basic 4, Microsoft has shifted the emphasis away from VBXs to OLE Control Extensions (OCXs). OCXs are like VBXs in functionality, but they are independent of any particular language. The existence of these affordable components has driven the sales of Visual Basic and greatly enhanced its usefulness. In this book, you will use several custom controls; however, learning how to author them is beyond the scope of this book.

A fifth reason for Visual Basic's popularity among professional programmers is its royalty-free distribution model. This means that if you write a program that is really good, you can distribute copies of it without paying a royalty fee to Microsoft or buying a special distribution kit.

Terms and Concepts

To succeed in the world of Windows programming, it is important to understand the jargon. Many of the terms used to describe Windows concepts have other meanings in other fields. This section lists several of these terms.

Object

An *object* is a piece of software equipment that has properties and a specific behavior. Objects behave much like data types, but they are normally much more complex. Access to objects is through properties, methods and events. The properties are the object's variables and constants. By changing the value of the properties you change the behavior of the object. Methods are the commands or functions that are associated with the object. Any operation that you want to perform against an object will be done in conjunction with its methods. Finally, events are the interrupts or action that occurs to give the object control. An example of an event is clicking the mouse. In Visual Basic objects can be forms, printers, windows, buttons, pictures, animations, and so on.

Window

A *window* is a rectangular area on the screen that contains an application or part of an application. The window is analogous to a sheet of paper lying on a desktop. You can overlay one sheet with another one, put it away, throw it away, bring it to the top, write on it or read off it.

User Interface

The *user interface* is the part of a computer program that the user actually sees. It contains all of the controls that are available to the user, such as buttons, windows, graphics, sound bites, and so on.

Events

Events are activities that occur which are of potential interest to an application. These events are normally caused by user action, but they can result from a timer expiring, or under program control (for example, forms loading, comm data coming in, and so on).

Event-Driven Programming Languages

These are languages that are designed to wait for one of a large number of user actions and react to it. This is in contrast to procedural programming languages, which react to a very limited number of possible user actions, often just a menu selection.

Tools

Tools are classes of objects that can appear in Visual Basic programs. These tools are used to create instances of themselves, called *controls,* on forms.

Controls

Controls are instances of tools that have been created. These controls provide functionality to the forms and enable the user to create events for the program to respond to.

Project

A *project* is a collection of files that make up an organized effort to create a working program. The result of a Visual Basic project is an executable program, called an *application.*

Application

An *application* is a completed program.

Executable File

An *executable file,* which is sometimes called simply an "executable," is a file that contains a program that has been translated into a set of machine-readable instructions. Executables are intended to run outside the environment in which they were created. Executables are written in virtually every computer language, although much more quickly in some than others. Under Windows, an executable normally has an .EXE suffix.

Custom Control

A *custom control* is a program that is written to enhance the power of Visual Basic, but that is not a built-in part of the language itself. These controls are frequently written by small software firms and sold through the mail.

If a calendar is needed for an application, instead of developing one, it is probably available as a custom control. These controls are used exactly like Visual

Basic objects except that they are not included with Visual Basic; they must be purchased separately.

Icon

An *icon* is a little picture that represents an application that has been minimized. Sometimes, you have to minimize all applications to see all of the icons.

Example: Installing Visual Basic

Install Visual Basic if you have not already done so. Start Visual Basic by clicking the Start button on the left of the Taskbar and then move the mousepointer to the Programs selection at the top of the list. A second menu list will then appear. Now, move the mouse pointer to the Visual Basic 4 option and a third menu will appear. At this point, click the option that says Visual Basic 4.0 as shown in figure 1.1.

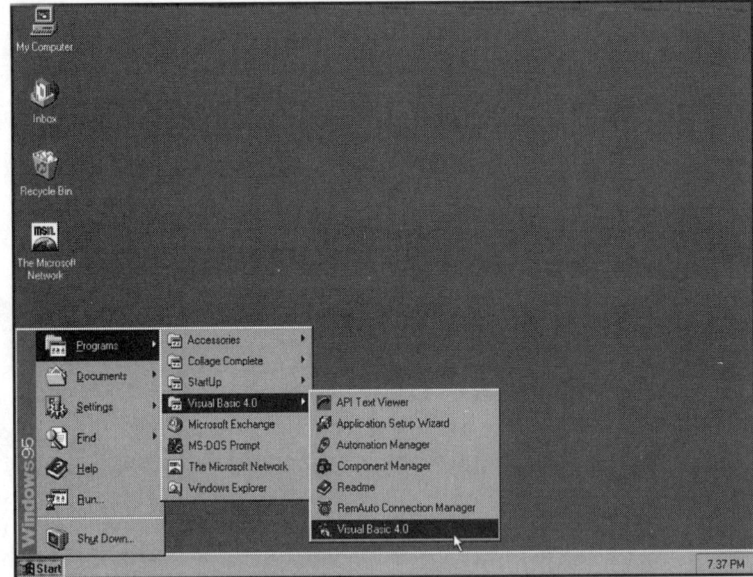

Figure 1.1
The Start list menus.

When a bunch of windows appear, choose Run, then Start. This command turns the current application into a running program. This creates a window that looks like figure 1.2.

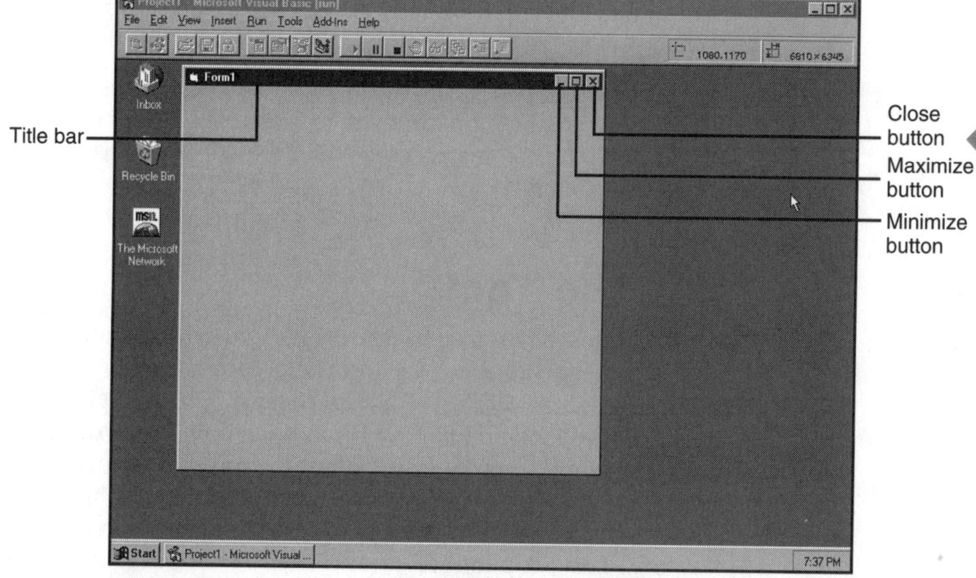

Figure 1.2

The simplest Visual Basic program.

Even though this window contains no Visual Basic controls, it is still a very capable program. Perform the following experiments on this window to see how it behaves:

- Click on the button with the full box on it in the far right corner (the *maximize button*). Doing so stretches the window until it fills the screen completely.
- Turn the full-screen version back into a window by clicking on the button in the top-right corner that has two boxes overlapping on it (the *middle-size button*).
- Double-click on the *title bar*. This will toggle the application between a full-screen and its windowed state.
- Turn the window into an icon by clicking on the button with the dash on it (the *minimize button*) in the top-right corner of the window.
- Turn every window that you see into an icon. Double-click the icon that has *Form1* written on it.
- Drag the window by pressing down on the mouse button while the mouse cursor is over the colored bar at the top of the application. While still holding down the button, move the mouse to a new location and let go of the button. This moves the window to a new spot on the screen.

- Terminate the application by clicking on the *close button* that has an X in it, which is located in the top-right corner of the window.

It is amazing that you can create a window that contains so much functionality without writing a single line of code or including one control. Throughout this book, you will find other instances in which a small effort on your part yields a large amount of functionality.

Using the Tools

Becoming proficient in Visual Basic requires you to learn some very different skills. The first skill is user-interface design. Microsoft Visual Basic is sometimes called a GUI (Graphical User Interface) builder. Using a rich set of visual tools, a programmer lays out the "look and feel" of his application. This is done using menus and toolbars that remind you of other Windows programs such as CorelDRAW! or Microsoft Write. Windows power users will feel right at home with this kind of interface. Parts I and II of this book concentrate on this aspect of writing Visual Basic applications. This book introduces these user interface tools one at the time until you understand them all.

Every object or "control" (such as a button, label, or text box) has associated with it a set of *properties*. These properties are different for every different type of control. Properties are concerned with characteristics such as color, size, and text caption. Much of the need to write code is removed by the availability of these properties. Although the setting of properties seems like a strange activity to a C programmer, it is a powerful way to get results with a minimum of effort.

Once you know how to build user interfaces, you will learn how to write the BASIC statements that make the interface come alive. These statements, called *code*, are associated with the buttons and controls of Visual Basic. This code gives your program detailed instructions about how you want each control and event to behave. The BASIC language working under Visual Basic makes VB a powerful tool because it allows you to exercise much more control over your computer than you can with a database package. Part III of this book covers the BASIC language constructs in detail.

Using an Event-Driven Language

Visual Basic is an event-driven programming language. This means that Visual Basic programs contain code to handle all meaningful user events or actions. When the user triggers an event, the operating system tells the program the exact nature of the event (for example, a keypress or mouse movement). The programmer can cause the program to react in the appropriate way by the code he writes. After the processing is finished, the Visual Basic program goes back into a waiting mode ready to process the next event.

Armed with both the interface-building and coding skills, you then learn how to combine them to produce some really neat applications. Part VI of this book leads you through the creation of a number of short but interesting applications. Following along with the text as these programs are written will help you become more that just a "cookbook programmer." You will learn what a professional programmer thinks about as she is developing an application.

Summary

In this chapter, you were introduced to Visual Basic. You read about how the language has evolved. The advantages of learning Visual Basic were explained, including some economic considerations, such as royalty-free distribution.

Several terms were introduced that are key to understanding the concepts in this book. You will see all of them again as you progress through the chapters.

Finally, you saw a simple program running in development mode. You had a chance to use the controls that are an integral part of a window. In the chapters that follow, you learn the concepts that form the foundation for the integration of code and objects to produce an application.

Review Questions

1. What is an object?
2. What is code?

3. What is an icon?
4. What is a custom control?

5. Explain the difference between a VBX and an OCX.
6. What is a property?

Review Exercises

1. Create a new Visual Basic project and run it by using the Start command from the Run menu.

2. Using the previous application, use the minimize, maximize, and restore buttons to change the size of the window.

3. Using the same application, use the mouse to move the form to various parts of the screen.

CHAPTER 2

Visual Basic Programs

When you tell a programmer about a new language, she normally says something like, "Let me see some code, then I'll figure it out." In traditional programming languages such as COBOL, Pascal, or C, the programmer writes instructions in the language. These instructions are kept in files that contain the entire program. If you want to know how the program works, you read the code and comments and figure it out. It is important to realize that code writing is not the central activity in Visual Basic program development. It is only one part of the process.

In Visual Basic, programmers have to adopt a totally new mind-set, because Visual Basic is a complete development system that includes a language. The code makes up only one part of the application and the built-in objects make up the rest, which means that the entire structure of a program is different. In this chapter, we will look at some of these differences by working through examples.

Starting Visual Basic

Before you can construct a Visual Basic application, you need to start up the Integrated Development Environment (IDE). The first step is to start Visual Basic by clicking on the Visual Basic 4 option in the Start menu, as shown in figure 2.1.

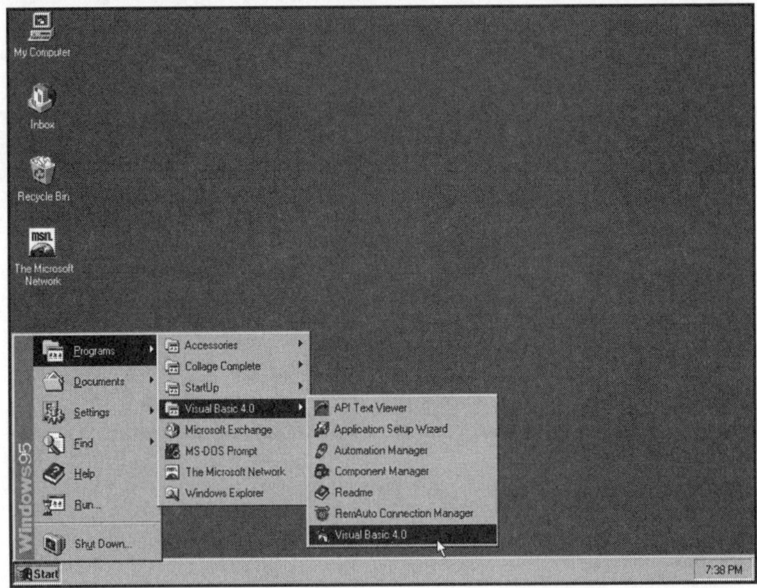

Figure 2.1

The Visual Basic Start menu option.

Choose Help, Contents. The screen, as shown in figure 2.2, appears.

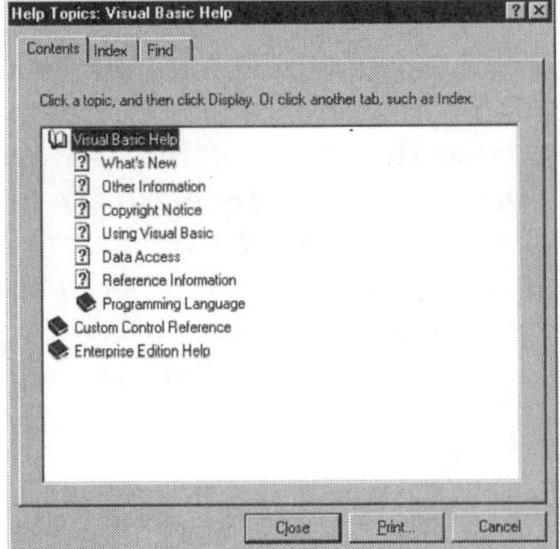

Figure 2.2

The Help screen.

The Help facility is designed to provide online information about how to use the system. For a full explanation of the Help facility, see Chapter 4, "The Windows Environment."

Now examine the Visual Basic working environment as shown in figure 2.3.

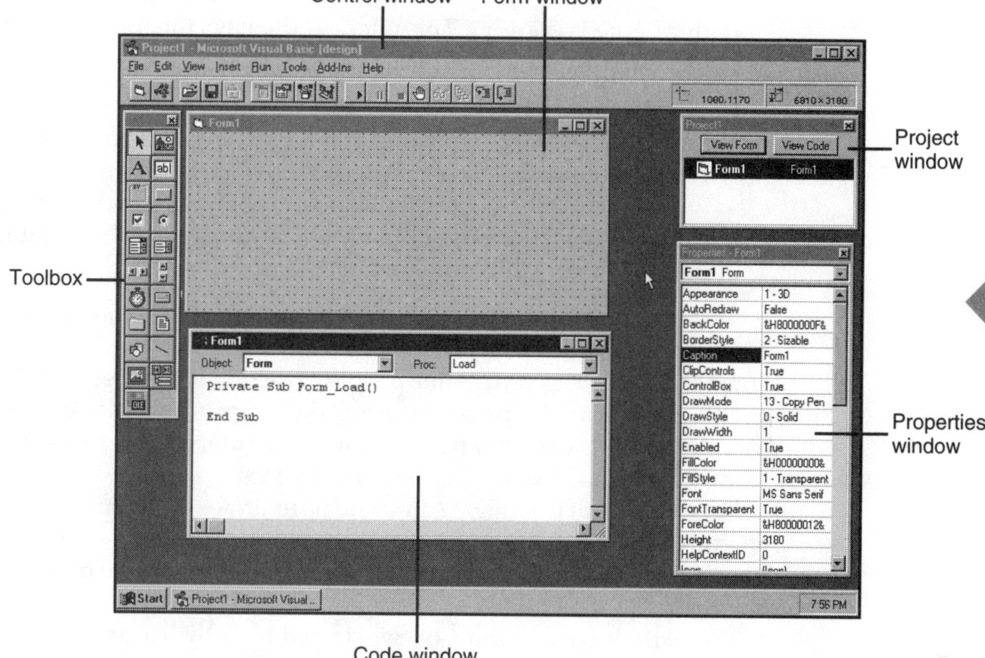

Figure 2.3

The six windows of Visual Basic.

- *The Form window*—This window is in the center of figure 2.3. The window caption (the text across the top of the window) is `Form1`. This window contains a clear area, called a form, that holds buttons, boxes, pictures, and so on. Each form becomes a window in a running program.
- *The Properties window*—This window is located on the right of figure 2.3. The window caption is `Properties-Form1`. This window contains settings that control the look and behavior of objects such as forms, buttons, picture boxes, and so on.
- *The Control window*—This window is located across the top of figure 2.3. The window caption reads `Project1-Microsoft Visual Basic (design)`. This window contains the Visual Basic Menu bar and Toolbar. It is through this window that activities that affect the entire application (such as adding a form or running the application) are initiated.
- *The Toolbox*—This window is located on the far left of figure 2.3. There is no caption on the Toolbox. As its name implies, the Toolbox contains the tools, also called *controls,* that you will use to build your applications. These tools allow you to add text, pictures, list boxes, buttons, and so on to your forms.

- *The Project window*—This window is located at the upper right of figure 2.3. The caption for this window is simply the name of the project, which in this figure is `Project1`. This window displays the forms, modules, and class files from which this application will be built.
- *The Code window*—This window is located in the lower center of figure 2.3. Its caption is `Form1`, indicating that it contains code for Form1. Any event code (program instructions you write which will be automatically executed whenever an event linked to the form—or object on the form—occurs) and general code (subprograms and functions contained in the form, but not linked to any events occurring on that form) appear here.

You can already see that this is not your father's old station wagon. But fear not, because by the time you get finished with this book, these screens will seem as familiar as your backyard. Some people's reaction when they first see these screens is "I'll never learn to program using this interface." Although it does look as complicated as the control panel on an F-16 fighter jet, it is really not very difficult to learn what each button and menu item does.

Take a moment to navigate through the interface by opening menus and clicking on icons to see how they act. Don't worry about messing up—you can always create a new project by choosing New Project from the File menu, to make your screen look like figure 2.3 again.

Visual Basic has a number of elegant and friendly features—such as ToolTips—to help you learn the environment. Whenever you position your mouse cursor over a tool, a ToolTip (a little balloon) appears to tell you the name of the tool or button. Everything that you need to create really good applications is here, thus allowing you to concentrate on the design and functionality of your program.

A Global Perspective of Windows

When you look at the screen as it is shown in figure 2.3, you see six distinct windows. Look at each of these to get a feel for its role in bringing new Windows programs into the world. In Part II of this book, you will study each of these windows in turn. For the purposes of this discussion, however, we will gloss over some of the details in order to keep the discussion at a more global perspective.

The sixth window, the Code window, will play an important role in program development. You can bring up this window by clicking the View Code button, which is near the top of the Project window, or by double-clicking on the object (form, or any control on a form). Later in this chapter, you will use the Code window to add some logic to a program.

The Form Window

In the middle of your screen is a window with the caption `Form1`. This is the Form window. Forms are the stars of your Visual Basic productions. Because you are working with a visual tool, and you are creating Graphical User Interfaces (GUIs), it stands to reason that something visual, the form, fills the leading role. The purpose of the form is to serve as a container for other stuff, known formally as *controls*. When completed, each form represents one window in your application. If your application requires five windows, you will construct five forms.

The forms serve as an interface between the users and the functionality of your application. Some forms are designed to contain a graphic, a document, an animation, or a combination of these. By organizing an application around the forms, you can design a program from the user's perspective.

The Properties Window

On the right of the page is a window that has the caption `Properties`. This is the Properties window. Properties are details about a component of Visual Basic. Each component has certain characteristics that are "hard-wired" into Visual Basic, such as the rectangular shape of a form. These characteristics are not under your control as a programmer, so you can't change the shape of the form to a polygon. However, the components have other characteristics or properties that are under your control. These characteristics are listed along with their current values in the Properties window. So far, you know of only one kind of component, the form. In figure 2.3, the properties that you see pertain to the form called `Form1`. For some of these properties (such as color, size, or location), you can enter a number, or string text, whereas others (such as visible or enabled) can hold only True or False values.

One of the properties of a form is its `Caption`, the words written in the title bar at the top of the window. In figure 2.3, the caption's value is `Form1`. If you look over at the Properties window, you will see that a property called `Caption` has that value `Form1`. To liven up this discussion a bit, let's change its value to something more meaningful, such as `Hello Screen`, by clicking on this row in the Properties window.

Note: Whenever you highlight a row in the Properties window, the value of that row appears in an editable text field called the setting box. Some settings boxes contain a multiple-choice field located next to the property setting when the property is highlighted. If you click on the multiple-choice box, you can choose a setting from a list box or dialog box.

Type **Hello World** on this line, as shown in figure 2.4.

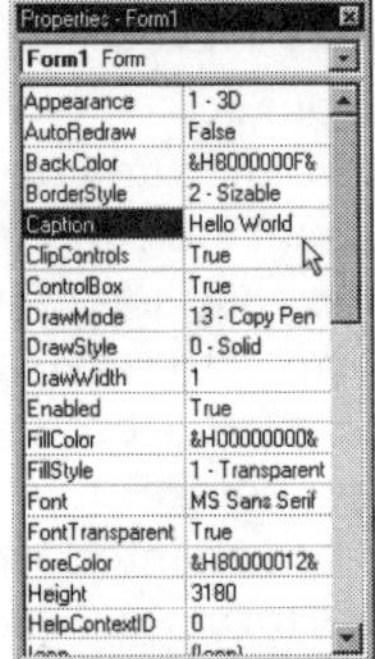

Figure 2.4

The Properties window.

You will observe immediately that when you type **`Hello World`** into the field, the caption on the Form window changes to `Hello World` also. Figure 2.5 shows the changed form.

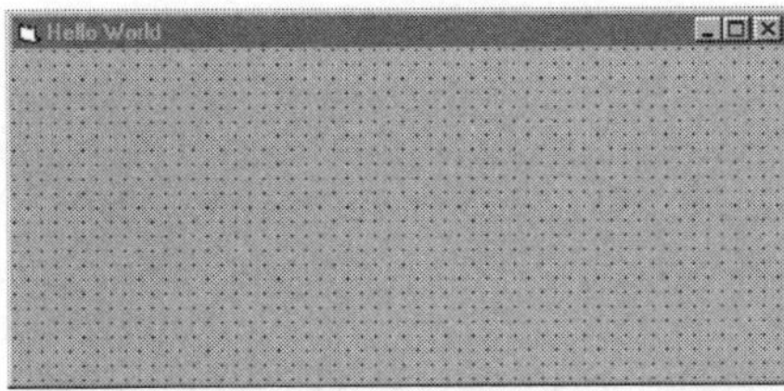

Figure 2.5

The Form window with the changed caption.

This change applies only to the form's caption, however; the name of the form is still `Form1`. It is a form's name, not its caption, that you refer to in the code when you want to refer to the form in code. The nice thing about properties is that they give you a quick way to change the look and feel of your application without programming.

The Control Window

At this point, you have a complete, although fairly boring, program. Let's run it and see what it does. Figure 2.6 shows the Toolbar, which you will use to run the program.

Figure 2.6

The Start button on the Toolbar.

On the Toolbar, you see three buttons that look like the ones on your VCR. If you click the button with the right-facing triangle, as shown in figure 2.6, the program starts. You can also start the program by pressing F5, or by choosing Run, Start from the menu bar (this isn't nearly as cool as using the button, though). This will cause almost all of the windows to disappear except the Form window. The Form changes into a real window and runs on your screen. The result of this program, an empty window, is shown in figure 2.7.

Figure 2.7
An empty window.

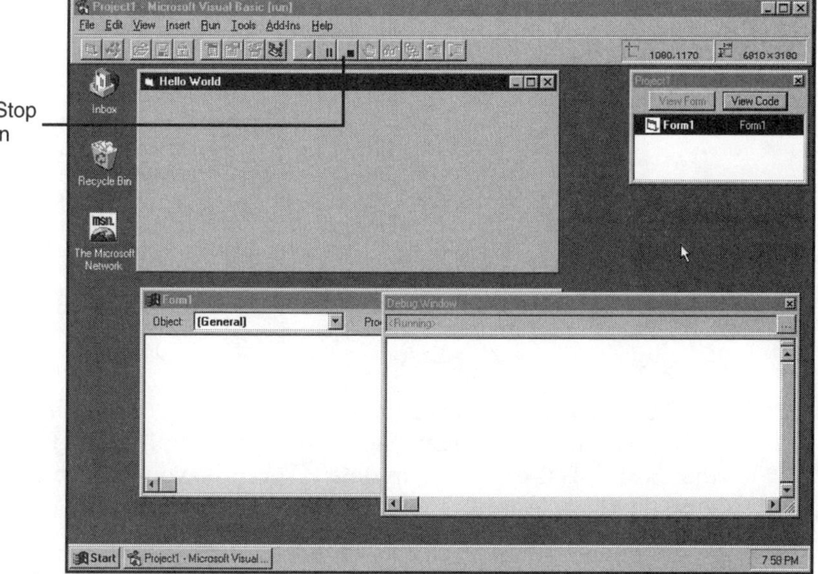

If you have written Windows 3.x programs in C using the Windows API, you will be amazed at how easy that was. If you are new to programming, you may not appreciate what you have just done. This window is fully functioning. It can be moved, resized, shrunk to an icon, restored to regular size, maximized, and closed just like any other window that you have ever used. You don't even remember writing all of the code to handle this, because you didn't have to write anything. The most valuable feature of Visual Basic is that it handles so many of the messy details of Windows programming and allows you to operate at a comfortable level of detail. To stop your application, you can click the Stop button—the button that contains a black box (see fig. 2.7). However, it is more preferable to click the X button on the upper-right of the form to end the program or to use the program's control icon.

You could also have stopped the application by choosing Run, End, but that takes all of the fun out of it.

The Toolbox

At this point, you know how to create enough empty Windows programs to fill the back of a pickup truck. But because they don't do any real work, no one will pay you for them. So, let's increase your risk in this venture by adding a control or two to the form. Before you can do this, you need to learn about the Toolbox window. The Toolbox window is pictured in figure 2.7 with annotations that show the name of each control. If you purchased the Enterprise version of Visual Basic, you will see more tools than this.

Figure 2.8

The Toolbox.

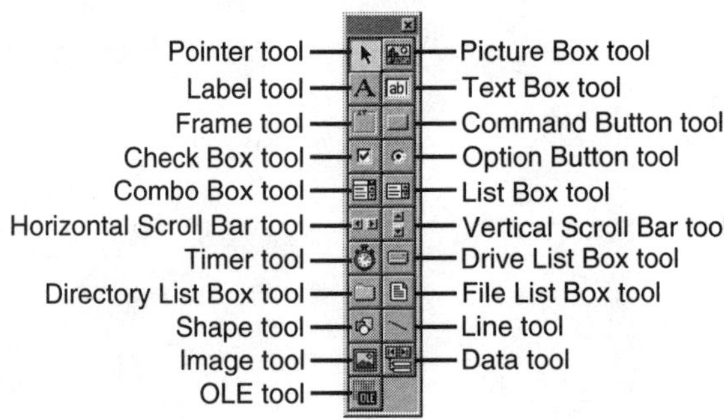

The Toolbox window contains a set of small icons, each of which represents a type of control that you can use to build your application. Later, in Part II, each of these controls is explained in detail. For now, you can see how a couple of them work in a simple application.

Example

To add a button to your form, you can either click once on the control button on the Toolbox and then move the mouse over to the form and draw the control in the desired position on the form, or you can use a shortcut by double-clicking on the icon for the Command Button control, which was shown in figure 2.8.

A button appears in the center of the form. Move the button out of the center by placing the cursor over the top of the button, holding down the mouse button with your index finger, and dragging the button to another spot nearer the border of the form. Now double-click on the Text Box tool, which was shown in figure 2.8.

Your form should now look something like the one shown in figure 2.9.

At this point, you should run the program by clicking the Run button on the Control window Toolbar.

Click the command button, Command1, that you just added to the form. When you click the button, it reverses the shadowing to give the impression that it has been pressed in. The button doesn't have any real effect though, because you haven't yet written any code to tell it what you want it to do. Click the Stop button on the Toolbar to return to design mode.

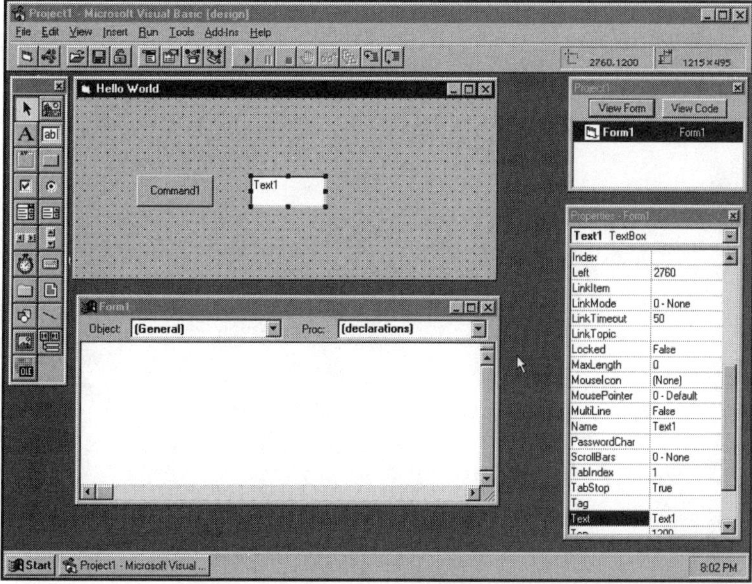

Figure 2.9

The window with a text box and a command button.

You'll add some code in a minute, but first let's give the button a new caption by selecting the button with your mouse and then looking at the Properties window.

You may notice that the Properties window, shown in figure 2.10, looks different when the button is selected than it did when the form was selected. This is because buttons are inherently different than forms, so it wouldn't make sense to use the same properties on both. Each time you select a component, you get the list of properties and current values that apply to that type of component.

Let's change the caption of the command button by selecting it with your mouse and then locating the `caption` property in the Properties window. Select the caption property and then type **Display Hello**. This changes the text that is written on the button itself.

While you are in the Properties window, change the `name` property of the button to `btnDisplay`. Any name will work for Visual Basic's purposes; however, meaningful names are easier for programmers to remember.

Next, select the text box in the form by putting your cursor over it and clicking once. In the Properties window, change the text box's `Name` property to `txtHello`. When you write the code for these components, you will refer to them as `txtHello` and `btnDisplay`. Remember that the name is what the code uses to refer to the button and the caption is what appears on the button itself. The name of the button is not always the same as the caption on the button because of the need for flexibility. You might want several buttons with the word Help written on them. You can name them `btnHelp1`, `btnHelp2`, `btnHelp3`, and so on because there is no requirement that the names and captions be identical. That way, when the user clicks on one of the buttons marked Help, your code knows which kind of Help the user wants to invoke.

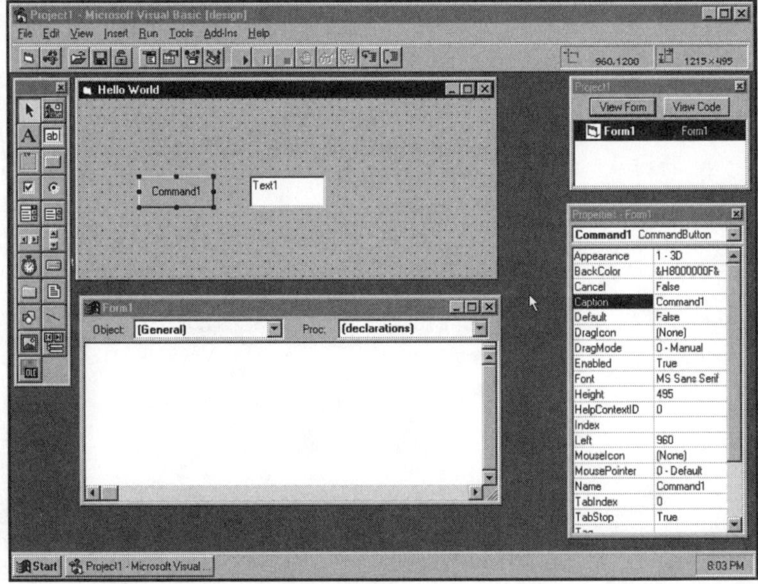

Figure 2.10

The properties for the command button.

Run the program again and observe that the form now looks similar to the one shown in figure 2.11.

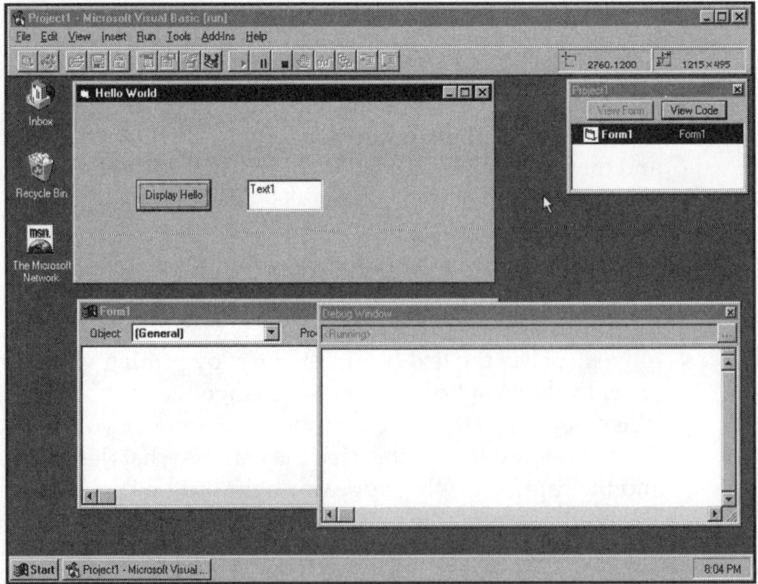

Figure 2.11

The running program.

Click the Stop button on the Toolbar in the Control window to end the run.

The Code Window

Without further delay, let's add some code to the example. To do this, you need only double-click the command button. The Visual Basic development environment is smart enough to know that what you want to do is bring up the Code window associated with that button. After you double-click, you will see the Code window, which is shown in figure 2.12.

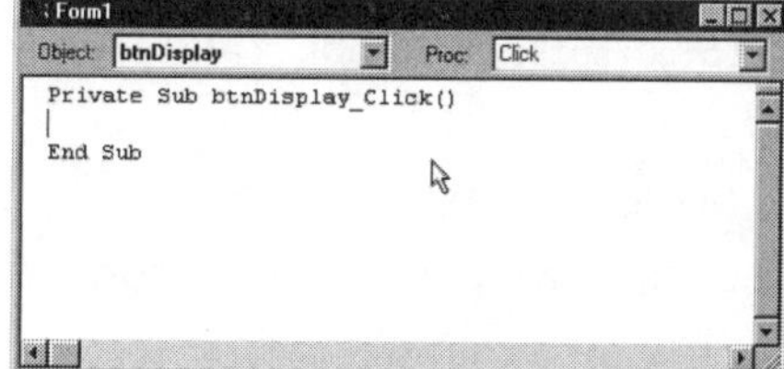

Figure 2.12
The Code window.

The Code window looks a little more complicated than you might have expected. In addition to a nearly blank screen, you get a couple of list boxes, one labeled `Object` and the other labeled `Proc:`. The relationship between objects and events is the basis of Chapter 3, "Event-Driven Programming." For now, it is sufficient to know that you can add code to the application in this window. This approach of adding a separate window for code allows the programmer to keep all of his code in one place.

Example

In addition to the two list boxes, you also see some lines of code that look like this:

```
Private Sub btnDisplay_Click ()

End Sub
```

Visual Basic is trying to help you by doing as much of your work for you as possible. It knows that the object in the list is the `btnDisplay` and that the event in the Proc list box is `Click`, so it created a skeleton *subroutine* for you. At this point, the name that you chose for the button becomes important. In C and COBOL, the names of the subroutines are totally the decision of the programmer, because he will be the one to call them. In Visual Basic, Windows will call the subroutine for you when the event named in the subroutine occurs. In order to do this, Windows has to know which subroutine to call for which event. Visual Basic accomplishes this by naming event subroutines according to the following convention:

```
Sub ObjectName_EventName()
```

in which `ObjectName` is the name of the object that was acted on, and *`EventName`* is the type of event that occurred. Sub indicates that this is a subroutine and not a function. The () is required even if no parameters are being passed as part of the syntax.

Note: If you change the name of a control after having edited any of that control's event-code routines, Visual Basic will move the existing routines to the general section of the form, and create new empty event routines under the control's new name.

Select `btnDisplay` as the object and `Click` as the event. Place your cursor on the line following:

```
Sub btnDisplay_Click ()
```

Add the following lines to this routine:

```
txtHello.text = "Hello, World!"
```

Run the program and see what happens. At first, the form looks like it did before. When you click the button, however, the text box displays the phrase `Hello, World!`. The form should now look similar to the one shown in figure 2.13.

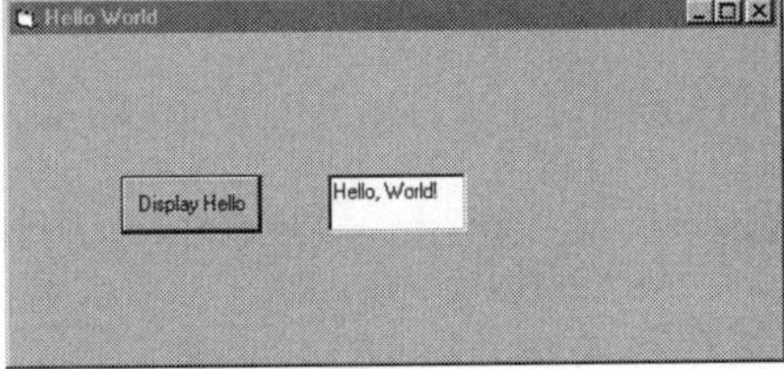

Figure 2.13
The form with the `Hello, World!` text box.

The Project Window

The final window that you need to be familiar with is the Project window. This window enables you to manage your project from one place instead of by managing a multitude of files. Figure 2.14 shows a simple project's Project window.

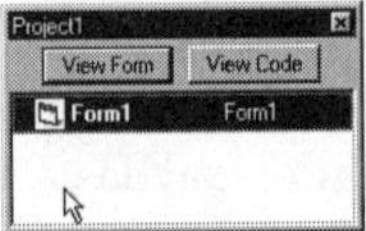

Figure 2.14
A simple Project window.

The caption for the window is the name of the project's make file, `Project1`. Because of the unimaginative name of this file, let's name it something like `TextProj`. To change the name of the project, you must save the project by choosing File, Save.

Visual Basic will first ask you to save any forms in the project. After choosing Save, it will then ask you for the Project File Name. Type **TextProj** and click Save. Notice that the Project window's caption changed to TEXTPROJ.VBP, as shown in figure 2.15.

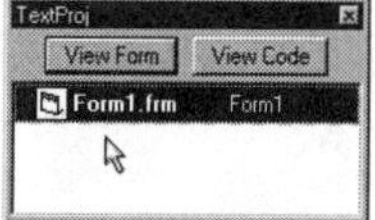

Figure 2.15
The saved Project window.

The name of the file that contains the project data is called TEXTPROJ.VBP. You will use this name to find the project later when you use the Open Project command on the File menu. The make file (.VBP) contains information that Visual Basic uses to load a project into memory when you want to work on it.

The make file is really a simple text file that can be viewed with a text editor. Figure 2.16 shows the contents of TEXTPROJ.VBP.

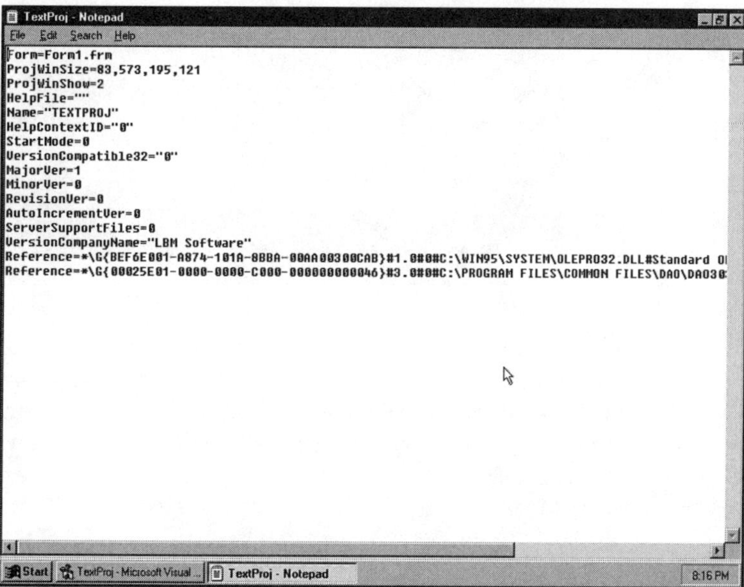

Figure 2.16
Looking inside a .VBP file.

This make file was viewed by opening it in Notepad. The first few lines list which forms and custom controls to load. The next few refer to the settings for the application. Toward the end, you see the name of the reference libraries that are included in this project.

Example

Let's create an example where you add a second form to the project. You do this by selecting Form from the Insert menu or by clicking on the left-most button on the Toolbar, the one with the picture of a window on it. This causes a new form window to appear with the caption `Form2` on it. Notice that as soon as you added that form, the contents of the Project window changed to refer to this form also, as shown in figure 2.17.

Figure 2.17

Adding a second form.

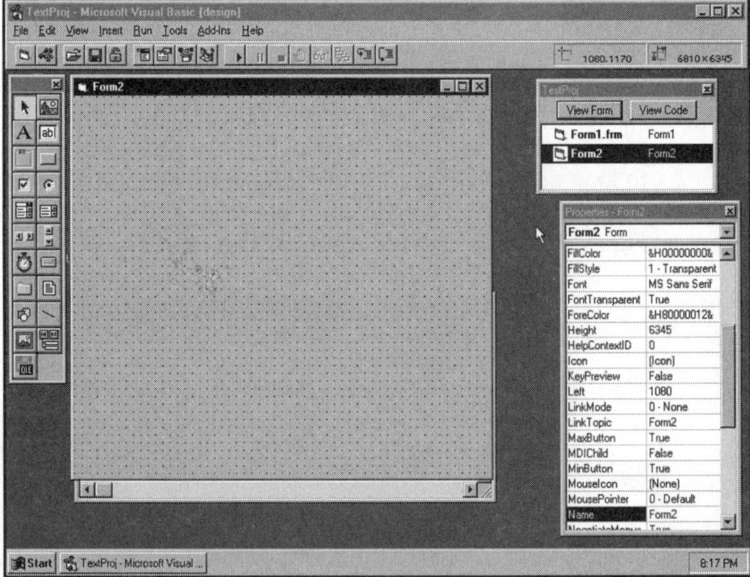

Now that you have a second form in your project, you want to access it during the running of the program. To do this, you can add a command button to each form. On Form1, add a command button named `cbForm2`, and on Form2, add a command button that is called `cbForm1`. The caption for `cbForm2` should be `Goto Form2` and the caption for `cbForm1` should be `Goto Form1`. Next, enter these two following lines in the `cbForm1_Click()` event:

```
Private Sub cbForm1_Click()
    Form1.Hide
    Form2.Show
End Sub
```

And add the following code to the `cbForm2_Click()` event:

```
Private Sub cbForm2_Click()
    Form2.Hide
    Form1.Show
End Sub
```

Next, run the program and verify that when you click on a command button, the form disappears and the other form appears. The words `Hide` and `Show` are called methods for the forms. Methods are like subroutines, except that they are associated with a kind of object, such as forms, and normally affect the object associated with them. In this example, the code tells the system to `Hide` Form1 and then to `Show` Form2. Hiding means that you want to keep the form in memory but make it invisible. Show means that you want to load a form into memory if necessary and then make it visible on the screen.

Next, add a module to the project by selecting Module from the Insert menu or by clicking on the Toolbar button second from the left (the one that looks like a picture of a human nerve shredded by too many hours on the computer). This again adds a line to the Project window, as shown in figure 2.18.

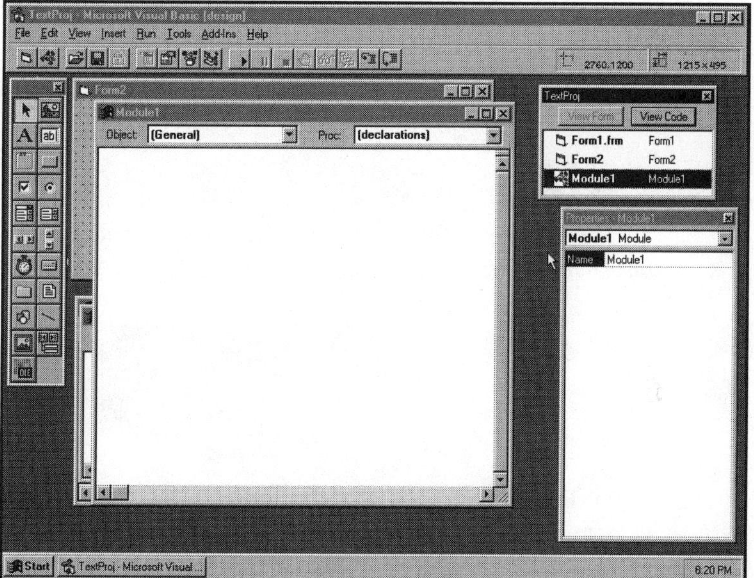

Figure 2.18
Adding a module to the project.

A module is a collection of subroutines and functions that are not associated with a specific form. Normally, these subroutines and functions are useful in more than one form. Let's add a subroutine to the module and then run a program that calls it. Add the following code to your module:

Listing 2.1 Subroutine Example to Display a MsgBox Prompt

```
Sub MsgText()
    Msg = "Do you want to continue ?"
    Style = vbYesNo + vbCritical + vbDefaultButton2
    Title = "MsgBox Demonstration"
    Help = "DEMO.HLP"
    Ctxt = 1000
    Response = MsgBox(Msg, Style, Title, Help, Ctxt)
    If Response = vbYes Then
        MyString = "Yes"
    Else
        MyString = "No"
    End If
End Sub
```

You don't need to pay much attention to the code details at this point. You will learn what it all means in later chapters. At this time, all you need to know is that the code causes a message box to be displayed when called.

Now add the following code to a command button on Form2 named `cbMsg`:

```
Private Sub cbMsg_Click()
   MsgText
End Sub
```

You can now run this program and observe that clicking on the `cbMsg` command button on Form2 causes the message box to appear as shown in figure 2.19.

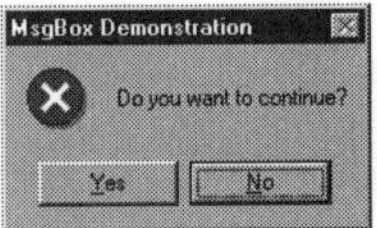

Figure 2.19

The message box from the module.

It is important to note that the code for the message box could have been placed in Form2 also. The use of a module was for the purpose of making this sub available to multiple applications. If you choose, you can add this same module to dozens of applications.

If the subroutine is only intended for a single application, it can be placed in the appropriate form. It is still possible to call a subroutine in one form from another form. The calling conventions are different when calling a routine that is in a form from a routine that is outside the form. For example, to call `MsgText` from inside the same form, the code would look like the code in figure 2.16. However, if you are calling this routine from another form, the code would look like the following:

```
Form2.MsgText
```

This informs Visual Basic which form the routine can be found in.

Summary

Just as the old saying goes that you learn everything really important in kindergarten (for example, don't push people, or wander off into the street when cars are coming), it could be said that you have now learned the most important lessons in Visual Basic. Compared with getting one simple program to run, all of the fancy features of the language are a breeze. By the time you reach the end of the book, you will be saying, "Hey, that wasn't as hard as I thought it would be." The other things that you will learn in the remainder of this book are simply details on the basic themes of designing the interface, setting the properties, writing the code, and running it to verify that it works correctly. The next chapter expands on the basic concept of events and event-driven programming.

Review Questions

The answers to the review questions are in Appendix A.

1. What is a project?
2. What is a make (.VBP) file?
3. Name the five windows that come up when you create a new project.

4. What is the Code window?
5. Name three ways to bring up the Code window.

6. What is a module?
7. What kind of information is in a .VBP file?

Review Exercises

1. Create a form and save the project.
2. Create a second form and add a button to bring it up.

3. Write a program that outputs the phrase `"Good-bye, World"` in another text box when you press `btnDisplay`.

4. Write a program that contains a button that turns the text in the text box to blanks when clicked. When you press this Clear button, it should assign `""` as the value of the `Text` property of the `Text1` text box.
5. Create a module and put a sub in it. Create three forms, each of which calls the same routine.

CHAPTER 3

Event-Driven Programming

As you learned in Chapter 1, Visual Basic is an event-driven programming language. The purpose of this chapter is to build a clear concept of what event-driven programming is and how it differs from traditional programming. In this chapter, you learn what constitutes an event by creating a simple application and examining a number of Visual Basic events.

Understanding Events

To understand event-driven programming, you must first understand the concept of an event. In your non-technical life (presumably, you have one), you think of events as unique occurrences, such as graduation, the World Cup, and the birth of a child. In reality, an event can be any ordinary happening. A ringing phone, a commercial on the television, and a heart attack can all be considered events, although some are more interesting than others. You handle events according to their importance. When the phone rings, you answer it. When you hear a commercial on TV, you go make a sandwich. When someone has a heart attack, you call the ambulance. When a plane flies overhead, some of us look up, whereas others do not even notice it. In truth, you are surrounded by thousands of events at all times. You selectively act on the ones you deem important at the moment.

You can carry this analogy to your programming life. When users are running a program under Windows, they do lots of things. They press the keys, move the mouse, click objects, drag objects, cut, paste, and so on. Your programs are expected to understand what the user just did (that is, what event occurred) and to react rationally in response to it. Given the variety of possible events, this task is not easy.

In the early days of programming, way back in the mid-eighties, most programs fell into one of two categories: batch or on-line. Batch programs executed without user interaction. They normally responded to only one event, the "program start" event. On receipt of the command to start the program, the operating system loaded the program into memory and began execution. The program then ran to completion (most of the time). In contrast, the on-line systems of that era assumed that a person was sitting in front of the computer. The person usually had a keyboard but no mouse, no touch screen, and no voice recognition system. As a result, a program could behave in a sequential fashion. It could require that the user choose from a very limited set of choices by pressing a certain key. Menus like the following were common:

1. Create an Invoice
2. Post a Payment
3. Send Out Late Notices
4. Exit

Please select one of these options.

Because the user had only four choices and only one way of interacting with the system—through the keyboard—the programming was very simple. The program contained some sort of input command such as `READ` or `GET`. As soon as the user responded with a 1, 2, 3, or 4, the program branched to the appropriate code block or subroutine, satisfied the request, and returned to the menu for the next request. At times, the program had several levels of menus, but the complexity was about the same. Although this approach was functional, it was fairly limiting. Graphical user interfaces such as those on Apple computer systems were much more interesting to use and seemed more natural than menus and keyboards.

Users started clamoring for better human-computer interfaces than programmers were giving them. These users liked pointing, dragging, and clicking, so Microsoft developed the Windows operating system to give customers what they wanted. The designers of the Windows product decided that the best way to handle this more complicated type of user input was to have Windows receive each message and then pass it to the program for which it was intended.

In effect, whenever an event occurs, Windows notices it and decides what kind of event it is. If an event intended for a program that is currently running occurs, Windows "hands the event over" to that application. This process of notifying the program that it has received an event is called *message passing*. The user action—for example, clicking the mouse in an application's window—is noticed by Windows. Windows then sends the application a message indicating that the event occurred, along with some additional information about the event (such as the coordinates of the occurrence) if necessary. If a program is not currently running, any event intended for it will be discarded by Windows.

Example

Creating a simple application will help you understand the concept of an event. First, create a new application by choosing File from the Visual Basic menu bar and then choosing New Project. Next, double-click the Command Button icon in the Toolbox. This puts a button in the center of the form. At this point, your form should look like figure 3.1.

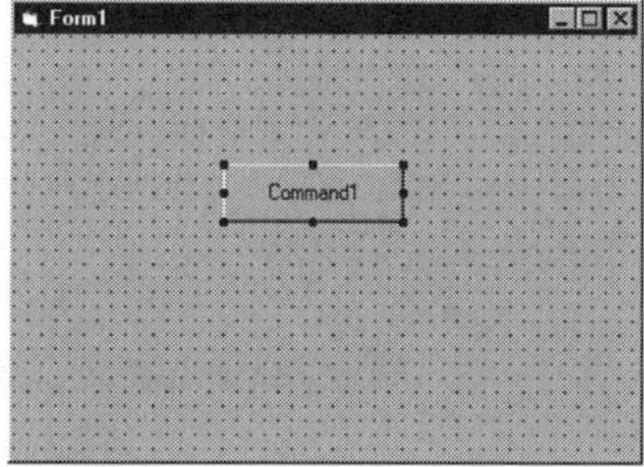

Figure 3.1
A form with a command button.

Double-click the command button to bring up the Code window (see Fig. 3.2). Now add a new line so that the subroutine looks like this:

```
Private Sub Command1_Click ()
   Command1.Caption = ""
End Sub
```

This code instructs Visual Basic to change the caption on that object (the button) to a null string "" (without a space), if the mouse is clicked while the cursor is over the button object named Command1.

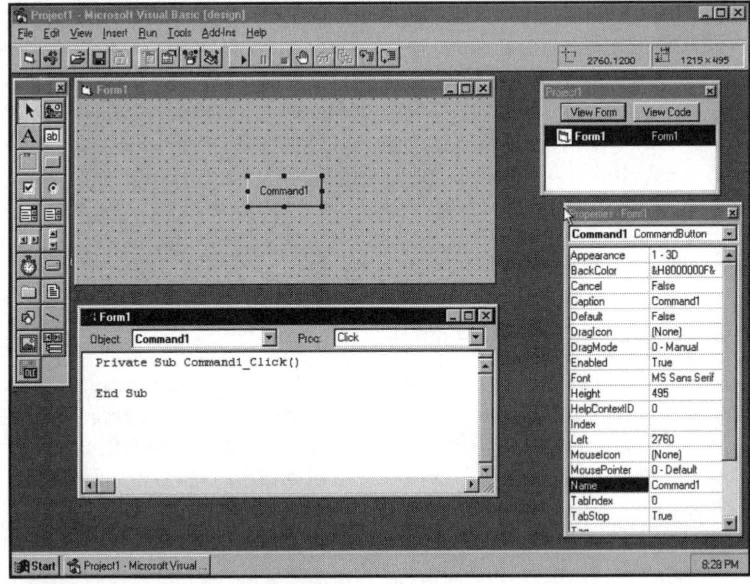

Figure 3.2
The Form1 Code window for the command button.

Run the program by clicking the Run button on the toolbar. Then click the command button. Its caption changes from `Command1` to nothing. The form should now look like that in figure 3.3.

Figure 3.3
Form1 containing a blank command button.

The button went blank because the subroutine that you wrote told it to go blank.

Event Procedures

The subroutine that you just wrote is called an *event procedure*, which is associated with an object and event pair. An event procedure executes only when its object has the focus (the object is highlighted), and its event occurs. In the preceding example, the object is the button `Command1`, and the event is the clicking of the mouse. Just for fun, stop the program (if it is still running) and then run it again. This time, click the form instead of the button. Nothing happens! The reason is that there is no event procedure associated with the `Click` event and `Form1 object` pair.

Example

To add that event procedure, stop the program again and double-click anywhere on the form. This brings up the Code window but with the `Form_Load()` subroutine.

Click the drop-down menu arrow next to the "Proc:" on this code window. This list shows events to which forms can respond. Choose Click from the list, and the Form_Click() subroutine appears in the window.

Add the following line to this subroutine:

```
Sub Form_Click ()
  Form1.Caption = ""
End Sub
```

This subroutine tells Visual Basic to change the `Caption` property of the form to blank whenever the form is clicked. The `Caption` property changes the title of the form. Run the program now to see how it works. After you have clicked both the form and the button, `Form1` should look like figure 3.4.

Figure 3.4

A form without a caption.

Now reexamine the previous examples to understand clearly the events that took place. In the first example, you created a button and defined an event procedure for the click event. When you ran the application and then clicked the button, Windows noticed that a click had taken place in a Visual Basic application's window, so Windows passed the event to Visual Basic. Visual Basic observed that the location of the cursor at the time the event occurred was over an object named `Command1`. Because Windows had identified the event as a `Click`, Visual Basic looked to see whether an event procedure existed called `Command1_Click()`. It did, so Visual Basic executed this procedure. The instructions in the procedure told Visual Basic to change the caption of the object called `Command1` to blank, so Visual Basic made this change. When the processing for this event was completed, control passed back to Windows to wait for the next occurrence of an event.

After that, you ran the application and clicked outside the command button, but still on the form. Windows detected the occurrence of this click also and passed it on to Visual Basic. Visual Basic checked and found that the form itself was the object being acted on and that the event was a click. Visual Basic looked for an event procedure for this combination of object and event, only to find that there was none. At this point, Visual Basic decided to do nothing, so it passed the control back to Windows, which also decided to do nothing.

In the second example, the same sequence of events took place, but by this time, you had defined an event procedure for `Form_Click()`. When you clicked this time, Windows passed a message about the event to Visual Basic, which executed the `Form_Click()` event procedure and then passed control back to Windows. This example illustrates that Visual Basic event procedures execute in response to object-event pairs, and not just to events.

Some events never reach the event procedure at all, because they are the responsibility of Visual Basic itself to handle. For example, run the preceding application again and turn the form into an icon by clicking the Minimize button in the upper-right corner of the window (see Fig. 3.5).

Figure 3.5
Using the Minimize button.

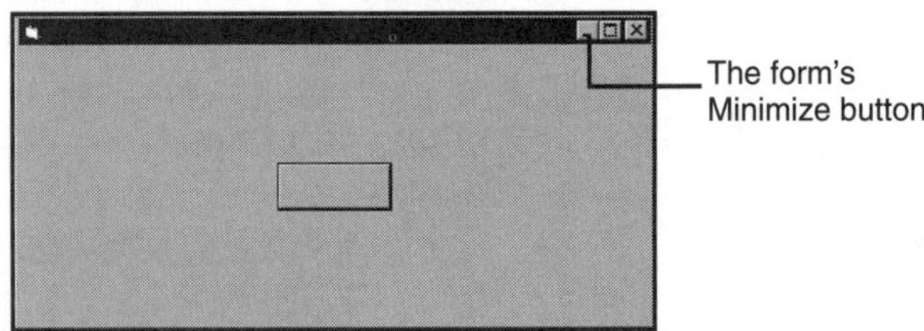

The window is minimized to the icon shown in figure 3.6.

Figure 3.6
The default icon for a minimized form.

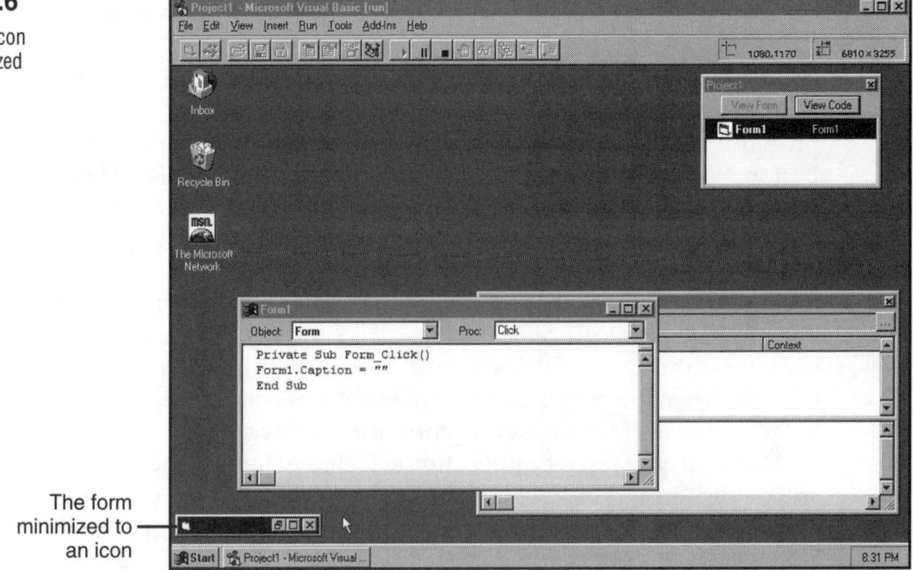

In this case, Visual Basic knew what to do without having to run any event procedure. Visual Basic received a message from Windows that a minimize event had occurred and knew how to decide which icon to use to represent the form. It decided that the appropriate place to handle this event was in Visual Basic, so it executed an event procedure that is internal to Visual Basic.

Other events never reach Visual Basic but are handled by Windows itself. When you move a window to a new position on-screen, Windows itself knows how to do this without having to bother your application or Visual Basic. Windows decides that this event is within its jurisdiction and handles it with one of its own internal routines.

In this way, you can see how the entire Windows system operates as an event-driven hierarchy of programs that respond to events. At each level in the hierarchy, the software handles events that belong to it and passes on (to a lower level) the events that don't belong to it.

The Triggering of Events

It should be clear by now that, in an event-driven architecture, the triggering of events controls all the action. At first blush, this approach would seem very restrictive because no action can occur without the appropriate event happening. Furthermore, because users differ in their preferences for the keyboard or the mouse, it would seem necessary to implement some event procedures twice—once for keyboard users and once for mouse users. Luckily, the developers of Visual Basic realized this need long ago. They have expanded the number of ways of triggering the same event so that it is almost always possible to do what you want.

Consider, for example, the number of ways you can trigger the click event. You saw earlier that this event occurs whenever you press the left mouse button. The click event can occur in response to a number of other events as well:

- ♦ On certain controls, the pressing of the right mouse button triggers the click event. This happens when the object under the cursor at the time of the click is the form itself. If, however, the object is a command button, a check box, or an option button, only the left mouse button will work.
- ♦ When a command button has the focus (the button is highlighted), pressing the space bar triggers the click event.
- ♦ If a command button's `Default` property is set to True, pressing the Enter key triggers the event.
- ♦ If a command button's `Cancel` property is set to True, pressing the Esc key triggers the event.
- ♦ If a hot key has been defined in the `Caption` property of an object, like `&Help` on a help key, the combination of Alt+H triggers the event.

- You, as programmer, can set a command button's `Value` property to True and thus trigger the event in the code.

From this list, you can see that there are a variety of ways to trigger the click event. This variety gives a programmer the control that she needs to complete a project, while still remaining faithful to the event-driven programming paradigm. The online Help facility built into Visual Basic provides similar information about the other events.

Mouse Events

A number of events can result from the user's interaction with the mouse. Each of them behaves somewhat differently. The following list briefly summarizes how each mouse-oriented event is triggered:

- `Click` occurs when a user presses the left mouse button while the mouse cursor is positioned over a control.
- `DblClick` occurs when a user presses the left mouse button twice in rapid succession, without moving the mouse. If the second click doesn't occur within the system's double-click time limit (set through Control Panel in Windows), Windows will interpret the user's actions as two separate `Click` events.
- `DragDrop` occurs when a user presses and holds down the mouse button, drags one control over another, and then releases the mouse button.
- `DragOver` occurs when a user is in the process of dragging one control over another. A special variable called `state` changes its value when the object being dragged is over a valid target. `DragOver` is used to change the cursor when the object being dragged is in the correct place to be dropped.
- `MouseDown` occurs when a user presses a mouse button.
- `MouseUp` occurs when a user releases a mouse button.
- `MouseMove` occurs when a user moves the mouse, even when no buttons are pushed. Because of `MouseMove`, your system appears to slow down when you jiggle the mouse back and forth while drawing a graphic on-screen. Windows notices every movement and communicates it to the application, giving it a chance to respond if needed. Perhaps the response should be a message box like that shown in figure 3.7.

Figure 3.7

A message box with an appropriate response.

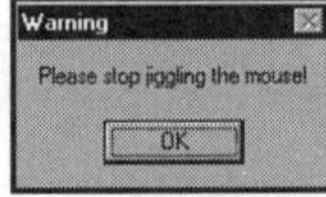

Example

In this example, you will create an image control by clicking on the Image tool in the Toolbox. Chapter 2 contains an annotated Toolbox in case you are unsure of which tool creates images. Set the value of the image's `Picture` property to the Bullseye icon. This icon can be found in the ICONS\MISC directory in the main Visual Basic directory. Add a text box to the form to allow a message to be written on the screen. Your form should now look like Figure 3.8.

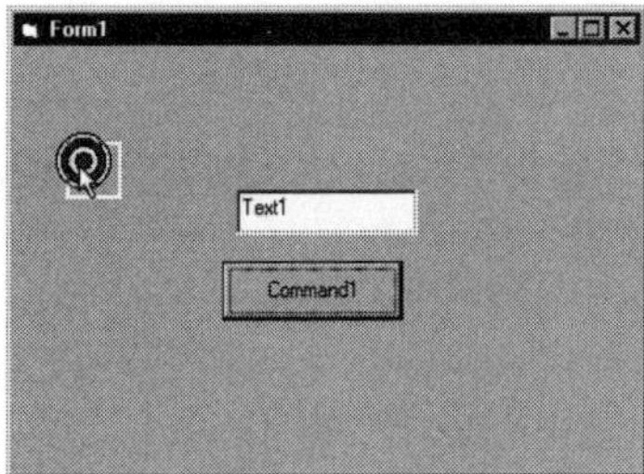

Figure 3.8
An image waiting to be dragged.

Change the image's `DragMode` property to `1 - Automatic`. This enables you to drag an outline of the bullseye around without programming. Next, add the Listing 3.1 code to the code window:

Listing 3.1 3LIST01.TXT Routines for Two Drag Events

```
Sub Image1_DragOver (Source As Control, X As Single, Y As Single,
➥State As Integer)
      Text1.Text = "You are dragging me!"
End Sub


Private Sub Image1_DragDrop (Source As Control, X As Single, Y
➥As Single)
      Text1.Text = "You dropped me!"
End Sub
```

Now, you are ready to run the program. Click on the Run button on the Toolbar. When the window appears, place your mouse pointer over the bullseye. While holding down the mouse button, move the mouse around within the form and see that a square moves with it. Also notice that the text in the text box now reads "You are dragging me!" Finally, drop the square over the bullseye where it came from by releasing the mouse button. Observe that the text in the text box changes to "You dropped me!"

What is happening in this example is fairly simple. When you pressed the mouse button, you triggered an event called `DragOver`. The instruction that you put in the `DragOver` event procedure for this object, `Image1`, is to change the text in the text box to the phrase "You are dragging me!" When you were finished dragging and released the mouse button over its original location, the event `DragDrop` was triggered by Windows. Your instruction in this event procedure was "You dropped me!"

The number of different mouse events may seem like overkill. However, they provide the programmer with the degree of control necessary to produce applications with the professional look and feel expected by today's users.

Keyboard Events

Keyboard events enable the application to monitor the keyboard input that is being passed to a program, and to modify that input if necessary. The main purpose of these events is input validation. This category has the following three main events:

- `KeyPress` occurs when a key is pressed (note: the event occurs on the downstroke and will, in fact, repeat as the keyboard auto-repeats characters). `KeyPress` is directed to the object that currently has the focus. If no object has the focus, or if the form's KeyPreview property is set, the event is directed to the form. The `KeyPress` event's parameter is the ASCII code for the key that was pressed. Because the codes of lowercase characters are different from those of uppercase characters, you could write an event procedure to capitalize the input if desired.
- `KeyDown` occurs when a key is pressed.
- `KeyUp` occurs when a key is released.

The keyboard events give the programmer the control needed to verify input in a professional manner. If a user presses a letter key when a numeric key is required, the program is expected to give the user an error message and an opportunity to respond correctly. The keyboard events provide an easy way for a programmer to exercise low-level jurisdiction over a program without having to write in a low-level language.

If the form's `KeyPreview` property is set, then all keystrokes are passed to the form's keystroke handler event routines before being passed on to controls. This can be very useful. For example, you may want to have a dialog with a group of command buttons, and allow your users to select one by pressing a letter. Normally, they have to press Alt+letter. However, if you intercept the keystrokes at the form layer, you can test for the keystrokes you want to act on, and execute whatever code you wish when they are pressed.

Example

This is a simple example of how these events work together. Create a form that contains two text boxes, `Text1` and `Text2`. Add the Listing 3.2 code to the form:

Listing 3.2 3LIST02.TXT Keyboard Event Routines

```
Sub Text1_KeyDown (KeyCode As Integer, Shift As Integer)
   Text2.Text = "The KeyDown Event Occurred"
End Sub

Sub Text1_KeyUp (KeyCode As Integer, Shift As Integer)
   Text2.Text = "The KeyUp Event Occurred"
End Sub
```

Run this program by clicking on the Run button in the Toolbar. This brings up a window that looks like the one shown in Figure 3.9.

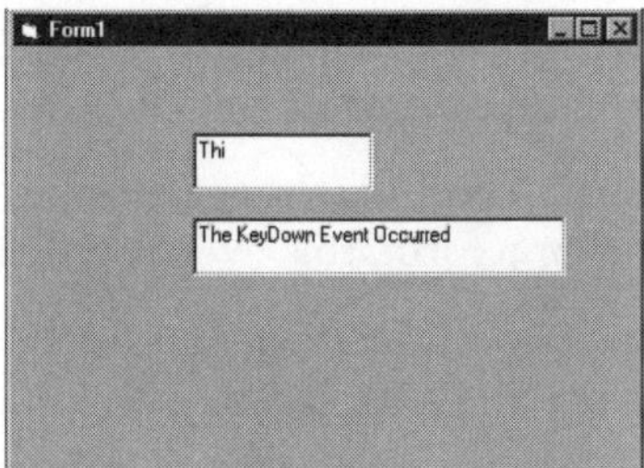

Figure 3.9
Running the KeyDown example.

Notice that every time you press a key while editing the first text box, `Text2`'s text reads `The KeyDown event occurred`. When you release the key, `Text2` reads `The KeyUp event occurred`. In both of these events, the parameters passed are KeyCode and Shift. The KeyCode parameter is the ASCII code of the key that was pressed, and the Shift parameter is the state of the modifier keys (for example, Alt, Shift, Ctrl).

This example shows how much control Visual Basic gives the programmer to respond to any number of events that users create while running Windows.

State-Change Events

Programmers find it useful to perform certain actions when something starts or changes. Visual Basic was written to trap certain state-change events so that you, as programmer, have a chance to perform actions if you choose. Here are the events in this category:

- `Activate` occurs when a form becomes the active window. Normally, a Visual Basic application is a set of one or more windows. Each of these windows is represented by a Visual Basic form. When a window is selected by a user to be the active one (usually by clicking on it), this event occurs, and the event procedure associated with it executes.

- `Deactivate` occurs when the user moves from one form to another. The `Deactivate` event gives the programmer a chance to tie up any loose ends that may exist in the first form.

- `GotFocus` occurs when an object becomes the one in focus, usually through a user action like clicking or tabbing. The form receives the focus by default whenever the form is the active window, yet no control on the form has the focus.
- `LostFocus` occurs when an object loses the focus, which normally happens when another control gets the focus.
- `Load` occurs when a form is loaded. This event is trapped so that you, as programmer, have an opportunity to do some processing whenever a form is loaded. If the form being loaded is the startup form, you will have a routine that runs every time the application starts.
- `Unload` occurs when a form is being unloaded from the program by a user action like closing a Control menu or by an `Unload` statement in code.
- `Initialize` occurs when an application creates an instance of a form or class. For a form, this event occurs before the `Load` event.
- `Terminate` occurs when all references to a form or class is removed from memory. For a form, this event occurs after the `Unload` event.
- `Paint` occurs when a form needs to be repainted (anytime a form that was covered up has been exposed). The `Paint` event occurs also when a window has been moved or enlarged if that change exposes part of the window previously covered.
- `Resize` occurs whenever a form has changed size. `Resize` normally is used as an opportunity to recalculate the size of objects contained within a form when its size changes.
- `Change` occurs when the contents of a control have changed.
- `QueryUnload` occurs when an application is closing. The `QueryUnload` event is typically used to make sure that all cleanup has occurred, such as saving data before closing. This event occurs on every form before any form is actually unloaded.

By using these state-change events, you can manage your applications to a fine level of control and appearance.

Link Events

Links are instances of object linking and embedding (OLE) technology. Linking is fully covered in Chapter 15, "The Data, Grid, and OLE Tools." Using linking, you can display data from other applications, such as Microsoft Excel and CorelDRAW!, in your Visual Basic applications. Linking gives your application a very sophisticated look and feel. The link events that support OLE are these:

- `LinkOpen` occurs when another application initiates a dynamic data exchange (DDE) conversation with the form. `LinkOpen` occurs for controls when they initiate a DDE session with a source application.
- `LinkClose` occurs at the end of a DDE session when the conversation terminates.
- `LinkExecute` occurs when one application sends a command to the Visual Basic application in a DDE conversation.
- `LinkError` occurs when an error condition develops during a DDE session.
- `LinkNotify` occurs when the source application changes the data that is connected to your Visual Basic application.

These link events enable you to manage the embedded and linked objects in your programs.

Miscellaneous Events

Another group of events exists to service very specific requirements. The events in this category include the following:

- `Timer` occurs when a preset timer event elapses. `Timer` is associated with the Timer control only. It enables you to write an application that sends itself an event at some future time.
- `Scroll` occurs when a user drags the little box inside a scroll bar. `Scroll` is meaningful only to scroll bars.
- `PathChange` occurs whenever the default path for file lookup changes. `PathChange` applies to only the File list box.
- `PatternChange` occurs when the listing pattern changes. This pattern includes wild cards (such as *.*) that users put into a File list box to designate which files they want to see displayed. This event only applies to the File ListBox.
- `Validate` occurs before a record becomes the current record (that is, just before an `Update`, `Delete`, `Unload`, or `Close` operation). One of the parameters tells the routine what action caused the event. `Validate` allows the programmer to make sure that the data is being handled properly.
- `SelChange` occurs when a Grid control is being used. A Grid control displays data in a matrix. One of its uses is a table of possible picks, like the big board in a Jeopardy game. One place in the matrix might be "Famous Places for $200," whereas another cell could be "Authors for $100." The `SelChange` event would occur whenever the user clicked on a different square.

- `Scroll` occurs whenever a scroll bar's thumb (the little box) is moved. This enables you to move the text of a window up and down continuously as the user is manipulating the scroll bar. Because this event fires so many times for even a short movement, it is important to avoid complicated event procedures when using this class of event procedures.

Summary

The event-driven programming paradigm enables you to develop systems that fit more naturally the way people want to do their work. It enables you to concentrate on one control and the events that can affect it. By tying code to events, you can write programs that monitor (and react to) not only the mouse and keyboard but system activities as well. By taking advantage of event notifications, you can produce systems that are much more complex than can be managed effectively with linear programming techniques.

Review Questions

Answers to the questions can be found in Appendix A.

1. What is an event?
2. What is an event-driven programming language?

3. What is an event procedure?
4. How are events triggered?

5. What is a state-change event?
6. How do timer events differ from the other Visual Basic events?

Review Exercises

1. Write a program that contains a command button that displays your name when it is clicked.

2. Write a program that changes the `Caption` property of a form to blanks whenever a key is pressed, but then returns it to normal when the key is released.

3. Write a program that changes the caption of the form to "You are a dragger" whenever an image control is being dragged.

The Windows Environment

In 1990, when Microsoft announced Windows 3.0, most programmers were very comfortable writing programs for the DOS environment. Although they loved the look and feel of the Windows graphical user interface, they feared the increased complexity that this new programming environment imposed on them. Instead of learning a few programming language statements, programmers now had to learn a complex application programming interface (the notorious Windows API) and a strange new architecture. At the time, BASIC was one of the most popular languages available for the PC. However, there was no Windows version of it. All flavors of BASIC were DOS-based compilers. At one point, there was an OS/2 version of Microsoft's, Professional Development System, but the support was dropped at the release of version 6.0. Prior to the release of Visual Basic, the only available Windows programming languages were either slow, difficult to learn, or both.

In this chapter, you learn what Windows programming is like so that you can appreciate better what Visual Basic is doing to help you, as a programmer. You review the basic terms and concepts associated with Windows, and most importantly, you learn about the online Help system.

The History of Windows

Many programmers don't realize that Microsoft first announced Windows back in 1983. The company released the first version, Windows 1.01, in November of 1985. The product was not a great success in those days, nor did it create much of a ripple in 1987 when release 2.0 came out. Windows, in its early years, was more of a user interface than an operating environment. Several factors slowed its acceptance, but the main one was the massive base of DOS applications that had been written for the PC. The programmers of the PC's first decade were creating good programs that were selling well. They didn't have much incentive to change their main-line programming environment for the purpose of improving only the look and feel of their applications.

In May of 1990, Windows 3.0 was released. Starting with this release, Windows could use the protected mode of the Intel 80286, 80386, and 80486 microprocessors. What this meant to programmers was that they now had access to 16 megabytes (M) of addressable memory instead of 640 kilobytes (K). By this time, the user community was demanding that more features be put in the programs than could fit naturally in 640K of memory. Many convoluted schemes had been devised to circumvent this limitation, but none of them was really satisfying. The combination of the ever-improving user interface, this memory management innovation, and a ton of hype by Microsoft enabled Windows to reach critical mass and explode onto the desktops of the world.

The success of Windows has resulted in a huge increase in the demand for applications. Thousands of users who had resisted learning DOS readily embraced Windows. Many users refused even to consider purchasing or developing new DOS applications. Software vendors, always sensitive to user preferences, have scrambled to meet this demand. The success of a few vendors (Microsoft included) in producing blockbuster Windows applications placed incredible pressure on the entire software industry to knock the user community's socks off every 10 or 12 months.

Writing Windows programs by using C or C++ and the applications programming interface (API) is not easy. There are over 1,000 separate function calls in the Windows API, each with five or six parameters. To make matters worse, C++ is a difficult language for many people to master. This difficulty, coupled with the need to write applications quickly, has created a huge market for products like Visual Basic.

With Visual Basic, a programmer can produce an application that is as rich as the C or C++ version about 90 percent of the time. A programming team made up of application specialists like accountants or industrial engineers, along with a few heavy C++ programmers, can knock out applications using Visual Basic. In this scenario, the application specialists use Visual Basic to design screens that users will like. These specialists call on the C++ programmers to develop customs when extensive low-level access, or extremely speed-sensitive code is required.

Windows Anatomy 101

To understand the Windows operating system, you have to understand the anatomy of a window. The concept of the Windows operating system is based on the desktop metaphor. On your desk, you normally have a large surface on which you place documents, photographs, magazines, and so on. When you want to focus on one of the documents, you bring it to the top and look at it. When you are finished with it, you either file it, set it aside, or throw it away. At times, you want to use three or four documents simultaneously, so you lay them side by side, or put one document on top of the others for a few minutes and then pull another up to the top.

Windows was written with a close mapping to this desktop analogy. The entire face of your screen represents your desktop. Each window represents a document. If you click a partially covered window, you bring it to the top of the pile. The scroll bars allow you to "turn the page" of multipage documents. To file a document away, you access the Save As properties sheet, give the document a name, and put it in a folder. To find the file later, you click the File Manager icon and retrieve the document from the folder back to the desktop. When you want to keep a document nearby, you minimize it so that it will be a click away when you need it. All these actions involve the use of the controls built into Windows itself. Figure 4.1 shows an annotated window. The paragraphs that follow describe the basic parts of the window.

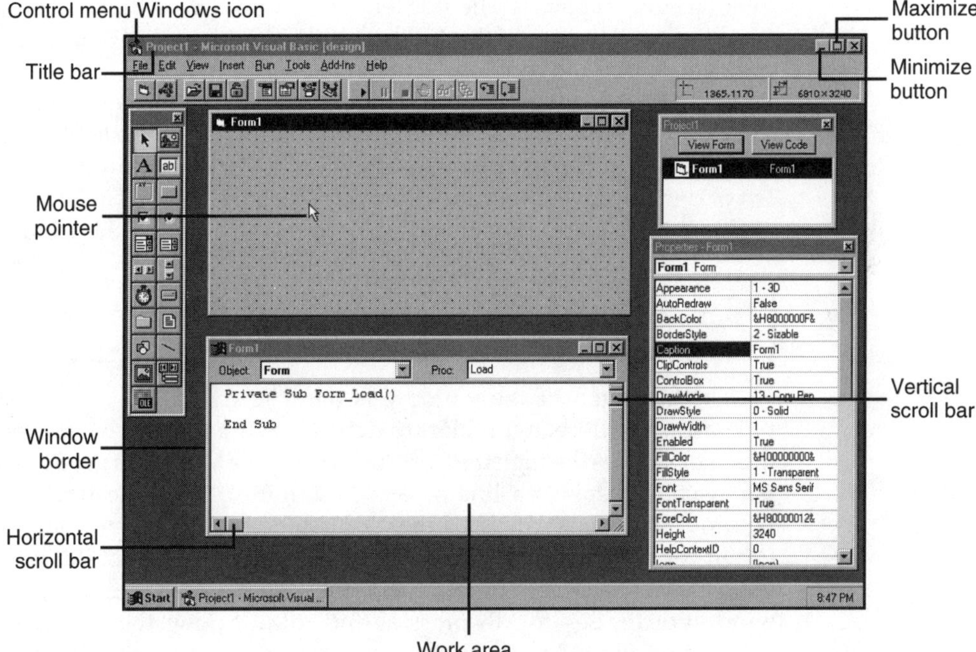

Figure 4.1
The basic parts of a window.

You use the *control menu icon* to access the Control menu, which gives the user a way to manipulate the window as a whole. The icon that is displayed is dependent on the program that is running (for example, Word would have the Word icon displayed). By using the Control menu, you can restore, move, size, minimize, maximize, close, or switch to another window. All these actions can be performed in other non-menu ways, but some users prefer to use the Control menu. In a Multiple Document Interface (MDI) application, a smaller icon appears in the corner of each child window as well.

An important part of a window is the *border* surrounding it. Each window can contain eight controls. These controls are used to change the size and shape of the window. Four of the controls, one in each corner, allow you to stretch the window in two directions at once. By placing the cursor on one of these corners, you can change both the height and the width at the same time. The other four controls are the four sides of the rectangular window. By placing the cursor on one of the side controls, the user can change the width but not the height of the window. By placing the cursor on the top or bottom control, the user can change the height but not the width of the window. As you move the mouse around the border, it will change according to the location on the border. In Visual Basic, you can create an application that has no border controls if you want.

The *window border outline* appears only when a window is being resized or moved. When a user grabs one of the resizing controls and moves it, a shadowy-looking border appears. This border outline moves with the cursor and lets the user visualize what the size of the window will be if he lets go of the mouse button at any moment during the resizing.

The *scroll bars* are really part of the application, but they are so prevalent that most people think of them as parts of the window. With the *horizontal scroll bar*, you can display a document that is much wider than the window itself; you simply pan left or right to view the entire document. Using the *vertical scroll bar*, you can pan up or down to display a document that is much longer than the window itself.

Note: It should be noted that MDI forms can also have scroll bars.

Across the top of the window is the colored *title bar*, which serves several purposes. First, it changes colors to signify that the window has the focus. You make the color choices through the Control Panel in the Main icon group. Second, the title bar usually displays a line of text describing the application that created the window. The bar normally shows something like `Microsoft Word - CHAPTER4.DOC`. When you are creating a Visual Basic application, the text of this bar is fully under your control as programmer. Third, the title bar provides a way to relocate the window on the desktop. By pressing and holding down the mouse button while the cursor is positioned on the title bar, the user can drag the window to a new location and drop it there. The window border outline follows the cursor to show the user where the window will be moved.

> **Note:** The title bar of an MDI parent will automatically display the contents of the title bar of a maximized child to the right of the contents of the parent caption.

The primary means of control for the window environment is the *mouse pointer*. The current location of the mouse is indicated by the location of the mouse pointer, whose default shape is that of an arrow. The mouse pointer changes shape to indicate that the CPU is busy (an hourglass), the pointer is over a border control (a double-arrow), or the pointer is in an area where text entry is legal (an I-shaped bar). These are but a few of the many types of mouse icons that you will encounter while using different Windows applications.

You use the *Maximize button* to change the size of the window to the maximum size possible on your screen. The maximum size is the familiar full screen. When a window is maximized, this button changes to the Restore button (discussed a bit later). In addition, you can toggle a form between maximized and restored states by double-clicking on the title bar.

You use the *Minimize button* to reduce the window to an icon placed near the bottom of the desktop. In Visual Basic, you can differentiate your form icons by changing the Icon property of the form. A default icon that looks like the one in figure 4.2 is used if you, as programmer, have not given a specific instruction about which icon to use.

The *Restore button* restores a maximized window to its original window size. This button enables a user to switch easily between full-size and window modes. Figure 4.2 shows the Restore button.

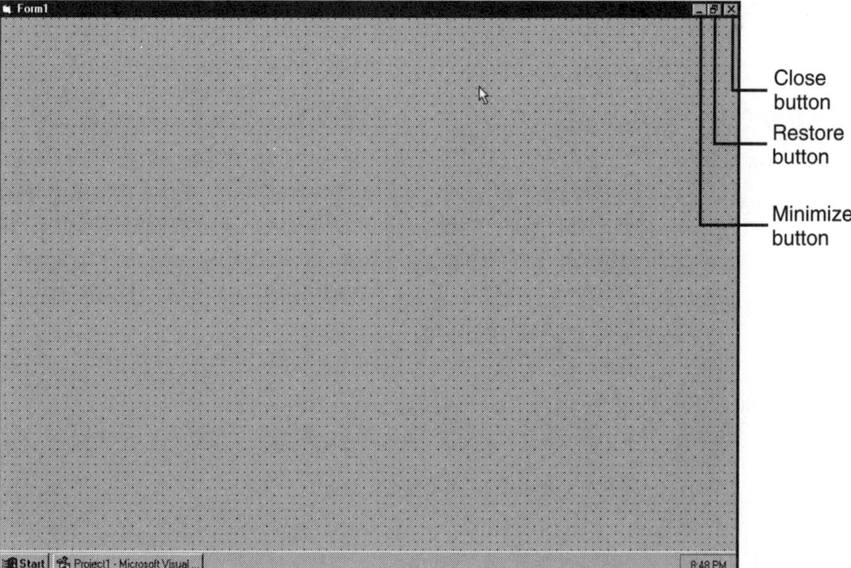

Figure 4.2

The Restore button.

In most applications, the *menu bar* gives the user a number of menu commands. What happens after a menu choice is made is the responsibility of the application programmer who created the window.

Windows makes extensive use of *icons*. An *icon* is simply a small bit-mapped picture. Programs usually are started with the click of an icon, but minimized windows are represented as icons, too. Clicking a minimized icon restores it to the size and state it was in when it was minimized.

Figure 4.3 shows the default Visual Basic form icon. Visual Basic has a slew of icons that you can choose from, but, if none is specified, it defaults to this one.

Figure 4.3
The default Visual Basic form icon.

A *properties sheet* is another window that displays the available options when some commands are entered. Sometimes properties sheets are used to warn or notify the users of an event that has occurred. At other times a properties sheet is used to give the user a set of controls to perform an action like opening a file. Visual Basic gives you, as programmer, considerable control over the placement of properties sheets in your applications. Generally, properties sheets cannot be resized and must be acted upon before the application can continue. Figure 4.4 shows an example of a properties sheet.

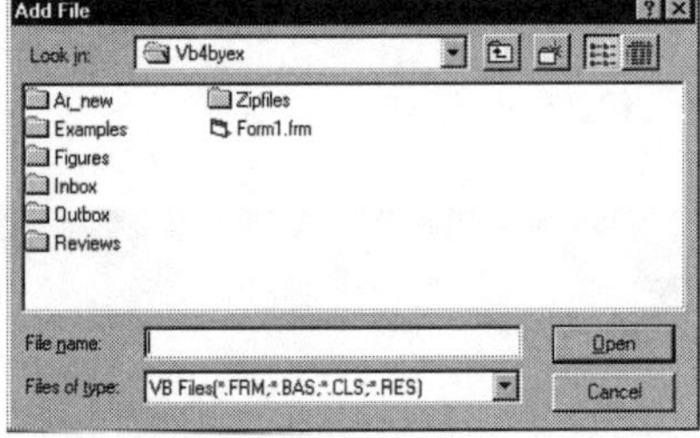

Figure 4.4
An example properties sheet.

The part of the window located below the menu bar, above the bottom border, and within the window borders is called the *client area*. This is the area available for working on your program or creating child windows. In this area, you draw pictures, write text, display bitmaps, and perform other tasks.

Windows Processing

To further your general education, consider for a moment how Windows works. You learned about the concept of events in Chapter 3, "Event-Driven Programming." The entire Windows system is based on handling events like keypresses or mouse clicks, and then interpreting the user's intentions to determine what the resulting state of the application should be. The resulting state has three components:

- The appearance of the screen
- The values of the variables in your program
- The contents of the disk files associated with the application

Thinking of Windows with this *event-resulting state model* in mind makes it much simpler to understand and to program. When writing programs, you need to decide only three things:

1. What is the state of the program?
2. What events should the program react to?
3. What resulting action should each event cause? What state should the program be in after this action completes?

After you make these decisions, you return to question 1 for each of the resulting states for each event. Eventually, when you have written code to handle every possible event in every possible resulting state, your program is ready to test. After the testing has verified that your program is reacting properly to every event, you are ready to release the program and become a millionaire (that's why you bought this book, isn't it?).

Using Help

Buying this book is a very good way to get a jump start on Visual Basic. After you have made your first solo flight in Visual Basic, however, you will need a source of continuing education. In Visual Basic, as in most well-written Windows programs, the online Help system is that source. You're contemplating a world-class set of automated documents here, not just another tired old set of tips and boring text. Over time, as the Help system has gotten better and manuals have gotten skinnier, the Help system has become a superior source of information to the manuals. In fact, some CD-ROM software is being shipped without manuals at all. Everything needed is included in the Help system on the CD itself. To survive in a world of electronic Help, you need to be very good at finding what you want through the Help system interface.

To start the Help system, follow these steps:

1. Start Visual Basic and click Help on the menu bar.
2. Choose Contents. The Help window shown in figure 4.5 appears.
3. Choose the type of help you want.

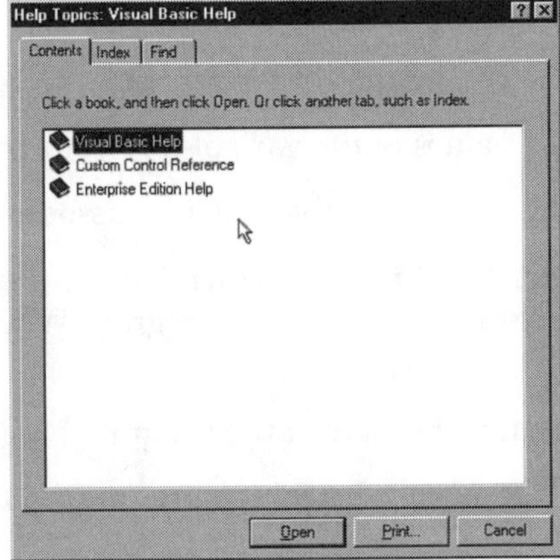

Figure 4.5
The Visual Basic Help window.

The Help Menu Bar

In figure 4.5, you see a window with three Book icons on it. To open the Visual Basic Help Book, click on the Open button at the bottom of the form. You will then get several Topic icons for Visual Basic Help as shown in figure 4.6. Since these figures were captured using the Enterprise Edition of Visual Basic, there is a Help topic for it. Each version of Visual Basic will include its own Help topic.

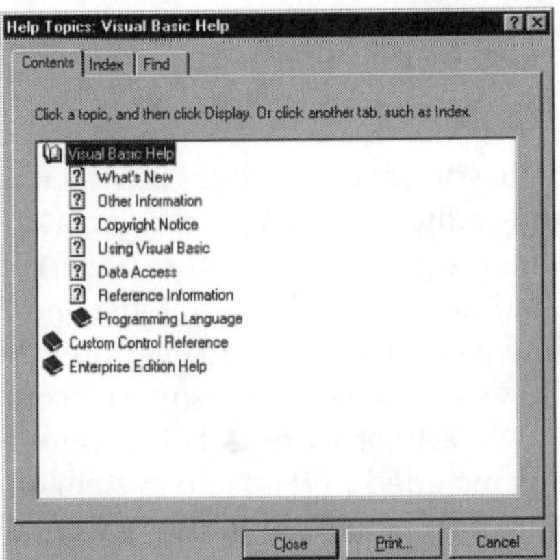

Figure 4.6
The Help Topics: Visual Basic Help window.

The Help system will show you through several different selection screens until you get to the topic you need, as shown in figure 4.7.

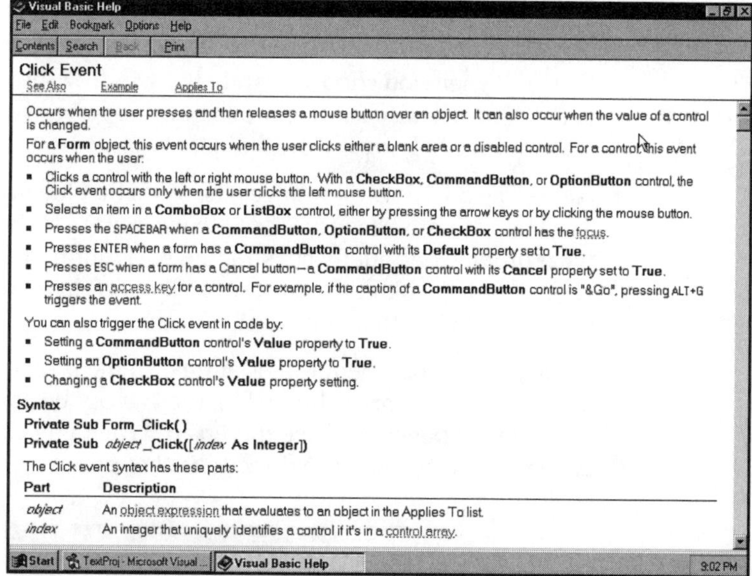

Figure 4.7

The `Click` event Help window.

At the top of the window is a menu bar with the following choices:

- *File*—The File menu enables you to Open a different help file, Print a topic, set up your Printer, and Exit from the Help system.
- *Edit*—You use the Edit menu to copy text to the Clipboard. Copying to the Clipboard is especially useful when you find a piece of code in the Help system and you want to include it in one of your event procedures. Another option on the Edit menu is Annotate. It displays an electronic pad where you can make notes to yourself. These notes will be marked with a paper clip in the upper-left part of the Help page that they pertain to. If you click on the paper clip icon, you can read, edit, or delete the annotation.
- *Bookmark*—The Bookmark menu enables you to perform a function analogous to placing a bookmark in a book. You can go to an interesting screen, choose Define from the Bookmark menu, and give the bookmark a name like *Section on the Grid Control*. This name becomes a new menu pick under the Bookmark menu. If you select this new name from anywhere in the Help system, you jump immediately to the place where you were when you created the bookmark. You can create several bookmarks for each Help file.

The Toolbar

Below the menu bar is a Toolbar. Note the first two buttons:

- *Contents*—When you choose Contents, you see the window shown earlier in figure 4.5.
- *Search*—When you choose Search, the window shown in figure 4.8 appears. You will also see a tab for Find. This gives you a more detailed search of the help text instead of just keywords.
- *Back*—The Back button retraces the steps that led you to the current screen. The Help system keeps track of what screens you have viewed, and in what order. Continually clicking the Back button traverses your path in reverse order. This feature is especially useful when you have made an unfruitful choice that you want to undo.
- *History*—The History button is similar to the Back button, but instead of taking you to the preceding page, the History button provides a window listing every page you have traversed. When you click the name of the page you want, you jump directly to that page.

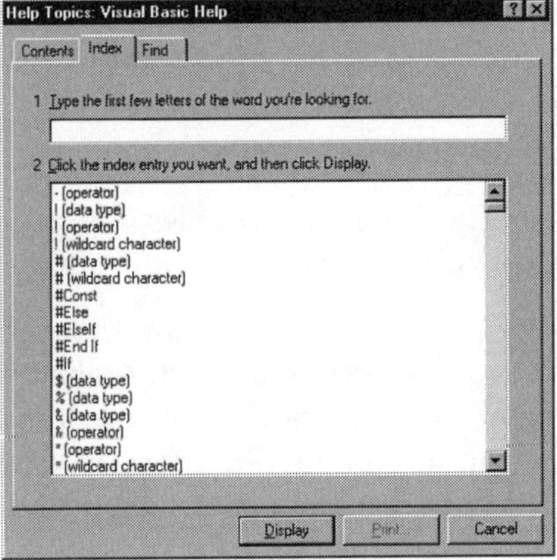

Figure 4.8

The Index tab search window.

The Search window gives you a powerful keyword-search capability. Run a test search as follows to see how to use it:

1. While in the Contents window (refer to fig. 4.5), click the Index tab at the top of the form. A window appears like that in figure 4.8. The cursor is in the input box.
2. Type the word **click** and watch the keyword box change its values as you type each of the letters. When you finish typing, the keyword box will be filled with references starting with the `Click` event.

3. Select the Click Event topic and then click the Display button. This takes you to the Help page shown in figure 4.7 above.

The Click Event Help window gives a lot of detail about how to use the `Click` event. You can click "See Also" for a list of related topics, and you can click Example to bring up a code example. Figure 4.9 shows what happens when you click Example in the Click Event Help window.

The Applies To link tells the reader which tools can respond to this event. *Links* are special commands to the Help system; a green word with solid underline is a jump type link (jumps to a related page) and a dotted underline is a pop-up link (short description pops up over current page).

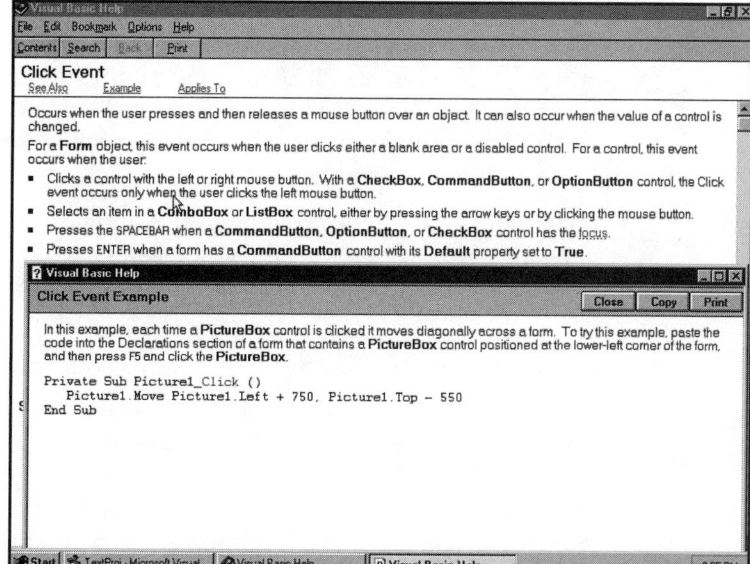

Figure 4.9
The Example window.

At this point, you can copy the code to the Clipboard and then include it in your program. This is a great way to get a jump start on a new feature that you want to use in a program.

Other Topics

Now, refer back to figure 4.6 to continue the discussion of the Help window features. The section just below the window's title, Visual Basic Help, contains seven sub-topics. You can access these by double-clicking the words themselves. The following information is available:

- *What's New*—This section summarizes the new features of this version of Visual Basic. It contains information on the following topics: Visual Basic, Applications Edition, OLE Automation, Creating Custom Objects and Collections, Property Procedures, 32-Bit Support and Conditional Compilation, Build Your Own Object Applications, and JET 3.0.
- *Other Information*—A list of additional help files that are available on other topics, such as data storage and custom control development.
- *Copyright*—This is the obligatory claim to various rights that software lawyers always make programmers put into our software packages. None of us knows what any of it means, and the lawyers like it that way.
- *Using Visual Basic*—This section allows a user to get information about how to perform certain common tasks such as setting properties and creating user interfaces. It also contains a tutorial on how to learn Visual Basic. The best time to use this section is when you are interested in looking for information on an activity like debugging, and not on a single command or property.
- *Data Access*—This topic provides information on topics related to the use of databases from within Visual Basic. It contains sections on ODBC, bound controls, the JET Database Engine, and other related topics.
- *Reference Information*—Reference information pertaining to the user interface, constants, the character set and keywords are provided in this section.
- *Programming Language Summary*—This section provides you with an alphabetized listing of Visual Basic features. This section contains subheadings that break the list of language features into smaller topics like Functions, Properties, Methods, Statements, Events, Objects, and Keywords. The real value of this section is when you know the name of an element of the language, but are not sure of the syntax or usage.

The Contents page contains one more main topic:

- *Custom Control Reference*—This topic contains information pertaining to all the available custom controls that come with Visual Basic.

  This kind of information can be very helpful to a developer because it frees him/her from the time-consuming chore of thumbing through manuals for obscure details. Next, we will run an example of using the Help facility to speed up the writing of a program.

Example

This example uses the online Help system to write a `Form1_Click` event procedure that uses the `MsgBox` function. Start by creating a new project that has an empty main form, Form1. Since we want to attach the `MsgBox` function to the `Click` event, simply double-click on the form anywhere. When the Code window comes up, choose the `Click` event from the list box labeled Proc:. This will cause an empty `Form1_Click` subroutine to appear in the body of the Code window.

Next, choose Search For Help On from the Help menu. When the Index tab window appears, type **MsgBox** in the text box on the dialog box. When the topics appear at the bottom of the Search window (see fig. 4.10), highlight the MsgBox topic and click the Display button or press Enter.

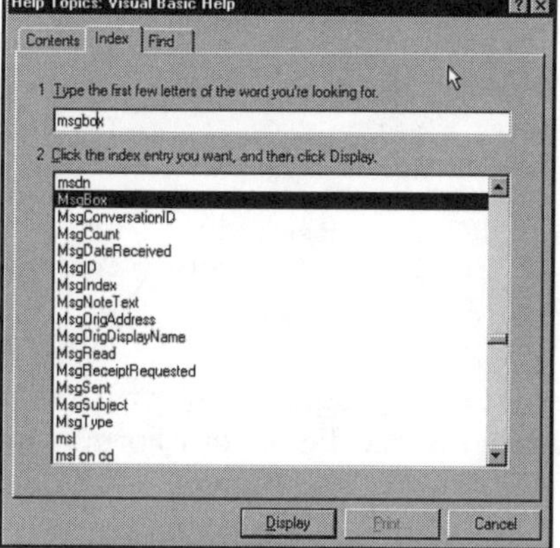

Figure 4.10

Using the Index tab search window.

The Help Topic associated with the `MsgBox` function appears in a window. By clicking the green text that reads Example, you bring up an additional window that displays some sample code that uses the `MsgBox` function (see fig. 4.11).

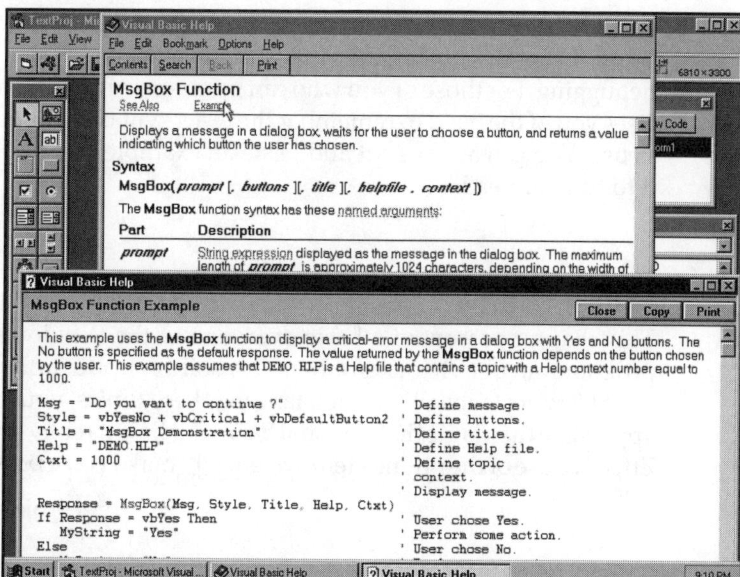

Figure 4.11

Looking at a Help topic.

Highlight the code portion that you wish to copy and click the Copy button. This moves the highlighted text to the clipboard. Next, open the code window to the `Form1_Click` event procedure and paste the code from the Clipboard. The result will look like the following code:

```
Private Sub Form_Click()
Msg = "Do you want to continue ?"    ' Define message.
Style = vbYesNo + vbCritical + vbDefaultButton2 ' Define buttons.
Title = "MsgBox Demonstration"   ' Define title.
Help = "DEMO.HLP"    ' Define Help file.
Ctxt = 1000 ' Define topic
        ' context.
        ' Display message.
Response = MsgBox(Msg, Style, Title, Help, Ctxt)
If Response = vbYes Then      ' User chose Yes.
    MyString = "Yes"     ' Perform some action.
Else    ' User chose No.
    MyString = "No" ' Perform some action.
End If
End Sub
```

Next, run the program and verify that when you click the form the message box appears in the middle of your Form1 window as shown in figure 4.12.

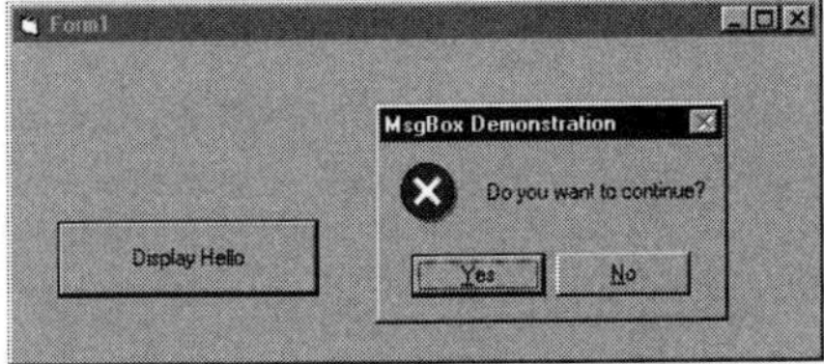

Figure 4.12

Running the example with the borrowed code pasted in.

By using this technique, you can save yourself many hours of typing and debugging. For those of you who can program in four or five languages, this facility frees you of the need to remember the exact syntax of the commands that you want to use. You can always cut and paste an example into your code and then modify it to fit your needs.

Summary

This chapter presented a basic overview of the Windows operating system as a programming environment. It gave a solid introduction to its architecture and a brief historical view. By understanding these topics, you are in a better position to appreciate the magic that is Visual Basic and how it really does make your job easier. Effective use of the online Help system will make you a power programmer sooner.

Review Questions

1. What is a dialog box?
2. What is the Control menu?
3. What is the Windows API?

4. What are the three components of a program's state?

Review Exercises

1. Use the online Help system to find the support phone numbers for Visual Basic.

2. Use the Search button on the button bar to look up the help topic on the `MouseMove` event.

3. Use the online Help system to find the meaning of error code 11. (*Hint:* This is a trappable error.)
4. Use the online Help system to look up the `Print` method. Copy the code from the Help window and paste it into the code for a command button's `Click` event. Run the program.

Projects

A Visual Basic application is composed of a number of different files, each filling a specific role. Visual Basic creates a complete application by processing these files to form an executable file. Because keeping up with so many component files is such a chore, the Visual Basic designers have provided you, the programmer, with a tool called the Project window. In this chapter, you examine the role of the Project window in application development.

The Value of Projects

As applications have become more sophisticated, so has the task of managing their components. Much of this complexity results from the fact that Visual Basic components are stored in separate files. A project consists of the following types of files:

- *Form files (FRM)*. As discussed in Chapter 2, "Visual Basic Programs," an application is made up of one or more forms. Stored with each form is its property settings (such as color, size, and location) and the controls you have placed on the forms. In essence, the form file records the details of the form you designed, exactly as you saved it when you were in design mode. All the code that you wrote for each control is stored there also, along with any variables and general procedures. If your application has multiple forms, each of the forms has its own FRM file.

- *Code module files (BAS)*. Sophisticated applications often contain complex logic and calculations. Many times, this code is independent of any particular control or form and can be called from a number of places in the same application. Code of this sort usually is stored in a separate file called a *code module*. These files end in the BAS extension, which is short for BASIC. Routines that are useful in more than one application normally are stored in code modules to minimize duplication of effort. You can build many executable files using the same code module file.

- *Class module files (.CLS)*. You can create new, custom objects using Visual Basic. These objects are instances of *classes*, and are stored in *class modules*. These objects have their own methods and properties. For a complete discussion of classes, see Que's *Using Visual Basic 4.0*.

- *Resource files (.RES)*. Each Visual Basic application can have, at most, one resource file. Resource files contain strings and bitmaps that can be displayed at runtime. The most common use of resource files is to provide different languages in the user interface to users in foreign countries. There also are performance advantages to using resource files, because storing the strings in a file removes the need to store literals within the program itself.

- *Custom control files (.OCX)*. Custom controls or add-ins are extensions to the functionality of Visual Basic and are typically written by third-party developers. The authors of these custom controls must follow strict coding practices so that the controls will look and act as if they are a natural part of Visual Basic. Many different custom controls come with the standard edition of Visual Basic: the grid control (GRID.OCX), the OLE control (OLE.OCX), and the common dialog control (CMDIALOG.OCX). When a custom control is added to a project, an icon is added to the toolbox, and an OCX file is added to the Project window. Each separate control is stored in its own file, with an .OCX extension.

  A brisk market in third-party custom controls has recently developed. Companies specialize in creating and marketing these controls, which are called Visual Basic extensions, or simply VBXs. Generalized versions of custom controls are called OLE control extensions (OCX). An OCX will work with any OLE-compliant environment, such as Visual C++ or Borland C++, as well as with Visual Basic. The purpose for VBXs and OCXs are the same, however. The OCX version is more general. Microsoft's plan is to shift from VBX files to OCX files as quickly as possible to simplify the support on only one standard.

- *The project file (.VBP)*. The project file contains information about the project, including component files that you, the developer, have chosen for creating your application. This file also contains the settings for the options you chose for this project. Project files contain the extension .VBP.

Microsoft Visual Basic enables you to combine and process all the preceding types of files into an *executable file (.EXE)*. The goal of a Visual Basic project is to produce a file that can be run directly under Windows. When you have finished the development of your application, you instruct Visual Basic to create the executable file. This file can then be distributed to your customers, and they can use it to do their work. Executable files end with the extension .EXE. Figure 5.1 shows the relationships of the files in a project.

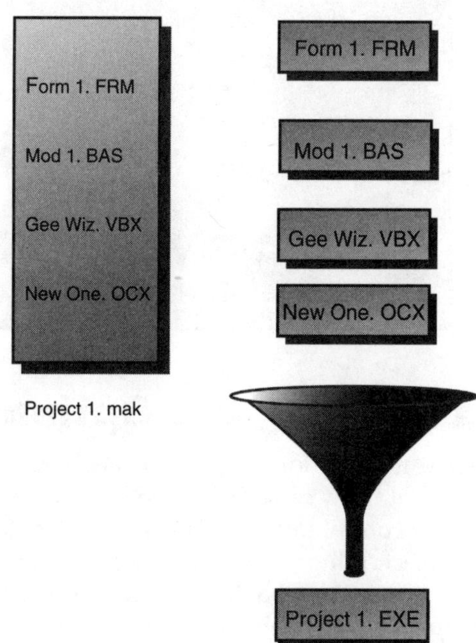

Figure 5.1
The application building process.

This chapter gives you instruction on the mechanics of creating a project. In Chapter 29, "Planning an Application," you learn how to plan a successful project.

Creating a New Project

To create a new project, all you have to do is start Visual Basic by double-clicking the Visual Basic icon in the Visual Basic application group. The Visual Basic screens will appear with a new project, called Project1, on-screen. The title bar contains the name of the project. As a rule, give your projects names other than Project1 to avoid possible confusion (see fig. 5.2). The Project window contents become the components of the executable.

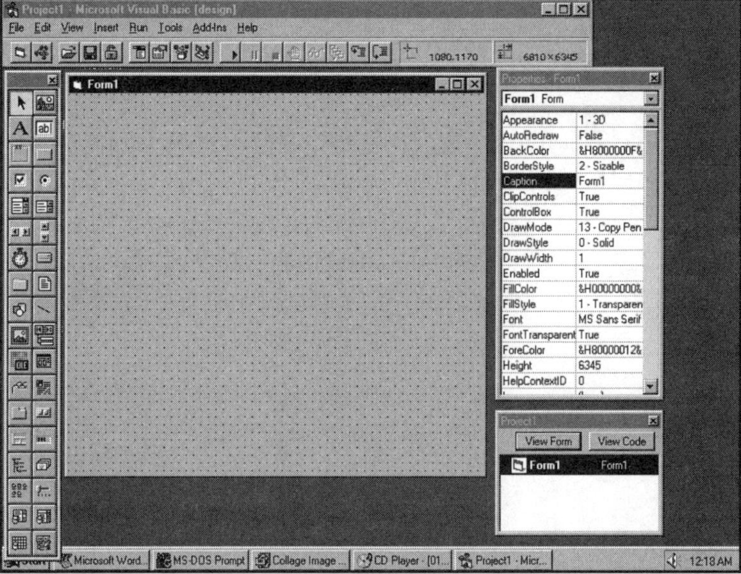

Figure 5.2

The default Project window.

Customizing the Options

There are four option categories that you can customize in the Visual Basic environment. They can be accessed by choosing Tools, Options. This will bring up a notebook control for the options. There are four tabs on the notebook: Environment, Project, Editor, and Advanced. The Options properties sheet is shown in figure 5.3. These notebook pages enable you to customize your workspace and project to meet your personal requirements.

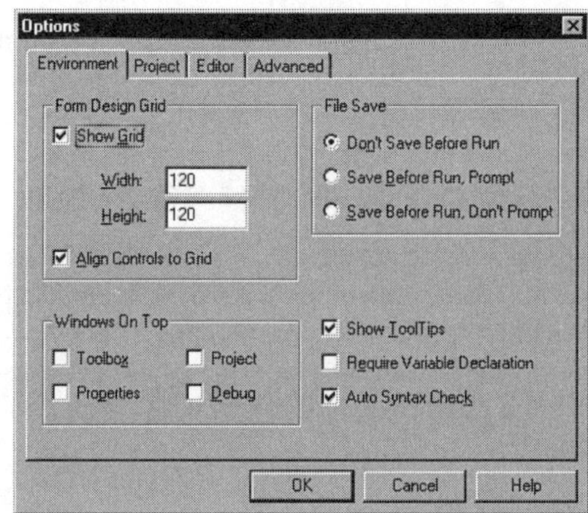

Figure 5.3

The Options properties sheet.

The Environment Options

You can control the way that your environment looks through the Environment Options notebook page, as shown in figure 5.3.

The settings on this page let you control some of the more mundane tasks handled by Visual Basic. The Environment Options deals mainly with the development environment. On this page, you can do the following:

- Turn on the grid and determine the distance between points on the grid. The grid determines how the controls on forms will be laid out. The smaller the integer value, the closer the controls.
- Make the controls align to a grid point. The easiest way to ensure that the controls on your forms are aligned is to choose Yes for this option. This will cause your controls to automatically move to the nearest grid point.
- The Auto Syntax Check controls the kinds of error messages that you see. When this is box is checked, you get immediate feedback from the system when you leave a line of code without writing it legally.
- Specify that certain development windows will always be on top. This keeps the important windows, such as the Toolbox and Properties box visible at all times.
- Turn ToolTips on or off. ToolTips are little yellow messages that tell you the name of a control if you leave your mouse cursor over that control for more than a second or two. These tips can save trips to the manual.
- Require that all variables be declared explicitly. Visual Basic can declare variables without a declaration when it encounters them in the code, as long as this option is not checked. Checking the box requires that the programmer declare each variable before it can be used.
- Save automatically every time you run the program. Options allow for auto save, prompt to save, and no save when run.

These choices allow you to customize the environment to suit the way you like to work.

The Project Options

Project options determine the behavior of an application during application development and at runtime. The Project Options notebook page is shown in figure 5.4.

Figure 5.4
The Project Options notebook page.

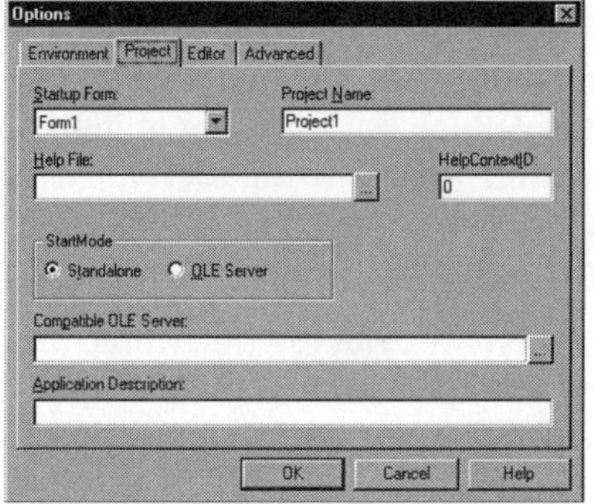

This page contains the following options:

- *Startup Form*. Visual Basic applications usually start with a form being loaded. This is where you specify which form is to be loaded first. Another way is to run a routine called `Sub Main` and load the first form from there if you prefer.
- *Project Name*. You enter here the name of your choice for the project.
- *Help File*. If you write a custom help file for your application, you enter the name here. Building a help file requires the Microsoft Windows Help Compiler, which comes with the Professional Developer's version of Visual Basic. Many developers are embedding quite a bit of information about their business in the help file, and not just information about running the program.
- *HelpContextID*. Here you enter the ID that this application will use in the Object Browser. The Object Browser is an information source that helps you keep track of the properties and methods associated with the objects in Visual Basic. This topic is covered in Chapter 8, "The Object Browser."
- *Application Description*. Here you supply a brief English description of the purpose of this application. This kind of information is very useful when others are given the job of maintaining a system you created.
- *Compatible OLE Server*. This is the name of the executable file if this is an object application (a topic beyond the scope of this book). OLE Servers provide objects to other applications. For more information on this subject, see Que's *Using Visual Basic, Special Edition*.

- *StartMode*. Here you indicate how the application is started. Leave this setting as the default StandAlone mode. (The OLE Server mode is beyond the scope of this book.)

These options allow your Visual Basic program to have that professional look and feel by giving you the control you need at the start of the application.

The Editor Options

You can control the fonts and colors of your environment through the Editor page of the Options properties sheet (see fig. 5.5).

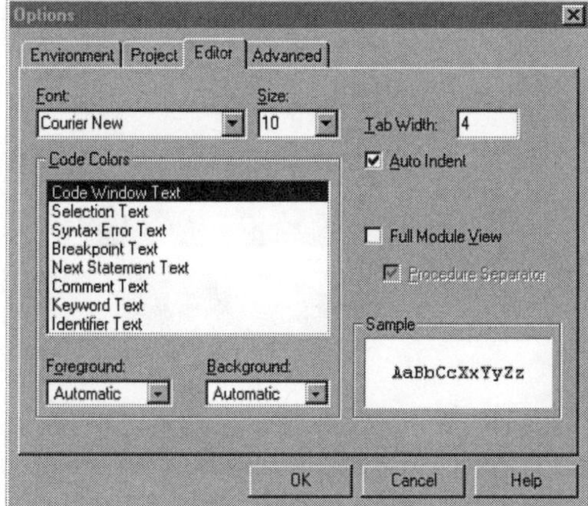

Figure 5.5

The Editor Options notebook page.

Like the Environment Options page, the Editor Options page deals mainly with the development environment. On this page, you can do the following:

- Change the colors of the different kinds of text in the environment. This enables you to use colors to highlight the code the way that makes sense to you.
- Change the font of the text. This option enables you to display code in your favorite font style.
- Change the size of the text for the far-sighted programmer. This makes the text easy to read.
- View your procedures all in one window, or as separate functions by choosing the Full Module View option.
- Control the spacing through automatic indention. This enables you to customize the indention of code.

Again, these choices enable you to customize the environment to suit the way you like to work.

The Advanced Options

The Advanced Options page deals with the more advanced project options (see fig. 5.6). This page contains the following options:

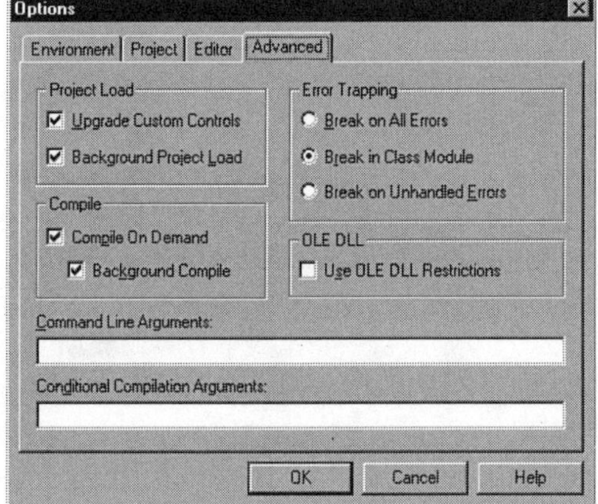

Figure 5.6

The Advanced Options notebook page.

- *Project Load options.* You have the ability to upgrade custom controls when the project first loads. You can use the Background Project Load option to allow the project to be loaded in the background.
- *Error Trapping options.* The options here enable you to customize how errors are handled during the execution of your program. You can have the program break on all errors, break in class modules when an error occurs, or break on all unhandled errors.
- *Compile Options.* There are two compile options that you can set. If you check the Compile on Demand box, then Visual Basic will compile only parts of your project when they are executed. If you do not check this option, the entire project will be compiled when you run it from the IDE. The advantage of Compile on Demand is that your program will begin to run more quickly in the IDE—the disadvantage is that certain compile-time errors will not be detected until they are encountered during a run of your program, which may make debugging more difficult. The Background Compile option allows you to run a program that is not fully compiled and allows Visual Basic to complete the compile in the background when the program is idle. You can use Background Compile only if you have selected Compile on Demand.

- *OLE DLL options*. This option runs a DLL in the development environment with the same restrictions that apply to the DLL when it is used outside of the development environment.
- *Command Line Arguments*. This line allows parameters to be passed to your application at startup during the development phase. At runtime, the parameters will be passed by choosing File, Run in Program Manager. The parameters can then be typed on the same line as the file name.
- *Conditional Compilation Arguments*. This box lists the constant declarations used for conditional compilation (a topic beyond the scope of this book). Conditional Compilation enables you to insert platform-specific commands into your code using a `#if... Then` syntax. When you build your application, you can specify which platform is the target. In this way, one body of code can contain all versions that you wish to support. For more information on this subject, see Que's *Using Visual Basic, Special Edition*.

These advanced options allow you to customize the behavior of your Visual Basic projects.

Saving a Project

Before you can save a project, it has to have a make file (.VBP). Call this project Hello. It is important to choose a name that indicates the purpose of the application you are creating. Calling it something like Proj1 or PJ1 is like naming your variables x and y. You are sure to be confused later.

Examples

The easiest way to name a project's make file is to save the project and name the make file. To accomplish this, follow these steps:

1. Choose Save Project As from the File menu. You then see a properties sheet that asks you to specify a name and location for the form. Next, you will see a properties sheet that asks you to specify a name and location for the project. This location is where the .VBP file for the project will be stored.
2. Name the form HELLO.FRM when prompted.
3. Call the project file HELLO.VBP and store it wherever you want in your directory system.

The file HELLO.VBP will look something like the following if you look at it in a text editor like Notepad:

```
Form=hello.FRM
Object={F9043C88-F6F2-101A-A3C9-08002B2F49FB}#1.0#0;
➥ COMDLG32.OCX
Object={BDC217C8-ED16-11CD-956C-0000C04E4C0A}#1.0#0;
➥TABCTL32.OCX
Object={3B7C8863-D78F-101B-B9B5-04021C009402}#1.0#0;
➥ RICHTX32.OCX
Object={6B7E6392-850A-101B-AFC0-4210102A8DA7}#1.0#0;
➥ COMCTL32.OCX
Object={FAEEE763-117E-101B-8933-08002B2F4F5A}#1.0#0;
➥ DBLIST32.OCX
Object={00028C01-0000-0000-0000-000000000046}#1.0#0;
➥ DBGRID32.OCX
Object={F6125AB1-8AB1-11CE-A77F-08002B2F4E98}#1.0#0;
➥ MSRDC32.OCX
ProjWinSize=308,458,179,128
ProjWinShow=2
Name="Project1"
HelpContextID="0"
StartMode=0
VersionCompatible32="0"
MajorVer=1
MinorVer=0
RevisionVer=0
AutoIncrementVer=0
ServerSupportFiles=0
VersionCompanyName="SoftWare Alchemy"
Reference=*\G{BEF6E001-A874-101A-8BBA-
00AA00300CAB}#1.0#0#F:\WIN95\SYSTEM\OLEPRO32.DLL#Standard
➥ OLE Types
Reference=*\G{00025E01-0000-0000-C000-000000000046}#3.0#0#F:
➥\PROGRAM FILES\COMMON FILES\DAO\DAO3032.DLL#Microsoft
➥DAO 3.0 Object Library
```

At the top of the file, each of the modules and forms in the project is listed. This project is very simple and has only one form. Next comes a list of the Visual Basic extension (OCX) files. This list can be rather lengthy if you saved the project with every OCX file included. In practice, you will want to remove every unneeded custom control from your project before you build the executable file in order to save space. In the middle of the file, the `ProjWinSize` setting specifies the size and location of the Project window. The `ProjWinShow` setting tells Visual Basic whether the Project window was visible when you last saved it. You also see many more settings and names of things like references in the code. These lines exist as the result of the settings in the Options menu picks. By virtue of what was stored in this file, Visual Basic knows how to bring up the development environment and how to build the executable.

You can remove unused form and module files from the project by following these steps:

1. Make the project window visible (if it isn't already) by choosing View, Project.

2. Click the name of the file that you want to remove from the project.

3. Choose File, Remove File.

4. Repeat this procedure for each unwanted file.

You can specify which files you want to automatically load in a new project. Having files loaded automatically is important if you have a number of custom controls and modules that you use in nearly every application, because adding them one at the time on every project can be tedious. To specify the files, you Open a special project called AUTO32LD.VBP. This is a special .VBP file that serves as a kind of template from the creation of new projects. Anytime that a project is created, Visual Basic includes in its Toolbox every custom control that is in AUTO32LD.VBP's Toolbox, and every form, module, class, and resource file that is in AUTO32LD.VBP's Project window. Use the following procedure to add custom controls to the AUTO32LD project:

1. Choose File, Open. The File Open properties sheet appears.

2. Select the project file called AUTO32LD.VBP. It can usually be found in the main Visual Basic directory (in effect, C:\VB4).

3. Click OK to open this project.

4. Add every file that you want to automatically load whenever you create a new project by clicking on the Add File pick from the File menu.

5. Choose File, Save Project to save these changes.

The next time you create a new project, you will start with the files specified in the AUTO32LD.VBP file.

If you load only the files from the AUTO32LD.VBP file at project creation, you may be missing some custom controls that you need for the new project. For example, many programmers make such heavy use of the databound controls that they load the Databound Grid and DBList controls for every project. To add these controls to the project, use the following procedure.

Example

1. Choose Tools, Custom Controls.

2. Click on the check box beside each custom control that you want to include in the Toolbox of every project that you create.

3. Click OK. Notice that one new icon appears for each new control that you added.

4. Choose File, Save Project.

Now, every time that you create a new project, these custom controls will be present in the Toolbox.

Making and Running the Executable File

After you complete the development and testing of your application, you are ready to distribute it to users. To distribute it, you need to create an executable file—a program that can run without the assistance of the development environment. When you ran programs in earlier chapters, you were simulating what the real run would be like. The Visual Basic integrated development environment was interpreting the code that you wrote for your application. (This is fine for debugging, but requiring your users to buy a copy of Visual Basic, open the development environment, and click the Run button on the toolbar is too much to ask.) An executable file is the final product that the end-user for whom it was built (such as the data entry person) will use as an interface to perform their work. By creating an EXE file, you enable users to start your program with a click of the mouse.

The executable files that are created with Visual Basic need several other files called runtime Dynamic Link Libraries to run properly on the user's machine. Some of these files ship with Windows, but others will not be found on a machine that does not have Visual Basic, or the custom controls (OCX files) that you used installed on that machine. In order to make sure that you are distributing everything that the user will need to run your application, Visual Basic comes with a special program called SetupWizard. This wizard guides you through the steps needed to create a distribution disk. For detailed instructions on how to use this wizard, refer to Que's *Using Visual Basic, Special Edition*.

Example

The creation of an executable file is quite easy. Follow these steps:

1. Choose File, Make EXE File. A Save properties sheet appears, asking you to choose the name and location of the new executable.

2. You answer the questions, and voilà, you have a program.

You are now ready to run SetupWizard and distribute your application to the masses.

Summary

In this chapter, you learned that *project* is the set of all files necessary to build an application. If you can use the project features of Visual Basic well, you will be able to create applications that are virtually indistinguishable from Windows applications written in C++ with the Windows API.

In addition, you learned how to customize a project using the Project options properties sheet. You also learned how to change the colors and fonts that you see while working on an application.

Next, you learned how to manipulate the makeup of new projects by using the AUTO32LD.VBP file. You added and removed files and controls from this project to affect the initial makeup of all new projects created on your computer.

Finally, you learned how to create an executable file that will run by itself, outside of the Visual Basic development environment.

Review Questions

Answers to the review questions appear in Appendix A.

1. What is the purpose of a Visual Basic project?
2. What kinds of files can be included in a project?

3. What is the purpose of a module file (.BAS)?
4. What is an executable file?

5. How do you start an executable file?
6. How do you control the initial makeup of new projects?

Review Exercises

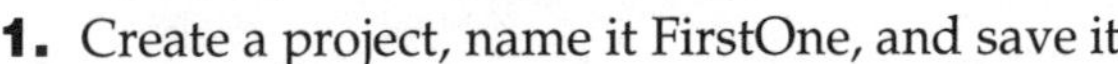

1. Create a project, name it FirstOne, and save it.

2. Create two forms, Forma and Formb, for the project and save them both. Designate Formb as the startup form. Run the application and verify that Formb comes up first.

3. Open your AUTO32LD.VBP file and add several custom controls to it. Create a new project and verify that these new custom controls appear in its Toolbox.
4. Create an executable file for the application FirstOne and add its icon to your Visual Basic program group. Run the file by double-clicking the icon.

CHAPTER 6

The Development Environment

To a real computer lover, nothing feels better than a great development environment. The feeling that comes from working in a well-designed, logical, convenient environment is similar to that of driving a new luxury car. You are amazed at the smoothness of the ride, ease of handling, and features available. But unlike cars, where a significant innovation comes along only once every few years, software tools seem to evolve into a new generation every 12 to 18 months. This release of Visual Basic is one of those giant jumps forward.

The purpose of this chapter is to give you the power to comprehend the Visual Basic machine as you begin driving it. All the information in this chapter can be found in other places, but here it is presented the way a programmer sees it—through the eyes of those who love a good machine. If you want to skip around and use this chapter as an easy-to-read reference, note that the chapter follows the organization of the menu bar. The first major topic is the File menu, followed by the Edit menu, and so on. No attempt has been made to give equal treatment to each menu selection. On the contrary, some options like Cut and Paste warrant no more than a passing mention. Others, such as the Make EXE File command on the File menu, are discussed more thoroughly. Still others, like the Help menu, deserve your attention but are covered in another chapter to which you are referred for details.

The Visual Basic menu bar is filled with powerful tools to make your programming life more productive and enjoyable. The menu bar contains 8 menus, 77 menu options (not counting projects added to the File menu), and 17 Toolbar buttons (see fig. 6.1).

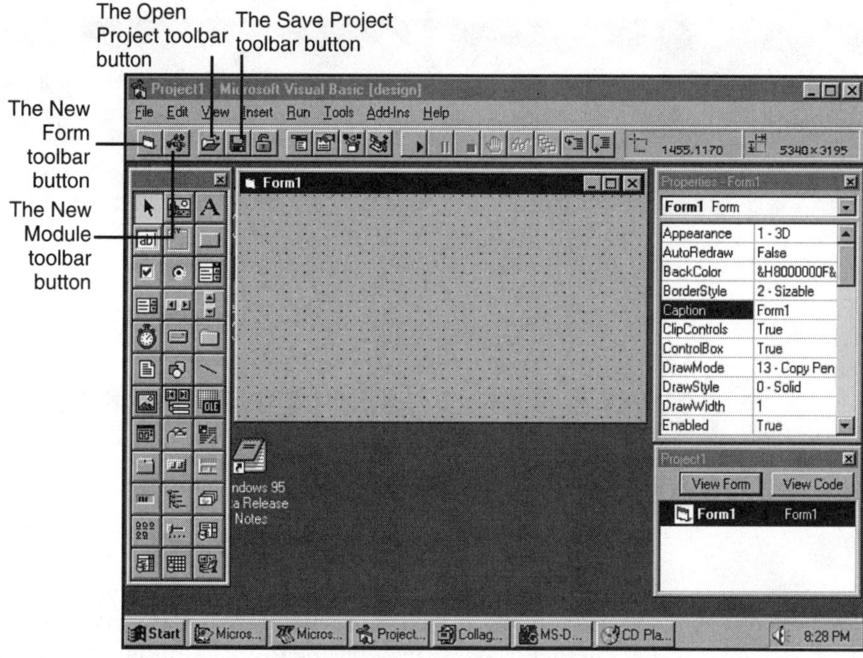

Figure 6.1
The Visual Basic menu bar and Toolbar.

Some of the menu choices, such as Edit, Copy, are very simple. Others, like Tools, Menu Editor, launch sophisticated applications to perform their tasks.

The File Menu

The first item on the menu bar, File, is familiar to most users, but several options on the File menu are not familiar at all. In theory, all of the options should have something to do with file processing, and, for the most part, they do. A few of them, such as Print Setup, seem to be included more for consistency with other Windows applications than for any logical grouping. Take a look at these options in the order in which they appear on the menu.

New Project, Save Project, Open Project, and Save Project As

The New Project menu option creates a completely new *project*—the Visual Basic term for an application still in development. A project is like a container file that tracks other files used to create the application.

Before you choose File, Exit, you normally click Save Project to save all changes you have made to your project. Figure 6.1 shows the Save Project button on the Toolbar.

If the project is a new one, you can name it with the Save Project As command. Later (after unloading the project or exiting Visual Basic), when you return to work on the project, you will execute File, Open Project to return your work to the screen. The Save Project As will name the project file, but not the project. To name the project, use the Project tab from the Tools, Options menu.

For a complete discussion of the concepts associated with projects, consult Chapter 5, "Projects."

Save File and Save File As

The Save File and Save File As menu options work basically the same as in other Windows applications. You use them any time that you want to write the contents of a form or module out to the disk. This menu option is run automatically when you choose Save Project or Save Project As from the File menu. When you try to save the project, the Save File dialog box is displayed if you have forgotten to name any individual forms or modules.

Add File and Remove File

The Add File command is used by Visual Basic to add another file to the current project. The files that are legal to add are forms (FRM), BASIC modules (BAS), classes (CLS), and resources (RES). Adding a new blank form to the project is so common that a special Toolbar button has been created to accomplish the task in one click.

Also available is an analogous button for adding a module to the project, even though this action is not as common as adding a form.

After a file has been added to the project, it will remain a part of the project unless you delete it with the File, Remove File command or the pop-up menu in the project window.

When a new project is being created, Visual Basic examines the contents of a special project file called AUTO32LD.VBP to determine which files you want loaded initially. If you find, for example, that you are loading every custom control in the free world into every new project, there is an easy way to tell Visual Basic to "lighten up." All you have to do is choose File, Open Project and, when the Open Project dialog box appears, choose AUTO32LD.VBP (see fig. 6.2).

After you open the AUTO32LD.VBP project, you see the project window shown in figure 6.3.

From the project window, you can use the Add File and Remove File menu options to load files that you want to start your new projects with and to remove files. For more information about the project window, see Chapter 5, "Projects."

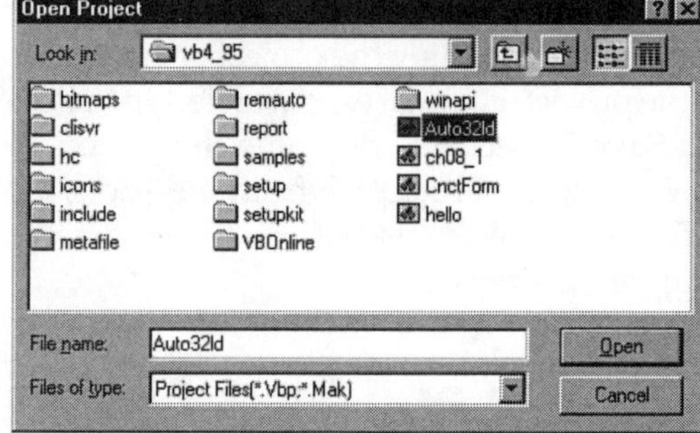

Figure 6.2
Opening the AUTO32LD.VBP file.

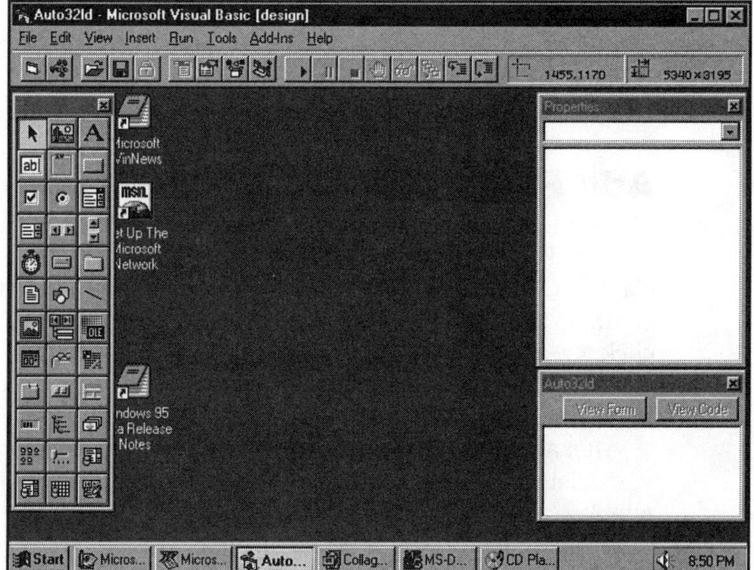

Figure 6.3
The AUTO32LD.VBP project window.

Print and Print Setup

The File, Print and File, Print Setup commands for Visual Basic work like print commands in other Windows applications, with the exception that you have to tell Visual Basic what you want printed (it defaults to current module). The Print properties sheet is shown in figure 6.4.

Normally, you want to print the event procedures for each of the forms. You also have the capability of printing an image of the form. Visual Basic programs are somewhat more difficult to maintain than procedural programs written in C or COBOL because the VB code is somewhat scattered. A number of third-party utilities and add-ons are available to enhance the documentation-generation capabilities of the system. These extensions can be a wise investment for companies that write systems with a long life ahead of them.

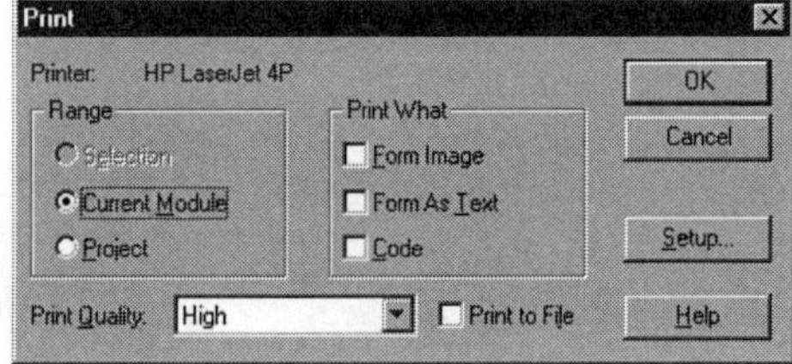

Figure 6.4
The Print properties sheet.

Make EXE File

One of the main reasons that Visual Basic has been so popular among independent consultants is because you can make an executable file and distribute it without paying royalties to Microsoft. To create this executable file, you use the File Make EXE File command. To see how this command works, let's create a simple application, attach it to an icon, and start it by double-clicking the icon.

Example

Your first task is to open a new project and add three command buttons to the form, as shown in figure 6.5.

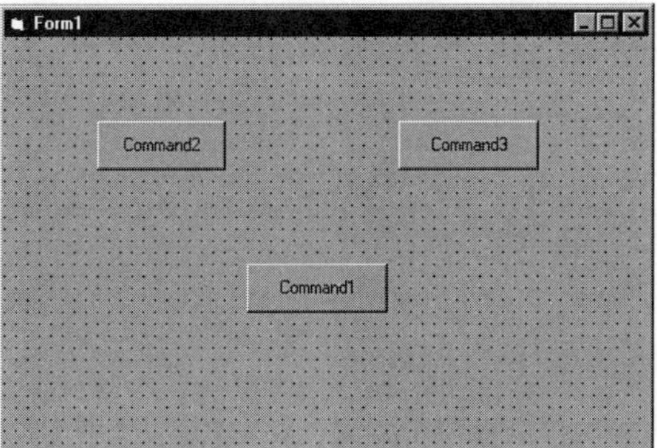

Figure 6.5
A simple application.

Next, make an executable file out of this form. You do this with the Make EXE File option. This command brings up the Make EXE File properties sheet (see fig. 6.6).

Figure 6.6

The Make EXE File properties sheet.

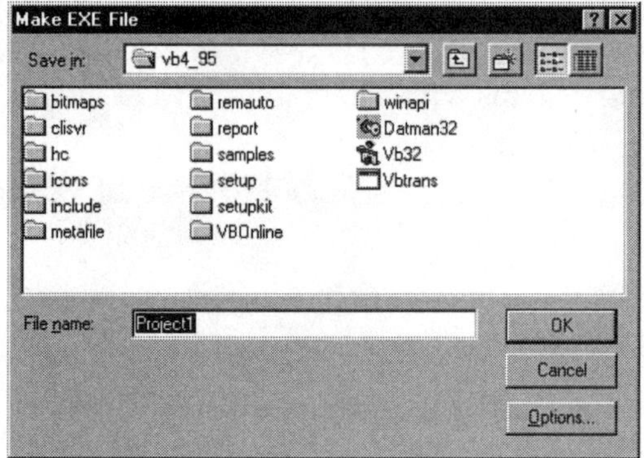

You can then run your program by using Explorer to locate the file, and then double-clicking the file to run it. The best way to run it, however, is to define an icon for the program and then run it by clicking that icon. Do that now. The name of the executable file is C:\VB\PROJECT1.EXE (C: is the drive where Visual Basic is installed).

To create the icon, go into Explorer, and choose File, New from the menu bar. A window like that shown in figure 6.7 appears.

Figure 6.7

The Create Shortcut window.

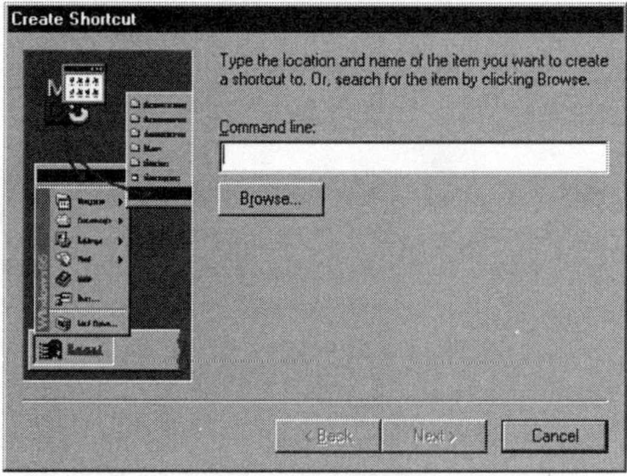

Choose the Shortcut menu item. At this point, you can type in the name of the file or use the Browse button to locate the file. When you have done this, select the Next> button. You are prompted for a name for the shortcut; you can name this anything you want to. Figure 6.8 shows the project with its shortcut highlighted. You can also drag the icon to the Windows 95 desktop to accomplish the same thing.

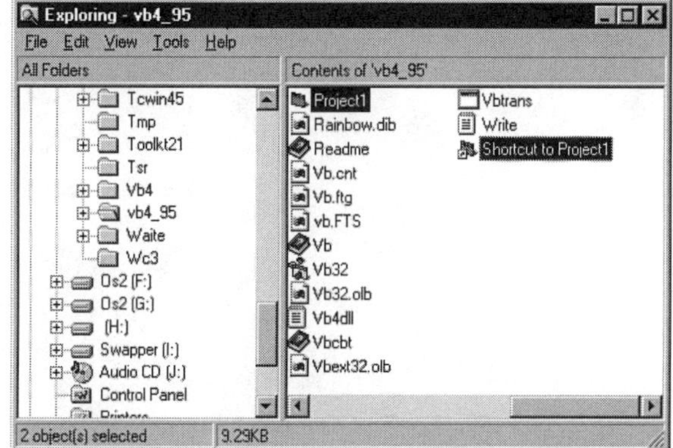

Figure 6.8

The project and its shortcut.

You can run the program by double-clicking either the program or the shortcut you just created. You may also want to have your program accessible from the Start button. You can drag the shortcut and drop it on the Start button. This adds an entry to the Start menu, as shown in figure 6.9.

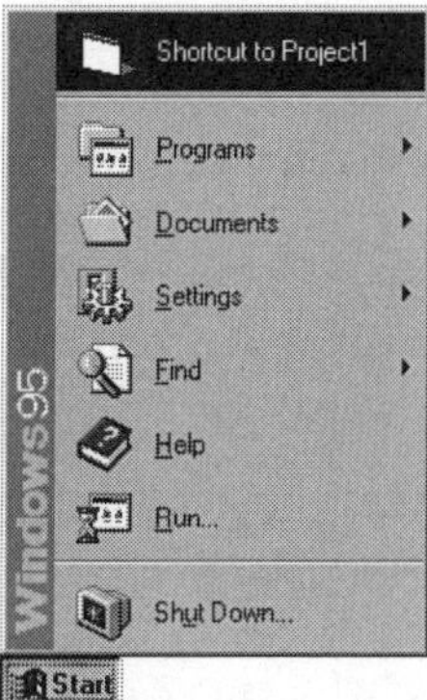

Figure 6.9

The Start menu with the shortcut added.

You probably are excited to see that you can create a Windows program that is virtually indistinguishable from those shipped with Windows or written by software vendors. Perhaps you will want to launch a development effort to become a new software vendor after reading this chapter. The software business is a great one; the only limits are your own intelligence and work ethic. Today's garage programmer is tomorrow's industry magnate.

Just to prove that you have accomplished the task, double-click your newly created menu item and observe that the main form of your humble project has now turned into a beautiful three-button application (see fig. 6.10).

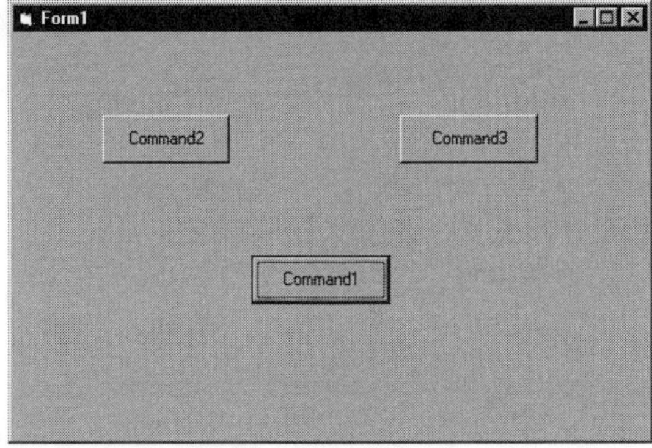

Figure 6.10
A beautiful three-button application.

It would be very helpful if you play with this application a little. Notice that you can press the buttons by clicking them. You can move the window to a new location by using the title bar. You can press the Tab key and see the focus shift from one button to the next. You can also maximize and minimize the window. Most old-time programmers who are new to the Windows environment are astounded that all this functionality can exist in a program that took so little time to develop. In the old days, you would have had to code all of this built-in window control by hand. In Chapter 9, "The Form," you learn how to design the form to include only the controls you want, removing such items as the Maximize button, Minimize button, window border, and title bar if you like. You close the application by double-clicking the Control menu box in the upper-left corner of your application's window, as shown in figure 6.10.

Most Recently Used VBP Files

The last several lines on the File menu hold the names of the most recently opened projects. By double-clicking one of these project names, you can move quickly to an open project. Because the references on the menu are fully qualified, you do not have to remember the name of the directory where the project's VBP file was stored. This advantage, coupled with the fact that the VBP file contains pointers to the files comprising the project, makes for a low-tech but highly productive feature of the system.

The Edit Menu

The Edit menu contains the usual set of critical but commonly found features. This menu can be a great time-saver, though, if you know how to use it well. Many parts of your code can be copied and pasted elsewhere, even from one application to another. How often have you have been saved by the Undo command when you accidentally blew out about an hour's worth of programming effort in one fell swoop? And who, in good conscience, could forget the contributions of Find and Replace?

Lest you be tempted to skip this section entirely, a couple of interesting menu options require a little explanation. Certainly, you won't want to miss these.

Undo, Redo, Cut, Copy, Paste, and Clear

To preserve the status of Visual Basic as a real Windows application, its developers have included the obligatory Edit commands of Undo, Redo, Cut, Copy, and Paste. You can use Copy and Paste to save time when you are using the Help menu to find information about a certain method, property, event, or feature. Most of the Help screens contain examples of these. Get in the productive habit of copying these examples onto the Clipboard with the Copy command and then pasting them into your form or module. That way, you can reduce the number of syntax errors and shorten your Visual Basic learning curve. Cut is also known as the shortcut Ctrl+X, Copy as Ctrl+C, and Paste as Ctrl+V.

Clear is a command that performs the same function as the Delete key. Clear removes the currently selected object from existence in the universe, unless you select the Undo command immediately afterward. Redo performs an undo on the Undo—it reverses the preceeding Undo command.

Paste Link

You can use Paste Link to link data from another application through the OLE container control. After you've copied valid data onto the Clipboard (such as a paragraph from a word processor or a range of cells from a spreadsheet), you can select the OLE container control on your form and then choose Paste Link to link the data.

The Paste Link command exists to support the connection of another application, which must also support OLE, to Visual Basic controls. Create an OLE container on your form by clicking the OLE control in the Toolbox. Then go to an OLE-compliant application, such as Microsoft Word 6.0, and copy a paragraph to the Clipboard. Go back to Visual Basic and Paste Link the Clipboard data into the OLE control. The paragraph is now linked to the OLE control so that when the paragraph changes, the Visual Basic application that is linked to this paragraph changes also. For more details on this feature, see Chapter 15, "The Data, Grid, and OLE Tools." This capability is useful when you want to add a piece of artwork into your application. Because the graphics capabilities of Visual Basic are limited, you might want to draw it in a graphics package, such as CorelDRAW!, and link it to Visual Basic.

Find and Replace

Find and Replace behave somewhat differently in Visual Basic than in other programs, such as a word-processing program. Here, these commands have to know more about where you want them to look for the keyword specified. Figure 6.11 shows the Find properties sheet.

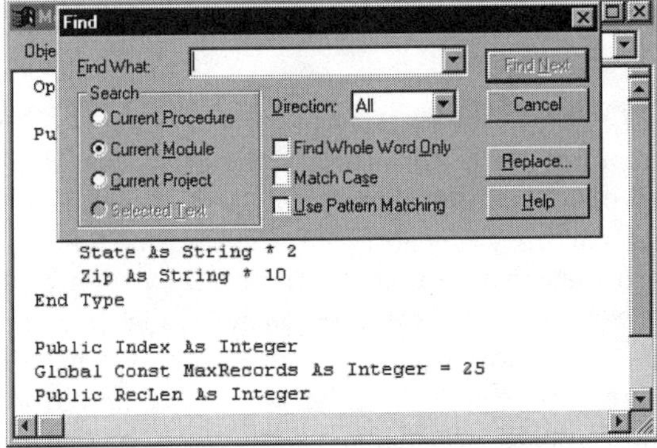

Figure 6.11
The Find properties sheet.

When you are searching for a string, you have the options of looking in the procedure, the current module, or the entire project. Otherwise, you have the standard directions to look—Up, Down, or All—as well as the usual matching of case and patterns.

Indent and Outdent

The Edit menu options Indent and Outdent (is that in the dictionary?) perform the function of indenting your code in fairly simple ways. The Indent and Outdent can be applied to blocks of text, much like the Tab and Shift Tab keys. Outdent performs the opposite action from Indent.

Using the Indent feature, you can make the procedure in Listing 6.1 look like that in Listing 6.2.

Listing 6.1 06LIST01.TXT—An Unindented Procedure

```
Private Sub Number_Click(Index As Integer)
If LastInput <> "NUMS" Then
ReadOut = "."
DecimalFlag = False
End If
If DecimalFlag Then
ReadOut = ReadOut + Number(Index).Caption
Else
ReadOut = Left(ReadOut, InStr(ReadOut, ".") - 1)
➥ + Number(Index).Caption + "."
End If
If LastInput = "NEG" Then ReadOut = "-" & ReadOut
LastInput = "NUMS"
End Sub
```

Listing 6.2 06LIST02.TXT—An Indented Procedure

```
Private Sub Number_Click(Index As Integer)
    If LastInput <> "NUMS" Then
        ReadOut = "."
        DecimalFlag = False
    End If
    If DecimalFlag Then
        ReadOut = ReadOut + Number(Index).Caption
    Else
        ReadOut = Left(ReadOut, InStr(ReadOut, ".") - 1)
        ➥ + Number(Index).Caption + "."
    End If
    If LastInput = "NEG" Then ReadOut = "-" & ReadOut
    LastInput = "NUMS"
End Sub
```

There can be no argument that the second listing is easier to read and comprehend. You might be lured into thinking that the Indent option would do this for the whole procedure with one click. Alas, that is not the case. You must go to the appropriate line and click the Indent menu option to move that line over essentially one tab stop. The Outdent option performs the inverse of Indent. You may want to continue using the Tab key and Shift+Tab to accomplish the same objective.

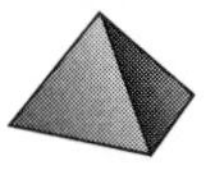

> **Tip:** You can also select a range of lines to indent or outdent as a group. Either select with the mouse, or position the cursor at the start of a line, hold down the Shift key, and use the up or down arrow keys to select the lines you want to work with.

Bring to Front

The objects that can appear on a form have a layering order. Closest to the form itself is the bitmap specified in the `Picture` property of the form. (See Chapter 9, "The Form," for more on the subject of form layers.) On top of the bitmap is any text written on the form itself. On top of that is the layer that contains the controls from the Toolbox. When these controls are created, they are put in front of any controls created before them. You can change this layering order with the commands Bring to Front and Send to Back on the Edit menu. Figures 6.12 and 6.13 illustrate how they work.

The problem with the two images in figure 6.12 is that the wrong image is in front. The smaller image should be on top of the larger one. To correct this, you either select the larger image and choose Send to Back, or choose the smaller image and choose Bring to Front. The result is shown in figure 6.13.

Figure 6.12

Two images that are incorrectly layered.

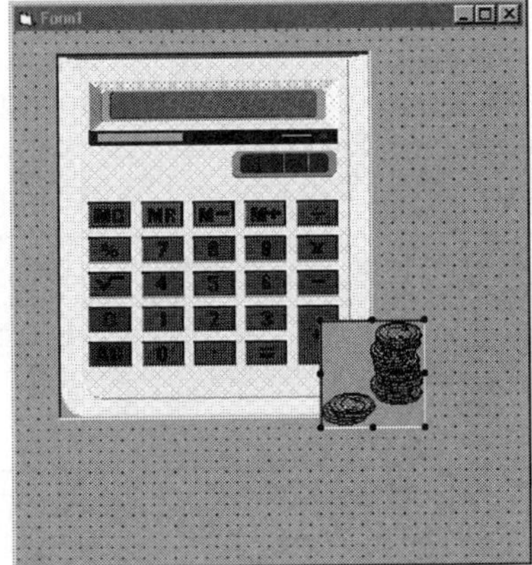

Figure 6.13

Two correctly layered images.

Align to Grid

The Align to Grid menu option enables the developer to align controls to the grid. This alignment is controlled by the Environment Options tab, accessed through the Tools, Options menu. A check box in this properties sheet controls whether the alignment to the grid is automatic. If the check box is selected, the Align to Grid option on the Edit menu can have no effect because the objects will have been placed on the gridlines at the time of creation and whenever moved or resized.

Lock Controls

The Lock Controls option allows the developer to lock a control or group of controls against movement. That way, one control cannot be moved inadvertently while another is being moved. Figure 6.14 shows the Toolbar button that corresponds to this menu option.

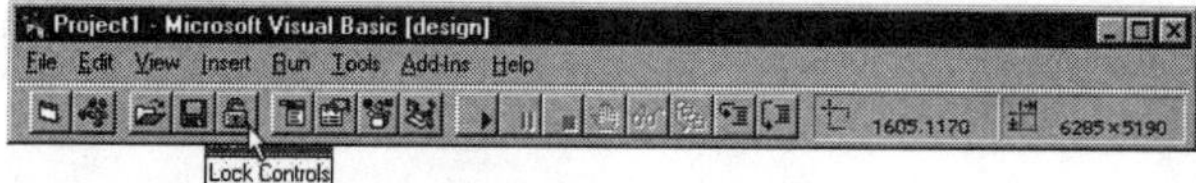

Figure 6.14
The Lock Control Toolbar button.

This Toolbar button is animated slightly. When it is set as locked, the button looks like a fastened padlock. When the button is set as unlocked, it looks like an unlocked padlock.

The View Menu

The View menu, as its name implies, enables you to see different parts of the development effort. Its goal is to provide the information that you need to make decisions about your applications.

Code

The Code command simply brings the code window to the front where you can write and edit code. This window is shown in figure 6.15.

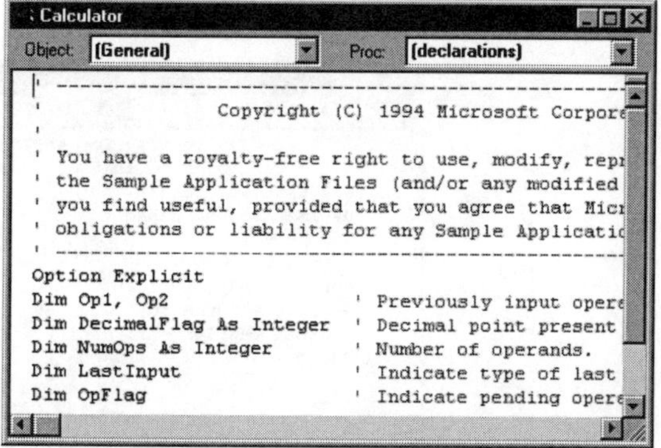

Figure 6.15
The code window.

The code window is covered in more detail in Chapter 2, "Visual Basic Programs." The coding of the procedures is explained in Part III, "Variables & Operators," Part IV, "Controlling Program Flow," and Part V, "Using Data Structures."

Form

The Form command finds the current form and displays it on the screen. A sample form is shown in figure 6.16.

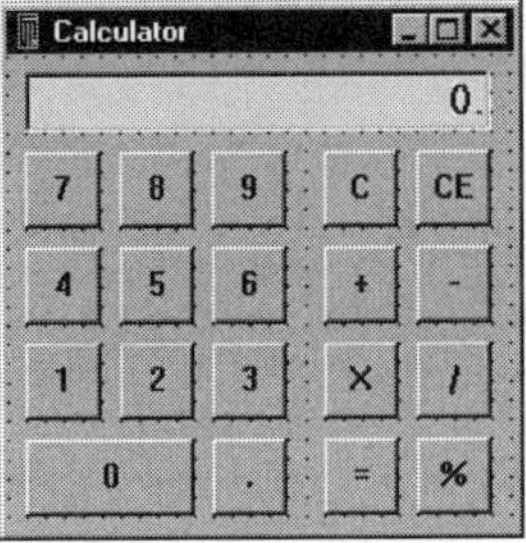

Figure 6.16
A form that looks like a calculator.

A complete discussion of forms and form design can be found in Chapter 9, "The Form."

Procedure Definition

When you are developing and debugging code, a very common activity is to go back and forth between the area you are testing and the definition of a procedure being called from that area. The Procedure Definition command looks at where your cursor is located in source code. If the word under the cursor is the name of a procedure, Visual Basic shifts the code window to display the body of that procedure. Figure 6.17 illustrates this concept.

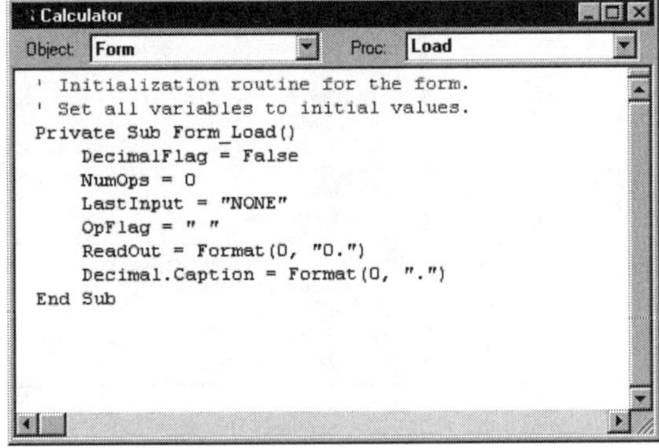

Figure 6.17
The code window with a procedure name.

If you choose Procedure Definition at this point, the code window displays the definition of `Form_Load`, as illustrated in figure 6.18.

With the code window in this position, the programmer can examine the source code for the `Form_Load` event procedure.

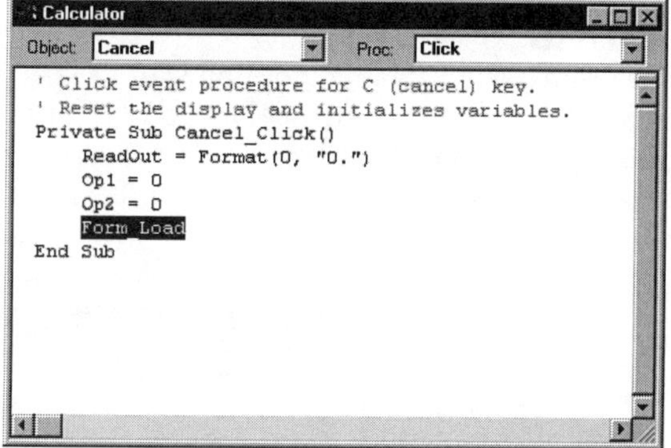

Figure 6.18

The `Form_Load` event procedure.

Last Position

After you have finished looking at the contents of the `Form_Load` procedure, you can choose Last Position from the View menu to return the code window view to your previous location. This is another way in which Visual Basic has automated an action that occurs frequently in the day of an applications developer.

Object Browser

One of the challenges of writing modern systems is to find out about all the code, properties, and methods available for your use. The Visual Basic development team has provided a utility, called Object Browser, for sifting through the mountain of information about these routines. The main screen of Object Browser is shown in figure 6.19.

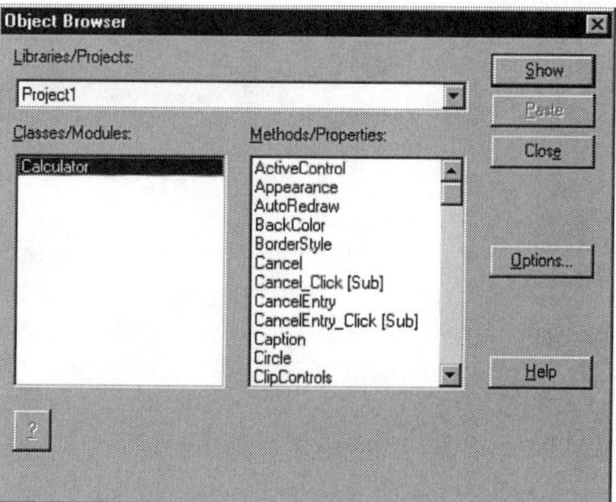

Figure 6.19

Object Browser's main screen.

A complete explanation can be found in Chapter 8, "The Object Browser."

Debug Window

The Debug Window menu option starts a special window used to find out about errors in your programs. It enables you to look at the values of variables during trial runs of your application. This window is especially helpful for annoying errors that cause your calculations to be off slightly. The Debug window is shown in figure 6.20.

Figure 6.20
The Debug window.

In brief, the upper half of the Debug window is where you examine the values of variables. The lower half allows you to enter commands or change variables as you step through the program. Chapter 35, "Debugging and Distributing an Application," deals with the art of debugging.

Project

The Project command in the View menu brings the project window to the front of the screen or opens it if it's closed. This window is shown in figure 6.21.

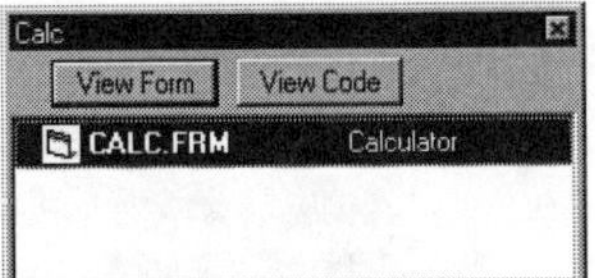

Figure 6.21
The CALC.VBP project window.

The purpose of the project window is to enable you to manage your project from one location. From this window, you can add or remove forms, modules, class and resource files to the project, view the forms, view the code, and perform a variety of other housekeeping chores. See Chapter 5, "Projects," for a complete discussion of projects.

Toolbox, Toolbar, and Color Palette

The last three commands in the View menu control whether the Toolbox, Toolbar, and Color palette are displayed on-screen. The Toolbar option is really a toggle switch; if you choose the option when it has a check beside it, the window disappears. If you choose the option when the window is not present, it appears. (The other two selections in this section of the View menu will simply show the item if it is not visible, but to close them, you must use the Close button on the actual window.) Figure 6.22 shows the palette window.

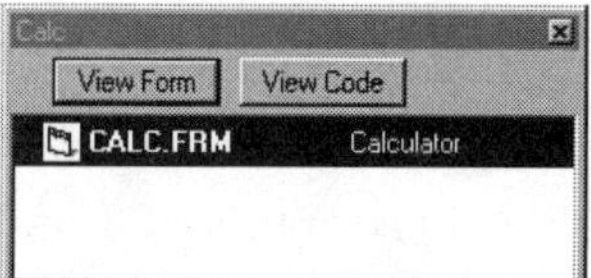

Figure 6.22
The palette window.

You can use the palette window to set the value of a color property. With the palette window, you can select an object and change the foreground, background, and text colors. Whenever you use this method, the appropriate values in the Properties window change automatically.

Properties

The Properties menu option brings the Properties window to the screen. You can set the values or properties for objects in your program from the Properties window. Figure 6.23 illustrates the Properties window.

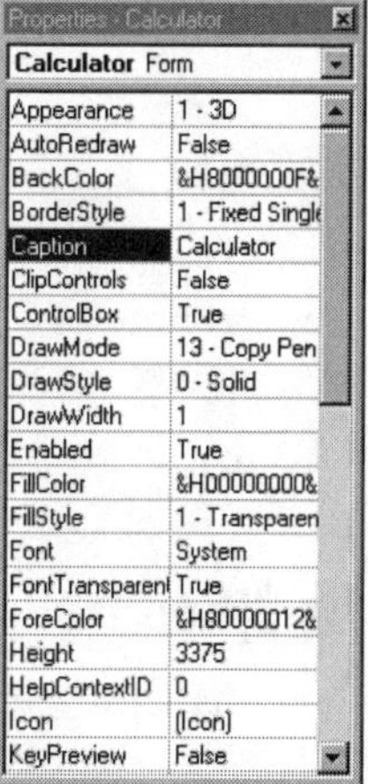

Figure 6.23
The Properties window.

A full treatment of properties and the Properties window can be found in Chapter 7, "The Properties Window."

The Insert Menu

The Insert menu, as the name implies, allows you to insert new objects in your projects and modules. The objects you can insert include the following:

- *Procedures*. When you select this menu option, a properties sheet appears where you can specify a procedure to be added to the current module.
- *Form*. This option adds a form to the project.
- *MDI Form*. This option adds a Multiple Document Interface (MDI) form to the project. An MDI form is one that can contain other forms. Explorer is an example of an MDI form. You can have a maximum of one MDI form per project.
- *Module*. With this option, you can add a new code module to your project. The code module holds procedures that are not associated with any specific events, and must explicitly be called from other parts of your program in order to be executed.
- *Class Module*. This option adds a new class module to your project. A new class creates new object types for your application. (The creation of new classes is beyond the scope of this book. See Que's book *Using Visual Basic, Special Edition* for detailed information on this topic.)
- *File*. You use this option to add a new file to the project.

The Run Menu

The Run menu contains options for testing your application while you are still in the development environment. You can, for example, start, end, and restart the application. Debugging is covered in detail in Chapter 35, "Debugging and Distributing an Application."

The Tools Menu

The Tools menu contains a number of choices that assist you in debugging. They are Add Watch, Edit Watch, Instant Watch, and Calls. These tools are covered in detail in Chapter 35, "Debugging and Distributing an Application."

Menu Editor

You invoke the Menu Editor by choosing that option from the Tools menu. The Menu Editor is a high-level tool you can use to create menus in a very intuitive manner. Figure 6.24 shows this utility.

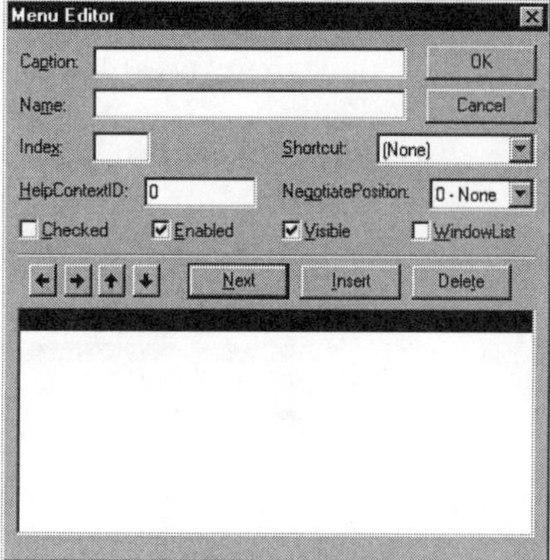

Figure 6.24
The Menu Editor.

Chapter 17, "The Menu Editor," tells you everything you ever wanted to know about creating menus with Menu Editor.

Custom Controls

Custom controls are software devices created by developers for inclusion in Visual Basic and other applications that comply with OLE 2.0. When you choose the Custom Control menu option, you access a dialog box that enables you to add and remove custom controls from the Toolbox. Figure 6.25 displays the Custom Controls properties sheets.

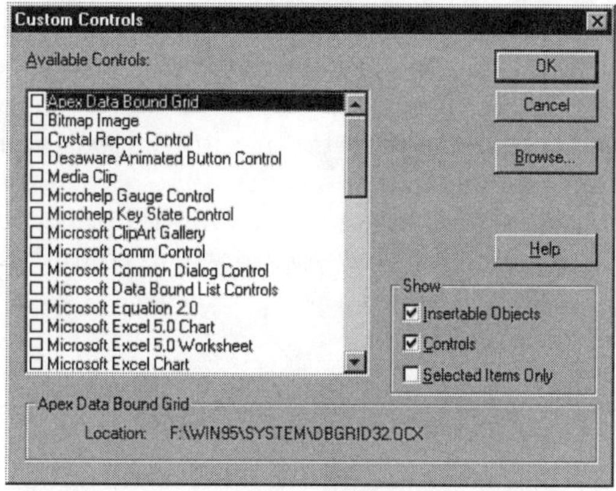

Figure 6.25
The Custom Controls properties sheets.

The subject of custom controls is treated in greater detail in Chapter 31, "Adding OLE Objects."

References

Visual Basic now allows references to objects outside the development system itself. By choosing the References command from the Tools menu, you invoke the properties sheets shown in figure 6.26.

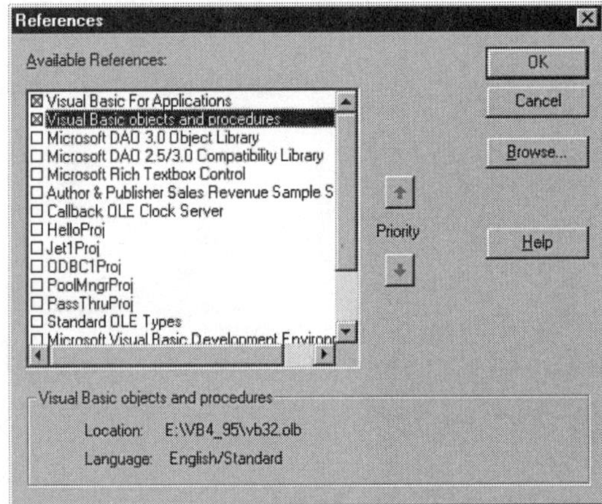

Figure 6.26
The References properties sheets.

For more complete information on references, see Chapter 8, "The Object Browser."

Environment, Project, and Format Options

Visual Basic has centralized the control of some options in a notebook control: Environment, Project, Editor, and Advanced Options. You can open this notebook by choosing Options from the Tools menu. The Environment options deal with customizing the grid on the forms, error trapping, and window logistics. The Project options enable you to capture global information about the project itself. The Editor Options allow you to customize the way your screen looks. The Advanced options allow you to access advanced project information. This release of Visual Basic has increased considerably your control over these kinds of features. Chapter 5, "Projects," covers these options in detail.

The Add-Ins Menu

The Add-Ins menu contains three menu options: Data Manager, Report Designer, and Add-in Manager. The Data Manager allows you to perform database maintenance activities from within Visual Basic. The Report Designer allows you to create custom reports. The Add-Ins Manager allows you to move other add-ins into this menu. All three of these options are covered in detail in Que's *Special Edition Using Visual Basic*.

The Help Menu

Visual Basic contains an extensive online Help facility. After you have mastered its use, you will find nearly all the reference material that you need at your fingertips. The Help menu is explained in Chapter 4, "The Windows Environment." Do yourself a favor and study that chapter if you skipped over it. You will save dozens of hours on your next project by copying code samples from Help and pasting them into your code.

Summary

This chapter has provided a whirlwind tour through the menu bar. You were introduced to some capabilities that will more than pay for the time invested in learning them.

You were introduced to many tools, like the Procedure Definition and Last Position options on the View menu, that enable you to move around the programming environment.

You also learned that the Run menu options enable you to move through a program while it is still in development.

Finally, you were introduced to Tools menu which provides functionality like menu editors and custom control managers.

Review Questions

Answers to review questions are contained in Appendix A.

1. What is the name of the file that controls the default components of a new project?
2. How do you add a file to a project after it has been created?
3. In which directory does Visual Basic keep icons?

4. How do you prepare an application for royalty-free distribution to your customers?
5. What distinguishes an MDI form from an ordinary one?

6. What is a custom control? Where do you get custom controls?
7. What functionality do the View menu options Procedure Definition and Last Position provide?

Review Exercises

1. Create a new project named BookProject1 and add a second form to it.
2. Change the background color of Form1 by using the color palette instead of the Properties window.
3. Create a form, add several buttons to it, and then make it into an executable file. Launch this application from the Explorer in Windows 95.

4. Create two command buttons and position them so that they overlap onscreen. Change the controls so that the other button is on top.
5. Create an application, make an EXE file out of it, attach an icon to it, and store it in the Visual Basic directory.

6. Use the Color Palette to change the background color of a form. Click around on the palette to look at different color possibilities.

CHAPTER 7

The Properties Window

Visual Basic is a language that deals with objects. It does not create new classes of objects in a manner similar to the way that C++ does, but it deals with creating instances of pre-defined set object types.

When you created the `btnDisplay` button in Chapter 2, "Visual Basic Programs," you really created an object (sometimes called an *instance*) of the class `CommandButton`. When you dragged or clicked on the Toolbox, a new button appeared on the form. This button was the same as every other button that you will ever create in Visual Basic in certain ways. For example, all buttons are rectangular and respond to the same events. But this button can have its own identity because it has a set of characteristics called *properties*. In this chapter, we will look at the role of properties in an application and learn how to change them to control the look, feel, and behavior of each object. You will also look at some of the properties that are commonly used in designing applications.

Objects and Properties

In a traditional programming language such as C or Pascal, the only object types that exist natively in the language are the fundamental data types such as integer and character. These simple objects are easy to learn. Every instance of these objects is virtually identical to every other instance of the same data type. Visual Basic contains these same kinds of simple objects, but it also contains quite a few higher-level objects such as forms, buttons, and text boxes. These higher-level objects are the source of increased productivity because they can be constructed more quickly and more accurately than an equivalent object written from scratch using C or BASIC.

In exchange for this rapid development, you lose some flexibility. For example, in C, you could create a round command button. In Visual Basic, the standard command button is rectangular. This inflexibility is part of the trade-off between ease-of-use and speed. To make this trade-off as painless as possible, the developers of Visual Basic asked themselves, "What are the variations on the basic command button that the programmers want?" Armed with this information, they defined a set of characteristics or properties that the programmer can change without altering the basic nature of the control. They repeated this process for every control in the Toolbox.

These developers decided to provide a special window that makes these values available for change during application development. This special window is called the Properties window.

Properties Window Anatomy

The Properties window is an ordinary window. It is shown in figure 7.1.

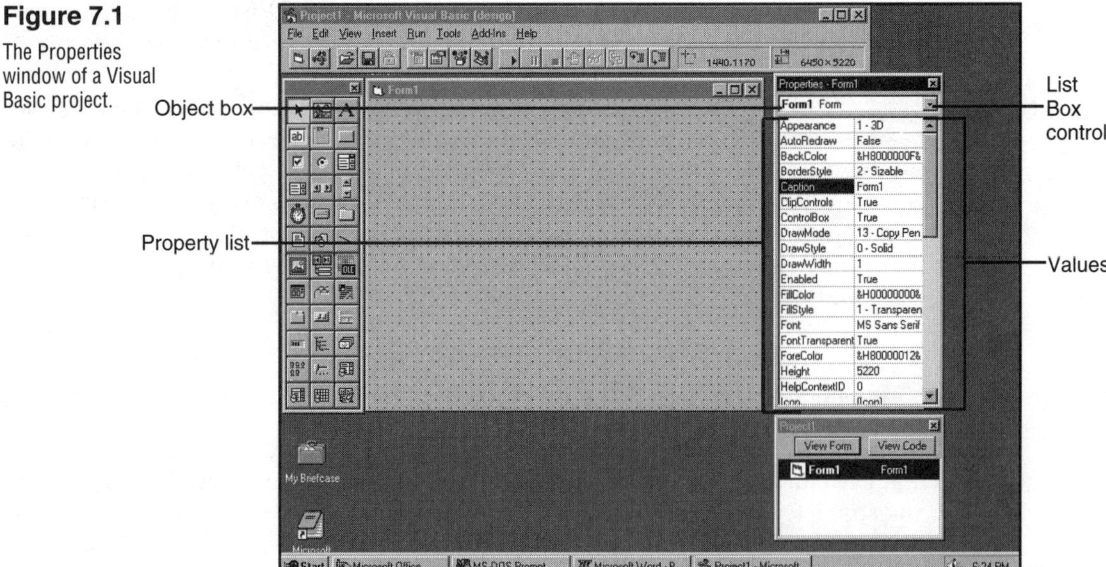

Figure 7.1

The Properties window of a Visual Basic project.

The window itself is slightly different than the ones that commonly appear in applications. You will notice immediately that there is a Minimize button but no

Maximize button. The Minimize button is there so that you can iconize the window if you choose to. The Maximize button is missing because the Visual Basic design team could see no advantage to a maximized Properties window. Therefore, to keep things simple, they removed the Maximize button.

The borders are active, however, and you can use them to lengthen or shorten the Properties window if you choose. Lengthening the window allows you to see more properties at the same time. That could be useful when you are looking at a complex object that has numerous properties. Making the Properties window wider is of value when you need to change properties that have values that do not fit in a short space. Also, you can move the Properties window to another location on the desktop, if necessary.

The Object Box

If a form is named `Starter`, the title bar of its Properties window will have the caption `Properties - Starter`. This indicates that the form `Starter` is the object that currently has the focus. Under the title bar is a List Box called the *Object box*, which contains the name and type of the object that has the focus. In the instance of the form called `Starter`, this line would contain the phrase `Starter form` with the former word indicating the name of the object and the latter word indicating that the properties displayed below it are properties associated with an object of type `form`.

If you click on the Object box, you will find that you cannot type text directly—you must choose from the objects in the list. Clicking on the List Box control (an arrow pointing downward to a line) displays a list of all current objects. By clicking on a different object, you can change the object whose properties appear in the window. You can also click on the object itself, and the result will be identical to choosing the object by name from the list. In figure 7.1, the Properties window shows the properties for an object called `Form1`.

Visual Basic Enterprise Edition comes with 26 built-in controls, each supporting a finite number of properties. When you purchase custom controls, you will find that each has a set of properties that are peculiar to that type of control. When you advance to the point of creating your own custom controls, you will be required to decide which properties the users of your control will be able to manipulate in order to customize that control for their own purposes.

The Property List

The property list is composed of one line for each property. On the left side of each line is the property name. Whenever you select a different object, the names of the properties change to those appropriate for an object of that specific type. Let's work through an example to illustrate this point. Create a command button on your form by double-clicking the Command Button control in the Toolbox window. This gives you a new button. Select this new button from the Object box.

Figure 7.2 shows the property list for a form and figure 7.3 shows the property list for a command button.

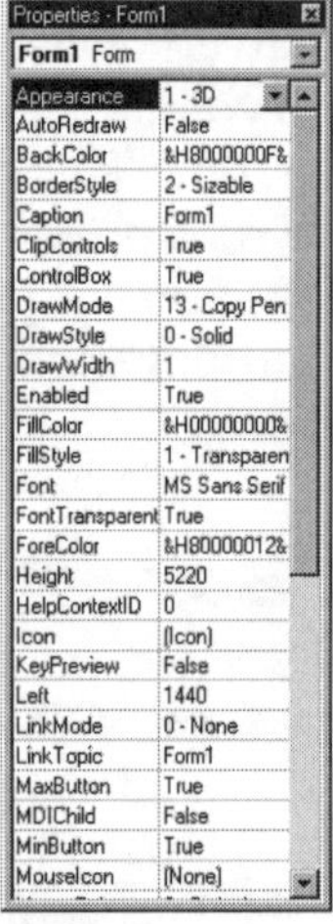

Figure 7.2

The Properties list for a form.

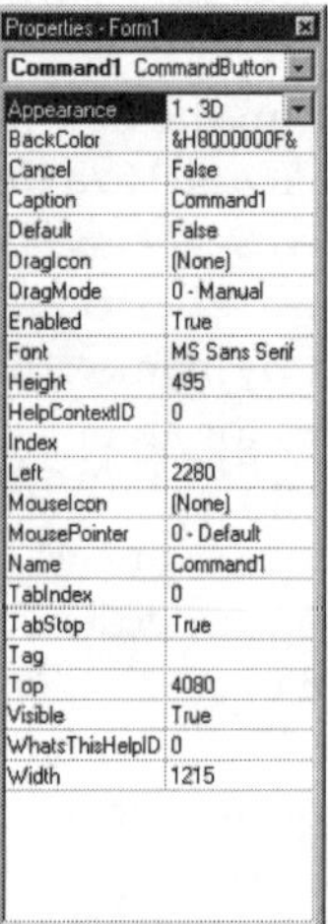

Figure 7.3

The Properties list for a command button.

Notice that the first property listed for both the `CommandButton` and the Form is Appearance. There are different properties for different types of objects. For example, a form has a property named `Icon`. This property contains the name of the file containing the icon that is to be used when a Minimize button is pressed while the application is running. A command button cannot be minimized, and therefore has no need for an icon.

In the right column on each line is the property's current value. If you change objects in the Object box while looking at the property's current value, you will notice that the value can be different for objects of the same type. Figures 7.4 and 7.5 show two command buttons whose property values differ in several respects.

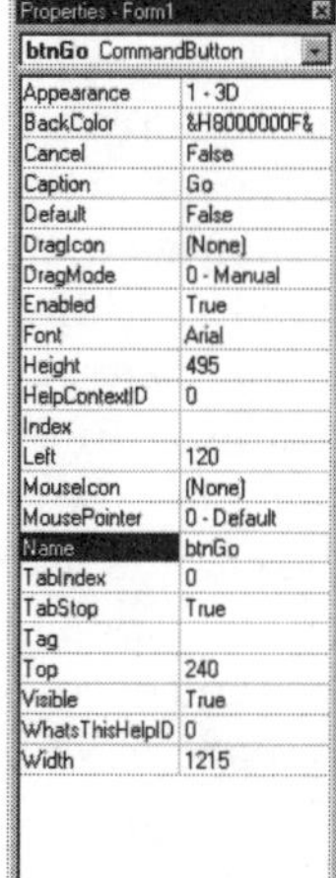

Figure 7.4
Property list for the Go button.

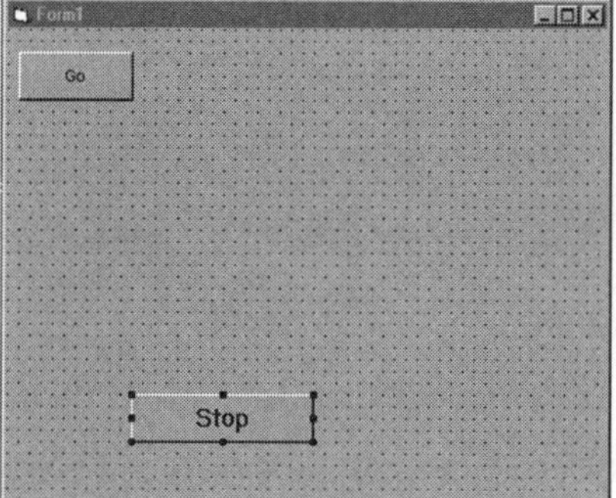

Figure 7.5
Property list for the Stop button.

The most obvious difference is the value of the `Name` property of the two buttons. The name of the button shown in figure 7.4 is `btnGo`, whereas the name of the one shown in figure 7.5 is `btnStop`. The value of the `Name` property becomes the name of the button in the source code of the application. Therefore, if you write code that refers to `btnGo`, Visual Basic knows exactly which button you are referring to. The names must differ or Visual Basic will attempt to treat the two buttons as an array. For details on how to create a control array, see Chapter 26, "Arrays."

Several other property values also are different. The `Caption` property, which controls the text that is written on the button, is `Go` on the left and `Stop` on the right. The buttons can be seen on the form in figure 7.5.

Notice also that there are several other property value differences. The Go button has a `Font` property value of `Arial`, whereas the Stop button has the value `MS Sans Serif`. This property value difference accounts for the difference in the way that the letters look on the buttons. The `Left` property controls how far from the left edge of the form the window is placed. The `Top` property determines the location of the controls relative to the top of the window's work area. In figure 7.5, you can see that the buttons are at different locations relative to the left and top of the window. The reason that these values differ is that the two command buttons are placed in different locations on the form.

To change the value of a property, you need only to click on the value displayed immediately to the right of the property's name. After you finish changing the value of the property, the change takes effect. You can see many of these changes while your form is still in development mode. Some properties will change automatically. The `Left`, `Top`, `Height`, and `Width` properties will automatically be changed whenever you move or size a control on a form.

Example

The following example illustrates how you can see changes take effect in design mode. Figure 7.5 showed the Go button positioned 240 units from the top of the form. (These units, called *twips*, are discussed in more detail in Chapter 9, "The Form.") To change the button's position on the form, follow these steps:

1. Create a command button on your form.
2. Select the button from the Object box in the Properties window. This should display a Properties window like the ones shown in figures 7.4 and 7.5.
3. Click on the `Top` property and type **0** (zero).
4. Press Enter and observe that your form looks something like the one shown in figure 7.6.
5. Now change the value of the `Top` property for this button to 2750. The change takes place while you are still in design mode, as shown in figure 7.7.

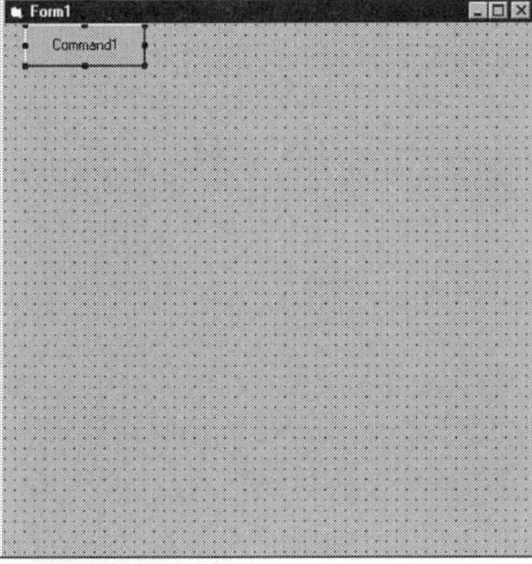

Figure 7.6

A button placed 0 units from the top.

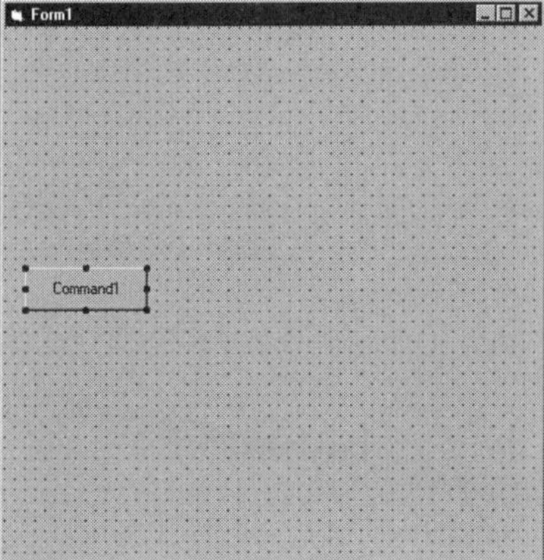

Figure 7.7

A button placed 2750 units from the top.

You use this method to change all of the properties that accept text input. Some of the effects, however, are not as easy to observe as the position of the button in the window.

Special Techniques for Changing Property Values

Not all properties are changed by entering text. Depending on the property, you may find that you are interacting with a list box, a combo box, a palette, or a dialog box instead of a simple text box. These other types of data input controls make it easier to select values for certain properties. The following sections look at some examples of this type of input.

Using List Boxes

Some properties are changed through the use of a list box, which is indicated by a small button with an arrow pointing downward at the right of the property value area. All the properties that can be only `True` or `False`, for example, are implemented as list boxes.

Example

This example shows you how to use the drop-down list box that is provided with some properties. Click `Form1` to give it the focus, then click the `Visible` property. You will notice the arrow pointing downward just to the right of the current property value, as shown in figure 7.8.

Figure 7.8

The `Visible` property of a form.

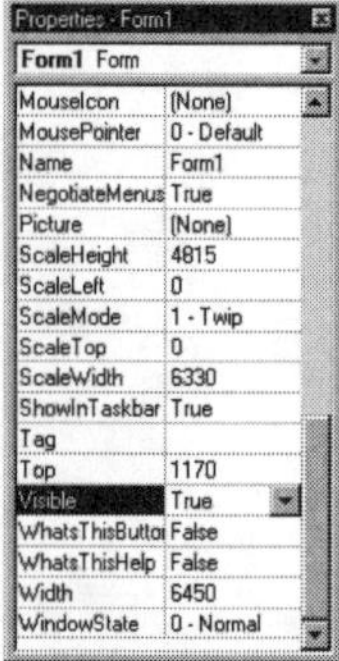

Pull down the list box and click to change the value to `False`. Pull it down again and change it to `True`. Just for laughs, try to change the value to `Undecided` by typing the word Undecided. You will notice that the List Box does not allow this update. You can, however, type the first letter of an item in the list (in this case, **t** or **f**), and the contents of the property will change to the appropriate value. You can also simply double-click the mouse on a list type property, and cycle through all the options in the list.

Using the Palette

You can enter all color properties by typing the hexadecimal value of a color. It is much easier, however, to change colors by selecting the new color from a palette.

Example

This example changes the background color of the form. Click on `Form1` and select the `BackColor` property. Click inside the text box anywhere beyond the last `&`. This places the cursor at the end of the string that represents the current color of the form's background. The default form color is `&H8000000F&`. Change the value to `&H000000C0&` and press Enter. The background color of the form now changes to look like what's shown in figure 7.9.

Figure 7.9
The form with a red background.

The easy way to do the same thing is to click the Choices button (the downward arrow) at the end of the text input line. This brings up a palette that looks like the one shown in figure 7.10.

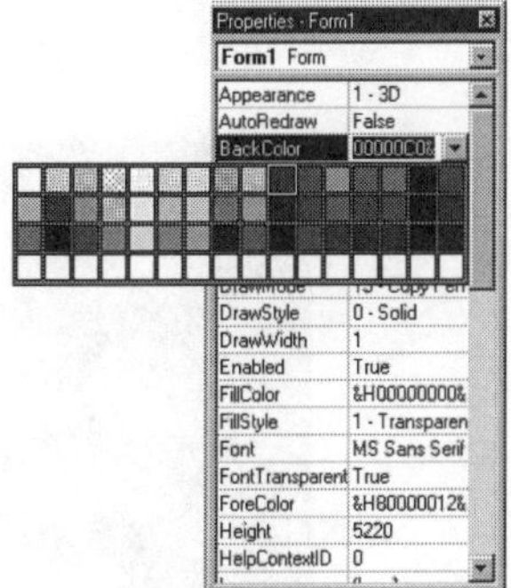

Figure 7.10
The color palette for a form's `BackColor`.

Change the color to any color you like by simply clicking the color squares in the palette. Notice that the hexadecimal value of the color in the text box changes accordingly, and that this color change is displayed immediately.

Using a Dialog Box

When the value of a property is the name of a file, the Choices button brings up a properties sheet rather than a simple list.

Example

Choose any form and click on its `Picture` property. Next, click on the Choices button and bring up the screen shown in figure 7.11.

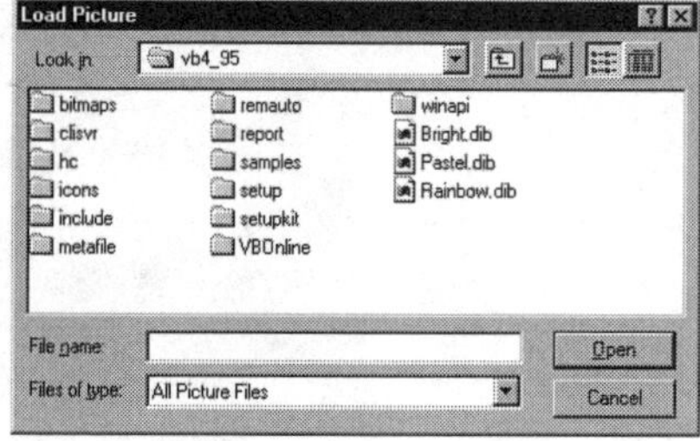

Figure 7.11
The Load Picture properties sheet.

You will immediately see that this window looks much like the one you normally see when you open a document in a word-processing or drawing system. Choose the file FOREST.BMP from your Windows 95 installation subdirectory.

You will then see your background change to look like the one shown in figure 7.12.

All the properties in Visual Basic that bring in a file from the operating system use a load file properties sheet. This includes the properties that determine the icons.

Figure 7.12
Loading a .BMP file onto a form.

Common Properties

Although each control has a unique set of properties that is designed specifically to support its functionality, several properties are common across a variety of property types. The following is a list of these common types and a brief description of their purposes:

- `Name`—Because every object in Visual Basic can be controlled by programs that you write, each must have a name, similar to a variable name, by which it is known to BASIC instructions that reside in the modules and event procedures.
- `Caption`—Objects that show text (such as the command button) need a way to control what is being displayed. The `Caption` property controls this. Objects that contain editable text, such as a text box, have a `Text` property instead of a `Caption` property.
- `Font`—Whenever text is displayed, the `Font` property determines the type of font to be displayed.
- `Enabled`—At times, the context of an application will make certain controls temporarily inaccessible (for example, a Close File button when no file is open). The `Enabled` property can be used to toggle the accessibility of a control.
- `BackColor`—Objects with backgrounds (such as forms) need to be able to control the color that is displayed. The `BackColor` property is used for this.
- `ForeColor`—Controls the color of text and graphics that are added at runtime.
- `Visible`—At times, you may want to hide and expose controls according to the logic of your program. Setting the `Visible` property to `False` and `True`, respectively, accomplishes this. Games make extensive use of this property.
- `Height`—Controls the size of a control from top to bottom.
- `Width`—Controls the size of a control from left to right.
- `Top`—The distance of an object from the top of its container. For a form, the `Top` is relative to the upper edge of the screen. For a button, the `Top` is relative to the upper edge of the form (or other container) containing the button.
- `Left`—The distance of an object from the leftmost edge of its container object. For a button, it is the left edge of the form, or other container containing the button.
- `TabIndex`—The order that the focus will follow when the Tab key is pressed. Visual Basic assigns this order to be the order in which objects were added to the form. This is probably not the best order for your users. You can change the tab order by assigning a TabIndex value to the controls on a form. Make the first item on the form have a TabIndex of 0, assign the next one as 1, and so forth.

- `DragMode`—It makes sense to drag and drop some objects. The `DragMode` property allows the developer to control how a control behaves during drag-and-drop operations. Setting this property to `Automatic` prevents normal operation of the control.
- `MousePointer`—This property allows the appearance of the mouse pointer to change while over an object, if desired.
- `AutoRedraw`—Tells Windows to restore the original look of a window if another is placed on top of it and subsequently moved. It is of use with images created with graphics methods. Other types of objects will be automatically repainted when uncovered by other windows, but images created with graphics methods will need to have the AutoRedraw property set to true if they are to be protected. AutoRedraw creates a copy of the image in memory, which is used to refresh the image when necessary. When AutoRedraw is false, VB uses the object's Paint event to repaint the object, which works for things like controls, but not for graphics drawn by code (i.e., using graphics methods).

In Part II, "Interface & Language Basics," each control in the Toolbox window is explained in detail. The properties that pertain specifically to each control are covered there in detail.

Summary

Visual Basic is an object-oriented language that emphasizes object creation rather than object class definition. It is powerful because it allows you, the programmer, to deliver functionality to your customers very quickly.

In an effort to provide as much flexibility as possible in a rapid application development tool, the developers of Visual Basic employed the notion of properties that can control behavior, in many cases, without programming. In this chapter, you learned about these properties in general and about the ways to change their values. You also stepped through a number of basic properties that apply to several of the controls to illustrate, through examples, the concepts presented here.

Finally, you examined the properties that are common to numerous controls in order to increase your understanding of the wide scope of this property-rich architecture.

Review Questions

Answers to the Review Questions are in Appendix B.

1. What is a property?
2. How are the values of the properties changed during development?
3. Why doesn't the Properties window have a Maximize button?

4. Name five common properties across the built-in controls in the Toolbox.
5. Name the three ways to change the values of properties during program development.

6. Assuming Windows 95 is installed in the C:\WIN95 subdirectory, tell what `Form1`'s background would look like if you placed the following value in its `Picture` property:

   C:\WIN95\ARGYLE.BMP

7. True or False?—You use an icon on the Toolbar to create an instance of that tool.

Review Exercises

1. Create a form that is located in the top-left corner of the screen. Using the Properties window, move it to the center of the screen.
2. Create a form that contains one button for each of your five best friends. Change the `Caption` on each button to display the name of one friend.

3. Create a form that uses an alternate mouse icon. (Hint: Use the `MousePointer` property of the form)
4. Create a form that contains six command buttons. Use the `MousePointer` property to change the way the mouse pointer looks when it is over each one.

5. Create your own bitmap using the Windows Paintbrush program. Create a form that uses this bitmap for its background.

CHAPTER 8

The Object Browser

In this chapter, we discuss Object Browser and Reference Manager, two components of Visual Basic, and which serve to simplify programming life. The utilities covered in this chapter are the Object Browser and the References properties sheet.

Each utility supports a certain aspect of developing applications in Visual Basic. Let's look at the utilities in the order you will use them.

Objects and Object Browser

As we discussed in earlier chapters, Visual Basic is a language that deals with objects. In the physical world, craftsmen create objects like refrigerators and chairs by using tools. They decide the precise type of object to create (for example, which model of refrigerator) and then follow a certain procedure to produce one. During construction, some of the features and properties of the refrigerator can be varied without changing the fundamental definition of the model. Some of these features might be the color and whether the door opens on the left or on the right.

A Visual Basic application uses similar construction reasoning. After analyzing the problem to be solved, you decide the precise type of form to be produced. You use the Toolbox to put the controls on the form. During construction, many decisions are made concerning the colors, size, and location, which alter the appearance without changing the fundamental definition of the control.

To understand objects, we need to define a few terms. The Toolbox contains *icons*. Each icon represents an object class or an object type. The *type* of an object is like the model of an automobile. The word "Mustang" represents a specific type or class of car, not a specific car. The model or class of a car defines it generally, but not specifically. For example, you could own a 1994 white Mustang 2-door convertible with an 8-cylinder engine. Your best friend could own a 1986 red Mustang hatchback with a 4-cylinder engine. Even though the two cars differ in a number of ways, they still are recognized by anyone who knows what a Mustang is. Each particular car, then, is an *instance* of the class "Mustang."

In the Visual Basic world, you can create two control buttons. They can be of different size, color, and location, yet they are still control buttons. Each button is an instance of the class "control button." Each button, then, is an object. Formally, we should instruct you with the phrase "create an instance of the class called control button" whenever we want a new control button on the form. It is simpler, however, to say "create a control button."

Methods

We have already learned that objects have a specific set of properties and respond to a specific set of events. Each object also has a finite number of procedures or methods that the programmer can use to control the behavior of objects. To better understand this concept, let's look at a method that applies to form objects. The `Move` method applies to all visible objects, including forms. To invoke a method, go into a form's code window, choose `Form` as the Object, `Click` as the event procedure (Proc:), and add the code in the following example.

Example—Beginner

```
Private Sub Form_Click ()
   Move 10, 10
End Sub
```

This method, `Move`, tells the form to move to a certain location (in this case, the location 10 units from the left side and 10 units from the top). Run the application and click anywhere on the form. You see how the `Move` method is used to reposition a form in response to a specific event.

The `Move` method can also be used to reposition objects within a form. Let's work an example of this also. Using the same form as above, add a command button by double-clicking on the command button tool. This will create an object of type command button and position it in the center of the form. Next, bring up the Code window for that form and choose `Form1`, the default name for forms, as the Object. Choose `DblClick` as the event procedure (Proc:) and add the code in the following example.

Example—Beginner

```
Private Sub Form_DblClick ()
   Command1.Move 10
End Sub
```

The syntax here is slightly different than it was in the `Move` method for the form. In this case, we see that the string `Command1.` was added to the beginning of the name of the method. Since `Command1` is the default name of the control button that we added, the command above could be paraphrased in the following pseudocode:

"Move the button called `Command1` to a position that is 10 units from the left-most edge of the form. Maintain the same position as before, relative to the top of the form."

Running this application and double-clicking anywhere on the form will cause this subroutine to execute and move the command button to a position near the far-left of the form.

The full implementation of the `Move` method will be presented when the Command button is presented in Chapter 10, "The Button Tools." Hundreds of methods are built into Visual Basic and the custom controls that are packaged with it, and hundreds more are available through the purchase of additional custom controls (.OCXs).

The existence of all of these objects, properties, and methods is a boon for someone who knows that they exist and knows how to use them. For the other two million developers, this avalanche of pre-written code represents a guilt trip of millennial proportions. We want to use these routines and avoid reinventing the proverbial wheel, but how do we find out about them and how to use them? This has been a problem in the software reuse arena since the beginning of coding. In this release of Visual Basic, Microsoft has made a pretty good stab at providing a tool to help programmers work through this difficulty.

Using Object Browser

The Object Browser is a special window that allows you to perform research on objects, their properties, and their methods. You invoke the Object Browser by choosing View, Object Browser from the Visual Basic menu bar. Alternatively, you can invoke Object Browser by clicking on the Toolbar button (see fig. 8.1).

Figure 8.1

The Object Browser Toolbar button.

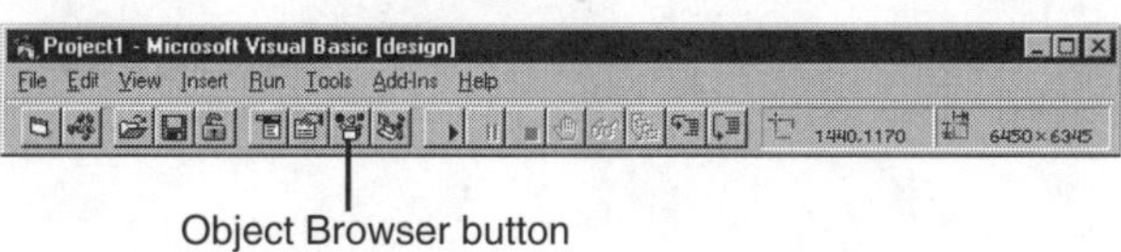

This will bring up the Object Browser window that is shown in figure 8.2.

This window looks a little complicated but it is really pretty straightforward. At the top of the form is the Libraries/Projects list box, which enables you to specify what objects you wish to browse. The placement of items in this list box is done using the References dialog box. We will cover this window later in this chapter. The following are three types of references that can reside in this list box:

1. *The Libraries*—These are collections of objects and methods. They normally ship with Visual Basic.
2. *Custom Controls*—These are libraries of controls that can be used in your applications as if they were built-in to Visual Basic.
3. *Projects*—These are the objects and methods that you create for yourself in the course of developing an application.

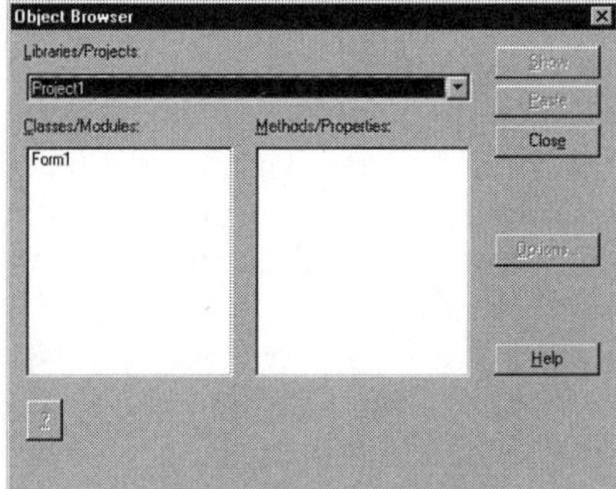

Figure 8.2
The Object Browser window.

Let's start by looking at an example where we will browse the objects in our own project. In figure 8.2, we see that Project1 is selected and that Form1, the only object, is selected. In the Methods/Properties list box, we see a list of the properties and methods that are associated with forms. Every way to affect the characteristics of the form is listed in the list box. Just for laughs, click on the word Icon in the Methods/Properties list box. You will see a few sentences of text appear at the bottom of the window. These lines represent mini-help on the `Icon` property (see fig. 8.3).

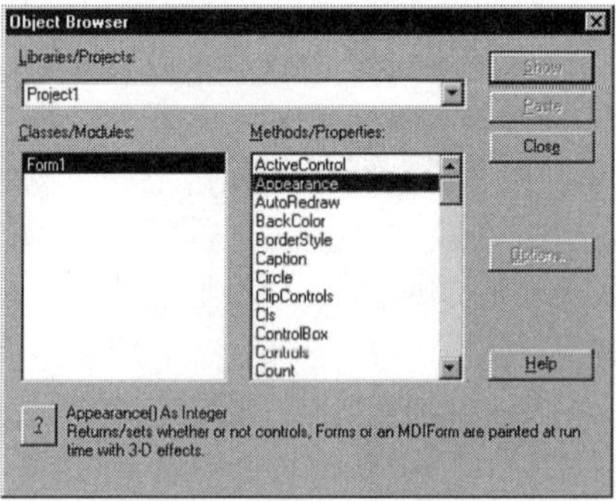

Figure 8.3
The mini-help in the Object Browser window.

Beside that text is a button with a "?" as its caption. This button gives you the full Help screen for the selected property or method. In order to prove that this really works, click on this button and view the Help window that is shown in figure 8.4.

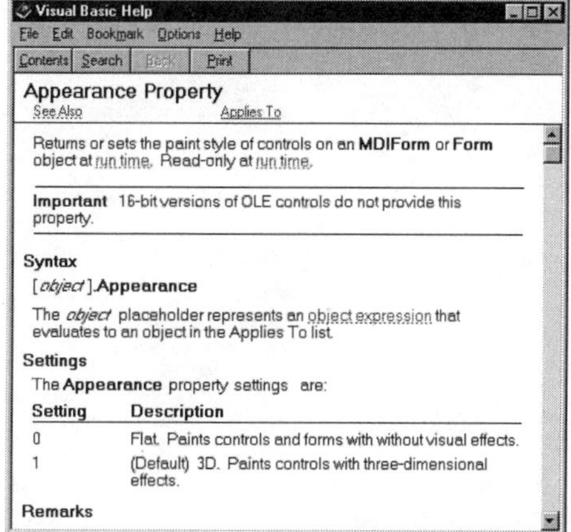

Figure 8.4

The help text.

If you need to look at the properties and methods that are associated with the built-in controls, select `VB - Visual Basic objects and procedures` from the Libraries/ Projects list box. This will populate both of the list boxes with the control classes and associated properties and methods (see fig. 8.5).

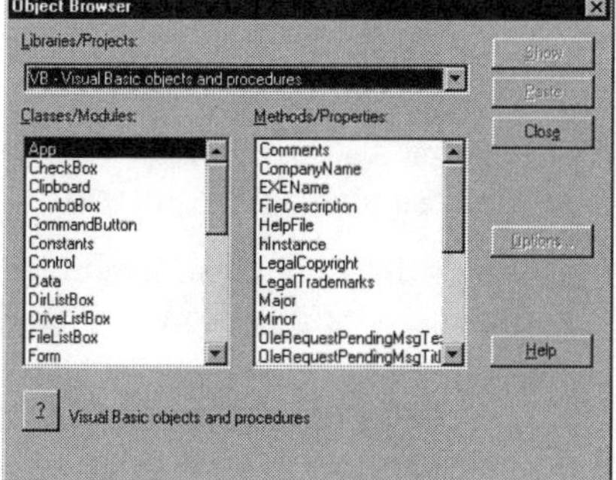

Figure 8.5

The Visual Basic objects.

Locate and select the Screen Class in the Object Browser. The screen has a number of properties and methods associated with it. As you select each one in turn, its explanation appears at the bottom, in the mini-help section of the window.

Another valuable use of Object Browser is in handling constants. Many methods and functions require that a constant be used to specify behavior. When your user selects Constants from the Classes/Modules list box, all of the constants that are defined for the object named in that particular Library or Project appear to the right. The details about this constant appear at the bottom of the window (see fig. 8.6).

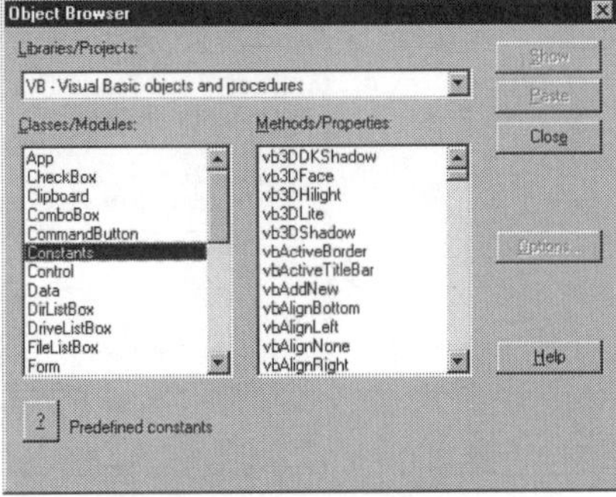

Figure 8.6

The Visual Basic constants.

In addition to the Libraries/Projects that we have looked at so far, there are several more that are in the list box. These are as follows:

- `VBA - Visual Basic for Applications`—These are the methods and procedures that pertain to VBA version 2.0, which is the language engine in Visual Basic.
- `MSComDlg`, `TabDlg`, `RichTextLib`, `ComctlLib`, `MSDBCtls`, `MSDBGrid`, and `MSRDC`—These seven are custom controls. The methods and properties associated with all custom controls in the current project also can be found in Object Browser. The exact number of controls you have will vary depending on your configuration of Visual Basic.
- `DAO - Microsoft DAO 3.0 Object Library`—This object library provides database access to bound controls.

Figure 8.7 shows these choices. Remember that your listing may vary depending on your version and configuration of Visual Basic.

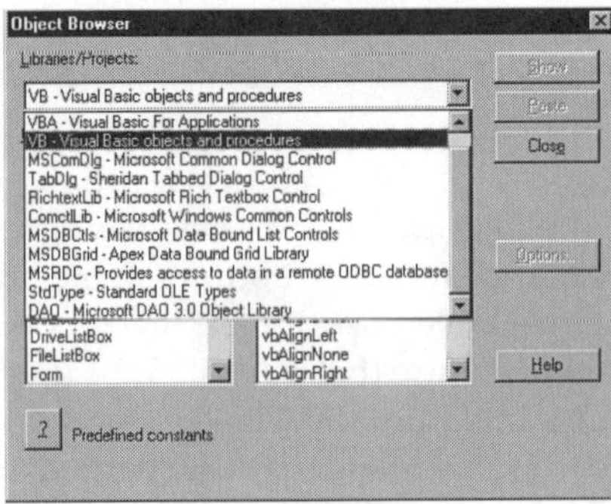

Figure 8.7

The Libraries/Projects drop-down list box.

It is best to limit the libraries and custom controls in a project to those being used. This reduces the chances for confusion, reduces the number of files needed to be distributed with the program, makes loading of the program faster, and reduces the time it takes for compilation. You control the inclusion and exclusion of these libraries individually by using the References properties sheet, which appears when you choose Tools, References from the Visual Basic main menu (see fig. 8.8).

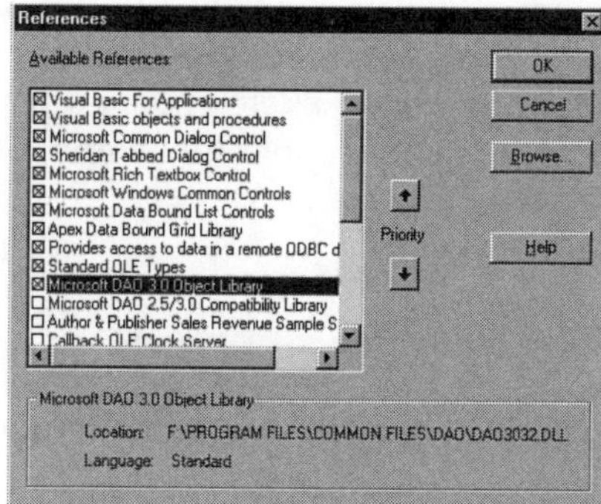

Figure 8.8

The References properties sheet.

You click on the check boxes to include or exclude these references from your project. The following are the only ones that are not optional:

- Visual Basic: objects and procedures
- Microsoft Visual Basic Environment

These are required in order to run the system at all. The others can be added or removed as you choose, or as your project requires.

The order of the items is important also. Whenever there is a name conflict between objects, the order of the placement of libraries in this list is used as a tie-breaker. The libraries that are listed higher will be used. Because of the potential significance of this rule, the References properties sheet provides a way to adjust the priorities via the arrows next to Priority in the References properties sheet.

The bottom of the properties sheet also displays the path and filename of the reference. This helps you associate the internal name of the library with its physical file name. You can use the Browse button to search for and add any other references that are not in the list.

Summary

In this chapter, we discussed the notion of objects and methods, two key concepts that serve as a major portion of the foundation of Visual Basic. We also discussed the difficulty of learning and managing the hundreds of objects that are included in the system.

We looked at the importance of Object Browser, a utility that can be of great help when you are trying to learn about a new object. Rather than being a duplicate of the online help system, Object Browser enables you to perform research on a topic from an object-centered point of view. It can also paste the name of a constant, or a skeleton for a call into your code. And, you can add descriptions for elements of your program by using the Options button. (You can easily bring up the Object Browser by pressing the F2 key, or by using the toolbar and menu.)

We also looked at the References properties sheet, which controls what objects are available to your applications and, as a consequence, which are viewable through Object Browser.

Review Questions

You can find the answers to the Review Questions in Appendix B.

1. True or False: All objects of the same class are identical.
2. True or False: Custom controls have properties, but no methods.

3. How do you find out what constants are defined in a project?
4. What is a reference?

5. Why not just include every library and .OCX in every project?

Review Exercises

1. Using Object Browser, find out the use of the `Picture` property of a form.
2. Using Object Browser, find out the properties and methods associated with the `Printer` object.

3. Use the online help system's Search facility to look up the `Icon` property. The result should look the same as what is shown in figure 8.4.
4. Remove a reference using the References properties sheet, then look for it in Object Browser.

5. Add a new custom control to your project. Use Object Browser to look at the properties and methods associated with this new control.

CHAPTER 9

The Form

The largest productivity gains that programmers enjoy when using Microsoft Visual Basic come when they use built-in objects. The most important of these built-in objects is the *form*. Forms are the canvas that programmers use to bring their ideas to life. But unlike the painter's canvas, which is white and lifeless until the picture is painted, forms can be very impressive when viewed in isolation. A form can be a simple gray rectangle, or it can be a beautifully colored and textured window complete with special icons and a menu bar. The purpose of this chapter is to make you aware of the options that you have when designing forms. Your job is to learn how to create forms that set the mood and ambiance that your applications require.

Customizing a Form

In Chapter 2, "Visual Basic Programs," you created a simple application with a common, boring form. Unfortunately, most of the applications that are written make such poor use of forms that you might not suspect that it is possible to create a good one. Let's start by creating a boring form and then make it more interesting in stages. Create your form by opening a new project. You will have a form on the screen called `Form1` by default for all new projects. Click the Run button and observe that the form looks like the one shown in figure 9.1.

Surely you can make it more interesting than it is here.

Figure 9.1
A boring form.

Adding Background Color to a Form

The first thing that you can do to this form is to change its color. You can do this in either of two ways. The first way is to change its property in the Properties window. To do this, click on the form to make it the selected object, and then click on the `BackColor` property in the Properties window. You will see that this property has a strange-looking number as its value, as shown in figure 9.2.

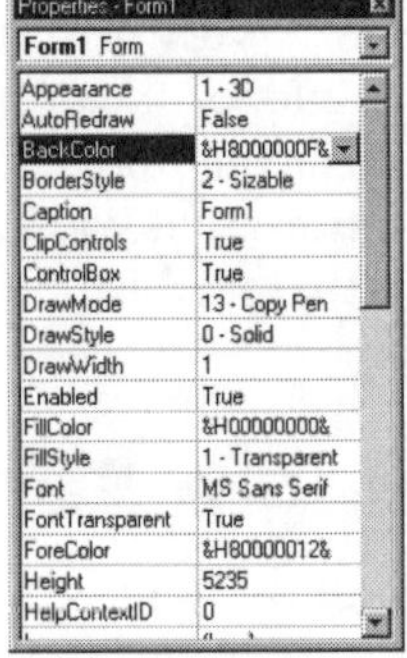

Figure 9.2
The Property window.

Because your form is currently gray, the string `&H8000000F&` appears as the value of the `BackColor` property. This string tells Visual Basic to make the background gray. Those of you who love obscure codes and symbols can change the color by changing the value of this string using the keyboard. Change the value to `&H00000000&` and see what happens. Your form now looks like the one shown in figure 9.3.

Although it is kind of fun to plug in a new number to this string and see what happens, it isn't very productive. Most of us would rather pick colors visually, so Visual Basic has provided a palette feature for color selection. You can access the palette by clicking on the little arrow to the far right of the `BackColor` property box. This brings up a palette that looks like the one shown in figure 9.4.

Figure 9.3
A solid black form.

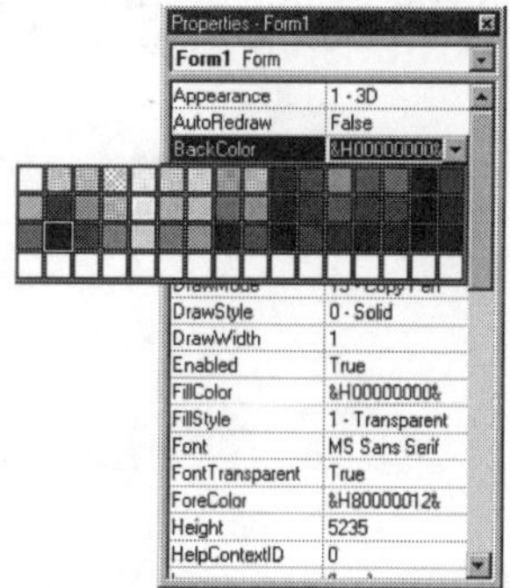

Figure 9.4
The color palette.

Click on the color that catches your eye. Your form now has a pleasing background color. If you choose a medium gray (`&H00808080&`) for your color, your form should look like the one shown in figure 9.5.

Figure 9.5
A medium gray form.

Notice that the character string representation of the color in the Settings box changes with each color. You can use this feature to put color changes in your code.

Click on the code window, choose Form1 as the object, and choose Click as the event. Include the following code in the Form_Click() subroutine:

Example

```
Private Sub Form_Click ()
   Form1.BackColor = &HFFFF00
End Sub
```

There is an easy way to get the string code for the color that you like. To get the string that specifies the desired color, just bring up the palette and click on the color that you like. The string code for that color will appear in the Settings box for the BackColor property. You can then type that value into the code in the event procedure that you want. Alternatively, you could cut and paste it into your code using the Clipboard. Your code window should now resemble figure 9.6.

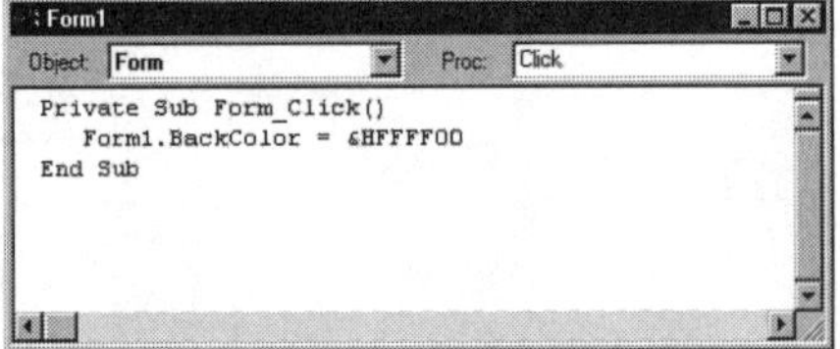

Figure 9.6
The code window for a color change.

Run the program and click anywhere on the form. Your form background should now be a lovely cyan color.

When you use the Properties window to set the BackColor property, the color that you choose will be the color of the form when the application is started. Whenever your application assigns a new BackColor to your form in the program, the color changes in concert with the event that triggers the code.

> **Caution:** Exercise judgment when using colors in Visual Basic. When used tastefully, colors can add to the atmosphere of an application. When used poorly, colors can make a program look cheap and homemade. Enlist the services of artistic people when deciding which colors to use. One of the methods I employ is to ask for the opinion of co-workers who are not programmers. They can usually provide a good insight from a user's perspective.

Changing the Form's Size

Now that you know how to change the color of a form, you are ready to learn how to alter other characteristics. One useful action to perform on a form is to change its size. To present a form in the right way, it is important that it be the correct size. Just as you can change the color in more than one way, you can change the size in more than one way. Let's look at controlling the size of a form by changing the Properties settings. To do this, start Visual Basic and display a form. Go to its Properties window and change the value of the `Height` property to 1500 and the `Width` property to 5000. The result is a form that looks like the one shown in figure 9.7.

Figure 9.7

A form that is 1500 twips by 5000 twips.

You may be wondering what units of measurement Visual Basic is using. It is clear that it isn't inches or feet. It is a nerdy little unit called the *twip* (not to be confused with a twerp). A twip is equal to 1/1440 of an inch. This unit frees you somewhat from using pixels. Pixels (picture elements) are difficult to use because there are varying numbers of them, depending on the resolution of the monitor and video card that is displaying the application. This means that a window that was designed for one resolution will change size when run on a system that is using another resolution. Twips are defined in terms of an absolute, the inch, and are therefore independent of the resolution of the display device. They have another advantage in that twips avoid the need for fractional math. If Visual Basic described sizes in terms of inches, you would find it very familiar, but you would be expressing sizes in terms such as .033 inches. This would be a pain. It is hard to conceive of a size smaller than 1/1440 of an inch; therefore, there is no need to define a fractional twip. All twip values can then be whole numbers.

Now that you are an experienced twip flipper, let's see how you can change the size of your window during program execution. Just for laughs, change the size of your form to 5000 twips (height) by 7000 twips (width). Now, create two buttons, `btnHeight` and `btnWidth`. Label them *Height* and *Width* respectively, and locate them in the top-left corner of your form as shown in figure 9.8. Change the `Name` property of the Height button to `btnHeight` and the `Name` property of the Width Button to `btnWidth`.

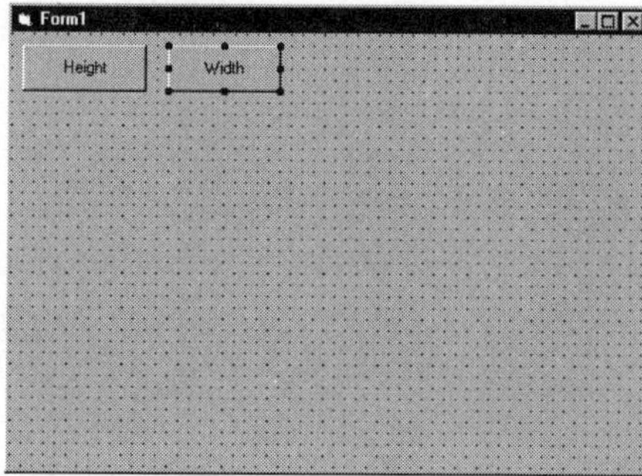

Figure 9.8

A form with two buttons.

Example

Double-click the button named `btnHeight` and add the following code:

```
Private Sub btnHeight_Click ()
   Form1.Height = Form1.Height - 500
End Sub
```

Next, add the following to `btnWidth`:

```
Private Sub btnWidth_Click ()
   Form1.Width = Form1.Width - 500
End Sub
```

Next, run the example and observe that each time you click the button labeled `Height`, the window gets shorter by about one third of an inch. The same occurs when you click `Width`—the window gets narrower by the same amount.

You know from using Windows applications that the user can normally change the size of a window using the mouse and the corners and sides of the window. You may be wondering why you should even bother to set the size when the user can override your actions by resizing the window with the mouse. You can remove these capabilities from your applications if you choose by changing the form's properties. Later in the chapter, in the section "Changing the Form's Border Style," you will see how to accomplish this.

Changing the Form's Location

It is often useful to control the location of a window on the desktop. When Visual Basic is started, all of the windows that form the development environment appear in a certain size and at a certain location on the screen. At times, you will want to have your application behave in much the same way. First, take a look at controlling the location of a form by changing the Properties settings. To do this, start Visual Basic and display a form. Go to its Properties window and change the value of the `Top` property to 1440 and the `Left` property to 144. The result is a form that looks like the one shown in figure 9.9.

Figure 9.9

A form located at 1440,144.

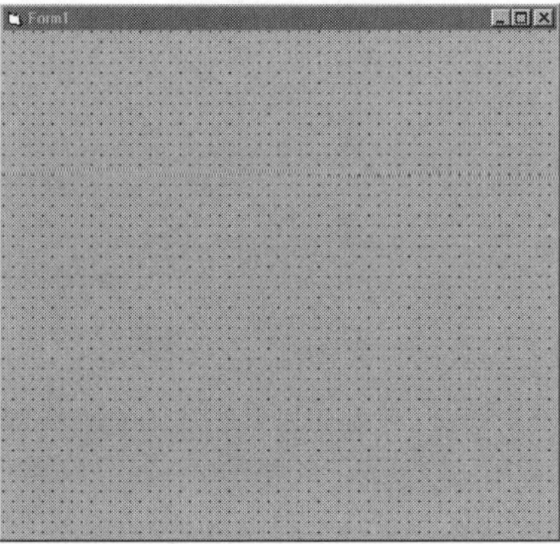

The reason for picking such odd numbers for the location is simple. Because one twip is equal to 1/1440 of an inch, 1440 twips equal one inch. Thus, your form is now located 1 inch from the top of the screen and 1/10th of an inch from the left. These measurements may not be exactly the same on different resolutions and different sizes of monitors, but are a fairly close estimation.

You could change the location of your window during program execution in the same manner that you changed the size. Create two buttons, `btnDown` and `btnRight`. Label them `Down` and `Right`, respectively, and place them as shown in figure 9.10.

Figure 9.10

A form with Down and Right buttons.

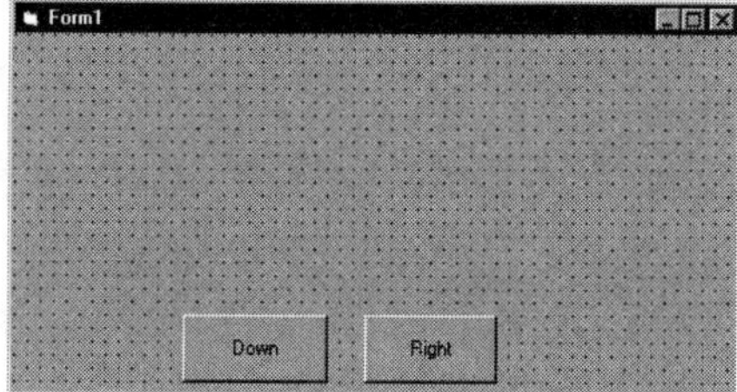

Double-click on the button named `btnDown` and add the following code to it:

Example

```
Private Sub btnDown_Click ()
   Form1.Top = Form1.Top + 720
End Sub
```

Next, add the following to `btnRight`:

```
Private Sub btnRight_Click ()
   Form1.Left = Form1.Left + 720
End Sub
```

Next, run the example and observe that each time you click the button labeled *Down*, the window moves down by about 1/2 an inch. The same occurs when you click on *Right*: the window moves right by the same amount.

Next, you will learn how you can make it impossible for the user to override the sizing and location of your windows.

Changing the Form's Border Style

When you run Windows applications, you are accustomed to seeing windows that look like the one shown in figure 9.11.

Figure 9.11
An ordinary window.

The most important features of the window are the following:

- The Control menu box—The Control menu allows the user to close, minimize, or maximize the window. It contains the programs icon (or a Windows default icon if the program does not have one) and is located in the top-left corner of most windows.
- The Window borders—These are used to change the size of the window in one direction.
- The Window corners—These are used to change the size of the window in two directions.
- The Title Bar—This contains the caption for the window. It is also used to move the window to a different location and to toggle the `WindowState` between Maximize and Restore (by double-clicking) if the window `BorderStyle` and `MaxButton` properties are set to allow these states.
- The Maximize button—This button causes the window to resize itself to fill the entire screen.
- The Minimize button—This button transforms the window into an icon.
- The Restore button—This button performs the same function as double-clicking the title bar.

This type of window is desirable in the majority of applications, but not in all of them. When writing a system that will be used by non-computer users, it would be nice to remove the resizing and moving capabilities, so that users are not confused by another worker's minimizing or closing the application. Systems that will be used by the general public, such as an office building directory system, can be easier to use if they don't have too many controls on the screen. Visual Basic's strategy for managing this kind of activity is to remove the controls from the window. If you want to fix the size, remove the border. If you want to fix the location, remove the title bar. If you want to eliminate the user's ability to close the application, remove the Control menu button. Take a look at how this is done.

Unlike most other properties of the form, the properties that control the presence or absence of the window controls cannot be altered at runtime. During design, the programmer specifies which of the controls to make available to the user at runtime. These are then fixed until the program is changed in design mode.

The first property that you will study is the `BorderStyle` property. The name of this property might fool you into thinking that it controls only the cosmetics of the window. It controls much more than that. In the window shown in figure 9.11, the `BorderStyle` property is set to `2 - Sizable`. What this really means is that you want this window to have all of the controls that you normally find in a garden-variety window. This includes resizing borders and corners, a Minimize button, a Maximize button, a title bar, and a Control menu button. Now, change this property on `Form1` to be `0 - None`. Next, run the application and observe that the window that is created looks like the one shown in figure 9.12. Be sure to include a way to end this program with one of the controls that you provide. Otherwise, you will find that you have invented a Windows version of the infamous infinite loop program. Remember, it isn't polite to make users have to use Ctrl+Alt+Delete to close your program.

Figure 9.12

A window without borders.

Although this window might look strange, it would be useful in a situation where you want the user to interact with the system only through the controls that you provide to him.

If the borderless window is too stark for your taste, take a look at one that is a little more luxurious. Change the `BorderStyle` property to `1 - Fixed Single`. The word *Fixed* means that the size of the window is fixed by the fact that there are no resizing handles on the border of the window. The word *Single* refers to the fact that the border is there, but it is of single width, or, in other words, fairly thin. Figure 9.13 shows a window that has been designated `Fixed Single`.

Figure 9.13

A fixed single window.

The most interesting feature of this window is the absence of any way to change the size of the window. Notice, however, that there is also no way to maximize, minimize, and middle-size the window (change it from full screen back to window mode). Note that it is possible to "grab" the title bar and relocate the window.

The third of the `BorderStyle` property values is `3-Fixed Dialog`. The word *Fixed* means that the resizable borders are missing, but in this case, it also means that the Minimize and Maximize buttons are missing. This means that this window will remain the same size for the duration of its existence. It can be moved, however, because it has a title bar. Figure 9.14 illustrates this kind of `BorderStyle`.

The fourth and fifth `BorderStyles`, (`Fixed` and `Sizable ToolWindow`) have a reduced-size title bar, no minimize or maximize buttons, and do not appear on the Windows 95 Task Bar.

Figure 9.14

A window with a fixed dialog `BorderStyle`.

Another way to control the functionality of the form itself is through the use of the `ControlBox` property of the form. When set to `True`, the Control menu box appears in the top left corner of the window. As stated earlier, clicking on this box brings up a menu which allows the application to be terminated, among other things. Figure 9.15 shows a window whose `BorderStyle` is set to `2-Sizable`, but whose `ControlBox` property is set to `False`.

Figure 9.15

A window with no Control menu box.

This form is missing not only the Control menu box, but is also missing all of the other window controls. You can set the `MaxButton` and `MinButton` properties to `True` or `False` in order to give or take away your user's power to turn your application into an icon or to make it become full-screen. The `ControlBox` property has to be set to True in order for the `MaxButton` and `MinButton` properties to be available, regardless of their settings. By learning to combine these flags and border styles, you can achieve nearly any level of control over what the user can do while running your application.

Writing on a Form

Having established yourself as a form-creating maniac, you are ready to enter the world of text. Many of us who grew up in the dark ages of computing (in other words, before the release of Windows 3.0) remember when computers could do very little more than display text on a screen. Freed from that indentured state by the introduction of the Graphical User Interface (GUI), you avoid text like the plague. There are times, however, when buttons and icons just don't communicate as well as the boring old alphabet that you learned by singing along with Big Bird and Ernie on Sesame Street. True, it is definitely uncool to actually use words on a GUI screen, but let's learn how to do it, anyway.

To put text on a form, you simply open the event to which you want to react, and write a few lines of code shown in the following example.

Example

```
Private Sub Form_Click ()
   Form1.Print "Hello,World"
End Sub
```

In this example, you have attached the printing to the `Click` event. It could have been attached to any other event that makes sense in the context of your program. Run the program and click on the form six times. The result is shown in figure 9.16.

Figure 9.16
A window containing "Hello,World" printed six times.

You should notice that the text started on a new line each time it printed. A question that comes to mind when printing on a form is, "Where on the form is the text that just printed? Is it above or below the other controls like buttons and text boxes?" Let's run an experiment to find out. Add a button and a text box to the form called `Form1`. The form should look like the one shown in figure 9.17.

Figure 9.17
A form with a button and a text box.

Now, run the application and click on the form itself about nine or ten times. Next, look and see that the words appear behind the button and the text box as shown in figure 9.18.

Figure 9.18

A button and text box with form text behind them.

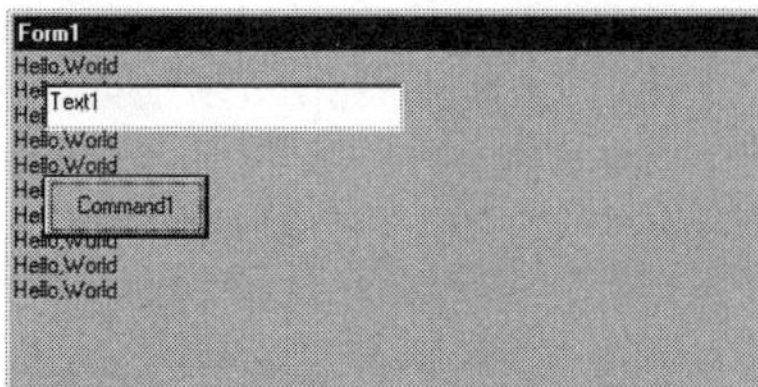

By way of analogy, you can think of the form itself as the wall. Text printed on the wall is like paint. The controls are hung on the wall like paintings.

Changing the Font

One thing clear from the preceding example is that the text is not very exciting. In fact, it is downright boring. Let's see if you can jazz it up a bit by throwing in a few fonts. Delete the button and text box from the form, then change the `Form1_Click` subroutine to look like the example that follows:

Example

```
Private Sub Form_Click()
   Form1.FontName = "Courier"
   Form1.Print "Hello,World"
   Form1.FontName = "Arial"
   Form1.Print "Hello,World"
   Form1.FontName = "MS Dialog"
   Form1.Print "Hello,World"
End Sub
```

These statements tell Visual Basic to print Hello,World three times. The first time, it is printed in Courier, which is an old-fashioned-looking typewriter font. The second time, it is printed in Arial, which is a modern-looking font. The third time it is printed in MS Dialog, which is bolder. Figure 9.19 shows the results.

Figure 9.19

Multiple fonts on one form.

Fonts come to computers from the world of the printing press. Each letter in the alphabet can be drawn in a variety of ways. They can be short and stout, or tall and skinny. They can be ornate or plain. Commercial printing companies have used fonts to create moods for their books. Computers have brought fonts to new heights in programs such as CorelDRAW!.

The tasteful use of fonts can be very effective in applications. Be careful, however, not to mix fonts that are too dissimilar. If you do, your user will see an unsightly mix of text on-screen that is hard on the eyes as well as hard to read.

There are other ways to alter the appearance of text on the screen besides the font style. You can also change the size and color of the letters. In addition, you can make your font bold, put it in italics, underline it, or strike through it with a line. To see this, change the code in the `Form_Click` subroutine to that shown in the example that follows:

Example

```
Private Sub Form_Click()
   Form1.FontName = "Arial"
   Form1.Print "Hello,World"
   Form1.FontSize = 24
   Form1.Print "Hello,World"
   Form1.FontBold = True
   Form1.Print "Hello,World"
   Form1.FontItalic = True
   Form1.Print "Hello,World"
   Form1.FontStrikethru = True
   Form1.Print "Hello,World"
   Form1.ForeColor = &h808080
   Form1.Print "Hello,World"
End Sub
```

The result of this example is shown in figure 9.20.

Figure 9.20

Multiple effects on a form's text.

Observe that the last line of the preceding example was formatted as Courier, 24 point, bold, italics, strikethrough, and gray.

At times, you will see the form name omitted from the property assignment. The line will be coded as follows:

```
Print "Hello,World"
```

instead of this:

```
Form1.Print "Hello,World".
```

If you type this code, you will find that it yields the desired result. What it doesn't do is help others understand your code. Relying on assumptions can make this task more difficult than it needs to be. Whenever possible, write code in the most readable form possible.

Adding a Custom Background

Earlier in this chapter, you learned how to change the color of the form's background. The next logical step in making your form more attractive is to give it a background design. This is a simple task in Visual Basic. Take a blank form, `Form1`, and add an attractive background to it. To accomplish this, you simply choose the `Picture` property in the form's Properties window. When you click on the ... box next to the `Picture` property's value, you see a properties sheet like the one in figure 9.21.

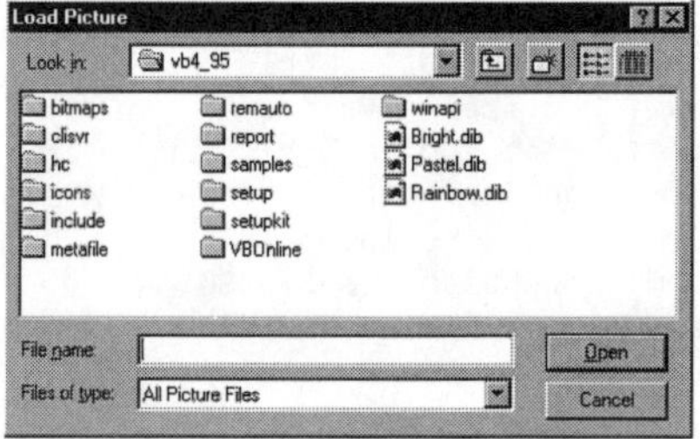

Figure 9.21
The file location properties sheet for pictures.

Use this properties sheet to find CLIPBOARD.WMF in the ?:\vb4\metafile\business directory (where *?* is the hard disk drive where you installed Visual Basic, and assuming you installed Visual Basic into the VB4 subdirectory). The background will look like the one shown in figure 9.22.

This pattern acts like the text that you put on the form earlier. It acts like paint that is put on behind the controls. Just to convince yourself that this is true, put a few controls on the form and see that it now looks like the one shown in figure 9.23.

You can see that buttons, labels, and clip art all appear on top of this form picture. Hopefully, this example will give you ideas for how to make your application more interesting.

Figure 9.22

The form with a metafile background.

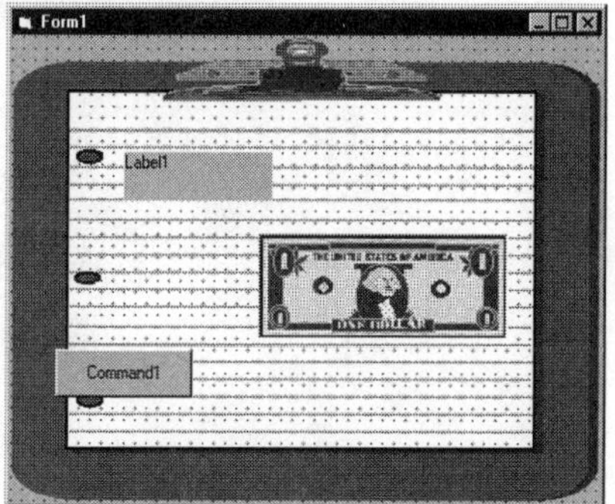

Figure 9.23

Several controls on the background.

It is also possible to change the background of a form at runtime. To do this, however, you will need to introduce a new Visual Basic feature called the *built-in function*. Later, in Chapter 25, "Sub-Procedures and Functions," you will learn how to write subroutines and functions. The authors of Visual Basic have supplied a number of functions for you. These functions include some simple ones like `Date$`, which returns the current date, and `Sin`, which returns the Sine of an angle (for you trigonometry-loving readers). There are more powerful functions such as `InputBox`, which pops up a dialog box for you, and the one that is needed now, `LoadPicture`. The `LoadPicture` function takes care of all of the processing necessary to remove the old background from your form and replace it with a new one. The following code sequence causes the clipboard background to change to a 3 1/2-inch floppy disk background.

Create a form that has two buttons on it, Command1 and Command2. Change Command1's `Caption` property value to `Clipboard` and Command2's `Caption` property value to `Disk`. Next, add the following code to these buttons (Note: Change the drive and directory in the `LoadPicture` function to match the drive and directory where you have loaded Visual Basic):

Example

```
Private Sub Command1_Click()
Form1.Picture=LoadPicture("?:\vb\metafile\business\clipbord.wmf")
End Sub

Private Sub Command2_Click()
Form1.Picture = LoadPicture("?:\vb\metafile\business\disk35.wmf")
End Sub
```

When you click the Disk button, the result of this code is a form that has a background like the one shown in figure 9.24, and when you click the Clipboard button, the result is like the one shown in Figure 9.22.

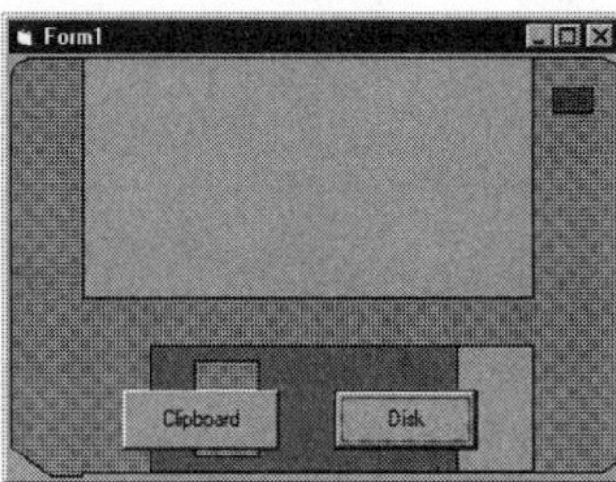

Figure 9.24

Changing backgrounds on a form.

The use of backgrounds can greatly enhance the perceived value of your software in the eyes of the buyer or user.

Changing the Icon

When your user minimizes your form, what icon does he see? Try minimizing `Form1`. What you see is an icon that looks like the one shown in figure 9.25.

Figure 9.25

The default icon.

Not very exciting, is it? Surely you can find a better icon than that one. To change the icon for a form, simply select the `Icon` property in the form's Properties window, and click the ... button. This brings up the properties sheet shown in figure 9.26, from which you can choose the name of an icon file (.ico).

Select the icon called FLGUSA01.ICO from the ?:\vb4\icons\flags directory (where *?:* is the hard drive where Visual Basic is installed and assuming you installed Visual Basic in the VB4 subdirectory). Figure 9.27 shows this icon.

Next, run the program and click the Minimize button. When you click the Minimize button, your application is minimized to an icon, which now looks like a flag. As you probably noticed when you were looking for the FLGUSA01 icon, a bunch of icons ship with Visual Basic. You can use any of these or any other icon-sized bitmap in your applications. There are several icon editing tools on the market, as well as commercial icon libraries available in both retail and shareware forms.

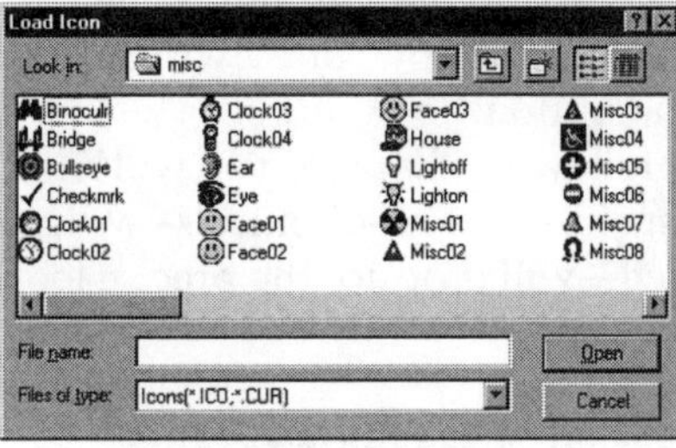

Figure 9.26
The icon selection dialog box.

Figure 9.27
The flag icon.

Miscellaneous Form Properties

Although this chapter is not intended to be a reference on all of the properties of forms, there are a few more that deserve mention. The first is the `Enabled` property. This property controls whether a window will accept events and respond to them. If you set `Enabled` to `False`, it ignores all inputs. If you set it to `True`, it behaves normally.

Another important property is called `Visible`. As the name implies, you can cause an active form to be hidden from view simply by changing this property.

`WindowState` is a property that controls how a form is displayed when it is loaded. If the value of this property is `0-Normal`, the form comes up as a window. If the value is `1-Minimized`, it is loaded as an icon. If its value is `2-Maximized`, it comes up in full-screen mode. Also, set the `MinButton` property to `False`, the `MaxButton` property to `False`, and the `WindowState` set to `2-Maximized`. Finally, set `ControlBox` to `False`, and make sure there is nothing in the `Caption` property. This will create a full-screen version of your application that can't be minimized (if there is a title bar, the user can double-click it, which restores it, and it will no longer be full-screen).

This is how you create a full-screen application in Visual Basic. The user cannot turn the application into a normal window. If he wants to close the application, he could simply double-click the Control menu button. However, you could set the `ControlBox` property to `False`, also. Doing so makes the application permanently full-screen. This is normally done for systems that will be used by people who are not familiar with computers.

Summary

In this chapter, you learned how to use the form as a primary component of your application. Each form can have a variety of colors, sizes, locations, and backgrounds. You can control these properties by changing the value of the property in the Properties window, or by writing code and attaching it to a control such as a command button.

In the following chapters, you will be introduced to the built-in controls that ship with Visual Basic. These controls—when added to the form that you now understand well—will produce the precise look and feel that you desire.

Review Questions

Answers to the review questions can be found in Appendix A.

1. How do you change the background of a form during design?
2. How do you change the background of a form at runtime?

3. What is a twip?
4. How do you make it impossible for your users to resize a window?

5. What is the Control menu?
6. Is `LoadPicture()` a subroutine, function, or event procedure?

Review Exercises

1. Create a form that has six buttons called Blue, Gray, White, Red, Yellow, and Green. Cause the background color to change to the color that corresponds to the `Click` event associated with each button. When you click on the Red button, the background should turn red, and so on.
2. Create a form with four buttons called Up, Down, Left, and Right. When one of these buttons is clicked, move the form 100 twips in the direction indicated by the name of the button.

3. Design a form that occupies the full screen and has no Control menu, no Minimize button, no Maximize button, and no title bar. Be sure to include a button that allows you to exit when you are ready.
4. Create a form that can be resized but cannot be minimized nor maximized.

5. Using the `LoadPicture` function, create a form that has six different backgrounds and six different buttons. When a button is clicked, the background should change.

CHAPTER 10

The Button Tools

Growing up in the 20th century, you've been surrounded by machines. These machines have commonly been powered by electricity. The inventors needed a way to control the starting and stopping of these machines, so they designed pushbuttons. As the number of devices multiplied, inventors were challenged to invent new types of buttons to meet the different logical needs of their devices.

This chapter deals with the button controls that are patterned after the buttons and switches used in electrical devices. This chapter provides a number of examples of how you can use these buttons to perform tasks that are common in computing.

Three types of buttons became commonplace: the pushbutton, the toggle switch, and the radio button. When Windows developers were looking for ways to enable users to communicate with the computer, the developers took analogies from the physical world. This made sense because people accept the familiar more readily than the foreign.

The Command Button Tool

Think for a moment about the electrical devices in your home. Consider, for example, the microwave oven. The controls on the face contain perhaps a dozen buttons:

- The Start button turns on the microwave.
- The Stop button turns off the microwave.
- The buttons on the number pad allow you to set an amount of time for the microwave to operate.

You can create a form that emulates this interface by using only the Command Button tool. Figure 10.1 shows the Command Button tool in the Toolbox.

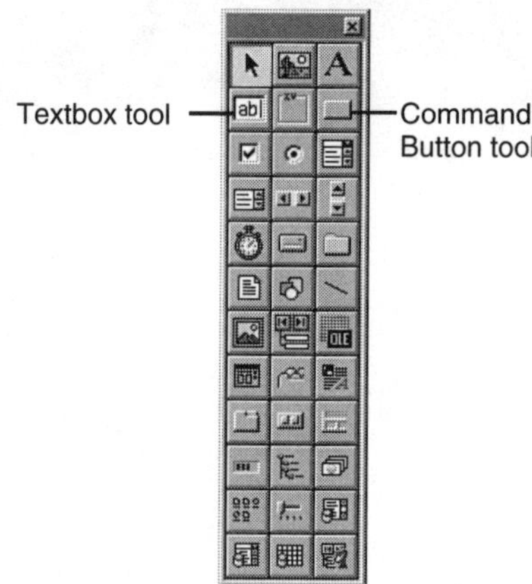

Figure 10.1
The Command Button tool.

If you double-click the Command Button tool, one button is placed in the center of the form (see fig. 10.2).

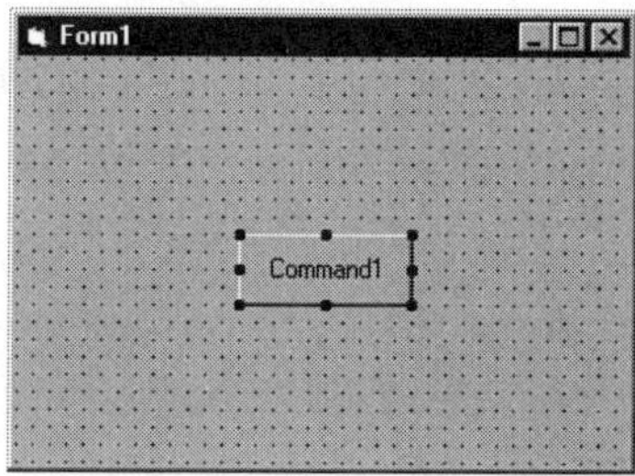

Figure 10.2
Putting a command button on a form.

The button appears on the form with a default caption of `Command1`, a default location in the center of the form, and a default size. You can change these default values once you have created the control. Now change the form to be more like what you might want. First change the `Caption` property of the `Command1` button to `Start`. (For information on how to change properties, consult Chapter 7, "The Properties Window.") Next, move the button to the lower-right corner of the form by dragging it with the mouse. Now change the name of the button itself to `btnStart`. This is the name that you will use to refer to this button in the event procedures. Change the `Font` property to `Arial 12-point bold`. Your form should now look like that in figure 10.3.

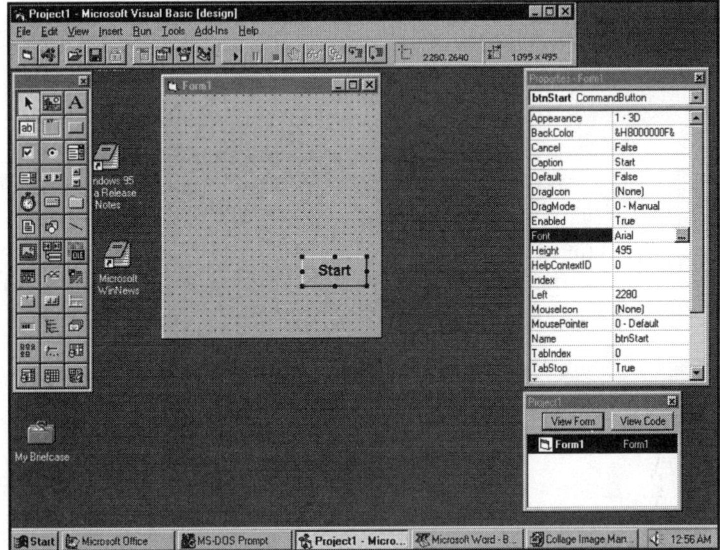

Figure 10.3

Changing the properties of the command button.

Example

You're now ready to add a text box to the bottom of the form so that you can test the buttons as you put them on the form. Double-click the Textbox tool (refer to fig. 10.1). Position the text box at the bottom of the screen, as shown in figure 10.4. Name the text box `txtOutput` and set its `Text` property to `blank`.

Now test the operation of the command button by writing a simple output routine. Double-click the command button to bring up the Code window. You will see some code that looks like the following:

```
Private Sub btnStart_Click()
End Sub
```

Add a line to the subroutine so that it looks like this:

```
Private Sub btnStart_Click()
   Form1.txtOutput.text = "You clicked Start"
End Sub
```

Run the program and verify that the result of clicking the Start command button looks like that in figure 10.4.

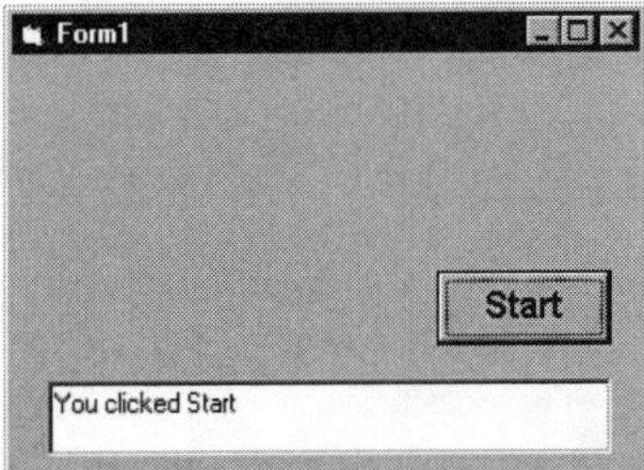

Figure 10.4

Running the sample program.

Next, create a new command button in the same way, but, this time, make it smaller. Name it `btnOne`. Choose 1 as its caption and position it in the upper-left corner of the form (see fig. 10.5). Then open the Code window and add the following code to the `Click` event for `btnOne`:

```
Private Sub btnOne_Click()
   Form1.txtOutput.text = "You clicked on 1"
End Sub
```

This code means that you want to display the sentence `You clicked on 1` in the text box at the bottom of this screen. Now run the program and click `btnOne`. The result should look like that in figure 10.5.

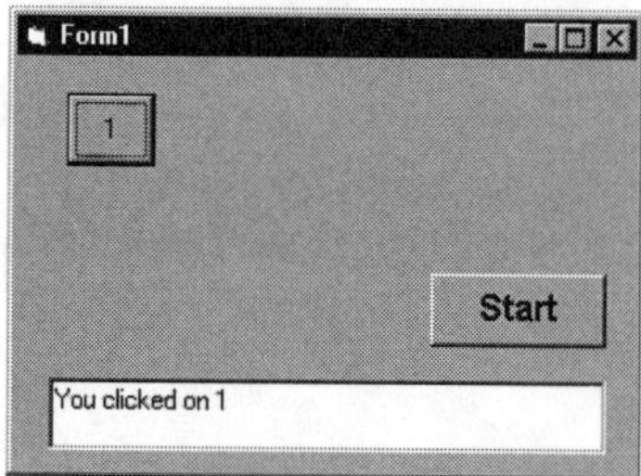

Figure 10.5

Clicking the 1 button.

Now that you've created the first several buttons of the interface, finish the interface by adding the command buttons labeled from 2 to 9, 0, and Stop, as shown in figure 10.6. Name them `btnTwo`, `btnThree`, and so forth; name the Stop button `btnStop`.

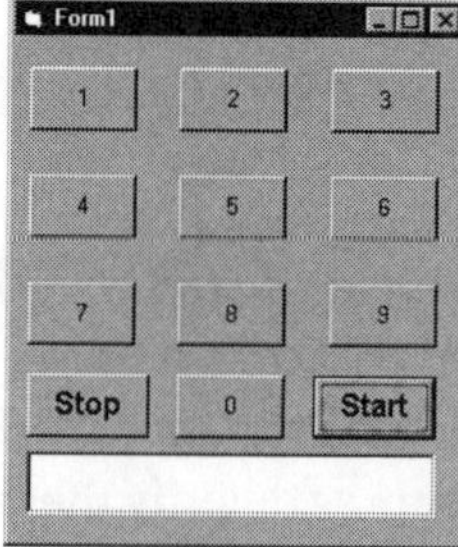

Figure 10.6

The finished application.

Run the application and verify that it works the way you planned. Whenever you press any button, the text box should display `You pressed ?`, where `?` is the caption of the command button you pressed.

The Check Box Tool

Another common type of button is the check box. When you are driving a car with cruise control, you press a lever that turns on the cruise control. The cruise has two possible options, on or off. When you fill out a form, you place checks in boxes to indicate a yes or no answer. The distinguishing features of check boxes are that they are binary (yes/no or true/false) and that each check box is independent of the others. Therefore, you could have any number from 0 to *n* of them checked, where *n* is the number of check boxes on the form.

To see how this control works, build an application that uses check boxes. The first step is to create a clean form (use the File, New Project menu selection if you currently have a project in Visual Basic) and double-click the Check Box tool in the Toolbox (see fig. 10.7).

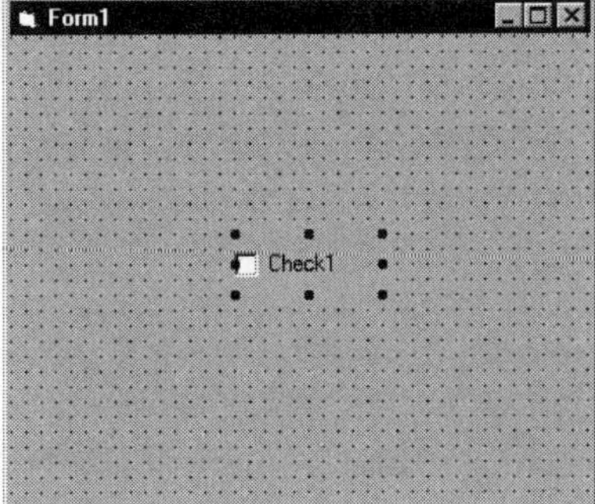

Figure 10.7
The Check Box tool.

A check box appears in the middle of your screen. Change the `Caption` property of the check box to `England` and the `Name` property to `chkEngland`. Next double-click the Picture Box tool (see fig. 10.8).

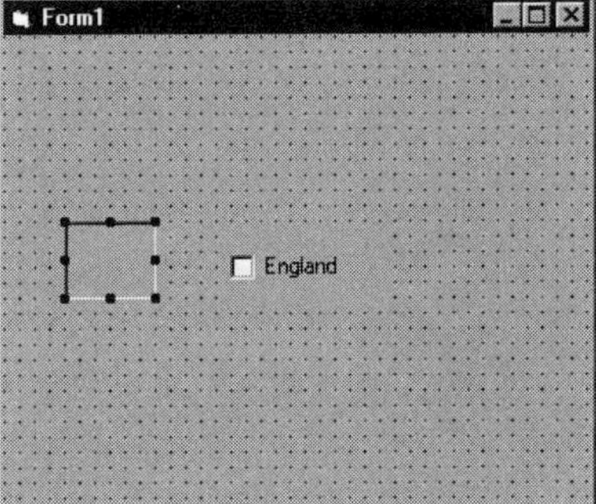

Figure 10.8
The Picture Box tool.

The picture box is formally discussed in Chapter 14, "The Graphics Tools." For now, think of the picture box as a container for pictures. Name the picture control `picEngland` and set its `Visible` property to `False`. Click the `Picture` property and select the file ?:\VB\ICONS\FLAGS\CTRUK.ICO (where ? is the drive where VB is loaded) in the properties sheet that appears. A picture will appear on-screen that looks like the one in figure 10.9.

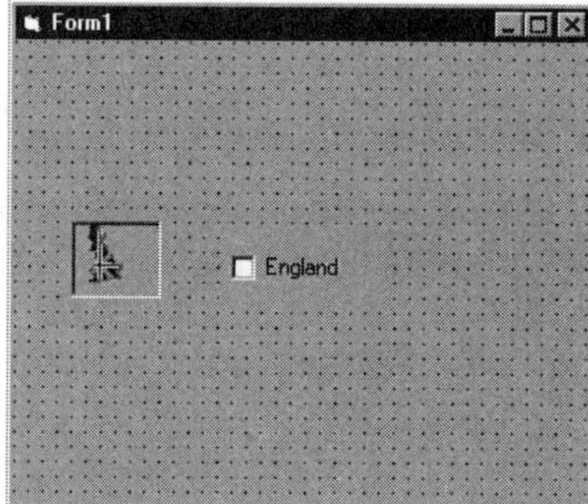

Figure 10.9
A picture of England.

Now combine the picture with the check box to create a small application.

Example

Add the following code to the `Click` event associated with the check box:

```
Private Sub chkEngland_Click()
    If chkEngland.Value = 1 Then
        picEngland.Visible = True
    Else
        picEngland.Visible = False
    End If
End Sub
```

Run this application and click the England check box. The picture of England alternately appears and disappears.

Now create the full-blown application. Create five more check boxes and five more picture boxes according to the information in Tables 10.1 and 10.2. Make certain that you set the `Value` property of the check boxes to 0. This will make the default startup state of the check box as unchecked.

Table 10.1 Check Box Properties for the Countries Example

Control Type	*Control Name*	*Value*
Check box	`chkEngland`	0
Check box	`chkItaly`	0
Check box	`chkSpain`	0

Control Type	*Control Name*	*Value*
Check box	`chkMexico`	0
Check box	`chkFrance`	0
Check box	`chkUSA`	0

Table 10.2 Check Box Pictures for the Countries Example

Control Type	*Control Name*	*Visible*	*Picture**
Picture	`picEngland`	False	CTRUK.ICO
Picture	`picItaly`	False	CTRITALY.ICO
Picture	`picSpain`	False	CTRMEX.ICO
Picture	`picMexico`	False	CTRUSA.ICO
Picture	`picFrance`	False	CTRSPAIN.ICO
Picture	`picUSA`	False	CTRUSA.ICO

Note: *All pictures come from the directory* ?:*VB**ICONS**FLAGS*.

Assemble these new controls in the order shown in figure 10.10.

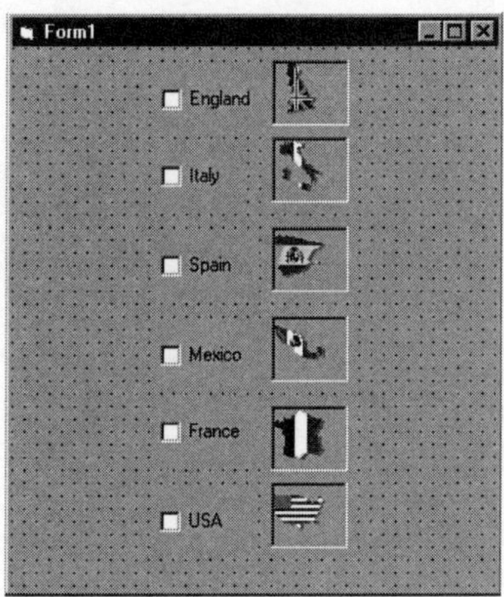

Figure 10.10
The completed application.

Now add the source code in Listing 10.1

Listing 10.1 10LIST01.TXT—Code for the Flags Check Box Controls

```
Private Sub chkEngland_Click()
    If chkEngland.Value = 1 Then
        picEngland.Visible = True
    Else
        picEngland.Visible = False
    End If
End Sub

Private Sub chkFrance_Click()
    If chkFrance.Value = 1 Then
        picFrance.Visible = True
    Else
        picFrance.Visible = False
    End If
End Sub


Private Sub chkItaly_Click()
    If chkItaly.Value = 1 Then
        picItaly.Visible = True
    Else
        picItaly.Visible = False
    End If
End Sub


Private Sub chkMexico_Click()
    If chkMexico.Value = 1 Then
        picMexico.Visible = True
    Else
        picMexico.Visible = False
    End If
End Sub


Private Sub chkSpain_Click()
    If chkSpain.Value = 1 Then
        picSpain.Visible = True
    Else
        picSpain.Visible = False
    End If
End Sub

Private Sub chkUSA_Click()
    If chkUSA.Value = 1 Then
        picUSA.Visible = True
    Else
        picUSA.Visible = False
    End If
End Sub
```

The logic in this program is fairly simple. Each of the `Private Sub` lines represents the start of an event procedure. The `Value` property is equal to 1 when the check box is checked, and 0 if it is unchecked. When a picture box's `Visible` property is set to `True`, you can see it. When it is set to `False`, you cannot. The logic of these procedures is explained here:

```
Private Sub chkEngland_Click()
```

This line is the start of a subroutine that is called when a check box with the `Name` property value of `chkEngland` is clicked (either checked or unchecked).

```
    If chkEngland.Value = 1 Then
```

This line tests to see whether the `Value` property of `chkEngland` is 1 (checked).

```
        picEngland.Visible = True
```

This line sets the `Visible` property of the picture box (with the `Name` property set to `picEngland`) to `True`. This tells Visual Basic to display the picture whose file name is located in the `Picture` property of the picture box.

```
    Else
```

This line means *otherwise*.

```
        picEngland.Visible = False
```

This tells Visual Basic to make the picture invisible.

```
    End If
```

This line tells Visual Basic that the `If` statement is completed.

```
End Sub
```

This tells Visual Basic to end the subroutine.

`If-Then-Else` statements are covered in more detail in Chapter 22, "The If Statement." With this new code, when you run the program, the pictures will appear and disappear based on whether the corresponding check boxes are checked or unchecked.

The Frame and Option Button Tools

Suppose that you were happy with the application you designed in the preceding section. You showed it to the customer, who liked the basic flow but said that only one box could be checked at a time. You could add considerable logic to the event procedures and turn the other boxes off and on, based on which check box was most recently checked. There is an easier way, however. It involves the use of two new controls from the Toolbox.

The first is the option button, or more correctly, the option buttons (because if you have only one, you don't have much of an option, do you?). Some people call option buttons *radio buttons* because they operate like the buttons on some car radios. The second is the Frame control, which groups option buttons together. The OptionButton tool used to create the option button control (see fig. 10.11) and the Frame tool used to create the Frame control (see fig. 10.12) are located in the Toolbox.

Figure 10.11

The OptionButton tool.

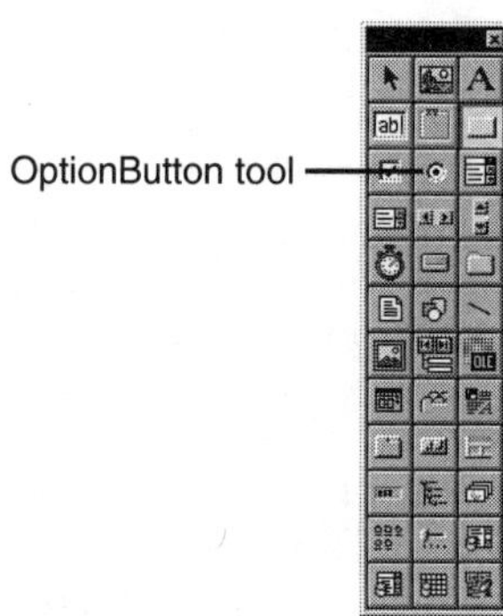

Figure 10.12

The Frame tool.

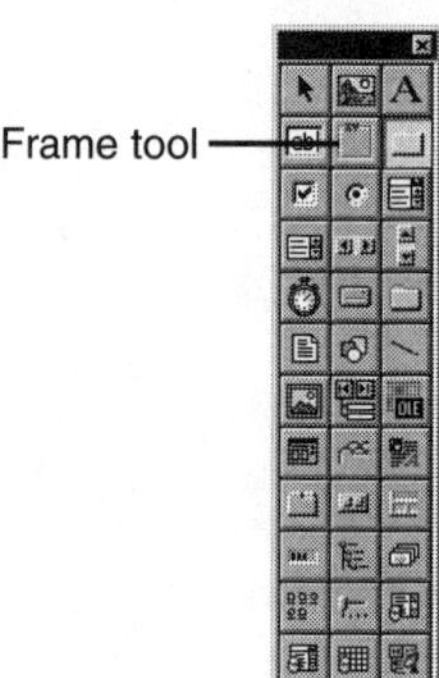

You can modify the last example to show only one picture at a time. You do this by deleting the check box controls and adding a Frame control with the Frame tool from the Toolbox.

> **Note:** When you delete a control, you also have to delete the event code that was associated with the deleted controls. When a control is deleted, VB moves any event code to the General section of the Code window.

Example

The purpose of the Frame tool, when used with option buttons, is to tell Visual Basic which options to group together. Only one of the buttons may be checked at a time, so it is important sometimes to have several groups on the same form. Now the form will look like figure 10.13.

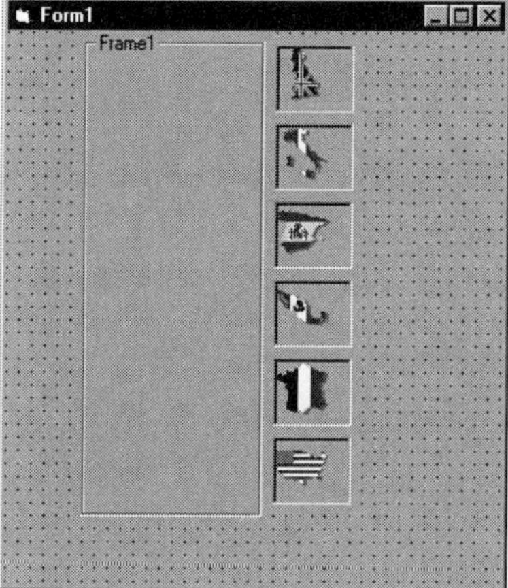

Figure 10.13
Adding a frame to the flag application.

Now add the six option buttons. For each one, click the OptionButton tool in the Toolbox and then show where you want the control to appear by dragging a small rectangle inside the frame.

> **Caution:** Double-clicking the Option Button tool places the button on the form, but not inside the frame where you need it. In Visual Basic, you cannot drag a control onto or off of a container. You must instead cut and then paste it to move it from form to container, container to container, or container to form.

Next, change the value of the `Name` property for each of the six new option buttons, using the values contained in Table 10.3. Then set the `Value` property to `0` for all six buttons.

Table 10.3 Property Values for the Option Buttons

Control Type	*Control Name*
Option button	`optEngland`
Option button	`optItaly`

continues

Table 10.3 Continued

Control Type	*Control Name*
Option button	`optSpain`
Option button	`optMexico`
Option button	`optFrance`
Option button	`optUSA`

Now you're ready to add the following code to the example:

Listing 10.2 10LIST02.TXT—Code for the Option Button version of the *Flags* program

```
Private Sub optEngland_Click()
    Clear_Flags
    If optEngland.Value = True Then
        picEngland.Visible = True
    End If

End Sub
```

Create five other routines that are like this one, but change the country name. Then add a routine to clear the flags off the screen when their option button isn't selected. You add this routine to the general declarations page of the form.

```
Public Sub Clear_Flags()
        picUSA.Visible = False
        picSpain.Visible = False
        picMexico.Visible = False
        picFrance.Visible = False
        picEngland.Visible = False
        picItaly.Visible = False
End Sub
```

The only part of this exercise that makes it unique from a coding perspective is the need for the `Clear_Flags()` subroutine. Visual Basic automatically sets the value of all option buttons except one to `False` when another one is selected. This doesn't clear the pictures from the screen, however. To clear all pictures from the form, you write a simple subroutine that sets the `Visible` property of every flag to `False`. This subroutine is called in the first line of each option button's `Click` event procedure. Then each of the procedures sets the appropriate picture's `Visible` flag to `True`, causing a flag to be displayed. Figure 10.14 shows the complete application.

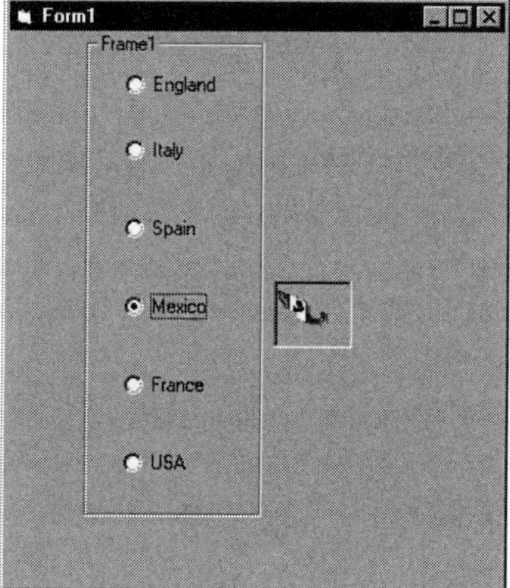

Figure 10.14

The option button version of the flag application.

Try the application and see how the flags appear and disappear according to the option button that is chosen.

Summary

This chapter discussed the thought behind the various kinds of buttons available in Visual Basic 4. The three kinds of buttons—command, check box, and option—form a powerful addition to your personal skills repertoire. They enable you to create some very powerful effects in your programs.

Review Questions

Answers to the review questions can be found in Appendix B.

1. What is the difference between a command button, a check box, and an option button?
2. What is an event procedure?
3. Where did the idea of using pushbuttons originate?

4. How do you make a control disappear?
5. Why do you have to include all the option buttons that logically belong together in the same frame?

6. Why did you write a `Clear_Flags()` subroutine in the last example?
7. What's the purpose of the `Visible` property for pictures?

Review Exercises

1. Create a form with all three kinds of buttons on it.
2. Make a command button that moves the form to a new location on-screen when you click it.

3. Remove the subroutine `Clear_Flags()` from the last example in the chapter and the calls to it from the event procedures. Run the example and see what changes.
4. Create a radio front containing option buttons for each of the radio stations you listen to. Create an event procedure for each button that displays the call letters of that station in a text box when it's clicked.

5. Create an application that contains three different groups of option buttons. (Reminder: Each group must have its own frame.) Make the first group for models of cars (such as Eldorado, Accord, and Taurus), the second for different car body styles (such as four-door, convertible, and hatchback), and the third for colors. Allow the user to choose one button from each group. Create a text box that summarizes what was chosen.

CHAPTER 11

The Scroll Bar Tools

Another great control that has been borrowed from the world of electrical devices is the scroll bar. These switches, called sliders on electrical devices, are commonly found on sound mixers, such as those on "boom boxes." As you slide them up and down, you vary the amount of bass and treble. In any application where you need to provide a "tuning" capability, scroll bars are ideal. The most common use of scroll bars in the Windows programs is to allow the user to control the display of text on a form. The best example of this is Microsoft Word for Windows.

Types of Scroll Bars

Actually, there are two varieties of scroll bars: horizontal and vertical. They are identical in the way that they operate; only their visual presentation is different. Figure 11.1 shows the buttons in the Toolbox for both varieties of scroll bar.

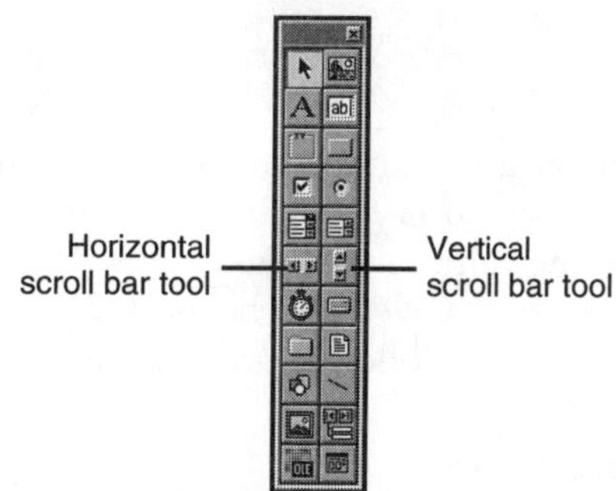

Figure 11.1
The scroll bar icons in the Toolbox.

Example

Let's start an example and work through it so that you can discover how to incorporate scroll bars into your applications. On a new form, add one horizontal scroll bar and one vertical scroll bar. Accept the default names of `HScroll1` and `VScroll1` for them. Add two Text boxes to the form and name them `txtHScroll` and `txtVScroll`. Arrange them on the form, as shown in figure 11.2.

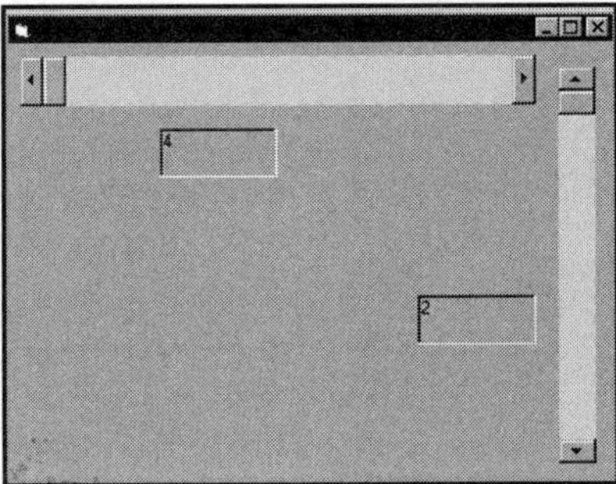

Figure 11.2

Two scroll bars.

Next, change the `Max` property of both scroll bars to `100`, but leave the `Min` property at `0`. The `Max` and `Min` properties determine the range of the scroll bar. The `Value` property of a scroll bar changes as the user moves the little box, called the *thumb* (who thought up that name?). The `Max` property specifies what the `Value` is when the button is all the way down (`VScroll1`) or to the right (`HScroll1`). So, in this example, you are deciding to make the range of the `Value` property from `1-100`.

Next, set the `Text` property of the Text boxes to `0`. This will be the text displayed when the application first starts up. Now, add this code which assigns the value of each scroll bar to its appropriate Text box.

```
Private Sub HScroll1_Change ()
   txtHScroll.Text = HScroll1.Value
End Sub

Private Sub VScroll1_Change ()
   txtVScroll.Text = VScroll1.Value
End Sub
```

Now, run the application and move the thumb on both of the scroll bars around with your mouse. Observe the change in the values displayed in the Text boxes. You will see that the values in the Text boxes do not change until you stop moving the scroll bar. The `Scroll` event can be used to get constant feedback on the movement of the scroll bar. The following code demonstrates this:

```
Private Sub Hscroll1_Scroll()
     Hscroll1_Change
End Sub
```

Changing Scroll Bar Properties

There are a few other scroll bar properties that are worthy of mention. The `Height` and `Width` properties change the appearance of the scroll bars without having any effect on their operation. Figure 11.3 shows some scroll bars that look different from those in figure 11.2.

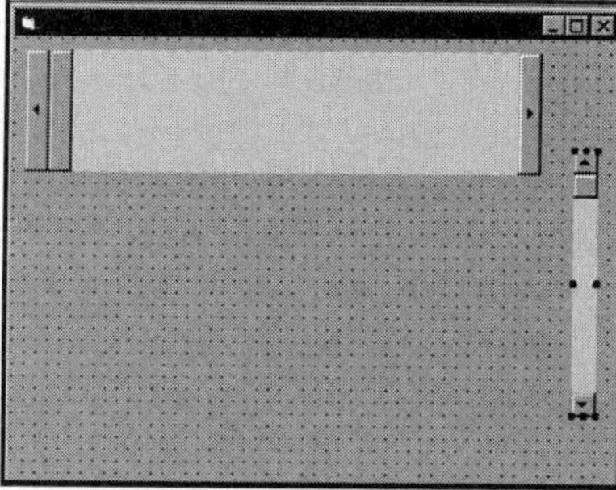

Figure 11.3
Strangely shaped scroll bars.

Another feature that you should try (while the application is running) is the end arrows. With each click, these arrows increment or decrement the `Value` property by one. The size of this increment can be altered by changing the `SmallChange` property of the scroll bar, but it is normally left at `1`.

Next, try clicking the scroll bars, but not on the thumbs. You will notice that the default behavior is just like that of the arrow buttons: plus or minus one. If, however, you alter the `Value` of the `LargeChange` property for the scroll bars, you can make this act more meaningful. Change the `Value` of the `LargeChange` property to `10`, and try clicking the open area of the scroll bar again. Now the changes are in steps of 10 instead of steps of one.

The `Height` property of `HScroll1` has been increased from 255 twips to 735 twips. The `Height` property of `VScroll1` has been changed from 3855 twips to 1855 twips. Notice that the same property name, `Height`, can have a different meaning on the two different controls. Increasing the `Height` of the horizontal scroll bar made it fatter. Decreasing the `Height` of the vertical scroll bar made it shorter, but not narrower. The inverse is true when using the `Width` property.

A good use of fat scroll bars is in systems designed to run on touch-screen terminals. Instead of a nice pointed mouse icon, the user has a dull fat finger. Trying to touch a normal scroll bar with your finger is like trying to thread a needle. The fat scroll bars are much easier on your users.

The `MousePointer` property allows you to specify the look of the mouse pointer when positioned above the scroll bar. The `MousePointer` property is a list box of about a dozen pointer choices. Each of these choices is an alternate pointer. Picking 99-Custom from the mouse pointer options allows you to specify an icon.

Let's do this to see how it works. Select a scroll bar by clicking on it.

Change the `MousePointer` property to 99-Custom. Next, change the `MouseIcon` property to ICONS\MISC\BULLSEYE.ICO in the VB directory. Now, run the program and move the mouse pointer over the horizontal scroll bar. The mouse pointer now looks like a little bull's-eye. This feature can give your user a visual confirmation that the mouse is indeed positioned over the scroll bar.

The scroll bars are controls just like command buttons and text boxes in the eyes of Visual Basic. In an application, you often want the user to think of them as part of the support structure, not as part of the application, per se. The `TabStop` property makes this possible by allowing you to remove the scroll bars from the Tab key's destination list. Let's test that. Change the `TabStop` property to `False` on `HScroll1`. Now, run the program and verify that you are no longer able to tab to `HScroll1`, but you are able to tab to `VScroll1`.

Example

Let's derive a more interesting example in order to illustrate the usefulness of the scroll bars. Create a new form and add our old friends `HScroll1` and `VScroll1`. Make their `Max 6000`, their `LargeChange 500`, and the `SmallChange` equal `100`. Now add a Picture box called `picBike` and change its `BorderStyle` property to `none`. Change its `Left` property to `0` and its `Top` property to `0`. This will make `picBike` borderless and place it in the upper left-hand corner of the screen. To add the picture to the control, click the `Picture` property of the Picture box and select ICONS\INDUSTRY\BICYCLE.ICO in the VB directory. Now add the following code to the example:

```
Private Sub HScroll1_Change ()
   picBike.Left = HScroll1.Value
End Sub

Private Sub VScroll1_Change ()
   picBike.Top = VScroll1.Value
End Sub
```

This code is telling the system to move the bike one twip for every one unit change in the `Value` property of one of the scroll bars. This makes the bike move enough to be easily viewed.

Run the program and observe that, as you manipulate the scroll bars, the bike moves around on the screen, as shown in figure 11.4.

Notice that as you move the thumb by dragging it with the mouse, only the bike moves when you let go of the mouse button. If you use the `SmallChange` arrows on the ends of the scroll bars, the movement is smoother.

Figure 11.4
Using scroll bars to move a bike.

Panning with Scroll Bars

Another common use of scroll bars is to move across a document or picture that is too big to fit in a window. This type of movement is called *panning*. When you pan across a picture, only a portion of the picture shows at any one time. The following example will show how this works.

Example

Create a new form with two scroll bars: `VScroll1` and `HScroll1`. Add a Frame control to the form and size it to fill the entire form except for the two scroll bars. Now, add a Picture control called `picMoney` inside the frame and make it larger than the frame itself. In the `Picture` property of `picMoney`, choose the file that is called METAFILE\BUSINESS\DOLLAR.WMF in the VB directory. Since it is a metafile, it can be enlarged by changing the `Width` property to 12,000 twips and the `Height` property to 8,500 twips.

Set the `Maximum` property of the `HScroll1` scroll bar to `12000` and the `Maximum` property of the `VScroll1` scroll bar to `8500`.

Next, add the following code to the application:

```
Private Sub VScroll1_Change ()
  picMoney.Top = VScroll1.Value * 10
End Sub

Private Sub HScroll1_Change ()
  picMoney.Left = HScroll1.Value * 10
End Sub
```

Run the code and observe that you can move the Picture box over the top of the dollar metafile by manipulating the scroll bars. Figure 11.5 illustrates this.

This type of user interface is ideal for viewing blueprints and other large documents that will not fit on a normal size screen.

Figure 11.5
Panning with scroll bars.

Using Scroll Bars for Data Output

Scroll bars can also be used to display results. In reality, a scroll bar is a lot like a bar on a bar graph. By changing the values of the scroll bars, they can be made to display these changes in data for simple types of functions. The position of the scroll button on the scroll bar can be thought of as a value position and where it is on the scroll bar gives the user vital information. The following example will show this by creating a gas tank display using the scroll bar.

Example

We will use a vertical scroll bar to represent the gas gauge on an automobile. In place of a sensor that measures the level of fluid in the gas tank, you can substitute a simple Timer control. (Timer controls are discussed in detail in Chapter 12, "The Timer Tool.") For this example, it is sufficient to know that a Timer control receives a `Timer` event whenever a specified period of time expires. Create a screen that looks like figure 11.6.

Figure 11.6
The gas tank example.

The first control to add is the Timer. Call it `Timer1` and give it an `Interval` property of `1000` (1 sec). Next, add a vertical scroll bar and call it `VScroll1`. Make its `Max` property equal `100`. Add some labels with "`Empty`," "`Full`," and a cute title, such as "`The Software Gas Tank`." Next, add the following code to the application:

```
Dim Counter as Integer
Private Sub Timer1_Timer()
  Counter = Counter + 10
  If Counter < 101 Then
    VScroll1.Value = Counter
  End If
End Sub
```

This subroutine is telling Visual Basic to create a variable outside the sub and call it `Counter`. The reason that it is declared outside the sub is so that it won't be reinitialized to zero every time the sub is called. It is set to zero at the start of the application only.

Next, every time the timer goes off, the counter is incremented, and this increment is added to the `Value` property of `VScroll1`. This value controls the position of the scroll bar on the screen. Figure 11.7 shows the application running.

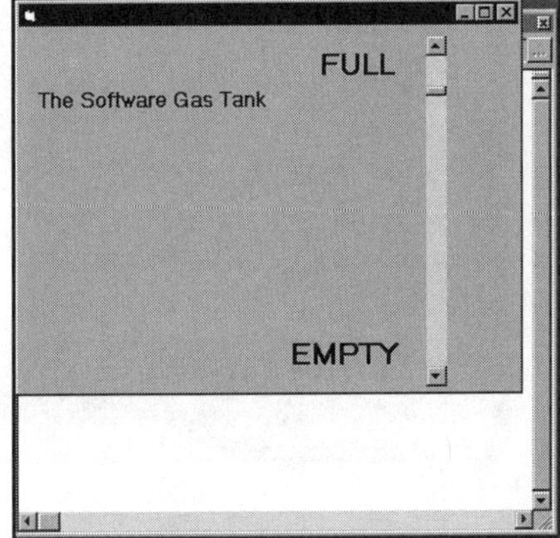

Figure 11.7
The running gas tank example.

As the Timer continues to fire, the value of the counter gets larger and larger. This causes the value of the scroll bar to be greater and greater, leading to the movement of the thumb down the scroll bar's body.

Using Scroll Bars for Data Input

There are many times when scroll bars can be used for data entry. Instead of asking the user to type in a number with the keyboard, it is possible to design a scroll bar that accomplishes the same result, but in a more user friendly fashion. Here's an example to illustrate this point.

Example

Create a new project that allows a user to select the amount of money that is to be deducted from each paycheck for a variety of categories. The `Value` properties of these sliders are summed and displayed in the `Deductions` Label field at the bottom of the form. Create the form by adding the vertical scroll bars and trim, as shown in figure 11.8. The names of the scroll bar and Text box controls should relate to the usage of each. An example of a name is vscDental for the Dental scroll bar.

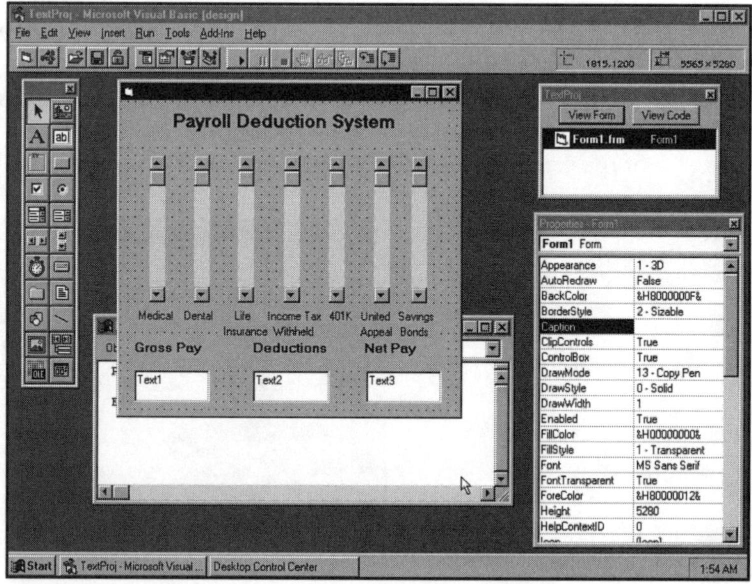

Figure 11.8
Developing the payroll deduction system.

Each of the scroll bars has some unique properties. The `Max` property is set to `0` and the `Min` is set to `100`. This is mathematically absurd, but it makes perfectly good sense in Visual Basic. All that it means is that you want the upward movement of the scroll bar to generate an increase in the `Value` property instead of the default downward direction. The upward direction is more intuitive when using the scroll bars for numerical input.

The purpose of this design is to allow the users to fine-tune their deductions until they balance exactly with one another and help users maximize their take-home pay. In order to accomplish this, seven vertical scroll bars were added, each one representing a type of deduction. As the user moves a thumb up, more money is given to that deduction, and the `Net Pay` box shows a smaller value. You can examine the code for this application below.

```
Dim Gross as Integer
Dim Deductions as Integer
Dim Net as Integer
```

These variables are declared outside of a subroutine so that they will have a duration that will last for the processing of the entire form. If they had been declared inside a subroutine, they would have been reinitialized each time an event procedure executed.

```
Private Sub txtGross_Change()
Calc_Net_Pay
End Sub

Private Sub vsc401k_Change()
Calc_Net_Pay
End Sub

Private Sub vscBonds_Change()
Calc_Net_Pay
End Sub

Private Sub vscDental_Change()
Calc_Net_Pay
End Sub

Private Sub vscLife_Change()
Calc_Net_Pay
End Sub

Private Sub vscMedical_Change()
Calc_Net_Pay
End Sub

Private Sub vscTax_Change()
Calc_Net_Pay
End Sub

Private Sub vscUA_Change()
Calc_Net_Pay
End Sub
```

Because of the need to recalculate the totals anytime any one of the scroll bars changed, it made sense to combine all of the calculations into one subroutine and simply call it from the `Change` event procedures for each scroll bar.

```
Public Sub Calc_Net_Pay()
   Gross = txtGross
   Deductions = vscLife.Value + vsc401k.Value + vscTax.Value
_vscDental.Value + vscMedical.Value + vscUA.Value + vscBonds.Value

   lblDeductions.Caption = Deductions
   lblNet.Caption = Gross - Deductions
End Sub
```

The result is both visually pleasing and satisfying to the user. Instead of doing a lot of typing, you can use the mouse. The relationship between the various deductions is represented graphically by the positions of the thumbs on the scroll bars themselves. Finally, the user can view the result on the screen immediately after it is made, as shown in figure 11.9.

Figure 11.9
Running the payroll deduction system.

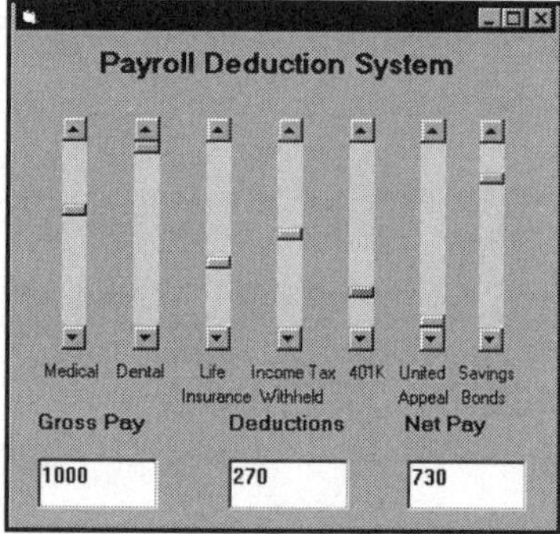

The advantage of using Visual Basic is clear in applications, like this one, that make full use of the interactivity and graphical nature of the tools.

Summary

In this chapter, you learned about two new tools: the horizontal scroll bar and the vertical scroll bar. You learned how to add them to your screens and interconnect them to other objects. You learned how to alter the increments that each manipulation of the scroll bar causes, as well as the range that the entire scroll bar can travel. You saw how to use scroll bars to control the positioning of a picture on the screen, thereby creating a crude form of animation. You also learned how to use scroll bars to pan around a picture that was larger that the window containing the scroll bars. This example also demonstrated how to generate a negative number with a scroll bar.

In the example involving the software fuel gauge, you learned how to use the scroll bars to output data graphically to the user. You also became familiar with the `Change` event and the event procedures associated with it.

Finally, you learned how to use scroll bars to substitute for text input. This example also demonstrated how to use data generated by scroll bar manipulation to perform calculations.

Review Questions

1. What event is triggered when a scroll bar is moved by the user?
2. What is a thumb?

3. What scroll bar property contains the location of the thumb?

4. What properties determine the range of values generated by the scroll bar?
5. Which properties work differently in vertical and horizontal scroll bars?
6. What is the purpose of the `SmallChange` property?
7. What is the purpose of the `LargeChange` property?

8. How do you cause the thumb to move without the mouse?
9. How do you get a scroll bar to yield increasing values as you move it upward instead of downward?

Review Exercises

1. Write a program that displays a Text box that gets bigger as you manipulate a scroll bar to the right and smaller as you manipulate it to the left.
2. Write a program the turns the mouse pointer into the American flag whenever it passes over a scroll bar.

3. Create a program with a scroll bar that gets fat as you move the thumb down and skinny as you move it up.
4. Create a program with a scroll bar that gets skinny as you move the thumb down and fat as you move it up.

5. Create a program that moves a bicycle through an obstacle course by manipulating scroll bars to determine direction.
6. Create a program that uses the same obstacle course as the previous program, but moves on its own based on a timer. Add another scroll bar to adjust the speed from slow to fast.

The Timer Tool

Have you ever seen a video game or a graphics-laden application, and just marveled at the effects? The animated characters seemed to move so smoothly and at just the right pace. The trees moved and the animals in the background all acted in a seemingly normal, random fashion. Chances are that they were being controlled by timers.

In the "olden days," programmers got the bright idea of setting up long `Do` loops that wasted time until they completed, an animated movement took place, and the `Do` loop started over. This alarming but effective scheme worked well on the early PCs (it made a lot of enemies on mainframes) until newer and older versions of the PC were being run by different users. The newer machines, being faster, could execute the `Do` loop in a fraction of the time that the old machines needed, making the animation look unrealistically quick.

What was needed was a way to tie the animation to the same temporal frame of reference that the user lives in: earth time. (You Einstein fanatics could easily confuse the issue by introducing relativity into the argument, but remember, this is an introductory text.) Visual Basic provides such a timer, appropriately named the *Timer tool* (see fig. 12.1).

Creating a Timer Tool

The Timer tool allows users to create as many timers in the same Windows program as they might need, each completely independent of every other. The user can then attach one or more activities to each timer, and create a remarkably complex animation. Start out simply, though, and create an application with just one timer. In the following example, you will add a timer control to a form and then program it to do something.

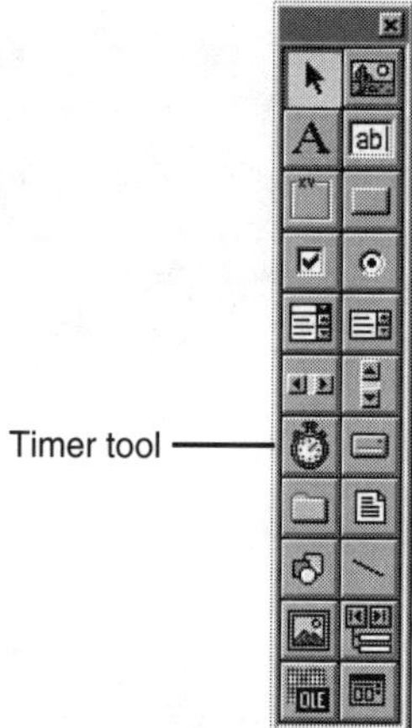

Figure 12.1
The Timer tool.

Example

Start by creating a new project called CH12.VBP. Next, add a timer to the main form by double-clicking the Timer icon in the Toolbox. At this point, your form should look like the one shown in figure 12.2.

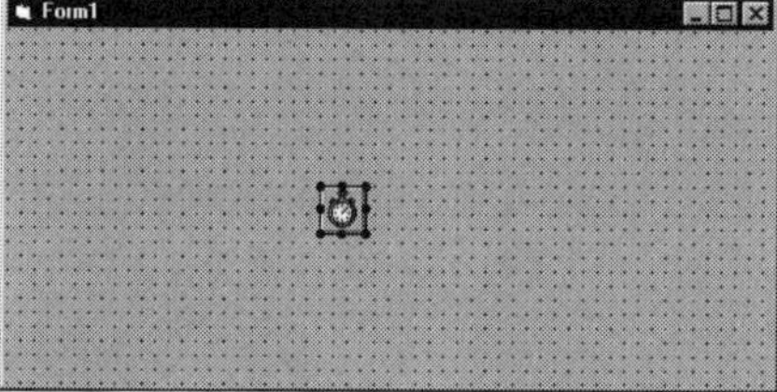

Figure 12.2
The Timer tool on a form.

The Timer control is unique in that it is always invisible while the program is running. It is also different in that it only responds to one event, the `Timer` event. The `Timer` event occurs every time a number of milliseconds (one one-thousandth of a second) passes that is equal to the value of the `Interval` property for that event.

Let's continue on with our example and illustrate this. Set the `Interval` property for the timer to be equal to 1,000 (1 second). Next, create a text box called `Text1` and place it on the form, as shown in figure 12.3. Add the following code to the `Timer` event for `Timer1`:

```
Private Sub Timer1_Timer ()
    Counter1 = Counter1 + 1
    Text1.Text = Counter
End Sub
```

This will work fine except that `Counter1` is a local variable here. Every time the timer fires, `Counter1` will be created anew and initialized to zero. The cure for that is easy, though. All that you need to do is to declare the variable `Counter1` in the Declarations section of `Form1`'s code section as follows:

```
Dim Counter1 as Integer
```

This makes `Counter1` a global value within this form and it will increment each time the `Timer1_Timer()` subroutine fires. Now, run the program and observe that the text box contains an integer that is increasing by one every second. Figure 12.3 shows the result.

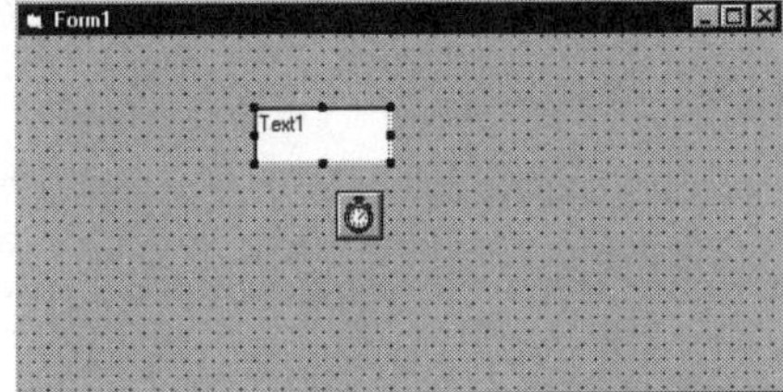

Figure 12.3
Running the Timer program.

Notice that the timer is updating the text box once per second. Let's add a second timer that updates once every 500 milliseconds (one-half second). Add another Text box to display the results and a second counter variable, `Counter2`, to the Declarations section. Now, run the program and observe that the first text box updates only half as often as the second one.

Using Timers to Control Animation

Text boxes are fine, but rather unexciting. Let's create a new project that will incorporate a Picture control into the form and then have a Timer control manipulate the picture to make it appear and disappear, and then to animate the picture.

Example

Create the Picture control by double-clicking the Picture tool in the Toolbox. In the `Picture` property, specify the icon file MAIL01A.ICO, that is found in the Icons\Mail subdirectory within the Visual Basic directory. Now, add a Timer control to the form by double-clicking the Timer tool in the Toolbox. Next, add the following code to the `Timer1_Timer` procedure:

```
Private Sub Timer1_Timer ()
If Picture1.Visible = True Then
   Picture1.Visible = False
Else
   Picture1.Visible = True
End If

End Sub
```

Finally, change the `Timer1 Interval` property to 1000. The form should now look like the one shown in figure 12.4.

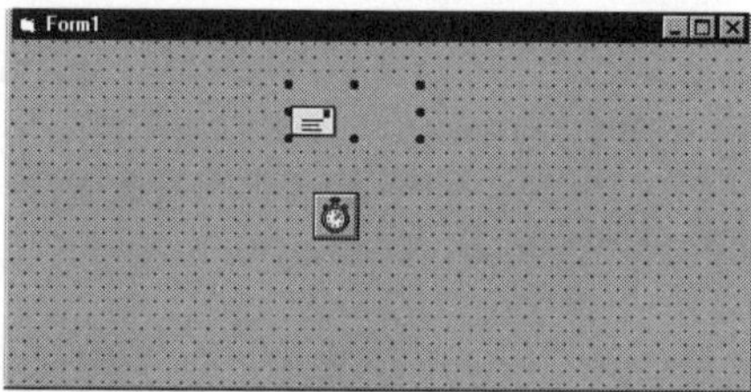

Figure 12.4
The timer and envelope picture.

Running the program causes the envelope to disappear for one second and to appear in the next second. This process repeats until the program is stopped.

Now that you have the basics down pat, let's complicate life a little by animating the opening and closing of the envelope in alternating seconds. To do this, you need to create two new pictures: `Picture2(0)` and `Picture2(1)`.

Note: An array of controls is very simple to create. Create all of the controls that you want in the array, and name them all the same `Name` property. The system will ask you if you intend to make this an array. If you answer "Yes," the new control will be assigned an `Index` property value that is different from the other members of that array. The control is then referenced by the name and the `Index` property combined. For example, if a control had a `Name` property value of `Array_of_Flags` and an `Index` of `3`, then this control would appear in code as `Array_of_Flags(3)`.

These pictures will contain the individual cells of the animation. Set the Picture property of the Picture2(0) to equal our main icon, MAIL01A.ICO. Set the Picture property of Picture2(1) equal to the icon, MAIL01B.ICO. Again, these icons can be found in the Icons\Mail subdirectory within the Visual Basic directory on your PC. Now, set the Visible property of both members of the array to False. The form should now resemble figure 12.5.

Next, include the following code to the Timer1_Timer event procedure after removing the existing code:

```
Private Sub Timer1_Timer ()
If Counter = 1 Then
   Picture1.Picture = Picture2(1).Picture
   Counter = 0
Else
   Picture1.Picture = Picture2(0).Picture
   Counter = 1
End If

End Sub
```

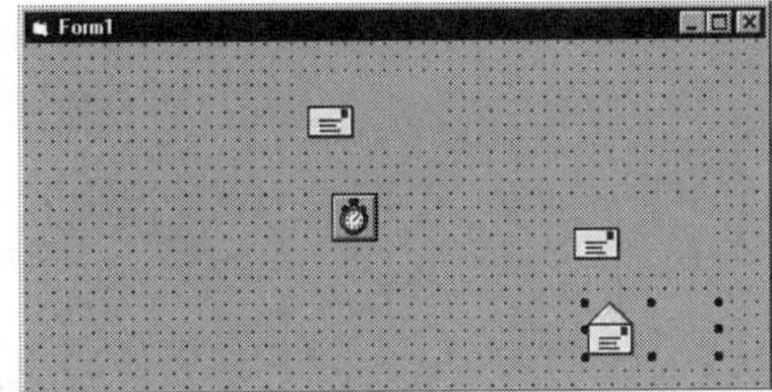

Figure 12.5
The animation development screen.

Place a `Dim` statement for `Counter` in the Declaration section of the form. The purpose of the `Counter` is to "remember" which icon was last displayed so that the other icon can be displayed at the next iteration. Before running the program, set the `BorderStyle` property of `Picture1` to `0` (None) to remove its border. Now, running the program will cause the timer and the two `Picture2` controls to disappear and the envelope icon to open and close in a very simple animation.

The *Enabled* Property

While it is great to have a timer that runs continuously, it would be better for some applications to start and stop the timer according to the user's input. Visual Basic has provided a way to do exactly that with a property called `Enabled`. Simply stated, when the `Enabled` property is set to `True`, the `Timer` event procedure executes just as you have seen. When the `Enabled` property is set to `False`, no `Timer` event procedure can execute for that timer.

Example

In accord with our custom, let's create a simple example to illustrate the point. Building on the preceding example, add a command button and call it the default name `Command1`. Set its caption to `"Animate"` and then add the following code to the `Click` event procedure for this button:

```
Private Sub Command1_Click ()
If Counter2 = 0 Then
   Command1.Caption = "Stop"
   Timer1.Enabled = True
   Counter2 = 1
Else
   Command1.Caption = "Animate"
   Timer1.Enabled = False
   Counter2 = 0
End If

End Sub
```

Change the `Enabled` property on `Timer1` to `False`. In addition, add the variable `Counter2` to the Declarations section for the form. The form should now look like the one shown in figure 12.6.

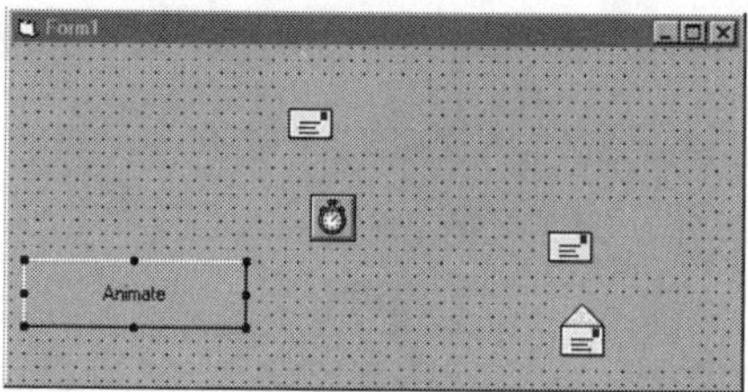

Figure 12.6
The form with the command button added.

Now, run the program and see what happens. The envelope will sit still until you click the command button. When you click the button, the animation starts and the caption on the command button is changed to `Stop`. Whenever you click the command button when it reads `Stop`, the animation stops. When you click the button when it reads `Animate`, the motion begins again. You are probably already thinking of a new video game using these techniques.

Arrays of Timers

Just as you used an array of pictures in an earlier example, you are going to use an array of timers in this section. Before you do, though, let's discuss the `Tag` property. The `Tag` property has no effect on the outcome of the program. Rather, it gives you a place to store any information about any object—in this case, the purpose of the timer. Suppose you had a "Three Stooges" video game. You would probably want to uncouple the movements of Curly, Larry, and Moe from each other to add realism. Let's also suppose that you created `TmrMoe`, `TmrLarry`, and `TmrCurly` to pace this animation. It would be useful to store the name Curly in `TmrCurly.TAG`, Larry in `TmrLarry.TAG`, and Moe in `TmrMoe.TAG`. Then you would have a way of tracking which timer is responsible for each character.

Example

First, start a new project and create an array of 16 timers, then name them all `TmrArray` and allow the system to assign the `Index` property for each.

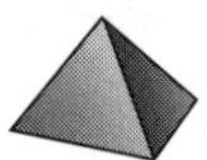

> **Tip:** The easiest way to create a control array is to start with one control and then use the Copy/Paste function of Windows to copy the control and paste it as many times as needed for the array.

Next, assign them intervals according to Table 12.1.

Table 12.1 The TmrArray Intervals

Index	*Interval*
0	200
1	300
2	500
3	600
4	700
5	800
6	900
7	1000
8	2000
9	10000
10	20000
11	30000
12	40000
13	50000
14	60000
15	100

Next, create an array of pictures called `Picture2` with 16 controls, and assign their `Picture` properties according to Table 12.2. The actual location of the icons depends on where Visual Basic was installed.

Table 12.2 The Picture Properties

Index	*Icon*
0	ICONS\MISC\CLOCK01.ICO
1	ICONS\MISC\CHECKMRK.ICO
2	ICONS\COMPUTER\TRASH01.ICO
3	ICONS\MISC\MISC14.ICO
4	ICONS\MISC\BULLSEYE.ICO
5	ICONS\MISC\HOUSE.ICO
6	ICONS\MISC\FACE02.ICO
7	ICONS\MISC\LIGHTON.ICO
8	ICONS\MISC\FACE01.ICO
9	ICONS\MISC\EAR.ICO
10	ICONS\COMPUTER\MOUSE01.ICO
11	ICONS\MISC\BINOCULR.ICO
12	ICONS\MISC\EYE.ICO
13	ICONS\FLAGS\FLGJAPAN.ICO
14	ICONS\MISC\MISC13.ICO
15	ICONS\MISC\BRIDGE.ICO

Your form should now resemble the one shown in figure 12.7.

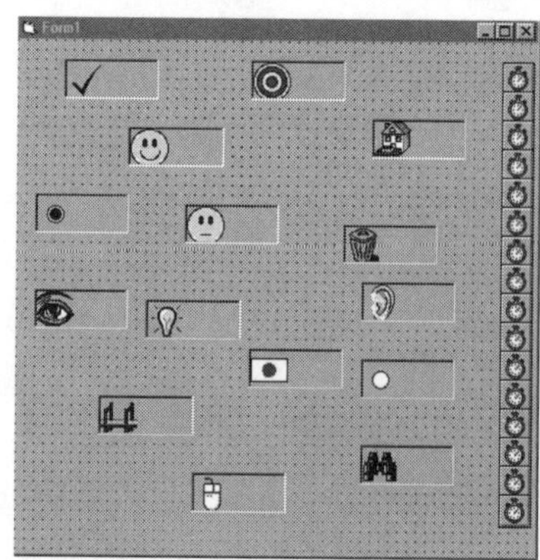

Figure 12.7
An array of pictures.

Now, all that is left is a little code. Don't be put off by control arrays. The logic is all very simple; every time a timer fires, reverse the display of the picture associated with that timer. In addition, set the `BorderStyle` property of all the `Picture2` array controls to `0` (None) to remove its border.

```
Private Sub TmrArray_Timer(Index As Integer)
If Picture2(Index).Visible = True Then
   Picture2(Index).Visible = False
Else
   Picture2(Index).Visible = True
End If
End Sub
```

Now, run the program and see how each picture on the form is timed differently—kind of like how the real world is timed. Figure 12.8 shows a snapshot of the application running.

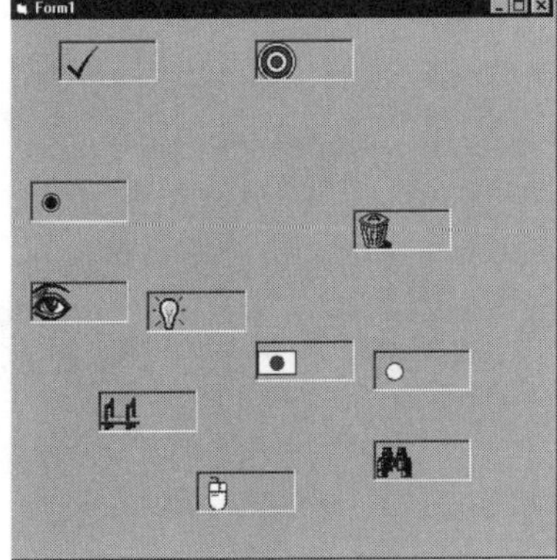

Figure 12.8
Running the timer array application.

The look was changed at each instant as different timers fired. This fact is important in applications where you are trying to simulate the real world in some fashion for your users.

Summary

In this chapter, you learned how to use a timer to generate events according to the passing of time. You learned how to tie these events with other controls to generate interesting forms. You also learned how to form an array of timers, each of which can drive its own functional process. I hope the subject of animation is a little less mysterious than it was before.

Review Questions

Answers to review questions are in Appendix B.

1. What purpose does a timer serve?
2. What is the unit of time used by the `Interval` property?
3. Why did we declare the `Counter` variables in the Declaration section instead of in the procedures themselves?
4. What is the purpose of the `Tag` property?

Exercises

1. Create an envelope example capable of moving, as well as opening and closing. (Hint: Use the `Top` and `Left` properties of the picture.)
2. Add a command button to Exercise 1 that enables and disables the timer.

3. Create an envelope example that moves according to one timer and animates according to another timer.

4. Choose a flag from ICONS\FLAGS in the Visual Basic directory. Edit it using Paintbrush or an icon editor to create three more icons to act as animation cells. Animate a flag blowing in the wind.

CHAPTER 13

The List Tools

The list box tools are important components of a graphical user interface because they relieve the user of the burden of typing. They present the user with choices from which to pick. This allows you to exercise a greater degree of control over the data that is input by the user. Using a list box, depending on the type and style selected, can allow a user to select from a list and/or enter data.

List boxes come in a variety of styles:

- The *list box*—This is a simple list of choices defined by the programmer. No data entry is possible and the user must choose one of the choices provided.
- The *combo box*—This is kind of a cross between a text box and a simple list box. A user can pick from three different styles: `0 - Dropdown Combo` (like a text box, with a list that drops down), `1 - Simple Combo` (essentially a text box and list box combined), and `3 - Dropdown List` (the user can select from list entries, but cannot edit any of them).
- The *directory list box*—This is a special list box that is customized to facilitate the selection of a directory by the user.
- The *drive list box*—This is a special list box that is customized to facilitate the selection of a drive by the user.
- The *file list box*—This is a special list box that is customized to facilitate the selection of a file by the user.

We will look at each of these controls in turn, in order to understand which one to use to accomplish a specific task.

Creating a List Box

The simplest list box control is the simple list box. You create an instance of the list box by clicking the List Box tool from the Toolbox and then drawing it onto a form. Figure 13.1 shows the List Box tool on the Toolbar.

Figure 13.1

The List Box tool is located on the Toolbar.

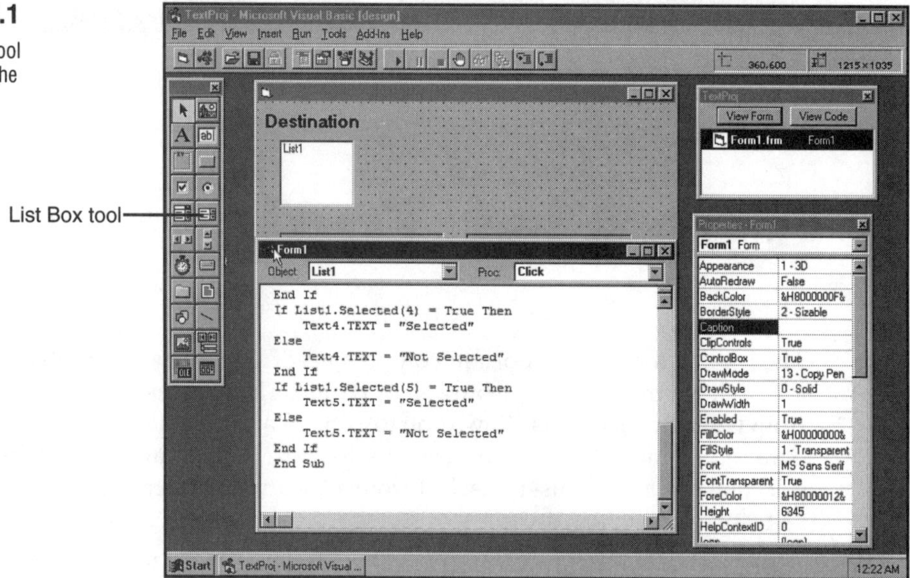

A list box is a way of selecting one or more items from a list of choices. Let's work through an example to show you how it works.

Example

Create a form and add a list box to it by double-clicking on the List Box button on the Toolbar. Add a label above the list box with the string "Destination" in it. Next, double-click on the form itself to bring up the code window. Add the Listing 13.1 code to the form.

Listing 13.1 13LIST01.TXT—Initializing the List Box

```
Private Sub Form_Load()
    List1.AddItem "Chicago"
    List1.AddItem "Dallas"
    List1.AddItem "Seattle"
    List1.AddItem "Washington"
    List1.AddItem "Houston"
    List1.AddItem "Dayton"

End Sub
```

This subroutine is tied to the `Load` event on the form which contains the list box. `List1` is the name of the list box. `AddItem` is a method that is associated with list boxes. Whenever you see an object name like `List1` followed by a period (".") and a verb like `AddItem`, you can bet dollars to doughnuts that the code is invoking a method. *Methods* are subroutines that are written by the developers of the object. Think of them as requests that an item makes to itself. `List1` is saying "add an item to me" that looks like "Chicago." `List1`, being a list box, knows how to react to this request because its authors provided code to handle it. *Functions* are different because they are not invoked by affixing their names to a control; they are standalone procedures, which return a value in their name. An example of a function might be some sort of date conversion routine.

Once we have added all of these items to the `List1` list box, we are ready to run it and see how it behaves. You might decide to resize the list box to display more lines at one time. Run the program that you have created and observe that it now looks like the one shown in figure 13.2.

Figure 13.2

Running the list box screen.

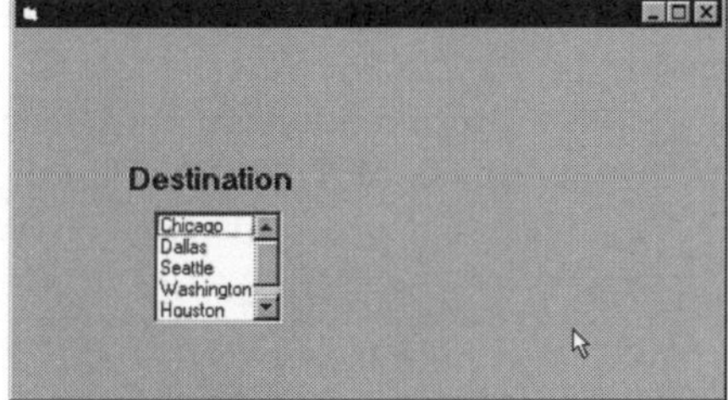

Notice that only part of the list is displayed at any instant. The list box size is controlled by the `Height` and `Width` properties just like the scroll bars and buttons are. At runtime, Visual Basic decides how many rows to put in the list box based on its size. If there are more rows that this, then a small scroll bar appears that allows you to look at the rest of them. Practice using the scroll bar on the side to move through the example.

The displaying of data in a list box is all very nice, but you would rather want to find out which item or items the user has chosen so that your application can react properly to it. One way to do this is with the `Text` property. Whenever your user selects one of the items in the list box, several things happen. First, the selection changes color to confirm the fact that the selection has been made. Second, Visual Basic copies the selection into a property called `Text`. Thus, `List1.Text` will contain the current selection in the `List1` list box. Let's change our sample form to show this. Add a text box to your form and call it `Text1`. Add the following code to the form:

```
Private Sub List1_Click()
    Text1.Text = List1.Text

End Sub
```

This code is saying to take the result of the selection and copy it into the `Text` property of the text box. Because text boxes display the value of the `Text` property, the value of the list box selection will appear immediately. The text box's font size and boldness have been changed for cosmetic reasons. Figure 13.3 shows this window running.

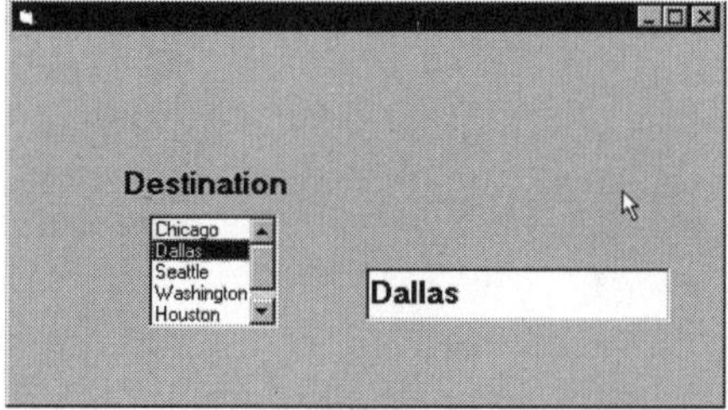

Figure 13.3
Displaying the `Text` value.

Another useful feature of list boxes is the `ListIndex` property. Whenever an item is added to the list box, it is assigned a number that represents its place in the list box. Some methods, like the `RemoveItem` method, require that you give this number to it whenever you want to remove an item from the list. Let's modify our sample once again to display this field. To do this, simply add another text box to the form and change the `Click` event procedure for the list box to the following:

```
Private Sub List1_Click()
    Text1.Text = List1.Text
    Text2.Text = List1.ListIndex

End Sub
```

Now when you click on the list box item, its text appears in one text box and its `ListIndex` appears in the other. This is illustrated in figure 13.4.

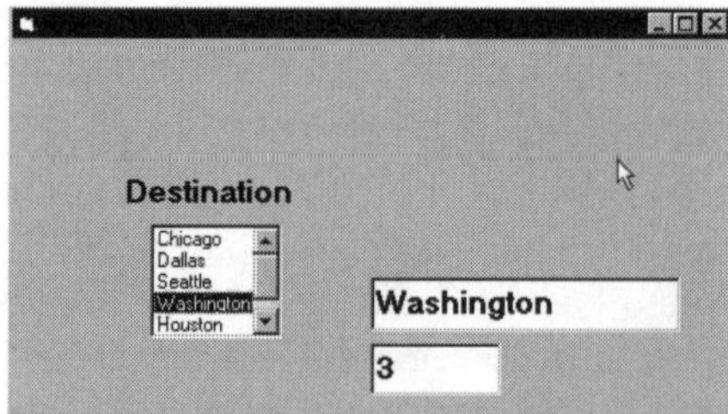

Figure 13.4
The `ListIndex` value.

In the following sections, we will see how important the `ListIndex` property is.

Selecting Multiple Items

In the ideal world, users only want to choose one item at a time. Here in the real world, it's not that easy at all. Users will inevitably want to choose more than one item from some list box that you create, and will threaten violence if you refuse to provide this capability. So, let's learn how to do this. The first part is easy; just set the `MultiSelect` property to `1 - Simple`, which allows them to select multiple items by clicking on them only. But let's be really brave. Select `2 - Extended`, which also allows you to use the Shift key to select a range of items and the Ctrl key to select them randomly. It also allows you to click and drag over a range of list items to select them.

Example

Having done that, let's again enhance our sample application to obtain visual feedback whether this indeed works. Let's start by deleting the existing text boxes and then add six new text boxes to the form, one for each item in the list box. Next, code these boxes so that they display "Selected" when the corresponding list box item is selected and "Not Selected" when the list box item is not selected. We do this by replacing the previous example code in the `List1_Click` event with the code in Listing 13.2.

Listing 13.2 13LIST02.TXT—Code to Display When a List Item Was Selected

```
Private Sub List1_Click()

If List1.Selected(0) = True Then
    Text6.Text = "Selected"
Else
    Text6.Text = "Not Selected"
End If

If List1.Selected(1) = True Then
    Text1.Text = "Selected"
Else
    Text1.Text = "Not Selected"
End If

If List1.Selected(2) = True Then
    Text2.Text = "Selected"
Else
    Text2.Text = "Not Selected"
End If
```

continues

Listing 13.2 Continued

```
If List1.Selected(3) = True Then
    Text3.Text = "Selected"
Else
    Text3.Text = "Not Selected"
End If

If List1.Selected(4) = True Then
    Text4.Text = "Selected"
Else
    Text4.Text = "Not Selected"
End If

If List1.Selected(5) = True Then
    Text5.Text = "Selected"
Else
    Text5.Text = "Not Selected"
End If

End Sub
```

The workings of this code will take some explanation. When a list box is created, Visual Basic creates an array called `Selected`. The `Selected` array contains one element for each item in the list. If you add an item, the `Selected` array becomes longer. Visual Basic monitors the actions of the user in selecting one or more items in the list box. It then updates the `Selected` array to reflect the current state.

If an item is selected, then Visual Basic will set the value of the corresponding element of the Selected array to `True`. Otherwise, it will set it to `False`. By testing this array in the code above, we can learn the selection status of each item in the list box. If there is a need to know how many items were selected in the list box, the property `Selcount` will contain the number of selected items.

The final step in the example is to add six Label controls, one for each text box that you added. Each Label should contain the string from the corresponding list box item. This tells the user which item was actually selected. The Label controls also have the `Backcolor` property set to the same color as the form.

Run the example and experiment with the various ways of selecting items. Press down the mouse button and drag. Press down the Ctrl key and click. Hold down the Shift key and select a range of items. Convince yourself that this logic does indeed work, as shown in figure 13.5.

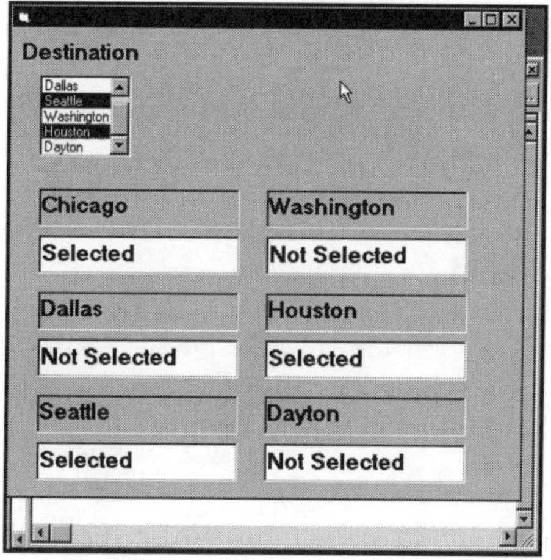

Figure 13.5
The multiple selection example.

Look for ways to use multiple selection in your programs.

The Combo Box

A variation on the list box is a control called the *combo box*. This control allows the user to pick from a list of options just as the list box did, but it also allows her to type in a response, if one of the existing ones doesn't fit the need. The Combo Box tool is shown in figure 13.6.

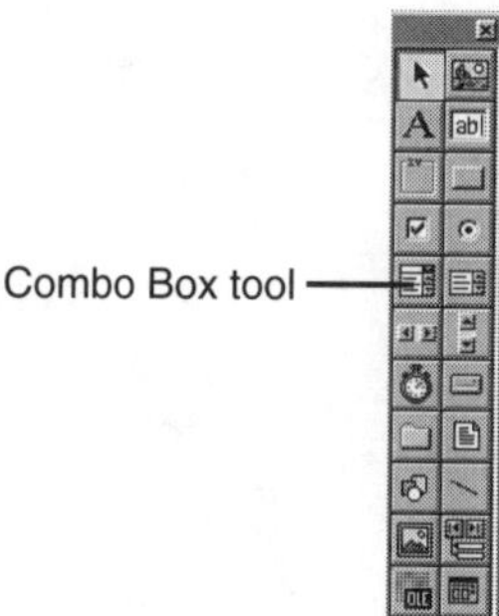

Figure 13.6
The Combo Box tool.

As is our custom, let's cut to the chase with examples of how to use the three different styles of combo boxes.

The Drop-Down List Combo Box

There are three styles of combo boxes. The first one, the *drop-down list combo box*, is like the simple list box except that it pulls down when selected instead of occupying precious window real estate at all times. To demonstrate the operation of this box, you need to create a form with a combo box. Set the style property of the combo box to `2 - Dropdown List`, which will create a combo box that looks like the one shown in figure 13.7.

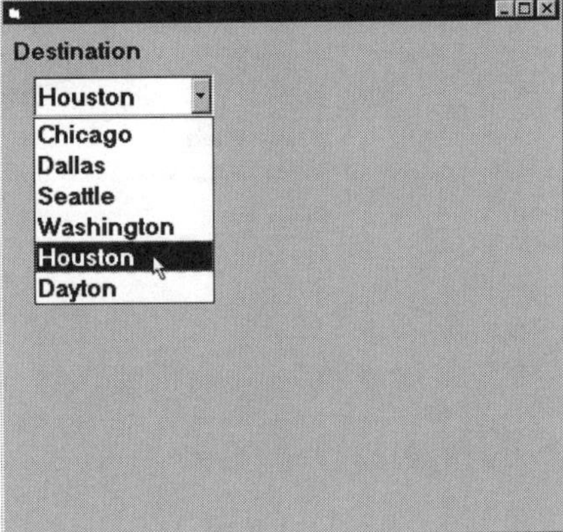

Figure 13.7
The drop-down list combo box.

The code to populate the choices, which resembles the code used to populate the simple list box in the previous section, is as follows in Listing 13.3:

Listing 13.3 13LIST03.TXT—Code to Initialize the Combo Box

```
Private Sub Form_Load()
    Combo1.AddItem "Chicago"
    Combo1.AddItem "Dallas"
    Combo1.AddItem "Seattle"
    Combo1.AddItem "Washington"
    Combo1.AddItem "Houston"
    Combo1.AddItem "Dayton"

End Sub
```

In the rest of its operation, the drop-down list combo box functions like a simple list box.

The Simple Combo Box

The *simple combo box* is a text box attached to a list box. To create one of these controls, simply create the combo box by double-clicking on the Toolbox button and then set the `Style` property to `1 - Simple Combo`. This combo box behaves like the drop-down combo box, except that the list box portion is visible at all times (see fig. 13.8). You will have to resize the combo box to display more than one line when running the application.

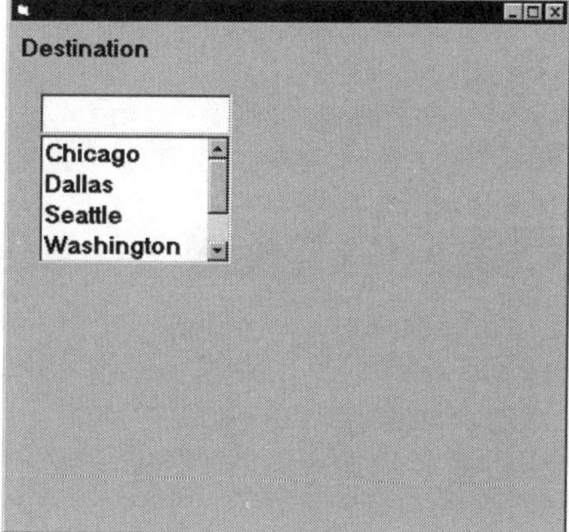

Figure 13.8
The simple combo box.

Otherwise, the simple combo box behaves like the list box except that the `Text` property can be either a string that the user has typed in, or an item from the list box portion. Often the combo box is coded in such a way that new items are added to the list box immediately when they are added to the text box. This is done by placing the following line of code in the combo box `LostFocus` event.

```
Comb1.AddItem Combo1.Text
```

The Drop-Down Combo Box

The final style of combo box that we will study in this chapter is the *drop-down combo box*. This combo box is like the drop-down list box in that it occupies only one line when not in use. It is like the simple combo box in that keyboard entry is accepted into the `Text` property. Figure 13.9 shows an example of this kind of combo box.

All three types of combo boxes provide functionality that gives your applications a very professional look and feel. One of the widely used properties of the combo box is the `Sorted` property. By setting this property to `True`, all the entries in a list will be sorted.

Figure 13.9
The drop-down combo box.

The Specialized List Boxes

There are three other types of list boxes that are so commonly needed that they are provided as built-in controls. Conceptually, they are simply list boxes and combo boxes. They contain a considerable amount of code that has been written for you. These controls are available the minute you install Visual Basic. They are the Drive, Directory, and File list boxes. These three controls are shown in figure 13.10.

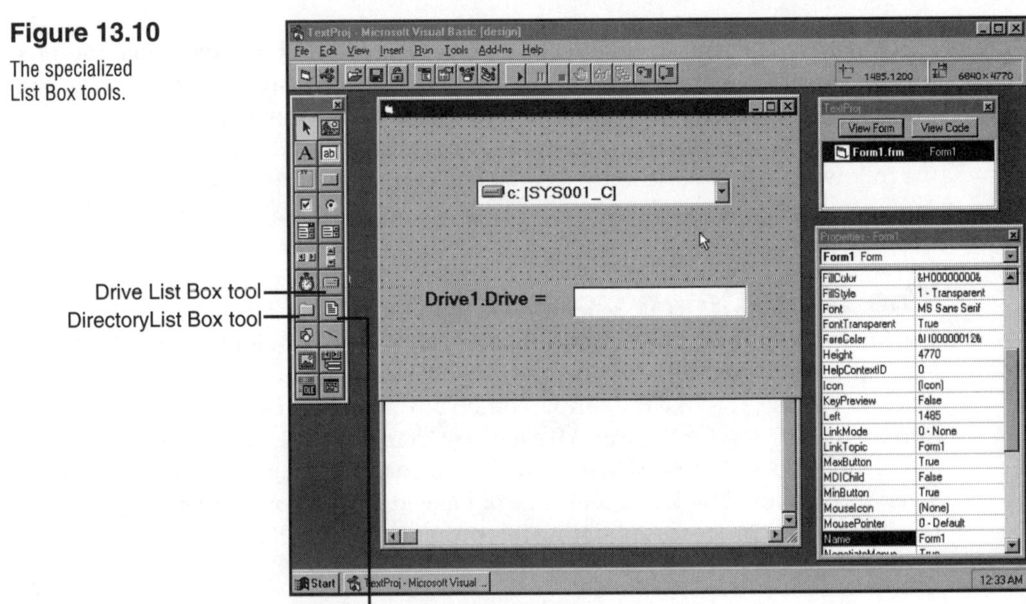

Figure 13.10
The specialized List Box tools.

Let's look at each of these special tools.

The Drive List Box

The *Drive list box* is used to allow a user to select a drive. The Drive list box is smart enough to go and search the host computer system and determine which drives—local and remote, floppy, rigid, and CD-ROM—exist on the system. It displays these choices graphically, as shown in figure 13.11 below.

Figure 13.11

Using the Drive list box.

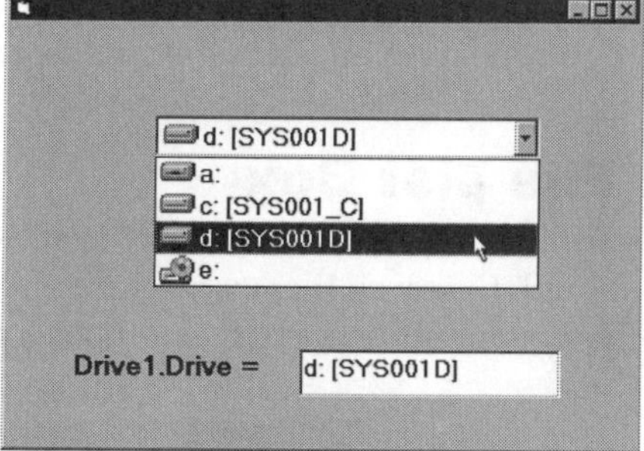

The selection that the user makes is recorded in a special property called `Drive`. The text box shown in figure 13.11 was displayed using the following code:

```
Private Sub Drive1_Change()
    Text1.Text = Drive1.Drive
End Sub
```

The `Drive` property contains the drive letter that was chosen by the user of the form. By assigning it to a text box, we can display it on the screen or it can be used within a routine to open a file, execute a program, and so on.

The Directory List Box

The *Directory list box* is used to allow a user to select a directory. The Directory list box is also smart enough to search the host computer system and determine which directories exist in the system. It displays these choices graphically, as shown in figure 13.12.

Figure 13.12

Using the Directory list box.

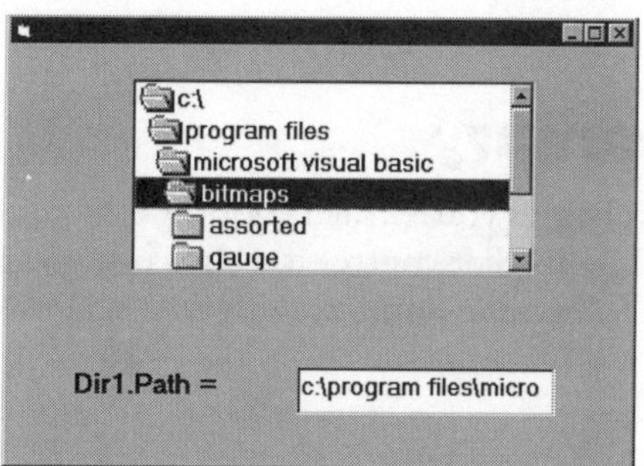

The selection that the user makes is recorded in a special property called `Path`. The text box shown in figure 13.12 was displayed using the following code:

```
Private Sub Dir1_Change()
    Text1.Text = Dir1.Path
End Sub
```

The `Path` property contains the directory location that was chosen by the user of the form. By assigning it to a text box, we can display it on the screen or it can be used within a routine to open a file, execute a program, and so on.

The File List Box

The *File list box* is used to allow a user to select a specific file. The File list box is also smart enough to search the host computer system and determine which files exist in the file system. It displays these choices graphically, as shown in figure 13.13.

Figure 13.13
Using the File list box.

The selection that the user makes is recorded in a special property called `FileName`. The text box shown in Figure 13.13 was displayed using the following code:

```
Private Sub File1_Click()
    Text1.Text = File1.FileName
End Sub
```

The `FileName` property contains the name of the file that was chosen by the user of the form. By assigning it to a text box, we can display it on the screen or it can be used within a routine to open a file, execute a program, and so on.

Summary

In this chapter you learned about special controls called list boxes. You learned how to add items that control the choices users have when running your application. You also became familiar with the `ListIndex` property.

You learned how to allow the user to select multiple items from the same list box. This chapter also covered the subject of combo boxes, and the three available styles of combo boxes.

The simple combo box allows the user to choose between entering text and picking from a list of choices. The drop-down list is only one line in height until it receives focus; it then enlarges to show all its choices. The drop-down combo box also is very small, but is different from the drop-down list box because the former accepts text input.

Finally, you learned how to create instances of the Directory list box, the Drive list box, and the File list box. These are the list boxes used by the File, Open dialog box that appears in nearly every Windows application that you purchase.

Review Questions

Answers to review questions are in Appendix B.

1. How does a list box know what to display?
2. What is a method? How is it different from a function?

3. What are the differences between the three types of combo boxes?
4. How do you enable multiple selection of items in a list box?

5. How can your program find out which items have been selected?
6. By looking at the following code sample, decide what the contents of the text box's `Text` property will be after your user changes the drive:

```
Private Sub Drive1_Change()
        Text1.Text = Drive1.Drive
End Sub
```

7. How do you create a Directory list box?

Review Exercises

1. Write a program that lists the members of your family in a list box.
2. Change the program that you wrote for Exercise 1 to allow multiple selections.

3. Modify Exercise 2 to make use of array processing for the text boxes.
4. Display the results of Exercise 2 by causing a picture to be visible or invisible based on whether or not an item was selected.

5. Write a program that performs the same function as the File, Open property sheet found in most Windows applications.

6. Write a program that uses all three kinds of combo boxes on the same form. When one combo box changes, reflect the changes in the two combo boxes on the form.

7. Use the `Sorted` property to change the order of appearance for items in a list box.

CHAPTER 14

The Graphics Tools

The picture and graphics tools are important controls in the Visual Basic system because they add pleasing visual effects to your applications. The power of a graphical interface is wasted if all that you do is write text on the screen. The addition of icons, bitmaps, metafiles, and drawings to an application's user interface is critical to achieving professional status for your system.

These graphical elements enable Visual Basic to break out of the "front end" paradigm and into the interactive graphics, or "game," paradigm.

These tools come in a number of flavors:

- The Line tool allows you to draw straight lines on forms.
- The Shape tool allows you to draw circles, ovals, rectangles, and rounded rectangles on the form.
- The Image tool displays bitmaps on the form.
- The PictureBox tool also displays bitmaps on the form, but is more flexible than the Image tool. Picture boxes are best suited for dynamic environments where a picture is being moved or animated. The PictureBox tool can also be used as a tool to create graphics, by using its Methods, and it can also be used as a container for other controls. Forms (except MDI Parent) can also be used with graphics methods.

By using the animation techniques available in the system, you can produce some stunning visual images. Figure 14.1 shows the Toolbox with these tools.

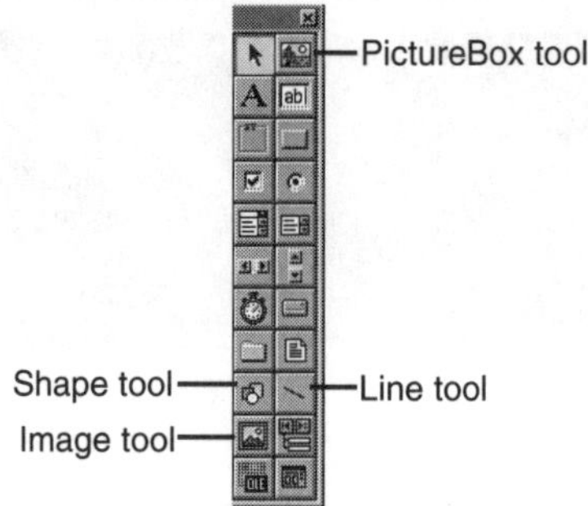

Figure 14.1
The Line, Shape, Image, and PictureBox tools.

Each of these controls will be looked at in turn so that you'll understand which one to use to accomplish a specific task.

The Line Tool

Let's start with the simplest way to add graphics to a screen: drawing a line. The Line tool is used to draw a simple line between two points. These lines are not, however, ordinary lines like the ones that you draw in Windows Paintbrush. These have properties that can be manipulated to produce motion.

Example

Let's run an example to demonstrate this. Create a line like the one in figure 14.2.

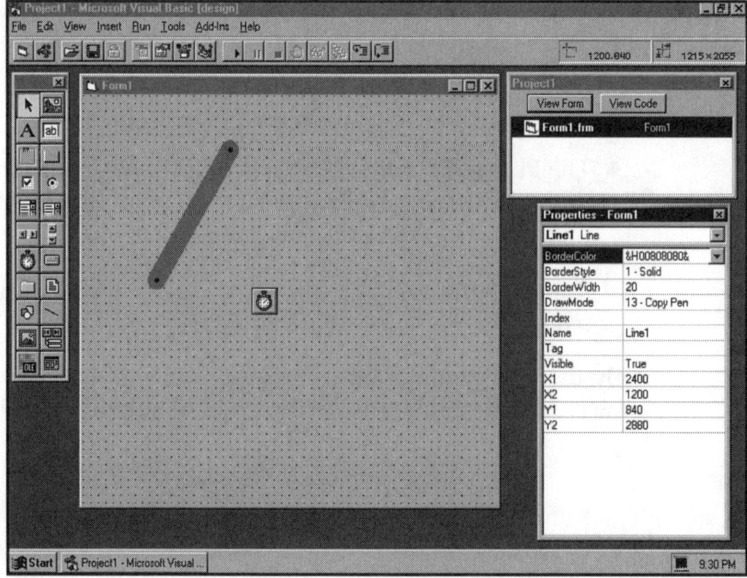

Figure 14.2
A walking line.

This line is unusual in that it has been made thick by changing its `BorderWidth` property from one to 20. Its color has also been changed by setting its `BorderColor` property to a gray. The properties `X1`, `Y1`, `X2`, and `Y2` determine the location of the line on the form. Using the form as a frame of reference, the line runs between the points `(X1,Y1)` and `(X2,Y2)` on the form. By altering these point values during the execution of a program, you can create animation. Now, add a Timer control to the form and then add the following code to the form:

```
Dim Turn as Integer

Private Sub Timer1_Timer()
If Turn = 1 Then
    Line1.X1 = Line1.X1 + 300
    Turn = 2
Else
    Line1.X2 = Line1.X2 + 300
    Turn = 1
End If
End Sub
```

A timer was included in order to make the animation independent of the speed of the CPU running it. To create the animation, the Timer's `Interval` property was set at 100 milliseconds (0.1 second). A variable, `Turn`, was declared in the Declarations section of the form to act as a switch so that a different end of the line moves each time the Timer fires. (For a complete discussion of the Timer control, see Chapter 12, "The Timer Tool.") The initial settings for the Line properties are as follows:

```
X1 = 720
Y1 = 600
X2 = 360
Y2 = 1995
```

By increasing the `X1` position by 300 twips and then increasing the `X2` position by 300 twips in alternating fashion produces animation. It appears that the line is walking across the screen, as shown in figure 14.3.

Another interesting property of the Line control is the `BorderStyle` property. This property allows you to alter the appearance of a line either at design time or at runtime. There are seven choices of line styles. These are illustrated in figure 14.4.

The setting of these styles is not limited to design time. By reassigning the `BorderStyle` to another value, you can create interesting effects.

Note: The `BorderStyle` properties (other than `Solid`) are mutually exclusive with a `BorderWidth` value larger than one. If the `BorderWidth` is larger than one, the line will be solid, regardless of the `BorderStyle` setting.

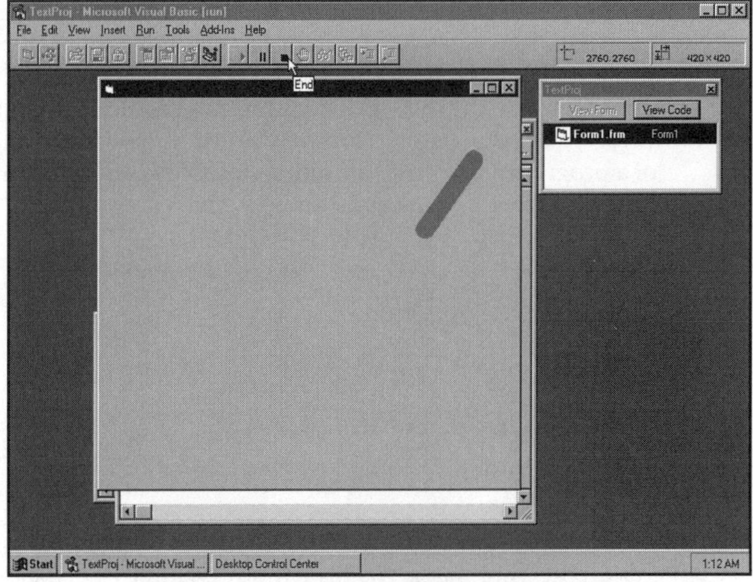

Figure 14.3

Running the walking line example.

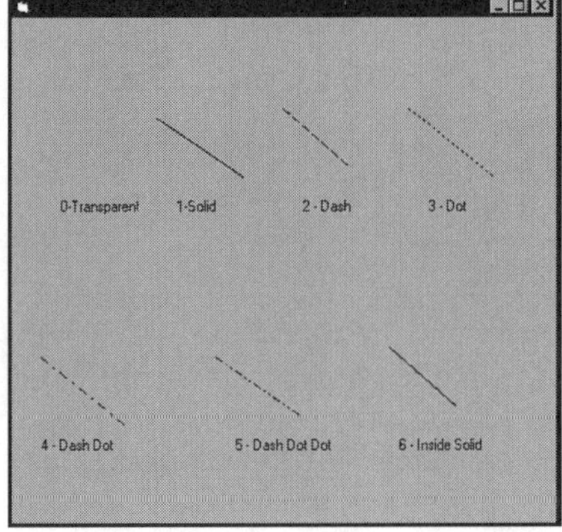

Figure 14.4

The seven border styles for lines.

In addition to adding motion to lines, you can also change the `DrawMode` property to give it special color changes at runtime. Because shapes have the same property and because examples are easier to understand when demonstrated with shapes, the `DrawMode` property will be discussed in detail in the section on the Shape tool.

The Shape Tool

The Shape tool allows you to add a variety of geometric patterns to the form. You have the following six different shapes to choose from:

- 0—Rectangle
- 1—Square
- 2—Oval
- 3—Circle
- 4—Rounded Rectangle
- 5—Rounded Square

You designate which shape that you want the object to show by choosing the `Shape` property and selecting one of the choices from the pick list. Each of these types is illustrated in figure 14.5.

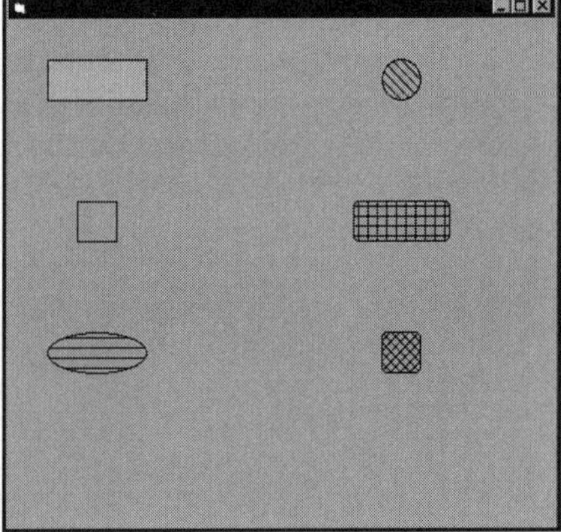

Figure 14.5
The Visual Basic shapes.

Along with the different shapes comes a choice of how to fill each of them. This is done by setting the `FillStyle` property. You have the following eight choices of fill styles:

- 0—Solid
- 1—Transparent
- 2—Horizontal Line
- 3—Vertical Line
- 4—Upward Diagonal

- 5—Downward Diagonal
- 6—Cross
- 7—Diagonal Cross

In Figure 14.5, the shapes are filled with the following styles:

- Rectangle: Solid
- Square: Transparent
- Oval: Horizontal Line
- Circle: Upward Diagonal (Looks downward, doesn't it?)
- Rounded Rectangle: Cross
- Rounded Square: Diagonal Cross

You can use the properties of shapes to create animated sequences.

Example

Let's start a new project to create an example to demonstrate this. Start by creating a shape control that has a `Shape` property of `3-Circle` and name it `Circle1`. Next, make it large enough to fill the window and add a timer to the form. Set the timer's `Interval` property to 200 (0.2 seconds). Your example should look like figure 14.6 at this point.

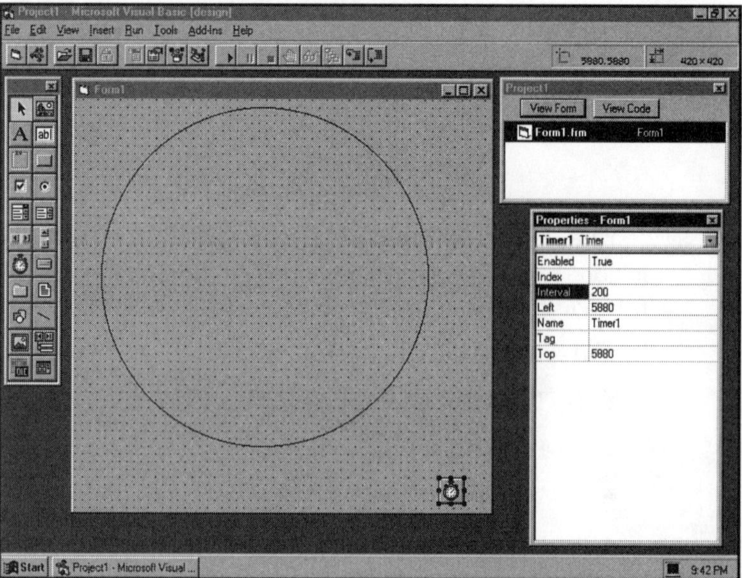

Figure 14.6
The shrinking circle example.

Now, add the following code to the form:

```
Private Sub Timer1_Timer()
While Circle1.Width - 1 > 2000
    Circle1.Width = Circle1.Width - 1
Wend
End Sub
```

The code for this example is fairly simple. You get a runtime error if the `Width` property of a shape is less than zero, so only continue until a certain size is reached. In this case, 2000 twips is the chosen size. `Timer1` is set to fire five times per second. When it fires, it shrinks the circle by one twip. This shrinks the circle, right before your eyes, until it looks like the one shown in figure 14.7.

Figure 14.7

Running the shrinking circle example.

Changing the size of objects is one way to give the appearance of distance. When an object is becoming smaller in a smooth animation, it appears to be getting further away from the user. This fact is exploited by video game writers to create three-dimensional effects.

It is important to note that this animation is fundamentally different from the cell animation described in Chapter 12, "The Timer Tool." In cartoon animation, each new picture replaces the previous picture to form a sort of electronic cartoon. The animation in the shrinking circle example was done by calculating what the next step was going to look like (in effect, a smaller value for `Width`). When the circle was rendered by Visual Basic, the newly sized circle was rendered each time. Cell animation takes more memory than calculation-based animation, but is less CPU intensive. The future direction of animation favors calculation-based techniques.

In addition to modifying the size of shapes, you can alter several other interesting properties associated with shapes. This is done through a seemingly strange property called the `DrawMode`. The `DrawMode` property allows Visual Basic to make wholesale changes in the shape based on a single setting. This is useful because of the speed at which this operation can take place. Table 14.1 lists the valid `DrawMode` property values.

Table 14.1 The Valid DrawModes

Setting	*Name*
1	Blackness
2	Not Merge Pen
3	Mask Not Pen
4	Not Copy Pen
5	Mask Pen Not
6	Invert
7	Xor Pen
8	Not Mask Pen
9	Mask Pen
10	Not Xor Pen
11	Nop
12	Merge Not Pen
13	Copy Pen (Default)
14	Merge Pen Not
15	Merge Pen
16	Whiteness

In essence, the `DrawMode` property allows the occurrence of several types of animation that can be learned from a book specifically written to address this subject. You can look at one of these values to get a feel for the concepts.

Figure 14.8 shows two shapes that illustrate the effects of changing the `DrawMode`. The first is a circle with a patterned fill and a thick border. The second shape is a large, black square.

Example

For the purposes of this example, choose a conceptually simple operation: Invert. This setting means that wherever the two objects overlap, make the circle the inverse (opposite) color from the background. To do this, set the `Drawmode` property to `6 - Invert`. Figure 14.9 shows the result of moving the circle so that it partially covers the square.

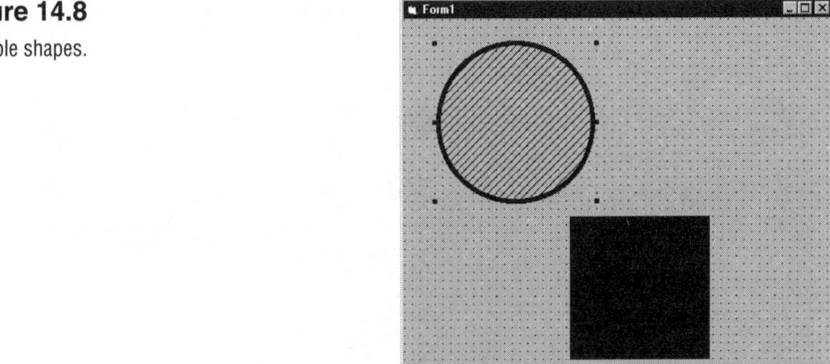

Figure 14.8
Example shapes.

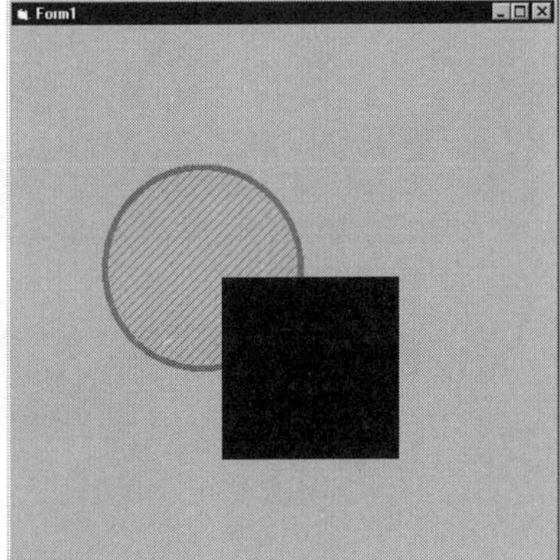

Figure 14.9
Overlapping the shapes.

The Image Tool

Image controls are the little brothers to Picture controls. They have the ability to display images on the screen, but they lack some of the properties that are found in Picture controls. The following section will introduce the Picture control and expound on the advantages and disadvantages of Picture controls verses those of Image controls. Images have a `Picture` property that can accept a metafile (.WMF), an icon (.ICO), or a bitmap (.BMP). The `Picture` property can then display the image on a form, as you see in figure 14.10.

There is one property of the Image control that is unique to it: the `Stretch` property. If `Stretch` is set to `True`, then the bitmap or metafile that is being displayed is "stretched" to fit the size of the control on the form. If it is set to `False`, then the borders of the Image control are adjusted to fit the size of the bitmap or metafile.

Figure 14.11 shows the icon from figure 14.10 after it has been stretched to fit the Icon control.

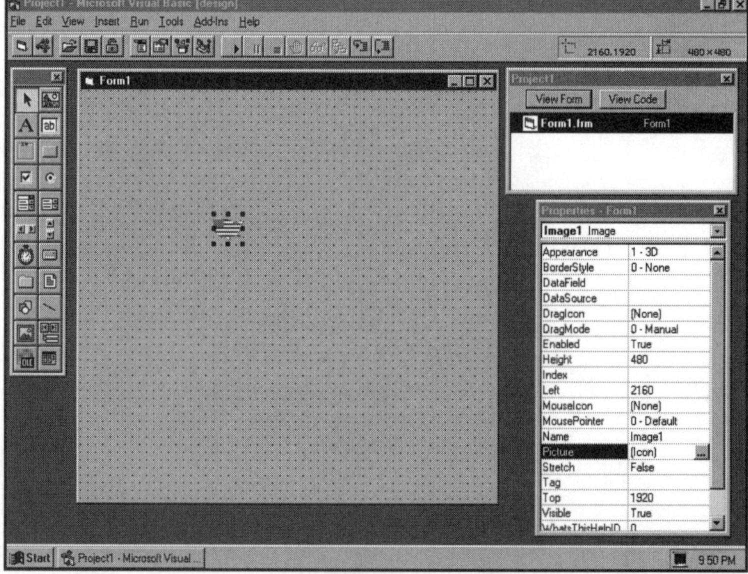

Figure 14.10

An image on a form.

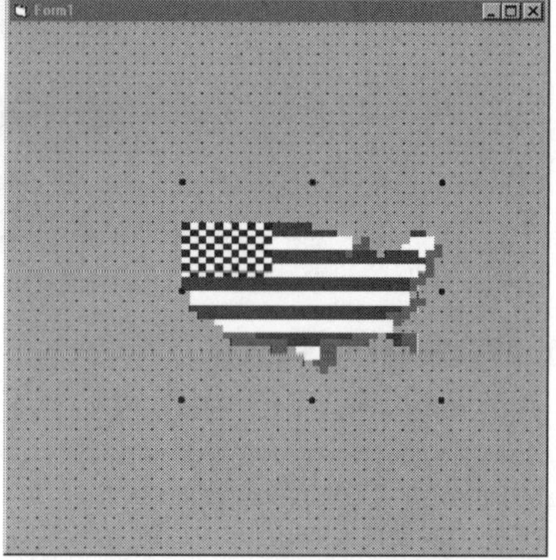

Figure 14.11

The stretched icon.

The Stretch property was set to `True` before the Image control was enlarged. Visual Basic increases the size of the icon to match the size of the Image control.

The PictureBox Tool

As mentioned in the previous section, the PictureBox tool is just the Image tool on steroids. You can create a Picture control and use its `Picture` property to specify which metafile, bitmap, or icon to display. The PictureBox also has an `Align` property, which means that it can be placed on a MDIParent form. Since only controls with an `Align` property can be placed on a MDIParent, this makes the PictureBox very useful—since once it's placed on the MDIParent, you can still use it as a container for other controls. This makes it handy for things like Toolbars, Status bars, and so on. This will be covered in Part VI, "Building Complete Applications."

Note: A *container control* is simply any control that can have other controls placed inside of it.

The resources required by Picture boxes exceed significantly the resources required by Images. The reason for this is due to the nature of the PictureBox control. Picture boxes are really mini-forms within a form. You can draw on them, write to them, and place controls on them. When they are moved, the controls and graphics move with them. Figure 14.12 illustrates how this works.

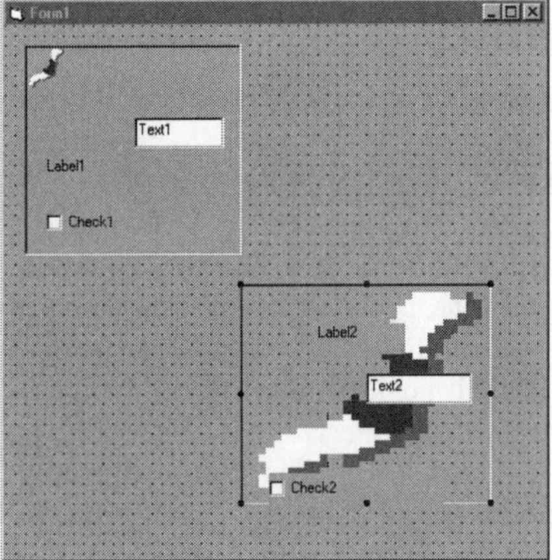

Figure 14.12
The PictureBox and Image controls.

The picture box was created first and then a shape, label, and a check box were added. The same procedure was followed for the Image also. The difference between the two controls becomes obvious when you move the two controls. Figure 14.13 illustrates this difference.

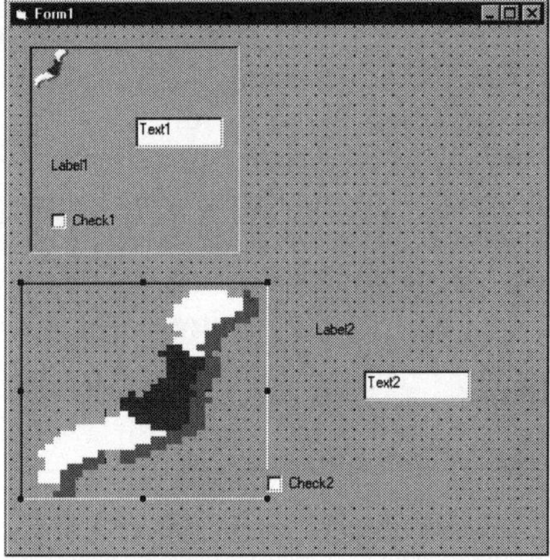

Figure 14.13
Moving an image and a picture box.

The picture box, being essentially a small form, contains the graphics and controls which were placed on it. The image, on the other hand, is merely art work, and incapable of containing objects. Remember, the Image control consumes fewer resources than the PictureBox control, and, therefore, Image control should be used whenever it is capable of doing the job.

Summary

In this chapter, you learned how to add lines to your forms. You learned how to vary the thickness of lines and how to produce animation by combining the properties of lines with the properties of timers.

In addition, you learned how to create different types of shapes and then how to create different fill patterns for these shapes. You were introduced to the concept of the `DrawMode` property, and you saw one example of how this property affects the appearance of shapes. You practiced animating a shape by altering the value of its properties with calculations.

The topic of Images was discussed, and an example of how to use them to stretch a bitmap was shown. The PictureBox tool was introduced, and the differences between it and the Image tool were explained.

Finally, you examined the resources consumed by various picture and graphics tools, and you learned how to decide whether an Image control or a PictureBox control is a better choice for a particular application.

Review Questions

Answers to review questions appear in Appendix A.

1. What property of a Line control determines its thickness?
2. How do you change the fill pattern of a shape?
3. How do you enlarge a bitmap using an Image control?

4. What would you do to the "walking line" example to speed up the walking?
5. What would you do to the "shrinking circle" example to cause the circle to grow instead of shrink?

6. What is the basic difference between the Image tool and the PictureBox tool?
7. What is the purpose of the `DrawMode` property?

Review Exercises

1. Write a program that moves a line across the screen while lying on its side.
2. Write a program that causes a line to move around its center axis point.

3. Modify the "shrinking circle" example to make the circle pulsate (grow larger then smaller in alternating fashion).
4. Create a program to enlarge a bitmap that you created by using Windows Paintbrush at the pixel level (zoom in closely). Stretch it and examine how the Image tool handled the addition of new pixels to the bitmap.

5. Write a program that looks like the "overlapping the shapes" example in this chapter. Add a command button that changes the `DrawMode` of the circle by one every time it is clicked. Run the program, and step through the different `DrawModes` to examine the effects.

The Data, Grid, and OLE Tools

There are times when you, the developer, would like to access objects and systems outside of your current program. These objects might be databases, pictures, word processing documents, sound bites, or any other piece of data that is of interest to your users. This chapter introduces you to a number of controls which will help you accomplish your goal. The following controls are shown in figure 15.1:

- The Data control
- The Grid control
- The OLE Container control

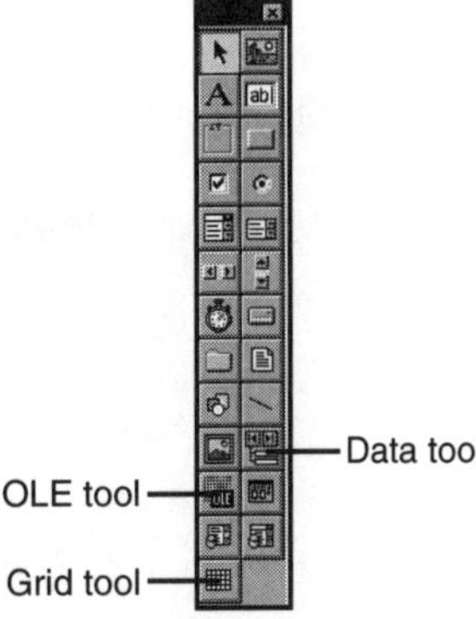

Figure 15.1
The Data, Grid, and OLE controls.

Let's look at each one of these tools in order to understand how to include them in your applications.

The Data Control

One of the most common activities of a Visual Basic program is accessing a database. The designers of Visual Basic created a control especially for that purpose. That control is called the Data control. Let's run an example that uses the Data control to access a database.

Example

Create a new form with the control shown in Table 15.1.

Table 15.1 The Controls for the Database Example

Control Type	*Name*	*Caption*
Label	Label1	Name
Label	Lable2	CompanyName
Label	Label3	City
Text	Text1	
Text	Text2	
Text	Text3	
Data	Data1	

Set all three Label controls' `Backstyle` properties to `0 - Transparent`. Next, change the `Picture` property of the form to C:\WINDOWS\CLOUDS.BMP. This will give your form the cool background. Your form should look like the one in figure 15.2.

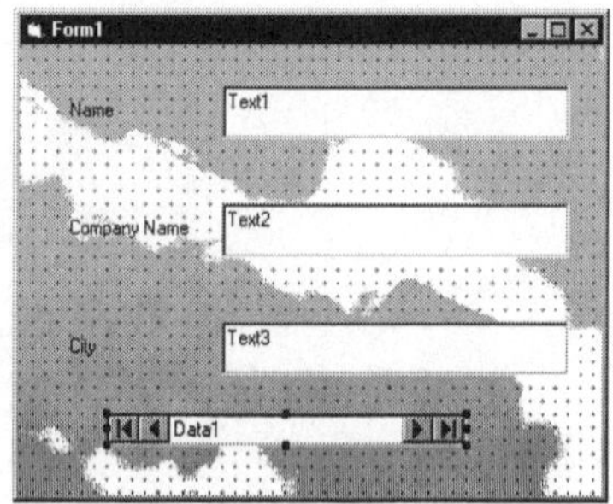

Figure 15.2
The form with the clouds bitmap.

Next, set the properties of the `Data1` Data control as follows:

Set the `Connect` property to `Access`. This means that you will connect to an Access database (*.MDB). Set the `DatabaseName` property to BIBLIO.MDB. This database ships with every copy of Visual Basic. It is populated and contains several tables. Set the `RecordSource` to `Publishers`. This is the name of the table where the data that you want to display resides.

Next, go to the first text box, `Text1`, and bind it to the database by changing its `DataSource` property to `Data1`, which is the name of the Data control on this form. Finally, change the `Datafield` property to `Name` for `Text1`, `CompanyName` for `Text2`, and `City` for `Text3`. Thus, Data controls bind to databases and Text boxes bind to Data controls. Now, when you run the program, you will see data in the Text boxes. As you click on the little arrows that are attached to the Data control, you can move around in the database. The arrow buttons on the far right and far left of the control will position the database to the beginning or the end of the referenced table. The inside buttons will move to the next or previous record, respectively.

This example will display every record in the Publishers table. Most of the time, you will be interested in a subset of the data from a table. This example can be made more "real world" by adding a selection criteria to the Data1 control. You add this criteria by changing the `RecordSource` property from `Publishers` to the `SQL` string, as follows:

```
Select * From Publishers Where PubId  > 5
```

Translated, this string means that you want to see all of the columns from the Publishers table if the `PubId` field is greater than `5`. This reduces the number of rows that are attached to the `Data1` Data control. This setting is shown in figure 15.3.

Figure 15.3

Adding an SQL query.

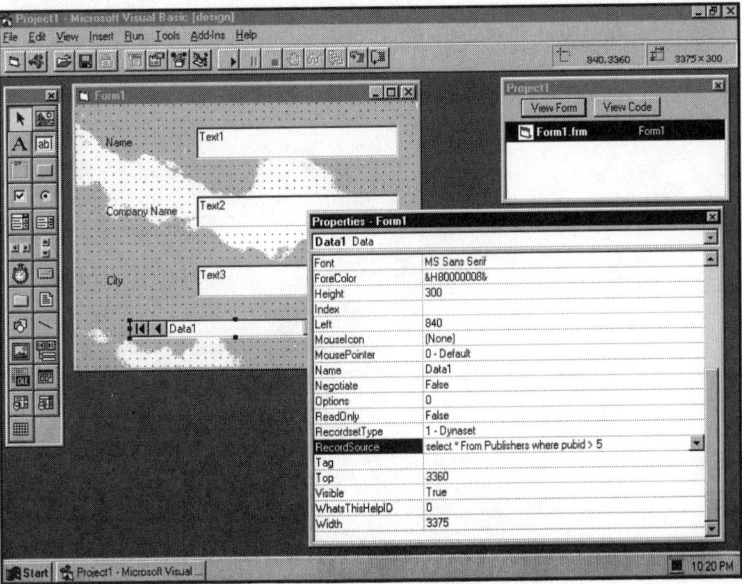

Now, when the application is run, you will see only those records that were retrieved by the data source based on the SQL statement. Running the program causes the data to be retrieved, as shown in figure 15.4.

Figure 15.4
Running the SQL example.

You can use the same controls as before to move from record to record. Chapter 33, "Adding Data and Grid Controls," provides additional examples of the Data control.

The Grid Control Tool

The Grid Control tool is not a built-in part of Visual Basic, but is an OLE control extension (.OCX). It is a useful control to own because it can display data in a tabular format. The real power of the Grid control is in its capacity to accept large amounts of data from a database and display it in a relatively small space.

Normally, your Toolbar will not have the Grid Control tool present unless you explicitly tell Visual Basic to load it. You give this instruction by clicking on the Tools, Custom Control menu pick. This brings up the Custom Controls window, as shown in figure 15.5.

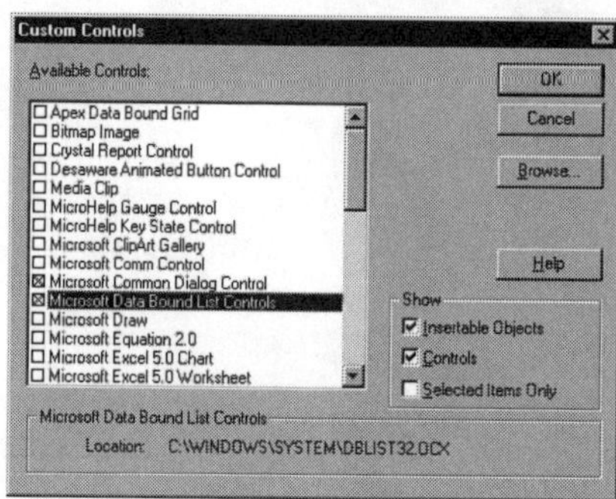

Figure 15.5
Adding custom controls to a project.

Click on the control that you want to add, `Microsoft Grid`, and then click on OK. Like magic, the Grid Control tool now appears in your Toolbox. Now you are ready to create a form that uses this control. First, start a new project.

Highlight `FORM1.FRM` in the project window and click on the View Form button. The Properties window should now be in view.

Select Toolbox in the Window menu to bring the Toolbox into view if it isn't already. Double-click on the Grid Control tool icon in the Toolbox window to add `Grid1` to the form. Position it to the top-left corner of the form. Drag the lower-right corner of the grid to a position near the lower-right corner of the form. In the properties for the grid, change the `Rows` property to `3` and the `Columns` property to `4`. Now save the project. The form should now appear similar to the one shown in figure 15.6.

Figure 15.6

The Grid control.

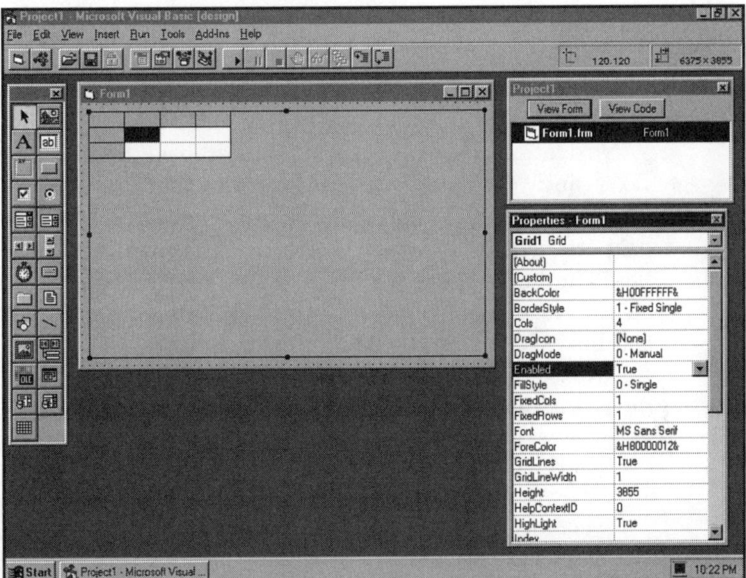

The grid control is normally associated with a database. In order to give your application easy access to the database, you need to create a Data control. Call it `Data1`. In addition, create three text boxes, `Text1`, `Text2`, and `Text3`.

These text boxes simplify the example somewhat since they can be bound to the fields in the database without coding. They also provide some visual feedback on the status of the Data control as you progress through the example. The last thing needed is a command button which can be used when you attach the code to the form. At this point, your example should look like the one shown in figure 15.7.

Figure 15.7
Adding additional controls.

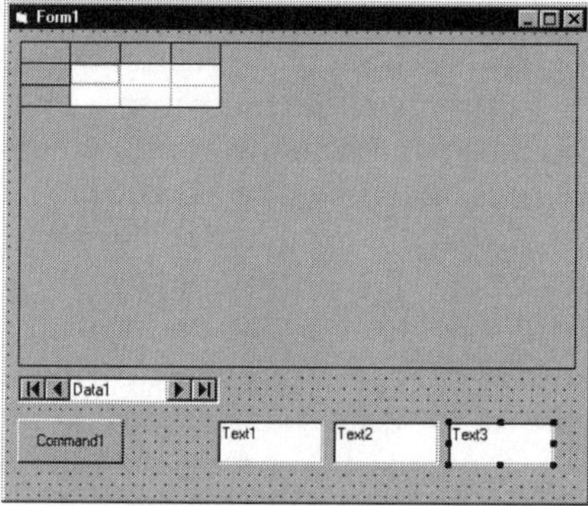

Example

In this example, you need to set the value of Data1's `DatabaseName` property to BIBLIO.MDB. Next, set the `DataSource` property to `Publishers`, which means the Publishers table in the BIBLIO.MDB database.

Next, attach the Text boxes to the database. Set the `DataSource` property of `Text1`, `Text2`, and `Text3` to `Data1`. This indicates that the Text boxes will be bound to the Data1 control and, by association, to the BIBLIO.MDB database. Set the `DataField` property of `Text1` to `Name`, of `Text2` to `Company Name`, and of `Text3` to `City`. These are the fields in the Publishers table that contain the data that you want to display. The built-in functionality of these controls will handle the details of populating these text boxes based on the data in the database.

Now, supplied with a form full of the appropriate controls, you are ready to add the following code to the application:

```
Private Sub Command1_Click()
    Grid1.Col = 1
    Grid1.Text = Text1.Text
    Grid1.Col = 2
    Grid1.Text = Text2.Text
    Grid1.Col = 3
    Grid1.Text = Text3.Text
Data1.Recordset.Movenext
Grid1.Row = Grid1.Row + 1
Grid1.Rows = Grid1.Rows + 1
End Sub
```

The way that the Grid control is populated is illustrated in this example. The `Col` property determines which column in the grid has the focus. Since `Text1.Text` is bound to the `Name` field in the database, it will contain the data in that field of the current row of the database. You assign that field in the database to the grid by assigning its value to the `Text` property value of the grid.

Next, change the `Col` property's value to `2`, and assign the value of `Text2` to the `Text` property. Finally, change the `Col` property to `3`, and assign the value of `Text3` to the grid. Having done this, increase the value of the `Row` property in preparation for the next time a row of data is added to the grid. Each time the button Command1 is clicked, a grid row is added that contains the data from a row in the database. Then the database is moved to the next record. After a number of rows have been added, your form should resemble figure 15.8.

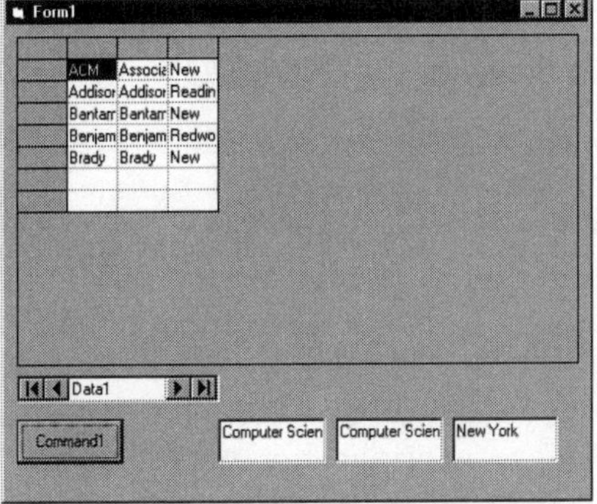

Figure 15.8
Populating the grid.

Now that the grid is populated, you can put it to use. One of the nice features of the Grid control is that its `Text` property will always contain the value of the cell in the grid that has the focus. Now, add a fourth text box to the form. Figure 15.9 shows how this works.

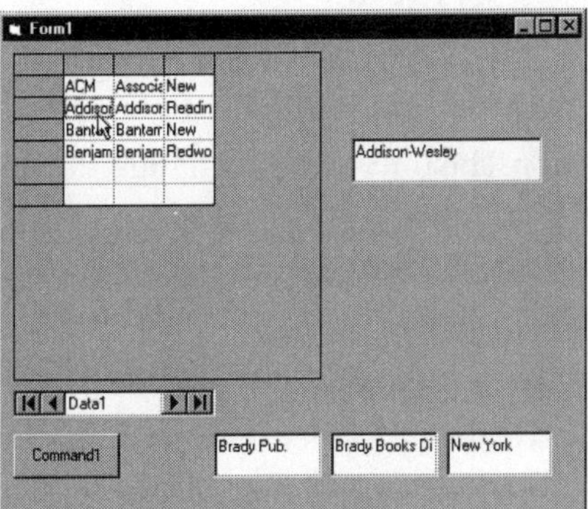

Figure 15.9
Accessing the grid's data.

In this example, the value that appears in the `Text4` text box is assigned by the following code:

```
Private Sub Grid1_SelChange()
    Text4.Text = Grid1.Text
End Sub
```

The `SelChange` event occurs whenever the user changes from one cell in the Grid to another. Whenever this happens, the value of the cell is copied to the `Text` property of the Text box. This will give you a control in which you select from a grid the same way that you select a color from a palette.

The OLE Control

OLE, the common acronym for Object Linking and Embedding, is the cornerstone of Microsoft's software reuse strategy. By designing their applications according to the OLE standard, independent software vendors can create programs that fit seamlessly into Visual Basic and other Microsoft products.

This strategy promises to greatly increase programmer productivity by allowing the integration of these components into an application. OLE is capable of connecting to an outside application via either linking or embedding.

Linking to an application means that your Container control contains a link to a document that was created by that application. If another application changes that document, your document will show those changes.

Embedding a document means that your Container control contains a document that was created using an OLE-compliant application. It does not, however, maintain any links back to any external document.

The biggest difference will be that an embedded object appears to be part of the Visual Basic application (almost as if it were a custom control placed on a form) whereas a linked object will, when activated, call up another program (the one it's linked to), which the user will use to work on the document. When finished, that (linked) application will end, and the user will be returned to the Visual Basic application.The only way to change the document that is contained in your OLE control is to open your application and activate the OLE control—normally by double-clicking on the control itself. When the OLE application comes up, you can alter the contents of the document, and then do a File, Close and Return to Unnamed. This will show the changed document in the changed window. You will see how this works in this section.

One way to use Object Linking and Embedding is via the OLE Container control in Visual Basic. This tool allows a rectangle to be opened on a form that is capable of displaying data from another application. Let's run an example to illustrate this concept.

Example

Double-click on the OLE Container icon in the Toolbox. This action will place a rectangular object on the form and display the Insert Object window. If you select the Create from File option, you can enter an existing OLE object file name (or browse for it). The form would look like the one shown in figure 15.10.

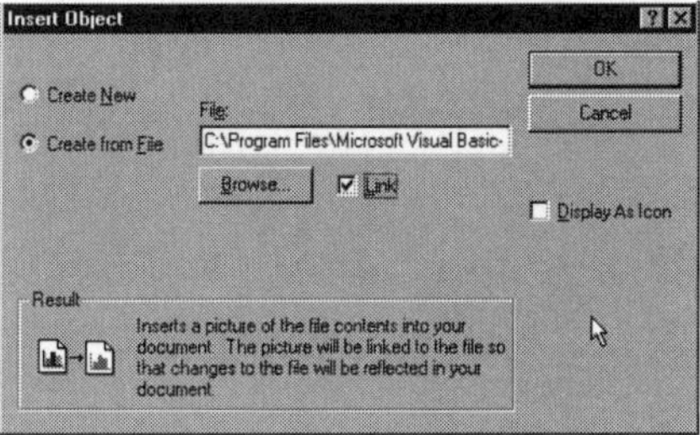

Figure 15.10

The Insert Object window.

This window is asking for instructions from you on what object you want to link or embed into this control. You can either specify an existing file or create a new object at this time. The latter case is more interesting, so click on the option button marked Create New. This will bring up a window that looks like figure 15.11.

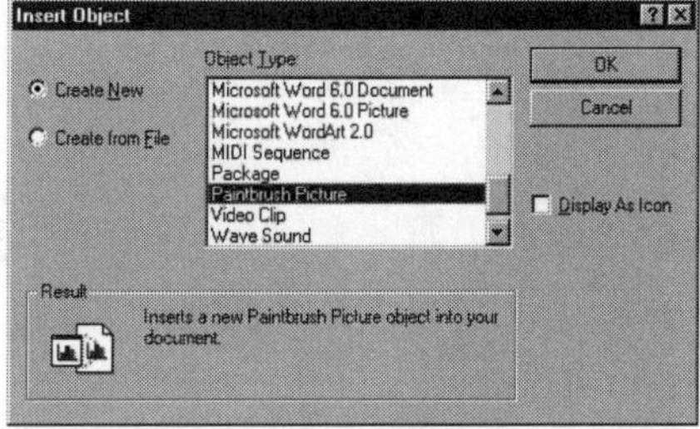

Figure 15.11

Specifying an OLE application.

The various OLE compliant applications are listed in a scrollable list box for you to select from. This list will vary according to the software that is installed on your system. Normally, one shrink-wrapped product will yield three or more custom controls. In this example, let's choose `Paintbrush Picture` and see what happens. The result of that selection is shown in figure 15.12.

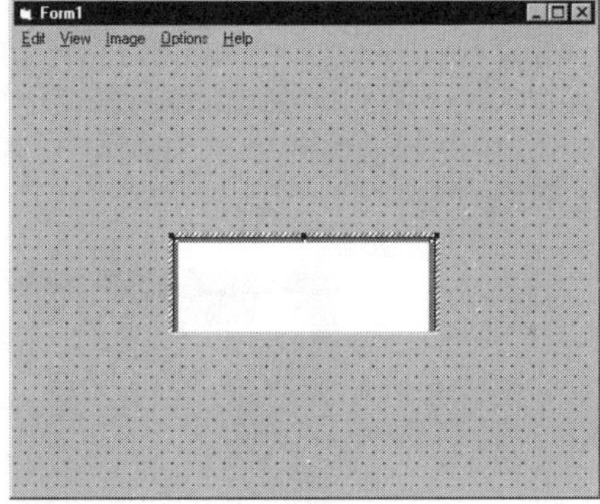

Figure 15.12
An application started by OLE.

Notice that you did not simply import a simple graphic, but rather a completely different application started—Win95 Paint.

Now, using the command set provided by Paint, create a picture like the one shown in figure 15.12. When you finish, select File, Close and Return to Unnamed. This is instructing Paint that you have finished and that you want to go back to the Visual Basic development environment. When you do this, your original form will reappear with a display that looks sort of like the drawing that you created in Paint. This is illustrated in figure 15.13.

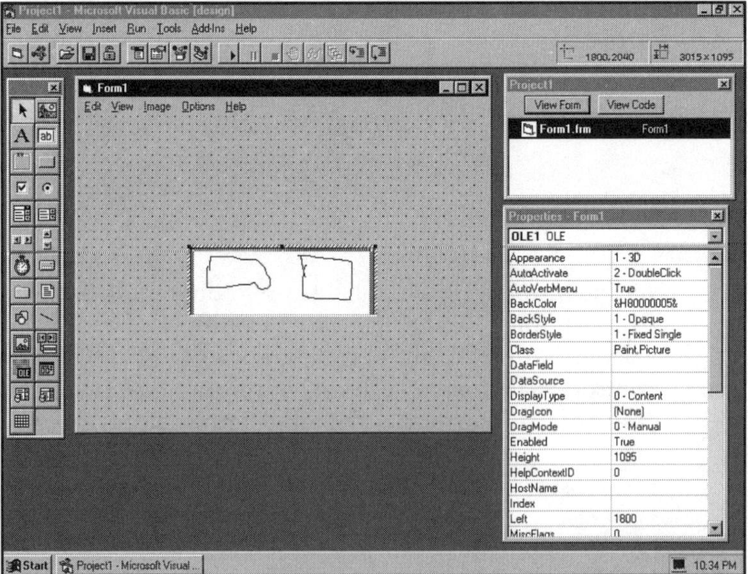

Figure 15.13
A form with an OLE container.

The only problem is that you can see only a small portion of the picture that you drew. This problem is easily remedied by changing the value of the `SizeMode` property to `2 - AutoSize`. This will expand the borders of the OLE control so that your picture automatically fits the drawing perfectly. The result of this change is shown in figure 15.14.

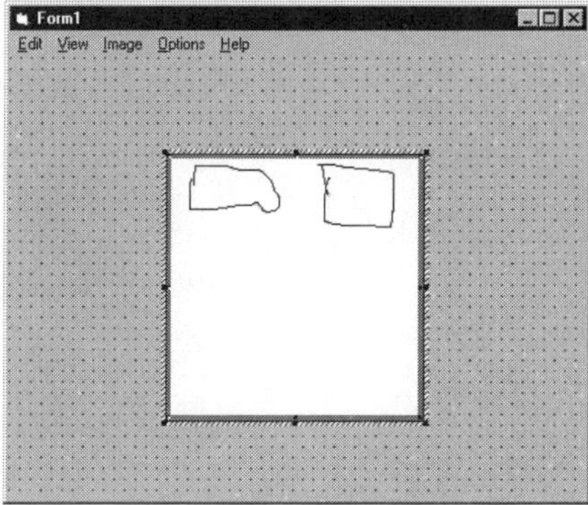

Figure 15.14
The AutoSized OLE Container control.

Having done this, you could save your work and deliver it to the customer. There is one other important aspect of the OLE control called activation. If you double-click on the OLE picture itself, you will invoke Microsoft Paint. What this means is that your users can start their OLE-compliant applications from within an application, bypassing the Program Manager.

In this scenario, the user would change the drawing and return to the original document by choosing Exit & Return To, as shown in figure 15.15.

Figure 15.15
Closing the OLE application.

Now that the user is exiting the OLE session, you see that the changes that were made while in Paintbrush Picture are automatically reflected in the original document, as shown in figure 15.16

Figure 15.16
Updated data in the OLE container.

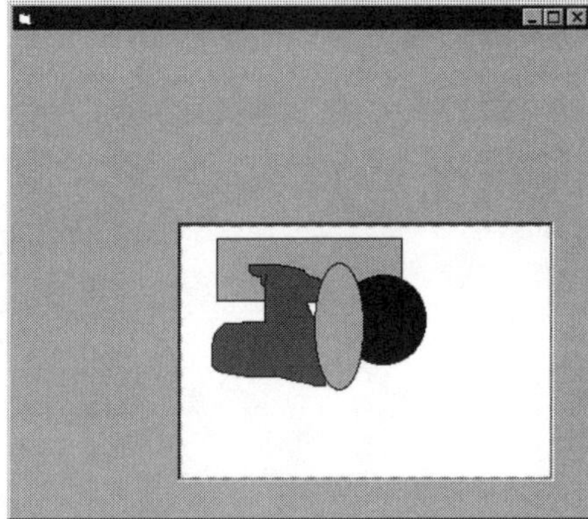

You can see in figure 15.16 that the new shape is included in the drawing. It would also be included in any other applications that contained this same link to this picture. One thing that you may have noticed was that the File menu in figure 15.15 looked a little different from the normal Paintbrush Picture menu, which is shown in figure 15.17 for purposes of comparison.

Figure 15.17
The normal Paintbrush menu.

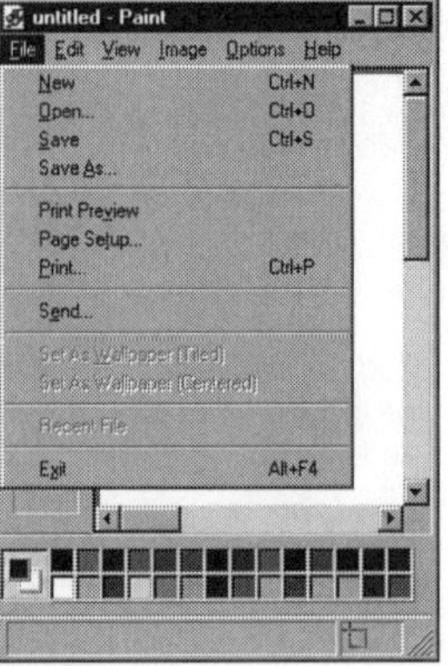

The reason for this difference is that when an application is being accessed via an OLE control, its goal is to produce the linked or embedded object in the Visual Basic form. This document may or may not ever be stored in a separate file and used for other purposes. This requires that the menus contain extra commands, such as Exit and Return To Unnamed, Update, and Save Copy As. These commands would make no sense in the normal Microsoft Paint context, so the designers had to decide how to present this functionality when the goal was to support the OLE access to the OLE 2.0-compliant application.

Summary

In this chapter, you were introduced to tools that can be used to connect your application to other applications on your computer. These connections allow you to "borrow" functionality from existing applications without writing the code yourself. This greatly enhances the productivity of programmers because they have more time to devote to the functional area being addressed.

The first control that you looked at was the Data control. This control allows Visual Basic to connect to an existing database engine. This connection allows you to interact with a database with little or no coding required. Using this technique, you can create a "front-end" application that shows the database data to the user in a highly customized format.

The Grid control gives you an opportunity to display your data in a compact format. It also gives you the ability to pick from the Grid control to select from a large list of choices.

Finally, the OLE control was discussed. This control allows your program to interoperate with other applications. There are two types of interaction allowed:

- *Linking* "ties" your program to an external program.
- *Embedding* makes an external program seem to be part of your program.

By using these techniques, you can greatly increase the value of the applications that you provide to your customers. You can create applications that have professional-quality graphics, word processors, and spreadsheets embedded in them, even if you don't know anything about how to write these kinds of programs.

Review Questions

Answers to the review questions can be found in Appendix A.

1. What does OLE stand for?
2. What is the purpose of the `DatabaseName` property in a Data control?

3. What purpose does the SQL query serve when used in the Data control?
4. What is an .OCX file?

5. Why do you have to explicitly load the Grid tool to the Toolbar using the Tools, Custom Control menu pick?

6. What is an OLE container?

7. What is the difference between *Object Linking* and *Object Embedding*?

Review Exercises

1. Write a program that adds a Data control to a form and displays data in a set of bound Text boxes.

2. Write a program that displays the same data as in Exercise 1, but displays it in a Grid control.

3. Create a Grid control that contains six rows and four columns. Populate the grid with the name of basketball teams. Create another grid that contains dates and times for basketball games. Create a set of Text controls that allows you to select teams for a specific game time.

4. Write a program that contains one OLE container for each type of program on your computer.

CHAPTER 16

The Common Dialog Tool

When users run programs, there are several activities that happen frequently. They open files, save files, select colors, and change fonts over and over during their work sessions. The designers of Windows 3.1 realized this and created special windows to perform these and other tasks. They created a set of "prefabricated" windows that query the user for the data needed to perform these functions, and save you, the developer, a lot of time. In addition, these windows, called *Common Dialogs*, serve as a kind of defacto standard for the operation of these activities in Windows programs in general. If you decide to bypass these dialogs (also called properties sheets) and create your own forms to perform these functions, your users may resent the fact that you have strayed from the beaten path. Even worse, they may conclude that you are really a DOS or UNIX developer who doesn't know his way around.

To make these common dialogs available in Visual Basic, Microsoft has distributed a special tool with the product called the *Common Dialog tool*. This tool can be found in the Toolbox (see fig. 16.1).

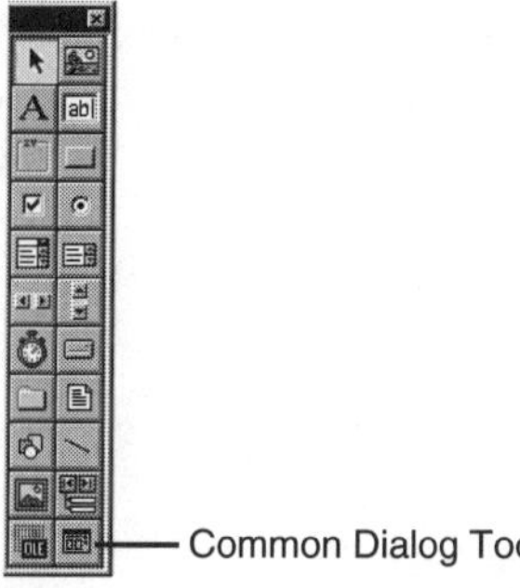

Figure 16.1
The Common Dialog tool.

The fact that it is so difficult to tell an add-in (OCX) from a built-in is a tribute to the Visual Basic architects. The subject of custom controls is covered in more detail in Chapter 15, "The Data, Grid, and OLE Tools." There are five properties sheets that can be invoked by using the Common Dialog tool and one function that is used to invoke Help:

- The Open properties sheet
- The Save As properties sheet
- The Color properties sheet
- The Font properties sheet
- The Printer properties sheet
- The Windows Help System

Let's look at each property sheet to understand how to include them in your applications.

The Open Properties sheet

One of the most common user interactions with the operating system is the opening of a file. Nearly every application opens at least one file on a hard drive. In applications like CorelDRAW, a user works with dozens of different drawings in a single day. She is constantly opening a file that contains a drawing, then closing it. The same is true of most Visual Basic applications. Your user will tell the system which file is to be opened. Your application will then open the correct file and connect your user to it via your application. To make the communication between the user and your application easier, you can use the *Open properties sheet*. Let's work an example to show you how to do this.

Example

Create a new form and add a Common Dialog control, text box, and command button to it, as shown in figure 16.2.

You will also notice the presence of a command button and a text box. The purpose of the command button is to invoke the Open properties sheet. Unlike most of the other controls that we have seen in Visual Basic, the Command Dialog control never appears on the screen, except in design mode. It is always invisible when the program is running. The text box has been added to give us a way to display the results of the user's interaction with the properties sheet.

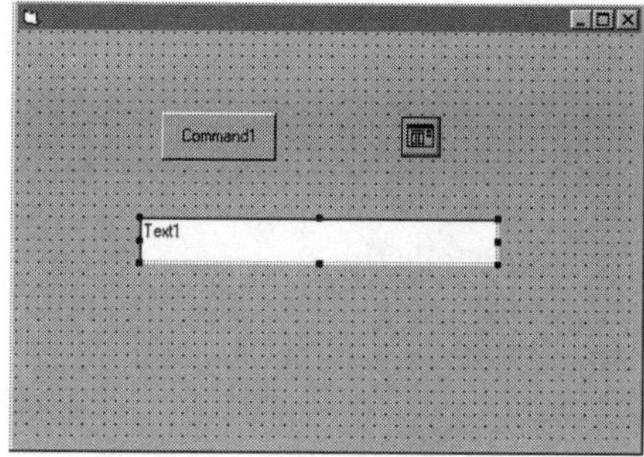

Figure 16.2
The Common Dialog control.

The properties sheets themselves do not open any files. They are simply front-ends that allow the user to operate in a fairly sophisticated environment in order to discover and specify the file that he would like your application to open. You must open the file yourself after the Open properties sheet has given you the name of the file. File Processing is explained in Chapter 28, "Files and I/O."

At this point, rename the Common Dialog control to `dlgCommon`. Now you are ready to run the program and click on the command button. When you click, the `Click` event for that button is invoked, as shown in Listing 16.1:

Listing 16.1 16LIST01.TXT—Common Dialog Open Sample Code

```
Private Sub cmdButton_Click()
    dlgCommon.FileName = ""
    dlgCommon.Filter = "Icons (*.ico)|*.ico|All Files (*.*)|*.*"
    dlgCommon.FilterIndex = 1
    dlgCommon.Flags = cdlOFNFileMustExist Or cdlOFNPathMustExist
    dlgCommon.Action = 1
     Text1.Text = dlgCommon1.FileName
End Sub
```

This routine has three main sections. The first section sets up the parameters for the command box. It has four lines. The first line tells the Open properties sheet that you do not want to put a file name in the File Name box on the form when it first comes up. The second line tells which files you want to display.

The phrase `Icons (*.ico)` tells this custom control that you want to display these words in the List Files of Type box. The phrase `|*.ico` is a separator followed by a string that tells which files are to be displayed in the list box. The string `All Files (*.*)|*.*` is telling the custom control that there is a second filter that is to be available to the user.

The `FilterIndex` property tells this .OCX to use the first filter. The following line causes the properties sheet to require that the user select a file that must already exist from a path that must already exist:

```
dlgCommon.Flags = cdlOFNFileMustExist Or cdlOFNPathMustExist
```

Flags are used to tell the Common Dialog control how to procede. The values of the flags (See Visual Basic Help Topic "COMMONDIALOG constants") are binary values and can be added together using a binary `OR` command.

The next line tells the control to specifically start the Open common properties sheet instead of one of the other common properties sheets. By setting the `Action` property to `1`, the Common Dialog control will display the Open Properties sheet.

```
dlgCommon.Action = 1
```

The result is shown in figure 16.3.

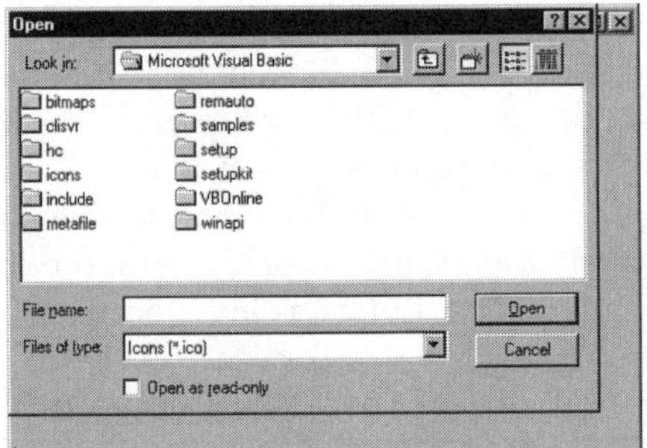

Figure 16.3

The Open common dialog control.

Using this properties sheet, the user can browse the entire directory structure and locate the file that she wants to open. Upon pressing the OK button, the `FileName` property of the Common Dialog control receives the name of the file that was chosen. The last line of the following event procedure displays the file name so that we can convince ourselves that the dialog worked:

```
Text1.Text = dlgCommon.FileName
```

The final result of this exercise is shown in figure 16.4.

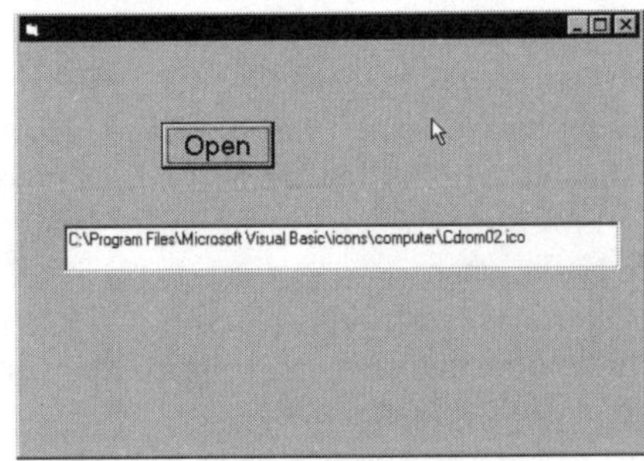

Figure 16.4

Running the Open properties sheet example.

The Save As Properties Sheet

Another common activity of Windows application is file saving. Again, Windows provides a common properties sheet, the *Save As common properties sheet*, to assist you in coding this functionality. Let's alter our previous example and make it into a Save As properties sheet. All that we have to do is change the `Click` event procedure and run it again.

Example

The new procedure is shown in Listing 16.2

Listing 16.2 16LIST02.TXT—Common Dialog Save As Sample Code

```
Private Sub cmdButton_Click()
 dlgCommon.DefaultExt = "ICO"
 dlgCommon.FileName = "DEFAULT.ICO"
 dlgCommon.Filter = "Icons (*.ico)|*.ico|All Files (*.*)|*.*"
 dlgCommon.FilterIndex = 1
 dlgCommon.Flags = cdlOFNOverwritePrompt Or cdlOFNPathMustExist
 dlgCommon.Action = 2
    Text1.Text = dlgCommon.FileName
End Sub
```

The `DefaultExt` property tells Visual Basic to assume an extension of ICO if none is given. The `Filename` property fills in the File Name box as a default. The other properties are similar to the previous example. Figure 16.5 shows the result of running this application and clicking on the Save button.

> **Note:** When displaying files for the Open or Save As properties sheets, Windows 95 hides the file extensions by default.

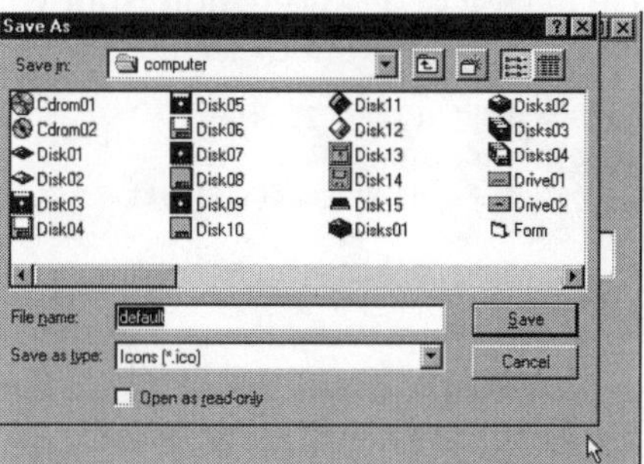

Figure 16.5
The Save As properties sheet.

Notice the effects of the property settings on the output. Figure 16.6 shows the window after the File Name has been selected.

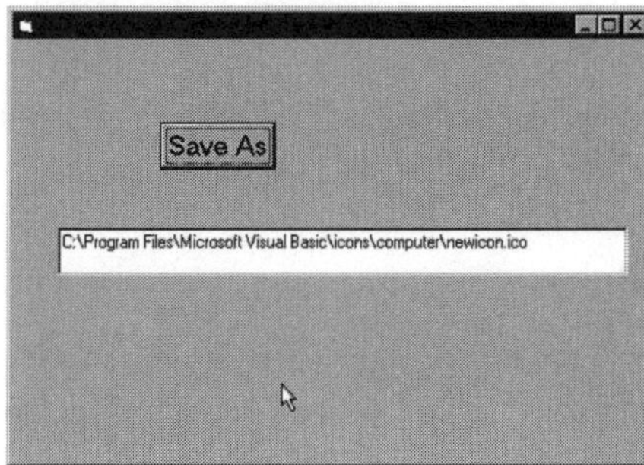

Figure 16.6
Running the Save As properties sheet example.

The file name that you chose is displayed in the text box in order to verify that the properties sheet operates as advertised.

The Color Properties Sheet

The *Color common properties sheet* is slightly different than the other common properties sheets in the way it interacts with the user. It gives the user the ability to pick from any color in the spectrum. It allows the user to select a color from a palette. The dialog then informs your application what the user picked. Like the Open and Save As properties sheets, the Color properties sheet is invoked by setting the `Action` property of the Common Dialog custom control. The settings that are important are assigned in the event procedure as they were in the previous example.

Example

The assignment of the `Color` properties in the first line is so that the same color will be in force in case of a cancellation from within the properties sheet. The `Action` property says that we want to see the Color properties sheet.

```
Private Sub cmdButton_Click()
    dlgCommon.Color = BackColor
    dlgCommon.Flags = cdlCCRGBInit
    dlgCommon.Action = 3
    Text1.Text = dlgCommon.Color
End Sub
```

Figure 16.7 shows the properties sheet itself.

The last line in the procedure displays the RGB value of the color selected as a string for us to inspect. The result of choosing a bright green color is shown in figure 16.8.

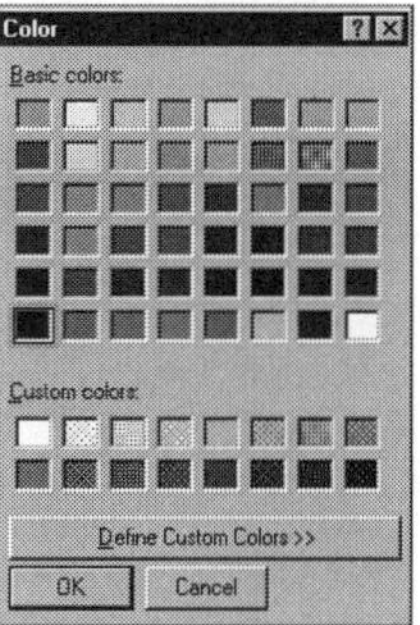

Figure 16.7
The Color common properties sheet.

The responsibility for changing the application in such a way that it reflects the color choice remains with the application developer. This properties sheet simply queries the user as to her desires and communicates that to the application.

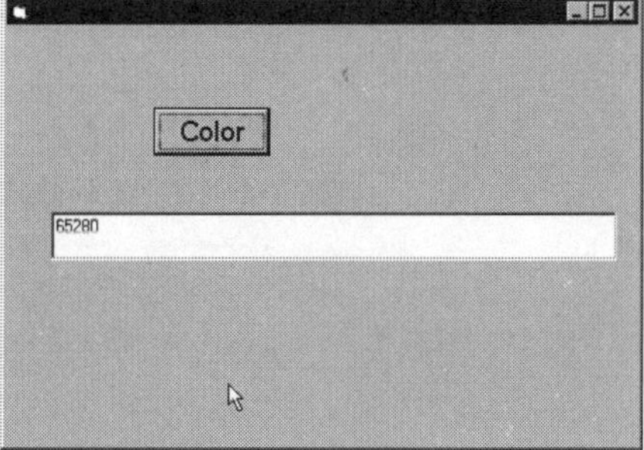

Figure 16.8
Running the color example.

The Font Properties Sheet

Next, we investigate the capabilities of the *Font properties sheet*. Fonts allow the user to select a typeface and size that fits his needs. The properties sheet then informs your application what the user picked. Like the Open and Save As properties sheets, the Font properties sheet is invoked by setting the `Action` property of the Common Dialog *OLE Control Extension* (also known as an OCX file). The settings that are important are assigned in the event procedure as they were in the previous example. The Font properties sheet is normally attached to a Text control in order to control the look of the text.

Example

The flow of this common properties sheet is somewhat different since you are choosing font attributes for a specific text box, `Text1`. The first seven lines of code (see Listing 16.2) copy the current settings into the properties sheet's properties. The `Action` properties sheet says to run the Font property sheet. Figure 16.9 shows the properties sheet itself.

Listing 16.3 16LIST03.TXT—Common Dialog Font Sample Code

```
Private Sub cmdButton_Click()
    dlgCommon.Color = Text1.ForeColor
    dlgCommon.FontBold = Text1.FontBold
    dlgCommon.FontItalic = Text1.FontItalic
    dlgCommon.FontStrikethru = Text1.FontStrikethru
    dlgCommon.FontUnderline = Text1.FontUnderline
    dlgCommon.FontName = Text1.FontName
    dlgCommon.FontSize = Text1.FontSize
    dlgCommon.Flags = cdlCFEffects Or cdlCFForceFontExist Or
    ➥cdlCFBoth
    dlgCommon.Action = 4
    Text1.ForeColor = dlgCommon.Color
    Text1.FontBold = dlgCommon.FontBold
    Text1.FontItalic = dlgCommon.FontItalic
    Text1.FontStrikethru = dlgCommon.FontStrikethru
    Text1.FontUnderline = dlgCommon.FontUnderline
    Text1.FontName = dlgCommon.FontName
    Text1.FontSize = dlgCommon.FontSize
End Sub
```

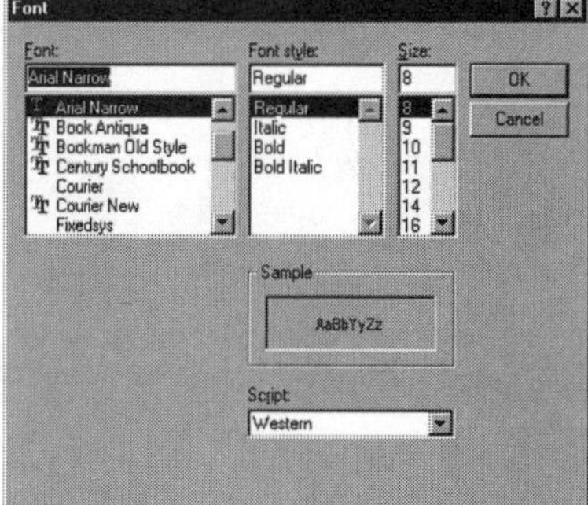

Figure 16.9

The Font common properties sheet.

The last seven lines tell us to assign the values generated by the user's interaction with the properties sheet back to the user for display. Experiment by changing some of the `Font` properties. The display changes to reflect the property values that you have changed. Figure 16.10 shows the Font has been changed to Arial, the Font Style has been changed to bold, and the Size has been changed to 12.

The responsibility for changing the application in such a way that it reflects the new font attributes remains with the application developer, but was handled at the time that the Font common properties sheet was invoked.

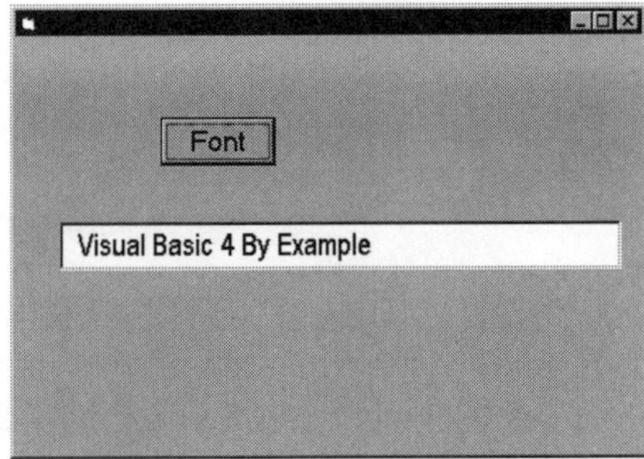

Figure 16.10
Running the font example.

The Print Properties Sheet

Another old friend of yours from Windows applications that you have purchased is called the *Print properties sheet*. Nearly all Windows applications use this properties sheet to find out what printer the user would like to use. The settings that are important are assigned in the event procedure as they were in the previous example.

Example

The `Action` property says that we want to see the Print properties sheet.

```
Private Sub cmdButton_Click()
    dlgCommon.Action = 5
    dlgCommon.Print "Testing 1 2 3... Testing"
    dlgCommon.EndDoc
    Text1.Text = "Printing is completed"
End Sub
```

Figure 16.11 shows the properties sheet itself.

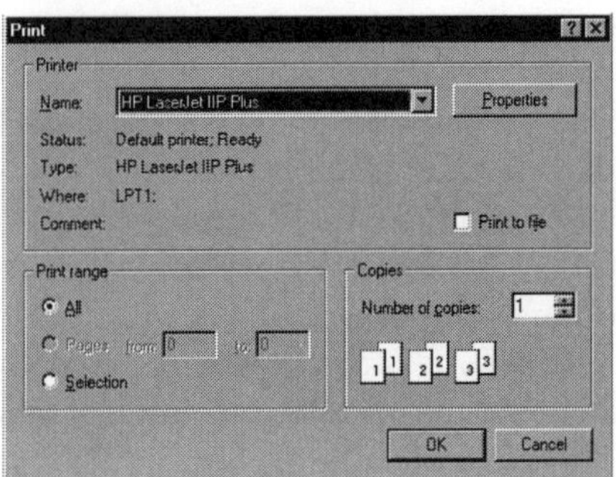

Figure 16.11
The Print common properties sheet.

The last three lines of the example print the test string on the screen and then notify us that it has completed. The screen should look like the one shown in figure 16.12.

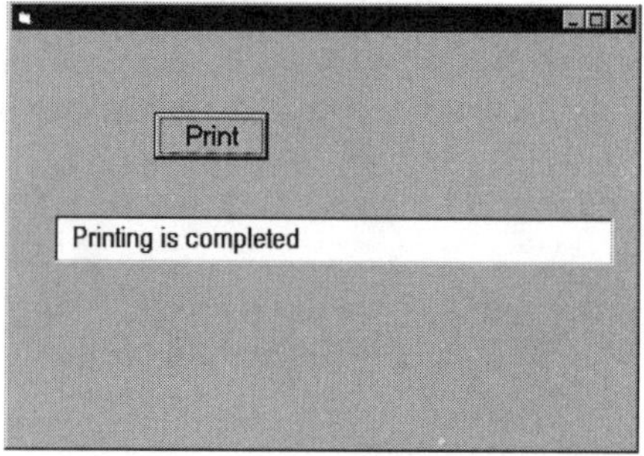

Figure 16.12
Running the print example.

The responsibility for actually printing the document took place outside of the properties sheet. This properties sheet simply queries the user as to his desires and communicates that to the system. When the Print properties sheet is displayed, the user can click on the Properties button to access the Printer properties form.

Summary

In this chapter, you were introduced to the concept of the Common Dialog control. You were instructed that a common properties sheet is implemented as an OLE Control Extension (also known as an OCX). An OCX is a custom control—often written by an independent software vendor—that fits seamlessly into the Visual Basic development environment.

In addition, you learned how to use the Open common properties sheet control to gather a file name from the user. This file name can be used to open the desired file.

The Save As properties sheet is very similar to Open properties sheet in the way the file names and directories are displayed. However, the Save As properties sheet is used to obtain the name to use when saving a file.

The Color properties sheet allows users to select a color from a palette. Can you imagine how long it would take to develop that kind of properties sheet from scratch? The Font properties sheet also was discussed; it differs from the other properties sheets in that it's normally attached to any control in order to control the look of the text that is displayed in that control.

Finally, we discussed the Printer properties sheet. This properties sheet is interesting because it communicates with the operating system to learn which printers are on the system. Armed with these common properties sheets, you can begin to create applications that are as professional looking as those that come from Microsoft.

Review Questions

1. What purpose does the Common Dialog control serve?
2. Name the five different types of common properties sheets.

3. True or False: The Open properties sheet doesn't open anything.
4. What role does the `Filter` properties play in the Open properties sheet?
5. What role does the `FilterIndex` properties play in the Open properties sheet?

6. What is the purpose of the `Flags` properties? What does it control?
7. Where does the Font common properties sheet find out about the fonts on your system?

Review Exercises

1. Create a button that invokes the Open common properties sheet that defaults to finding metafiles (*.WMF).
2. Write a program that invokes the Color properties sheet.

3. Create a text box that is written in Courier 12-point font. Using the Font common properties sheet, change it to Arial 18-point font.
4. Create a Print common properties sheet and print a test string in Landscape mode (if your printer supports Landscape mode).

5. Write a program that has a Command button for each common dialog type. Code them so that each uses the `Action` properties to invoke the required function.

CHAPTER 17

The Menu Editor

The menu bar is an important part of nearly every Windows application that you purchase. Even when the application is equipped with a toolbar, those buttons are simply shortcuts that duplicate the actions caused by a menu pick. If you think about the Windows applications that you are accustomed to using, they normally have a menu bar across the top of the window just under the title bar. Figure 17.1 shows the menu bar for the Windows Paint program that ships with every copy of Windows 95.

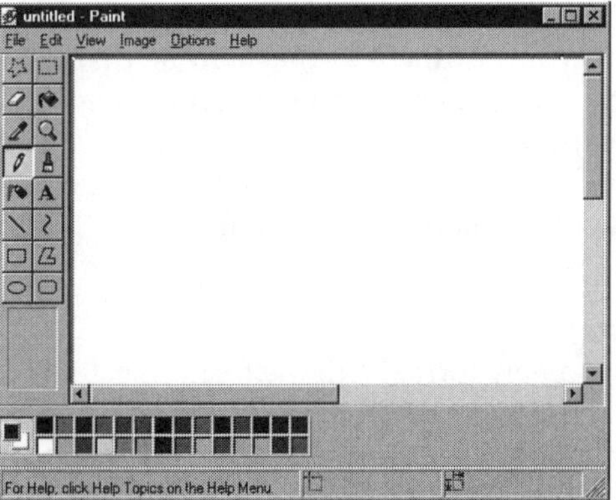

Figure 17.1
The Windows 95 Paint program.

In reality, the line of words across the top of the window is called the menu bar. Normally, the words that appear on the menu bar are not menu items, but menu names. If you click on one of these menu names, you get a pull-down menu with anywhere from three to ten or more menu items. These items can be thought of as command buttons that only support one event, the `Click` event.

The Menu Editor Window

Because Visual Basic is sold as a Windows program development environment, one would expect that it contains a facility for adding menus to applications. This is indeed the case. In fact, it has a rather convenient facility called the Menu Editor to assist you with this. You invoke the Menu Editor by selecting the form to which you wish to add a menu, and then choosing Tools, Menu Editor from Visual Basic's own menu. This can also be accomplished by pressing Ctrl+E on the keyboard. The window shown in figure 17.2 appears.

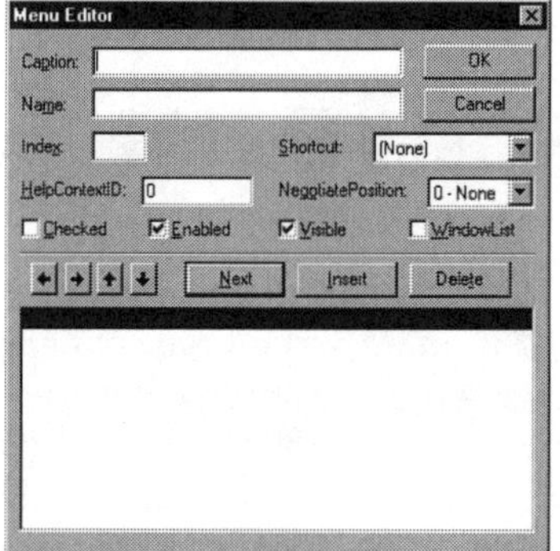

Figure 17.2
The Menu Editor.

The Menu Editor is a very efficient tool to produce the menus that are needed by your programs. The large blank area at the bottom of the Menu Editor window displays the current menu structure. The Caption box at the top of the window is where you put the text that will be displayed during the form's execution. The Name box contains a name that represents the menu pick in your code. This name serves the same function as the `Name` property of the command buttons that you have created. The menu picks respond to the click events associated with their names. Let's create a simple menu to illustrate this concept.

Example

Create a new form. With the form selected, choose Tools, Menu Editor or alternatively, press Ctrl+E from the keyboard. This will bring up the Menu Editor screen. At this point we want to add two menu names, each having the menu picks as outlined in Table 17.1.

Table 17.1 The Menu Structure for the Example

Menu Name	*Menu Item*	*Name*	*Event Procedure*
Fly		mnuFly	
Fly	Delta	mnuFlyDelta	mnuFlyDelta_Click
Fly	American	mnuFlyAmerican	mnuFlyAmerican_Click
Fly	ValuJet	mnuFlyValuJet	mnuFlyValuJet_Click
Fly	Southwest	mnuFlySouthwest	mnuFlySouthwest_Click
Drive		mnuDrive	
Drive	Truck	mnuDriveTruck	mnuDriveTruck_Click
Drive	Cadillac	mnuDriveCadillac	mnuDriveCadillac_Click
Drive	Tractor	mnuDriveTractor	mnuDriveTractor_Click

The word on the left (in effect, Fly or Drive) is the name of the menu. There is no event procedure associated with this word in this example. It is not common to have the top-level menu perform any other task than simply showing the submenu. The second column represents the word written on the menu item that triggers an event procedure. The programmer chooses that word. The next column is the name of the menu item in the code. This name is chosen by the programmer, and normally follows some naming convention. Here, the "mnu" stands for menu item, followed by the menu name and the menu item name. Following some sort of naming scheme allows a programmer to work on a more complex application than would otherwise be possible. (It is easy to lose your religion after a few days working on a program with arbitrary naming practices.)

The fourth column is the name of the event procedure. This procedure is automatically named by concatenating the name of the menu pick to Click, which is the name of the event. Let's start by adding in a menu caption, "Fly". Enter it in the Caption box on the Menu Editor window. Next, enter **`mnuFly`** in the Name box. For now, ignore the rest of the controls that you see. Click on the Next button. Enter in the next item in Table 17.1, **`Delta`**, in the Caption box. Enter **`mnuFlyDelta`** as the name and click on Next. The screen should look like the one in figure 17.3.

Notice that the word Delta is directly under the word Fly in the work area at the bottom of the window. The bottom area shows the menu in an outline form. That means that Visual Basic thinks that Delta is a menu instead of a menu item. If you click on the OK button, you see that `Form1` looks like the one shown in figure 17.4.

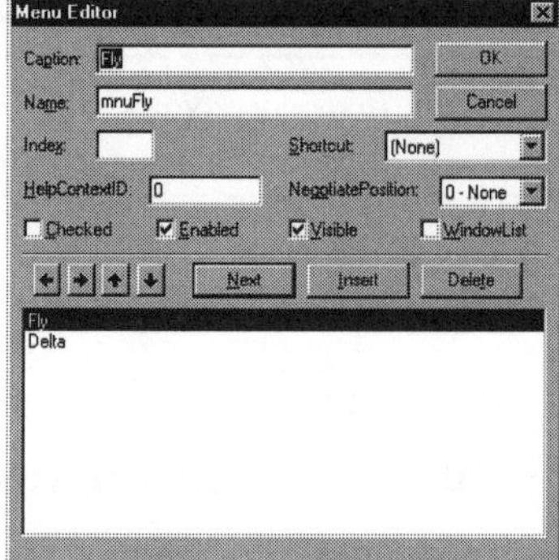

Figure 17.3
Entering the sample menu to the Menu Editor window.

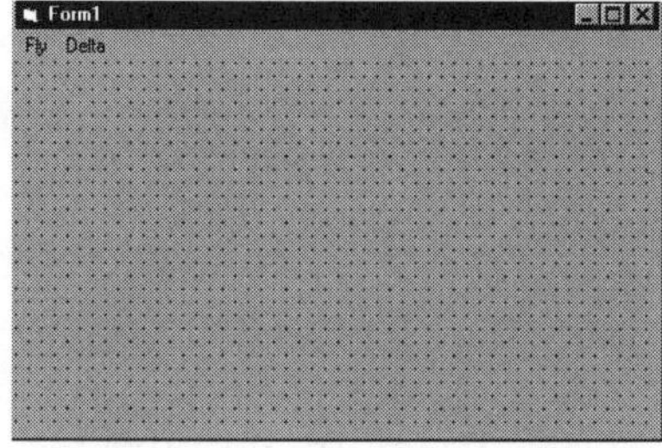

Figure 17.4
The incorrect menu.

This menu is not correct. We wanted Delta to be under the Fly menu, not to be a menu of its own. We can correct this very easily. All that we need to do is to indent the word Delta in the work area at the bottom of the Menu Editor window. We indent by clicking on the right-arrow button, as shown in figure 17.5.

The arrow pointing to the right makes the selected menu item one place more subordinate than it previously was. The left arrow makes the item less subordinate. The up arrow moves the selected item higher up in the list, and the down arrow moves it down in the list. The Next button creates a blank item waiting to be filled. The Insert button creates a blank item just above the one that is selected at the time. The Delete button, as you might expect, destroys the selected item.

So, armed with this new knowledge, let's fix our problem with the Delta menu pick. Click on the word Delta and then press the right arrow, thereby making it subordinate to the Fly menu. Now, continue to add the other members of Table 17.1 until your Menu Editor window looks like the one shown in figure 17.6.

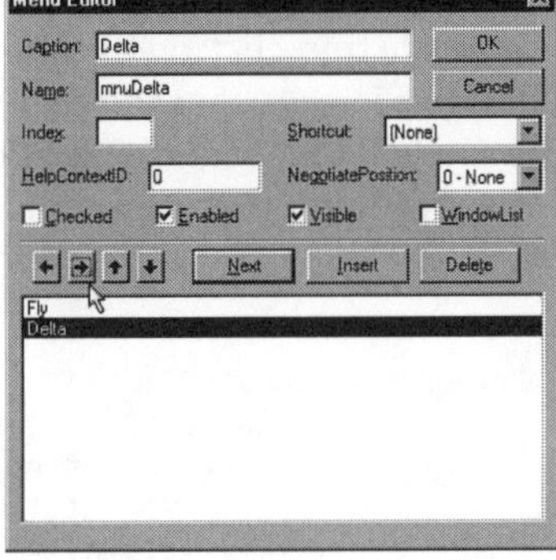

Figure 17.5

The indenting arrows in the Menu Editor window.

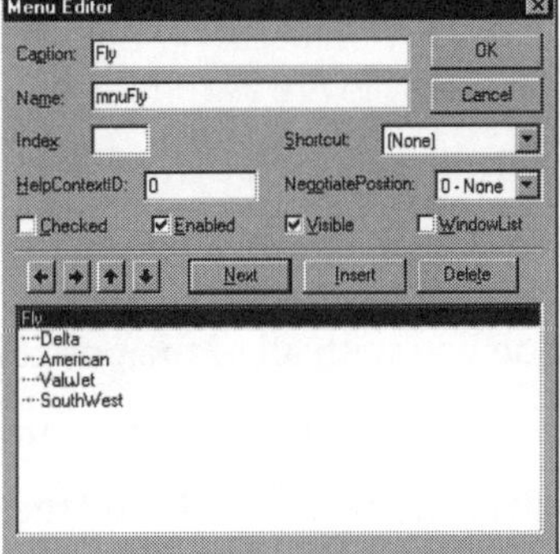

Figure 17.6

Entering the sample menu.

Now, let's add the Drive menu to the form. Add the Drive menu as a menu and not as a subordinate menu item of Fly. Then add all of the menu items and make them subordinate to the menu Drive. The finished menu system should look like the one shown in figure 17.7.

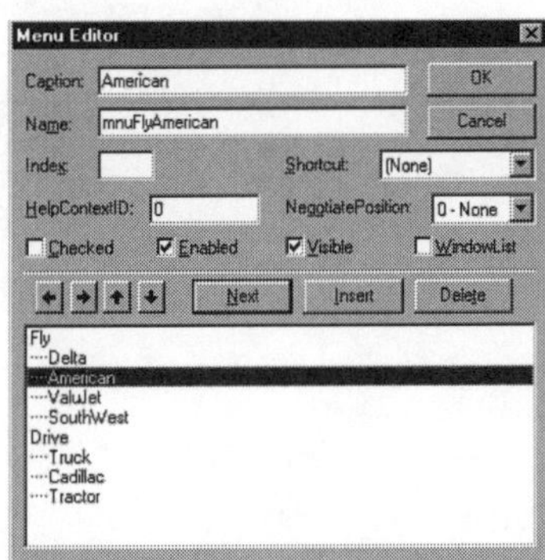

Figure 17.7

The completed menu system.

Now, let's add a few command procedures and see if the menu structure works as advertised. To do this, click on the OK button to close the Menu Editor. Now play with the menus and verify that they are in the correct place in the menu structure.

Access the Code window and add an event procedure by highlighting the menu item ValuJet and clicking on it. This will bring up the Code window with the routine called `Sub mnuFlyValujet_Click` in the work area. Now, add the following code to the procedure:

```
Private Sub mnuFlyValuJet_Click()
    Msg = "You Choose ValuJet"    ' Define message.
    Style = vbOKOnly ' Define buttons.
    Title = "ValuJet"  ' Define title.
    Response = MsgBox(Msg, Style, Title)
End Sub
```

This code sets several parameters and then calls a built-in function called `MsgBox()`. The function `MsgBox()` accepts a number of parameters. The interesting ones for this example are as follows:

- Msg—This is the text that is to be displayed on the screen.
- Style—This gives you a choice of buttons and icons. In this example, we want an OK button so we fill in **`vbOKOnly`**. The On-line Help system can provide you with all of the possible choices.
- Title—This is the text that goes in the title bar of the window.

The result of adding this code and then selecting ValuJet from the menu is shown in figure 17.8 .

Next, add similar code to each of the events and verify that all of the menu picks work properly.

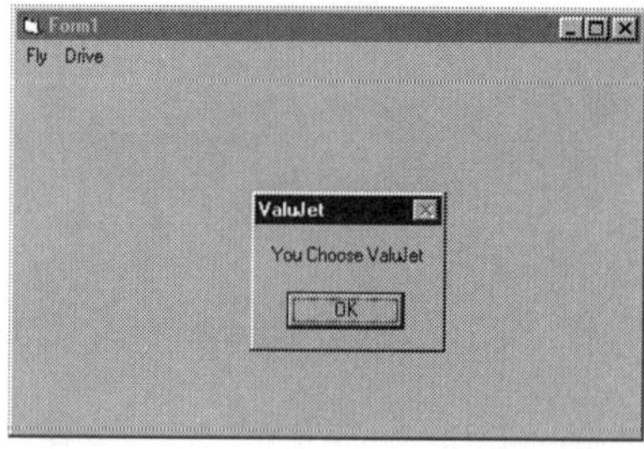

Figure 17.8

The message box for ValuJet.

Hotkeys

In Windows, it is common to use keystroke combinations instead of mouse manipulation to accomplish a task. For example, to save a file, you can either choose File, Save from the menu bar of most applications, or you can press Alt+F+S. These key combinations are called *hotkeys* (or *accelerator keys*). When you are developing Windows applications with Visual Basic, you will want to make your menus seem as professional as possible. Adding hotkeys is one way to add that professional touch.

Example

Luckily, the Menu Editor makes the task of adding these keys nearly trivial. All that you have to do is decide which letter will be the hotkey for each menu and menu pick. You designate this key by placing an ampersand (&) in front of that letter. Visual Basic then knows how to deal with the keystrokes in such a way as to invoke the same event procedure that is invoked by the equivalent mouse actions. Figure 17.9 shows the Fly and Drive menus with a full set of hotkeys added.

Figure 17.9

Hotkeys in the Menu Editor.

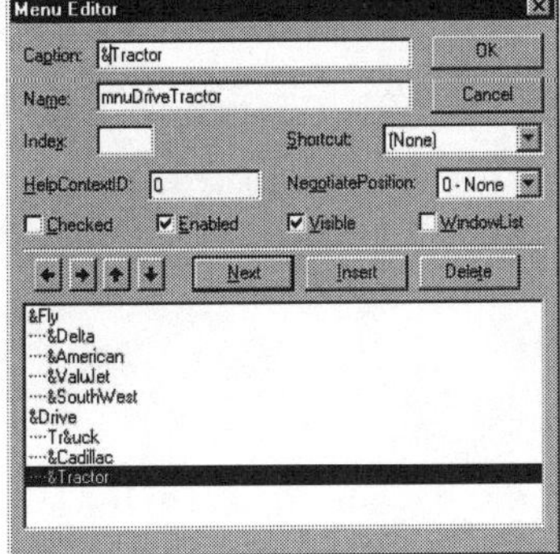

Notice that the normal case is to choose the first letter if possible. When two menu items have the same first letter, we normally go to another unique letter. The & may be placed anywhere in the caption, not just before the first letter. The keystroke sequence for Fly, Delta would now be Alt+F+D. Try it and verify that it works. Notice also that the hotkey is underlined in the menus themselves, in case you forget which keys you selected for a given pick.

Shortcut Keys

Similar to the hotkeys are the *shortcut keys,* for the times when you want to use keystrokes in your menu design, but would rather deviate from the Alt+Key1+Key2 regimen. Visual Basic allows you to do this through the Shortcut box on the Menu Editor window. Figure 17.10 shows some of your alternatives.

Figure 17.10

The shortcut keys.

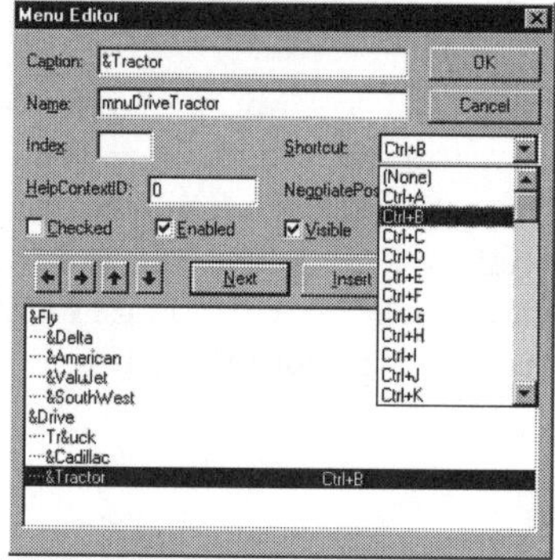

You will notice that a number of Ctrl+Key forms are in the list. In addition, there are a number of F3 type keys, as well as Shift+F3 and a few strange ones like Alt+Backspace. When you select a shortcut key for a menu pick, the shortcut keystrokes appear beside the menu pick in the menu, as shown in figure 17.11.

Figure 17.11

The shortcut keys on the menu.

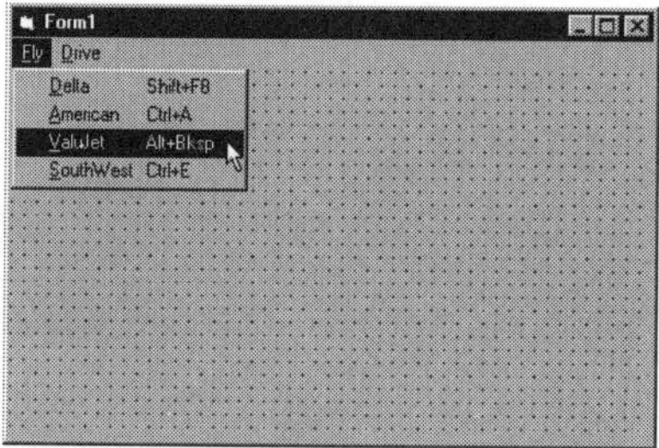

All that you have to do is use the shortcut key that is written beside the menu item, and Visual Basic will interpret this in the same way as if you had used the mouse.

Note: Accelerators or hotkeys are used to navigate the menus; shortcuts bypass the menus. A properly designed menu *must* have an accelerator for *each* menu item, so that the user can effectively navigate the menus by using the keyboard in lieu of the mouse. Shortcuts, however, are generally reserved for most-used commands; they are easier to remember and key in, but assigning them to every menu item would be overkill.

The Other Critical Fields

There are a few other critical fields in the Menu Editor window. The HelpContextID is important when you are going to add a complete Help system to your application.

The check boxes, labeled Checked, Enabled, and Visible, determine the default value for the menu when a form is loaded. Checked means that a check will be placed beside the pick in the menu. Enabled means that the pick is not "grayed out," and is therefore available as a pick. Visible means that it actually appears in the menu at start time. During the execution of your program, you normally change the value of the properties associated with these check boxes to guide your user's choices to the ones that make sense at each instance.

The Index, NegotiatePosition, and WindowList boxes are useful in special situations. Check the on-line Help system for information about these.

Subordinate Menus

Another useful feature of the Menu Editor is the ability to create cascading subordinate menus. Let's look at an example of what this means. Let's add the following menu picks under the Fly, Delta menu pick. To do this, change the Menu Editor window to look like the one shown in figure 17.12.

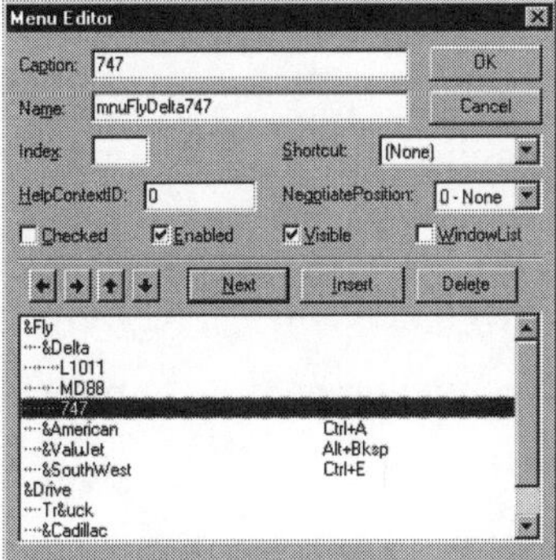

Figure 17.12
The cascading menu.

You will notice that there are three new menu picks, and that they are listed under Delta, but indented one more time. This means that they are subordinate to the Delta menu pick. Figure 17.13 shows this menu in action. The shortcut key for the Delta menu must be removed in order to add a subordinate menu.

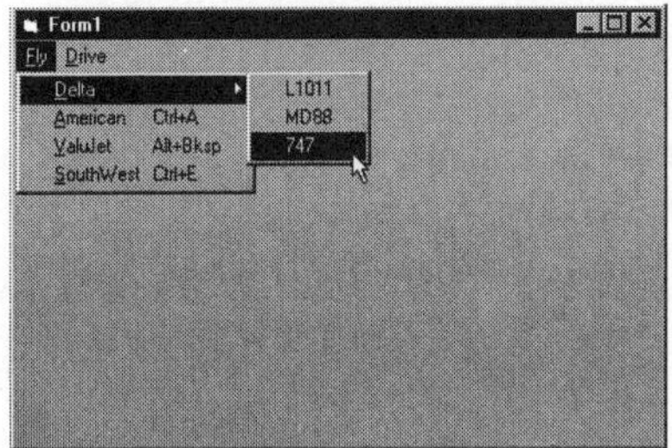

Figure 17.13
Cascading menus.

These cascading menus allow for a more logical grouping of commands in a hierarchy.

Example

Now that you have seen the basic menu building features, let's combine them in an example. For this example, input the menu system in Table 17.2.

Table 17.2 A Sample Menu Structure

Caption	*Name*	*Shortcut*
&Order	mnuOrder	
------ &Meatball Sandwich	mnuMeatball	
------ -	dummy	
------ &Pizza	mnuPizza	
----------- &Cheese	mnuCheese	
----------- &Pepperoni	mnuPepperoni	
------ &Spaghetti	mnuSpaghetti	
&Tip	mnuTip	
------ &Fifteen Percent	mnuFifteen	Ctrl+W
------ &Twenty Percent	mnuTwenty	Shift+F4
------ &Stiff	mnuStiff	Alt+Bksp
&Pay	mnuPay	
------ &Cash	mnuCash	
------ &Credit Card	mnuCredit	F5
------ &Sneak Out	mnuSneak	Ctrl+F11

Table 17.2 only *looks* intimidating. In reality it is very simple. The words on the left are the captions that we want to include in our menu. The next column shows the names of the menu picks within the code. The third column is a list of shortcut keys that are in addition to the keys assigned by the "&" in the name.

Let's look at each line in order to understand what each is doing:

&Order mnuOrder

You create this line by entering **&Order** as the caption and **mnuOrder** as the name. No shortcut key is defined.

---- &Meatball Sandwich mnuMeatball

The Meatball line is subordinated once to the Order line.

---- - dummy

The dummy line is added to provide a separator between the Spaghetti pick and the Meatball pick.

> **Note**: Although separator lines never generate any events, they nonetheless have event code sections. Each separator must therefore have a name that is different from any other routines (for example, `sep1`, `sep2`, and so on).

---- &Pizza mnuPizza

The Pizza line is identical to the Order line except that the right-arrow button was pressed, which made the Pizza pick subordinate to the Order Pick. This means that the user would first click on Order, then on Pizza.

---------- &Cheese mnuCheese

The Cheese line has been subordinated (indented by clicking on the right arrow button) twice. This makes the Cheese pick subordinate to the Pizza pick.

---------- &Pepperoni mnuPepperoni

The Pepperoni line is identical in functionality to the Cheese line.

---- &Spaghetti mnuSpaghetti

The Spaghetti line is subordinated once to the Order line.

&Tip mnuTip

Because the Tip line is not subordinated, it will appear on the menu bar.

---- &Fifteen Percent mnuFifteen Ctrl+W

The Fifteen line is similar to all of the other menu items created so far except that it can be activated by Ctrl+W as well as by choosing it with the mouse.

---- &Twenty Percent mnuTwenty Shift+F4

The Twenty line is similar to all of the other menu items created so far except that it can be activated by Shift+F4 as well as by choosing it with the mouse.

---- &Stiff mnuStiff Alt+Bksp

The Stiff line is similar to all of the other menu items created so far except that it can be activated by Alt+Bksp as well as by choosing it with the mouse.

&Pay mnuPay

The Pay line is like the Order and Tip items. This menu will appear on the menu bar.

---- &Cash mnuCash

The Cash line is a subordinate of the Pay menu.

---- &Credit Card mnuCredit F5

The Credit line is like the Cash item, except that it can be activated by F5 as well.

---- &Sneak Out mpSneak Ctrl+F11

The Sneak line is like the Cash item, except that it can be activated by Ctrl+F11 as well.

The resulting Menu Editor window will look like the one shown in figure 17.14.

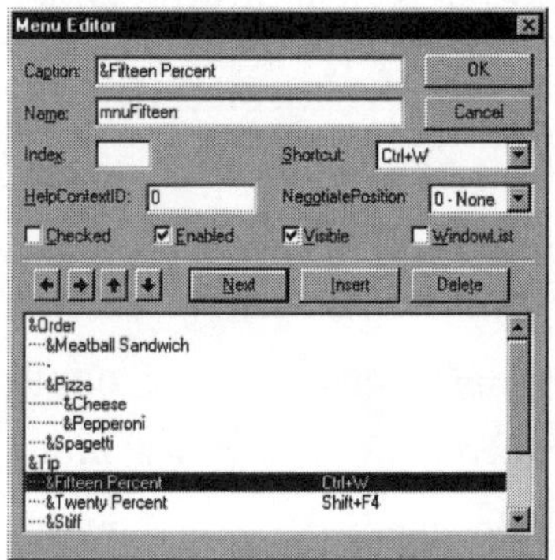

Figure 17.14
The Menu Editor window with the menu.

After these menu items have been entered in, run the program and see the menu items work. They won't do any real work because we haven't implemented any event procedures, but the menu system will operate. Notice that there are three items on the menu bar, Order, Pay, and Tip. The reason that they are on the bar is that they were not subordinated to any other items. Click on each of them and observe that the items below them are exactly the ones that were subordinated one time in the Menu Editor.

The Order menu has a pick called Pizza. Pizza has an arrow beside it that indicates that it also has subordinates. Clicking on Pizza reveals that the name of the subordinates are Cheese and Pepperoni. Therefore, if you wanted to order a pepperoni pizza, you would choose Order, Pizza, Pepperoni with the mouse, or by pressing Alt+O+P. Notice also that there is a line between Meatball Sandwich and Pizza. This line resulted from the addition of the dummy line above. It serves a purely cosmetic purpose—to separate one set of items from the other.

Next, click on the Tip menu item. It reveals a set of menu items with key sequences beside them (Ctrl+W, and Shift+F4). These sequences were added to these menu items via the shortcut box in the Menu Editor.

Now you are ready to run the program. Figure 17.15 shows the program while running.

This program demonstrates how to bring all of the Menu Editor's main features together in one menu structure.

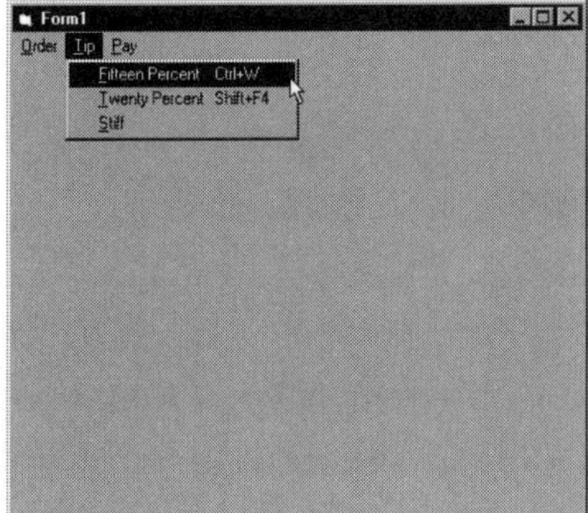

Figure 17.15
Running the program.

Summary

In this chapter you learned how to add menus to your windows. You learned also how to attach menu items to these menus and how to add event procedures to these menu items. You learned how to add accelerator keys (or hotkeys) and shortcut keys to the menu structure so that your customers will have choices of how the menu items are selected.

Finally, you learned how to create a multilevel, cascading menu that organizes the menu items in a hierarchical fashion.

Review Questions

Answers to the Review Questions can be found in Appendix A.

1. What event does a menu button respond to?
2. What purpose is served by the name of the menu item?
3. What is the difference between a hotkey and a shortcut key?

4. How do you make a menu item appear on a menu?
5. How is a function different from an event procedure?

6. Based on the following code sample, what button would be presented on the MsgBox?

```
Private Sub mnuValuJet_Click()
    Msg = "You Choose ValuJet"    ' Define message.
    Style = vbOKOnly ' Define buttons.
    Title = "ValuJet"   ' Define title.
    Response = MsgBox(Msg, Style, Title)

End Sub
```

7. How do you create a cascading menu?

Review Exercises

1. Write a program that creates the same menu structure that is in the Windows Paint program.
2. Write a program that puts the message boxes on the Fly/Drive menu.

3. Create a menu that cascades to four levels.
4. Using the up and down arrows, rearrange the menu items for the Fly/Drive menu where items normally on the bottom are on the top, and the items normally under Drive appear under Fly.

5. Create a menu for a form that includes items at three levels. The menu should include the following items:

Caption	*Name*	*Shortcut*
&Cars	mnuCars	
---- &American	mnuAmerican	
---------- &Ford	mnuFord	
---------- &Dodge	mnuDodge	
---- &French	mnuFrench	
---- -	dummy	
---- &Japanese	mnuJapanese	
&Motor Cycles	mnuMoto	
---- &American	mnuAmericanCy	Ctrl+W
---- &Japanese	mnuJapanCy	Shift+F4
---- &Russian	mnuRussianCy	Alt+Bksp

CHAPTER 18

Constants and Variables

In this chapter, you will learn about constants and variables, which are flexible and invaluable components that help you write top-notch programs. *Constants* allow you to store an unchanging number into a named location and refer to it throughout your program just by its name. *Variables* allow you to store data into a named location and use or change it at will.

Constants eliminate the need to hardcode values into programs. Hardcoding values into a program refers to placing a number—sometimes referred to as a *magic number*—throughout your application. If you are creating a program that calculates a discount on a product, for example, you may be tempted to insert the discount value throughout the program wherever it is needed. What happens, then, when you need to change the discount rate from 7 percent to 9 percent? You would have to find all occurrences of the discount rate and manually change each one from 7 to 9. In this type of situation, constants can ease your programming and maintenance burden.

Variables can store information of any kind; they allow access to this information as often as it's needed, just by referencing the variable's name.

What Is a Constant?

A constant is a value that will not change throughout the execution of the program. A constant, as its name implies, cannot be changed. If you have a value that you will need to use in several places throughout your program, it is a good idea to declare this value as a constant. A constant cannot be changed during the running of a program.

The benefits of utilizing constants are twofold. First, you don't have to remember a number such as 32.7915, and type that number in every section of code that requires use of the number. You can declare a constant to be equal to 32.7915 and just reference the constant wherever you would reference the number.

The second benefit to using constants is the ability to change one value in your program, re-compile, and have all references be made to the new value, rather than the old value, automatically.

For example, if your program prints out envelopes, it may well calculate the total postage required for a particular batch of envelopes printed. You print out 100 envelopes, and the cost of each stamp is 29 cents. By simple multiplication, the total would be $29.00. You could code this line as follows:

```
100 * .29
```

But what happens to your application when the price of a stamp increases to 35 cents? You would have to go through your entire application and change every reference to stamp price from .29 to .35. This may not seem like a major problem, but in very large applications it could be a nightmare. It would be very easy to miss one reference to the old value, and thereby introduce a bug into the application. If you make the current value of the stamp a constant, you only have to change the value once, and re-compile your program. All references to the stamp price will then contain the new value. The code segment below shows the declaration of a constant (several variables are included so that the code makes sense):

```
.
.
Dim MailingCost As Currency
Dim TotalEnvelopes As Integer
Const StampPrice As Currency = .29
.
**Program process here**
.
MailingCost = StampPrice * TotalEnvelopes
.
** Use the calculated variable MailingCost here**
.
```

This example shows how you can declare and use a constant. Constants can have all the same properties as any other variable, except that their value cannot be changed during the running of the program. See the next section for a complete explanation of what a variable is. Keep in mind that a constant is just a variable that cannot be changed during the running of the program. Constants cannot be arrays or User-Defined Types (UDT).

What Is a Variable?

Data and the ability to manipulate it play an important role in computer programs. When a program needs to count the number of times a certain task is performed, the computer must be able to store and manipulate this information.

So, how do variables figure into this equation? A variable is a named storage location for information. Think of the variable as a storage locker: you can reference the information stored in the locker just by using the locker's name. You can name the variable anything you want within the Visual Basic variable-naming conventions. Naming conventions are discussed in detail in this chapter in the "Naming Variables" section.

Take, for example, a household budget program. The program needs two numbers, the total income and the total debt. The program will use these two numbers to calculate a debt-to-income ratio which the bank has requested. This is overly simplistic for a budget application, but it illustrates the point of variables.

> **Note:** To declare a variable is to tell the compiler the name of the variable, and possibly what type of variable it is. To initialize a variable is to give the variable a value, whether it is a zero for numeric fields, a certain date, a dollar amount, or a string.

The following lines declare and initialize the two variables the program needs:

```
TotalIncome = 45000
TotalDebt = 17000
```

The program now can refer to `TotalIncome` and `TotalDebt` just as if they are numbers. Any mathematical operation that can be performed on a number can be performed on a variable. The variables will only be declared and initialized if this is the first time the variable is referenced (and Option Explicit is off).

Variables don't store numbers only. The following section takes a look at the different types of variables available in Visual Basic.

Variable Types

There are variable types for each of the data types available in Visual Basic. I would be putting the cart before the horse if I didn't delve into the different types of data that can be stored in a variable. The basic data types and the characters used to declare the types are shown in Table 18.1.

Table 18.1 Visual Basic Fundamental Types

Data Type	*Description Character*	*Declaration*	*Range*
Byte	1 byte	[None]	0 to 255
Boolean	2 bytes	[None]	True or False

continues

Table 18.1 Continued

Data Type	*Description Character*	*Declaration*	*Range*
Integer	2-byte integer	%	-32,768 through 32,767
Long	4-byte integer	&	-2,147,483,648 through 2,147,483,647
Single	4-byte floating-point number	!	-3.402823E38 through -1.401298E-45 (negative values) 1.401298E-45 through 3.402823E38 (positive values)
Double	8-byte floating-point number	#	-1.79769313486232D308 through -4.94065645841247D-324 (negative values) 4.94065645841247D-324 through 1.79769313486232D308 (positive values)
Currency	8-byte number with fixed decimal point	@	-922,337,203,685,477.5808 through 922,337,203,685,477.5808
Object	4 bytes	[None]	Any Object reference
Date	8 bytes	[None]	January 1, 100 to December 31, 9999
String	String of characters	$	0 through approximately 65,500 characters
String (fixed-length)	Length of string	$	1 to approximately 65,400.
Variant	Date/time floating-point numbers, or strings	[None]	A Variant can contain numeric data in the same range as a Double variable, or any character string

Data Type	*Description Character*	*Declaration*	*Range*
User-defined	Number required by elements	[None]	The range of each element is the same as the range of its data type.

All data types can be stored as a variables. The default storage type for a variable is the `Variant`. If you do not expressly tell the compiler that you want the variable to be of a different type, it assumes that you want a Variant.

`Variant` is the most flexible type of variable. It can be used to hold most of the other data types, except for fixed-length strings and User-Defined Types. With this flexibility also comes some risks. For example, you could have two Variant variables, one that is a string and the other that is a numeric. The compiler would let you try to multiply these two variables, because they are both `Variants`, but because the values are not the same type, this would result in an error.

Now that you have seen the different data types available in Visual Basic, you can move on to see the different methods of declaring a variable for use in a Visual Basic program.

Declaring Variables

The declaration of a variable simply means that the program knows that the variable exists, and knows what values are valid for the variable. There are certain restrictions concerning the names Visual Basic allows to be used for variables.

Naming Variables

Visual Basic, like all programming languages, has a set of rules that apply to all aspects of the language. The names that you are allowed to use for variables are no exception. The rules for naming variables are as follows:

- The name *must* begin with a letter.
- The name can contain only letters, numbers, and the underscore character (_). Punctuation characters and spaces are not permitted.
- The variable name must not exceed 255 characters.
- The variable name must not be a Visual Basic reserved word. It can contain a reserved word, but cannot solely consist of a reserved word. (For example, `PrintThis` is okay, `Print` is not).

This list is pretty easy to follow, but let's take a look at a few valid and invalid names to make sure that you have no questions. The following are some valid variable names:

```
Total_Income

X

LoopCounter

A_Very_Long_Variable_Name
```

The following are some invalid variable names:

```
6_Month_Income

Baseball Scores

ByVal
```

The variable name `6_Month_Income` is invalid because a variable cannot begin with a number. The second name, `Baseball Scores`, is not valid because spaces aren't allowed in variable names. The "extremely long" variable name is invalid for just that reason: a variable cannot be longer than 255 characters. Finally, you cannot use `ByVal` as a variable name because `ByVal` is a Visual Basic reserved word.

Tip: When naming variables, try to use descriptive names. This makes your code easier to understand, and easier for you—or someone else—to modify later.

Example: Bad and Good Variable Names

The following example shows three variables being declared. The `X` and `Y` variables have numbers placed into them at the time they are declared. The `Z` variable is declared to be equal to the product of `X` and `Y`. The final line prints the value of `Z`.

```
Sub Form_Click ()
    X = 5
    Y = 7
    Z = X * Y
    Form1.Print Z
End Sub
```

Although `X`, `Y`, and `Z` are valid names for variables, they certainly don't provide any information about what might be stored in them. Take a look at the following example to see how using descriptive variable names makes the code much more readable.

```
Sub Form_Click ()
    Weeks = 5
    DaysInWeek = 7
```

```
    DaysElapsed = Weeks * DaysInWeek
    Form1.Print DaysElapsed
End Sub
```

Using descriptive names for variables helps to reduce the amount of comments your code needs. The more descriptive the variable names are, the easier it is to understand what each variable represents.

Dimensioning Variables

The `Dim` statement tells the compiler that you want to *dimension* a variable. This tells the compiler the name (and optionally the type) of the variable that you intend to use. If you omit the type, the compiler assumes the Variant type. The syntax for the `Dim` statement is as follows:

```
Dim Variable_Name [As Variable_Type]
```

`Variable_Name` is the descriptive name that you have chosen for the variable. The `As` *`Variable_Type`* is optional. If you do not declare the variable as a specific type, the compiler assumes that the variable type is a `Variant`. The following example illustrates using the `Dim` statement.

Example: Using the *Dim* Statement

Listing 18.1 18LIST01.TXT—Using the *Dim* Statement

```
Sub Form_Click ()
    Dim A_String
    Dim A_Long
    Dim An_Integer
    Dim Total
    A_String = "Visual Basic 4"
    A_Long = 987654321
    An_Integer = 256
    Total = A_Long + An_Integer
End Sub
```

This code dimensions the variables prior to using them. Even though all these variables hold different types of information—a `String`, a `Long`, an `Integer` and a `Variant`—the compiler still uses the `Variant` data type for all of them. This can waste memory because the `Variant` data type requires eight bytes of storage, whereas an `Integer` requires only two.

The following code listing employs a more memory-efficient method of dimensioning the variables:

Listing 18.2 18LIST02.TXT—Using a More Memory-Efficient Method of Dimensioning Variables

```
Sub Form_Click ()
    Dim A_String As String
    Dim A_Long As Long
    Dim An_Integer As Integer
    Dim Total As Long
    A_String = "Visual Basic 4"
    A_Long = 987654321
    An_Integer = 256
    Total = A_Long + An_Integer
End Sub
```

Although this may seem like a lot of extra steps to take when declaring a variable, it will help reduce the size of your programs and speed them up. The other benefit of dimensioning variables is type-checking by the compiler. If you declare a variable of one type and attempt to store data of another type in it, the compiler will usually generate a `Type Mismatch` error.

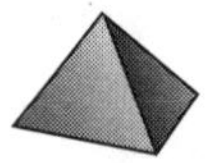

Tip: If you dimension every variable as a specific type, `Type Mismatch` errors will usually be spotted by the compiler, thus preventing erroneous code from reaching the final program.

Declaring Variables Implicitly

In Visual Basic there are several ways that variables can be declared. The first of which is simply to type the variable name into your code. The variable can be assigned a value immediately, but value assignment is not necessary. Variables declared in this manner are always `Variants`, since the compiler does not know what type of variable you want unless you use a type declaration character in the name of the variable. This is a perfectly valid method for declaring variables. Type a variable anywhere in the code, and Visual Basic assumes that you want a new variable when it encounters the new name.

Example: Implicit Variable Declaration

Listing 18.3 shows an example of declaring variables implicitly.

Listing 18.3 18LIST03.TXT—Declaring Variables Implicitly

```
Sub Form_Click ()
    A_String = "Visual Basic 4"
    A_Long = 987654321
```

```
    An_Integer = 256
    Total = A_Long + An_Integer
End Sub
```

All the variables in the above example are said to be declared "on the fly."

Declaring Variables Explicitly

Declaring variables using the implicit method may seem like a very easy way to create a variable. After all, you just type the name of the variable into the code whenever you need it. If the compiler sees a new name, it creates a new variable for you. This is not without its drawbacks, though.

Example: Problem with Implicit Variables

Consider the subroutine in Listing 18.4.

Listing 18.4 18LIST04.TXT—Implicit Variables

```
Sub Calc_Totals ()
    Dim SubTotal As Currency
    Dim Tax As Currency
    Dim Totals As Currency
    SubTotal = 500#
    Tax = 37.5

    Totals = SubTotal + Tax
    Form1.Print Total
End Sub
```

This subroutine calculates and prints the sum of `SubTotal` and `Tax`. The subroutine will, however, always print 0. Do you see the problem? The subroutine correctly adds `SubTotal` and `Tax` and places that result into the `Totals` variable. The line `Form1.Print Total` prints out the result but has the word `Totals` misspelled, with the `s` missing. The compiler thinks that `Total` is a new, implicitly declared variable, and prints its value (0) to the form. Change the print statement to the following:

```
Form1.Print Totals
```

Now the program will work as expected.

Visual Basic provides a means to eliminate these types of errors. You can tell Visual Basic to generate an error message whenever it runs into a name that has not been explicitly declared as a variable. In order to do this, place the following statement at the beginning of a code or form module:

```
Option Explicit
```

This directs the compiler to check all variable names it encounters strictly, and to stop and generate an error message whenever a name is encountered that has not been declared.

Example: Using *Option Explicit*

To illustrate this point, begin a new project.

1. Double-click the form to bring up the procedure definition window for Form1.
2. Choose `(general)` from the Object pull-down, and make sure that the Proc pull-down is at `(declarations)`.
3. Type **Option Explicit** as shown in figure 18.1. Choose the `Form` from the Object pull-down and choose `Click` from the Proc pull-down.

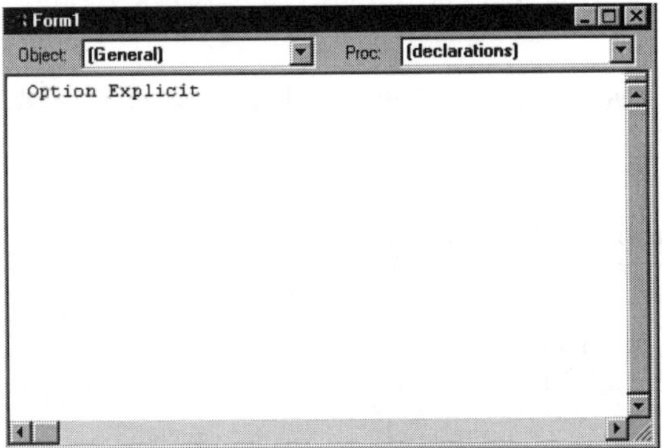

Fig. 18.1
The general declarations page of a form.

4. Type the following information:

```
Sub Form_Click ()
    Calc_Totals
End Sub
```

Now that you have set up the program to require all variables be explicitly declared, the next step is to create the `Calc_Totals()` subroutine. Use the Object pull-down to bring up the general declarations page. You should see the `Option Explicit` statement you entered earlier (refer to fig. 18.1). Enter the program listing exactly as shown in Listing 18.5 (see the following tip). You will notice that after you type in the first line containing the subroutine name, it will appear that the `Option Explicit` option has disappeared. Never fear, Visual basic maintains the declarations page for all variables and directives, and a separate page for each subroutine. Pay careful attention to the fact that the word following the `Print` statement is `Total`, and not `Totals`.

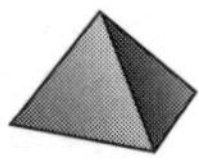

Tip: You can find Listing 18.5—as well as each Listing in this book—on our Internet site. If you cut and paste, you won't have to type in any code!

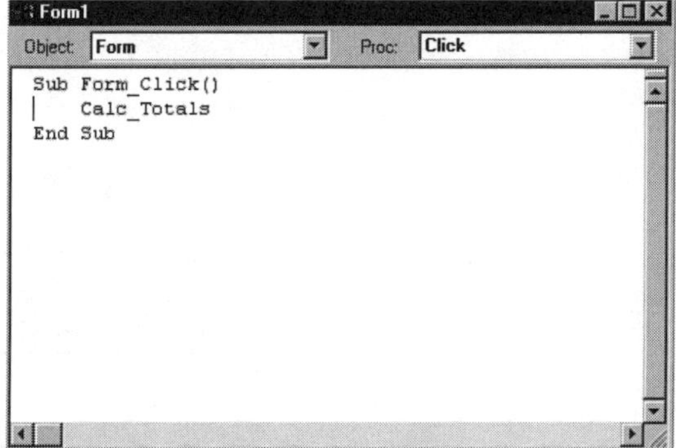

Figure 18.2
The general section of a form.

Listing 18.5 18LIST05.TXT—*The Calc_Totals()* Subroutine

```
Sub Calc_Totals ()
    Dim SubTotal As Currency
    Dim Tax As Currency
    Dim Totals As Currency
    SubTotal = 500#
    Tax = 37.5

    Totals = SubTotal + Tax
    Form1.Print Total
End Sub
```

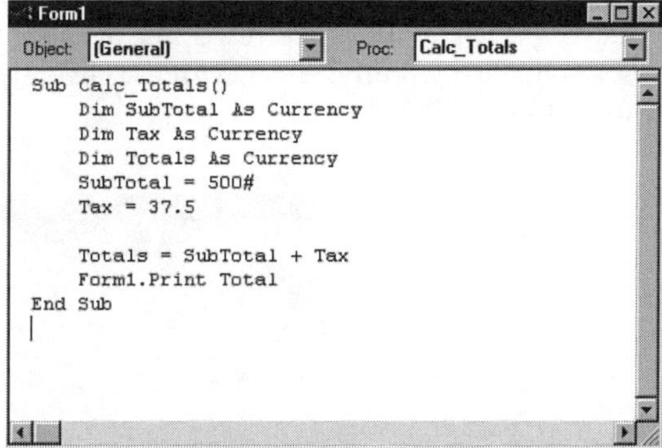

Figure 18.3
The Calc_Totals() Subroutine

You are ready now to run your program. Choose Run, Start from the Toolbar. The program will not run because the variable `Total` has not been explicitly declared. You will see an error message like that shown in figure 18.4.

Click OK and the offending variable will be highlighted (see fig 18.5.) The word `Total` has been highlighted to indicate that this variable has not been declared prior to use. Correct the error by changing `Total` to `Totals` and run the program again. You can also press F5 to continue running the program without restarting the application.

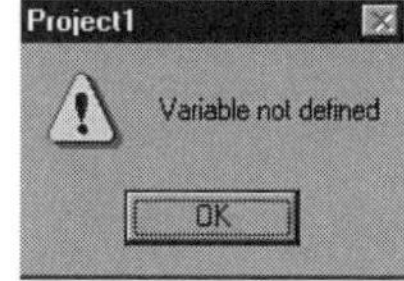

Figure 18.4
The `Variable Not Defined` error message.

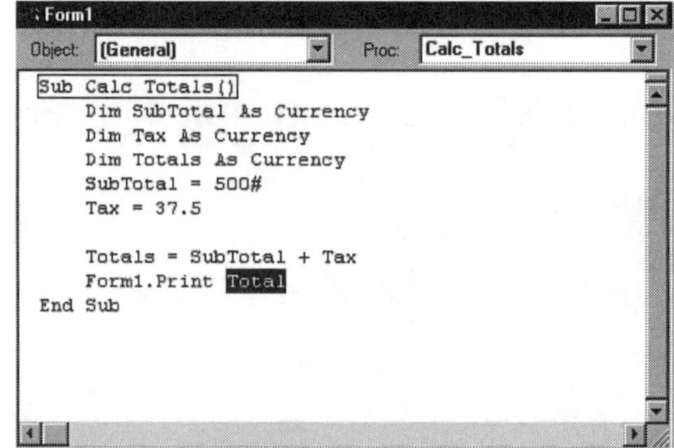

Figure 18.5
The undeclared variable is highlighted.

The program should compile and run without problems at this point. You will be presented with a blank form. When you click the form, the number 537.5 should be displayed in the upper-right corner of the form. If you click several times, the number will be presented several times. The output from this application is shown in figure 18.6.

Figure 18.6
Program output with no errors.

Variable Scope

The scope of a variable refers to its life and visibility. There are three different types of scope a variable can have: *local*, *module*, and *global*. These may seem like foreign concepts, but let's look at each term in turn to see what it means.

Local Scope

When you declare a variable within a function or subroutine, only the code within the procedure can see that variable. This is referred to as *local scope*. The example in Listing 18.3 illustrates this point. Create a new project named VarScope. Draw two buttons on the form and change the title of the buttons to Sub1 and Sub2. The form now should look like the one shown in figure 18.7.

Figure 18.7

A VarScope form with Sub1 and Sub2 buttons.

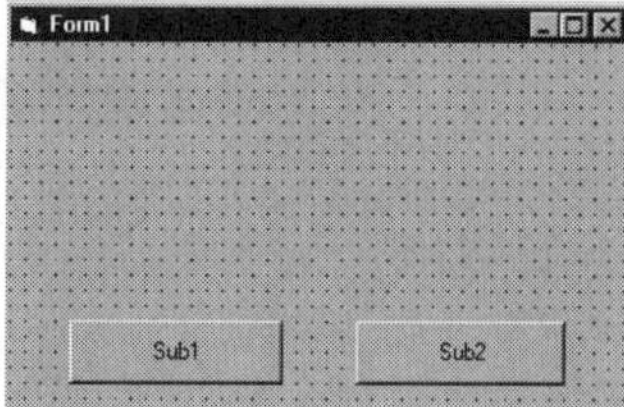

Double-click on the `Sub1` Button and enter `Sub1` in the `Command1_Click()` subroutine that follows. Do the same thing for the `Sub2` button, this time entering `Sub2` into the subroutine. We have now connected the buttons to the `Sub1()` and `Sub2()` subroutines.

```
Sub Command1_Click ()
    Sub1
End Sub

Sub Command2_Click ()
    Sub2
End Sub
```

The next step is to enter the subroutines that are referenced by the buttons. Bring up the general declarations section of the form by choosing `(general)` from the Object pull-down and `(declarations)` from the Proc pull-down. Enter the text as shown in Listing 18.6. When you have finished entering the `Sub1()` subroutine, begin entering the `Sub2()` routine directly under the `End Sub` of `Sub1()` (see fig. 18.8). After typing in the name of the subroutine and pressing enter, Visual Basic will create a new page for you to complete the entering of `Sub2()`.

Listing 18.6 18LIST06.TXT—The *Sub1()* and *Sub2()* Subroutines

```
Sub Sub1 ()
    Dim Var1 As Integer
    Dim Var2 As Integer
    Var1 = 5
    Var2 = 3
    Form1.Print "Var1 in Sub1 = "; Var1
    Form1.Print "Var2 in Sub1 = "; Var2
End Sub
```

continues

Listing 18.6 Continued

```
Sub Sub2 ()
    Dim Var1 As Integer
    Dim Var2 As Integer
    Form1.Print "Var1 in Sub2 = "; Var1
    Form1.Print "Var2 in Sub2 = "; Var2
End Sub
```

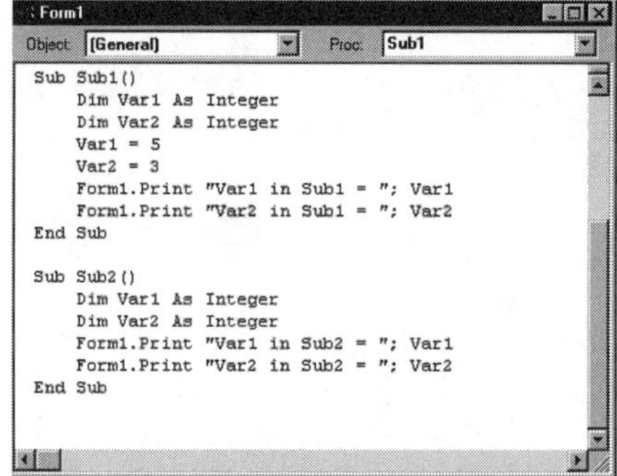

Figure 18.8
Entering the `Sub1()` and `Sub2()` subroutines.

After you have completed entering `Sub1()` and `Sub2()`, you can run the program. Choose Start from the Run menu. Click the Sub1 button and the output will be like that shown in figure 18.9.

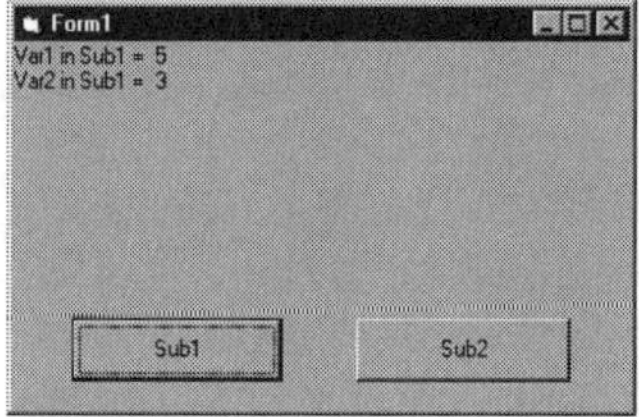

Figure 18.9
VarScope output after pressing the Sub1 button.

As you can see from the program output, in `Sub1()`, `Var1` is equal to 5 and `Var2` is equal to 3. Now press the Sub2 button. The output will be like that shown in figure 18.10.

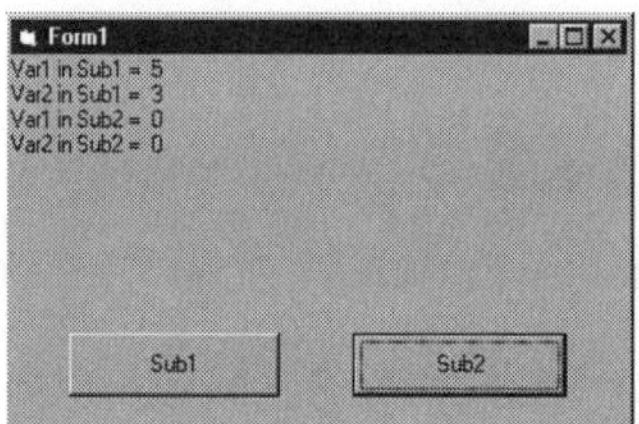

Figure 18.10
VarScope output after Pressing the Sub2 button.

So what does this tell us? In both `Sub1()` and `Sub2()` we declared variables with the same name. In `Sub1()` we put values into these variables and printed them out. In `Sub2()` we simply printed out the variables without initializing them to any value.

Module Scope

The next type of scope is called *module scope*. Variables declared with module scope can be seen by all procedures within that module. Let's take a look at how module scope can be used with the `VarScope` program.

The first thing we need to do is to delete the variable declaration lines from both the `Sub1()` and `Sub2()` subroutines. Figure 18.11 shows the new `Sub1()` routine. Make certain that you perform the same steps for `Sub2()`.

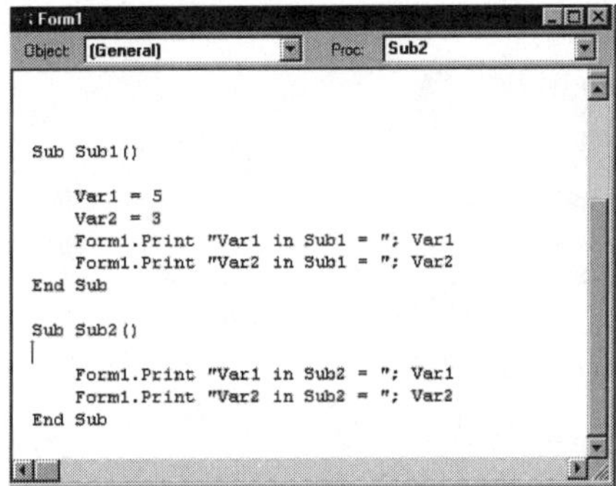

Figure 18.11 Removing the variable declarations from `Sub1()`.

Now place the variable declarations on the declarations page of the module. This is illustrated in figure 18.12.

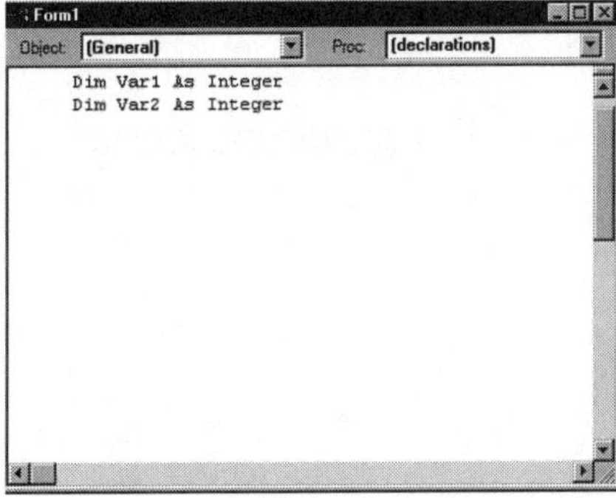

Figure 18.12 Adding the variable declarations to the module.

Now, run the program again. If you click on the Sub1 button, the results are the same as they were when the variables had local scope. If you click on the Sub2 button, however, the results are a little different from the prior example. The output from this program is shown in figure 18.13.

Global Scope

There is one other type of scope that a variable can have: *global scope*. By using the word `Global` in place of the `Dim` statement, the variable is visible to all modules. A `Global` variable can only be declared inside a code module. Any attempt to declare a `Global` variable in a procedure or a form module will generate an error.

Example

To illustrate this point, change the `Sub1()` and `Sub2()` procedures so that they match the code in Listing 18.7.

Listing 18.7 18LIST07.TXT—*Sub1()* and *Sub2()* Referencing a Global Variable

```
Sub Sub1 ()
    Var1 = 5
    Var2 = 3
    Var3 = Var1 * Var2
    Form1.Print "Var1 in Sub1 = "; Var1
    Form1.Print "Var2 in Sub1 = "; Var2
    Form1.Print "Var3 in Sub1 = "; Var3
End Sub

Sub Sub2 ()
    Var3 = Var1 + Var2
    Form1.Print "Var1 in Sub2 = "; Var1
    Form1.Print "Var2 in Sub2 = "; Var2
    Form1.Print "Var3 in Sub2 = "; Var3
End Sub
```

Next, click on the New Module button on the Toolbar. This adds a code module to the Varscope program. Add the line declaring a global variable named `Var3`, as shown in figure 18.13.

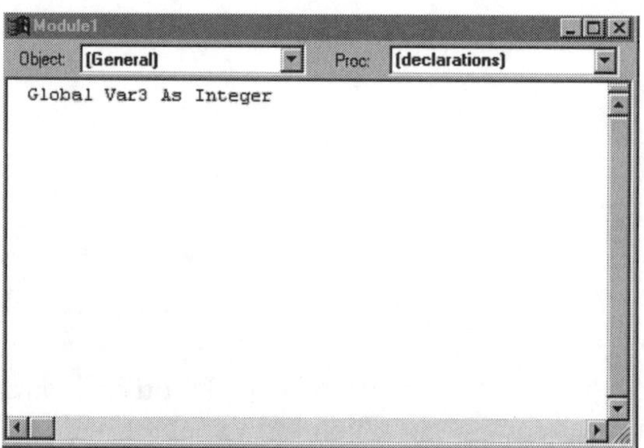

Figure 18.13

Adding a global variable to a code module.

Now you can run the program. The variable `Var3` is available to all procedures throughout the entire VarScope program. If you wished to add code to one of the forms procedures to print out the value of `Var3`, you could do that since `Var3` is visible to all procedures, while `Var1` and `Var2` are only visible to `Sub1()` and `Sub2()`.

> **Note:** `Global` variables *must* be declared within a code module. `Global` variables are visible to all procedures within a program, regardless of the module in which they are located.

Name Shadowing

There is one final point to consider when naming variables. A variable declared with local scope that has the same name as a module or global variable will *shadow* the variable with the broader scope. This may seem confusing at first, but really it is quite simple.

> **Note:** When two variables have the same name, a given procedure sees only the variable that has the scope nearest to the procedure. Local scope overrides both module and global scope. Module scope overrides only global scope.

Consider a subroutine named `Shadow()` that has declared a variable named `Counter`. There is also a variable named `Counter` that is declared within the module. When the `Shadow()` procedure accesses the `Counter` variable, it sees only the variable that has been declared locally. The local variable is shadowing the module-level variable.

Example: Searching the Shadows

To further understand name shadowing, create a new project and add two buttons, as shown in figure 18.14.

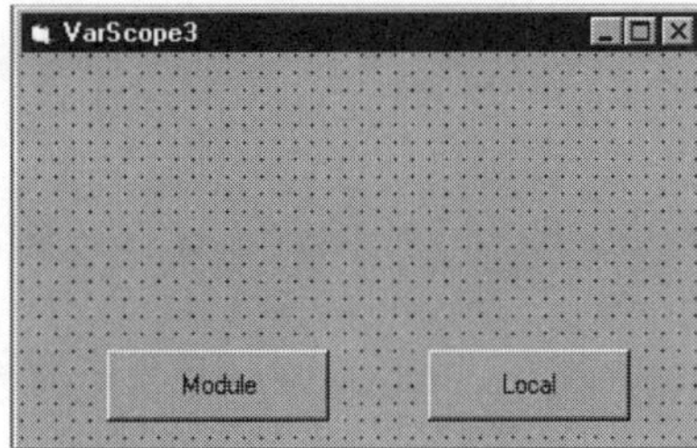

Figure 18.14
The form for the VarScpe3 program.

Now add the code shown in Listing 18.8 to the program. The `Command1_Click()` and `Command2_Click()` procedures should be attached to the Module and Local buttons, respectively. The `Form_Load()` procedure assigns the value of 10 to the module-level variable `Counter`. The `Shadow()` procedure declares its own `Counter` variable and then prints it out.

Listing 18.8 18LIST08.TXT—The VarScpe3 Program

```
' Place in the general declarations section
Dim Counter As Integer

' Place in the Module Buttons Click Procedure
Sub Command1_Click ()
    Form1.Print "Module Variable = "; Counter
End Sub

' Place in the Local Buttons Click Procedure
Sub Command2_Click ()
    Shadow
End Sub

' Place in the Form_Load() Procedure
Sub Form_Load ()
Counter = 10
End Sub

' Place in the General Definitions Page
Sub Shadow ()
    Dim Counter As Integer
    Form1.Print "Local Variable = "; Counter
End Sub
```

Run the program. When you click the Module button, the variable `Counter`, which has module scope, is printed to the screen. This produces a 10 on-screen. When you click the Local button, the `Shadow()` procedure is called and it prints out its `Local Counter` variable which has not been assigned a value yet, so it prints a 0. The output from this program is shown in figure 18.15.

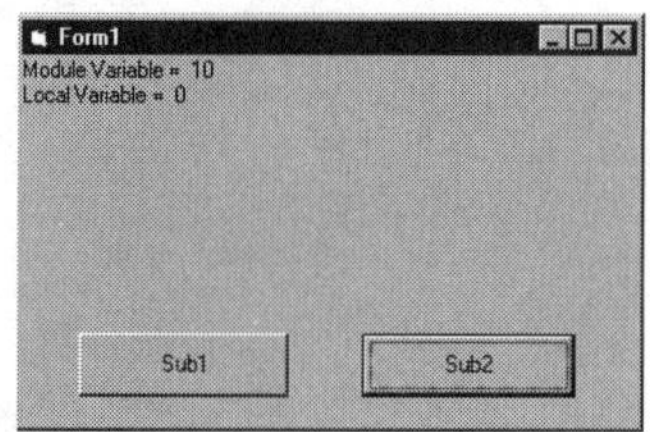

Figure 18.15

The output of the VarScope3 program.

Variable Modifiers

There are special states for variables. These are the `Static` and `Constant` types. Static variables allow a subroutine to maintain the value of a variable even when the scope, or life, of the variable normally would have ended. Constants provide the means to define an unchangeable variable once, and then use it throughout your program.

Static Variables

When dealing with variables, you have to be concerned with their scope, but each variable also has a lifetime—this is the period of time that the variable exists. Variables that are declared with either module- or global-level scope exist throughout the entire execution of your program. Local variables, on the other hand, maintain their values only throughout the execution of the procedure in which they are declared.

But what if you want a local variable to maintain its value even after the procedure containing the variable has ended? The solution to this problem comes from using the `Static` keyword in place of the `Dim` statement to declare a static variable. An example of this follows:

```
Static Counter As Integer
```

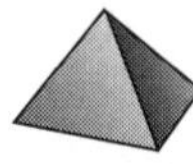

Tip: Declare a variable as `Static` when you want to maintain its value after the procedure it is declared in has ended.

Example: Implementing Static Variables

Let's look at an example to see just how this concept works. The program shown in Listing 18.7 illustrates the use of `Static` variables. To create this program, first create a new project. Then add a button to the form, as shown in figure 18.16.

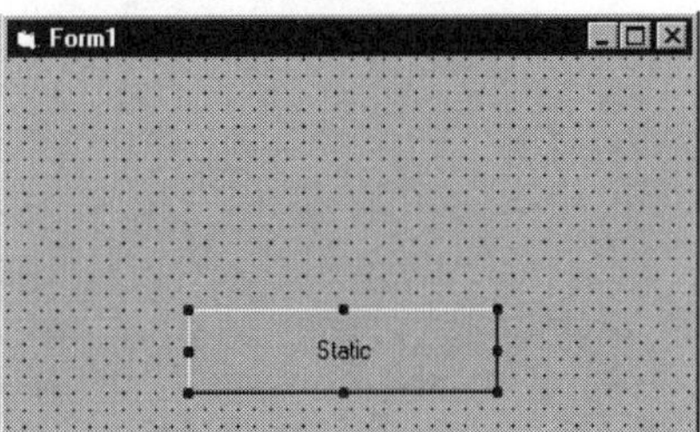

Figure 18.16

The form of the static program.

Then add the code shown in Listing 18.9. The code for the `Command1_Click()` routine calls the `Static_Var()` procedure every time the button on the form is clicked. The `Static_Var()` procedure declares 1 variable as static. Every time this procedure is called it adds 1 to the value of the `Counter` variable and then prints the value to the form. If the `Counter` variable were not declared as `Static`, the `Static_Var()` procedure would print a 1 to the form on each button click.

Because the `Counter` variable is declared as `Static`, it maintains its value even after the procedure has ended. This means that the second time the procedure is called, adding 1 to the variable actually increments the variable. You can make all of the variables static by making the procedure static. This can be done by prefacing the `Sub` keyword with the `Static` keyword. The output from this program is shown in figure 18.17.

Listing 18.9 18LIST09.TXT—Using Static Variables

```
' Place this code in the Command1_Click()
Sub Command1_Click ()
Static_Var
End Sub

' Place this code in the General Declarations Section
Sub Static_Var ()
    Static Counter As Integer
    Counter = Counter + 1
    Form1.Print Counter
End Sub
```

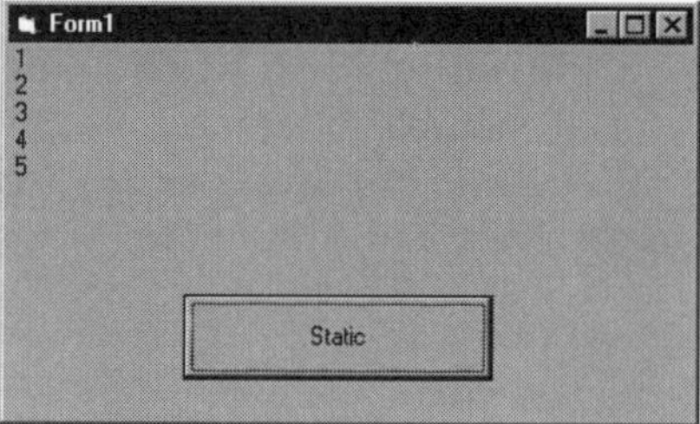

Figure 18.17
The output of the static program.

Constants

Constants were discussed earlier in this chapter, but since they are a type of variable modifier, let's take a look at how they can be used to modify variables.

There will be times when your program contains numbers. Certain numbers will be used throughout a given program, or the program may make reference to a certain string of characters in several places. These situations call for the constant type, which allows you to define a value only once, and have the value available for use by all procedures.

This would also make changing the value much easier. You could change the value in one place, re-compile your program and the new value would be recognized everywhere the variable is referenced.

You may also want to display a certain string of characters at different places in your program. Visual Basic offers a simple method for handling all of these cases. Variables can be declared as constants. The value of a constant is unchangeable. The syntax for declaring a constant is as follows:

```
[Global] Const constantvariable = expression
```

A constant can be global by prefacing the word `Const` with the optional word `Global`. Just as with global variables, global constants must be declared within a code module, and not in a form. Note that all rules of scope and lifetime apply to constants as they do to all types of variables. The value of `expression` can consist of numbers, operators, and strings. See the following samples for valid constants:

```
Const Discount_Rate = 5.7
Global Const Total_Cats = 5
Const Book_Title = "Visual Basic 4 By Example"
```

You can reference a constant just as you would reference any variable. Just remember that the constant's scope depends upon where in your program you declared the constant. The constant will maintain its value for the duration of the program's execution.

Summary

This chapter showed you the key differences between constants and variables. You learned what a variable is, and what the different types of variables are. You saw different methods that are available for declaring variables. You have learned about the scope and lifetime of variables, name shadowing and the different modifiers that can be applied to variables.

The variable is one of the building blocks that will help you create a solid foundation for your Visual Basic programs. The next chapter introduces you to simple input and output.

Review Questions

Answers to the review questions appear in Appendix A.

1. What is a variable?
2. What are valid data types for storing in a variable?
3. Which of the following are valid names for variables?

   a) `12_Month_Projection`

   b) `Integer`

c) `BombShell!`

d) `A_LONG_VARIABLE_NAME`

e) `Arc`

f) `Discount_Rate`

4. What is the keyword for declaring local variables?
5. How do you make sure all variables are declared prior to their use?
6. What is the scope of a module variable?
7. What is the scope of a global variable?

8. What values will the following procedure print each time it is called?

```
Sub Print_Total()
     Static Total As Integer
     Total = Total + 2
     Form1.Print Total
End Sub
```

9. What variables are affected by name shadowing?
10. Where do all global variables have to be declared?

Review Exercises

1. Write a program that implicitly declares three variables in a procedure named `Print_Vars()`. Tie this procedure to a button on the form, and have the values print on the form every time the button is clicked.
2. Change the previous program to explicitly declare the variables, making one of them static. Increment the static variable by one every time the procedure is called.

3. Write a program that declares all variables explicitly. Create a module-level integer variable. Create a procedure that declares a variable by the same name as the module level one you created. Print both values to the form by making a call to one procedure.

4. Create a program that contains global variables, global constants, and module-level variables. Have one procedure print out all of the values of the variables.

CHAPTER 19

Simple Input and Output

In this chapter, you learn about program *input* and *output*. These two basic principles are the foundation for users interacting with programs. When a program asks you for a response to a question that it prints on the screen, the question is output. Your response to it is input.

Program Output

When a program needs to tell the user that something has happened or needs to happen, the program displays this information to the user. This information can take several forms. The information can be in the form of a line of text written on-screen, or it can be in the form of a message box. This chapter looks at each of these different methods.

Using the Print Method

If you want to print a line of text, Visual Basic provides the `Print` method for all objects that can support text. The `Print` method applies to Forms, PictureBoxes, the Printer object, and the Debug object. The easiest of these objects to use to illustrate this example is the *form*. Take a look at the `Print` method and the various ways it can be used for providing output on a form window. The following example shows the simplest type of program output: the printed line.

If you open a new project and double-click the Form1 window, you see a dialog box containing the objects and procedures in your project. This is referred to as the Code window of a form. Because you just opened the project, there are no objects available to use other than the *Form* and *(General)*. All predefined procedures that the form can recognize are shown in the Proc drop-down list box. Choose Click from the list. In the `Form_Click()` subroutine, type the code shown in the example.

Example

This example shows simple output to a form whenever the form is clicked with the mouse.

```
Private Sub Form_Click()
    Dim A_String

    A_String = "Visual Basic 4"

    Form1.Print A_String
End Sub
```

You now can run the sample program. The form will appear and nothing will happen. Remember that you entered code into the `Click()` subroutine, so until you click the form, nothing should happen. Click the form several times. You will see results similar to that in figure 19.1.

Figure 19.1

Simple output on a form.

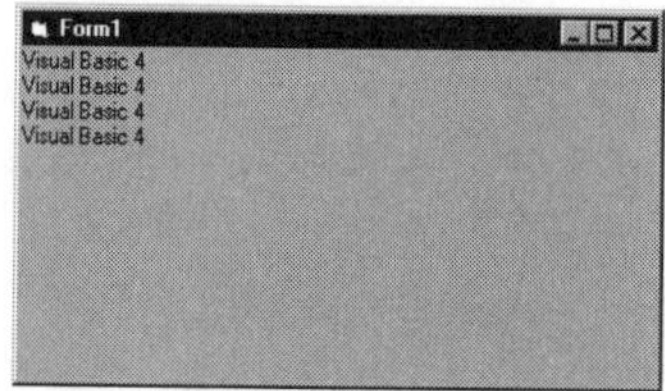

This is the one of simplest methods you can use to output information from your program. The program uses the Print method of the form to do this. To print on any form in your program, you just need to reference the form name followed by the Print function separated by a period. The syntax of this command is as follows:

```
FormName.Print "What you want to print"
```

`FormName` is the name of the form on which you want to print; `Print` is a built-in method of the form, and the text string `"What you want to print"` is the data to be printed. This method can be used to place text onto a form. Note that the quotes are used only to define the beginning and end of the string; they are not printed.

You may be asking yourself how you can position the text on the form. If you run the previous example and click on the form multiple times, the line will be repeated beginning on the next line. A Print Zone is 14 columns. You can skip Print Zones by using the optional `Tab` keyword or by using a comma.

The full syntax for the `Print` method is the following:

```
Object.Print Outputlist
```

The `Object` is the item on which you want to print. In the preceding example, this was the name of the form. `Print` is the method that is called to print to the named object. `Outputlist` can contain the following:

```
{Spc(n) ¦ Tab(n)} Expression Charpos
```

The `Spc` and `Tab` functions enable you to position the text on a line. These are optional and can be used if you want to place your text somewhere other than in the first column on the line. `Expression` is the text you want to display. `Charpos` tells Visual Basic where you want to leave the cursor for the next `Print` statement to be executed. If you want to continue to print on the same line, you place a semicolon immediately following the expression. The `Spc` and `Tab` functions also can be used for determining the `Charpos`.

The following three examples show how you can use these operators to format the output to the form.

Example

The code in Listing 19.1 shows how to use the `Spc` keyword and semicolon to print the two strings on the same line, as shown in figure 19.2. By using the `Spc(5)` command before the text string, the output begins in column six. Note that the first column is number 1, so column 1 + 5 spaces = column 6. The semicolon at the end of the first `Print` statement means that the next call to `Print` should begin printing where the previous call ended. The second call to `Print` prints two spaces and then the string again.

Listing 19.1 19LIST01.TXT—Using the Spc Keyword

```
Private Sub Form_Click()
    Dim A_String
    A_String = "Visual Basic 4"

    Form1.Print Spc(5); A_String;
    Form1.Print Spc(2); A_String
End Sub
```

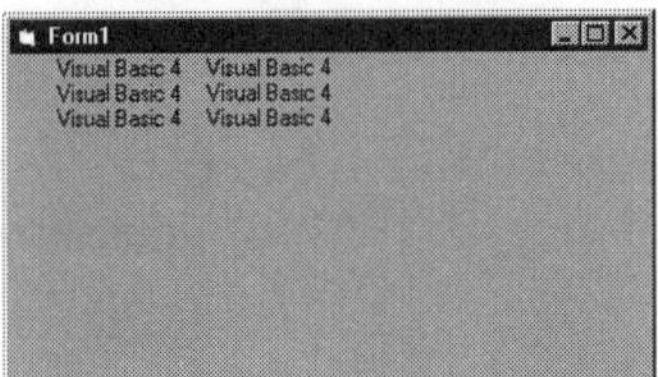

Figure 19.2

The output of the preceding lines of code.

What if you don't want to begin printing on the first line of the form? You can use the `Print` function with no parameters to move down as many lines as you want.

Example

Listing 19.2 demonstrates how to use the `Print` function to advance lines on a form. You will get the results shown in figure 19.3.

Listing 19.2 19LIST02.TXT—Using the Print Function to Advance Lines on a Form

```
Private Sub Form_Click()
Dim CurLine As Integer
Dim A_String As String
    A_String = "Visual Basic 4"
    CurLine = 1

    Form1.Print A_String & " Is on Line #" & CurLine

    For CurLine = 2 To 6
        Form1.Print
    Next CurLine

    Form1.Print A_String & " Is on Line #" & CurLine

End Sub
```

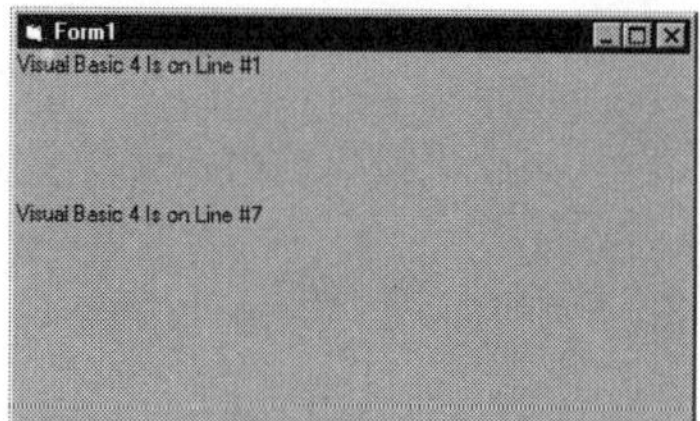

Figure 19.3

Using the `Print` function to advance a line.

From the preceding example and the output in Listing 19.3, you can see that when the `Print` function is used with no other parameters, it advances the cursor to the next line.

Example

The difference between the `Tab` and `Spc` keywords can be shown by the using the code in Listing 19.3. The output is shown in figure 19.4.

Listing 19.3 19LIST03.TXT—The Difference Between the Tab and Spc Keywords

```
Private Sub Form_Click()
    Dim A_String
    A_String = "VB 4.0"

    Form1.Print Tab(10); A_String; Tab(20); A_String
    Form1.Print Spc(10); A_String; Spc(20); A_String

End Sub
```

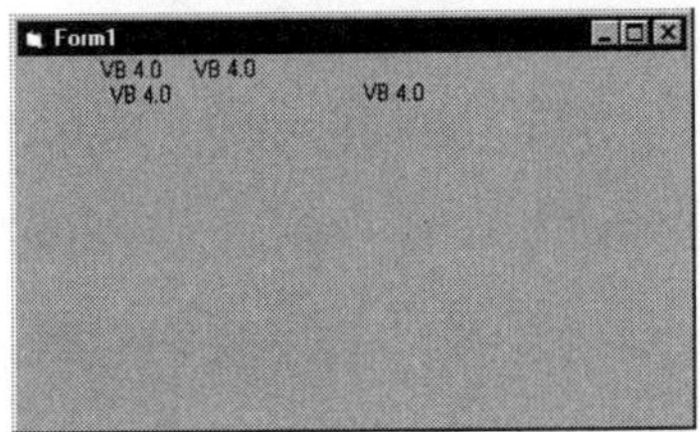

Figure 19.4
The output showing the use of Spc and Tab.

Note: `Spc(n)` will move the cursor `n` spaces from the cursor's current position. `Tab(n)` will move the cursor `n` spaces from the left margin.

By experimenting with the different keywords available to the `Print` method, you can place or change the information onto a form to inform your users or alert them that something has happened or changed.

There are several other properties that can be used to place text onto a form. These are the current position of the cursor. The information containing the location of the cursor is stored in the `CurrentX` and `CurrentY` properties. They allow you to determine exactly where you want your output to appear.

There is another property, `ScaleMode`, that affects how the `CurrentX` and `CurrentY` properties behave. If you recall from the discussion of the Form window in Chapter 9, "The Form," a form can have several different modes that it recognizes. These modes refer to the scale used for drawing graphics and text on the form.

The most common `ScaleMode` for text is character. This means that when `CurrentX` and `CurrentY` are both set to `5`, the next `Print` statement will begin at column and row 5. The starting position of the `ScaleMode` property is in the upper-left corner of the form and begins with 0/0. An example of using the `ScaleMode`, `CurrentX` and `CurrentY` properties is shown in Listing 19.4.

Listing 19.4 19LIST04.TXT—Using the ScaleMode, CurrentX, and CurrentY Properties

```
Private Sub Form_Click()

    Form1.ScaleMode = 4   'Character

    Form1.CurrentX = 20
    Form1.CurrentY = 6
    Form1.Print "Down and across"

    Form1.CurrentX = 0
    Form1.CurrentY = 0
    Form1.Print "Upper Left"

End Sub
```

The output from this example is shown in figure 19.5.

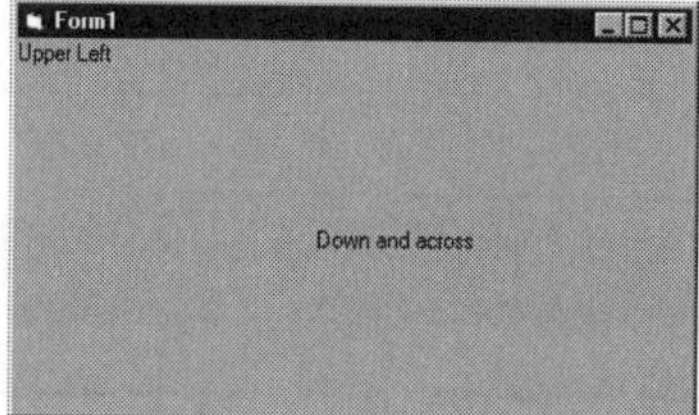

Figure 19.5
Using the `CurrentX` and `CurrentY` properties.

Printing to the Debug Window

The `Print` method can be used to display information in the Immediate pane of the Debug window. This type of program output is used during program development. If you need to know whether a calculation worked, you can print out the result to the Debug window. Think of the debug window as a programmer's scratchpad; it will never be seen by your users. If you need to know if a subroutine is being called when you intended it to, you can print information to the Debug window for your own information.

Example

This method is identical to printing to a form, except that you use the word `Debug` instead of the form name. See the following code and figure 19.6 for examples of how this is done:

```
Private Sub Form_Click()
    Debug.Print "Printing Debug Information"
End Sub
```

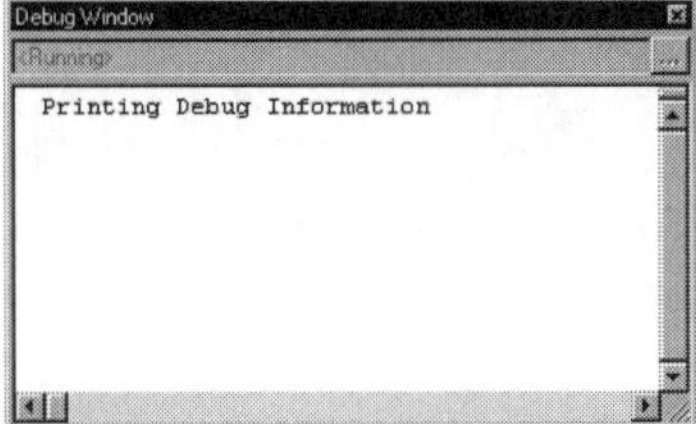

Figure 19.6
Printing to the Debug window.

You can use the Debug window and the Print method anytime you want to view information that you don't want to appear in your program. That information is displayed at runtime. You may be asking why you wouldn't just create another form and print those messages to the new form. You could do that, but you would have to remember to remove all references to that form prior to releasing your program.

Such a procedure is unnecessary when you use the Debug window, which is seen only in the Visual Basic development environment. You don't have to remove all references to the Debug window; Visual Basic does that for you.

The Debug window also has scroll bars; forms do not. This means that new things that are printed will not scroll off the bottom, as they do on a form, and that you can scroll back to see previous things that were printed.

The Message Box

If you are familiar with modern graphical operating systems such as Windows, OS/2, or Windows NT, you already have seen a message box. A message box can be used for both input and output. This section concentrates on the output aspects of the message box.

Visual Basic provides a built-in function for creating message boxes: the `MsgBox` function. When you need to inform users that something has happened, you can use a message box. The syntax of this function is the following:

```
MsgBox(prompt[, buttons][, title][, helpfile, context])
```

The `MsgBox` function displays the text contained in prompt. All other parameters are optional. For the purposes of the discussion of simple output, only the first two parameters of the function need to be considered. To illustrate the use of a message box, the next example shows how to create a very simple one.

Example

Create a command button on the form. Change the caption of the button to the word `Message` using the `Caption` item in the Properties window. Then double-click the button, which brings up the empty `Command1_Click()` subroutine. Type the following text:

```
Private Sub Command1_Click()
    MsgBox "Message Button Pressed"
End Sub
```

When you run the program, you will see your form with the message button on it. When you click the button, you see a result similar to that in figure 19.7.

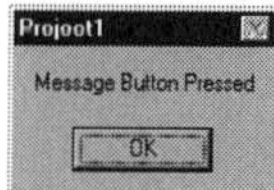

Figure 19.7
Creating a simple message box.

The length of the message that you can display is approximately 1024 characters. This number depends on the width of the font being used. A message box is a convenient way to display relatively short, simple messages that provide information.

There will be many times when you need to get your user's attention. The message box has many different ways to do this. Let's look at several of the other parameters for the `MsgBox` function.

The first parameter of the `MsgBox` function is the message to be displayed. The second is the buttons that are used. The icon to be displayed is also a part of the button parameter. If the button parameter is omitted, zero is assumed. This is the default setting: no icon and only an OK button.

If you want to change these default settings, you can use the Visual Basic arguments. These settings can be added together to include all of the attributes you want in your message box. The valid constants for creating a Visual Basic message box are shown in Tables 19.1, 19.2, and 19.3.

Table 19.1 shows the Visual Basic constants for creating buttons on a message box.

Table 19.1 Constants for Button Definitions

Constant	*Value*	*Description*
vbOKOnly	0	Display OK button only
vbOkCancel	1	Display OK and Cancel buttons
vbAbortRetryIgnore	2	Display Abort, Retry, and Ignore buttons
vbYesNoCancel	3	Display Yes, No, and Cancel buttons
vbYesNo	4	Display Yes and No buttons
vbRetryCancel	5	Display Retry and Cancel buttons

Constant	Value	Description
vbDefaultButton1	0	First button is default
vbDefaultButton2	256	Second button is default
vbDefaultButton3	512	Third button is default

You can use the constants in Table 19.1 to define the buttons that appear in your message box. The last three constants are used to change which button is highlighted by default.

Example

You may want to have an OK and Cancel button on your message box with the Cancel button being the default. You could accomplish this by adding the vbOKCancel and vbDefaultButton2 constants to create the desired results.

Example

The following sample code shows you how to do this.

```
Private Sub Command1_Click()
    MsgBox "Message Button Pressed", _
           vbOKCancel + vbDefaultButton2
End Sub
```

The output from this program is shown in figure 19.8. Try experimenting with the different combinations. Only one of the button choices and one of the default button choices can be used together.

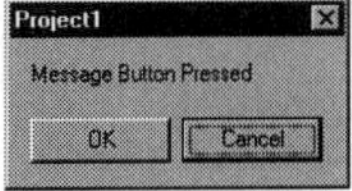

Figure 19.8

A message box with OK and Cancel buttons. The Cancel button is the default.

Table 19.2 lists the constants you can use to optionally display an icon in your message box. These constants are added into the button definitions to create the number that represents the choices you have selected for your message box. The next example illustrates this point.

Table 19.2 Constants for Icon Definitions

Constant	Value	Description
vbCritical	16	Display Critical Message icon
vbQuestion	32	Display Warning Query icon

continues

Table 19.2 Continued

Constant	*Value*	*Description*
vbExclamation	48	Display Warning Message icon
vbInformation	64	Display Information Message icon

Example

Expanding on the previous example, you can add an icon to the message box. The following code shows how to add the information icon to the message box (see fig. 19.9):

```
Private Sub Command1_Click()
    MsgBox "Message Button Pressed", _
           vbOKCancel + vbDefaultButton2 + _
           vbInformation
End Sub
```

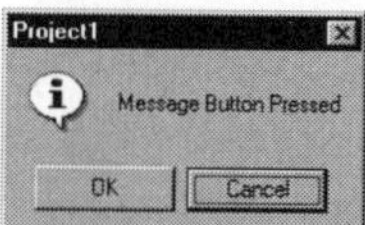

Figure 19.9

A message box with an information icon.

There is only one more set of constants to be considered when you create a message box. These constants are concerned with the *modality* of the message box.

The concept of modality is fairly simple. There are two types: *application modal* and *system modal*. Application modal means that nothing else can take place within the application that created the message box until the user responds to the message box. A system modal message box, on the other hand, suspends all applications currently running in the entire system until the user responds to the message box. The constants that affect modality are shown in Table 19.3.

Table 19.3 Modality Constants for Message Boxes

Constant	*Value*	*Description*
vbApplicationModal	0	The user must respond to the message box before continuing work in the current application.
vbSystemModal	4096	All applications are suspended until the user responds to the message box.

The default modality of a message box is application modal. If you need to prevent anything else from happening in the system, you can use the `vbSystemModal` constant. You should do this only when you have encountered an error that could cause problems in other applications within the system. For example, if you detect a problem with one of the disk drives, the application should pop up a system modal message box to prevent any other applications from accessing what could be a defective disk.

The `MsgBox()` function returns a constant indicating which button was chosen. For reference, these return values are listed in Table 19.4. To respond to these return values, you will need to know more about controlling program flow. These concepts are covered in detail in Part IV, "Controlling Program Flow."

Table 19.4 MsgBox Return Values

Constant	*Value*	*Button Chosen*
vbOK	1	OK
vbCancel	2	Cancel
vbAbort	3	Abort
vbRetry	4	Retry
vbIgnore	5	Ignore
vbYes	6	Yes
vbNo	7	No

Now you have the information you need to communicate with your users. The next section details the different methods that you can use to get input from the user.

Program Input

Visual Basic provides many different methods for requesting input from your users. All of the examples in this chapter have relied on the `Click()` method of the form to initiate the printing that appeared on the form.

Without the capability to interact with the user, any program you write would be virtually worthless. You have to be able to obtain information so your program knows what the user wants to do. Visual Basic provides a very simple method for querying the user for input. This function is the `InputBox` function.

The `InputBox` function is similar to the `MsgBox` function. The syntax for the `InputBox` function is the following:

```
InputBox(prompt[, title][, default][, xpos][, ypos]
               [, helpfile, context])
```

For the sake of simplicity, this discussion focuses on the first three parameters of the function. The `prompt` is the text that you want to display to the user. This should be descriptive of the type of information that you are asking for. The `title` is the text you want to display in the title bar of the input box. The `default` is the default value to be displayed in the box. If no default is specified, the entry field on `InputBox` is blank.

Example

An example of using the `InputBox` function is shown in the following lines of code.

```
Private Sub Form_Load()
    UserName = InputBox("What is your Name ?", _

                "Hello")
    MsgBox "Hello " + UserName
End Sub
```

The preceding program displays `InputBox` requesting the user's name. After the user responds, `MsgBox` displays the string `"Hello <Name>"`, in which `<Name>` is what the user typed. The input box is shown in figure 19.10. The message box used to reply to the user is shown in figure 19.11.

Figure 19.10

A simple input box.

Figure 19.11

A message box responding to input from an input box.

Unlike `MsgBox`, there are no icons that can be displayed on `InputBox`. By using `InputBox`, you can query the user for simple information—one piece at a time.

If you want to provide a default response to an `InputBox` query, you need to add the text to the `InputBox` function call. This text will be returned by the function unless the user changes it.

Example

Create a program to obtain a directory for storing files. You will want to provide a default directory so the user can simply click the OK button to answer the question.

To provide the user with a default response to the query, create a button on Form1 and change its caption to `Create`. In the `Command1_Click()` function for the Create button, type the following code:

```
Private Sub Command1_Click()
 Directory = InputBox("Location to Store Files:", _
                      "Create Directory", _
                      "C:\VB4")
 MsgBox "Directory Chosen " + Directory
End Sub
```

When you run this program, you see an input box with a default value of `C:\VB4` in the entry field. This is shown in figure 19.12. If the user wants to leave the default alone, he or she needs only click OK or press Enter. The input box is shown in figure 19.13. The program then displays the chosen directory using `MsgBox`.

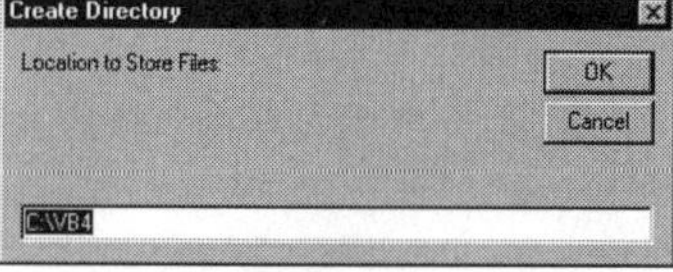

Figure 19.12

An input box displaying default information.

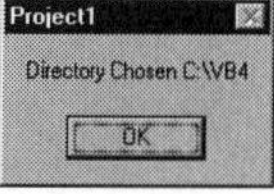

Figure 19.13

A message box showing the information input.

The previous example will work if the user presses the OK button. What happens when the user presses the Cancel button? The `MsgBox` function will return a blank string "". You can test for this to ensure that you don't try to process data that the user didn't intend you to. An example of checking for the blank string is shown in Listing 19.4.

Listing 19.4 19LIST04.TXT—Checking for the Blank String

```
Private Sub Command1_Click()
 Directory = InputBox("Location to Store Files:", _
                      "Create Directory", _
                      "C:\VB4")
if (Directory <> "") Then
    MsgBox "Directory Chosen " + Directory
Else
    MsgBox "No Information Entered"
End If
End Sub
```

By running the above example you will see results similar to those shown in figure 19.14 if you press Cancel instead of OK or Enter.

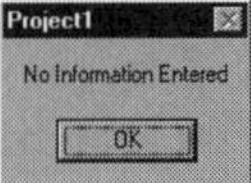

Figure 19.14
A message box trapping the Cancel button.

This covers the basics of user input. You should experiment with all the different options of the `InputBox` function to become familiar with its use. More advanced forms of input can be accomplished by using customized dialog boxes, which are discussed in Part VI, "Building Complete Applications."

Summary

In this chapter, you learned about the different methods you can use to communicate with the user. By using the `Print` method, you can place text or data onto a form or any other object that can accept text.

You learned how to use the `MsgBox()` function to give your users feedback. You also can customize the message box display by using different buttons, icons, and modes.

Finally, you saw how to get input from your users with the `InputBox()` function. You can customize this function by specifying the text, title, and any default information to be displayed.

Review Questions

The answers to the review questions are in Appendix B.

1. What is the method name for printing to a form?
2. What function is used to display a message box on-screen?
3. What function is used to get data from the user?

4. What window does not appear in a compiled program?
5. What does system modal mean?

6. What default value would the following code present in the entry field of `InputBox`?

```
Private Sub Command1_Click()
   InputBox("Messages to appear in What Language?", _
            "Enter Language", _
            "English")
End Sub
```

7. What is the difference between system modal and application modal?

8. What would be displayed in a message box if the button parameter were the following:

```
vbAbortRetryIgnore + vbDefaultButton3 + vbCritical
```

Review Exercises

1. Write a program that explicitly prints the days of the week to both the Form window and the Debug window.

2. Write a program that uses the `InputBox` function to ask the user's age. Print the user's age in a message box and on the Form window.

3. Write a program that presents a series of message boxes, each one different and using a different icon.

4. Write a program that presents a series of message boxes, each one different and each one using a different choice of buttons.

5. Write a program that creates a system modal message box. Attempt to click on any other application or icon you have on your system. Note the results. Create the same message box without the system modal attribute. Attempt the same things with other applications. How do these two attributes differ?

CHAPTER 20

Math Operators

Visual Basic provides a number of built-in operators for performing mathematical calculations—from addition and subtraction to squaring a number.

In this chapter, you learn about the math operators and functions provided by Visual Basic. You also learn about *precedence*—which determines the order in which the operations are performed—and how to use the MOD operator.

The Order of Precedence

The *order of precedence* is the order in which mathematical operations are performed. You can override the order by enclosing an expression or operation within parentheses. The order of precedence for mathematical operations is shown in Table 20.1.

Table 20.1 The Order of Precedence for Math Operators

Operation	*Operator*	*Order of Precedence*
Exponentiation	^	1
Negation	–	2
Multiplication and floating-point division	*, /	3
Integer division	\	4
Modulo arithmetic	Mod	5
Addition and subtraction	+, –	6

If two operations of the same precedence appear on the same line, the only two that have the same order are multiplication and floating-point division; they are evaluated from left to right.

The following sections discuss the different operators and their orders of precedence.

The Addition Operator

To add together several numbers on a calculator, you press the + between the numbers. This is the same principle behind the + operator in Visual Basic. The following is the syntax of the addition operator:

```
Result = Expr1 + Expr2
```

`Result` is a numeric variable type. `Expr1` and `Expr2` are expressions. An *expression* is any combination of keywords, operators, variables, and constants that produce a string, number, or object. An expression can perform a calculation, manipulate characters, or manipulate data.

Expressions are covered in detail in Chapter 21, "Expressions." In this chapter, you will use simple numeric expressions to illustrate the math operators in Visual Basic.

Example

If you have two variables that you want to add together, you can use the addition operator to achieve this goal. The following code shows a simple addition operation:

```
Private Sub Command1_Click()
    Result = 15 + 20
    MsgBox "Result = " & Result
End Sub
```

In this example, the numbers 15 and 20 are added together, and the result is returned and stored in the variable `Result`. This variable is then shown on the screen using a simple message box (see Fig. 20.1). You probably noticed that the `&` operator is used to concatenate the strings together for the string to print in the message box. You can use the + operator and the `&` operator interchangeably when dealing with only strings. This can lead to problems when using the + operator with a string and a numeric. This will result in erroneous data because Visual Basic will attempt to add a string and a number.

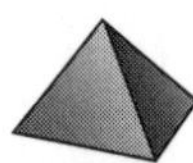

> **Tip:** I suggest using the `&` operator for string concatenation and saving the + operator for addition. This prevents confusion as to what type of variable is being used.

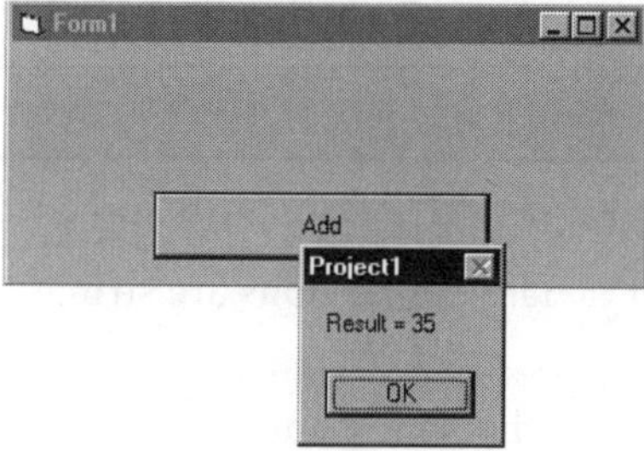

Figure 20.1
Using the addition operator.

You can use the addition operator with different types of variables. Table 20.2 shows the types of variables that can be added together; the types of results returned from these operations are shown in Table 20.3.

Table 20.2 Types of Variables That Can Be Added Together

Expression Type	*Action Taken*
Both expressions are numeric data types (`Byte`, `Boolean`, `Integer`, `Long`, `Single`, `Double`, `Date`, or `Currency`)	Add
Both expressions are String	Concatenate
One expression is a numeric data type and the other is any `Variant` (except `Null`)	Add
One expression is a `String` and the other is any `Variant` (except `Null`)	Concatenate
One expression is an `Empty Variant`	Return the remaining expression unchanged as result
One expression is a numeric data type and the other is a `String`	A `Type mismatch error` occurs
Either expression is `Null`	The result is `Null`

Table 20.3 Results Returned from Operators

Expression Type	*Action Taken*
Both `Variant` expressions are numeric	Add
Both `Variant` expressions are strings	Concatenate
One `Variant` expression is numeric and the other is a string	Add

Using the addition operator is a straightforward process. If you need to add variables, use the addition operator. The result does not have to be stored to be used.

Example

If you look at the following code, you will notice that the result is just shown in a message box without using another variable to hold the value.

```
Private Sub Command1_Click()
    MsgBox "Result = " & (15 + 20)
End Sub
```

The results from this example are identical to that shown in Figure 20.1. The only difference is that this example did not store the result of the addition into a variable and then print out the variable. The result was calculated and displayed at the same time.

Notice that there are no parentheses around the two numbers being added. You do not need parentheses as long as you use the `&` operator to concatenate the string and the result of the addition, although it is good programming practice to enclose all math operations within parentheses for clarity.

If you typed the line of code shown below, what would the result be?

```
MsgBox "Result = " + 15 + 20
```

As shown in Table 20.2, if you try to add a string and a number, you will get a `Type mismatch error`. The compiler cannot perform that operation, so the line of code does not work.

Practice using the addition operator with different types of variables to see the results. The next section discusses the counterpart to the addition operator.

The Subtraction Operator

The subtraction operator performs the subtraction of one number from another. Its syntax is as follows:

```
Result = Expr1 - Expr2
```

or

```
- Number
```

The subtraction operator, like the addition operator, actually has two different uses. In the first line of code above, it works as you might expect: it subtracts one number from another and returns the result. In the second line, however, there is only one number. This is because you can use the subtraction operator to change the sign of a number or variable. You can turn the number 5 into a negative 5, for example, just by preceding it with the subtraction operator, which when used in this context is referred to as the negative sign.

Example

If you run the following program, you will see a result similar to that shown in figure 20.2. The subtraction operator subtracted two numbers and returned the result. The negative sign was placed in front of the result to change the number from 24 to –24.

```
Private Sub Command1_Click()
    Result = 38 - 14
    Form1.Print "Result = " & Result
    Form1.Print "Negative Result = " & -Result
End Sub
```

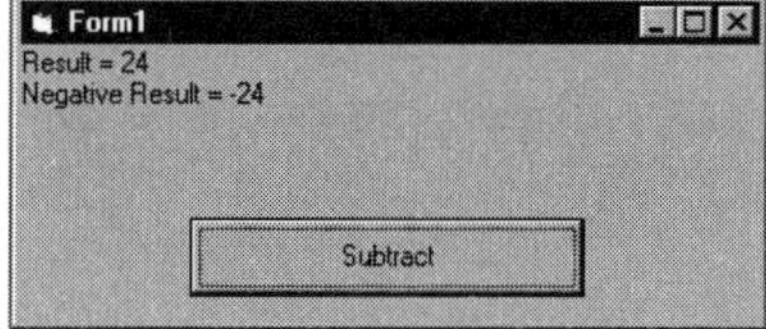

Figure 20.2
Using the subtraction operator to subtract and change the sign of a number.

Many expressions use both the addition and subtraction operator. The order of precedence is the same for both, which means that their operations can be done in any order and the result will be the same.

Example

Listing 20.1 uses both the addition and subtraction operators. The output is shown in figure 20.3.

Listing 20.1 20LIST01.TXT—Using Both Addition and Subtraction Operators

```
Private Sub Command1_Click()
    Expr1 = 100
    Expr2 = 75
    Expr3 = 90
```

```
    Result = Expr1 + Expr2 - Expr3
    Result2 = Expr1 - Expr3 + Expr2
    Form1.Print "Result  = " & Result
    Form1.Print "Result2 = " & Result2
End Sub
```

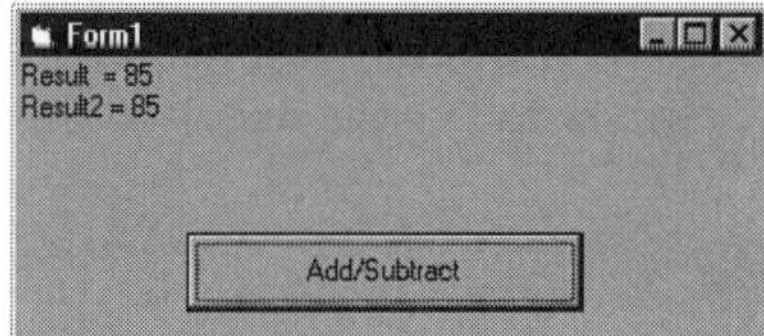

Figure 20.3
Combining addition and subtraction.

The order that the variables were added and subtracted made no difference in the result. You can change the order by using parentheses; the compiler will always begin at the innermost parentheses and work its way out to solve an expression.

Example

Listing 20.2 shows how parentheses can make a difference in the order in which the operators are executed and that changing the order can drastically change the result (see fig. 20.4).

Listing 20.2 20LIST02.TXT—Using Parentheses to Affect the Order of Operators

```
Private Sub Command1_Click()
    Expr1 = 100
    Expr2 = 75
    Expr3 = 90

    Result = Expr1 - Expr2 + Expr3
    Result2 = Expr1 - (Expr2 + Expr3)
    Form1.Print "Result  = " & Result
    Form1.Print "Result2 = " & Result2
End Sub
```

Figure 20.4
Changing the order of addition and subtraction operators.

The subtraction operator is very straightforward and simple to use. Remember to be careful when using parentheses to change the order of addition and subtraction operators; this can sometimes give you an undesired result.

The Multiplication Operator

Using the multiplication operator is very similar to using either the subtraction or addition operators, with two distinct differences. The first and most obvious is the result. If you add 5 and 7 you get 12; multiplying them, of course, yields 35. The second difference is the order of precedence that a multiplication operator has. Multiplication and division operations are performed first by the compiler. This means that if you have a line, such as the following:

```
Result = 5 + 7 * 3
```

you may expect the compiler to add 5 and 7, and then multiply that result by 3, giving you a result of 36. However, because multiplication has a higher order of precedence than addition, the 7 and 3 are multiplied to yield 21, and 5 is added to that number to produce a final result of 26. Try this in a program to see the results for yourself.

Example

This example shows how to change the order of precedence to change the final result.

If you run this program, you will get a message box like that shown in figure 20.5. As you can see from the result, the answer is 26.

```
Private Sub Command1_Click()
    Result = 5 + 7 * 3
    MsgBox "Result  = " & Result
End Sub
```

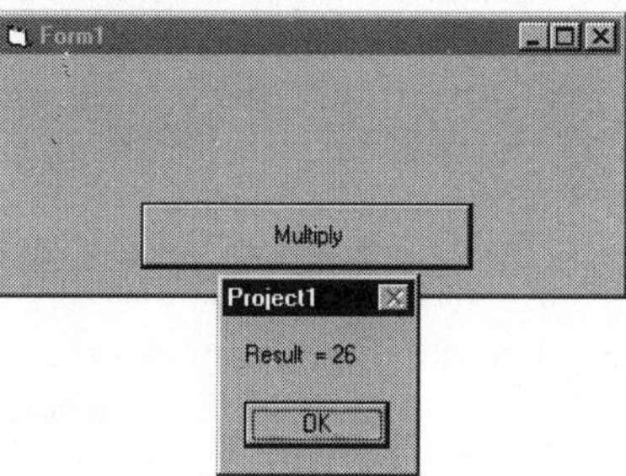

Figure 20.5

The multiplication takes place before the addition due to the order of precedence.

If you want to perform the addition first, place parentheses around the addition operation. Listing 20.3 performs both versions of the operation. Figure 20.6 shows the output.

Listing 20.3 20LIST03.TXT—Performing Both Versions of the Operation

```
Private Sub Command1_Click()
    Result = 5 + 7 * 3
    Result2 = (5 + 7) * 3

    Form1.Print "Result  = " & Result
    Form1.Print "Result2  = " & Result2
End Sub
```

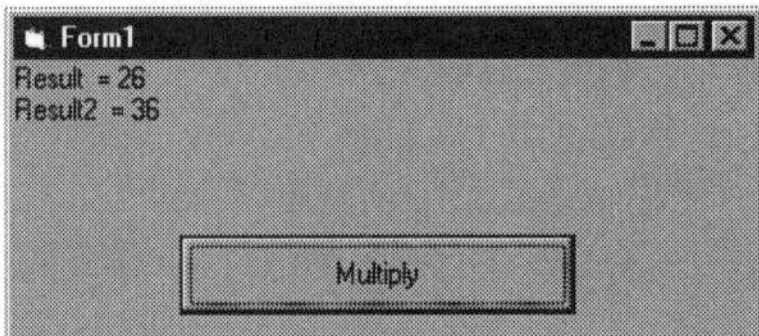

Figure 20.6

Using multiplication and addition and changing the order of precedence to produce different results.

Remember the order of precedence when using multiplication; all multiplication will be performed before addition and subtraction, unless you use parentheses to specifically tell the compiler to do otherwise.

The Division Operators

There are two separate and distinct division operators. One is for *integer division*, and the other is for *floating-point division.*

Integer division is the division of whole numbers; no decimal places are returned, and the fractional part is truncated. This can be useful, for example, when calculating the number of products that can be purchased for a particular price. You would not try to sell a customer 5.2 hard drives; rather, you would want to tell your customer that he could purchase five hard drives. The syntax for integer division is as follows:

```
Result = Expr1 \ Expr2
```

On the other hand, the floating-point division operator saves the decimal precision of the division and returns `Double`, `Double Variant`, `Single` or `Null` as the result type.

The syntax for floating-point division is as follows:

```
Result = Expr1 / Expr2
```

The order of precedence of a floating-point division operation is the same as that of a multiplication operation. If both division and multiplication appear in the same expression, the expression is evaluated from left to right.

Example

Take a look at how the different types of division work. This program shows an example of integer division.

```
Private Sub Command1_Click()
    Result = 15 \ 4

    MsgBox "Result  = " & Result
End Sub
```

By using the integer division operator, you lose the remainder. The value is rounded down to the nearest integer, and the remainder of .75 is discarded. Figure 20.7 shows the output.

Figure 20.7

Using the integer division operator.

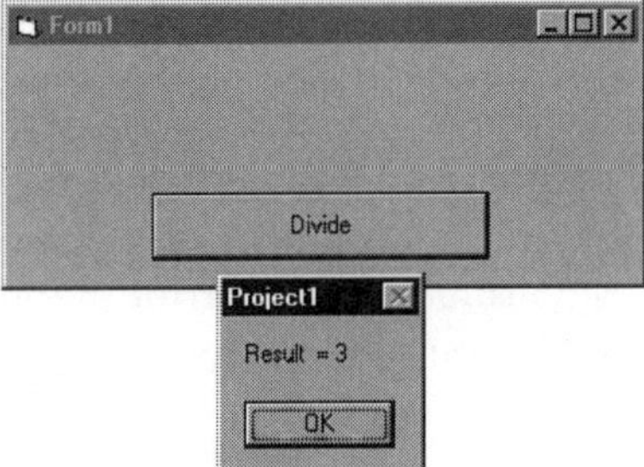

Example

If you need the number to be precise, use the floating-point version of the division operator. Take a look at the different effects the two versions of the division operator have on the same numbers.

Listing 20.4 20LIST04.TXT—Using the Floating-Point Version of the Division Operator

```
Private Sub Command1_Click()
    Result = 15 \ 4
    Result2 = 15 / 4

    Form1.Print "Result  = " & Result
    Form1.Print "Result2  = " & Result2
End Sub
```

Figure 20.8 shows the difference between these two operators. When you use division operators, be careful to choose the one that delivers the precision you need.

Figure 20.8

Using the integer and floating-point division operators.

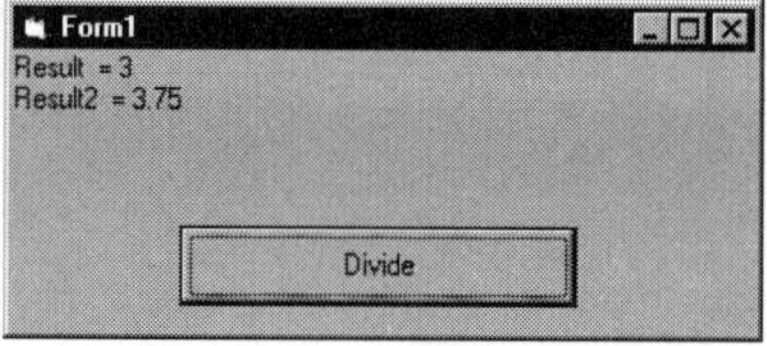

Example

Listing 20.5 combines the four different operators that you have seen so far and shows how their precedence plays a role in the outcome of the expressions they create.

Listing 20.5 20LIST05.TXT—Combining the Four Operators

```
Private Sub Command1_Click()
    Result = 15 \ 4 * 2 + 7 - 3
    Result2 = 15 \ 4 * (2 + 7) - 3

    Form1.Print "Result  = " & Result
    Form1.Print "Result2  = " & Result2
End Sub
```

The multiplication and division operators will be performed before any addition or subtraction unless you override the order of precedence with parentheses. Figure 20.9 shows the output.

Figure 20.9

Combining the four basic math operators.

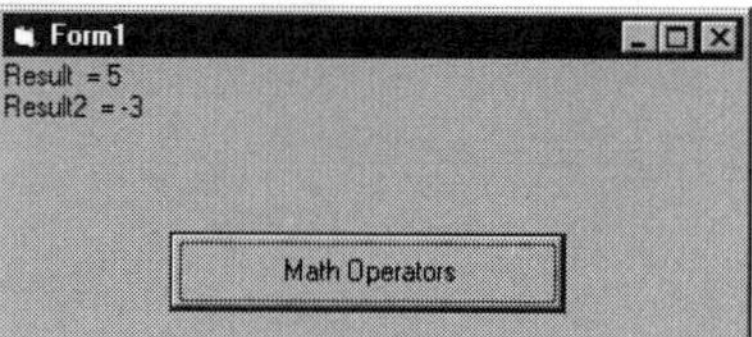

The *Mod* Operator

The `Mod` operator is another type of arithmetic operator that uses division. It returns the *modulo* (or remainder) of a division operation. If you want to use the integer division operator to obtain a whole-number result, you could get and examine the remainder by performing a `Mod` operation on the same expression.

The `Mod` operator is used just like the division operator. The syntax is the following:

```
Result = Expr1 Mod Expr2
```

Example

Now examine Listing 20.6 to see just how the `Mod` operator works.

Listing 20.6 20LIST06.TXT—Using the Mod Operator

```
Private Sub Command1_Click()
    Result = 17 \ 3
    Remainder = 17 Mod 3

    Form1.Print "Result  = " & Result
    Form1.Print "Remainder  = " & Remainder
End Sub
```

The integer division operator returns the largest whole number that can be divided into the denominator. The `Mod` function returns the remainder. The output is shown in figure 20.10.

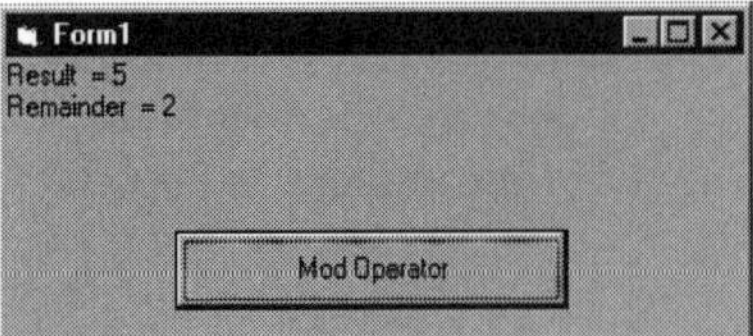

Figure 20.10

Using the `Mod` and integer division operators.

Armed with the integer division, floating-point division, and `Mod` operators, you should be able to perform any type of division that your program requires.

The Exponention Operator

One final operator completes the set of math operators available to a Visual Basic program: the *exponention operator.* It is used whenever you want to raise a number to a power. The following is the syntax of the exponention operator:

```
Result = Number ^ Exponent
```

`Number` is the base and *`Exponent`* is the power to which the base is raised. If you wanted to raise 5 to the 3rd power, for example, the syntax would be as follows:

```
Result = 5 ^ 3
```

This is equivalent to:

```
Result = 5 * 5 * 5
```

Example

This program raises 5 to the power of 7 and then prints the result on the form (see fig. 20.11).

```
Private Sub Command1_Click()
    Result = 5 ^ 7

    Form1.Print "Result  = " & Result
End Sub
```

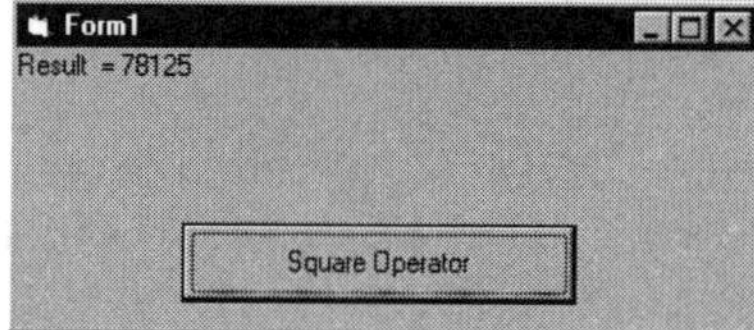

Figure 20.11
Using the square operator.

To use the square operator in your programs, you must understand its order of precedence. The square operator is the first operation that will be evaluated in an expression, but you can change this order by using parentheses.

Example

Listing 20.7 shows how you can get two vastly different results from the same expression just by changing the order of evaluation. Figure 20.12 shows the results.

Listing 20.7 20LIST07.TXT—Affecting Expression Results by Changing Order of Evaluation

```
Private Sub Command1_Click()
    Result = 100 * 2 ^ 3
    Result2 = (100 * 2) ^ 3

    Form1.Print "Result  = " & Result
    Form1.Print "Result2  = " & Result2
End Sub
```

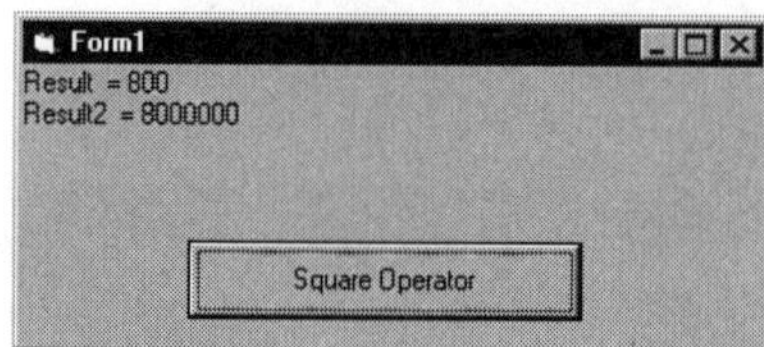

Figure 20.12
Changing the value of an expression by using parentheses.

Summary

In this chapter, you learned to use the basic math operators and how to combine them into one expression that produces one result. Also, you learned the order of precedence of each operator and how to override precedence. You also learned about the differences in floating point division and integer division.

In Chapter 21, "Expressions," you learn more about expressions and their order of precedence.

Review Questions

The answers to the review questions are in Appendix A.

1. What is the `/` operator used for?
2. For what is the `^` operator used for?
3. What does the `Mod` operator return?

4. Which two operators have the same order of precedence?
5. Which operator will be executed first, based on its order of precedence?
6. What value will this code sample print in the message box?

```
Private Sub Command1_Click()
    Result = 15 * 7 / 7 Mod 5 + 3 ^ 2
    MsgBox "Result = " & Result
End Sub
```

7. What value will this code sample print in the message box?

```
Private Sub Command1_Click()
    Result = 15 * 7 / (5 Mod 7) + 3 ^ 2
    MsgBox "Result = " & Result
End Sub
```

8. In what order are multiplication and division operations performed when they are in the same expression?

Review Exercises

1. Write a program that calculates the sum of five numbers. Show the result in a message box.
2. Write a program that uses both the addition and subtraction operators. Make sure that the program has at least three variables. Change the order of precedence of the variables using parentheses.

3. Write a program that divides two numbers using the `/`, `\`, and `Mod` operators. Compare the three answers.

4. What is the difference between integer and floating point division?

5. Create a program that uses all of the math operators in one calculation. Experiment with changing the precedence of each operation and compare the results.

Expressions

Expressions are one of the key elements of processing data within a program.

In this chapter, you learn about the different elements that can be used to make up an expression and the different ways to manipulate them. The Visual Basic online help defines an expression as "any combination of keywords, operators, variables, and constants that produce a string, number, or object." The help goes on to say that an expression "can perform a calculation, manipulate characters or data."

What exactly does all that mean? Simply put, expressions are the workhorses of the programming languages. Whenever any action occurs, it occurs because some expression somewhere was evaluated.

Simple Expressions

The simplest expression is made up of one component, such as the variable `X`. However, expressions can contain very elaborate formulas made up of numerous variables and functions. Even the most complicated of formulas is still just an expression. Expressions are used extensively in Chapter 20, "Math Operators," even though they aren't discussed as such.

There are three basic types of expressions:

- A mathematical comparison between two values having a result that is either true or false is an expression. For example, the statement `1=7` would equate to false because 1 is not equal to 7.
- An expression can be one or more values or variables joined by functions or functional operators.

- An assignment of a value to a variable using another variable, value, or expression is itself an expression.

Using these definitions, take a look at a few different examples to illustrate the different types of expressions.

According to the first definition, the statement `X < LoopCounter` is an expression of comparison. In English, the expression would read, "`X` is less than `LoopCounter`."

Using the second definition, the expression `(3 * X) Not+ (X^2 + 7)` joins one or more variables together by functions or functional operators. The `Not` in the formula is called a *logical operator*. (Logical operators are discussed later in this chapter.)

By the third definition, `Cost = NumPurchased * PurchasePrice` is an expression of assignment. The expression to the right of the equal sign is evaluated and assigned to the variable `Cost`.

Comparison Operators

Comparison operators play a major role in expressions. They are used to compare one expression to another, and there are only two ways the expression(s) can be evaluated: `True` or `False`. If you see `5 > 100`, you can safely assume that the expression is false because you know that 5 is less than 100. What if the expression were `100 > 100`? This too would be false because 100 is equal to 100.

Table 21.1 lists the comparison operators that are available in Visual Basic.

Table 21.1 Visual Basic Comparison Operators

Symbol	*Description*
<	Less than
<=	Less than or equal to
>	Greater than
>=	Greater than or equal to
<>	Not equal
=	Equal

As you can see in Table 21.1, the equal sign is a comparison operator. But hasn't it been used as an assignment operator, also? The answer is yes. The equal operator can be used for either comparison or assignment; it all depends on the context in which the operator is used.

The equal sign is used as an assignment operator when placed outside a comparison statement; otherwise, it is considered an assignment operator. Comparisons are covered in detail in Part IV "Controlling Program Flow."

Example

Listing 21.1 uses most of the comparison operators from Table 21.1. Look at the code before you run it. What do you expect to see for the results? The result of running this program is shown in figure 21.1.

Listing 21.1 21LIST01.TXT—The Comparison Operators

```
Private Sub Command1_Click()
    X = 7
    Y = 5

    Form1.Print Spc(3); "X < Y = ";
    Form1.Print X < Y
    Form1.Print Spc(3); "X > Y = ";
    Form1.Print X > Y
    Form1.Print Spc(3); "X <= Y = ";
    Form1.Print X <= Y
    Form1.Print Spc(3); "X >= Y = ";
    Form1.Print X >= Y
    Form1.Print Spc(3); "X <> Y = ";
    Form1.Print X <> Y
End Sub
```

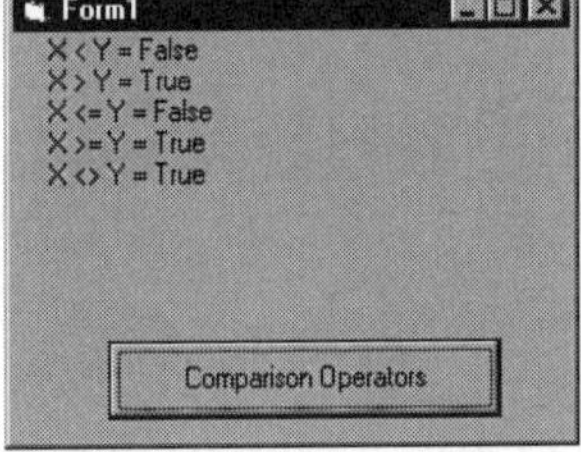

Figure 21.1
The output of Listing 21.1.

You will notice that this example does not use the equal sign. That is because the equal operator is used as an assignment operator unless it is used in a program control expression, such as the `IF...THEN` statement.

The values printed on-screen are either `True` or `False`, based on the validity of the comparison. The values `True` and `False` actually are represented by numbers: `True` is `-1` and `False` is `0`. To make your programs easier to understand, it is considered good practice to use the built-in constants `True` and `False`.

Comparison operators make up a good deal of the logic that your programs will use to make decisions. These decisions will usually be used to determine whether to execute some code based on the result of the comparison.

Table 21.2 shows the order of precedence for the comparison operators.

Table 21.2 Comparison Operator Precedence

Operator	*Symbol*
Equality	(=)
Inequality	(<>)
Less than	(<)
Greater than	(>)
Less than or equal to	(<=)
Greater than or equal to	(>=)

Logical Operators

Logical operators are used to manipulate and compare expressions, or to manipulate and compare data on a bit level. This chapter concentrates on the comparison aspects of the logical operators.

The logical operators are as follows:

```
And
Not
Or
Xor
```

Advanced logical operators, which are not covered in this chapter, are as follows:

```
Eqv
Imp
```

The syntax for each of these operators is described in the following sections.

The *And* Operator

The `And` operator is used to compare two values. If the two values are both true, then the return value is `True`. If they are not both true, then the return is `False`.

Example

Listing 21.2 shows the use of the `And` operator.

Listing 21.2 21LIST02.TXT—The And Operator

```
Private Sub Command1_Click()
    W = 15
```

```
    X = 7
    Y = 5

    Result = W > X And X > Y
    Form1.Print Spc(3); "W > X And X > Y = " & Result
    Result = X > W And X > Y
    Form1.Print Spc(3); "X > W And X > Y = " & Result
End Sub
```

The `And` operator used in the preceding example compares two comparisons. The results of this program are shown in figure 21.2. If both of the comparisons are true, the result is `True`. If either of the comparisons is false, the result is `False`.

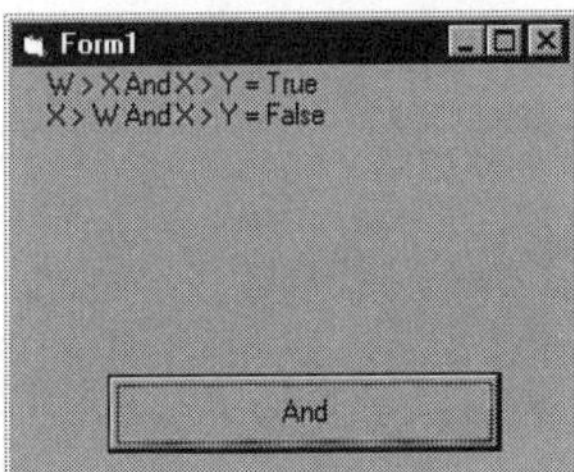

Figure 21.2
The results of using the And operator.

The *Not* Operator

The `Not` operator returns the opposite of a value. If a comparison equates to `True` and is combined with the `Not` operator, the result is `False`.

Example

Listing 21.3 illustrates the use of the `Not` operator.

Listing 21.3 21LIST03.TXT—The Not Operator

```
Private Sub Command1_Click()
    W = 15
    X = 7
    Y = 5

    Result = Not W > X
    Form1.Print Spc(3); "Not W > X = " & Result
    Result = Not X < Y
    Form1.Print Spc(3); "Not X < Y = " & Result
End Sub
```

This illustrates how the `Not` operator can be used to negate a value. If you were to evaluate `W > X`, you would get `True` because `15` is larger than `7`. But if you put the `Not` in front of the `W`, it becomes `-W`, or `-15`, which is less than `7`. The results of this program are shown in figure 21.3.

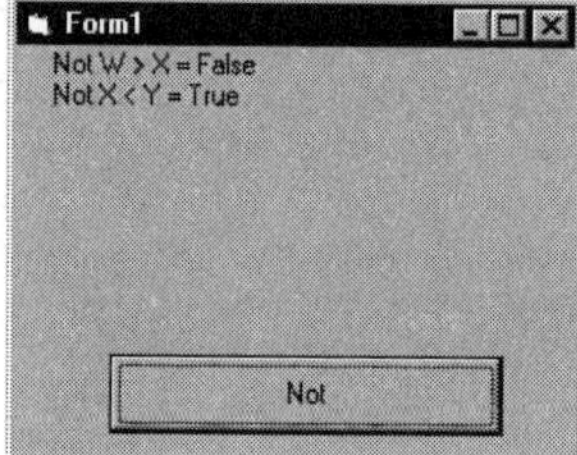

Figure 21.3
Using the `Not` operator.

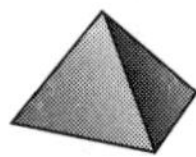

Tip: `Not` performs Logical Negation, which is not the same as Negation with the minus sign. `Not` reverses each bit in the expression result, and reverses True and False.

The *Or* Operator

The `Or` operator is used to determine whether any value is true. If either or both of the values that are being compared with `Or` evaluate to `True`, then the entire expression is considered to be true. In order to receive a `False` from `Or`, both expressions have to be false.

Example

Use the `Or` operator whenever you want to determine whether either or both expressions are True. The result of running Listing 21.4 is shown in figure 21.4.

Listing 21.4 21LIST04.TXT—The Or Operator

```
Private Sub Command1_Click()
    W = 15
    X = 7
    Y = 5

    Result = X > W Or Y > W
    Form1.Print Spc(3); "X > W Or Y > W = " & Result
    Result = X < Y Or Y < W
    Form1.Print Spc(3); "X < Y Or Y < W = " & Result
End Sub
```

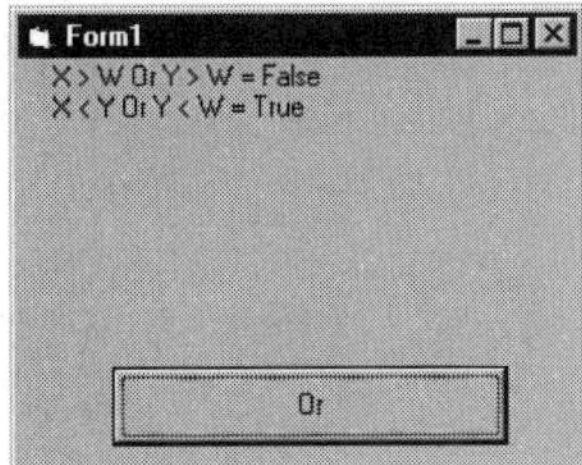

Figure 21.4
Using the `Or` operator.

The *Xor* Operator

The `Xor` operator is similar to the `Or` operator except that the `Xor` operator returns `True` only if one, but not both, of the expressions is true. This is referred to as an *exclusive-or:* the operator excludes the case where both expressions are true.

Example

Listing 21.5 illustrates the usage of the `Xor` operator. The output is shown in figure 21.5. As an experiment, use the same expressions with both `Xor` and `Or`, and compare the results.

Listing 21.5 21LIST05.TXT—The Xor Operator

```
Private Sub Command1_Click()
W = 15
    X = 7
    Y = 5

    Result = X < W Xor Y > W
    Form1.Print Spc(3); "X < W Xor Y > W = " & Result
    Result = X < Y Xor Y > W
    Form1.Print Spc(3); "X < Y Xor Y > W = " & Result
End Sub
```

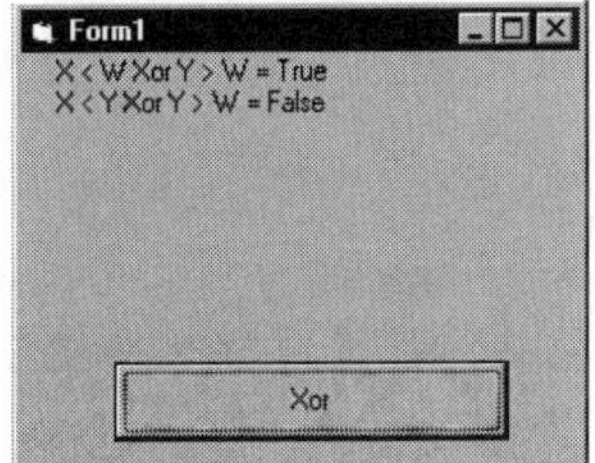

Figure 21.5
Using the `Xor` operator.

Logical Operator Precedence

Logical operators have their own order of precedence. This order is as follows:

```
Not
And
Or
Xor
Eqv
Imp
```

Using the logical operators can enable you to create expressions that you may need in your programs. You learn more about expressions as you progress through Part IV, "Controlling Program Flow."

Summary

In this chapter, you learned what an expression is and how to create one. You also learned about comparison operators and how to use them in your applications. You should become very comfortable with comparisons, you will be using them in every program that you write. You learned about logical operators and how they operate and can be used in expressions. You also learned about the order of precedence for logical operators.

Review Questions

The answers to the review questions are in Appendix A.

1. What is the <> operator used for?
2. What is the < operator used for?
3. What does the >= operator return?

4. Which logical operator returns `True` if either expression is true?
5. Which logical operator negates an expression?

6. Which comparison operator can be used for both comparison and assignment?
7. Assuming that W=15, X=7, and Y=5, what would the value of `Result` be after each of these expressions?

a. `Result = W < 20 Or Y > 5`

b. `Result = Not Y < 20`

c. `Result = Z < W And Y > Z`

d. `Result = X > Y Xor Y > Z`

Review Exercises

1. Write an expression that compares three numbers for equality. Print the result on the form and then show the result in a message box.

2. Write an expression that uses the logical `And` operator and four variables. Let the variables equal 2, 4, 6, and 8. Make the left side of the expression true and the right false. What is the result? Make both sides false and then true. What are the results?

3. Write an expression that uses the `And` operator. Print the result to the form. Add the `Not` operator to the expression. Are the results what you expected? Try using the `Xor` and `Or` operators in place of the `Not` operator. What results did this yield?

4. Write an expression that uses the `Xor` operator and experiment with each side of the expression. Try all combinations possible. For example, make the left side false and the right side true. Record your results. Does the `Xor` operator operate as you expected? Remember that the `Xor` operator is the exclusive-or operator. This refers to one or the other being true, but not both.

5. Create a program that uses the `And` and `Or` operators in one expression. Experiment with parentheses to see the results.

6. Create a mathematical formula that uses the math operators found in Chapter 20, "Math Operators," to create two expressions. Use the different logical operators to link the two expressions. Print the results to the form.

CHAPTER 22

The *If* Statement

In this chapter, you learn how to execute your programs based on the condition of an expression. This process is commonly referred to as *conditionally executing* the code.

To conditionally execute code, you must first have a test. This test is called the condition. If the test condition is passed, the code is executed; if the condition is not passed, the code is not executed. The reverse sometimes works instead: if the expression does not pass the test condition, you execute certain code. The Visual Basic construct for performing these types of conditional tests is the `If-Then-End If` statement, commonly called an `If` statement, or an `If` block.

Visual Basic offers other ways to check a value against a series of values. One way is to use the `Select-Case` statement. This chapter covers the use of the `If` statement and the `Select-Case` statement.

Conditional Execution

In Chapter 21, "Expressions," you learned that an expression can be either true or false, which is the premise on which conditional execution is based. If you need to know that a particular condition is true (or false) before performing some specific task, you can use conditional execution. The simplest form of conditional execution is the `If` statement.

If-Then-End If

You may have already guessed how the `If-Then-EndIf` statement works. The `If` statement tests for a value; if the condition is met, `Then` performs an action. The `End If` portion of the statement is a directive to Visual Basic that signals the end of the conditional test and execution.

Example

Look at a simple example that illustrates how this works:

```
If Cats = 5 Then
     AtMyHouse = True
     MsgBox "5 Cats? Could be my house !"
End If
```

The conditional test is whether the variable `Cats` is equal to `5`. If it is, the code between the `Then` and `End If` keywords is executed.

This type of control over program execution is vital to anything other than the simplest of applications. If you were to write the traditional Hello World program, conditional logic is unnecessary, although any programs beyond that level of simplicity would require at least some conditional logic.

The conditional tests performed within an `If` statement can be as elaborate as you need. Any expression that can be evaluated in terms of true or false can be used as a conditional. For example, this statement is valid:

```
If ((X / Y And W^3 * 5) / 7 > 32) Then
     ' Perform Logic Here
End If
```

The following statement, however, is not valid as long as the value of `TextString$` is not `True`:

```
If (TxtString$) Then
     ' Perform Logic Here
End If
```

The second example is invalid because the conditional cannot be expressed as either true or false. The key to creating and using conditional expressions is that the expression must evaluate to either a true or false value. Remember that the value of false is 0 and the value of true is -1. You could test for these values if you wanted to, but for readability of your code, it is recommended that you use the predefined constants if you need to make a true or false comparison.

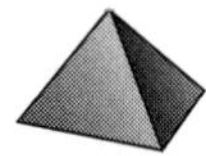

> **Tip:** You can assign a string the values of `True` and `False`. If a string has been assigned a value of `True` or `False`, that string can be used in a conditional statement.

By default, the `If` statement checks whether a condition is true. You could have a statement like this:

```
If (ErrCode = True) Then...
```

This statement really says, "If `ErrCode` is `True`, then perform the code below." But what if you wanted to test to see whether a statement is false? You could do it one of two ways. The easiest way is to check whether the value is false. But you could check whether the value is not true. Although checking for a value to be not true is the same as checking for a value to be false, you will want your code to be as easy to read and maintain as possible. The following two statements are equal and will perform the same, but which one is easier to read?

```
If (Value = False) Then...
If Value Then...
If (Value = Not True) Then...
```

At times, you will want to check for a certain condition to be met. In Chapter 19, "Simple Input and Output," you learned about using message and input boxes. When you use a message box containing more than one button, you will want to check to see which button the user pressed. If the choices are OK and Cancel, you will probably not want to perform the same tasks for both buttons.

If you are using an input box, you will want to check whether the return value is equal to `""`, which is an empty string. If an empty string is returned, the user either pressed the Cancel button or pressed the OK button without entering any text. Either way, you don't have the required input to process, and you need to take the appropriate action.

Example

Here is an example of using an input box and not checking the condition of the return code from the `InputBox` function.

```
Private Sub Command1_Click()
 Directory = InputBox("Location to Store Files:", _
                      "Create Directory", _
                      "C:\VB4")

 MsgBox "Directory Chosen " & Directory
End Sub
```

Run this code and choose the Cancel button in the message box. Your result should appear similar to that in figure 22.1.

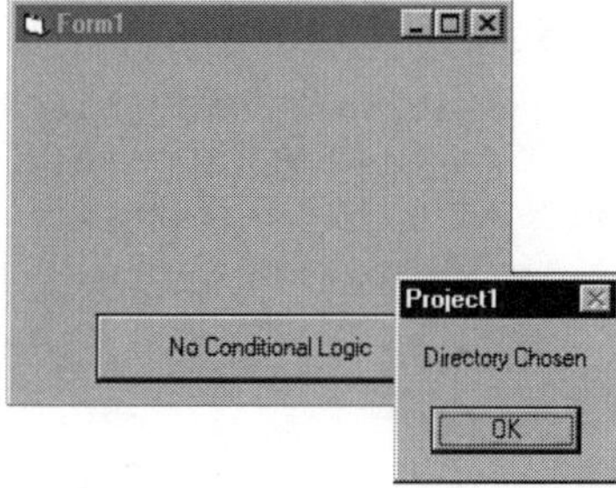

Figure 22.1

Output from `InputBox` after choosing the Cancel button.

Figure 22.1 shows that the program tried to print the chosen directory. Because the Cancel button was chosen, the program printed nothing. This could cause problems if you think that the variable `Directory` contains a valid string when it is actually blank.

Example

Listing 22.1 shows the same function, but uses the `If` statement to determine what happened in the `InputBox` function.

Listing 22.1 22LIST01.TXT—Using *If* Statement to Determine Outcome of *InputBox* Function

```
 Private Sub Command1_Click()
 Directory = InputBox("Location to Store Files:", _
                      "Create Directory", _
                      "C:\VB4")

If (Directory > "") Then
 MsgBox "Directory Chosen " + Directory
' Processing of the chosen directory could go in here
End If
End Sub
```

As you can see, the return value of the input box is checked. If this value is not equal to an empty string, then something was entered, or the OK button was clicked and the default string was returned. As long as the string is not empty, you can now continue processing using the variable `Directory`. If the Cancel button was chosen, or if the default string was erased and the OK button was pressed, the variable `Directory` will be empty and you should not attempt to process it.

Take a look at another instance in which you check the return code of a function. This time, you use the `MsgBox` function. Most Windows applications ask whether you are sure that you want to exit when you attempt to close down the application. This need for confirmation provides a perfect example of when to use the `If` statement.

Example

Listing 22.2 shows how not using an `If` statement when the user attempts to close an application can produce invalid results. Not checking can also be disastrous to your application if you need to perform some other tasks before shutdown. This example can be added to a form that you already have open, or you can start a new form, add the following code, and run the program.

Listing 22.2 22LIST02.TXT—Failing to Use an If Statement Produces Invalid Results

```
Private Sub Form_Unload(Cancel As Integer)

' The value of Cancel determines whether the App will
' terminate or not. If Cancel = 0 the app will exit.
' Any nonzero value will prevent the program from exiting

Cancel = 0

RetCode = MsgBox("Are You Sure?", _
          vbOKCancel, _
          "Quit Application?")

End Sub
```

This is an example of a common message box. The `Form_Unload` subroutine is called whenever the user chooses to close a form. In the case of a single form application, this means that the user wanted to exit the application, either by double-clicking the system menu or by choosing Close from the system menu.

Most applications present the user with a message box asking whether the user really intends to exit. That is what the preceding code does—except that this code has a problem. Because there is no conditional test to see what button was pressed, the button that is pressed won't matter; the form will exit anyway. The value assigned to the `Cancel` variable tells Visual Basic whether to exit the form. Any non-zero value causes the application to exit.

To make this code usable, you need to test the return value of the `MsgBox` function. By doing this, you can determine which button was pressed and act accordingly.

Example

Listing 22.3 shows an enhanced version of the exit routine presented in the previous example. In your code window, add the code that is missing to match this enhanced version of the exit routine, then run the enhanced program.

Listing 22.3 22LIST03.TXT—Enhanced Version of the Exit Routine

```
Private Sub Form_Unload(Cancel As Integer)

' The value of Cancel determines whether the App will
' terminate or not. If Cancel = 0 the app will exit.
' Any nonzero value will prevent the program from exiting
```

continues

Listing 22.3 Continued

```
Cancel = 1

RetCode = MsgBox("Are You Sure?", _
          vbOKCancel, _
          "Quit Application?")

' Code to Exit Application
If (RetCode = vbOK) Then
    ' If OK button pressed, change Cancel variable to 0 to exit
    ' otherwise, leave it set to 1 so the form will not exit
    Cancel = 0
     MsgBox "OK Button Pressed"
End If
End Sub
```

A message box is presented when you attempt to close the form. If you click the OK button, the form exits. If you click Cancel, you are returned to the form. Without the capability to test for certain conditions, a computer couldn't do much (except, of course, print `Hello World` to the screen).

The `If` statement has several optional parts, enabling you to test for more than just one condition. These additional statements are discussed in the following sections.

Else and *ElseIf*

What do you do if you want to test for more than one condition? You can use the `If` statement for testing multiple conditions, as well as have a default action performed if none of the conditions that are tested for are met.

As optional parts of the `If` statement, the `Else` and `ElseIf` statements extend its functionality. For a better understanding of how the `Else` and `ElseIf` statements work, the following is the complete syntax of the `If` statement:

```
If Condition Then
     [Statements]
[ElseIf NextCondition Then
     [NextStatements]]
[Else
     [DefaultStatements]]
End If
```

As the syntax shows, an `If` statement can have more to it than just the `If`, `Then`, and `EndIf` statements. You can have a default action that takes place whenever the condition defined by the `If` statement is not met. This default action is defined by the `Else` keyword.

Example

To illustrate this point, Listing 22.4 is an enhanced version of the earlier example that requested a directory name using `InputBox`. The enhanced version uses an `Else` statement to indicate when no directory was chosen.

Listing 22.4 22LIST04.TXT—Enhanced Version of Example That Requested Directory Name Using InputBox

```
 Private Sub Command1_Click()
Directory = InputBox("Location to Store Files:", _
                     "Create Directory", _
                     "C:\VB4")

If (Directory <> "") Then
 MsgBox "Directory Chosen " + Directory
' Processing of the chosen directory could go in here
Else
 MsgBox "No Directory Chosen....Processing will not continue."
End If

End Sub
```

This code produces one of two results: If the Cancel button is pressed, you see a message box like that in figure 22.2. If the OK button is pressed to accept the default directory, you see a message box similar to that in figure 22.3

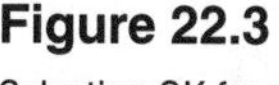

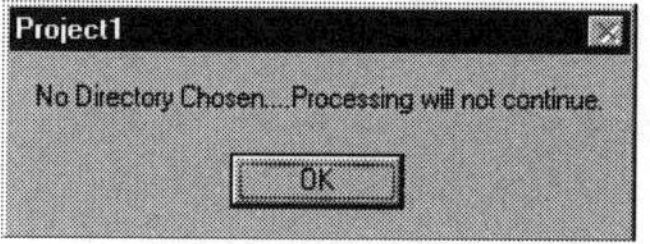

Figure 22.2

Selecting Cancel from the Input box.

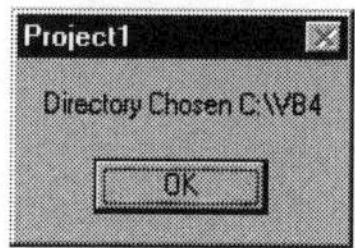

Figure 22.3

Selecting OK from the Input box.

As you can see from the code and output, you can have an either-or situation when using the `If-Then-Else` combination. This combination can be useful if you have to perform one of two separate acts based on the value, or condition, of an expression. What if you want to test more than one condition? The `ElseIf` statement is used for just that purpose.

`ElseIf` enables you to create conditions that check for multiple conditions. For example, if the variable `X` equals five, then the variable `Y` should equal 10. But if `X` equals 10, then `Y` should equal 17; otherwise, `Y` should equal `X`.

Example

The following code shows how you can perform this conditional test using the `ElseIf` and `Else` statements:

```
If X = 5 Then
     Y = 10
ElseIf X = 10 Then
     Y = 17
Else Y = X
End If
```

By using the `Else` and `ElseIf` statements, you can check for different conditions that require different actions to be taken. The `Else` statement is primarily used for a catchall default statement: If all other conditions have not been met, take the action in the `Else` statement.

Example

Now look at Listing 22.5, which uses the `ElseIf` and `Else` statements to check the value of a number that has been input.

Listing 22.5 22LIST05.TXT—Using the *ElseIf* and *Else* Statements to Check the Value of a Number

```
 Private Sub Command1_Click()

 Number = InputBox("Enter a number from 1 and 10", _
                  "Using the ElseIf/Else Statements")

If (Number = "") Then
 MsgBox "Operation Cancelled..."

ElseIf (Number >= 1 And Number < 5) Then
 MsgBox "Number Entered is greater than 1 and less than 5"

ElseIf (Number = 5) Then
 MsgBox "Number Entered is equal to 5"

ElseIf (Number > 5 And Number <= 10) Then
 MsgBox "Number Entered is greater than 5 and less than 10"

Else
 MsgBox "Number Entered is not from 1 to and 10"
End If

End Sub
```

When you run this program, you are presented with an `InputBox` requesting that you enter a number from one to 10. The first `If` statement checks to see whether the Cancel button was chosen; if it was, a box is presented stating that the operation was cancelled.

If you type a number from one to 10, the `If-ElseIf` statements will catch the number and show you a message box with the range in which your number falls. What if you type the number 17? The `If-ElseIf` statements will not catch the number, and it will fall through to the `Else` statement. The default for the `Else` statement is to inform you that you have not entered a valid number. The possible outputs from this code are shown in figures 22.4 through 22.8.

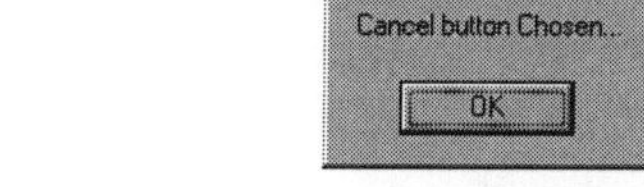

Figure 22.4
Result of selecting Cancel from the Input box.

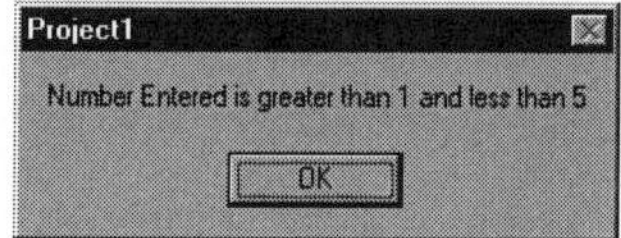

Figure 22.5
Result of entering a number from one to four.

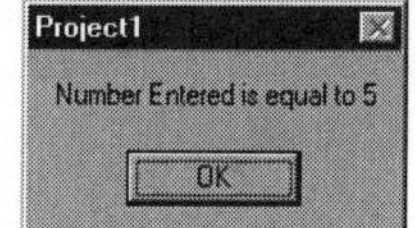

Figure 22.6
Result of entering the number five.

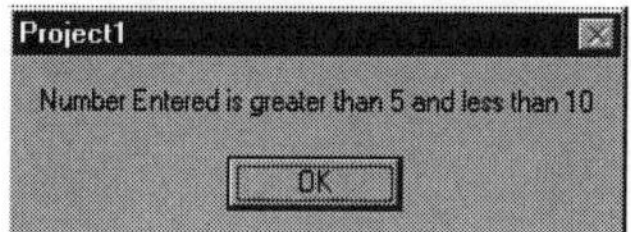

Figure 22.7
Result of entering a number from six to 10.

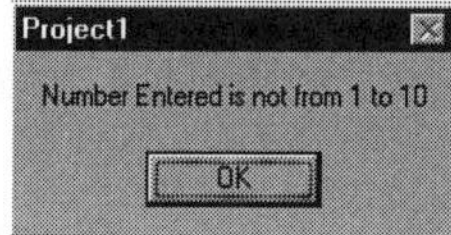

Figure 22.8
Result of entering a number that is not from 1 to 10.

You should now be able to use the `If-Then-ElseIf-Else-End If` statement to create any conditional statement you need. In the next section, you learn about the `Select-Case` statement. This specialized statement can replace the `If` statement if you need to check one expression for a variety of possible values.

The *Select Case* Statement

Another control statement available in Visual Basic is the `Select Case` statement. It is useful when you need to check one expression for a number of different values. If you had a variable called `PayTerms` and wanted to check the terms of an invoice, you could use an `If` statement. However, doing so would require checking the same value repeatedly for valid conditions.

Example

The following code fragment shows how you would do the check with an `If` statement:

```
.
.
.
If PayTerms <= 10 Then
  Terms = 1    ' Set Terms to Level 1

ElseIf PayTerms > 10 And PayTerms <= 30 Then
  Terms = 2    ' Set Terms to Level 2

ElseIf PayTerms > 30 and PayTerms <= 60 Then
  Terms = 3    ' Set Terms to Level 3

ElseIf PayTerms > 60 and PayTerms <= 90 Then
  Terms = 4    ' Set Terms to Level 4

Else
  Terms = 0    ' Not Known

End If
.
.
.
```

You would have to check continually the same variable for a variety of conditions. This kind of checking requires quite a bit of typing, and therefore can introduce errors. An easier way to write the same conditional statement is to use the `Select Case` statement.

With `Select Case`, you can select the expression you want to test and then list all the different cases, or values, for which you want to take special action.

Example

Look at the following code to see how the previous sample could be rewritten with the `Select Case` statement:

```
.
.
.
Select Case PayTerms
Case 0 To 10
   Terms = 1    ' Set Terms to Level 1

Case 11 To 30
   Terms = 2    ' Set Terms to Level 2

Case 31 To 60
  Terms = 3    ' Set Terms to Level 3

Case 61 To 90
  Terms = 4    ' Set Terms to Level 4

Case Else
  Terms = 0    ' Not Known

End Select
.
.
.
```

If you compare these two examples, you will see that the `Select Case` statement is much easier to read and requires less typing. Use `Select Case` only when you want to test one expression for a number of possible values.

Example

Listing 22.6 shows how you can rewrite the program shown earlier using the `If` statement:

Listing 22.6 22LIST06.TXT—Rewriting Program Using If Statement

```
 Private Sub Command1_Click()
 Number = InputBox("Enter a number from 1 to 10", _
                   "Using the ElseIf/Else Statements")
Select Case Number
     Case ""
          MsgBox "Cancel button Chosen..."
     Case 1 To 4
          MsgBox "Number Entered is greater than 0 and
          ➥less than 5"
     Case 5
          MsgBox "Number Entered is equal to 5"
     Case 6 To 10
          MsgBox "Number Entered is greater than 5 and
          ➥less than 11"
```

continues

Listing 22.6 Continued

```
     Case Else
          MsgBox "Number Entered is not from 1 to 10"

End Select
End Sub
```

As noted, you use the `Select Case` statement to check one value or expression for a variety of conditions. If you need to check the values of multiple expressions and perform different tasks based on the conditions of those expressions, use the `If` statement and its components.

Summary

In this chapter, you learned how to control program flow with the If statement and the Select Case statement. Both of these statements enable you to check the values of variables and expressions and act accordingly. You will be using these statements in your programs to help control how your programs act and react to different situations. In Chapter 23, "The *Do While* Statement," you learn how to perform repetitive tasks until certain conditions are met.

Review Questions

The answers to the review questions are in Appendix A.

1. What is the purpose of the `If-Then-Else` statement?
2. What are the parts of the `If` Statement?
3. What is used to end the `If-Then-Else` statement?

4. What code does the `Else` statement generally contain?
5. How many expressions or conditions can be checked with the `Select Case` statement?

6. Is there anything wrong with this code sample?

```
Select Case Number
Case 1
     MsgBox "1 Selected"
CaseIf 3
     MsgBox "3 Selected"
CaseIf 5
     MsgBox "5 Selected"
Case Else
     MsgBox "Number Is not a 1, 3, or 5"
End Select
```

7. When would you use the `Select Case` statement in place of an `If-Then` statement?

8. How many different expressions can be tested by an `If-Then` statement?

Review Exercises

1. Write an `If` statement that checks for these three values: X = 5, Y = 7, and Z = 3.

2. Write an `If` statement that checks for the value of Y to be from 1 to 10, 11 to 50, and 51 to 100. If the value is not in one of these ranges, use an `Else` to catch this. Test the `If` statement with different values of Y.

3. Write an `If` statement that checks whether X = 5 and Y = 3. How many different combinations can be checked with one `If` statement?

4. Write a `Select Case` statement that checks a variable for each number from 1 to 10. Include a default case for numbers that are out of this range.

5. Create a program that prompts the user for a number from 1 to 10. Create a `Select-Case` statement that tells the user whether they picked the right number. This program is like the old game in which someone says, "I'm thinking of a number from 1 to 10. What is it?"

6. Use both an `If` statement and a `Select Case` statement to perform a test on a number. This test should check the number for a series of different values. Make certain that both the `If` and `Select Case` statements perform the same tests. Which one is easier to read? Which one would be easier to maintain?

CHAPTER 23

The Do-While Statement

In this chapter, you learn how to use loops. A *loop* in programming is a set of instructions executed repeatedly until a certain condition is met. This form of repetitive execution can save time and space when you write your programs. Suppose that you wanted to print the numbers from 1 to 20 to the form. You could type 20 consecutive `Form1.Print` statements, or you could create a loop that contained one `Form1.Print` statement.

The premise behind loops is this: You can use a loop either to wait for something to happen (represented by a condition being met) or to perform repetitive tasks. Several different forms of loops are available. This chapter covers the `Do-While` loop.

The *Do-While* Loop

You use the `Do-While` loop to *do* something *while* or *until* a condition is met. For example, you may write a loop that requests a value in a certain range and then continues to request that value until a valid number is entered. This use of a `Do-While` loop is common.

Example

Now take a look at the syntax of the `Do-While` loop, as shown in following sample:

```
Do [{While ¦ Until} condition]
     [statements]
     [Exit Do]
     [statements]
Loop
```

Or the condition can be placed at the end of the loop, as follows:

```
Do
     [statements]
     [Exit Do]
     [statements]
Loop [{While ¦ Until} condition]
```

In the first syntax, the condition must be met for the loop to execute at all. In the second syntax, the loop is executed once, then the condition is checked to see if the loop should continue for another cycle before checking the condition again.

Here are the keywords used by the `Do-While` statement:

```
Do

Exit Do

While

Until

Loop
```

A `Do` loop must consist of three parts. All loops must begin with the `Do` keyword and end with the `Loop` keyword. They must have a third part as well: either the `While` keyword or the `Until` keyword. You can use two different types of `Do` loops, as shown by the preceding syntax.

The first syntax checks the condition before executing any of the code in the loop. The second syntax executes the code in the loop once and then checks the condition. The type of `Do` loop you use depends entirely on your needs.

Example

These lines of code show a simple `Do` loop. It prints the numbers 1 to 5 on-screen. Because you want this loop to perform an action before checking the condition, the example uses the second syntax of the `Do` loop.

```
Private Sub Command1_Click()
Int X = 1
Do
Form1.Print X
    X = X + 1
Loop Until X > 5
End Sub
```

If you run this code, you will see the numbers 1 through 5 printed on the form. Notice that the `Do` and `Loop` keywords were used with the `Until` keyword. The code reads, "Print the value of `X`, add 1 to `X` until the value of `X` is greater than 5, and continue processing after the `Loop` keyword." The output from this listing is shown in figure 23.1.

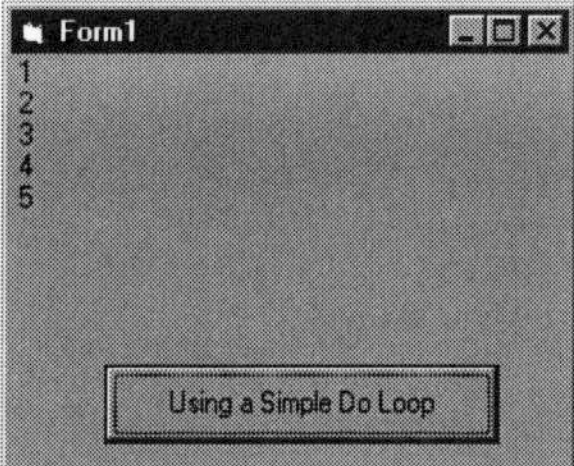

Figure 23.1
Output from a simple `Do-Until` loop.

Just how does this loop work? Everything between the words `Do` and `Loop` is the body of the loop. That code will be executed for each iteration of the loop. The keyword `Until` states the condition of the loop, which will repeat itself until the variable `X` is greater than 5.

Example

This loop could have been written as a `Do-While` loop instead of a `Do-Until` loop. To see the differences between the two, look at the following listing:

```
Private Sub Command1_Click()
Dim X As Integer
X = 1
Do
Form1.Print X
    X = X + 1
Loop While X <= 5
End Sub
```

If you look at the condition shown in this example, you will notice that it states `While X <= 5`, whereas the `Until` loop shown in the preceding example uses `Until X > 5`. Both loops perform exactly the same. The main difference is that a `While` loop executes continuously while certain conditions are met. The `Until` loop executes until a certain condition is met. Now take a look at a more illustrative example.

Example

Listing 23.1 illustrates how to use a loop to request information. If the number entered is not within the desired range, the condition for exiting the loop is not met and the loop will continue.

Listing 23.1 23LIST01.TXT—Using a Loop to Request Information

```
Private Sub Command1_Click()

Do
```

continues

Listing 23.1 Continued

```
Number = InputBox("Enter a number from 1 to 10",
        [ccc]"Using the Do Until Loop")

Loop Until Val(Number) >= 1 And Val(Number) <= 10

Form1.Print "Number Entered was " & Number

End Sub
```

If you run this code, you will be presented with an input box requesting that you enter a number between 1 and 10. If you enter the number 99 and choose OK, you will immediately see the input box again asking you for a number. The reason is that the conditions for exiting the loop were not met when you entered 99. To exit the loop, you have to enter a number from 1 to 10. When you do this, the number you entered is printed on the form.

The output from the preceding example is shown in figure 23.2.

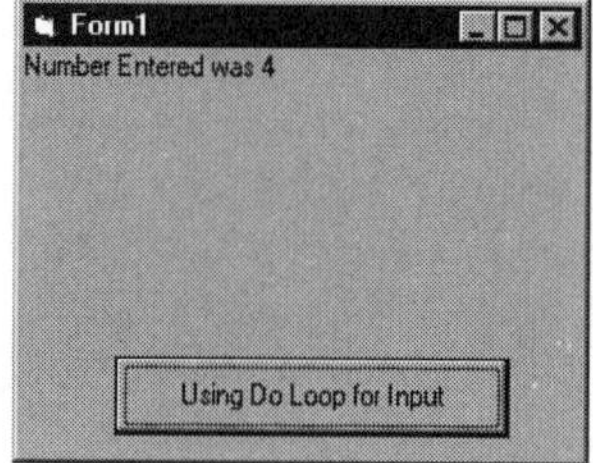

Figure 23.2
Using a `Do` loop for input.

This code is fairly simple. The loop continues to execute until the proper condition is met to exit the loop—entering a number from 1 to 10. What happens if you do not enter a number and choose OK, or choose the Cancel button? The variable `Number` will be assigned an empty string (`""`), which causes problems when Visual Basic attempts to use an empty string in a numeric conditional test. Try choosing the Cancel button and see what happens. You will generate a `Type-Mismatch` error.

How do you prevent such an error? One of the keywords in the `Do-Loop` statement is `Exit Do`. Whenever Visual Basic encounters an `Exit Do` statement, it immediately exits the loop; processing continues with the first line following the `Loop` statement.

By combining an `If` statement and the `Do` loop, you can stop execution quite easily.

Example

Listing 23.2 shows how to use the `Exit Do` statement to stop the execution of a loop.

Listing 23.2 23LIST02.TXT—Using Exit Do to Stop Loop Execution

```
Private Sub Command1_Click()
Do
 Number = InputBox("Enter a number between 1 and 10", _
                  "Using the Do Until Loop")

 If Number = "" Then
    Exit Do
 End If

Loop Until Val(Number) >= 1 And Val(Number) <= 10

Form1.Print "Number Entered was " & Number

End Sub
```

The `If` statement inside the loop checks the value of `Number` and, if it is an empty string, exits the loop. The call to `Exit Do` informs Visual Basic to stop the processing of the loop and continue execution on the line immediately following the `Loop` statement.

This program still has one flaw, though. The line that prints the value of the variable `Number` will still be called every time, regardless of whether there is a valid number to print. If you press the cancel button, you will see results similar to that shown in figure 23.3. You can easily correct this flaw by adding another `If` statement to the line that prints the value of `Number`. This is shown in the next example.

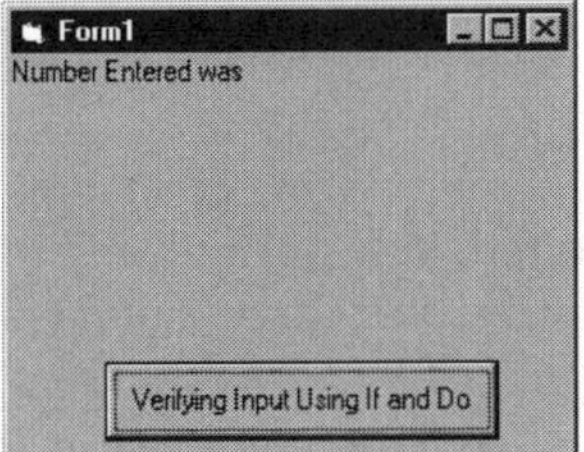

Figure 23.3
After choosing Cancel from the input box.

Example

Listing 23.3 adds onto the previous code by checking the return value from the input box. If that value is a blank string, it indicates that either the Cancel button was chosen or the OK button was pressed and no information was entered. This is one method for validating user input. Figure 23.4 shows the result of entering a 5 into the input box. Figure 23.5 demonstrates the result of canceling the input string.

Listing 23.3 23LIST03.TXT—Checking Return Value from Input Box

```
Private Sub Command1_Click()
Do
 Number = InputBox("Enter a number from 1 to 10", _
                   "Using the Do Until Loop")

 If Number = "" Then
    Exit Do
 End If

Loop Until Val(Number) >= 1 And Val(Number) <= 10

If Number = "" Then
    MsgBox "No Number Entered"
Else
    MsgBox "Number Entered was " & Number
End If

End Sub
```

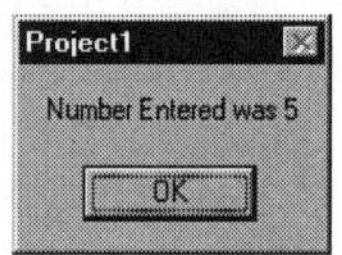

Figure 23.4

Showing a valid number entered.

Figure 23.5

Results of choosing Cancel from the input box.

By viewing the preceding code, you can see that the loop is exited whenever an empty string is returned from the call to `InputBox`. If an empty string is not returned, the condition is checked to see whether it is met. If it is not, the loop starts over again and a new input box is shown. If the condition is met, the loop exits.

After the `Loop` statement, the value of `Number` is tested. If it is an empty string, the loop is exited by the `Exit Do` statement, as shown in figure 23.5. If `Number` is not an empty string, you can assume that the value of the variable is from 1 to 10 and can print it. Entering a valid number will provide you with results similar to that shown in figure 23.4.

Now consider other ways to use a loop. If you have a section of code that needs to execute while a condition is true, you can use a `Do-While` loop. Until now, you have seen the use of the `Do-Until` loop. Both loops can be used interchangeably, but the subtle differences that are required in the conditional tests and execution are worth examining.

Example

The following code shows how you can use the `Do-While` loop:

```
Private Sub Command1_Click()
Number = 2
Do While Number < 1000
        Number = Number * 2
Loop
Form1.Print Number
End Sub
```

The output from this code is shown in figure 23.6. Notice how the variable went from 2 to 1024 before falling out of the loop and printing to the screen. The condition of the loop was to execute the loop as long as `Number` was under 1000. By making `Number` equal to `Number` times 2 for each iteration of the loop, you doubled the variable until it was greater than 1000 and then printed it to the form.

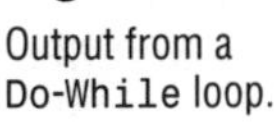

Figure 23.6

Output from a `Do-While` loop.

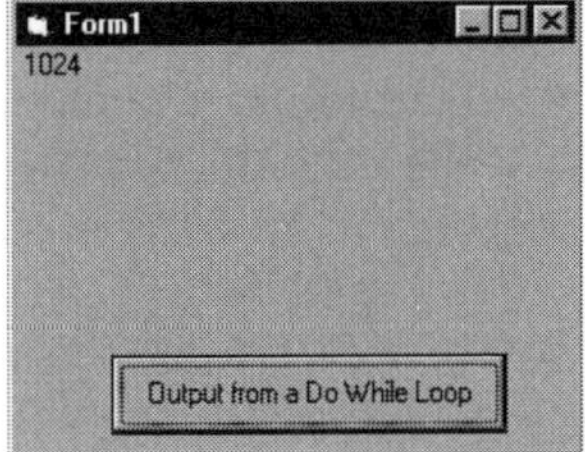

This type of loop can be useful for finding records that meet certain requirements. Suppose that you have a group of records to be processed. The records have in them an amount for total sales. You want to process all the records; however, an error condition that could cause your processing to fail is a record whose total sales figure is a negative amount. You could process the records in a `Do-While` loop and then fall out of the loop when an error occurred. The following example shows how this works:

```
.
.
.
Do While TotalSales > 0
' Process Records Here
Loop
.
.
.
```

You could take this a step further by processing all records from the first to the last, setting an error flag, and exiting the loop if a bad record is encountered. Look at this code to see how this might be done:

```
.
.
.
ErrorFlag = False
Do While RecordNumber < LastRecord
' Get the Record
if TotalSales < 0 Then
     ErrorFlag = True
     Exit Do
End If
' Process the Record
Loop
If ErrorFlag = True Then
' Process the error here
End If
.
.
.
```

As you can see, loops enable you to perform a repetitive process. Whatever processing you need to do, if you have to do it several times, you can place it in a loop and reduce the amount of code you have to write without reducing the functionality of your program.

Summary

In this chapter, you learned about `Do` loops, which perform some tasks repeatedly until a certain condition is met. When the condition is met, the loop ends and processing continues with the first line of code following the `Loop` statement.

`Do` loops can be exited with the `Exit Do` statement. `Exit Do` is useful for getting out of a loop when a condition other than that expressed by the `While` or `Until` statement requires you to end the loop. With the `Exit Do` statement, you can actually have a loop that exits on conditions other than those defined by the `Do` loop.

In Chapter 24, "The For Statement," you learn about another kind of loop: `For-Next`.

Review Questions

The answers to the review questions are in Appendix A.

1. What is the purpose of a loop?
2. What are the parts of the `Do-While` statement?
3. What line of code is executed after a loop exits?

4. How can you exit a `Do` loop other than by meeting the condition of the loop?

5. How many `Exit Do` statements can be inside a `Do` loop?

6. How many times will the following loop execute?

```
X = 1
Do
X = X + 2
Loop While X < 101
```

7. What is the difference between a `Do-While` loop and a `Do-Until` loop?

8. How many different expressions can be tested by a `Do` loop? What are the ways of testing the conditions inside a loop?

9. Does a loop have to perform a certain number of times before quitting? Can a loop never execute at all?

Review Exercises

1. Write a `Do` loop that prints the numbers 1 through 20 on a form. Print a line after the loop saying that the loop has finished.

2. Write a `Do` loop that counts down from 20 to 0 by 2s and prints out all the numbers on the form.

3. Write a `Do-While` loop that requests a user's name as input. If the correct name is not entered, stay in the loop until it is.

4. Add code to Exercise 3 that allows only three attempts at entering a correct name. If the correct name is not entered within three tries, show an error message box and exit the loop.

5. Create a `Do-While` loop that never gets executed. (*Hint:* If the condition is not true when the loop starts, it will end immediately.)

6. Create a `Do-Until` loop that checks for three different conditions: one that the `Until` statement checks and two others inside the loop. You can create these additional conditions using the `If` statement or the `Select-Case` statement. For a better understanding of conditional logic, use both the `If` and the `Select-Case` statements.

CHAPTER 24

The For Statement

In this chapter, you learn how to use the For loop. The For loop is an incremental loop, differing only slightly from the Do loop, which was explained in the preceding chapter.

For-Next Loop Syntax

The For-Next loop includes the incrementing of the loop counter as a part of the loop. Here is the syntax of the For-Next statement:

```
For Counter = Start To End [Step StepValue]
     [Statements]
     [Exit For]
     [Statements]
Next [Counter]
```

Look at the different elements that make up the For loop. The keyword For is the beginning of the statement. The variable Counter holds the current iteration number of the loop during execution. The Start value represents the starting value of Counter, and End represents when the loop should be exited. StepValue is the value that Counter should be incremented after each iteration of the loop. The loop ends with the Next statement. This statement checks the value of Counter; if it is less than End, StepValue is added to Counter, and the loop will repeat itself.

Another version of the For-Next loop is the For Each loop. The syntax for this statement follows:

```
For Each member In array or collection
     [statements]
     [Exit For]
     [statements]
Next [member]
```

The For Each loop does not use a counter variable; instead, it operates on an array or collection. The statements within the loop are carried out on each element of the array or collection. The counter variable that determines the number of times the loop executes is inferred by the size of the array or collection. If an array contains five elements, the loop will execute five times.

Example

Take a look at a simple For-Next loop to see how all these elements work. Listing 24.1 shows an example of a simple For-Next loop.

Listing 24.1 24LIST01.TXT—Example of Simple *For-Next* Loop

```
Private Sub Command1_Click()
For LoopCounter = 1 To 5 Step 1
    Form1.Print LoopCounter
Next LoopCounter
End Sub
```

The main difference between the For-Next loop and the Do-While loop is that, with For-Next, you can specify how the counter is to be incremented in the declaration of the loop, instead of having to increment a counter variable within the body of the loop.

Example

The preceding For loop could be written with Do-While syntax. Compare that example with Listing 24.2 to see just how these two loops vary.

Listing 24.2 24LIST02.TXT—*For Loop* Written With *Do-While* Syntax

```
Private Sub Command1_Click()
LoopCounter = 1
Do
    Form1.Print LoopCounter
    LoopCounter = LoopCounter + 1
Loop Until LoopCounter > 5
End Sub
```

As you can see by comparing these two loops, the For-Next loop enables you to declare the loop counter variable's starting value, the ending value of the loop, and the increment value of the counter variable. With a Do loop, all this work is not automatically done.

The Step Statement

The Step statement of the `For-Next` loop is optional and can be useful depending upon your needs. You do not have to define a step value when you write a `For` loop. If this value is not defined, the default value is 1, which means that all For-Next loops will increment by 1 unless otherwise instructed. To override this default behavior, the Step statement is used.

Example

Listing 24.3 demonstrates the use of a `For` loop to gather data from the user. Using a `For` loop for this task can present problems. Run the following code and enter a number that is not in the range of 1 to 10. The counter variable is automatically incremented, and the loop exits after five iterations, even if all the numbers entered were not valid. This loop should be written using a `Do` loop, but appears here to illustrate a point. `For-Next` loops should be used for repetitive tasks with distinct start and stop points.

Listing 24.3 24LIST03.TXT—Using *For Loop* to Gather User Data

```
Private Sub Command1_Click()
For Counter = 1 To 5
 Number = InputBox("Enter a number From 1 to 10", _
                   "Using the Do Until Loop")

 If Number = "" Then
    Exit For
 End If

If Number >= 1 And Number <= 10 Then
    Select Case Counter
    Case 1
       FirstNum = Number
    Case 2
       SecondNum = Number
    Case 3
       ThirdNum = Number
    Case 4
       FourthNum = Number
    Case 5
       FifthNum = Number
    End Select
 End If

Next Counter
```

continues

Listing 24.3 Continued

```
If Number = "" Then
    MsgBox "Cancel Selected"
Else
    Form1.Print "Numbers Entered = "
    Form1.Print FirstNum
    Form1.Print SecondNum
    Form1.Print ThirdNum
    Form1.Print FourthNum
    Form1.Print FifthNum
End If

End Sub
```

The output from the preceding example is shown in figures 24.1 and 24.2. In figure 24.1, five numbers in the proper range were entered. In figure 24.2, the second number entered was out of range, but the loop continued anyway. The continuation occurred because the counter was incremented automatically.

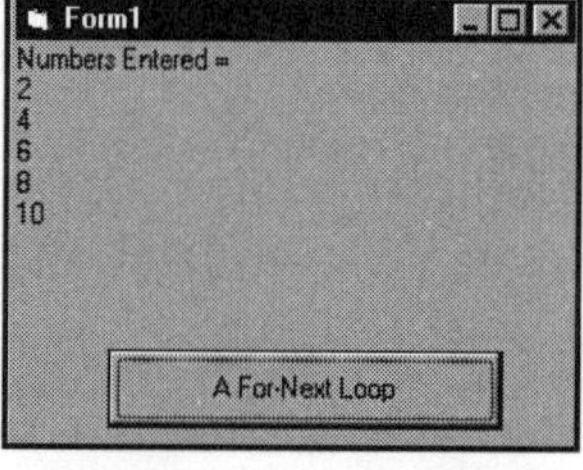

Figure 24.1
Output from a For-Next loop.

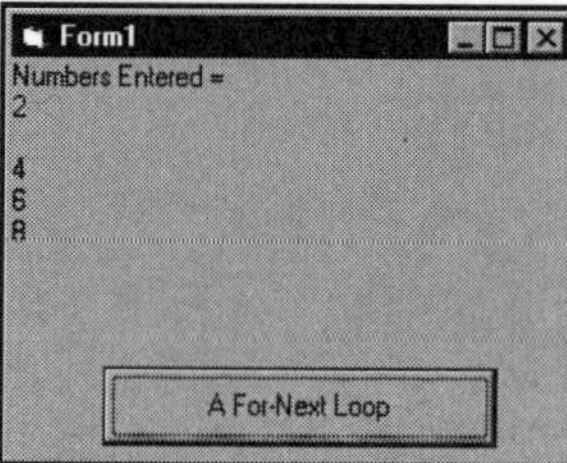

Figure 24.2
Output from a For-Next loop with incorrect data entered.

If you want to control just how the counter is incremented, you should use a `Do` loop. If you have an incremental loop that needs a starting point and an ending point, the `For` loop is probably the best choice.

You can override the default step value if you want. Maybe your loop needs to be incremented by 5 every time instead of by 1. If you wanted to print all the numbers from 1 to 50 by 5s, you could alter the step value of the `For` loop.

Example

Listing 24.4 shows you how to alter the step value.

Listing 24.4 24LIST04.TXT—Altering the Step Value

```
Private Sub Command1_Click()
For Counter = 0 To 50 Step 5
   Form1.Print Counter
Next Counter
End Sub
```

The output of this code is shown in figure 24.3. Notice that the counter variable is being printed. This use of the `For` loop is common. `For Each` loops are used extensively with arrays to increment through the indexes of an array. The use of `For` loops and arrays is discussed in detail in Chapter 26, "Arrays."

Figure 24.3 Output from a `For-Next` loop with a step value of 5.

Negative Increments of a *For-Next* Loop

`For` loops do not have to be incremented with a positive value. They can be decremented as well. If you specify a negative value for the step value, the counter will be decremented.

Example

Listing 24.5 shows how to decrement the counter in a `For` loop.

Listing 24.5 24LIST05.TXT—Decrementing the Counter in a *For Loop*

```
Private Sub Command1_Click()
For Counter = 10 To 1 Step -1
   Form1.Print Counter
Next Counter
End Sub
```

As you can see from the output in figure 24.4, `For` loops are versatile enough to be either incremented or decremented.

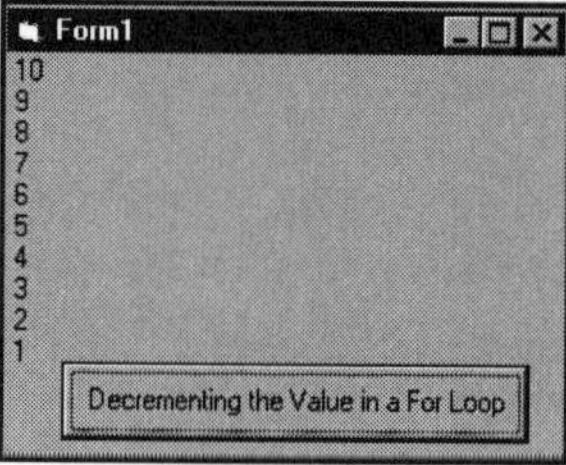

Figure 24.4
Decrementing the counter in a `For` loop.

The *Exit For* Statement

`For` loops can be exited before the counter is incremented to the end point. The use of the Exit For statement is optional. By using `Exit For`, you can instruct the loop to terminate and continue processing with the line of code that follows the `Next` statement.

Example

The `Exit For` statement is very similar to the `Exit Do` used to stop the execution of a `Do` loop. Listing 24.6 shows the use of the `Exit For` statement.

Listing 24.6 24LIST06.TXT—Using the *Exit For* Statement

```
Private Sub Command1_Click()
For Counter = 7 To 100 Step 7
   If Counter Mod 5 = 0 Then
      Form1.Print Counter & " Divided by 5 leaves a remainder of 0"
      Exit For
   End If
Next Counter
End Sub
```

The preceding example increments the counter variable from 7 to 100 by a step value of 7. The `Exit For` statement is called when the counter variable is evenly divisible by 5. Figure 24.5 shows that the counter was 35 when the program exited the `For` loop.

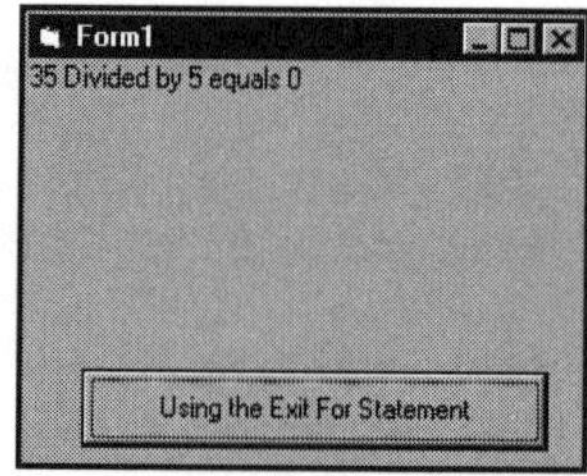

Figure 24.5
Using the `Exit-For` statement.

Nested *For* Loops

`For` loops can be nested. Nesting them can be helpful if you have several repetitive tasks that need to be done.

Example

Listing 24.7 shows how you could use a `For-Next` loop to increment through two different variables at the same time by nesting them.

Listing 24.7 24LIST07.TXT—Nesting a *For Loop*

```
Private Sub Command1_Click()
For X = 1 To 2
   Form1.Print "X  = " & X
   For Y = 1 To 5

    Form1.Print " Y = " & Y;
   Next Y
   Form1.Print ""
Next X
End Sub
```

The output from the preceding example is shown in figure 24.6. This example shows that the first loop, the `X` loop, executes once. The `Y` loop next executes 5 times. Then the `X` loop executes a second time, triggering the `Y` loop to run a second time. This nested loop is controlled by the outer loop. In other words, when the `X` loop's condition is met, the nested loop ends.

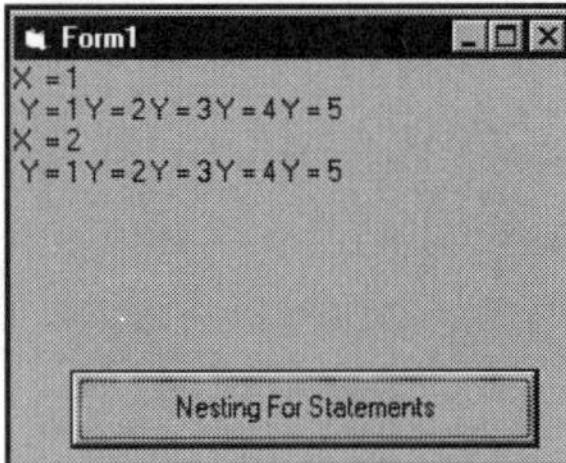

Figure 24.6
Nesting `For` loops.

`For` loops can be nested with as many layers as you want, although you will probably not need to go more than three layers deep. Nested `For` loops can be very useful when processing multidimensional arrays. These arrays are discussed in Chapter 26, "Arrays."

Chapter Summary

In this chapter, you learned about `For` loops. Similar to `Do` loops, `For` loops are used to perform repetitive tasks until the condition of the loop is met. `For` loops use a counter variable and a range in which to execute. They have a step value that indicates how the counter will be incremented. The step value can be either positive or negative, which causes the loop to increment or decrement, respectively.

You can exit `For` loops with the `Exit For` statement. This statement is useful for getting out of a loop when a condition other than that expressed by the counter, range, and step value requires you to end the loop. Using the `Exit For` statement, you can actually have a `For` loop that will exit on multiple conditions.

In Chapter 25, "Sub-Procedures and Functions," you learn how to create your own routines for performing tasks and returning values.

Review Questions

Answers to the review questions are in Appendix B.

1. What is the purpose of a `For` loop?
2. What are the parts of the `For-Next` statement?
3. Which parts of the `For-Next` statement are optional?

4. How can you exit a `For` loop other than meeting the conditions set by the counter, range, and step value?
5. How many `For` statements can you nest within each other?

6. If you have a loop that has a step value greater than the range, how many times will the loop execute? Note an example:

```
For X = 1 To 10 Step 10
   Form1.Print X
Next X
```

7. What is the difference between a `Do-While` loop and a `For` loop?
8. How many different expressions can be tested by a `For` loop? What are the ways of testing the conditions inside a loop?
9. Does a loop have to perform a certain number of times before quitting? Can a loop never execute at all?

Review Exercises

1. Write a `Do` loop that prints the numbers 1 through 10 on a form. Print a line after the loop indicating that the loop has finished.

2. Write a `For` loop that counts down from 20 to 0 by 2s and then prints out all the numbers on the form.

3. Write a `For` loop that requests a number as input and adds this number to the loop counter. What does adding the number do to the loop? How can adding or decrementing the counter variable affect the processing of the loop?

4. Change the code in Exercise 3 to show the value of the counter variable before and after the addition of the number takes place. Alter the code so that the rest of the numbers entered are added to the counter and the rest are subtracted from it.

5. Create a nested `For` loop that has two levels. The outer level should execute three times; the inner level, seven times. Print out a line when the counter variables are these:

   X = 1 and Y = 3

   X = 2 and Y = 7

   X = 3 and Y = 1

   Hint: You will need to use either an `If-ElseIf` or a `Select Case` statement within the inner loop.

6. Create a `For` loop that checks for two different conditions. The first is the range of the `For` loop; the second can be any condition you want. Use the `Exit-For` statement to terminate the loop when this condition is met. Have a variable that contains a value of True if the loop exited normally, and a False if the `Exit-Do` statement was executed. Use a `MsgBox` function to show how the loop exited.

CHAPTER 25

Sub-Procedures and Functions

In this chapter, you learn how to create and use your own sub-procedures and functions. Both sub-procedures and functions are commonly called procedures. They differ only slightly, and this chapter shows you the differences. You can create your own sub-procedures to perform any tasks you need. This chapter shows you how to write functions and sub-procedures, focusing on the subtle differences between them.

Sub-Procedures

One of the most common elements of a Visual Basic program is the sub-procedure. A *sub-procedure* is a procedure used to perform a certain task and return control to the program that called it. *Calling a sub-procedure* refers to transferring program control and execution to the sub-procedure. Suppose that you have a sub-procedure named `Sub1`. You want to print a line to the form, call the sub-procedure, and then print a second line to the form. An example of such a program is shown in the following example.

Example

Listing 25.1 is an example of a simple sub-procedure. When the `Command1_Click()` sub-procedure is called, it prints a line to the form, then transfers control to the `Sub1` sub-procedure. `Sub1` prints a line informing you where control is, then returns to the `Command1_Click` sub-procedure and program flow resumes on the line following the call to `Sub1`.

Listing 25.1 25LIST01.TXT—An Example of a Simple Sub-Procedure

```
Private Sub Command1_Click()
Form1.Print "Print First Line"
Sub1
Form1.Print "Print Second Line"
End Sub

Sub Sub1()
Form1.Print "Inside of Sub1"
End Sub
```

If you examine this code, you will actually see two different sub-procedures. The first is the default sub-procedure that is called when a button named `Command1` is pressed.

To better understand the use of sub-procedures, create a form with one button on it. Name the form `Form1` (the default) and name the button `Command1` (also the default). Double-click the button. You will be presented with a shell for the `Command1_Click()` sub-procedure. Enter the code as previously shown. Enter the code for the `Sub1()` sub-procedure below the `Command1_Click()` sub-procedure. You can now run this program.

When you run the program, you will see a standard form with your button on it. Click the button. You will see a result similar to that shown in figure 25.1. What exactly took place in the execution of this program?

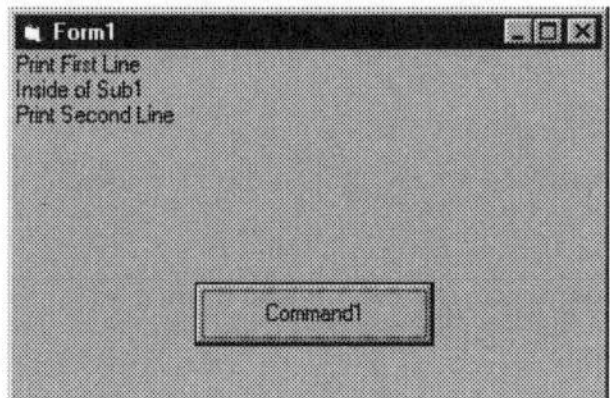

Figure 25.1

Using a sub-procedure.

Look closely at the program. When you clicked the button, the `Command1_Click()` sub-procedure was called by Visual Basic. This response to an event, such as the clicking of a mouse button, is the premise that Visual Basic uses to communicate between all of the objects available to a form. Each object in Visual Basic has its own predefined set of events to which it can respond. Your job is to insert code in these predefined sub-procedures to make them respond however you want.

This particular sub-procedure prints a line to the form, calls another sub-procedure, and then prints another line to the form. The third line in the code is just the name of the sub-procedure `Sub1`. By placing the name of a sub-procedure in another sub-procedure (or function), you cause control of the program to branch to the called sub-procedure, and execution continues until the program sees the `End Sub` statement. Control then reverts to the procedure that called the sub-procedure, and processing continues with the first line of code following the sub-procedure. This line of action created the output shown in figure 25.1.

The preceding example is very simple. You may ask why you couldn't just add another line to the code in the `Command1_Click()` sub-procedure to print out the extra line that was printed out by the `Sub1` sub-procedure, and eliminate the subroutine call to print the extra line. In this case, you could—and should. But for processing tasks that require quite a bit more code to accomplish, the use of sub-procedures makes your code much easier to understand and follow.

When creating sub-procedures, you should keep a couple of things in mind. First, try to group related tasks into one sub-procedure. For example, if you need to process a name and address, you should group these items together and process them in the same sub-procedure. Your program would be harder to understand and follow if you were to process the name in one sub-procedure and the address in another sub-procedure. Second, if you have a task that needs to be done repeatedly, place this code in a sub-procedure. That way, you can avoid typing the same set of instructions over and over.

> **Note:** Any code that you need to call from more than one location is a good candidate for its own sub-procedure or function.

Example

You can execute repetitive by just calling the sub-procedure when you need to process the code. For an example, take a look at Listing 25.2.

Listing 25.2 25LIST02.TXT—Calling the Sub-Procedure to Process the Code

```
Private Sub Command1_Click()

Get_Number

Form1.Print "Processing goes in here"

Get_Number

End Sub


Sub Get_Number()
Do
 Number = InputBox("Enter a number from 1 to 10", _
                    "Using the Do Until Loop")
```

continues

Listing 25.2 Continued

```
    If Number = "" Then
       Exit Do
    End If

   Loop Until Number >= 1 And Number <= 10

   If Number = "" Then
       MsgBox "No Number Entered"
   Else
       MsgBox "Number Entered was " & Number
   End If

   End Sub
```

This example shows how you can use a sub-procedure to isolate frequently used code into one central location so that it can be accessed by other procedures that need its functionality. One item is missing from the code in Listing 25.2. You have no way to pass information to the sub-procedure. How would the `Command1_Click()` procedure know what number was entered into the `Get_Number()` sub-procedure? This is where parameter passing comes into play.

Parameter Passing

You can write sub-procedures that accept different variables, called *parameters*. These values can be sent from the calling program to the called sub-procedure. The called sub-procedure can use parameters in several ways. The sub-procedure can use the parameters for calculation or for displaying them to the user, or the sub-procedure can modify the values so that the calling procedure knows what has happened in the sub-procedure. This explanation may sound like quite a mouthful, but it really is not. Look at the general syntax of a sub-procedure and its components:

```
Sub ProcedureName (Parameters)
     local variable and constant declarations
     Statements
End Sub
```

The structure of a sub-procedure provides the ability to pass values into a sub-procedure for that sub-procedure to use. They can modify these variables, and the variables may or may not be changed in the calling program depending on how the arguments are passed to the procedure. A variable can be passed by reference (`ByRef`) or by value (`ByValue`). Passing a parameter by reference means that you are providing the procedure with a reference to the calling procedures variable. If the variable is changed in the sub-procedure, that change will be reflected in the calling procedure. Passing a parameter by value provides the sub-procedure with a copy of the variable for its own use. Any changes made to a variable passed by value do not appear in the calling program.

Example

Listing 25.3 is an example of passing a parameter to a sub-procedure.

Listing 25.3 25LIST03.TXT—Passing a Parameter to a Sub-Procedure

```
Private Sub Command1_Click()

Dim number As Integer
number = 5
Get_Number number
Form1.Print "Number = " & number

End Sub

Sub Get_Number(ByVal number As Integer)
  number = number * 5
  Form1.Print "Number In Sub-procedure = " & number
End Sub
```

The output from this code is shown in figure 25.2. You may be surprised by the result. You might think that the newly calculated value of `Number` would be reflected in the calling program. This is not the case with sub-procedures when parameters are passed using the `ByVal` keyword. You can pass a variable into a sub-procedure, but even if the variable is changed within the sub-procedure, the sub-procedure changes only its copy of the variable. If you want to use a sub-procedure to change a variable, you will have to change the parameter modifier to `ByRef`.

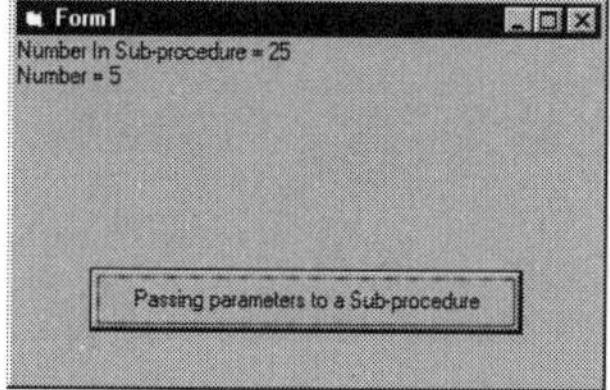

Figure 25.2

You can have the change made to a variable in a sub-procedure be reflected also in the calling program. For an example, see Listing 25.4.

Example

As mentioned earlier, variables passed as parameters to a sub-procedure by value are a copy for the sub-procedure to use. The sub-procedure can modify the variable but the change will only be seen by the sub-procedure. If you use variables passed by reference inside the sub-procedure and modify them, the changes can be seen by all other procedures that can see that variable (it is within the scope of the procedure) within the program. Variable scope is discussed in depth in Chapter 18, "Constants and Variables."

To use a variable by reference, you will have to add the `ByRef` keyword to the parameter definition of the sub-procedure (see Listing 25.4).

Listing 25.4 25LIST04.TXT—Adding ByRef Keyword to Parameter Definition of Sub-Procedure

```
Private Sub Command1_Click()
Dim Number As Integer
Number = 5

Get_Number Number
Form1.Print "Number = " & Number

Get_Number Number
Form1.Print "Number = " & Number

End Sub

Sub Get_Number(ByRef num As Integer)
  num = num * 5
  Form1.Print "Num In Sub-procedure = " & num
End Sub
```

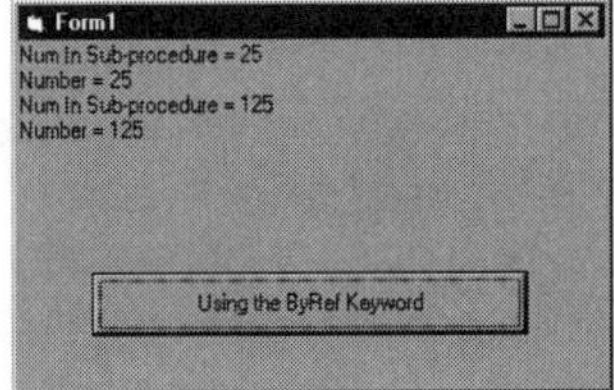

Figure 25.3

Using the `ByRef` keyword in a sub-procedure.

As you can see from figure 25.3, when a variable is used in a sub-procedure by value, all procedures that can see the variable will see the changes made to it within the sub-procedures that you write. If a variable is global, there is no need to pass the variable since all procedures can see the variable. While there may some need for global variables, their use can be dangerous since any procedure can change their values. When passing data to a procedure, try to use either the `ByVal` or `ByRef` keywords.

Passing parameters to a sub-procedure can be quite useful. For example, if you wanted a generic input routine that could be called from any number of places, you can create this sub-procedure and pass the prompt and title strings as parameters to the sub-procedure.

Example

Listing 25.5 shows how to pass strings to a generic sub-procedure.

Listing 25.5 25LIST05.TXT—Passing Strings to Generic Sub-Procedure

```
Private Sub Command1_Click()

Prompt_For_Input "Enter Your Name", "Name"
Call Prompt_For_Input("Enter Your Age", "Age")

End Sub

Sub Prompt_For_Input(Prompt, Title)

 Data = InputBox(Prompt, Title)
 MsgBox "Data Entered was " & Data

End Sub
```

The two separate input boxes created by this single sub-procedure are shown in figures 25.4 and 25.5.

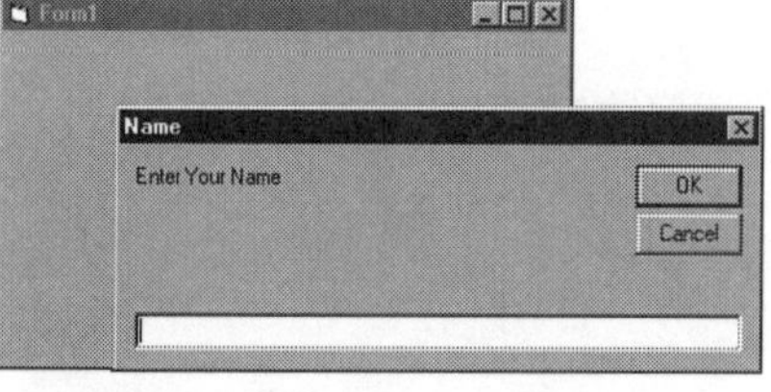

Figure 25.4

Calling a sub-procedure with a name prompt string.

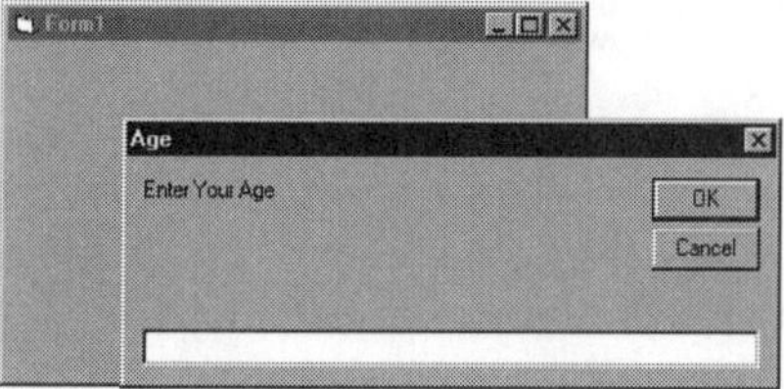

Figure 25.5

Calling the same sub-procedure with a prompt for the user's age.

If you look closely at the two different references to the `Prompt_For_Input` sub-procedure, you will notice that the first reference is made using no parentheses, whereas the second reference uses the `Call` statement and the parameters are enclosed in parentheses. You can use either of these formats to call a sub-procedure when passing parameters to it. Which one you use is purely a matter of preference.

The *Exit Sub* Statement

A sub-procedure can end before it encounters an `End Sub` statement. You can have a sub-procedure end early by including in it an `Exit Sub` statement. This statement functions much like the `Exit Do` and `Exit For` statements used to end a loop early. For a demonstration of the use of `Exit Sub`, see the following example.

Example

Listing 25.6 illustrates how you can use the `Exit Sub` statement to exit a sub-procedure before it has reached the `Exit Sub` statement.

Listing 25.6 25LIST06.TXT—Using Exit Sub to Exit Sub-Procedure Before it Reaches Exit Sub Statement

```
Private Sub Command1_Click()

Prompt_For_Input "Enter Your Name", "Name"
Call Prompt_For_Input("Enter Your Age", "Age")

End Sub


Sub Prompt_For_Input(Prompt, Title)

 Data = InputBox(Prompt, Title)
 If Data = "" Then
    MsgBox "Cancel Chosen"
    Exit Sub
 End If

 MsgBox "Data Entered was " & Data

End Sub
```

This code shows you how to check for a valid input. If no valid input is detected, the `Exit Sub` statement is called after a call is made to the function `MsgBox` to display the message shown in figure 25.6.

Figure 25.6
Using the `Exit Sub` statement to exit a sub-procedure.

Functions

A *function* is a specialized form of a sub-procedure. The only difference between a function and a sub-procedure is that a function can return a value. Both functions and sub-procedures can be passed variables, and they both accept the same types of arguments. A function can be called and a value can be returned that is not a modification to a parameter that has been passed in. The name of the function can be assigned a value in the function; if this is done, the function name will hold the return value. The syntax of a function is shown in the following code:

```
[Public ¦ Private] [Static] FunctionName [(arglist)] [As type]
     [statements]
     [FunctionName = expression]
     [Exit Function]
     [statements]
     [FunctionName = expression]
End Function
```

To return a value from a function, you assign the return value to the function name. Note the following example:

```
FuncName()
.
.
FuncName = 5
End Function
```

This code returns a value of 5 to the calling procedure. You could obtain this value with one of the following lines:

```
FunctionReturn = FuncName()

FunctionReturn = FuncName
```

If you do not have any parameters to be passed to the function, you don't need to include the parentheses. If you are passing any parameters to a function, you need to enclose them in parentheses, as shown here:

```
FunctionReturn = FuncName(Parm1, Parm2)
```

Example

You can use a function's return value a couple of ways. The return value can be assigned to a variable, as just shown, or the function call can be used in a statement. Both uses are shown in Listing 25.7.

Listing 25.7 25LIST07.TXT—Showing Both Uses of Return Value

```
Private Sub Command1_Click()

Ret = FuncName
Form1.Print "Return Value = " & Ret; ""

Form1.Print "FuncName = " & FuncName
End Sub

Function FuncName()

FuncName = 5

End Function
```

As you can see from this code, you can assign the return value of a function to another variable name; or you can use the function in the place where you want the return value to be used, such as in a print statement or a calculation. The output from this example is shown in figure 25.7.

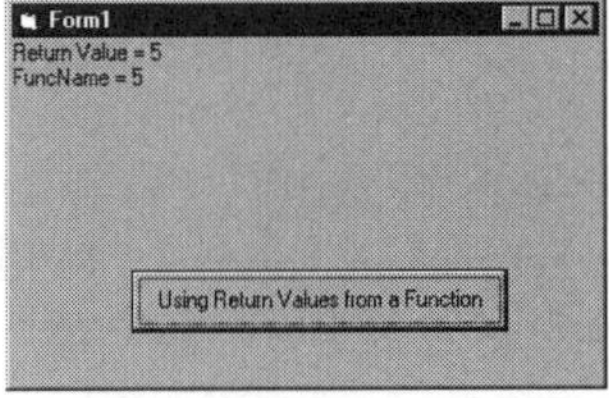

Figure 25.7
Using the return value of a function.

The syntax of a function is almost identical to that of a sub-procedure. A function contains an `End Function` statement; a sub-procedure uses an `End Sub` statement. The `Exit Sub` statement also has a counterpart, called an `Exit Function`, in a function. The purposes of `Exit Sub` and `Exit Function` are the same.

> **Caution:** Because a function returns a value in its name, its name will have a type. If it isn't set explicitly in the function declaration, it will have the default type (`Variant`, unless overridden by `Def[type]` statements). If you are expecting a function to return a specific type, then declare it with the `As Type` statement for the type you want to use.

The examples in this chapter illustrate the main differences between a sub-procedure and a function. Both are an integral part of programming in Visual Basic. You will use sub-procedures and functions extensively in your programs. Make sure that you become familiar with how to use them.

Summary

In this chapter, you learned about creating and using sub-procedures and functions. They are similar in their structure and execution, but there is one major difference: A function can return a value; a sub-procedure cannot.

You use functions and sub-procedures to isolate processing that is needed in more than one location, or by more than one control within an application. You can therefore avoid redundant coding, reduce code size, and eliminate potential errors from typing the same code more than once.

In Chapter 26, "Arrays," you learn about creating and using arrays of variables.

Review Questions

Answers to the review questions are in Appendix B.

1. What two types of procedures can you create to perform tasks in Visual Basic?
2. What are the different parts of a sub-procedure?
3. What are the different parts of a function?

4. How can you exit a sub-procedure before encountering the `End Sub` statement? How can you exit a function before encountering the `End Function` statement?
5. How many sub-procedures can you call from another sub-procedure?

6. What is the difference between a sub-procedure and a function?
7. What are the two different methods that you can use to call a sub-procedure? What are the differences between the two methods?
8. If *`sub-procedure1`* calls *`sub-procedure2`*, can *`sub-procedure2`* call *`sub-procedure3`*? How could you ensure that *`sub-procedure1`* would know the return value of *`sub-procedure3`* without using a module level or global variable?

Review Exercises

1. Write a sub-procedure containing a `For` loop that prints the numbers from 1 to 10. Call this sub-procedure from another procedure. Do not pass any parameters to the sub-procedure.
2. Modify the code in Exercise 1 to accept a parameter that will change the step value of the `For` loop. Pass in a 2, a 3, and a 5.

3. Write a function that accepts two parameters, both of them numeric. Return the sum of the numbers to the calling program. Modify the function to subtract the numbers and return the result. Then multiply both numbers and return the result. Finally, divide both numbers and return the result. Experiment with different numbers of parameters and different mathematical operations.

4. Write a sub-procedure that allows the calling program to know whether a value has been changed in the sub-procedure. Then use a function to perform the same task.

5. Make a function that prompts the user for a name and returns the name. Prompt for a password and return the password. Pass parameters to the function to change the message and title shown in the input box used within the function.

6. Create a series of four sub-procedures. Have each sub-procedure print a line on the form stating its number (`Sub1`, for example). Call the functions in this order: 1 calls 2, 2 calls 3, and 3 calls 4. After number 4 ends, what happens? In number 4, try adding a call to number 1. What happens when you do this?

Arrays

In this chapter you will learn about arrays. Arrays are a group of variables of the same type, all of which are referred to by a common name. Arrays can be used to hold related information without the need to have a large number of variables to hold them. For example, if you are building a program that performs income tax calculations, you need the program to know the tax rates for all 50 states. Depending on the application, you may also need the program to know the names of all 50 states. In either case, arrays are an efficient solution.

You could create 50 string variables for the states, and another 50 floating-point variables for the tax rates, but this would be almost impossible to program, let alone maintain. Instead you create an array of 50 strings and another of 50 floating-point variables, and you will only need to refer to the array and its subscript to obtain the correct variable. Don't worry about subscripts yet, for they are covered in the next section.

Simple Arrays

There are three different syntaxes for declaring an array. In this section you learn the simplest of these. Creating an array of a data type is almost the same as declaring a variable of the same data type. Below is the syntax for declaring an array of integers:

```
Dim ArrayVar(5) As Integer
```

You will notice that the only difference between declaring this array and declaring an integer variable is the set of parentheses containing the array size. The line above creates an array of five integers. These integers are stored one after the other in memory making it easy to access and treat them as one named variable with different subscripts to differentiate the different elements. Now that you have created a simple array, how do you use the individual components of the array? All arrays in Visual Basic begin with the zero element. This means that the first array variable is *ArrayVar(0)*, the second is *ArrayVar(1)*, etc.

Example—Beginner

Let's look at an example that illustrates this point. Listing 26.1 shows a simple array declared and used.

Listing 26.1 26LIST01.TXT—Simple Array Declared and Used

```
Private Sub Command1_Click()
Dim ArrayVar(5) As Integer

For X = 0 To 4
    ArrayVar(X) = X + 1
Next X

For X = 0 To 4
    Form1.Print "ArrayVar(" & X & " ) = " & ArrayVar(X)
Next X

End Sub
```

Listing 26.1 declares an array of 5 integers. The first `For...Next` loop places the values 1 through 5 in the array, the second `For...Next` Loop prints the values of the array on the form. `For...Next` Loops were covered in detail in Chapter 24. See the output of this program in Figure 26.1.

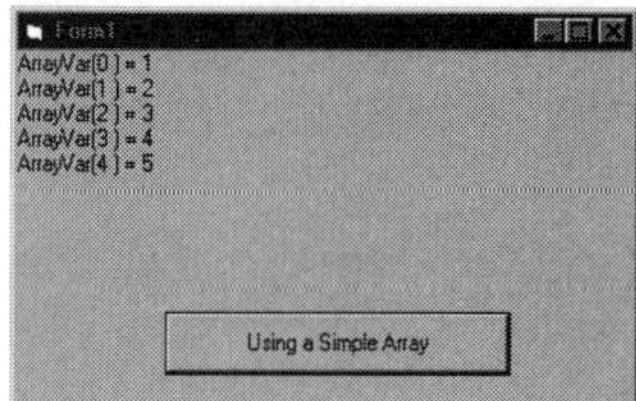

Figure 26.1 Using a simple array.

By looking at the output shown in figure 26.1, you can see that there is one variable called ArrayVar. It is an array of 5 integers, each one of these variables is distinguished from each other by the subscript of the array.

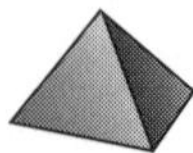

Tip: A *subscript* is the number used to refer to the location of a particular element within an array. If you want to reference the first element in an array called ArrayInt, you would use ArrayInt(0), The second element is ArrayInt(1), and so on.

Can you use arrays on different types of data? The answer is yes. If you wanted to create an array of all 50 states, you could declare an array as shown below.

```
Dim StateArray(50) As String
```

Now that you have an array of 50 strings, you can fill the array and use it in your program. For arrays that will probably be used by multiple subroutines, such as the state array above, you will probably want them to have module or global scope. This will allow all of your subroutines and functions to have access to the array.

Example—Beginner

Let's take a look at an example of using a string array. Listing 26.2 shows how to use a string array.

Listing 26.2 26LIST02.TXT—Using a String Array

```
Private Sub Command1_Click()
Dim CatArray(5) As String

CatArray(0) = "K.C."
CatArray(1) = "Sammy"
CatArray(2) = "Patches"
CatArray(3) = "Stik"
CatArray(4) = "Spaz"

For X = 0 To 4
    Form1.Print "CatArray(" & X & " ) = " & CatArray(X)
Next X

End Sub
```

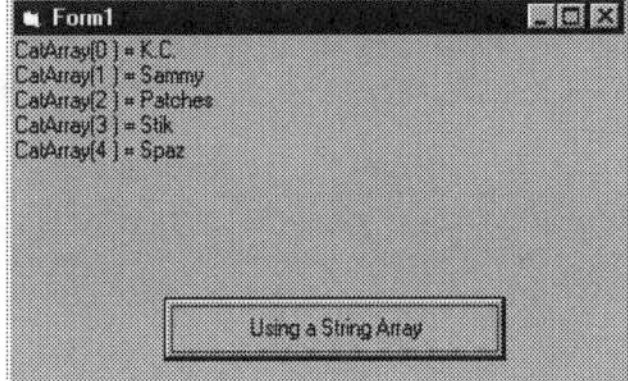

Figure 26.2
Using a string array.

As you can see from the code in the previous example, an array of 5 strings is dimensioned. This array is then filled with values. These values are then printed to the form using a `For...Next` loop.

Remember that all of the elements of an array are referenced by their subscripts. Array subscripts are the number of the array variable. Arrays begin with element 0, by default. This behavior may or may not be what you would like. You may want, for example, to begin your array with element 1 instead of 0. This can be accomplished by using the `Option Base` statement or by specifying the array elements you want. The `Option Base` statement is covered in detail in the following section.

Option Base

The base of an array is the first element of the array. Or in other words, the number that an array starts at. By default Visual Basic begins all arrays at zero. This may not be the number you'd like to start with. If you want the array to begin with the number 1, you can, of course, make your array 1 element larger than you need, and only use the array beginning at subscript 1. This method will waste the memory space of one element. This may not be a large waste, but you should learn early to practice the most efficient methods for all of your programming tasks, and arrays are no exception.

So, if you don't want to waste an array element in order to begin the array at 1 instead of 0, what do you do? Visual Basic provides the `Option Base` statement to allow you to begin your arrays at 1.

The syntax for the `Option Base` statement is as follows:

```
Option Base {0¦1}
```

The only valid values for the `Option Base` are either 0 or 1. Any other value will create an error.

Since 0 is the default base for all arrays, you do not need to use the `Option Base` statement if you are planning to use this default. If you want to change it, you need to include the `Option Base` statement in your module before any array declarations are made.

Example—Intermediate

Listing 26.3 uses the same `Integer` array example shown earlier and adds the `Option Base` statement to change the base of the array from 0 (the default) to 1.

Listing 26.3 26LIST03.TXT—Adding the Option Base Statement

```
' Placed on the Code page of the project
Option Base 1

Private Sub Command1_Click()
Dim ArrayVar(5) As Integer

For X = 1 To 5
    ArrayVar(X) = X
Next X

For X = 1 To 5
    Form1.Print "ArrayVar(" & X & " ) = " & ArrayVar(X)
Next X

End Sub
```

If you compare the code shown above with the earlier version of the integer array, you will see that there are a few differences. The array above begins with element 1, instead of 0. This allows the `For...Next` loops that process the array, to begin with 1 and end with 5. This makes the array more intuitive. If you have an array of 5 elements using `Option Base 1`, then the last element in the array is element 5 and not 4. The output from the above example is shown in figure 26.3. Notice how the subscripts and the values of the integers are the same; this is caused by using the `Option Base` statement.

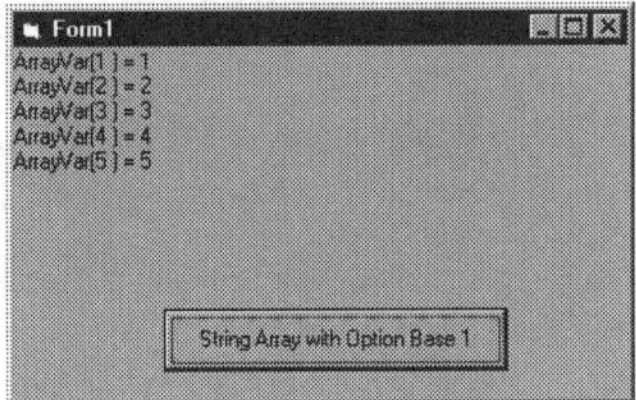

Figure 26.3
Using a simple array with `Option Base 1`.

You are not limited to only having 0 or 1 for the starting point of your arrays. You can specify any values that you want to, as shown in the following section.

Specifying an Array Range

What do you do if you want to create an array that doesn't start with 0 or 1? You can accomplish this by simply specifying the range that you want when you dimension the array. For example, if you wanted to have an array that went from 75 to 100, you would dimension the array as follows:

```
Dim MyArray(75 To 100)
```

This would create an array of 25 elements with a valid subscript range of 75 to 100. You can also use negative numbers in your arrays. The following code is also valid:

```
Dim MyArray(-1000 To 1000)
```

The preceding example would create an array whose range is from -1000 to 1000.

There are other ways to explicitly change the starting element of an array, as explained in the following section.

Complex Arrays

A simple array is one that declares a single array. You can create multiple arrays with one Dim statement if you need to. The method for doing this brings us to the second type of array definition. The second syntax for array declarations is as follows:

```
Dim ArrayVar([ArraySize])[,ArrayVar2([Array2Size])
    ..Array60Var([Array60Size]) [ As Type ]
```

It is important to note that only the last array declared in this fashion will have the `[As Type]` applied to it. All other arrays will be created with the default data type, which is a `Variant`. Be careful when using this type of declaration to ensure that you create arrays of the data types you want.

This method for declaring arrays can be helpful if you need to declare multiple arrays of the same type. For example, look at the following code. This example declares 2 `Variant` arrays and 1 `Integer` array.

```
Sub Command1_Click
Dim ArVar1(5) As Variant
Dim ArVar2(10) As Variant
Dim ArVar3(20) As Integer
.
.

End Sub
```

The code sample shown above declares 3 different array variables. The first 2 are the same type. You could declare the first 2 as shown below and save your self a bit of typing. The declarations shown in both examples are identical in function.

```
Sub Command1_Click
Dim ArVar1(5), ArVar2(10)
 Dim ArVar3(20) As Integer
.
.

End Sub
```

The code in the example above illustrates the second form of declaring variables. Up to 60 variables can be declared at one time using one `Dim` statement. You will probably not declare this many arrays using one statement, but if you need to, Visual Basic provides you with the means to do so. When you do use this method, be careful. You must use the `As Type` qualifier on every array declaration that you want to be any other data type than `Variant`.

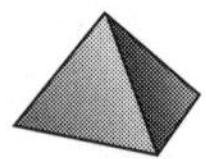

Tip: The range of an array is the numeric bounds of the array. If an array starts at 0 and goes to 200, this is the inclusive range of the array. Elements –1 and 201 are out of bounds, or non-existent, to this array.

Array variables do not have to begin with either a 0 or 1. You can use the `To` keyword to force an array to begin and end with any numbers you desire. The syntax for doing this is shown below:

```
Dim ArrayVar(FromInt To EndInt)
```

This syntax can be used with any of the array definitions, from the simplest to the most complex. If, for example, you wanted to have an array begin with the number 200 and end with the number 205, you could do that simply by specifying the starting and ending numbers for the array.

Example—Intermediate

Listing 26.4 shows how you specify a range for an array.

Listing 26.4 26LIST04.TXT—Specifying Range for an Array

```
Private Sub Command1_Click()
Dim ArrayVar(200 To 205) As Integer

For X = 200 To 205
    ArrayVar(X) = X
Next X

For X = 200 To 205
    Form1.Print "ArrayVar(" & X & " ) = " & ArrayVar(X)
Next X

End Sub
```

The output from this example is shown in figure 26.4. You can use this method if you need to create an array that does not begin with either 0 or 1.

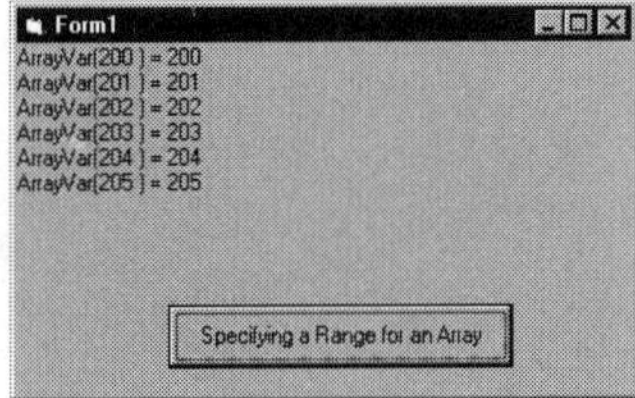

Figure 26.4
Declaring a range for an array.

The range of an array is the only valid set of values that can be used to reference the array. If you attempt to access an array beyond the bounds of the array, you will generate a `Subscript out of range` error.

Example—Intermediate

Listing 26.5 provides an illustration of an attempt to access an out-of-range subscript.

Listing 26.5 26LIST05.TXT—Accessing Out-of-Range Subscript

```
Option Base 1

Private Sub Command1_Click()
Dim ArrayVar(5) As Integer

For X = 0 To 5
    ArrayVar(X) = X
Next X

For X = 0 To 5
    Form1.Print "ArrayVar(" & X & " ) = " & ArrayVar(X)
Next X

End Sub
```

Attempt to run the example program shown above. What do you expect to happen? Look at the output shown in figure 26.5. The code in the above example makes an attempt to access the zero element of a 5 element array whose valid range is 1 to 5. This range was set by the `Option Base` 1 statement. Attempting to access a nonexistent element of an array generates a `Subscript out of range` error.

Figure 26.5

Attempting to access an out-of-range subscript.

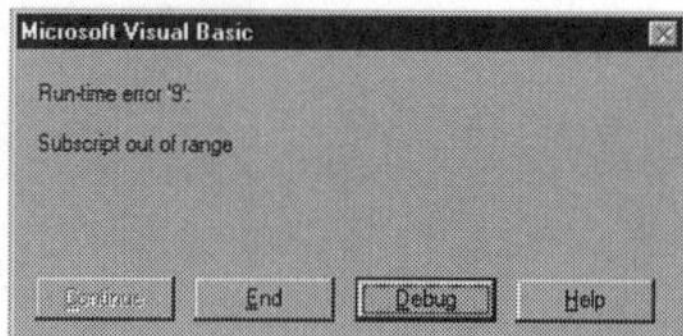

Visual Basic provides you with functions that allow you to query the range of an array. These are the `LBound` and `UBound` functions. The next section covers these two functions in detail.

LBound and UBound

The bounds of an array have two limits. The lower and upper bounds. These refer to the range of an array. An array that has 5 elements from 0 to 4, would have a lower bound of 0 and an upper bound of 4.

Visual Basic provides two functions that will allow you to test the upper and lower bounds of an array before you attempt to access the array and avoid generating an out of range subscript error.

The syntax for the `LBound` and `UBound` functions is as follows:

```
LBound (ArrayName, Dimension)
UBound (ArrayName, Dimension)
```

Using either of these functions is very simple. See the following example:

```
Result = UBound(ArrName,1)
```

This syntax can also be shortened to the following:

```
Result = UBound(ArrName)
```

If you are dealing with a single dimensional array, you can omit the dimension parameter. This is the preferred method for coding when dealing with a single dimensional array.

Result will contain the largest subscript available in the array `ArrName`. The second parameter refers to the dimension of the array that you wish to check for the range. All arrays that we have seen so far in this chapter have been single dimensional arrays. The next section covers arrays of more than one dimension. For all single dimensional arrays, the dimension parameter can be eliminated or a value of 1 can be used.

Let's take a look at an example of how you might use the `Ubound` function to prevent the out-of-range error from occurring.

Example—Advanced

The code that illustrates how to use `Ubound` to prevent out-of-range errors is shown in Listing 26.6.

Listing 26.6 26LIST06.TXT—Using Ubound to Prevent Out-of-Range Errors

```
Option Base 1

Private Sub Command1_Click()
Dim ArrayVar(5) As Integer

For X = 1 To 6
    Result = UBound(ArrayVar, 1)
    If (X <= Result) Then
       ArrayVar(X) = X
    Else
    MsgBox "Attempt to Access an Out Of Range Subscript." &
    ➥" Subscript attempted = " & X & _
           " and is greater than UBound Result of "
           ➥& Result
    End If
Next X
```

continues

Listing 26.6 Continued

```
For X = 1 To 6
    Result = UBound(ArrayVar, 1)
    If (X <= Result) Then
       Form1.Print "ArrayVar(" & X & " ) = " & ArrayVar(X)
    Else
    MsgBox "Attempt to Access an Out Of Range Subscript." &
    ➥" Subscript attempted = " & X & _
           " and is greater than UBound Result of "
           ➥& Result
    End If

Next X

End Sub
```

The code shown above uses the `UBound` function to check the upper array bounds before attempting to write and access the array element. This prevents the generation of the run-time error of `Subscript out of range`. The output from this program is shown in figure 26.6.

When the loop counter X exceeds the upper bound of the array returned by the `UBound` function, the message box shown in the example above is presented. You can use the `UBound` and `LBound` functions to insure that you are within the range of the array prior to attempting access to the array.

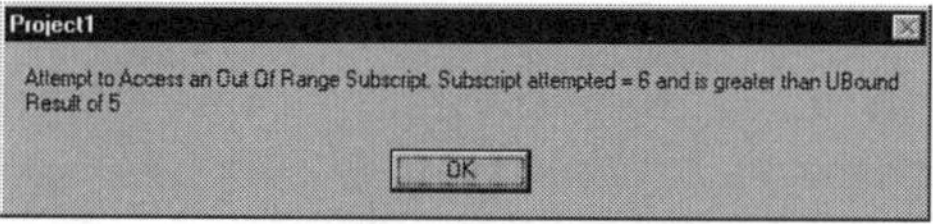

Figure 26.6
Using `Ubound` to prevent access to an out-of-range subscript.

The `Lbound` and `Ubound` functions act exactly the same and can be used to determine the upper and lower range of an array prior to accessing the array element.

Multi-Dimensional Arrays

So far in this chapter you have used single dimensional arrays. Arrays are not limited to only this single dimension. You can dimension an array so that it is multi-dimensional.

An array that is single dimensional can be considered to be just a column of data. By adding another dimension to an array, you can have columns and rows of data. For example, the pieces on a chess board are an 8x8 square. If you dimension an array of 8 integers, you have one of the 8 columns of data. You would need 8 different column arrays if you could not create a multi-dimensional array. Let's look at an example of a two-dimensional array that creates a 2x4 array.

Example—Intermediate

The following example shows the creation, initialization and use of a 2x4 array.

Listing 26.7 26LIST07.TXT—Creating, Initializing, and Using a 2x4 Array

```
Option Base 1

Private Sub Command1_Click()
Dim ArrayVar(2, 4) As Integer

For X = 1 To 2
    For Y = 1 To 4
        ArrayVar(X, Y) = X * Y
    Next Y
Next X

For X = 1 To 2
    For Y = 1 To 4
            Form1.Print "ArrayVar(" & X & "," & Y _
            & ") = " & ArrayVar(X, Y)
    Next Y
Next X

End Sub
```

The code shown in the example above illustrates the use of a two dimensional array. The nested `For...Next` loops are ideal for accessing a multidimensional array. The output from this example is shown in figure 26.7.

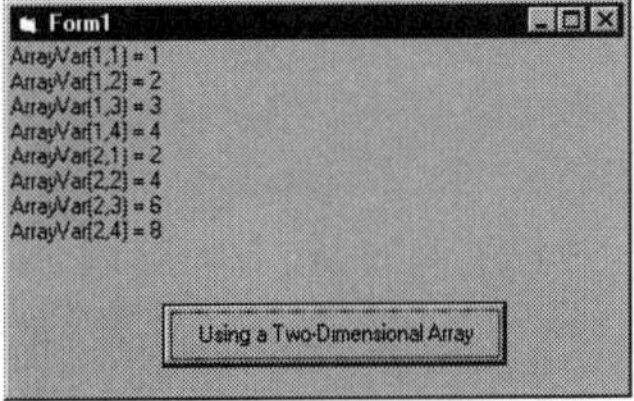

Figure 26.7
Using a two-dimensional array.

Arrays can contain more than two dimensions. Say, for example, you wanted to track the statistics for the football league. You could create one multidimensional array that tracks the statistics for one team, then turn this array into an array that encompasses all teams. Let's look at a simple example.

Example—Advanced

Listing 26.8 shows the creation of a three-dimensional array. This array consists of the same 2x4 array created in the above example, but adds a third dimension that creates two of the original 2x4 arrays.

Listing 26.8 26LIST08.TXT—Creating a Three-Dimensional Array

```
Option Base 1

Private Sub Command1_Click()
Dim ArrayVar(2, 4, 2) As Integer
Counter = 0

For X = 1 To 2
    For Y = 1 To 4
        For Z = 1 To 2
          Counter = Counter + 1
          ArrayVar(X, Y, Z) = Counter
        Next Z
    Next Y
Next X

For X = 1 To 2
    For Y = 1 To 4
       For Z = 1 To 2
          Form1.Print "ArrayVar(" & X & "," & Y &
     [ccc]"," & Z & ") = " & ArrayVar(X, Y, Z)
        Next Z
    Next Y

Next X

End Sub
```

The example shown above creates an array with 2 columns, 4 rows and 2 instances of this 2x4 array. This third dimension can be useful for tracking the other elements of the array. The output from the example program listed above is shown in figure 26.8. A counter variable is used to increment the value that is placed in each element of the array. Each element of the array contains numbers from 1 to 16.

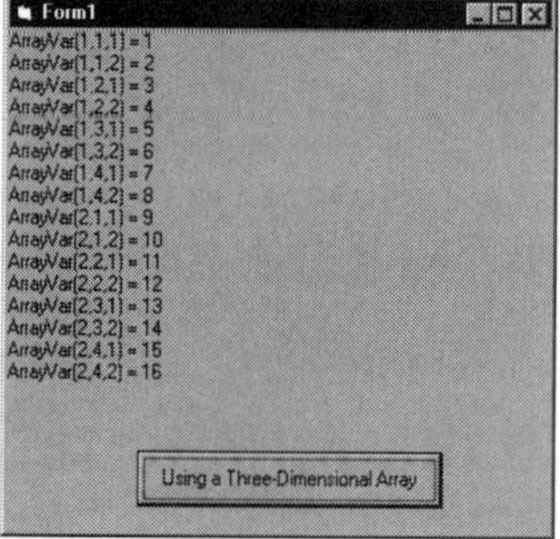

Figure 26.8
Using a three-dimensional array.

The *Array* Function

Visual Basic provides an easy method to create and load an array all in one step. This function will return a `Variant` that contains an array. The `Array` statement is new to Visual Basic 4. The syntax for the `Array` statement is as follows:

```
Array(ArgList)
```

`ArgList` is the listing of the elements that you want to be loaded into the array.

Example—Intermediate

An example of using the `Array` function is shown in Listing 26.9.

Listing 26.9 26LIST09.TXT—Using the Array Function

```
Option Base 1

Private Sub Command1_Click()
Dim ArrayVar As Variant

ArrayVar = Array(5,10,15,20,25)

For X = 1 To 5
    Form1.Print "ArrayVar(" & X & " ) = " & ArrayVar(X)
Next X

End Sub
```

If you run the previous example, you will see results similar to those shown in figure 26.9. Make note that the only valid base range values for the `Array` function are either 0 or 1 (as specified by the `Option Base` statement).

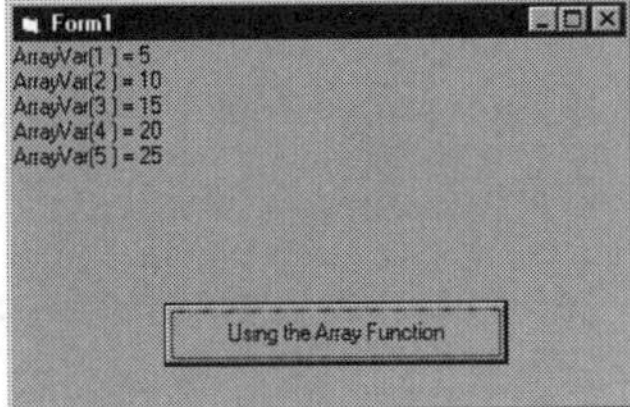

Figure 26.9
Using the `Array` function.

This can be a useful method for creating a `Variant` array. You may not want to use this method for creating large arrays; using loops for loading and using larger arrays is usually much more efficient.

Summary

In this chapter you learned about creating and using arrays. Arrays can be very useful for maintaining a single variable name that has access to multiple instances of a certain type of variable. You can create multidimensional arrays that give you a row-and-column style array.

By creating a three-dimensional array, you can create an array of arrays. There are functions, `Lbound` and `Ubound`, that allow you to test the lower and upper bounds of an array. They return the lower and upper limits for the range of a particular element in an array.

There are many facets to creating and using arrays. For more advanced information on arrays, including static and dynamic arrays and the use of the `ReDim` statement, please see *Special Edition Using Visual Basic 4* by Que.

In Chapter 27, "User-Defined Types," you will learn how to create your own variable types. These can be useful when you need more than one type of element to represent the data that you wish to use.

Review Questions

Answers to the Review Questions are in Appendix B.

1. What is an array?
2. Why would you use an array to hold the 50 different states rather than using different variables for each state?
3. What is the range of an array?

4. What is a two-dimensional array?
5. What statement is best suited for accessing an array?
6. How many arrays can be declared with one `Dim` statement?

7. Attempting to access subscript 15 in an array that has 10 elements will generate what type of error?
8. What are the two different functions that return the lower and upper bounds of an array?
9. What can arrays be used for? Can you have an array that contains integers and strings?

Review Exercises

1. Create an array large enough to hold 25 numbers. Initialize the array with the values 26 through 50 and loop through the array and print them to the form.

2. Modify the code in Exercise 1 to present the user with a message box asking for the direction to cycle through the loop. Cycle through the array based on the user's response and print from the lower-to-upper or upper-to-lower bound based on the user's input.

3. Write a two-dimensional array that will hold the batting averages for a baseball team of 15 players. Use an input box to fill the array. Calculate the average for all players on the team, and present this calculation in a message box.

4. Modify the program shown in Exercise 3 to include a second team of 15 players. *Hint:* You will have to create a three-dimensional array to do this.

5. Create an array of 20 integers. Use the `UBound` and `LBound` functions to ensure that you cannot exceed the upper or lower bounds of the array as you will the array. Try to load a value into the 25th and –5th element of the array. Make a message box appear stating which end (upper or lower) of the bounds for the array was violated.

6. Create a series of two arrays. Make them identical (except for the names of course). They can be of any type and size you choose. Fill them and display the values of each on the form. Save and/or print your code. Now take the two arrays and make them into one array. Perform the same processing on them as before. Compare the code from both attempts. How did the processing of two arrays compare to that of one three-dimensional array?

CHAPTER 27

User-Defined Types

In this chapter, you will learn how to create and use user-defined types. You have learned about variables and arrays in this book. In this chapter you will learn how to create your own data types consisting of multiple variable types. These user-defined types are referred to as *structures*, or sometimes *records*. For the sake of this chapter, I will refer to them as structures.

> **Note:** User-defined data types can also be called user-defined structures. This chapter will refer to them as structures.

If you wanted to create a program that would allow you to maintain an address book for all of your contacts, you could use individual variables for each field you needed. For example, you could use a string called Fname for the first name, a string called Lname for the last name, and so on. This would work; however, it may become cumbersome when you have a large number of contacts that you want to monitor. It would be much simpler to have a structure that contained all of this information that you could treat as one entity. In this chapter, you will learn how to create this structure.

Simple Structures

A user-defined structure is one that contains other existing data types grouped together to form a new data type. This grouping is referred to as a *composite declaration*. The new data type created is a composite of other pre-existing data types.

Note: A user-defined structure is composed of pre-existing data types. These can be data types integral to Visual Basic, or user-defined types.

The statement used for creating your own structures is the `Type` statement. The syntax of the `Type` statement is shown below.

```
Type TypeName
     VarName1[(ArraySize)] As ExistingType [* StringLength]
     VarName2[(ArraySize)] As ExistingType [* StringLength]
     .
     .
End Type
```

By looking at the syntax of the `Type` statement, you will notice that following the `Type` keyword is the name of the structure that you want to create. This can be any word that is not a reserved word, keyword, or a declared variable name. If you have declared a variable named *Client*, you will not be able to name a structure *Client*.

All user-defined types must be declared at the module level. It is invalid to declare them inside procedures. All user-defined types are public, by default. You can declare a type in a form, but this declaration must be Private, and this type will be private to the form.

Example

Let's look at an example of a simple user-defined structure. Open a new project. Add a module to the project. Type the code shown in Listing 27.1 onto the module page.

Listing 27.1 27LIST01.TXT—User-Defined Structure

```
' Module Page of the Project
Type UserType
    FName As String
    LName As String
End Type
Public Names As UserType
```

In the code shown above, you created a structure called *UserType*. It contains two strings, *Fname* and *Lname*. You also created a variable called *Names* that is of the type *UserType*.

You should now have a screen similar to that of figure 27.1

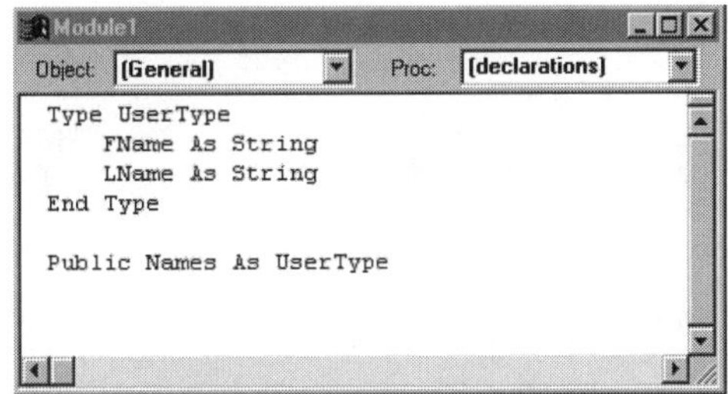

Figure 27.1
Declaring a user-defined type in a module

Close the module. You can do this by double clicking on the system menu. Add a button to the form as shown in figure 27.2.

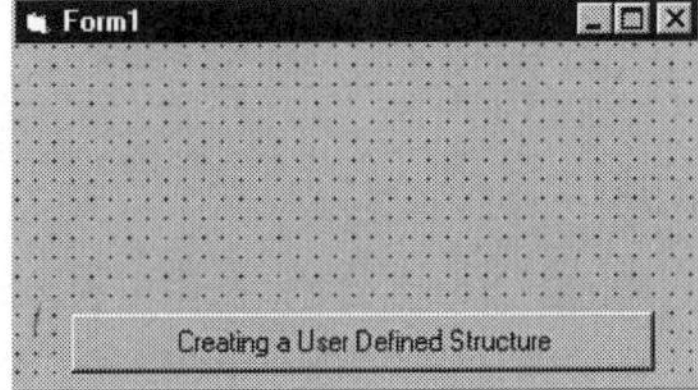

Figure 27.2
Add a button to the form.

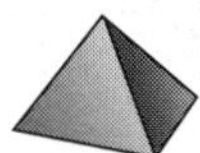

Tip: A user-defined type consists of data elements that can be of the same or different types grouped under one common name. These individual pieces of data are called members of the structure. To access the individual members, use the structure name, a period, then the member name. For example:

```
Structure.Member
```

Example

Double-click on this new button, and add more code from Listing 27.1 to the `Command1_Click` subroutine. Notice how you are referencing the parts of the structure you just created.

Listing 27.1 27LIST01.TXT—User-Defined Structure

```
Private Sub Command1_Click()

Names.FName = "John"
Names.LName = "Doe"
```

continues

Listing 27.1 Continued

```
Form1.Print "First Name = " & Names.FName
Form1.Print "Last Name  = " & Names.LName

End Sub
```

Run the program you have just created. You will see output similar to that of figure 27.3

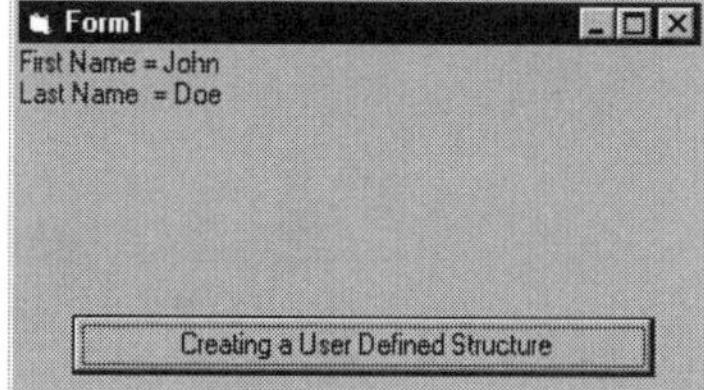

Figure 27.3
Output using a user-defined structure.

You can limit the size of string variables used in a structure by adding the * *StringSize* statement to the declaration after the *As String* type statement. This sets the absolute length of the string to *StringSize*. This is usually required when you are going to be randomly reading and writing your structures to a file. This is due to the fact that a fixed string length is needed to ensure that each record written to the file is of the same size.

Example

Let's change the previous example to make the string sizes constant. Bring up the module from the example you created earlier and change it to the code shown in Listing 27.2.

Listing 27.2 27LIST02.TXT—Making String Sizes Constant

```
' Module Page of the Project
Type UserType
    FName As String * 5
    LName As String * 25
End Type
Public Names As UserType
```

Example

If you run the program again, your results will be exactly the same. Why? The names placed into the structure did not extend past the string length maximum set in the structure definition. Change the code for the `Command1_Click` subroutine to that shown in Listing 27.2.

Listing 27.2 27LIST02.TXT—Exceeding Maximum Length of Structure Member

```
Private Sub Command1_Click()

Names.FName = "Jonathan"
Names.LName = "Doe"

Form1.Print "First Name = " & Names.FName
Form1.Print "Last Name  = " & Names.LName

End Sub
```

Run the program. What happened? You should have results similar to those shown in figure 27.4. Only the first five characters of the name Jonathan were loaded into the structure. This is because the absolute length of the variable was set to 5. All other characters were discarded. Setting the absolute length of a string can be a very valuable tool, but remember to leave enough room for the longest string that you anticipate your structure to need.

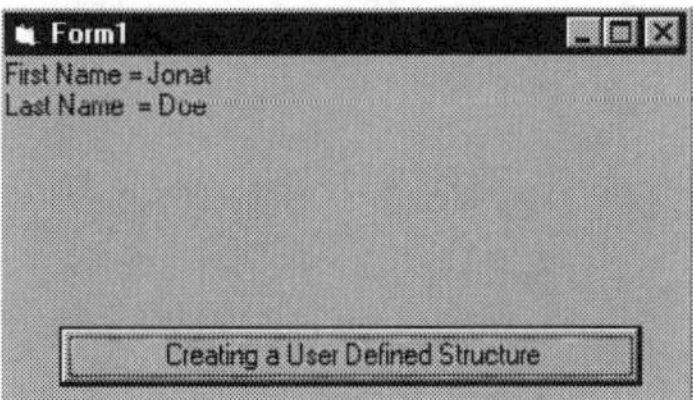

Figure 27.4
Exceeding the absolute length of a structure member.

You now have a basic knowledge of how user-defined structures work. You can group multiple variables into one structure and access them through the new structure. This can be very useful when reading and writing data to a file, as you will see in Chapter 28, "Files and I/O." Let's look at several more complex structure definitions and uses.

Structures within Structures

You have seen how to create a structure, but what if you want to include a structure that you created in another structure? This is accomplished by declaring the structure you want included prior to the structure you want to include it in.

Example

Both instances of Listing 27.3 show an example of how to declare the structure you want included before defining the structure you want to include it in. This example modifies the code from the previous examples to incorporate a structure within a structure.

Listing 27.3 27LIST03.TXT—Entered in Code Module

```
' Entered into the Code Module
Type Address
     Street As String
     City As String
     Zip As String
End Type

Type UserType
    FName As String * 10
    LName As String * 25
    Addr As Address
End Type

Public Names As UserType
```

Listing 27.3 27LIST03.TXT—Entered into the Command1_Click Event

```
'Entered into the Command1_Click Event
Private Sub Command1_Click()

Names.FName = "Jonathan"
Names.LName = "Doe"
Names.Addr.Street = "AnyStreet"
Names.Addr.City = "AnyTown"
Names.Addr.Zip = "00000-00000"

Form1.Print "First Name = " & Names.FName
Form1.Print "Last Name  = " & Names.LName
Form1.Print "Street     = " & Names.Addr.Street
Form1.Print "City       = " & Names.Addr.City
Form1.Print "Zip        = " & Names.Addr.Zip

End Sub
```

Enter the code shown in the above example and run the program. You should see results similar to those of figure 27.5.

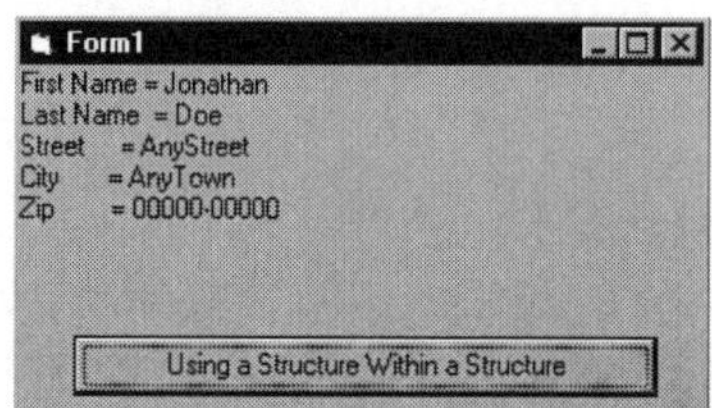

Figure 27.5
Using a structure within a structure.

As you can see from the code example above, the Names structure contains another user-defined structure, Addr. To access the Addr structure, you use the same method as accessing any other structure member, you use the structure name, a period, and then the member name.

The main point to remember with nested structures is that you will have to use the first structure name, a period, the second structure name, a period, then the member you wish to access. This is shown in Command1_Click subroutine in the example on the previous page. Notice the following line:

```
Names.Addr.Street = "AnyStreet"
```

This line is accessing the Names structure, of which the Addr structure is a member. Street is a member of the Addr structure. This is how you can nest one structure within another. You must remember to create structures that you want to include in other structures before you define them.

Example

Use the following code in place of the previous code. What happens?

```
Type UserType
    FName As String * 10
    LName As String * 25
    Addr As Address
End Type

Type Address
     Street As String
     City As String
     Zip As String
End Type

Public Names As UserType
```

You'll notice in the previous code that there is a reference to the Address structure in the Names structure, but the Address structure has not been defined yet.

Use of Complex Structures

Let's look at an example of a complex user-defined structure. For the example shown in Listing 27.4, the structure defined on the module page is called NameRec and contains a first name, last name, address, city, state, and zip code fields.

Example

A complex user-defined structure.

Listing 27.4 27LIST04.TXT—Complex User-Defined Structure

```
Type NameRec
    FName As String
    LName As String
    Address As String
    City As String
    State As String
    Zip As String
End Type

Public Contacts As NameRec
```

In the code above you have defined a structure called `NameRec` and declared a variable of type `NameRec` called `Contacts`. Now let's create a form that will use this structure and its members.

Create a form named `CnctForm` that looks like that shown in figure 27.6. Name the text boxes as shown below:

```
FirstName

LastName

Address

City

State

Zip
```

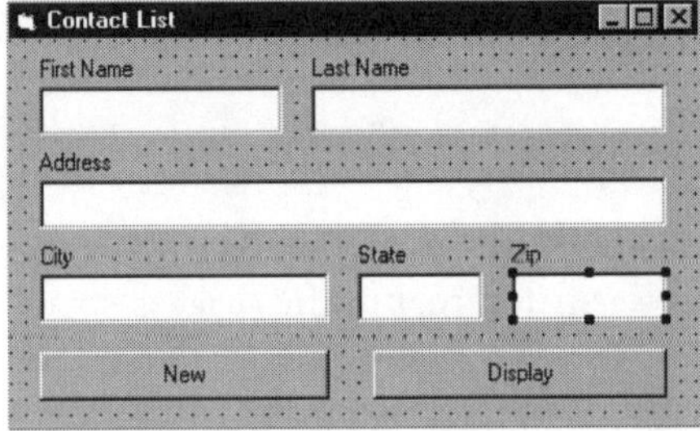

Figure 27.6
The form for the `CnctForm` project.

Add two buttons to the form. Change the captions on the buttons to `New` and `Display`. Now your form should look just like that shown in figure 27.6.

Example

Add more code from Listing 27.4 to the form.

Listing 27.4 27LIST04.TXT—Complex User-Defined Structure

```
Sub Get_Data()
    Contacts.FName = CnctForm.FirstName
    Contacts.LName = CnctForm.LastName
    Contacts.Address = CnctForm.Address
    Contacts.City = CnctForm.City
    Contacts.State = CnctForm.State
    Contacts.Zip = CnctForm.Zip
End Sub

Sub Clear_Record()
    Contacts.FName = ""
    Contacts.LName = ""
    Contacts.Address = ""
    Contacts.City = ""
    Contacts.State = ""
    Contacts.Zip = 0
End Sub

Sub Clear_Form()
    CnctForm.FirstName = ""
    CnctForm.LastName = ""
    CnctForm.Address = ""
    CnctForm.City = ""
    CnctForm.State = ""
    CnctForm.Zip = ""
End Sub

Sub Display_Info()
Dim CRLF As String
CRLF = (Chr(13) & Chr(10))

    MsgBox "Information Entered" & CRLF & _
           "First Name: " & Contacts.FName & CRLF & _
           "Last Name : " & Contacts.LName & CRLF & _
           "Address   : " & Contacts.Address & CRLF & _
           "City      : " & Contacts.City & CRLF & _
           "State     : " & Contacts.State & CRLF & _
           "Zip       : " & Contacts.Zip, , "Contact Entered"
End Sub

Private Sub Command1_Click()
    Clear_Record
    Clear_Form
End Sub

Private Sub Command2_Click()
Get_Data
Display_Info
End Sub
```

continues

Listing 27.4 Continued

```
Private Sub Form_Load()

End Sub
```

Run the program. Enter data into the entry fields on the form. You will see a form like that shown in figure 27.7.

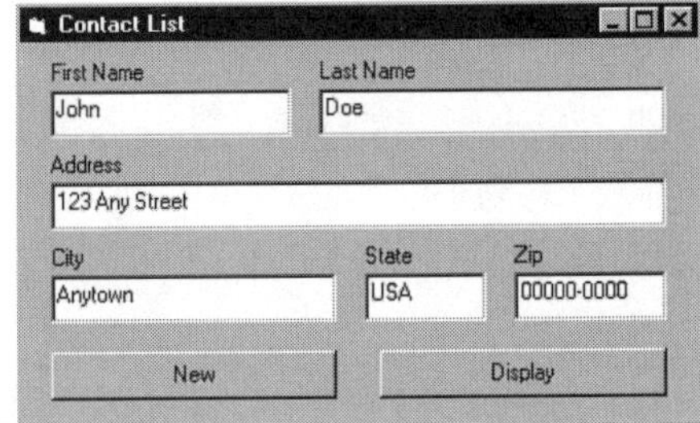

Figure 27.7
Running the `CnctForm` project.

This program performs several different functions. When you click on the new button the form and the structure are both cleared. This is accomplished with the `Clear_Record` and `Clear_Form` sub-procedures. If you click on the Display button, the `Get_Data` and `Display_Info` sub-procedures are executed. The `Get_Data` sub-procedure takes the information in each entry field and loads the corresponding structure member with the information. By clicking on the Display button you will see the information you entered in the entry fields shown in a message box, similar to that of figure 27.8.

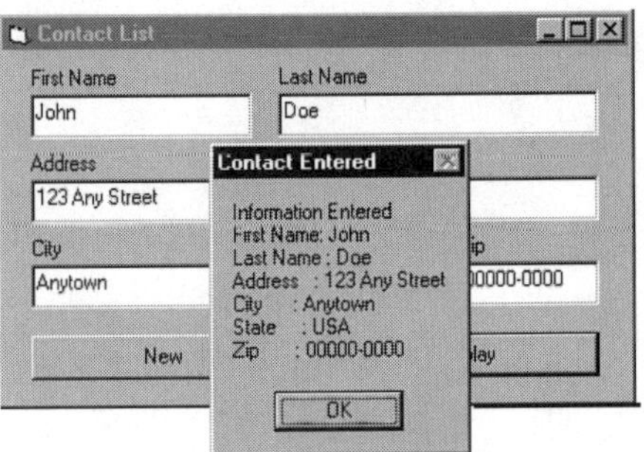

Figure 27.8
Displaying the information entered in the form.

This program could easily become the beginning of a personal rolodex. A few things are missing. For example, right now the program only handles one record, and there is no way to save the data entered. Saving the data for this program will be covered in Chapter 28, "Files and I/O." But let's look at modifying the code to include more that one record.

If you want to be able to track more than one user-defined structure, you can create an array of them. Just as with any other variable, an array can be created by using a user-defined structure as the variable type.

Example

Listing 27.5 creates an array of five `NameRec` structures named `Contacts`.

Listing 27.5 27LIST05.TXT—The Module Page of the CnctMod Form

```
Option Base 1

Type NameRec
    FName As String
    LName As String
    Address As String
    City As String
    State As String
    Zip As String
End Type

Public Index As Integer
Public Contacts(5) As NameRec
```

Now change the `CnctForm` form to look like the one shown in figure 27.9. The New button shown in figure 27.6 should only have its caption changed to read Clear Record, rather than New. Add two new buttons for Next Record and Previous Record. Add a label that says `Current Record #` : and a label called `RecordNum`. Your form should now look like the one shown in figure 27.9

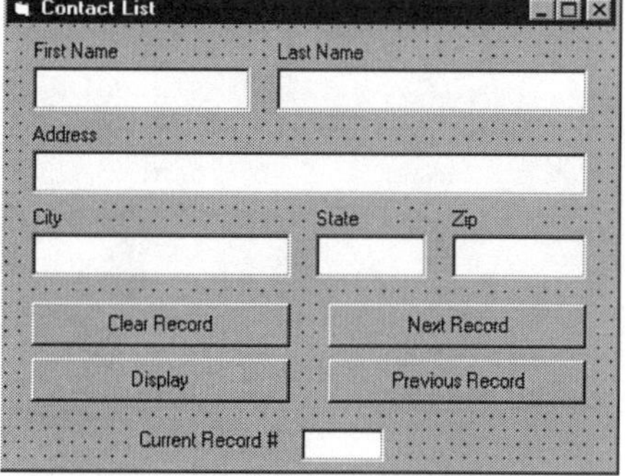

Figure 27.9
The form for the `CnctForm2` project.

Example

Use more code from Listing 27.5 to change the `CnctForm` form to look like the one shown in figure 27.9.

Listing 27.5 27LIST05.TXT—Altering the Form

```
Sub Get_Data()
    Contacts(Index).FName = CnctForm.FirstName
    Contacts(Index).LName = CnctForm.LastName
    Contacts(Index).Address = CnctForm.Address
    Contacts(Index).City = CnctForm.City
    Contacts(Index).State = CnctForm.State
    Contacts(Index).Zip = CnctForm.Zip
End Sub

Sub Clear_Record()
    Contacts(Index).FName = ""
    Contacts(Index).LName = ""
    Contacts(Index).Address = ""
    Contacts(Index).City = ""
    Contacts(Index).State = ""
    Contacts(Index).Zip = ""
End Sub

Sub Clear_Form()
    CnctForm.FirstName = ""
    CnctForm.LastName = ""
    CnctForm.Address = ""
    CnctForm.City = ""
    CnctForm.State = ""
    CnctForm.Zip = ""
End Sub

Sub Display_Info()
Dim CRLF As String
CRLF = (Chr(13) & Chr(10))

    MsgBox "Information Entered" & CRLF & _
           "First Name: " & Contacts(Index).FName & CRLF & _
           "Last Name : " & Contacts(Index).LName & CRLF & _
           "Address   : " & Contacts(Index).Address & CRLF & _
           "City      : " & Contacts(Index).City & CRLF & _
           "State     : " & Contacts(Index).State & CRLF & _
           "Zip       : " & Contacts(Index).Zip & CRLF & _
           "Record #  : " & Index, , "Contact Entered"
End Sub

Private Sub Command1_Click()
    Clear_Record
    Clear_Form
End Sub

Private Sub Command2_Click()
    Get_Data
    Display_Info
End Sub
```

```
Private Sub Command3_Click()
    If Index < 5 Then
        Get_Data
        Index = Index + 1
        Get_Record
    End If
    CnctForm.RecordNum = Index
End Sub

Private Sub Command4_Click()
    If Index > 1 Then
        Get_Data
        Index = Index - 1
        Get_Record
    End If
    CnctForm.RecordNum = Index
End Sub

Sub Get_Record()
    CnctForm.FirstName = Contacts(Index).FName
    CnctForm.LastName = Contacts(Index).LName
    CnctForm.Address = Contacts(Index).Address
    CnctForm.City = Contacts(Index).City
    CnctForm.State = Contacts(Index).State
    CnctForm.Zip = Contacts(Index).Zip
End Sub

Private Sub Form_Load()
    Index = 1
    CnctForm.RecordNum = Index
End Sub
```

The changes to the code to accomplish handling five structures have been fairly minor. The structure is no longer just a single variable, but an array of structures. All references to the `Contacts` variable now refer to `Contacts(Index)`. `Index` is the index number of the structure that is being displayed.

There are four new subroutines and one new global variable used to make this program handle five different structures. The first one to look at is the `Form_Load()` subroutine. This subroutine initializes the `Index` variable to `1` and places this number on the form in the `RecordNum` text field.

There are two other subroutines that are almost identical. They are for the Previous and Next buttons. These functions check the value of the `Index` variable. If it is possible to go either down or up (depending on which button is pressed), the subroutine calls the `Get_Data` subroutine to save the data on the form into the current record. Then the `Index` variable is changed to the desired value and the record matching the new value of the `Index` variable is displayed on the screen using `Get_Record`.

The `Get_Record` subroutine takes the data from the currently selected array member and places this data on the form. You now have a working contact list program. Save this project as `CnctFrm2.vbp`. Chapter 28, "Files and I/O," uses this same project and forms and builds on the knowledge gained here.

Summary

In this chapter, you learned about creating and using user-defined data types. These types are referred to as structures, and can be used to contain variables of different types, even other user-defined types. You can create variables or arrays using these new data types.

You saw how you can use one user-defined structure inside the definition of another. This nesting of data types is only possible if the structure being used is defined before another structure attempts to use it.

You also saw how to manipulate data in structures, and in arrays of structures. In Chapter 28, "Files and I/O," you will learn about another advantage to using user-defined types: writing entire structures to disk.

Review Questions

Answers to the Review Questions are in Appendix A.

1. What is a user-defined type? What are user-defined types commonly called?
2. What are the keywords used to define a structure?
3. What types of variables can be contained in a structure?

4. Can you create a structure that contains other structures? If so, what are the restrictions?
5. What will happen when you try to run the program containing the code below?

```
.
.
Type UserType1
     Str1 As String
     UserVar As UserType2
End Type

Type UserType2
     Str2 As String
End Type
.
.
```

6. What is the absolute length of a string? How do you specify this within a structure?

7. If you needed to track baseball players and their batting averages, which would you use and why?

   1) Two arrays. The first containing the players and the second containing the batting averages.

   2) An array of structures containing both the player and his average.

8. Of all the different data types, are there any that cannot be used within a structure?

9. Why should you specify the absolute lengths of strings within a structure that is going to be used for reading and writing to a disk?

Review Exercises

1. Create a structure that contains three different types of variables (i.e., `Integer`, `String`, `Double`). Fill these values in the structure, and then print them to the form.

2. Modify the code in Exercise 1 to use two different structures to hold the same three variables. *Hint:* Have one structure hold another structure. Fill the values in both structures, and then print them to the form.

3. Create a program that has a structure for holding information about a classroom of five students. The information in the structure should hold their first and last name, their last five test scores and the average of their test scores. The program should print out the students names and their average test scores. You can code the statistics directly into the program.

4. Modify the program shown in Exercise 3 to use a form that will query for each student and then present the information in a message box.

5. Modify the program shown in Listing 27.5 to include a company name and an e-mail address. After you do this, change the number of contacts that can be stored from 5 to 15.

6. Beginning with the program that you created in Exercise 5, add several more fields. The first field should be the middle initial, the next should be a second address line, and a third for a second e-mail address. When you display this information using the display button, do not display any information that is blank.

CHAPTER 28

Files and I/O

Virtually every program in existence today uses files. At the very least, even if a program does not use files, the program itself is a file that is executed when the program is run. Whether a program saves data into a data base, or just keeps information for its own use (such as a user's preferred color scheme or window position), most programs make use of files.

In this chapter, you will learn about file creation, access, and input and output procedures. There are three different types of file access: Sequential, Random, and Binary. Sequential access is the simplest file access, and as such it has its drawbacks. Sequential files are the simplest to create and read, but they can be slow and cumbersome.

Random access is a much faster and useful method of accessing files. However, these advantages come at the cost of complexity.

Binary files are a special type of random-access file. They are explained toward the end of this chapter.

Basic File-Handling Commands

Several commands in Visual Basic are common to all forms of file input and output. These commands open the files, specify the files mode, close the file, and check for free file numbers to be used. These commands are covered in the following section.

The *Open* Statement

There are commonalties between sequential files and random-access files. The `Open` statement is used for all types of files, with the difference being in the parameters (or arguments) used in the `Open` statement.

The `Open` statement initiates a channel for reading and/or writing to a file. Once the channel is open, the data *stream* can flow. The mode the channel was opened for, either read, write, or both, dictates how the stream of data can flow.

The syntax for the `Open` statement follows:

```
Open FileName$ [For Mode] [Access Restriction]
➥[LockType] As [#]Channel% [Len = RecordLength%]
```

All Open statements must include the Filename and Channel number. All of the other parameters are optional. A simple call to Open using only the required parameters would look like this:

```
Open "FileName.Txt" As #1
```

The `Open` statement above would open the file FileName.Txt as channel number 1. To reference this file for input or output, you would reference the channel number. This channel has been opened in random-access mode. The default for opening a file, if the `For Mode` statement is omitted, is `Random`.

Let's look at the optional parameters that the `Open` statement can accept.

For Mode

There are five different modes that a file can be opened for. These are shown and described in Table 28.1.

Table 28.1 Modes for Opening a File

Statement	*Description*
Output	Opens a channel to a file for sequential output, starting at the beginning of the file. If the file does not exist when the `Open` statement is called, the file is created; otherwise, the file is overwritten.
Append	Opens a channel to a file for sequential output, beginning at the end of the file. If the file does not exist, the file is created. Using Append will never overwrite an existing file.
Input	Opens a channel to a file for sequential input, starting at the beginning of the file. Data is read in the same order that is output.

Statement	*Description*
Random	Opens a channel to a file for random read and write access. This mode allows data to be read in and written to a file at any specific record boundary. This is the default mode for opening a channel to a file if the For Mode statement is omitted from the `Open` statement.
Binary	Opens a channel to a file for binary data access. In binary mode, a file can be accessed at the byte level. This means that you can read and write individual bytes to and from a file.

The `For Mode` command is not required when using the `Open` statement. The default mode for the `Open` statement is `Random`. If you do not include the type, Visual Basic will assume `Random` and will insert the `For Random` mode for you. Look at the following code samples for examples of how you would use each of the modes for opening a file.

Mode: `Input`

```
Open "Input.Txt" For Input As #1
```

Mode: `Append`

```
Open "Append.Txt" For Append As #1
```

Mode: `Output`

```
Open "Output.Txt" For Output As #1
```

Mode: `Random`

```
Open "Random.Txt" For Random As #1
```

or

```
Open "Random.Txt" As #1
```

Mode: `Binary`

```
Open "Binary.Dat" For Binary As #1
```

By using the `For Mode` statement you can explicitly choose the file mode that you wish to use. If you do not choose a file mode, `Random` is the default.

> **Note:** If you do not tell Visual Basic what mode you want to open a file as, it will assume `Random` and fill in the mode for you. If you type the following:

```
Open "Random.Txt" As #1
```

Visual Basic will change the line to the following:

```
Open "Random.Txt" For Random As #1
```

Access Restriction

The optional statement `Access Restriction` allows you to restrict access to a file. This access can be either `Read`, `Write`, or `Read Write`. This additional access restriction is often used when writing programs that will be run across a network.

Specifying a read-only access (`Read`) will allow users to see the contents of a file, but they will not be able to modify them. Specifying `Write` access will allow a user to modify a file and specifying `Read Write` will allow a user to read and update a file.

LockType

Use the `Lock` keyword to specify the operations permitted on the open file by other processes. This parameter is useful when writing network applications. You can restrict, or serialize, access to a file so that only one user at a time can have access to a file, or be writing to a file. This can prevent two users from attempting to make changes at the same time, and inevitably losing the changes that one of the users made.

The valid options for the Lock statement are:

`Shared`, `Lock Read`, `Lock Write`, and `Lock Read Write`

`Shared` allows all users access to the file simultaneously.

`Lock Read` will lock the file so that only the person who has the file open for reading can access the file.

`Lock Write` will lock the file so that only the person who has the file open for write access can open the file for writing.

`Lock Read Write` will lock the file from all users except the one who has the file open for read and write access.

Len = RecordLength%

The length specified by the `Len = RecordLength` statement is used by random-access files as the size of data that will be passed from Visual Basic to the file. This is necessary when accessing records from a file.

The first record in a file will begin at location 1. All subsequent records will be written at locations in increments of 1. The actual location in the file that the next record length will be `N * RecordLength`, where `N` is the record number.

This may seem similar to the way an array stores information by default, and it is. The first element in an array is stored in `Array(0)`. While the first element in a file is stored at record number 1. To make the index coordination between arrays and files easy, use `Option Base 1` or define the array to begin with element 1 for all arrays that are to be used to write to a file.

The *FreeFile* Function

When looking at the syntax of the Open statement, you may have asked yourself, "How do I know if a channel number is available for use?" Visual Basic provides a function that can be used to determine the next available channel number for you. By using the FreeFile function, you are guaranteed that the channel number you use will not be used by another open file. The syntax of the FreeFile function follows:

```
FreeFile[(RangeNumber)]
```

The optional parameter `RangeNumber` allows you to specify that you want the channel number returned to be in either the range of 1 to 255 or 256 to 511. The default range, if no `RangeNumber` parameter is specified, is 1 to 255. The following example shows how to use the `FreeFile` function to obtain a channel number and open a file using that number.

```
.
ChannelNumber = FreeFile
Open "FileName.Txt" For Output As #ChannelNumber
.
.
```

Use the `FreeFile` function whenever you want to ensure that a channel number is not already in use. This may not be necessary for very small applications that only use several files. However, even in small applications, the use of `FreeFile` will ensure that you do not accidentally use the same channel number by more than one file at the same time.

> **Caution:** Be sure to avoid the shortcut of using `Freefile` within the `Open` statement, as shown below:
>
> ```
> Open Filename$ For Output as FreeFile
> ```
>
> Although this will work, there will be no way to know what the file number is for actual operations on the file.

The *Close* Statement

All files that have been opened using the `Open` statement need to be closed. The statement for closing a file is `Close`. This statement takes the open channel number as its only parameter. The syntax for the `Close` statement follows:

```
Close #ChannelNumber% [,ChannelNumber2%..ChannelNumberX%]
```

As you can see from the syntax, you can specify any number of channels to close by using the `Close` statement. If you do not specify any channel numbers, all open channels are closed. This can be useful for terminating your applications, to ensure that all open files are closed and their data saved to the disk.

You may close as many files as you wish by using a single `Close` statement. The following sample code shows how to use the `Close` statement:

```
.
ChannelNumber = FreeFile
Open "FileName.Txt" For Output As #ChannelNumber
' Process File here
Close #ChannelNumber
.
```

Now that you have seen the basic statements required for opening and closing files, and setting their access modes, we'll look at several examples of how to output to and input from sequential access files. The next section covers the `Print #` statement, which is used to output text to a file.

Sequential-Access Files

Sequential file access means just that—it occurs sequentially. When you create a sequential access file, you are creating a file that must be read from and written to sequentially (for example, in order from beginning to end). This is the biggest weakness of a sequential file.

To use the file, you must process the entire file, from beginning to end. If you only need to update one byte of information in a 1,000-byte file, then you must process 999 extra bytes every time you want to perform this update.

Sequential file access can be very useful when you need to process a text file, such as your AUTOEXEC.BAT file, or if you are storing small amounts of data where speed is not a issue. We'll look at the functions that Visual Basic offers for handling all types of files.

The *Print #* Statement

Being able to open and close files is necessary to be able to use them. But how do you put information into a file? One method is the `Print #` statement. This statement is used when writing to a sequential access file. The syntax of the `Print #` statement follows:

```
Print #ChannelNumber, [OutputList]
```

The `#ChannelNumber` is the opened channel to the file that you wish to write to. `OutputList` can consist of the following (see Table 28.2):

```
[{Spc(n) | Tab[(n)]}][Expression][CharPos]
```

Table 28.2 Available Settings for the OutputList Parameter

Setting	*Description*
Spc(n)	Used to insert spaces in the output, where n is the number of spaces to insert
Tab(n)	Used to position the insertion point to an absolute column number, where n is the column number. Use Tab with no argument to position the insertion point at the beginning of the next print zone
Expression	Numeric or string expressions to print
CharPos	Specifies the insertion point for the next character to be printed. Use a semicolon to specify that the next character should be printed immediately following the last character printed. The Tab(n) function can be used here. The same functions Tab(n) performs at the beginning of a Print # statement apply here. If CharPos is omitted, the next character is printed on the next line.

Now we'll look at an example of using the `Print #` statement to print information to a file.

Example

Listing 28.1 opens a file named Print.txt and writes the numbers 1 to 5 into it. It then closes the file.

Listing 28.1 28LIST01.TXT—Using the Print # Statement

```
Private Sub Command1_Click()
CNumber = FreeFile
Open "Print.txt" For Output As #CNumber
Form1.Print "File Print.txt Opened"

For X = 1 To 5
    Print #CNumber, X
    Form1.Print "Writing a " & X & " to Print.txt"
Next X

Close #CNumber

Form1.Print "File Print.txt Closed"

End Sub
```

If you run the program shown in Listing 28.1 you will see output similar to that shown in figure 28.1. The program informs you that it has opened the file, then proceeds to write to the file and show you what has been written. Finally, the program closes the file and tells you that the file has been closed.

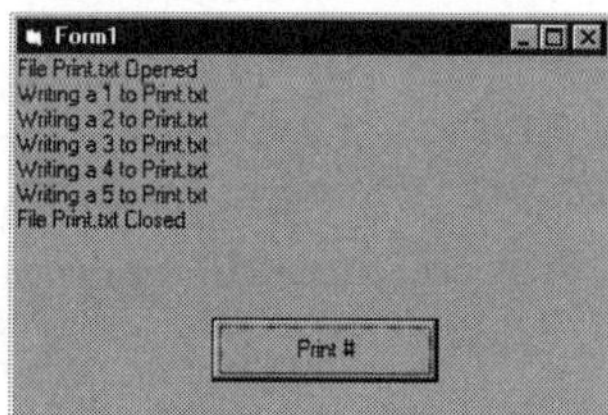

Figure 28.1

Using `Print #` to write to a file.

So, how do you know that the process worked? Go to a DOS prompt and look in the directory where you have Visual Basic installed. The default directory is VB on whatever drive you have VB installed on. Execute the following command and you should see the numbers 1 through 5 printed as shown by the following output:

```
E:\VB4>type print.txt
 1
 2
 3
 4
 5
```

This is a simple usage of the `Print #` statement. There were no statements included to position any of the output, so it defaulted to printing each character on a new line. If you wanted all of these characters printed on the same line, you could include a semicolon after the `X` variable and the numbers will print one after another on the same line.

Example

Listing 28.2 shows you how to do this.

Listing 28.2 28LIST02.TXT—Printing Numbers on Same Line

```
Private Sub Command1_Click()

CNumber = FreeFile
Open "Print.txt" For Output As #CNumber
Form1.Print "File Print.txt Opened"

For X = 1 To 5
    Print #CNumber,X;
    Form1.Print "Writing a " & X & " to Print.txt"
```

```
Next X

Close #CNumber

Form1.Print "File Print.txt Closed"

End Sub
```

If you run the program shown in Listing 28.2 and type the file from a DOS prompt as shown below, the file created will look like the following output:

```
E:\VB>type print.txt
 1  2  3  4  5
```

You probably noticed the space between the numbers when they are printed to the same line. This is done to allow the different data elements that have been written to the file to be distinguished from one another. This space is referred to as a delimiter. When attempting to read this data back in, it would be difficult to know how many elements were written if the file contained 12345 instead of 1 2 3 4 5.

You can experiment with the different parameters of the Print # statement and see what results you get when creating a file. Being able to create and write to a file won't do you much good if you can't retrieve the information when you want to. The following section covers retrieving information back in from a file.

The *Input* # Statement

After you have written data to a file, you need a method for retrieving that data. For sequential files the statement used is the Input # statement. This statement will allow you to read in the information that has been written to a file. The data must be read in exactly the same order and format as it was output. The syntax of the Input # statement follows:

```
Input #Channel%, Variable1 [,Variable2..VariableX]
```

`Input` requires an open channel number and the variables to hold the data being read in will be held in. The `Input #` statement and the `Print #` statement that wrote the data to the file should have the same format. If you used comma delimiters to write the data, you should also use the same delimiters on the `Input #` statement.

Note: If you write a series of variables on one line, and you want to be able to reliably read them in with the `Input #` statement, you must either use the `Write #` statement, (instead of `Print #`) or manually include comma delimiters. `Input #` reads up to the first space, comma, or end of line if it is reading into a numeric variable. It reads up to the first comma or end of line when reading in a string unless the strings are quoted.

Listing 28.3 provides and example of writing to a file and then reading the information back in.

Example

The code from the previous example has been used and modified for this example. The print function no longer prints information to the form, this information is printed to the form during the input functions.

Listing 28.3 28LIST03.TXT—Writing To a File and Reading Information Back In

```
Private Sub Command1_Click()

CNumber = FreeFile
Open "Print.txt" For Output As #CNumber

For X = 1 To 5
    Print #CNumber, X
Next X

Close #CNumber

End Sub

Private Sub Command2_Click()
CNumber = FreeFile
Open "Print.txt" For Input As #CNumber
Form1.Print "File Print.txt Opened"

For X = 1 To 5
    Input #CNumber, Y
    Form1.Print "Retrieved a " & Y & " from Print.txt"
Next X

Close #CNumber

Form1.Print "File Print.txt Closed"

End Sub
```

The code in this example uses the same function for writing the information to the file as the previous example. However, in this example another button was added for input. By pressing this button, the `Print.txt` file is opened and the contents are read in and displayed on the form. The output from this program is shown in figure 28.2.

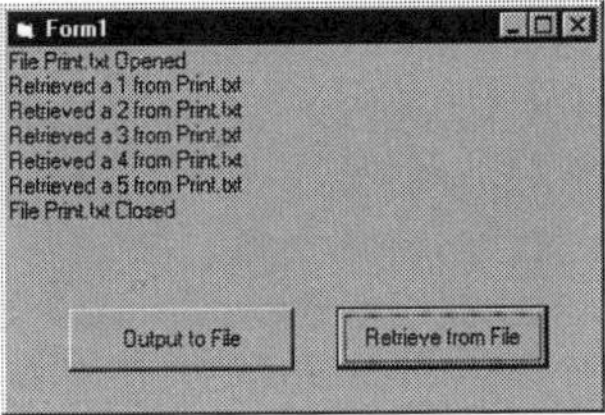

Figure 28.2

Using `Input #` to read from a file.

This covers the basics of using the `Input #` statement. There is one more statement that can be used for basic data file access. That is the `Write #` statement. The `Write #` statement is covered in the following section.

The *Write #* Statement

The `Write #` statement is another method for writing information to a file. The `Write #` statement and the `Print #` statement differ only slightly. All data written to a file using the `Write #` statement is comma-delimited, not space-delimited. This is required when writing files that will be used by certain mail-merge or spreadsheet programs that expect all data fields to be delimited by a comma.

Note: To read data correctly from a file into variables, always use the `Write #` statement instead of the `Print #` statement.

Run the program shown in the Listing 28.4.

Example

The program will create a file called Write.txt. After you have created the file, use the type command from the DOS prompt to display the file. What is different between the same file created by using the `Print #` statement?

Listing 28.4 28LIST04.TXT—Creating a Help File Called Write.txt

```
Private Sub Command1_Click()

CNumber = FreeFile
Open "Write.txt" For Output As #CNumber

For X = 1 To 5
    Write #CNumber, X;
Next X

Close #CNumber

End Sub
```

The contents of the Write.txt file follow:

```
E:\VB>type write.txt
1,2,3,4,5,
```

If you do not use the semicolon after the data being printed, each piece of data would be on its own line, and there would be no commas separating the data. In this instance both the `Write #` and `Print #` statements act identically.

Random-Access Files

In the section concerning sequential files, you learned about all of the statements that can be used with those files. The `Open` statement and the `Close` statement are the same for both types of files. The only difference between the two is the mode that the file is opened for. If the `For Random` statement is not used, or another mode is specified, the file will not be opened for random access.

> **Note:** If you do not tell Visual Basic what mode you want to open a file as, it will assume `Random` and fill in the mode for you. If you type the following:
>
> ```
> Open "Random.Txt" As #1
> ```
>
> Visual Basic will change the line to the following:
>
> ```
> Open "Random.Txt" For Random As #1
> ```

The following sample statement opens a file for random access.

```
Open "Random.txt" For Random As #1
```

You can open a file as a random-access file and use it as a sequential-access file. There is nothing wrong with doing this, although you will sacrifice the benefits of a random-access file. However, you will gain the new advantages of the `Get` and `Put` implementations in VB 4.

Just what is a random-access file? It's a file that you can read from or write to at any point in the file. A sequential file needs to be processed from beginning to end, whereas a random-access file can be accessed to read or write data at any place in the file—for example, when you create a file that contains 10 lines of code. In order to get the 6th line of the file in sequential mode, you would have to read all 10 lines. If you access the file in Random mode, you could go to line 6, read it in and close the file.

The same holds true for writing to a file. If you had the same 10-line file and you wanted to change the data on line 8, you would have to write out all 10 lines of the file in order to update line 8 in sequential mode. In random mode, you could just write out line number 8.

The `Random` method for file access has its distinct advantages. You can read in or write out only the data that you need to. This may not seem like much of a time savings with a file that has only 10 records. But consider the time that each file access would consume on a 10,000-line file.

Two statements are used for random-access files. These are the `Put #` and `Get #` statements.

The `Put #` and `Get #` statements are very similar to the `Print #` and `Input #` statements used for sequential file access. The major difference between these two sets of statements is that the `Print #` and `Input #` statements write out one piece of data at a time, to the file. There is no way for them to position to line 5 and just update that line.

The `Put #` and `Get #` statements syntax is a little different than that of `Print #` and `Input #`. The syntax for the `Put #` and `Get #` statement follows:

```
Put [#]Channel, [RecNumber], Variable
Get [#]Channel, [RecNumber], Variable
```

As you can see, these statements accept the record number as statements. By specifying the record number you want to write to, you can only update, or read in the data that you want. All record numbers begin with number 1. The `Variable` that is written can be of any data type, even an array or a user-defined structure. This can be one of the most powerful features of a random-access file. It will allow you to store and retrieve any block of data as a single unit.

Let's modify the last example to illustrate how a random-access file works. The modified code is shown in Listing 28.5.

Example

This example uses `Put #` to create a random-access file with a record length of 5. This is very important; if the record length is not known, the `Put #` and `Get #` statements would not know how far into the file to go to find a particular record. The formula for finding a record is `RecordNumber * RecordLength`.

Listing 28.5 28LIST05.TXT—Using Put # to Create Random-Access File with Record Length of 5

```
Private Sub Command1_Click() ' Create Button

CNumber = FreeFile
Open "Random.txt" For Random As #CNumber Len = 5

For X = 1 To 5
    Put #CNumber, X, X
Next X

Close #CNumber

End Sub
```

continues

Listing 28.5 Continued

```
Private Sub Command2_Click() ' Change Button
CNumber = FreeFile
Open "Random.txt" For Random As #CNumber Len = 5
NewVar = 9
Put #CNumber, 3, NewVar

Close #CNumber

End Sub

Private Sub Command3_Click() ' Display Button
CNumber = FreeFile
Open "Random.txt" For Random As #CNumber Len = 5
Form1.Print "File Random.txt Opened"

For X = 1 To 5
    Get #CNumber, X, Y
    Form1.Print "Retrieved a " & Y & " from Random.txt"
Next X

Close #CNumber

Form1.Print "File Random.txt Closed"

End Sub
```

This example uses three buttons. One creates the file, another displays the file, and a third changes the file. Run the program shown above. Press the Create button, then press the Display button. Your results should be similar to what's shown in figure 28.3.

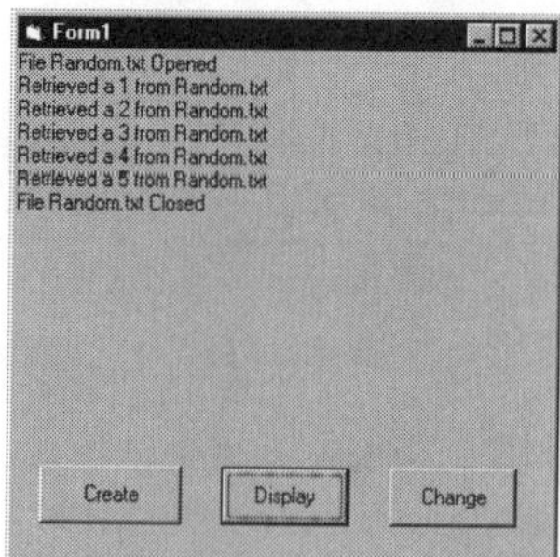

Figure 28.3
Using random access to create and read a file.

Now press the Change button. Press the Display button again. Your results should look like those shown in figure 28.4.

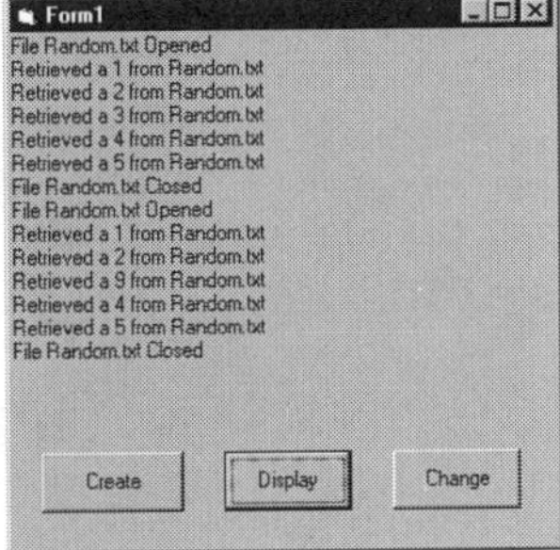

Figure 28.4
Changing one record in a random-access file.

The third record in the file is now a nine instead of a three. The subroutine that made this change simply did a `Put #` to record number three with a variable containing the new value to be written. That is all there was to it. Let's look at one final example that will illustrate how to use random access to store user defined structures.

This example expands on the contacts example from Chapter 27. Listing 28.6 shows the code required on the code page. The listing that follows that is more of Listing 28.6, showing the code required for all the buttons, entry fields, and so on. The form for this project should look like that shown in figure 28.5.

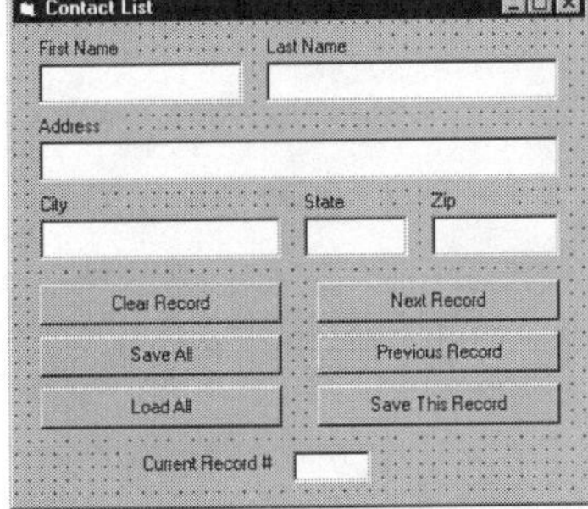

Figure 28.5
The form for the contacts program.

Example

Listing 28.6 shows the code required on the code page.

Listing 28.6 28LIST06.TXT—Code Page for the Contacts Program

```
Option Base 1

Public Type NameRec
    FName As String * 15
    LName As String * 25
```

continues

Listing 28.6 Continued

```
    Address As String * 30
    City As String * 15
    State As String * 2
    Zip As String * 10
End Type

Public Index As Integer
Global Const MaxRecords As Integer = 25
Public RecLen As Integer
Public Contacts(MaxRecords) As NameRec
```

Listing 28.6 28LIST06.TXT—More Code for the Contacts Program

```
' Load the data from the form into the current structure
Sub Get_Data()
    Contacts(Index).FName = CnctForm.FirstName
    Contacts(Index).LName = CnctForm.LastName
    Contacts(Index).Address = CnctForm.Address
    Contacts(Index).City = CnctForm.City
    Contacts(Index).State = CnctForm.State
    Contacts(Index).Zip = CnctForm.Zip
End Sub
' Clear out the Current Structure
Sub Clear_Record()
    Contacts(Index).FName = ""
    Contacts(Index).LName = ""
    Contacts(Index).Address = ""
    Contacts(Index).City = ""
    Contacts(Index).State = ""
    Contacts(Index).Zip = ""
End Sub

' Clear out the data on the form
Sub Clear_Form()
    CnctForm.FirstName = ""
    CnctForm.LastName = ""
    CnctForm.Address = ""
    CnctForm.City = ""
    CnctForm.State = ""
    CnctForm.Zip = ""
End Sub

' Clear Record
Private Sub Command1_Click()
    Clear_Record
    Clear_Form
End Sub
```

```
' Save All Records
Private Sub Command2_Click()
CNumber = FreeFile
Open "Contacts.Dat" For Random As #CNumber Len = RecLen
For X = 1 To MaxRecords
    Put #CNumber, X, Contacts(X)
Next X
Close #CNumber
MsgBox "All Records Saved", , "Save All"
Get_Data
Update_Form
End Sub

' Load All
Private Sub Command5_Click()
CNumber = FreeFile
Open "Contacts.Dat" For Random As #CNumber Len = RecLen
For X = 1 To MaxRecords
    Get #CNumber, X, Contacts(X)
Next X
Close #CNumber
Index = 1
Update_Form
MsgBox "All Records Loaded", , "Load All"
End Sub
'Next Button
Private Sub Command4_Click()
    CnctForm.RecordNum = Index
    If Index < MaxRecords Then
        Get_Data
        Index = Index + 1
        Update_Form
    End If
End Sub

' Previous Button
Private Sub Command5_Click()
    CnctForm.RecordNum = Index
    If Index > 1 Then
        Get_Data
        Index = Index - 1
        Update_Form
    End If
End Sub

' Save This Record
Private Sub Command6_Click()
CNumber = FreeFile

Open "Contacts.Dat" For Random As #CNumber Len = RecLen
```

continues

Listing 28.6 28LIST06.TXT—More Code for the Contacts Program

```
Put #CNumber, Index, Contacts(Index)

Close #CNumber
MsgBox "Record Number " & Index & " saved.", , "Save Record"

End Sub

' Updates the Form with the Chosen Record
Sub Update_Form()
    CnctForm.FirstName = Contacts(Index).FName
    CnctForm.LastName = Contacts(Index).LName
    CnctForm.Address = Contacts(Index).Address
    CnctForm.City = Contacts(Index).City
    CnctForm.State = Contacts(Index).State
    CnctForm.Zip = Contacts(Index).Zip
    CnctForm.RecordNum = Index
End Sub

' Initializes data needed for startup
Private Sub Form_Load()
    Index = 1
    CnctForm.RecordNum = Index
    RecLen = Len(Contacts(1))
End Sub
```

After you have created the form and typed in all of the code, run the program. You will have a functional address book that you can use to store information to disk. This exercise is meant to show you how to culminate all the knowledge that you have gained thus far in this book. It demonstrates the use of conditional logic, array processing, input and output, variables, controls, and finally file I/O.

Go through this example carefully. There are a lot of features and techniques that you can use in your own applications.

Binary Access Files

Binary access files are closely related to random access. Binary files have no record length associated with them. This makes them more difficult to manage, but they can save disk space.

If you had a file that was random access with a record length of 10, 5 records written to this file would consume 50 bytes, even if you only had 10 bytes of data stored in the records. The extra spaces will contain spaces as a marker for the allowable record size. If you were to write the same 5 variables out using binary mode, the file would only hold 12 bytes. This makes binary files similar to sequential and random-access files.

You can accidentally write over data by using the binary method. Binary files are usually reserved for reading and writing bitmapped images. An in depth discussion of binary files is beyond the scope of this book, but is mentioned here to provide a base understanding of their makeup.

Summary

In this chapter, you learned about the statements related to creating and using files. You also learned about the different file modes available, and the advantages and disadvantages inherent to each file type. You learned how to create and use sequential-access files, and then how to create and use random-access files.

Most importantly, you learned differences between random-access and sequential access files, especially what is necessary for updating and retrieving information from each type of file.

Review Questions

Answers to the Review Questions are in Appendix A.

1. What is a sequential-access file?
2. What are the keywords needed to open a file with the `Open` statement?
3. How many files can be closed with the `Close` statement? What happens if you do not provide a channel number when issuing the `Close` statement?

4. What is the main difference between random- and sequential-access files?
5. What type of file is being opened by the statement below? Where will the first record written to this file be written?

```
.
.
Open "TestFile" For Append As #1
.
.
```

6. Why do random-access files need to know the record length of the data that is to be written into them?

7. Why is accessing one record from a random-access file quicker than accessing the same record from a sequential file?
8. What formula does `Put #` and `Get #` use to determine the position of the file for each of their separate operations?
9. Why should you specify the absolute lengths of strings within a structure that is going to be used for reading and writing to a disk?

Review Exercises

1. Create a program that creates a sequential file that will hold the following information: name, age, and favorite color. Fill this file with five separate names, ages, and favorite colors. Use three `For...Next` loops to write this information to the file. *Hint:* You will need three arrays, one for each value.

2. Modify the code in Exercise 1 to use an array of structures that contains the same information. Which method is easier to use?

3. Create a program that uses a random-access file to store 20 numbers. Use an input box to query the user which value she would like changed, and to what. Print this information to the form or to a message box.

4. Modify the program shown in Exercise 3 to use sequential files.

5. Modify the program shown in Listing 28.6 to include a company name and an e-mail address. After you do this, change the number of contacts that can be stored from 25 to 50. *Hint:* The number of contacts possible is stored in the `Global` variable `MaxRecords`.

6. Beginning with the program that you created in Exercise 5, change the program to include a New Record button. Pressing this button should increase the size of the `Contacts` array by one and allow you to fill in this new structure. *Hint:* You will have to make the size of the array not a constant, but instead use the actual number of records in the file as your maximum number. This can be accomplished by tracking the number of records that have been filled out, and adding one to it.

CHAPTER 29

Planning an Application

Well, if you've read the book to this point, you have experience now with nearly every feature and language construct in Visual Basic. You have created dozens of short programs that illustrate one feature or another. At this point you probably are asking yourself, "What do I do with it all?" By using all the controls and objects discussed in previous chapters, you can amaze your friends with what you can make the computer do. But to get anything really useful done on your computer, you must create larger and more complex programs, called *applications*. Many things go into creating an application. Some of them are involved tasks, such as designing a form layout to use. Others can be easy, such as picking a color for the forms.

This chapter focuses on the planning stage of your application, during which you define all data structures the application needs, and identify functions that the application must perform. Later in the chapter, coding standards and naming conventions are discussed; you'll learn what a tremendous help these can be during application development.

The remainder of this book covers the rest of the application development process: application forms design, user interaction, data access, error processing, debugging techniques, performance, and how to distribute the application once it's finished. You will see how all the features of Visual Basic are brought together to create working, useful applications for yourself and other users.

What is an Application?

An application is a program or set of programs that perform some useful task. Generally, all of the programs that make up an application work against the same body of data, or database. In the past, programmers thought of applications as a few huge programs that work together toward the same goal. This has changed thanks to the introduction of Graphical User Interface (GUI) languages like Visual Basic. Programmers must now learn to think of an application as a large number of objects (that is, forms, controls, menus) and the small pieces of code that control these objects. By using these devices, the programmer can control his world of users, data, modems, printers, and so on.

Visual Basic has given us a new way of creating simple applications without the need for large amounts of Basic code. If we want, it also gives us the ability to create very complex applications that are easy to use. So, an application is a collection of functions that are combined together to perform a particular job in a uniform manner.

We will be creating our application by using the objects supplied by Visual Basic. Think of these objects as the building blocks of the application. As we design and create the application, we will constantly be adding more of these blocks to the pile. The pile must remain organized or it will fall apart. Because of these objects and what they do for us, we can now spend our time on the design and creation of our applications, instead of how to get the data in and out of the computer.

Designing an Application

The most difficult part of creating any application is deciding what it will do and how that should be done. The most important part of creating an application is the time spent in designing it. Unfortunately, most programmers do not spend as much time designing the application as they should. They would rather jump right in and start creating the application. For every hour that you spend designing your application, however, you could save as much as a day of debugging time. If you start with a good design, you will have considered more of the situations that might present problems later.

Note: As a general rule, it is always easier to fix a design problem before the program is created.

Building a good application is like building a house. When building a house, you would never put the walls up first. You need to have something to attach them to. If you start nailing wood together without a plan, your house would not be safe to live in. It's the same with building an application. The plan, or design, is the foundation that is needed. If you start with a good foundation, the house will stand up to a great deal of abuse; similarly, when you start with a good design, your application will hold up, even when people "live in it" more roughly than you'd like.

To arrive at a good design, you need to understand what makes up a good application. Both a house and an application must be built according to a carefully planned set of steps. Following this plan prevents the roof of a house from being built before the walls. In a Visual Basic application, you don't want to create any code before you create the forms.

If you build the application in the wrong order, or leave a part out, it will be very hard to code and even harder to test. It can take longer to complete, or never work at all. To design an application you must first understand what you want it to do.

In an application, the major parts are as follows:

- The database (if required)
- The program
- The user interface
- The reports and any other printed output
- The Help file

A typical application has its own folder in Windows (see fig. 29.1). This folder contains both the program icon and the help icon.

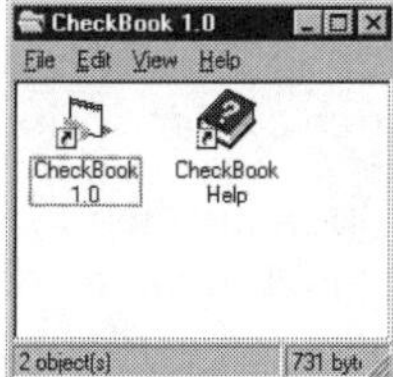

Figure 29.1

Application program group in Windows.

When you double-click the program icon, the Main Menu form is displayed (see fig. 29.2). This is the main application form, to which you must add all the program logic. In the next four chapters, you will learn how to add your logic to turn a blank main menu form into a functioning application. The finished application code can be found in the file CHKBOOK.ZIP on our Web site.

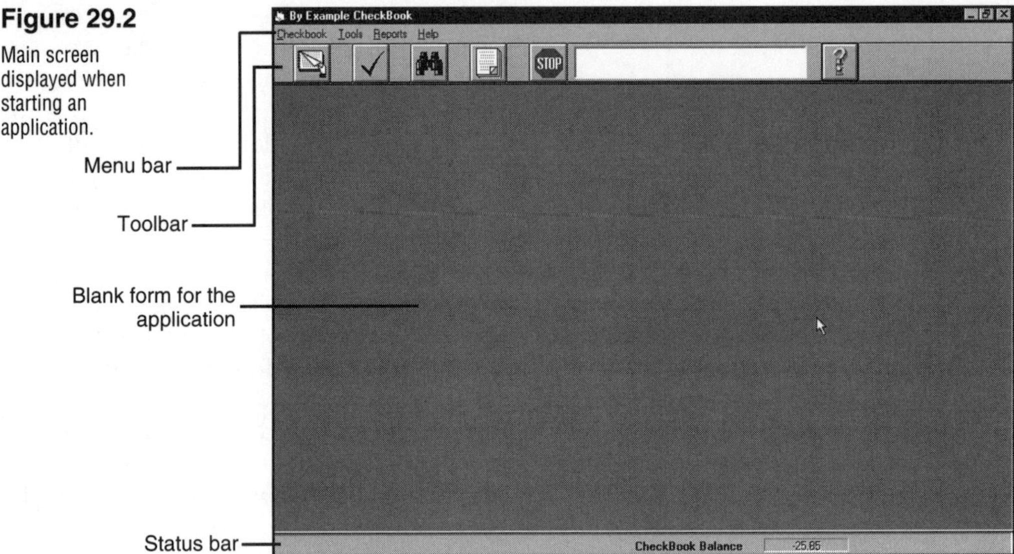

Figure 29.2
Main screen displayed when starting an application.

On this screen you see several Visual Basic objects required for an application. A typical application has a menu bar and toolbar at the top, a status bar at the bottom, and usually some initial form in the center of the screen. This *menu screen* generally is the starting point for all functions in the application. In the next few chapters you will learn how to create the form in figure 29.2, as well as some other forms you need for our example, a CheckBook application.

Describing the Application

Let's put our application into words. This is usually done by writing a short paragraph describing exactly what the application is and what it will be able to do. An example of such a description is:

> The CheckBook application will track checks and deposits from multiple bank accounts. For each account, it will keep a running balance. It also will allow an entry to be added, changed, or deleted. The user will be able to search for a specific entry using the payee, date, check number, or amount. This application can balance the checkbook against a bank statement. Finally, it can print an account statement.

This presents us with a good idea of what functions the application will do, giving you a final goal to aim for as you design the application. The next section discusses application functions in more detail.

Identifying the Necessary Functions

A programmed *function* is a small task that is part of the total application. Decide what major job you want the application to do. Then write down different tasks that are needed for that job. For our sample application, the major job is explicit in the name, it is an electronic checkbook. Now, let's take a closer look at some of the questions you need to answer during the design of the application.

First, how complicated will this application be? Only one bank account or many? Will it be able to print checks or just print statements (or not print at all)? Next, who will the users be? Families, small businesses, or both? Also, how many tasks will you include in it? Some tasks absolutely are required for the application to work; however, certain other tasks you can think of are nice to have, but aren't required. These tasks are called *features* because they make the application unique. Okay, let's list some of the more important tasks that must be in the application:

- ♦ Adding an entry
- ♦ Modifying an entry
- ♦ Deleting an entry
- ♦ Keeping a running account balance
- ♦ Balancing the checkbook
- ♦ Searching the checkbook for a specific entry
- ♦ Printing an account statement

This is far from a complete list of tasks or functions. However, from the menu list in figure 29.3, it is a good place to start because it specifies what the goal of each function should be. As the design progresses, you will find that there are more functions that should be added. When designing in Visual Basic you can start by designing the forms you might need, and then change them as you go along. This technique is called *prototyping*, or creating a demo as you design the actual programs. Prototyping also lets you decide what should happen when a given button on the form is clicked or when a menu option is selected.

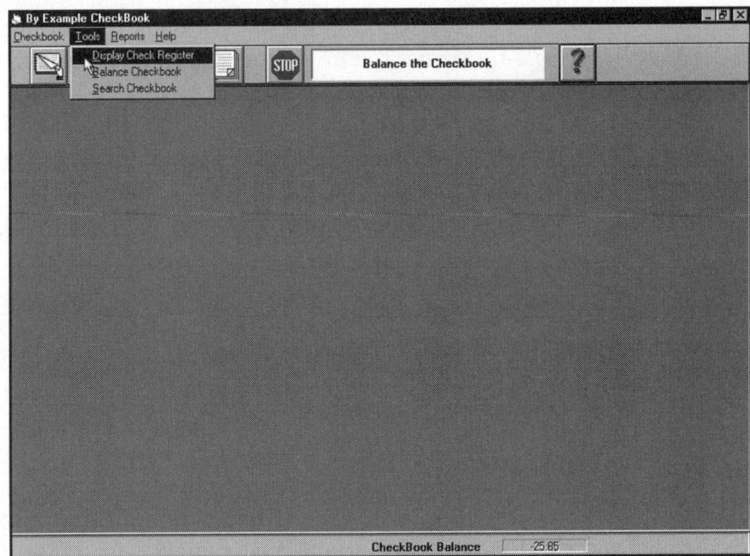

Figure 29.3

The menu bar showing some of the checkbook functions.

Describing Each Function Using Pseudocode

Like a good carpenter building a house, you must be able to bring all the elements together to form a working, usable, application package. Being able to bring together just the right number of forms, to make them look good, and to make it all easy-to-use, results in a good application.

A good method to use for designing an application is to write down in plain language what each function is going to do. This is called *pseudocode*. An example of a function described with pseudocode is the following:

```
GetNextCheck()
   Use a SQL call to the database to get the last check number
   in the LINE-ITEM table.
   Add 1 to the check number
   Return it to the calling routine.
```

When you use pseudocode, you should try to list all the events that will occur in the application. Then when you translate the pseudocode into an actual Visual Basic application, much of the code is already defined, this is much easier if the pseudocode is already in statement form, rather than a conversational-style paragraph.

This is not easy, because most of us do not think like a computer. But, it's still easier creating an application from pseudocode than from only ideas. Once you have the functions described in English, you can further break down the functions into subfunctions (a subfunction describes each step within a main function, such as, what will the program do when the save button on the deposit entry form is clicked).

You must always realize that the design you come up with is not set in cement. You should go back over it several times looking for possible problems in logic *before* you start building the application. This critical review of your plans is an important part of the design process. In addition, you will learn more about Visual Basic and programming this way, as you build the application. Some of these things will make the application better, but only if you could go back and rewrite some of the functions. Allow yourself to go back and change it, and the application will come out better.

Database Selection

Any application must have a way of storing the information that it will be working with. Selecting the method for storing the data is very important. The database is a collection of data for an application. It provides a single source of data. Because of the way data will be stored, it must be managed. In this section of the chapter we will discuss why we use databases, and how to design, create, and manage one.

Development of Databases

Over the years, databases were developed to handle more and more complex data retrieval requests. They arose because methods of data handling that were used earlier showed significant limitations.

Punch Cards

In the early days, data was kept in a simple format of 80 characters in a single line on a card (see fig. 29.4). These cards were read one at a time or sequentially, but once you had read a card, you could not go back to it. This created all sorts of problems in program design and creation. What if there was an error in the data? What happened if some of the data had to be updated? Following very close behind the punch card was punched paper tape.

These types of problems usually resulted in the application being run many times each time the process had to be completed. This causes delays and if there is only a certain amount of time to complete it, then there is a chance it would not finish in time.

Figure 29.4

Sequential record layout for the checkbook.

DATE	CHECK NUMBER	PAYEE NAME	AMOUNT

Sequential Files

These questions and others were the reasons to come up with a better solution. The next step in the evolution of data storage was the magnetic file on a disk. A file took all the data cards and stored them together on disk. This meant that the lines of data were no longer cards, but they were still read and processed in the same way. This still limited a program to a linear or straight line process. What was needed was a way to get a record from anywhere in the file when it is needed. The ability to read lines of data in any order was the first important step towards databases. This *random access* of data allowed the program to read and write the data in whatever order was needed to process the requests.

Relational Files

As the amount of data being stored increased, the need to have more efficient ways of storing and accessing the data became a priority. In the sequential file approach to data, every record needed to have all the data required for the process (for example, name, payee, and so on) included in the record. This duplication of data was a very large waste of disk space and processing time. What was needed was a way of *relating* or linking several separate files to each other. This ensured that data which was needed several times could be kept as a single entry in a related table. This *relational database* is an organized collection of data tables that can be accessed and updated in a variety of ways.

If we look at the database layout in figure 29.5, we can see how having certain information in separate tables makes it easier to control the data. Once the tables are created, we must link them together in order to get the data from the separate tables. This linking is called a table join. A table is *joined* by a field or fields in one table matching a field or fields in another table. While processing the data, an entire record of information can be constructed from the different tables in the database. Another thing that relational databases give us is the built-in capability of accessing our data using a variety of functions such as queries.

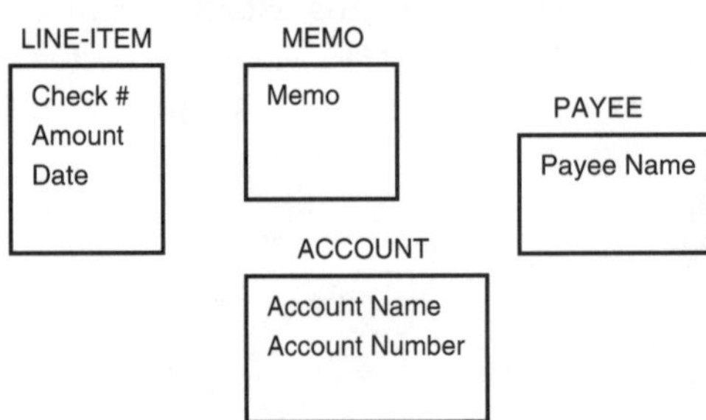

Figure 29.5

Relational table layout for the checkbook.

A *query* is a way of requesting certain records from the database. In most relational databases there is a standard language used to communicate with the database. This language is called SQL (Structured Query Language). An example of a SQL request is

```
Select * from line-item where date = '06/25/94' and amount > 25
```

Here, the date and amount parameters are used to restrict the records that will be retrieved to only certain, desired, records (in this case, those with an exact date of June 25, 1994 and an amount above 25).

Indexing speeds-up the retrieval process by putting the records in a particular order before they are searched. Although there are times when a sequential file is still used, most applications today use some form of relational database.

Designing the Database

To design the database, you use the same steps that you used to design the application. A good design lets you build a database that will provide you with faster, more accurate answers. The difference between designing the database, and designing the application, is generally determined by the type of application you are creating. Some applications have absolutely nothing to do with databases and others are more concerned with the user interface. To practice database design, we will actually build the database as we go. The time spent in designing a database is well worthwhile, as the process usually saves more time than it takes. Let's look at what is in a database and how it works.

What Makes up a Database?

A relational database lets you look at all of your data in the form of *tables*. A table consists of pieces of data, called *rows* that contain *columns*. What you would think of as a record is the *row*. Each row has at least one column that is unique to that row.

You might ask yourself, "Why can't I just start writing code?" The better you understand your data, the easier it will be to create a good design. If you design your database as you create the application, you will find that your application and database will have to be changed constantly to allow for changes in the design. Your database should contain whatever data you will need to produce the reports that you want. You should look at the reports and see what types of data you need to print out; from this, you can work backward to decide exactly what data you need.

In our checkbook application, for example, the reports may include such things as screen displays showing us the checkbook entries, statements, and checks. List the data that makes up those things. Once this is done, you should be able to list which *columns* are needed in the database. The CheckBook application needs the following columns:

Check Number

Entry Date

Amount Paid

Amount Deposited

Account Number

Account Name

Memo area

Check Payee or Deposit/withdrawal type

After you have all the data columns that you think you need, you will see that there are some data columns that are repetitive. The next step is to decide how many tables you will use for the data and what data columns go in what tables. It is during this process that you will combine certain data columns into one data column, such as the Amount Paid and Amount Deposited. In a simple application like the checkbook, you will probably need only 2-3 tables. One table will keep the actual data about the check, withdrawal or deposit; and another table should keep the data on who the payee is for the entry. As you go along you might see that there is a need for another table, but for now your database should look like the one shown in figure 29.6.

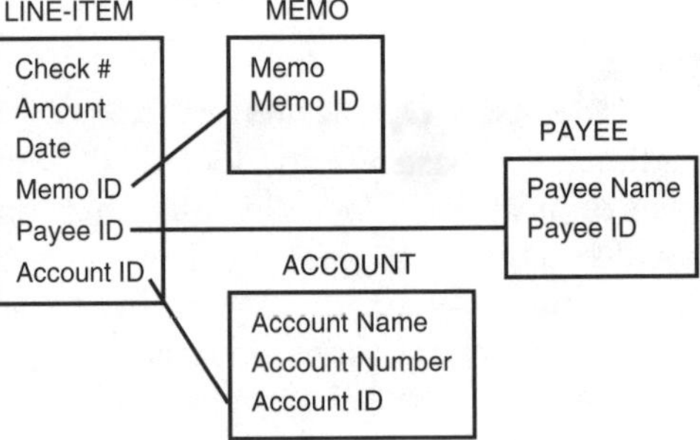

Figure 29.6

Database tables with the joins shown.

MS Access vs. ODBC databases

Which database should you use? There are dozens of commercial databases on the market today, dBASE, Paradox, and several others will work with Visual Basic 4, using the Data control. However, MS Access is connected to Visual Basic internally so that using it doesn't require anything special to be done. To connect to some other databases such as Watcom, Visual Basic requires Open Database Connectivity (ODBC) drivers to be installed on your PC. For more information, search for ODBC in the Visual Basic Help system.

Note: Choosing a database is entirely up to you. However, since MS Access connects directly to Visual Basic, I use it throughout these examples for simplicity's sake.

Using the Data Manager

Visual Basic comes with a program named Data Manager that allows you to manage several different databases including MS Access. Start Data Manager by choosing Data Manager from the Add-Ins menu on the Visual Basic menu bar.

Data Manager is a Visual Basic program used to manage the databases that you will use with your application. Data Manager allows you to create new Access databases and to attach several different types of existing databases to an Access database. These database types are listed below.

dBASE

Paradox

Btrieve

FoxPro

With this program you can add columns to existing tables, modify data in the tables for testing purposes, create indexes for the data, and delete data, columns, or tables from the database. When adding columns to a table you must specify what type of data will be in the column (that is, numeric, text, true/false, and so on). In addition, the size of the field is specified so that the database knows how much space it needs for the data.

Now you can create the database for our checkbook application. Start Visual Basic, then choose Data Manager from the Add-Ins menu. Once you get the Data Manager screen, choose New Database from the File menu. In the File Name area of the New Database properties sheet (see fig. 29.7), enter **Chkbook.mdb** as the database name and then click Save.

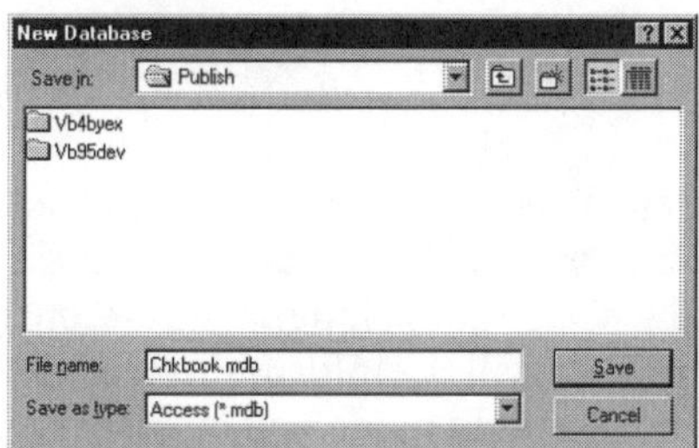

Figure 29.7

Entering a new database file name.

You should see the blank table form displayed (see fig. 29.8). At this point, you can add the tables you need for the checkbook.

Figure 29.8

The table list box for a database.

Now, you can add the first table, **LINE-ITEM**. Click the New button, and when the Add Table properties sheet appears (see fig. 29.9) enter the new table name.

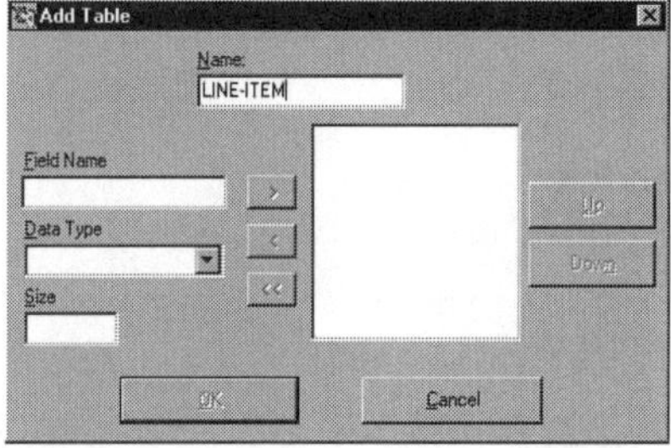

Figure 29.9

Adding a new table to the database.

Fields also can be added to the table in this properties sheet. Enter the Field Name **Chknum**, as shown in figure 29.10.

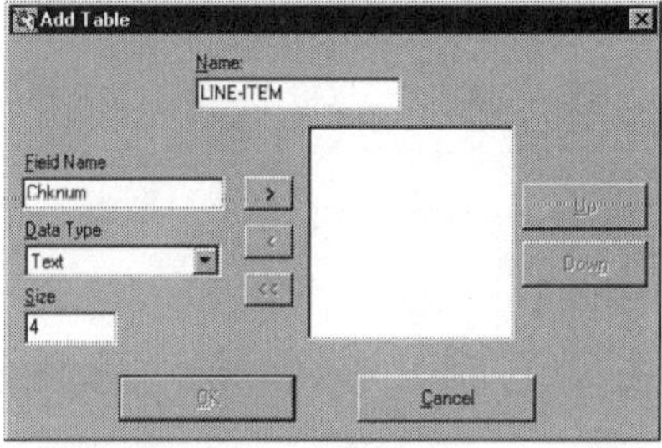

Figure 29.10

Adding a field to the table.

The Data Type drop-down list box (see fig. 29.11) displays the list of available field types from which you can select. For a complete description of the data types, refer to the Visual Basic language reference manual.

After entering all the information for the field, click the > button to add this field to the table. The field name will be displayed in the box on the right half of the Add Table properties sheet (see fig. 29.12). You can enter as many fields as you want using this properties sheet. Then, using the up/down buttons, you can reposition the fields in any order you want. Save the table by clicking the OK button.

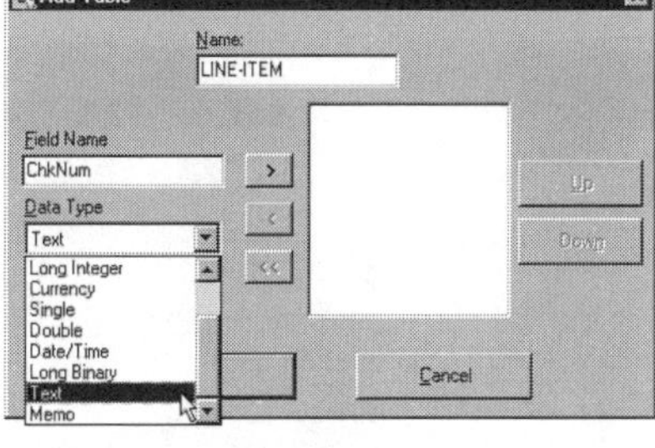

Figure 29.11

Add Table form showing the Data Types.

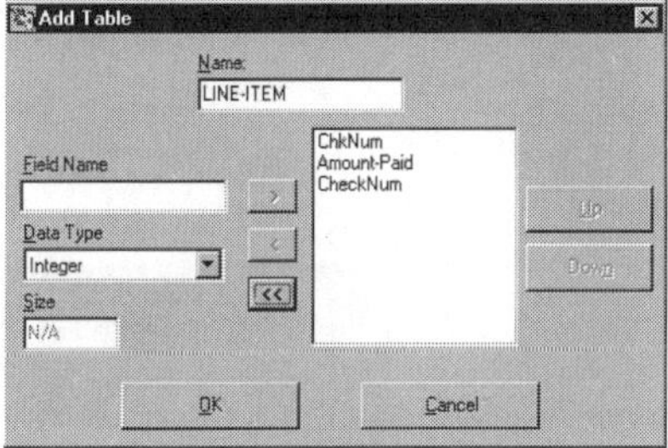

Figure 29.12

Field entry form showing the field list.

After you add the table, it will be displayed on the Tables form (see fig. 29.13).

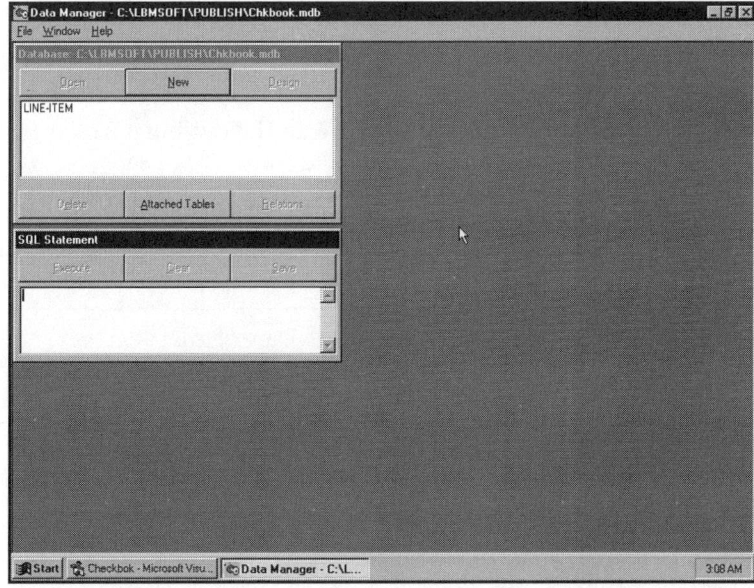

Figure 29.13

Tables form showing existing table name.

Click the Design button to display the Table Editor (fig. 29.14).

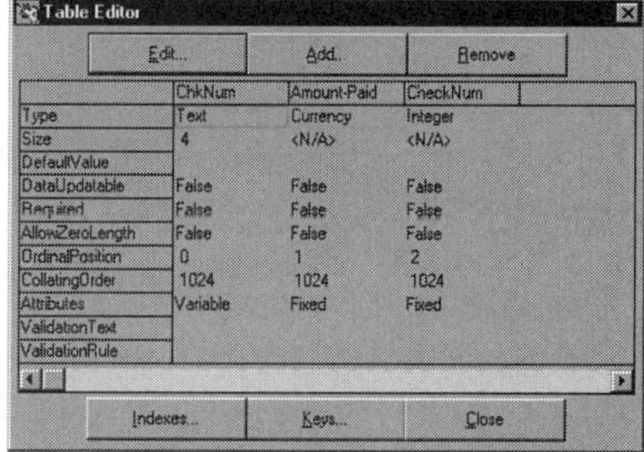

Figure 29.14
The Table Editor showing data field properties.

Click the Add button to add another field to the table (see fig. 29.15).

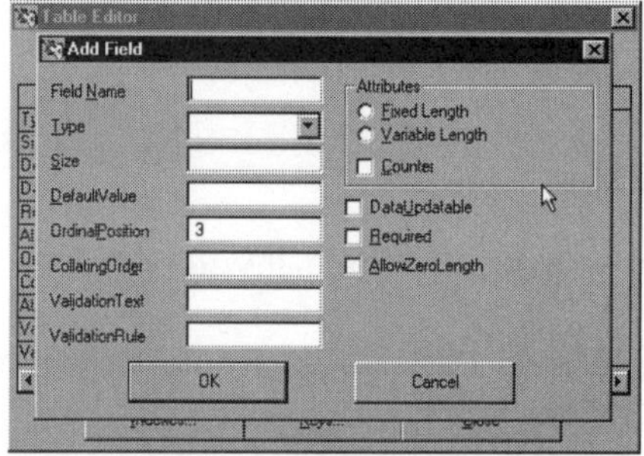

Figure 29.15
The Add Field properties sheet is accessed through the Table Editor.

Now, add the fields that are listed below, but it is okay to ignore the other settings that are shown on the Add Field form.

Table 29.1 LINE-ITEM Table

Column name	*Field type*	*Size*
EntryDate	Date/Time	
ClearRecv	Text	1
AmtPaid	Currency	
AmtDeposit	Currency	
AccountKey	Integer	
PayeeKey	Integer	
MemoKey	Integer	
ItemKey	Integer	

After we have entered the fields, we have to create an index for the table. An *index* is used by the database to order and search the data, just as the index of this book can be used to find the page containing a certain topic. Database indexes allow for very fast access of the data. In fact, most databases allow multiple indexes so that you can search the database in various ways.

To create an index, click the Indexes button on the Table Editor to open the Indexes form, and then click the Add button to create a new index.

In the Index Name field of the Add Index properties sheet (see fig. 29.16), enter the index name **ChkIndex**. The fields in the index should be `AccountKey` and `ItemKey`. We want it to be a primary *index* and to be unique. Making it *unique* means that there cannot be more than one combination of `AccountKey` and `Itemkey` in the table. Click the OK button to close and save the new index entry. When you return to the Indexes form, the new entry is listed (see fig. 29.17).

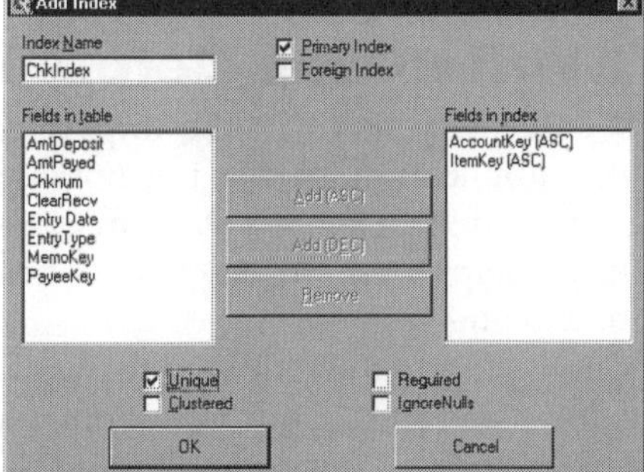

Figure 29.16

Adding an index to the table.

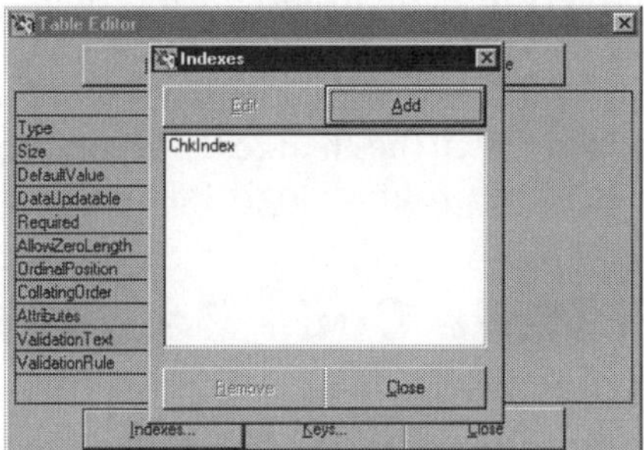

Figure 29.17

The Indexes form listing the index you just added.

After you have entered all the information for this table, close the Table Editor by clicking the Close button. Then close the Data Manager by choosing File, Exit. This saves all the work you did within Data Manager.

Data Manager is a very powerful tool for creating the database. Data Manager also can repair, compact, encrypt and decrypt the database. All of these functions are Visual Basic object *properties* for a Data control. In addition, Data Manager allows you to add data to the database to test your application. Application testing is discussed in Chapter 35, "Debugging and Distributing an Application."

What Not To Do

This may seem like a strange topic to include in a chapter on how to create Visual Basic applications, however, knowing what not to do when creating an application is just as important as knowing what you should do. Why applications begin with designing, and also why standards are important when building an application will be discussed in this section.

Don't Write Code Before Designing!

It should be clear by now why it is important to have a good design before starting to create an application. In case it is not, here are the reasons stated another way: Having a good design keeps you from guessing what to do next. Paying attention to the design helps to minimize changes to an application after the building of the application begins.

What if you forgot a window in the wall of a house? You would have to knock the wall down and start again, or cut out a window after-the-fact, which probably won't look as good as the planned windows. The same idea applies to programming. If you find that you have forgotten something in a section of program logic, it may be very difficult to add the forgotten logic without completely rewriting the section of code. However, if you find a logic problem, you can change the program logic and simply move on. Finally, if you find a design problem, you have to alter the design to match the change. To accommodate the design change, you may have to remove some program logic that's already written.

Don't Write Code Before Establishing Standards!

Having programming standards when creating any computer program is very important. The better you name the routines and program variables, the easier it will be to understand the code and find errors while you are testing code. You can see, for example, that the routine in Listing 29.1 is easier to follow than the one in Listing 29.2 (these listings aren't included on the Web site because they're only examples).

Listing 29.1 Routine Without the Use of Conventions

```
Function function1 (ByVal var1) As Integer
Dim x, y As Integer
Dim z As String
If Right$( var1, 1) <> "\" Then
var1 = var1 + "\"
End If
On Error Resume Next
ChDrive var1
If Err <> 0 Then GoTo label1
ChDir "\"
x = 3
y = InStr(4, var1, "\")
Do While y <> 0
z = Mid$( var1, x + 1, y - x - 1)
Err = 0
MkDir z
If Err <> 0 And Err <> 75 Then GoTo label1
Err = 0
ChDir z
If Err <> 0 Then GoTo label1
x = y
y = InStr(x + 1, var1, "\")
Loop
function1 = True
Exit Function
label1:
If Err = 71 Then
MsgBox "Please insert Disk in Drive"
Resume
End If
function1 = False
End Function
```

Listing 29.2 Routine Showing the Use of Conventions

```
' Create the path contained in DestPath$
' First char must be drive letter, followed by
' a ":\" followed by the path, if any.
'-----------------------------------------------
Function CreatePath (ByVal DestPath) As Integer
Dim backpos, forepos As Integer
Dim temp As String
    '
    ' Add slash to end of path if not there already
    '-------------------------------------------
    If Right$(DestPath, 1) <> "\" Then
        DestPath = DestPath + "\"
    End If
```

continues

Listing 29.2 Continued

```
    '
    ' Change to the root dir of the drive
    '--------------------------------
    On Error Resume Next
    ChDrive DestPath
    If Err <> 0 Then GoTo errorOut
    ChDir "\"
    '
    ' Attempt to make each directory, then change to it
    '-----------------------------------------------
    backpos = 3
    forepos = InStr(4, DestPath, "\")
    Do While forepos <> 0
        temp$ = Mid$(DestPath, backpos + 1, forepos - backpos - 1)
        Err = 0
        MkDir temp
        If Err <> 0 And Err <> 75 Then GoTo errorOut
        Err = 0
        ChDir temp
        If Err <> 0 Then GoTo errorOut
        backpos = forepos
        forepos = InStr(backpos + 1, DestPath, "\")
    Loop
    CreatePath = True
    Exit Function
    '
errorOut:
    If Err = 71 Then
        MsgBox "Please insert Disk in Drive"
        Resume
    End If
    CreatePath = False
End Function
```

First of all, you should be able to tell exactly what a given routine is doing, just by its name. You should make variable names as long as necessary so that the use of each variable is plain (for example, `chk_amt_input` is the variable name for the data field that holds the check-amount-input value). In addition, each subroutine name should reflect the task the subroutine performs (such as, `Add_Deposit_to_Balance()`). This makes the subroutines in the application easy to read and to understand.

Summary

So, designing and building an application is easy. Right? Not really. As we have seen, there are a great many things to think about and many pitfalls to watch for. You may have noticed that I have mainly avoided the term *coding*. This is because I believe that an application is designed, created, and built rather than coded and written. We can never spend too much time designing an application. Of course, we have to balance design time with the overall schedule, and make sure we get the application finished when it needs to be finished.

In addition, the database must be flexible enough to allow changes in design and function. We have seen that—given enough thought—a database can be created that leaves us the ability to add more fields. If the addition of new fields to a table (or the addition of a new table) does not affect the database, then we have succeeded in designing a good database.

Also, using good names for data fields and subroutines will make our life easier when reading and debugging an application. If you can look at a subroutine or variable, and understand its function just by reading its name, you are one step closer to having a very maintainable application.

In the next chapter, you are going to design the forms needed for the checkbook application. In addition, you will see how to interact with the user through menus and command buttons.

Review Questions

Answers to review questions are in Appendix A.

1. What is an application?
2. What are the major parts of an application?
3. What is pseudocode?

4. What is the difference between sequential and relational files?
5. What does the acronym SQL stand for? What is SQL used for?
6. How does Visual Basic connect to a database?
7. What is Data Manager used for?

8. What are the benefits of using programming standards?

Review Exercises

1. List some other features you might want to add to the checkbook application.

2. Using Data Manager, add the remaining tables to the CHKBOOK database. Listed below are the table names and data fields for each of the remaining tables. Also add an ascending index for each table on the counter field in the table.

Column Name	*Field Type*	*Length*
	Payee Table	
Payeeid	Integer	
PayeeName	Text	20
	Memo Table	
Memoid	Integer	
Memo	String	20
	Account Table	
Accountid	Integer	
AccountName	Text	20
AccountNumber	Text	15

3. Using good naming standards, finish the design description below. Write pseudocode for the routines described in the design.

```
Checkbook Main Form
Menu: Checkbook; Tools; Reports; Help
     Checkbook: Add entry; Update entry; Delete entry; Change
account; Exit
     Tools: Balance Checkbook; Search checkbook
     Reports: Print account statement
     Help
Toolbar: Add; Delete; Delete; Reports; Reconcile account;
➥Search; Exit; Help
```

The button bar should also have a caption box to display what the buttons do. In the middle of the form a grid should display the current account's check register. The status bar should be shown at bottom of form and it should always have the current account's balance.

When the Add Entry menu or button is selected, show the `Entry` form with all input fields blanked out. When the `Update/Delete` function is selected an entry from the grid must have been selected for action.

When the `Reports` function is selected, print the checkbook with a running balance. When the `Search` function is selected, display a form asking for the data to search for.

When the `Balance` checkbook function is selected, then what? When account selection is selected, then display the account list form. When `Exit` is selected, then close all forms and end application.

Creating Forms

A windows application is a collection of related forms that allows a user to interact easily with the data. As you might have seen in other Windows applications, some applications can be very useful, but boring to look at or use. In Chapter 9, "The Form," you brought many Visual Basic objects together to create simple applications that were interesting to look at. Using what you have learned about the features of Visual Basic, in addition to some design standards that we will discuss, you can create a useful application that looks good, and is easy to use. However, no matter how closely standards are followed, an application's forms will to some degree reflect the personality of the programmer who created them.

What we are going to cover in this chapter is how to design a form, what should be placed on it, where the objects should be placed and how the Multiple Document Interface (MDI) forms enable us to create very complex looking applications. Also, we will see how the menus, Toolbars and Help features that we see all the time in Windows applications are created and how they enhance the application.

Forms, The User Interface

The form is *the* most important part of any application. If the interface is not easy, or it just doesn't look good, then nobody will want to use it. The GUI interface offers us a wide variety of ways of making the user 'feel' comfortable with the application. The experience of the user has to be taken into account when considering the layout of the forms.

The Principles of Good Form Design

Designing a form is a little different than the design process we have already covered in the previous chapter. When we design a form we want to keep in mind the following design concepts.

- Make all of the forms in an application consistent.
- Use the same standards throughout the application.
- When possible, have the command buttons located in the same positions on all forms.
- Use color to make important information stand out.
- Make the form easy to read.
- Don't clutter up the form with too much information.
- Make data entry simple.

Now that we have listed the principles, let's go over them one at a time.

- Make all of the forms in an application consistent.

A good form should display the same information in the same way all the time (see fig. 30.1). This makes it easier to understand the data. If the same information is displayed differently on different forms, then it should be for a good reason and not because it looks good.

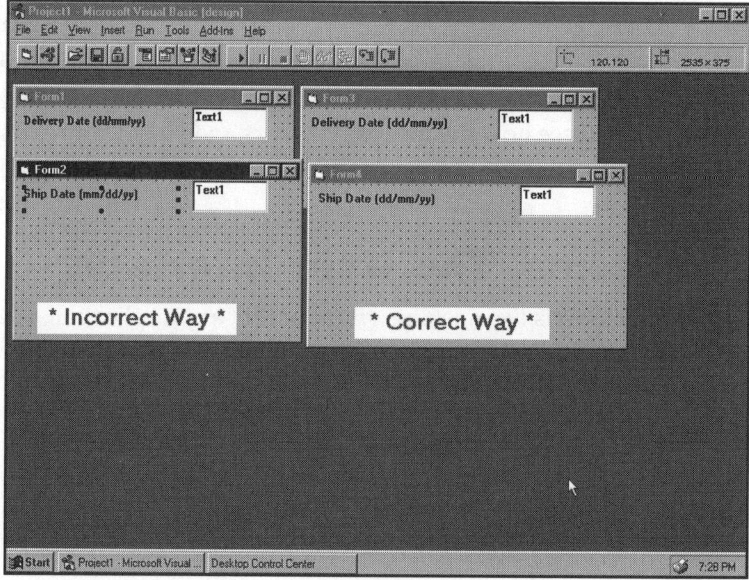

Figure 30.1

Use the same format when displaying data.

- Use the same standards throughout the application.

  Keeping the same standards means that if you use a particular word to describe something, continue to use the same word on all forms (see fig. 30.2). Also, don't change labels on command buttons or prompts. If the command button on a form is Cancel, don't change it to Quit on the next form.

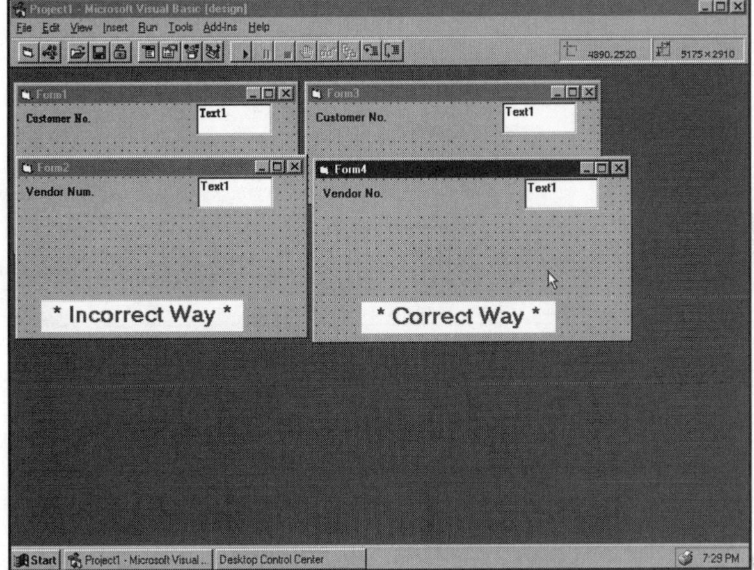

Figure 30.2
Standardize the words you use on a form.

- Have the command buttons located in the same positions on all forms.

  If you move command buttons around from one form to the next, you can confuse the user (see fig. 30.3). If you have a Delete button on Form1 where a Save button is on Form2, the user can delete data by accident.

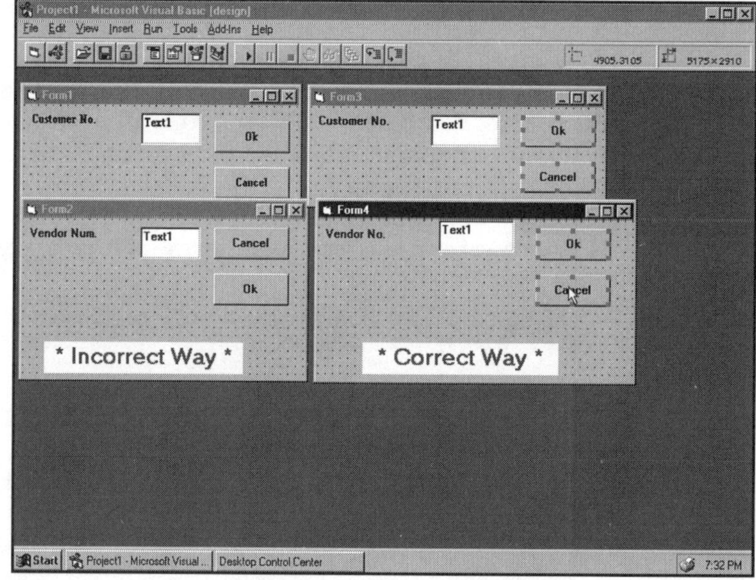

Figure 30.3
Keep the buttons in the same position.

♦ Use color to make important information stand out.

Color is the best way of making a point. To have something stand out, change its color (see fig. 30.4). For our checkbook, if the balance becomes negative, we will change the color of the number to red.

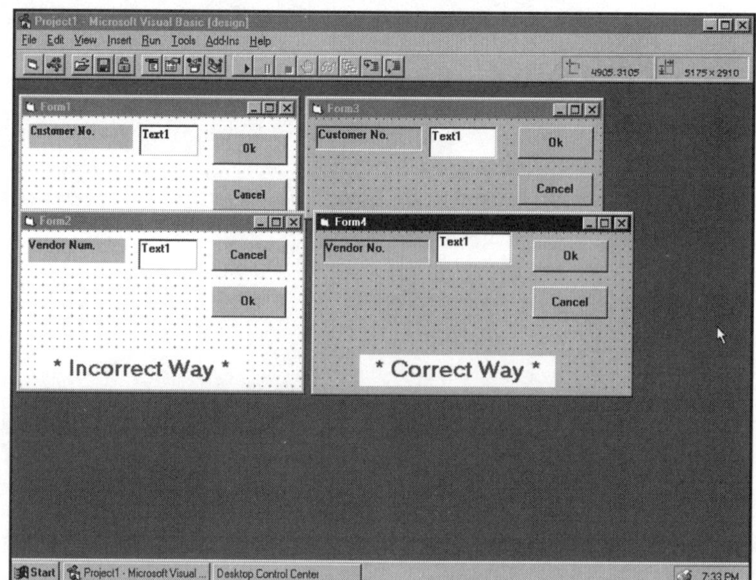

Figure 30.4
Color makes things stand out.

- Make the form easy to read.

  Don't confuse the user by using many different fonts or font sizes to display prompts and data (see fig. 30.5). You should choose a specific size and font for data fields that stand out well. In addition, you should use a different font for the labels and prompts. This will let the user know what are labels and what are data fields on the form. Only use 1-2 different fonts on a form. Finally, underline might look good on paper but, on a screen it is very hard to read.

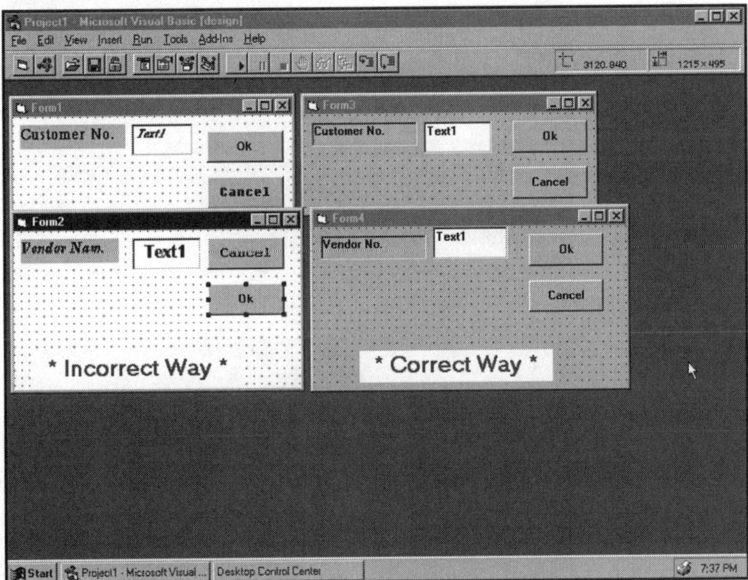

Figure 30.5

Different fonts can be confusing.

- Don't clutter up the form with too much information.

  Many programmers feel that they need to have all the information on the same form. Don't feel that you have to do this. As you can see from figure 30.6 this will only clutter up the form and confuse the user. What you should do if there is too much information is either use the Windows 95 Tab property sheet control to your form or separate the form into two different forms.

- Make data entry simple.

  The user should be able to enter his information easily and quickly. The data fields on the form should flow smoothly in a logical direction of input (see fig. 30.7). You should make use of combo boxes for list selection, option buttons for multiple options and check boxes for Yes/No questions.

Figure 30.6

Too much information is not good.

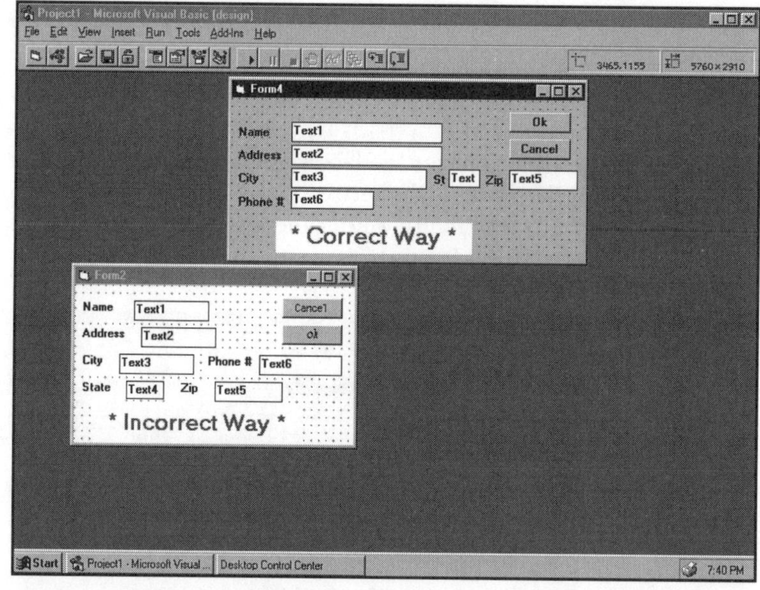

Figure 30.7

Data entry should be easy.

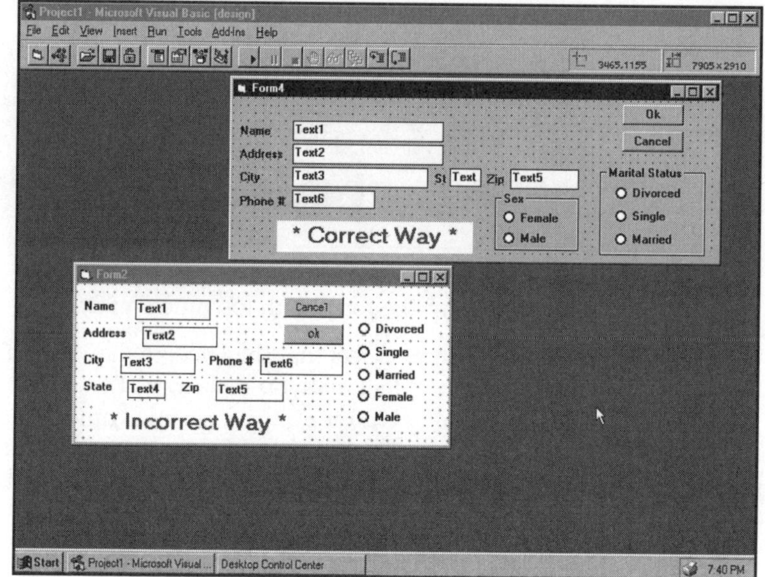

Deciding What Should Be on Each Form

Each form in the application should be looked at as having a distinct job to do. In most applications there are many different types of forms. The *main form* is the exception to this view of single function forms. The main form, or *parent* form, is the frame of the application. All other objects and forms will be selected and displayed on the main form.

Your checkbook is a fairly simple application, so it will have only a very few forms. To start off, let's list the forms that you are going to want. Even after you have these forms created, you will still make changes as you go along. You must also look at each form and list the data elements and functions that are associated with each of them.

The main menu form (see fig. 30.8) only has the menu bar, button bar, and the status bar on the form. Within the status bar the checkbook balance displayed. The button bar contains buttons to add, delete and change an entry, a button to print a report, one to balance the checkbook, another to search the checkbook, and of course one for Help and one to exit the application. In addition, there is a Label object on the button bar that displays what each button does.

Figure 30.8

The main form is where the check register, Toolbar, status bar and menu list will always appear.

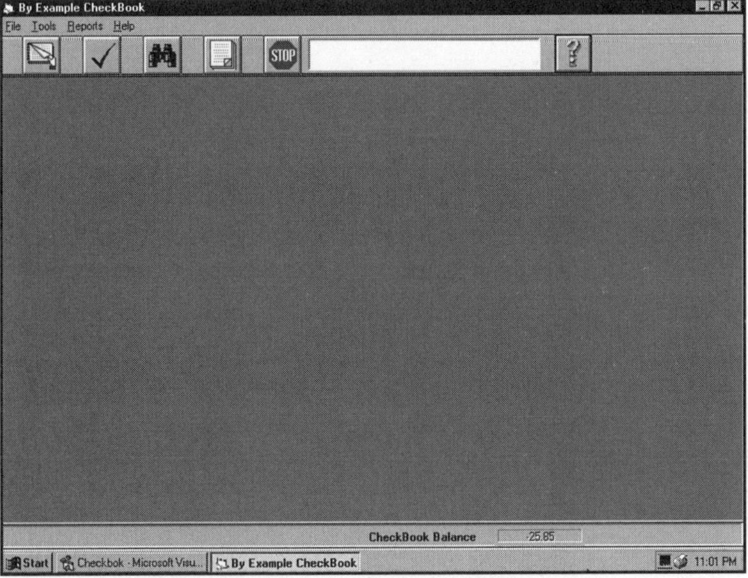

The Line Item Entry form (see fig. 30.9) will contain all the fields for a checkbook entry. This will include the Entry Date, Check Number (if it is a check), the Payee, the Amount, an area to enter a note about the entry, and two option buttons to tell the application whether the entry is a Check or a Deposit.

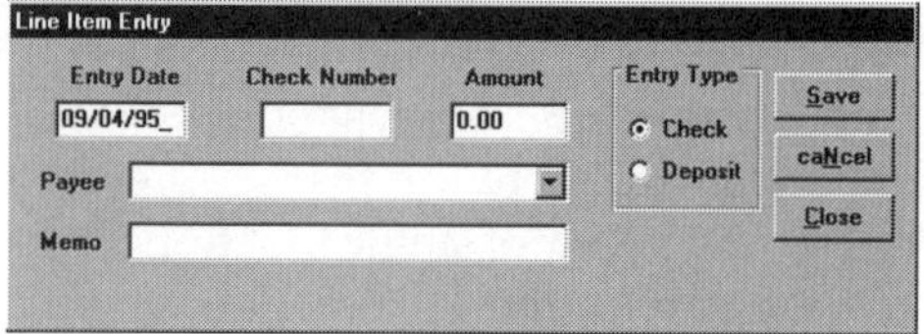

Figure 30.9
The Line Item Entry form is where both the Check and Deposit entries will be done on this form.

The account selection form (see fig. 30.10) is a very simple form. It only contains a data control to display the account name and number for selection.

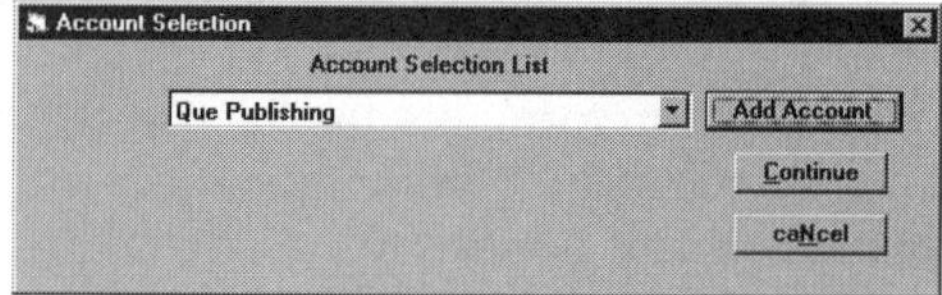

Figure 30.10
The Account Selection form will prompt for the account the user wants to work with.

The Checkbook Balance Display form (see fig. 30.11) will let us balance a checkbook account. To do this we need to enter the ending balance and also mark the entries that have been cleared. We will then need to display the checkbook in a Grid control.

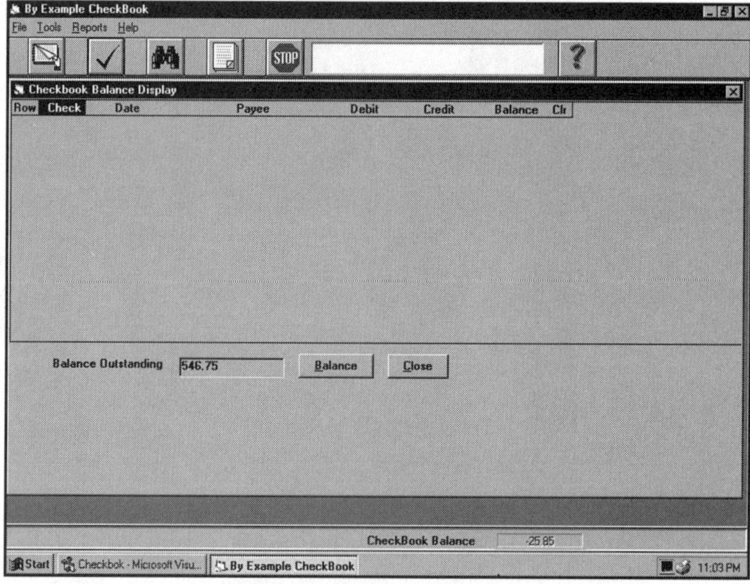

Figure 30.11
The Checkbook Balance Display form will let the user balance the checkbook.

The Check Register Display form (see fig. 30.12) will display the entire account information. It will use a Grid control to do this.

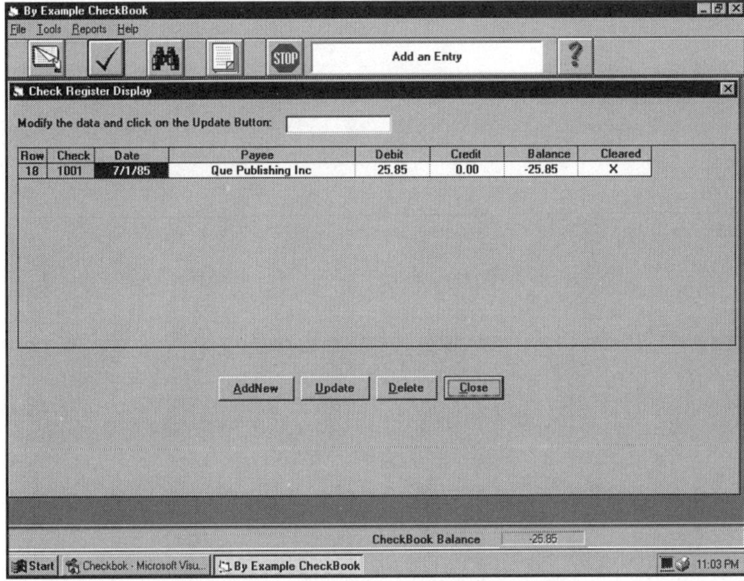

Figure 30.12
The Check Register Display form will display the current account's check register.

The Checkbook Search form (see fig. 30.13) will search the current account for the text entered. It will have a text box in which to enter the search information, and several option buttons to select which field to search.

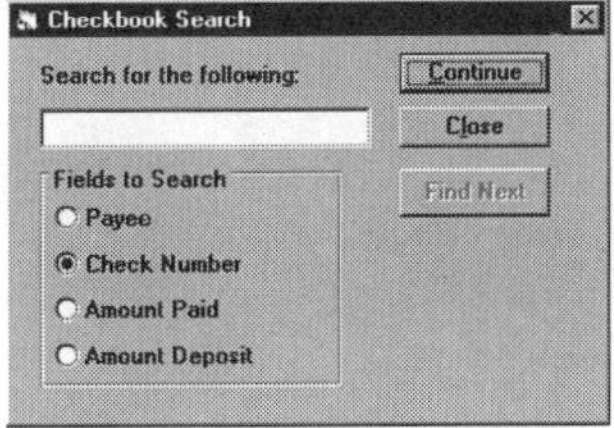

Figure 30.13
The Checkbook Search form is all the user needs to ask for a specific entry in the checkbook.

Let's Create the Forms

Whenever you start Visual Basic, it opens a new project. A *project* is nothing more than how Visual Basic keeps track of what is in your application. In addition to the project, you must also select the custom controls that you want in your application. To do this, select Custom Controls from the Tools menu list and then select the Available Controls you want from the list (see fig. 30.14). In this application, you will use the 3D, Grid, Masked Edit and Common Dialog controls. Click the OK button to close the form.

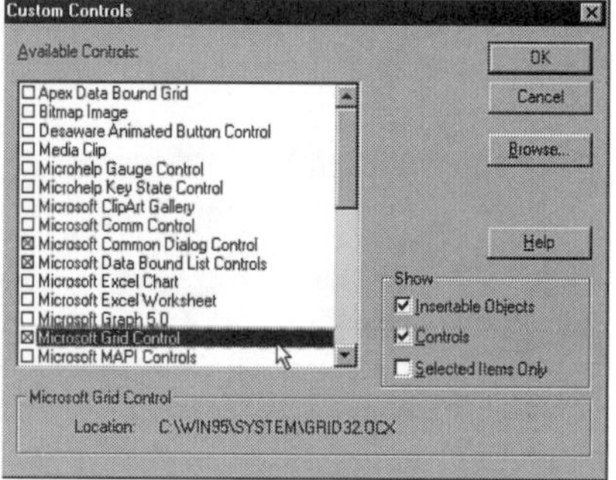

Figure 30.14
Custom Controls selection form.

The first form, named Form1, is already displayed (see fig. 30.15).

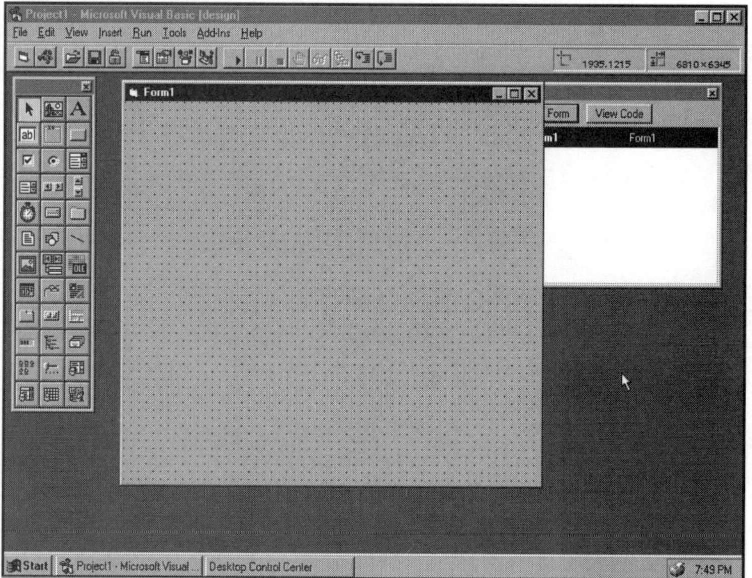

Figure 30.15
Visual Basic screen with Form1 open.

However, since you are creating a new application and will be using MDI forms, you must first remove the default form (Form1) from the project and then add a new form from the Insert pull-down menu (see fig. 30.16). This new form is called an MDIForm. Select MDI Form from the Insert menu to open it.

You will be adding several objects to this form. In addition, you will be adding a menu and also making changes to some of the *properties* of the form. These properties are displayed on their own form (see fig. 30.17) and will be modified in the following section.

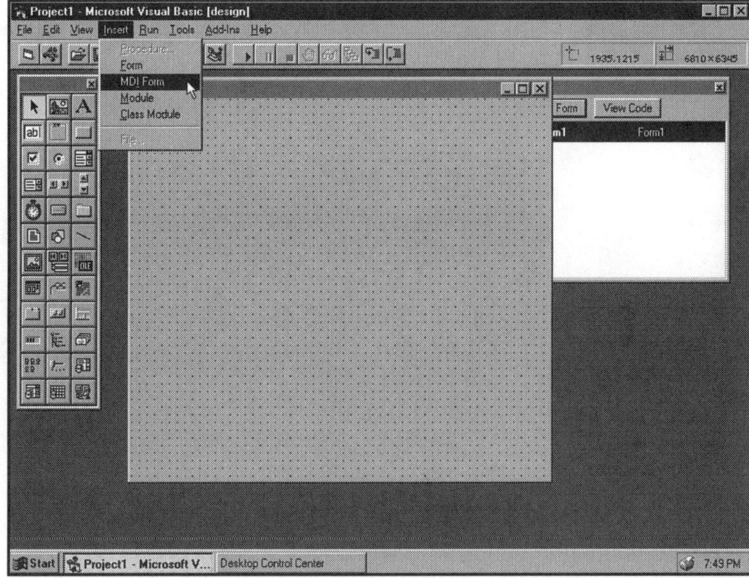

Figure 30.16
MDI Form menu selection.

The first thing we want to change is the `Name` of the form and the `Caption`. Let's change the form's name to `CKBKMAIN` and the caption to `By Example Checkbook`. To do this, click on the properties form and find the `Caption` line (see fig. 30.17), then click on the word `Form1` and type in the new caption. Changing the `Name` of the form is done the same way.

The status bar is an SSPanel box.

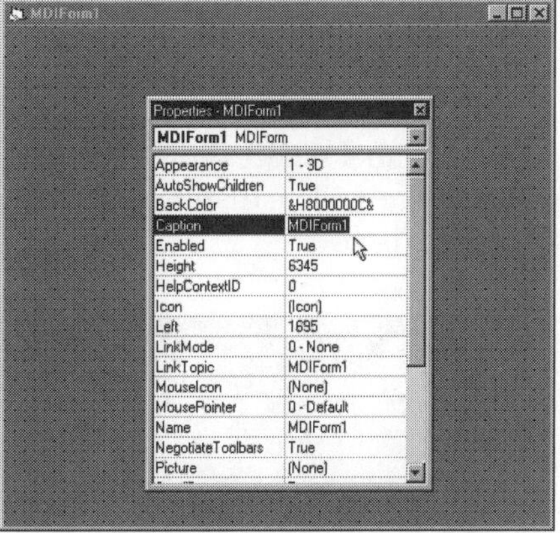

Figure 30.17
`Caption` property of form.

Example

To add a status bar to our application main form, we will first click on the SSPanel control in the Toolbox.

Then we will draw the SSPanel object on the form (see fig. 30.18).

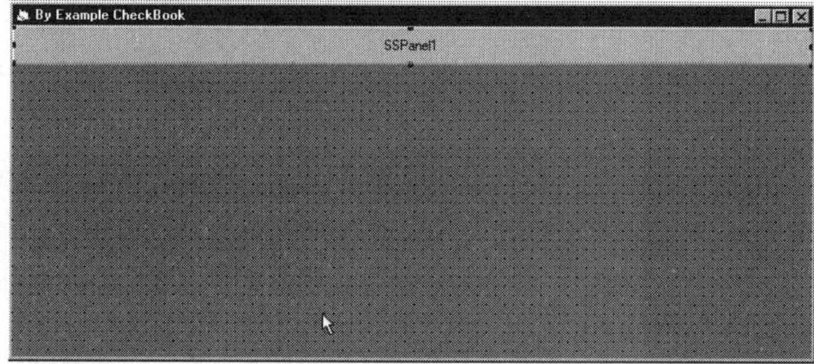

Figure 30.18
SSPanel control drawn on the form.

Click on the Properties form and then click on the `Align` property for the SSPanel box to change it to `2 - Align Bottom` (see fig. 30.19).

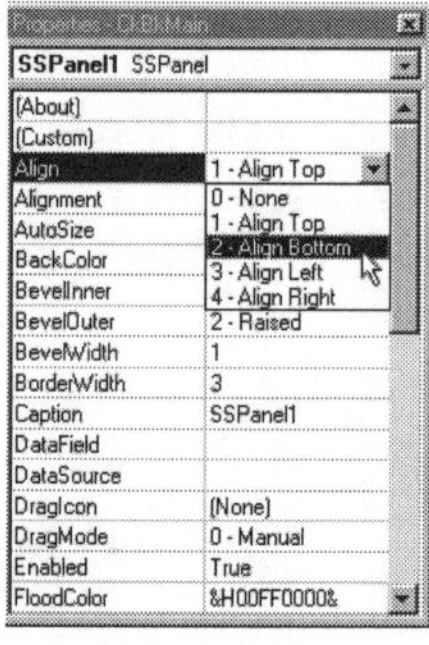

Figure 30.19
`Align` property of SSPanel box set to `2 - Align Bottom`.

Now draw a label object on the status box. This label box will be where the checkbook balance will be displayed (see fig. 30.20). The label should have a `Name` property of `lblbalance`.

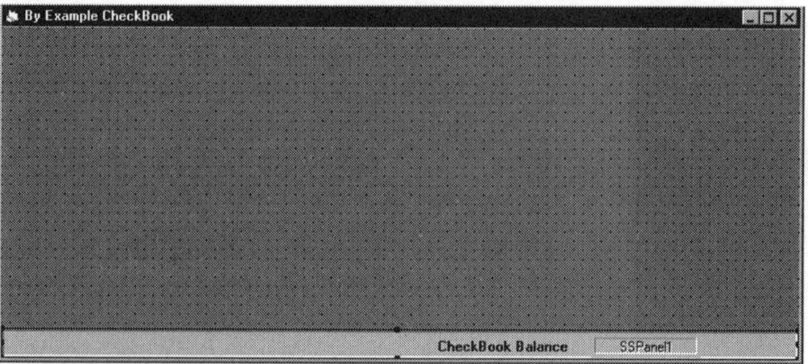

Figure 30.20
Checkbook form with the status bar and balance label.

We will be putting the Toolbar on the MDI form later in this chapter. When using a database, we also need Data control and Data Aware controls on the form. A Data control is the method that Visual Basic uses to connect to the database. Data controls will be discussed in detail in Chapter 33, "Adding Data and Grid Controls." The forms that need Data controls and Grid controls will be created in the same chapter.

At this point, we can build only parts of the forms we need for the application. All of these forms we create will have a Cancel button. The forms that allow data entry will have a Save button and forms like the search form will have a Continue button. The next form we can build is the Line Item Entry form. Click on the New form button.

This will create another form in our project. The project is the way Visual Basic keeps track of what is in our application. Change this forms caption to `Line Item Entry` and the form name to `LineItem`. In addition, change the `MDIchild` property to `True` and set its `Borderstyle` property to `1–Fixed Single`. Now we can draw the objects that we need on the form. The objects that are on the form are shown in the following table.

Screen Label	*Control Type*	*Control Name*
Entry Date	Masked Edit Box	mskdate
Check Number	Text Box	txtchknum
Payee	ComboBox	cboPayee
Amount	Masked Edit Box	mskAmt
Memo	Text Box	txtMemo
Deposit	Optionbutton	optDeposit
Check	Optionbutton	optCheck

When you are finished, the form will look like the one shown in figure 30.9. Add the Date field by clicking on the masked edit button.

Draw a box on the form. This is our date field, so change the `Name` property to `mskDate` and also change the `Mask` to `##/##/##`. This mask or format will only allow numbers to be entered in a date format. Next add a label next to the date field that has a caption of Entry Date (see fig. 30.21).

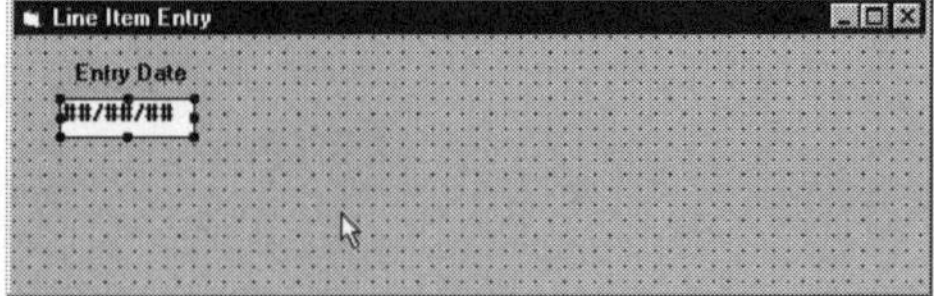

Figure 30.21

Line Item Entry form with only the Entry Date field on it.

The Amount field is also a masked edit box so add it the same way as the date field. Name it `mskAmt` and the mask should be `#,###.00`. This will allow dollar amounts to be entered.

The Check Number and Memo fields are only text boxes. The difference between a text box and a masked edit box is that there is no `Mask` property in the text field. However, you must set the `Maxlength` property of the text box to match the length of the field in the database. Draw the two text boxes on the form as shown in figure 30.22.

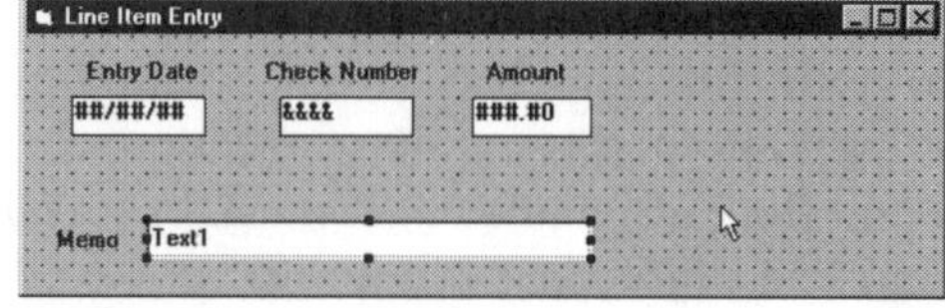

Figure 30.22
Line Item Entry form with the fields on it.

The Payee field will allow the user to enter a new payee to the application or select one from `dbCombolist`. To add the Payee field, click on the dbCombo button (figure 30.23).

Figure 30.23
The dbCombo button in the Toolbox.

Then draw the combo box on the form. It should be named `cboPayee`. The other property we have to set is the `Style` property to make this a combo box. Your form should now look like the one shown in figure 30.24.

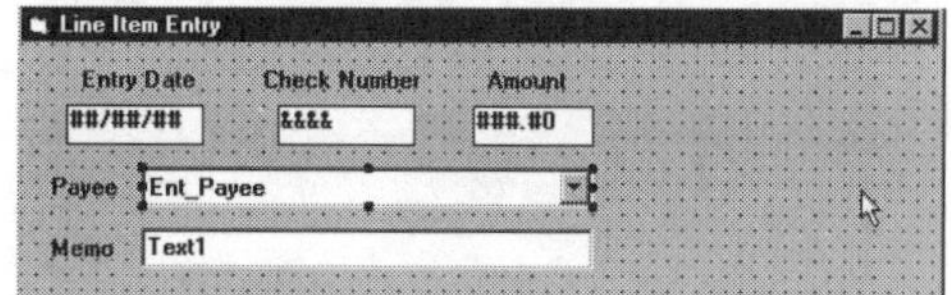

Figure 30.24
Line Item Entry form with the combo box on it.

The final object is the option buttons for the Check and Deposit selections. These buttons are in a frame. First, add the frame and then add two option buttons to the frame. The buttons should have captions that say `Check` and `Deposit`, respectively (see fig. 30.25).

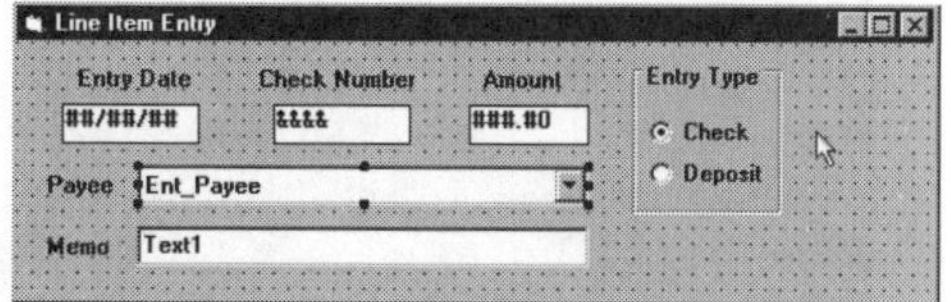

Figure 30.25
Line Item Entry form with all the fields on it.

As I mentioned before, you will also need several command buttons. Add the Save button by clicking on the command button in the Toolbox and then drawing it on the form. The caption should be `Save` and the name should be `btnSave`. All the command button names should start with `btn`. Now add the Cancel and Close buttons to the form. Your form should now look like the one shown in figure 30.9.

Even though you will be adding the Data controls and Grid controls to the other forms later, you can still create the forms with only command buttons on them. Add a new form to the application and name it `CHKBAL`. Change the caption to `Checkbook Balance Display`. Then add the Balance and Close command buttons to the bottom of the form. You now have an empty form to use later (see fig. 30.26). Now add the remaining three forms to the application. Change the `Name` and `Caption` properties for each so that they follow the naming standards you have been using.

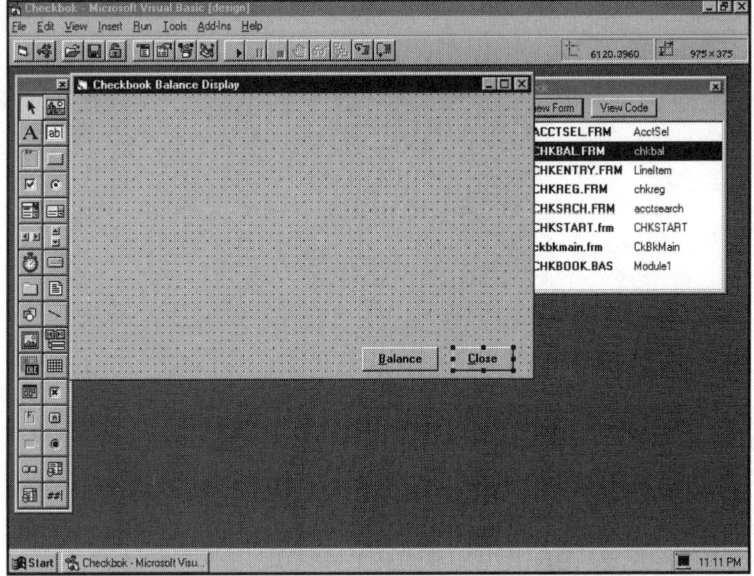

Figure 30.26

An empty form with only command buttons.

MDI Forms

An MDI form gives us the ability to give the user an application that can display multiple child forms within one parent form. A *child* form is an ordinary form that can only be displayed within the parent form's border. When a child form is minimized, its icon appears on the MDI form's desktop instead of the Windows desktop (see fig. 30.27).

In addition, when a child form is maximized, its title is combined with the MDI form's and is displayed in the MDI form's title bar (see fig. 30.28).

Most application designs use the MDI form to control access to parts of the application at any given time. Also, when the application is closed or ended, all of the child forms will be closed and any close functions will be performed *before* the application actually ends. When a non-child form is minizmized, its icon will appear on the Windows desktop instead of the MDI forms desktop (see fig. 30.29).

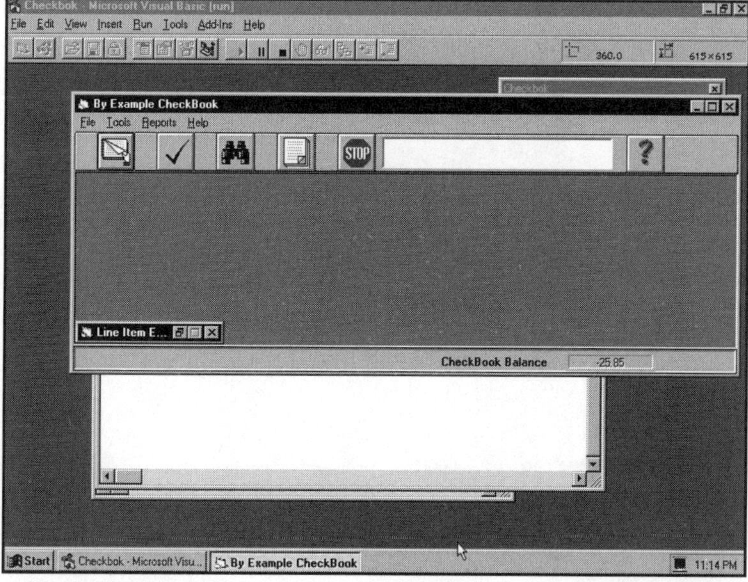

Figure 30.27
Child form icon on the MDI form desktop.

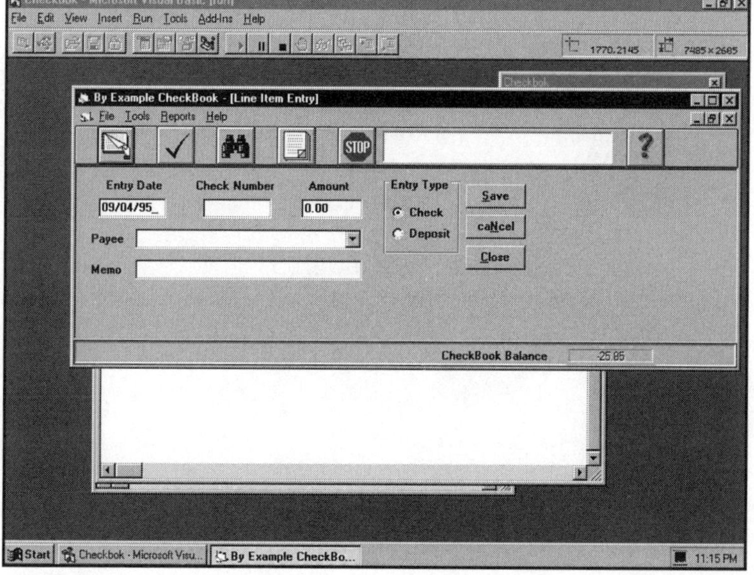

Figure 30.28
Child form title on the MDI form.

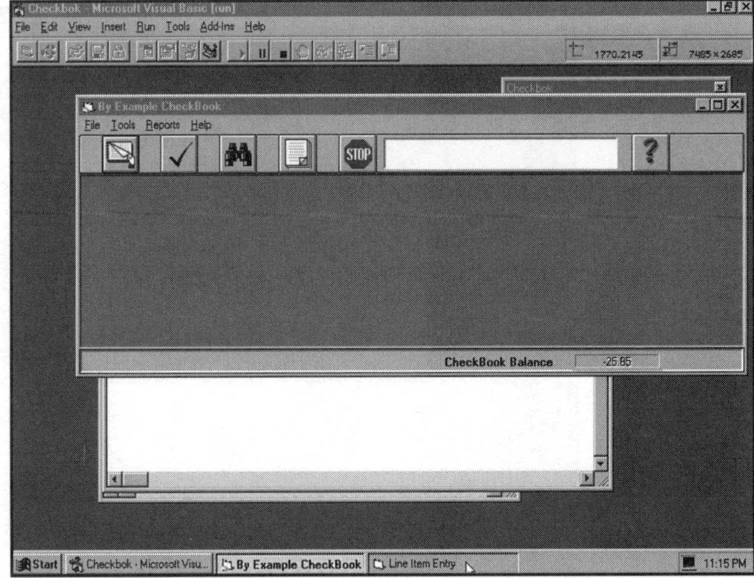

Figure 30.29
Minimized non-child form.

MDI Forms—Parent and Child

In any application, there can be only one parent MDI form and any number of child forms. What you want displayed in the main form will help you decide whether to use the MDI interface or not. The only objects that you can place directly on the MDI form are the ones that support the `Align` property. The Picture Box and SSPanel controls both support the `Align` property. In addition, the Timer and Command Dialog controls can be placed on a MDI Form.

In the Checkbook application that you designed in Chapter 29, you have a Grid control being used on the form, so you have a choice. You can either put the Grid control on a child form or not use MDI forms at all. The choice is yours, however, for the purpose of this book. I will be using MDI forms. This will allow you to have more then one form open at a time (see fig. 30.30).

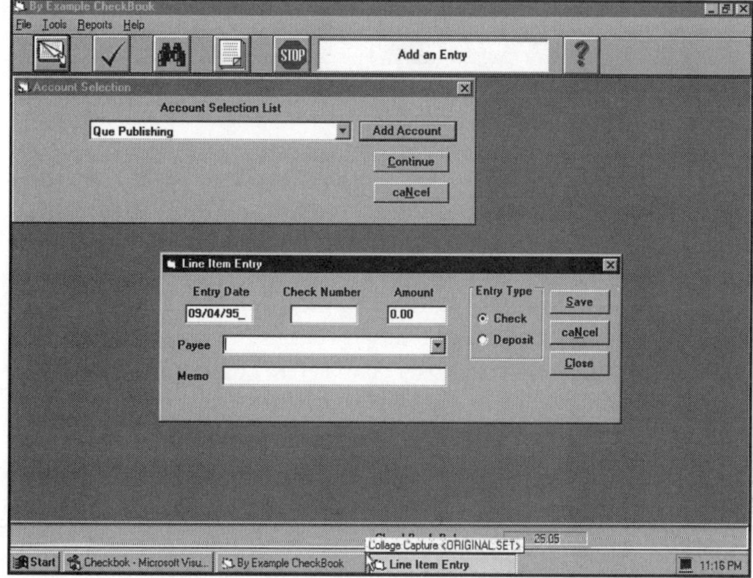

Figure 30.30
Checkbook with two child forms open at once.

When and Why to Use Child Forms

Even when you are using multiple forms, there are times when you want a standard form, not a child form. A child form cannot be displayed modal. This means that we will have to have a combination of forms. Some forms will be child forms while others will be non-child-modal forms.

When a modal form is displayed, its function must be performed and the form closed before you can continue with any other task within your application or Windows. This type of form is used to request information that is needed before any other processing in the application can be done. On the other hand, a modeless form allows you to display information and still continue with other functions within the application.

Menus, Buttons and Help

Menus and Toolbars are the way that users select functions simply by clicking with the mouse. Menus are created by using the Menu Editor. The Menu Editor is part of Visual Basic's features. To add a menu to the application, open the Menu Editor by clicking on the Menu Editor button of the Visual Basic Toolbar (see fig. 30.31).

Figure 30.31
Menu Editor button on the Toolbar.

A Toolbar will give the user quick access to the most frequently used menu selections and commands in an application (refer to fig. 30.31). A button bar is added to a form in a series of steps. You must first put an SSPanel object on the form and then place button controls on the SSPanel. Buttons make it easier and faster for the user to access features of the application.

Finally, the Help facility is very important for answering questions on how to use the application (see fig. 30.32). The Help menu allows the user to access different areas of the Help file by selecting the topic he wants from the menu.

Figure 30.32
Visual Basic's Help menu.

Main Menus

The menu bar across the top of the form is the doorway into the application. To make your application easier to use, you should group the menu selections according to their functions. This menu can be modified to display only those functions that are allowed at a given moment. A menu bar can be displayed on a MDI parent form as well as a non-MDI parent form. To add a menu to the MDI form, click on the form and then click on the Menu Editor button (refer to fig. 30.31). The Menu Editor appears (see fig. 30.33). This form allows us to enter each of the menu selections.

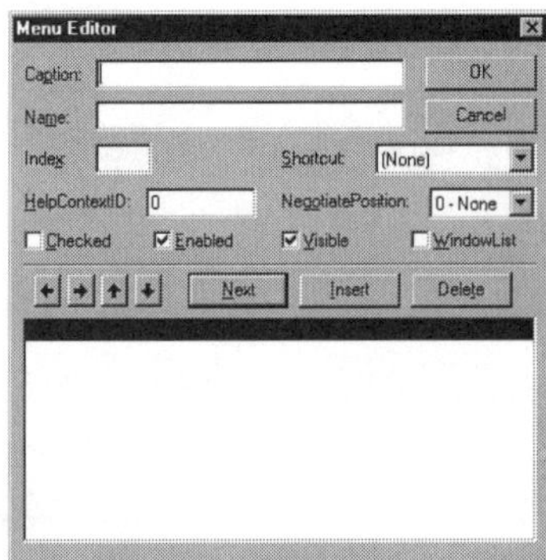

Figure 30.33
The Menu Editor form.

A menu selection requires a Caption and a control Name. The caption is what you will see on the menu when the application is excecuted. The variable name is how we access the menu selection within the program code. Some menu selections perform an action directly, while others display a lower-level menu list (see fig. 30.34).

Figure 30.34

Menu bar with a lower-level menu.

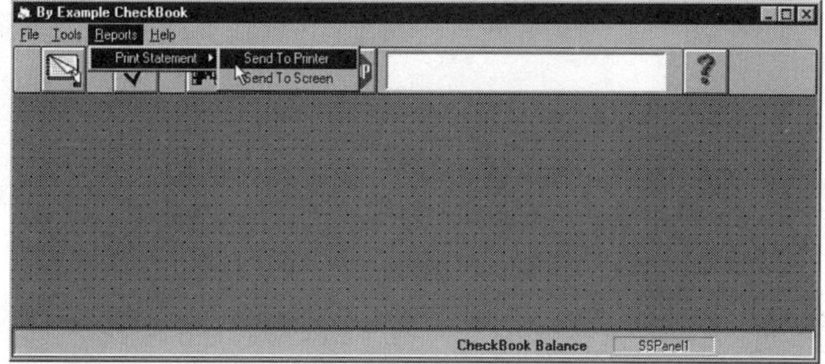

To add the File menu selection, type **&File** in the Caption field. The & tells the program to underline F on the menu. This allows the user to access the File menu list simply by pressing Alt+F. Now type in the variable name `MnuFile`. The prefix `Mnu` tells us that this variable is associated with a menu. As you entered the caption you should have noticed that it also appeared in the menu area display at the bottom of the Menu Editor (see fig. 30.35).

Figure 30.35

File has been added to the menu.

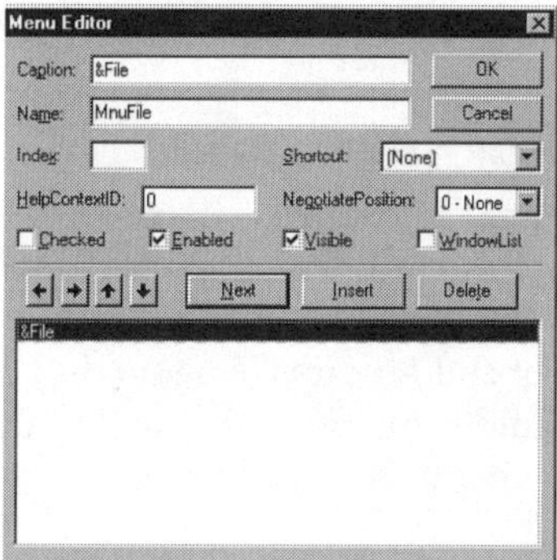

Now, to add another entry, click on the Next button. This will clear the Caption and Name fields to allow you to add a new entry. Add the menu selections for `&Add an Entry`, `&Account Selection`, and `&Exit Checkbook` (see fig. 30.36). After clicking on the Next button, click the right-arrow button. This will make the next entry a lower-level selection under File. To enter a higher-level menu item, click Next and then click the left-arrow button.

Figure 30.36
File menu with the lower-level items.

The main MDI form menu should have the functions that are in the Menu Editor shown in figure 30.37.

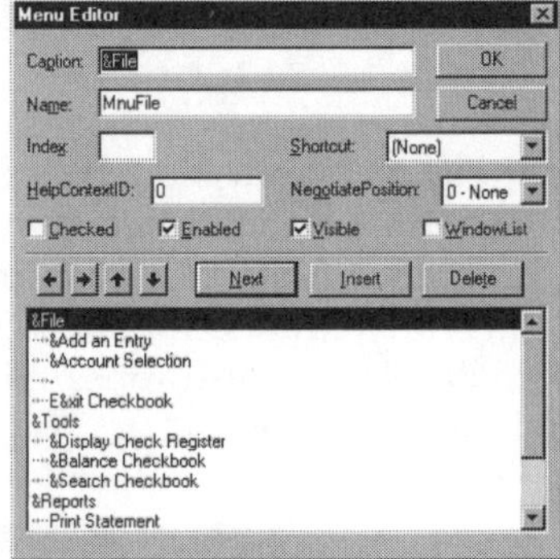

Figure 30.37
Menu Editor showing completed menu for a MDI form.

Child Form Menus

Whenever a child form is displayed, it can have its own menu bar definition. If a child form has a menu bar it will replace the parent menu bar when displayed (see fig. 30.38).

The use of child menus lets you display the menu options that are available for the active child form. Since this will be done automatically by Visual Basic, you do not have to create code to do this.

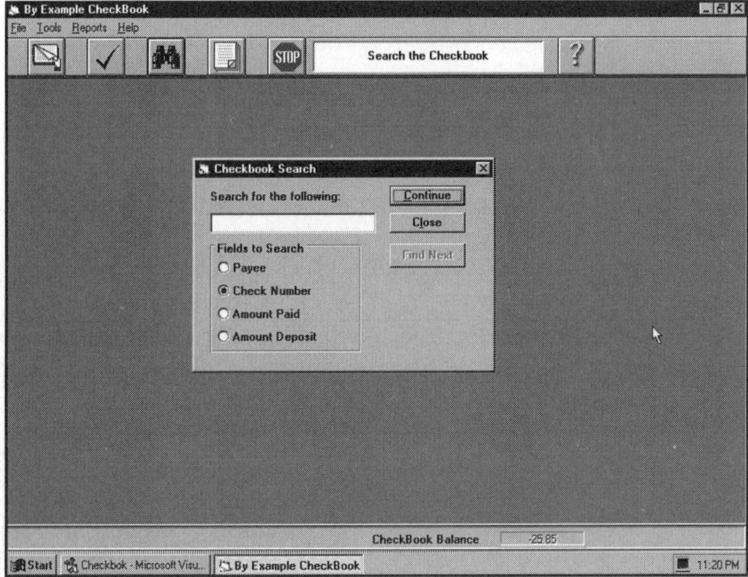

Figure 30.38

MDI form with a child form with a menu.

Using Toolbars Instead of Menus

All of the controls that start with SS that are used in this section are included in the Sheridan 3D Controls Custom Control. A Toolbar gives much the same capabilities as the menu bar. However, it is a more graphic depiction of the function. Visual Basic itself uses the button bar to allow fast access to certain capabilities of the development environment. To add a Toolbar to our application main form you will first click on the SSPanel button in the Toolbox.

Then we will draw the SSPanel object on the form (see fig. 30.39).

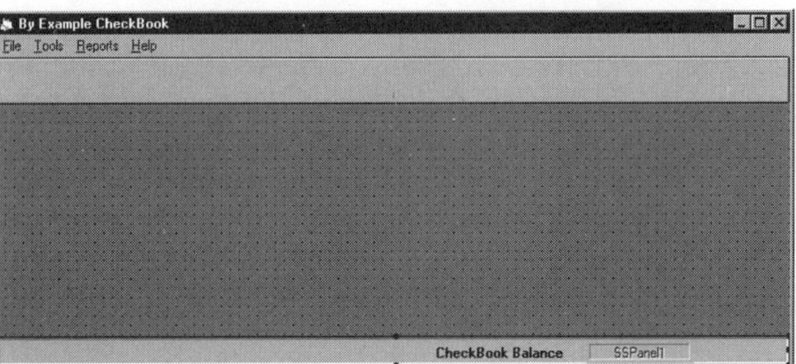

Figure 30.39

SSPanel box drawn on the form.

Once you have the SSPanel aligned to the top of the form you should clear the text from the `Caption` property. You can now add the buttons. Click on the SS command button in the Toolbox.

Now, draw a SScommand button on the SSPanel box for each feature you want to access from the Toolbar (see fig. 30.40).

Figure 30.40
The CheckBook button bar.

For each button, click on the `Picture` property to add a picture to the button (see fig. 30.41). You will be prompted for the picture to place on the button. These pictures are icons and can be found in the Icon subdirectory in the Visual Basic main directory. Since this application is yours, choose whichever icons you want to have on the Toolbar buttons.

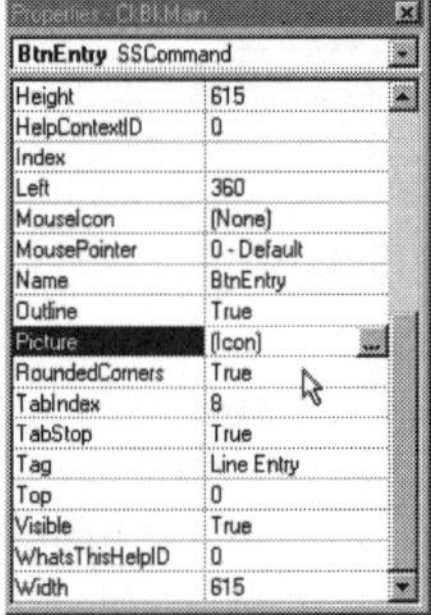

Figure 30.41
SSPanel property of command button.

The last object on the button bar is the Label object that displays each button's function. Draw a label box on the SSPanel control and change the name to `btnMemo`.

To see how the application will look when it runs, you will add two Visual Basic commands for each form you create. In each child form that was created, add the command `Unload Me` to the Cancel button's `Click` event (see fig. 30.42). This will close the form and return to the form that loaded it.

In the MDI menu, add the command `lineitem.Show` to the `Click` event for the corresponding menu selection (see fig. 30.43). This will display the child form that is specified in the `Show` command when the menu item is selected. You can also add this command to the `Click` routine for the button on the Toolbar for that function.

Figure 30.42

Command button `Click` routine with `Unload Me` command.

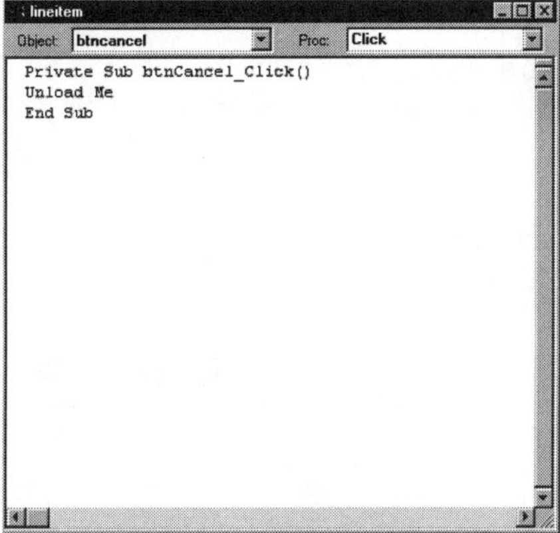

Figure 30.43

Menu item routine to show child form.

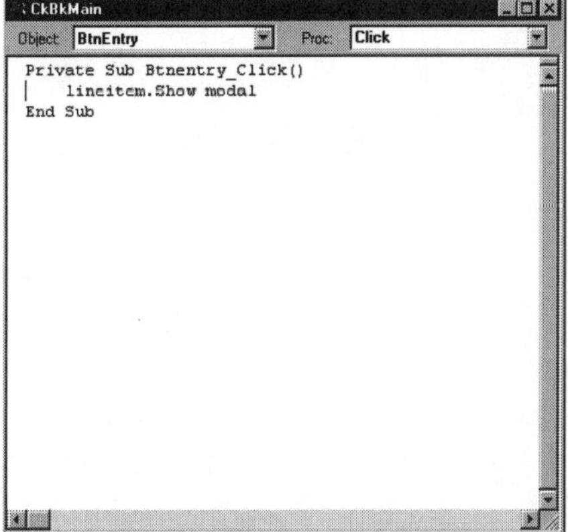

Finally, on the MDI form, add the command `End` to the `Click` routine for the menu selection to exit the application. You can also add the command to the Toolbar button to exit the application. This will end the application whenever they are clicked. The Cancel and Close buttons both have the `Unload` command in them; however, what is performed in each of the two routines is completely different. The `Close` routine will unload the form and save any work that was done. The Cancel button, on the other hand, will unload the form and throw away any of the work done. The code for these events will be created in Chapter 33, "Adding Data and Grid Controls."

What you have done with these few commands is to make the application executable. This means you can run the application, however, it still will not do anything. But now you can see how the forms look when you select them from the menu. This allows you to check your design.

What To Do About Help

The Help system appears as part of your final application. It consists of both text and graphics, which are displayed in the Windows Help box (see fig. 30.44). Visual Basic includes the Microsoft Help Compiler system which allows you to compile these files into a Help system file. The compiler takes word documents from a word processor and graphics and combines them into a finished Help file that can be accessed by the Windows Help program.

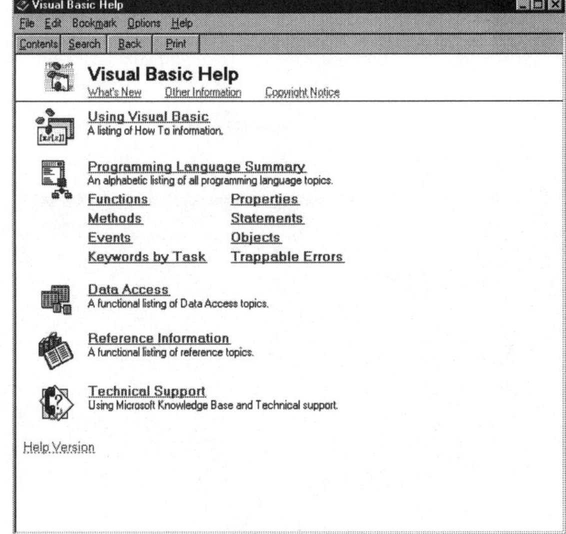

Figure 30.44

Contents menu from the Help system.

Creating the Help system is not an easy task. It is almost as complex as creating the application. You have to decide what to put into the Help file and then how to present it. A single unit of information in the Help file is called a *topic*. A topic is a complete unit of information that consists of text and graphics. A topic can hold as much information as you need in order to explain the subject. If the information takes up more room than a single screen, then the Help system will display scroll bars to allow you to scroll through the topic.

You also should have a Table of Contents as part of the Help file. This allows the user to see a list of all the topics in the Help file and to choose a particular one. In addition to the Table of Contents, you can have context-sensitive help. This means that if you click on an object and then hit the F1 key you would get the Help screen for that object. To create the Help file, you must have a word processor that can work in *Rich Text Format* (RTF) (see fig. 30.45). This is the only format that the Help compiler will work with.

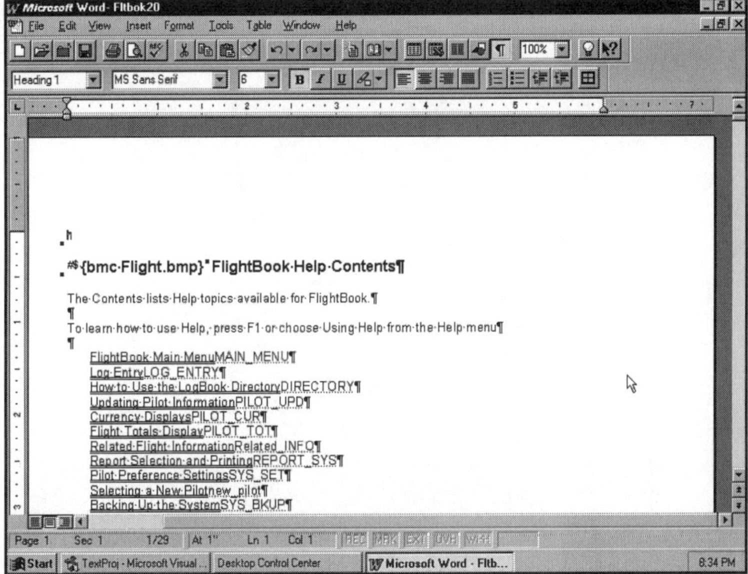

Figure 30.45

Content menu in the word-processor format.

The Help file has several types of hot spots on the screen. A *hot spot* is an area of the help text or graphic that allows the user to ask for more information. When a word or phrase is underlined with either a solid line or a dotted line, it denotes a Jump window. When you move the mouse pointer over one of these, it changes into a hand.

If you double-click on this area it will cause the Help system to either display a *pop-up window* or *jump* to another topic. A pop-up window is generally used to display the definition of a word or phrase. A jump (see fig. 30.46) will actually display an entirely new topic.

To create a Help topic, you must write the text, format it, and insert the required codes using underlined text, hidden text, and footnotes. The footnotes in the text contain the control information the Help compiler uses to link the information with the help commands. The Help system is usually accessed from the menu bar. However, the Help menu list usually has several special selections in it. For more detailed information on the creation of a Help file for your application see the Visual Basic Help Compiler Guide. In addition, there are several help authoring systems available that will greatly reduce the misery of Help file creation.

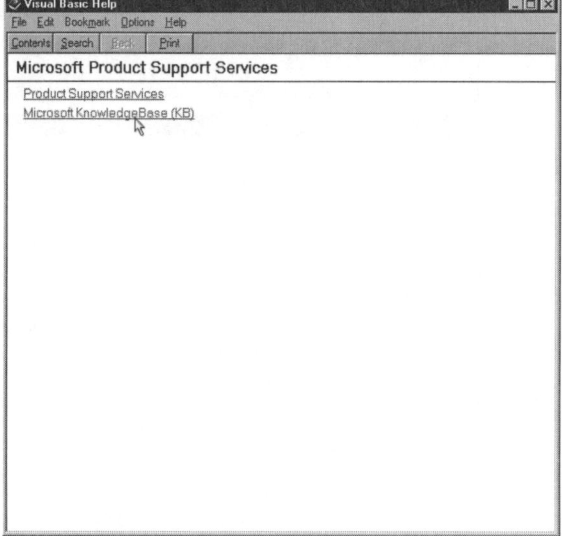

Figure 30.46
Help topic with jumps.

Summary

In this chapter you have looked at how to make the interface with the user work better. You can see that Visual Basic gives us a quick and easy way to create forms that you need for the application. The creation of a form is nothing more than drawing boxes on an empty form and positioning them where you want them. Choosing the correct type of object to use is what takes the time and effort when creating the form. You also have seen that it is very important to have your forms stick to a standard for placement, color, naming and labeling for the objects that you place on them.

Besides forms, you have created the menu bar that your application will use to interact with the application. The menu bar lists all of the available functions in the application. Menus can have many levels to them, allowing the user to step down through specific levels of function to get to the one they want. In addition to the menu bar the user also has a Toolbar for quick access to some of the more frequently used functions. These Toolbars have become one of the most used objects on a form. This is because of the use of pictures on the buttons to describe what the buttons function is. Most of the newer versions of familiar applications use these Toolbars (for example, Word for Windows). The code for the entire application that is dicussed in this section of the book can be found in file CHKBOOK.ZIP on the Web.

Finally, you looked at what it takes to create the Help file for the application to use. Building the Help file requires a lot of time and effort to decide what and how the information should be accessed by the user. Because of the time needed to do this properly we did not create one in this application.

In the next two chapters, we will create the remaining forms and add the database access to them. This will complete the forms that you need for the application to execute. Your application has slowly been taking shape, but you still only have some very pretty forms without any program logic behind them. Without the logic to execute when you click on the menu, Toolbar or command button, your application will not do anything. As you continue, you will add program logic to the forms to allow them to perform the functions that you want.

Review Questions

Answers to review questions are in Appendix A.

1. What is a form?
2. How do you add a control to a form?

3. What are the principles of good forms design?
4. What is an MDI form?

5. What is the difference between a menu and a Toolbar?
6. What does it take to create a Help file?

Review Exercises

1. Create the initial Checkbook Search form using the skills from this chapter.

2. Complete the application menu bar (as shown in fig. 30.37). The remaining menu selections are:

Menu Label	*Control Name*
Tools	mnuTools
Display Check Register	toolsDisplay
Balance Checkbook	toolsBalance
Search Checkbook	toolsSearch
Reports	mnureports
Print Statement	rptPrint
Help	mnuHelp

3. Add the code to the Line Item Entry menu routine to show the Line Item Entry form. Then, in the Line Item Entry form, add the code to close the form.

CHAPTER 31

Adding OLE Objects

In Chapter 15, "The Data, Grid, and OLE Tools," you learned how to use Object Linking and Embedding (OLE) to attach other applications to your forms. The combined use of these features can really boost your users' acceptance of your applications. Because the built-in graphics tools are quite powerful, but mastery of them is non-trivial, we will be using OLE to bring easier graphics to our sample application.

In this chapter, we are going to delve more deeply into the use of OLE by creating an application that combines multiple features in the same applications. First, we are going to learn how to include the custom controls that ship with other applications as icons in our toolbar. Next, we are going to add objects created with these new tools to a form. The result will be a form that has a fair amount of sophistication to its controls.

Free Custom Controls

Independent software vendors create custom controls which act like built-in controls. These controls sell for hundreds of dollars, and are normally worth every penny. They can save you so much time creating and debugging applications that they're a bargain. Suppose that someone were to give you a dozen of these controls at no charge. Wouldn't that be great? The designers of Visual Basic have done just that by enhancing the product so that it can find all of the OLE 2.0 controls that already exist on your system. This means that by purchasing Excel, Word, CorelDRAW!, or any other OLE 2.0-compliant applications on the market you get a free set of controls. In fact, Windows 95 comes with several OLE 2.0-compliant applications that you can use without spending any money on expensive applications.

Let's tap into this "mother-lode" without further digression. All that you have to do to discover this hidden treasure is click on the Tools, Custom Controls menu selection as shown in figure 31.1.

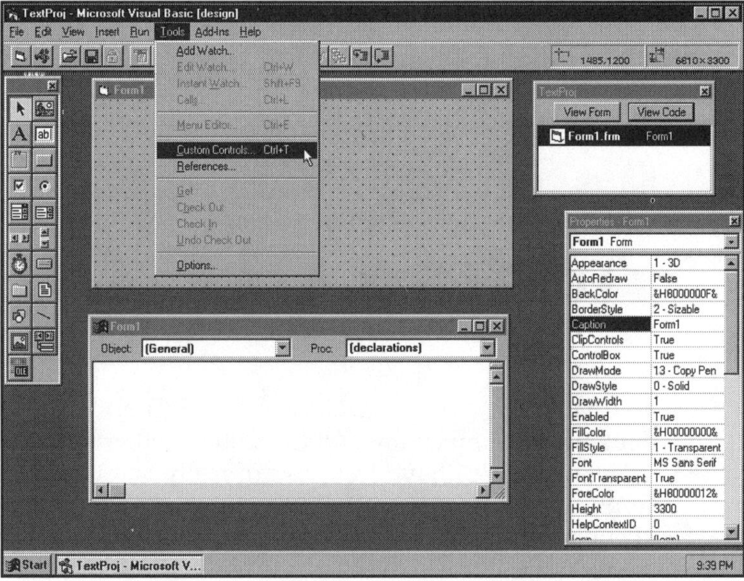

Figure 31.1
The Custom Controls menu selection.

Be sure Insertable Objects is checked. Then by selecting Custom Controls, you invoke a properties sheet that looks like the one shown in figure 31.2.

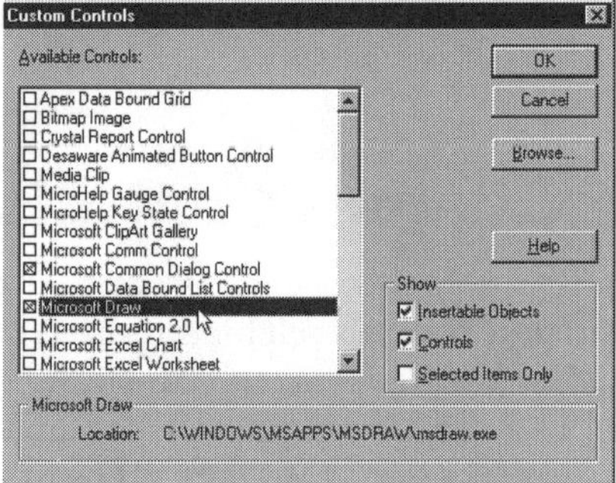

Figure 31.2
The Custom Controls properties sheet.

The Custom Controls properties sheet displays all of the custom controls on your system. There are four basic sources of custom controls:

- Those that ship with Visual Basic. We have already looked at the Grid tool and the Common Dialog tool. These are not built in.

- Those that come when you buy application software. Included in this category are the controls that come with Microsoft Draw that we used in an example in Chapter 15, "The Data, Grid, and OLE Tools."
- Those that are sold by independent software vendors. These are often sold by mail-order houses that specialize in programming tools. They are beginning to show up on the shelves of computer stores, though.
- Those that you write for yourself. This topic is beyond the scope of this book; in fact, writing OCX controls is generally regarded as fairly difficult—even by experienced VBX developers. There are a number of packaging details that you must learn; but, the real magic is in what the control does, not in the fact that it is a custom control. If you are interested in doing this, be brave, buy a book and give it a shot. Familiarity with C/C++ and the Windows application programming interface (API) is required for this kind of programming.

You should see all of your custom controls, regardless of source, in the Custom Controls properties sheet. Click on several of these and then click the OK button. What happens next is really impressive. An icon for each of these custom controls appears on your Toolbar. Figure 31.3 shows the custom icon for the Microsoft Draw Picture tool.

Figure 31.3

The custom control for Draw Picture.

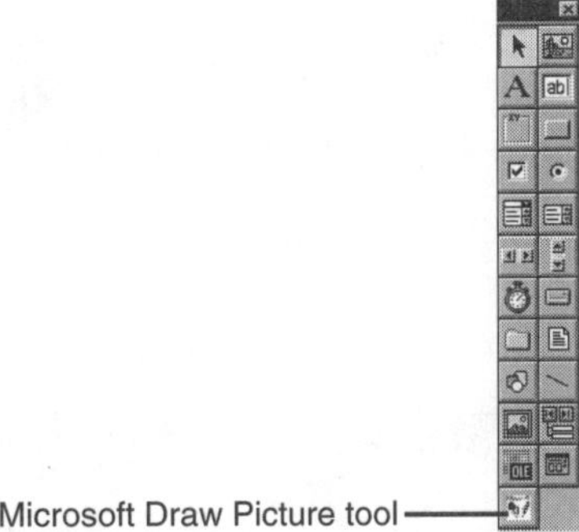

Double-clicking on this custom control causes a rectangular control to be placed on your form, and immediately transfers control to Microsoft Draw as shown here in figure 31.4.

At this point, you can create a drawing by using the facilities available in Microsoft Draw. There are considerably more choices available to you by using this application than exist natively in Visual Basic. Draw a logo-style picture as shown in figure 31.4. Now, choose Exit from the File menu to return you to your Visual Basic form as shown in figure 31.5.

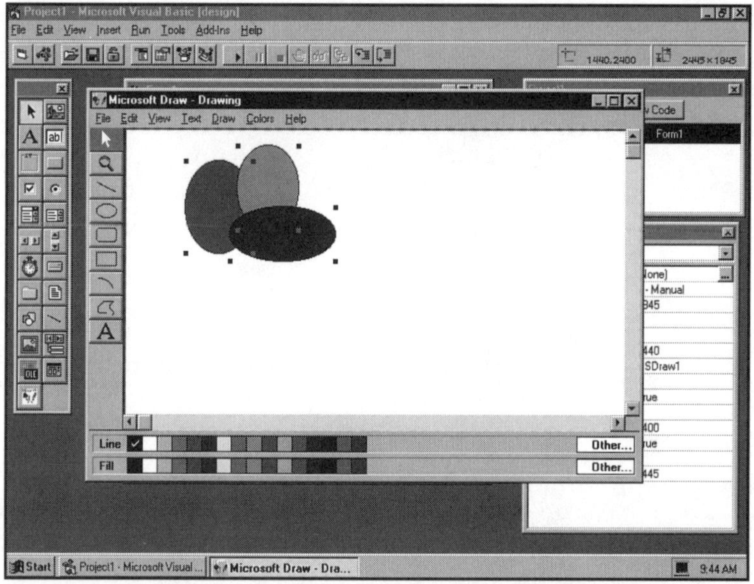

Figure 31.4

The Windows Draw picture editor.

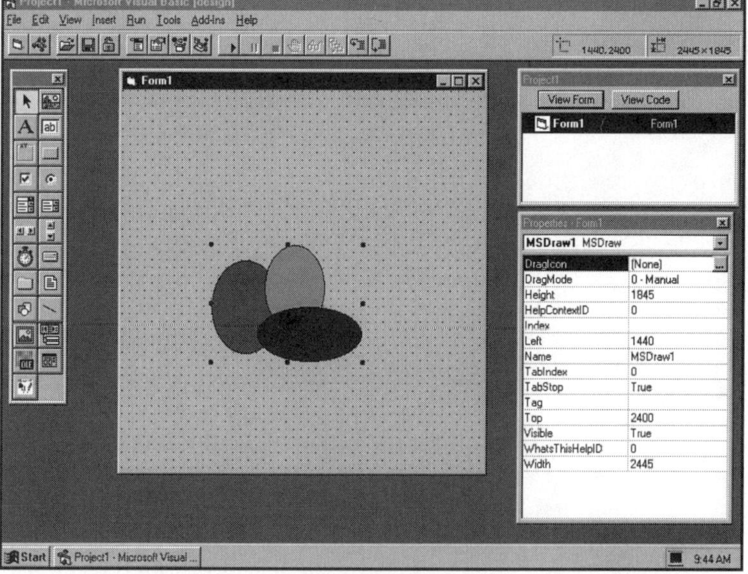

Figure 31.5

The form with a logo.

At this point, you have a drawing on your form that was created by using another application accessed through a Visual Basic custom control. When your application is running, you can change the contents of the custom control by double-clicking on it, just like you change the documents that are created with the built-in OLE

Container tool. Let's experiment with it in order to assure ourselves that it really does work. Start your application and then double-click on the OLE control rectangle in your form to bring up the Microsoft Draw Picture editor again. Lo and behold, it works like Microsoft said that it would. The result is shown in figure 31.6.

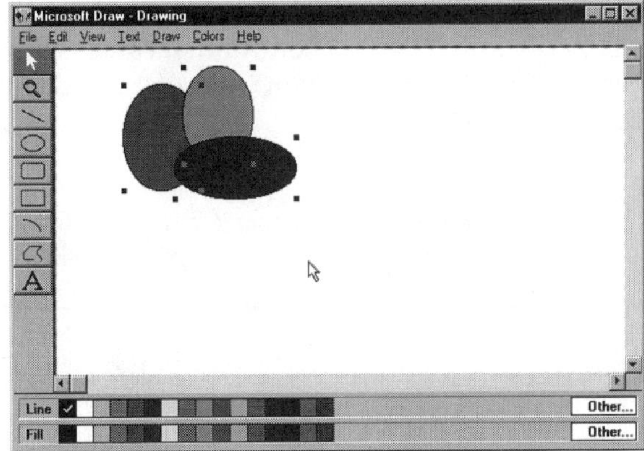

Figure 31.6
Invoking the application by double-clicking.

In reality, our set of ovals doesn't look much like a logo, so let's clean it up by making them a little longer and adding strings to them to make them look like balloons. After you do this, choose Exit from the File menu. This will make our form look like the one shown in figure 31.7—except for the lettering.

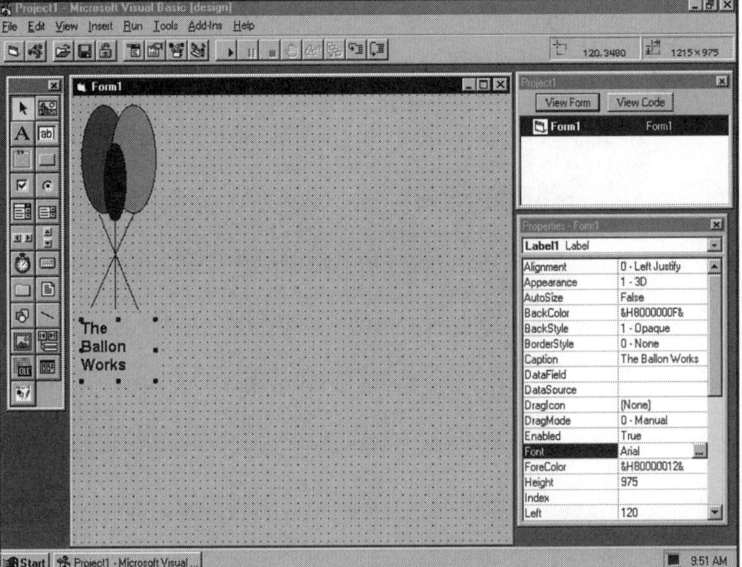

Figure 31.7
The improved logo.

Add the lettering by creating a Label control and setting its caption to "The Balloon Works," the name of our fictitious company. Change its font, make it bold and italicized by using the Font property of the Label control.

Having accomplished this, we are ready to fill out our application and turn it into a great memo from upper management to the owners of this company. In order to give it a professional look, let's add a graph. An easy way to do this is by using the Microsoft Graph custom control that comes with Microsoft Access and Microsoft Word. Choose Tools, Custom Controls and select Microsoft Graph 5.0 from the list box in the window. A new tool, shown in figure 31.8, appears in your Toolbox.

Note: Depending on the version of the Microsoft Products that you have on your computer, some of the menus and program labels may be different.

Figure 31.8

The Microsoft Graph 5.0 tool.

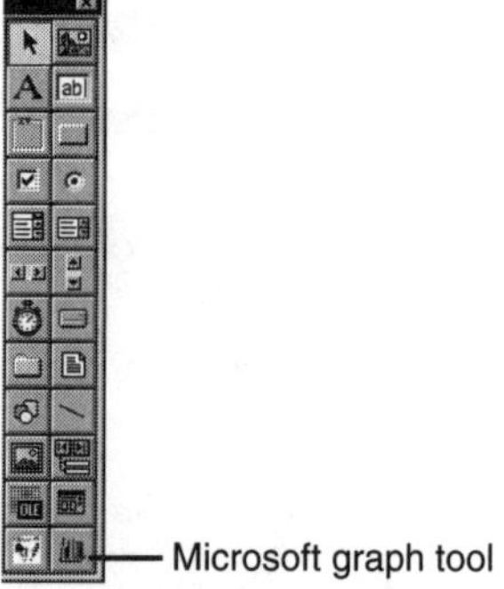

Double-clicking on this tool will bring about a surprising result. Your form seems to have been taken over by this new control. A menu bar appears at the top, a spreadsheet-like window appears that is full of numbers, and a sample graph appears on the screen. What has occurred is OLE 2.0's in-place activation feature. Because we are adding a chart to the form, chart design functions appear everywhere. The first thing that you can do is edit the Datasheet window to provide data to the chart. This application takes the data from the Datasheet window and graphs it in the control. This form and these objects are shown in figure 31.9.

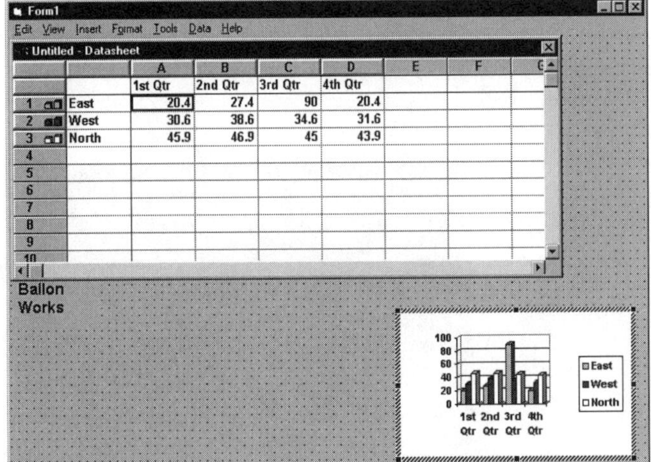

Figure 31.9

Creating a graph.

The left column shows the colors that will be assigned to each city's data. Across the top is a row that designates what the x-axis of the graph will say. The data in the cells provides the information that the Graph control must have to draw the graph. This window is pictured in figure 31.10.

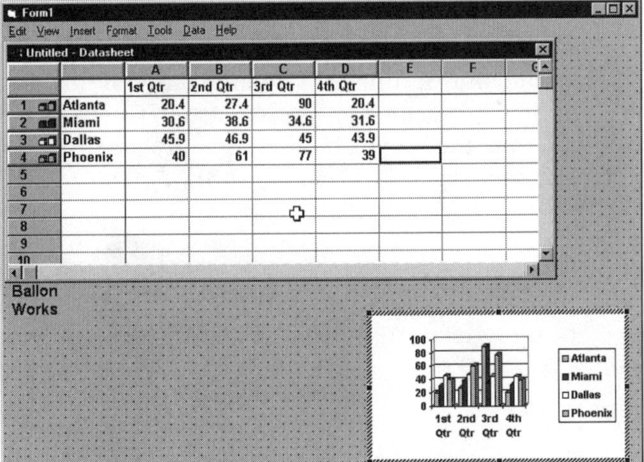

Figure 31.10

The Microsoft graph Datasheet.

After filling out the Datasheet, the Graph control paints the graph on your window as shown in figure 31.11. Notice how all of the controls and menus that were needed to specify the layout of the chart have vanished. All that is left is the graph itself.

Figure 31.11

The form with the graph.

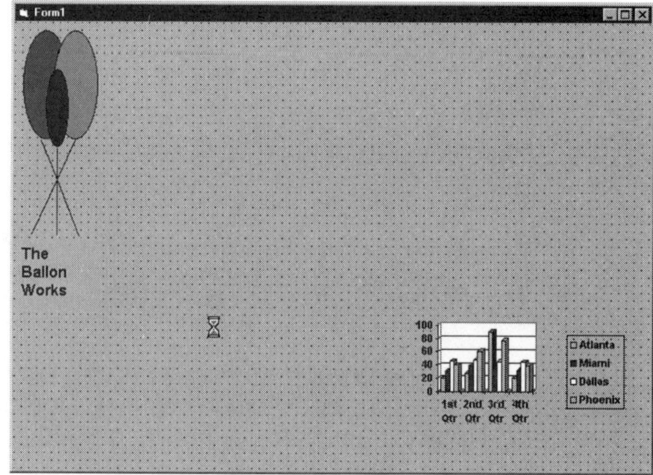

Flushed and heady with success, we are now ready to add another tool to the Toolbar, the Microsoft Wordpad tool. This tool will allow us to insert a rectangle of text into our document. To gain the use of this tool, go into the Custom Control window by clicking on Tools, Custom Controls. Choose the Microsoft Wordpad item from the list box by clicking and then press OK. Your Toolbox will receive a new member as shown in figure 31.12.

Figure 31.12

The Microsoft Wordpad tool.

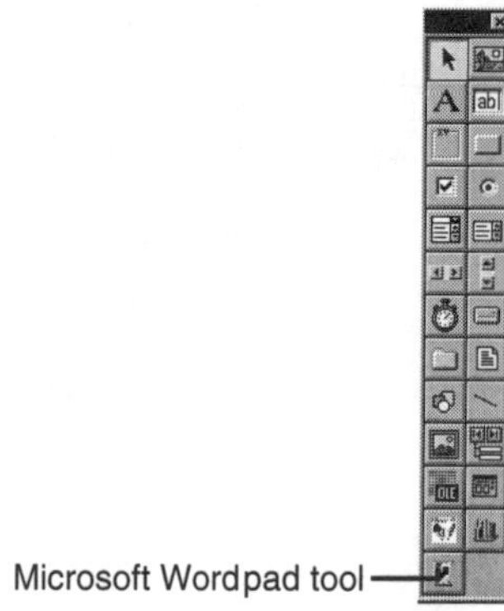

Double-clicking on this new tool brings more surprises. Your form is now taken over by a different menu. What you now have is the Microsoft Wordpad application in the middle of your own application as shown in figure 31.13.

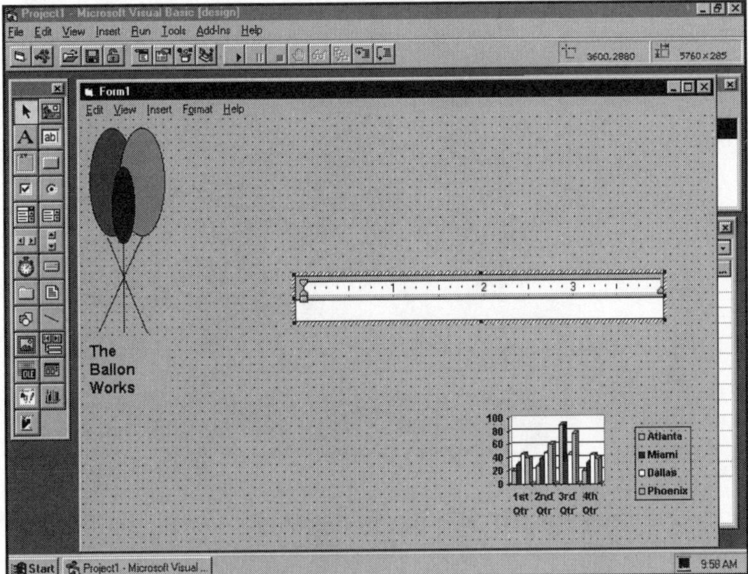

Figure 31.13
Adding a Microsoft Wordpad text box.

All of the standard functions of Wordpad are available to your application. The improvement of this control over the simple Text Box control is hard to overstate. Suddenly, all of the code that has been written for the Wordpad application is available to Visual Basic via this custom control.

Armed with all of this power, let's add a summary of the company's progress and highlight the best-selling item as shown in figure 31.14.

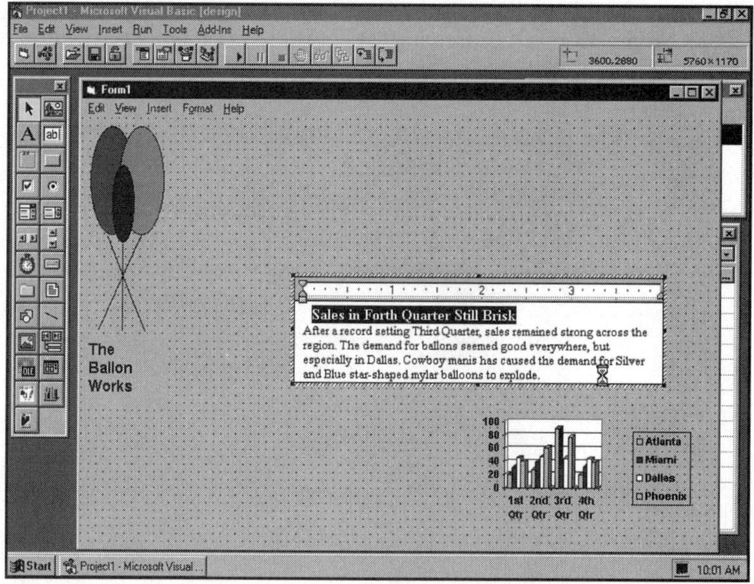

Figure 31.14
The form with the Wordpad text box.

Now, let's run the application and see how it looks. As you can see in figure 31.15, the form is looking pretty complete.

Figure 31.15
Running the application.

Let's try adding some predefined pictures. We can do this now by calling on ClipArt Gallery to provide a Toolbox tool. We follow the same procedure of choosing Tools, Custom Controls and choosing ClipArt Gallery from the list box. This will add the ClipArt Gallery tool as shown in figure 31.16.

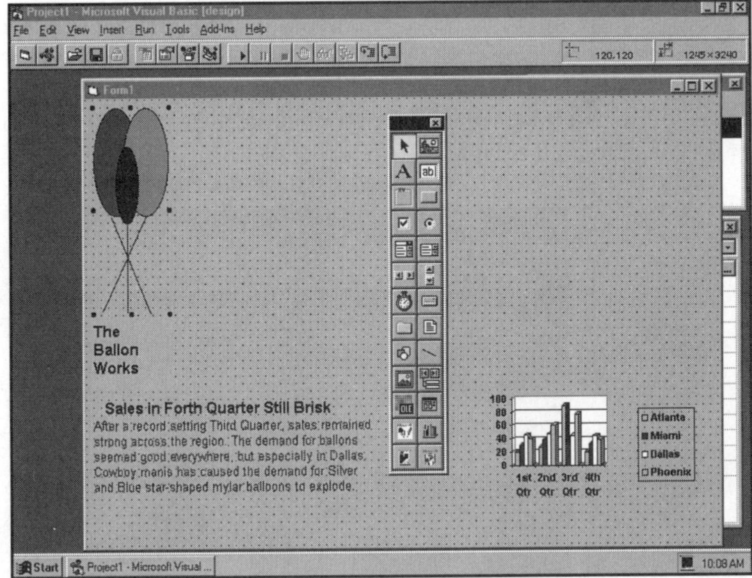

Figure 31.16

The ClipArt Gallery tool.

Double-clicking on the ClipArt Gallery tool will take you into the Clipart Gallery Image window. Now, you can choose a picture and Insert it into the object as shown in figure 31.17.

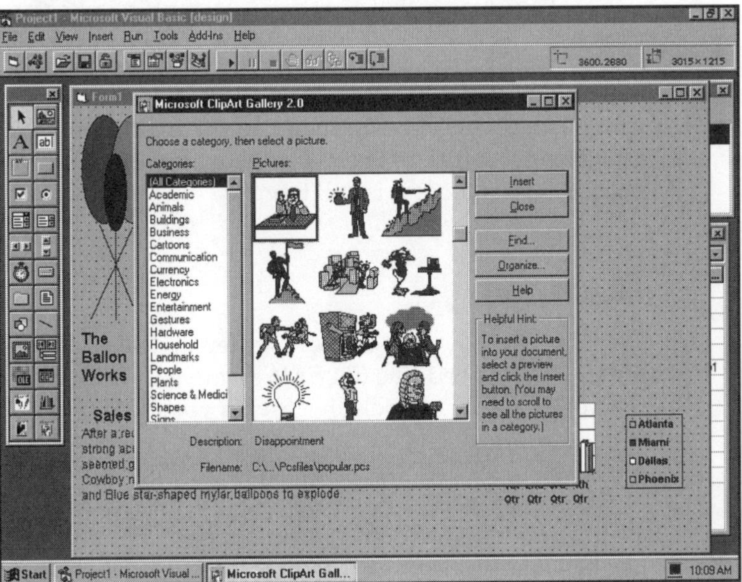

Figure 31.17

The ClipArt Gallery drawing environment.

Having done this, all that you need to do is to click Insert, then click Close. The control will now get this picture placed into its rectangle on your screen. The report is now finished. It contains a basic form and four controls, one from Microsoft Draw, Microsoft Wordpad, Microsoft Graph, and ClipArt Gallery. The finished product is pictured in figure 31.18.

Figure 31.18
The completed report.

This report is very special because it can be updated for next month by simply running the application and clicking on each one of the OLE objects in the window. This greatly simplifies your user's life because all she has to do is change what is needed—even the text is still there.

Summary

In this chapter, we took the next step in developing an understanding of Object Linking and Embedding (OLE). We started by learning how to find and include, on the Toolbar, OLE 2.0 tools that are on your system. This gave you custom objects from applications you already own. Next, we started work on an application that contained four OLE controls, each created by adding a tool to the Toolbar.

First, we created a logo by using a control called Microsoft Draw Picture. This is a fairly simple art package that ships as part of Word. This logo was designed to look like balloons on a string.

Next, we used Microsoft Graph 5.0 to create a graph of some sales data.

Following this, we added a text box that was a Microsoft Wordpad. The Wordpad control is far superior to the built-in TextBox tool because it provides all of the functionality of a word processing system.

Finally, we added a drawing of the fictitious president of our company. This picture was created in ClipArt Gallery using its extensive library of artwork.

Review Questions

1. What is an OLE object?
2. What menu pick adds OLE controls to your Toolbox?

3. What language are custom controls normally written in?
4. What advantage did the Wordpad object give you over using the built-in TextBox control?

Review Exercises

1. Write a program that uses one of these controls.

2. Write a program that contains both a Text Box control and one from Word (or another word processor, if you own one). Try to identify the advantages of having the word processor instead.
3. Write a program that uses the built-in graphics controls to draw a picture. Draw another picture with an OLE 2.0-compliant graphics package like Visio or ClipArt Gallery. Identify the differences in functionality.

4. Write a program that uses the ClipArt Gallery OLE object to add a control with a complex drawing to your form. Create another application that uses the built-in OLE container control to add the same complex drawing. Make the .EXE file for both of them. Run each program and see if one is faster than the other. Examine the size of the two of them. Which is larger? Is the difference small?

Adding Message Boxes and Scroll Bars

Message boxes are something that anyone who has ever used Windows is familiar with. This is how Windows lets us know that something has happened or wants us to answer a question or even enter some piece of information that it needs in order to continue processing (see fig. 32.1). Whenever a message box is displayed, you have to respond to it before continuing what you were doing. This is because a message box can only be displayed as a modal form. Message boxes are very good ways for you to tell the user when something goes wrong in the application or when you want the user to choose a course of action.

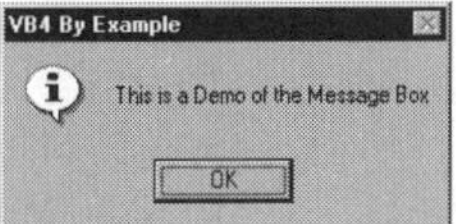

Figure 32.1
A message box displaying a message.

Scroll bars will appear whenever there are MDIChild forms that at least partially extend beyond the border of an MDIForm. This will allow the MDIChild forms to be moved back into the client area of the MDIParent. This feature allows you to browse through the information by scrolling the visible portion of the form up/down and right/left (see fig. 32.2). However, in a situation in which forms are placed on a non-MDI parent form in such a way that they extend beyond the borders of a form, or, if a form is resized by the user in such a way as to move controls beyond its borders, scroll bars will *not* be displayed.

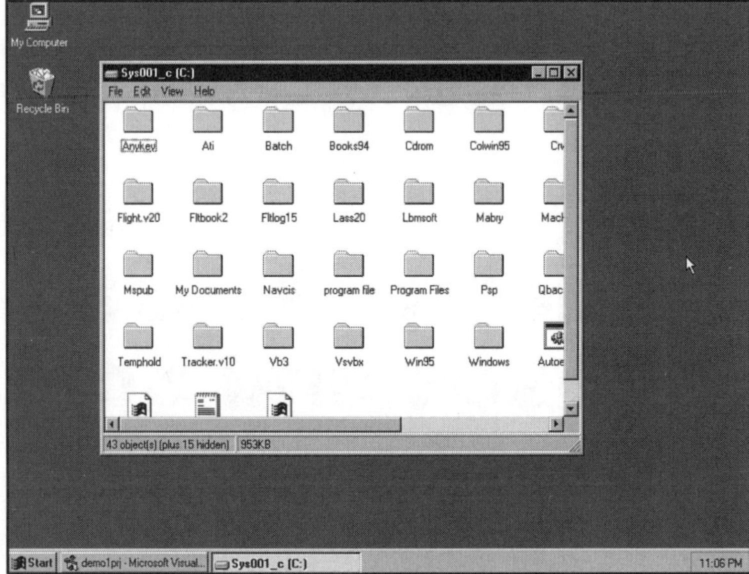

Figure 32.2
Scroll bars in use on the Windows desktop.

In this chapter, you are going to see how to use message boxes and scroll bars. Also, we will discuss why you should use these features in your application. Not only will message boxes help you control the flow of the application, but it will also enhance the overall look of the application. This means that your application appears like any other Windows application you might use.

When To Use Message Boxes

A message box is a very powerful feature of Visual Basic. It allows you to communicate with the user during the normal processing of the application. You can ask the user if it is okay to continue or tell them that there is a possible problem. Message boxes appear throughout any Windows application. If there is an error, the user is informed of it by the use of a message box. When the application has a warning or a message for the user, a message box is used to inform the user. Also, if the application has a question, then a message box is displayed to ask the question and wait for the response (see fig. 32.3).

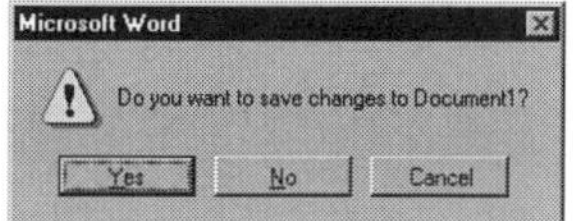

Figure 32.3
A message box asking a question.

Finally, there is a special type of message box that allows the user to input a single piece of data. This is called an *input box* (see fig. 32.4). An input box will display a prompt in a dialog box, then it will wait for the user to input text and/or click a button, and return the contents of the text box to the program.

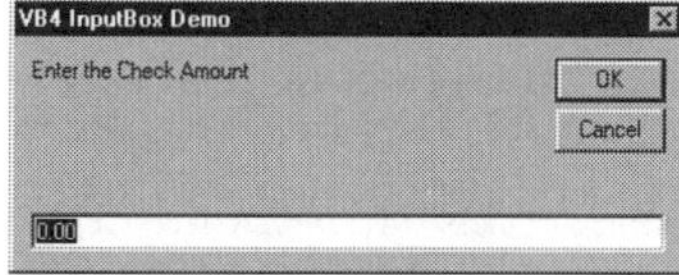

Figure 32.4
An input box asking for data

Both the message and input boxes are really part of the Windows environment and can be accessed by using the Windows API or the convenient Visual Basic statements. They are included so that you do not have to build our own versions of these functions. Can you imagine what it would look like if every application had their own variety of a message box figure?

These forms are sometimes called *pre-defined dialog boxes*. A pre-defined dialog box makes it possible for us to use it without worrying about designing it.

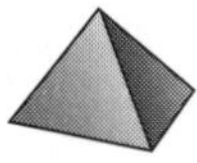

Tip: The only thing that you have to remember is that you have very little control over these dialog boxes.

Displaying Information To the User

To display a message to the user, you need to understand the formats of the message box command. There are two variations of the message box: there is a statement type and a function type. The statement type pauses until the user clicks the button, but returns no user information to the program, and is used only to inform the user of something without offering any choices. This is generally used to display a message that requires only an OK button to be clicked by the user. These messages are usually warnings or informational in nature (see fig. 32.5). The function type `MsgBox` allows the user some choice, via a selection of buttons, and returns a value to the calling program. The function type of the `MsgBox` call, however, requires parenthesis around the parameters to the `MsgBox`.

Figure 32.5

A message box displaying a warning.

The message box is displayed by the following Visual Basic program line:

```
MsgBox "There is not enough money in Account", 48,
➥ "Checkbook System", "Check.HLP", 1000
```

Let's break down this line by looking at a generic definition of the MsgBox command statement.

```
MsgBox    <Message to display>, <Message type>,
➥<Message box title>, <Help, Context>
```

The <Message type> corresponds to a number that gives the MsgBox three pieces of information. It tells the MsgBox what buttons to display and what their captions should be. Also it defines what icon should be displayed on the form. In addition, you can specify which of the first two buttons is the default and finally, whether it should be displayed as an application modal form or a system modal form.

An application modal MsgBox means that the user must respond to the message box before continuing work in the current application. However, the user can switch to another application without continuing the current one. Depending on the message, the user might want to check something out using another Windows application. In contrast, a system modal MsgBox means that all applications are suspended until the user responds to the message box.

The message that is displayed can be up to 1024 characters long for both an application modal message box and a system modal message box.

When there is a need to supply Help to the user for a given error, you can add the Help file name to the MsgBox call. Also, the context number lets you specify what topic in the help file to display. The context number refers to an existing location in the Help file. The Helpfile and Context parameters are a matched pair—if one is used, both must be used.

Note: The message box automatically breaks the message line at the right edge of the dialog box. If you do not want this, you would have to set line breaks yourself by using a line feed character (chr$(13)).

When using the MsgBox, we can either use numbers to define the type or use the constants that are defined in the VBA object library. The available object libraries can be viewed and/or pasted into the code using the Object Browser from the Visual Basic View menu list. The Object Browser displays the available objects and their definitions (see fig. 32.6).

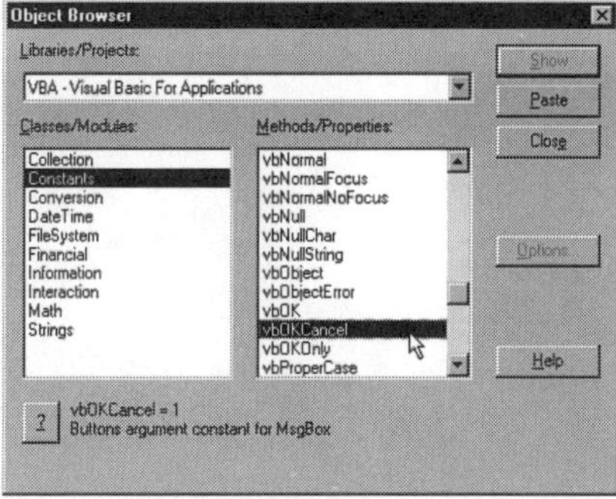

Figure 32.6
Object Browser Form showing `vbOkCancel` parameter.

The constants that can be used with a message box are shown in Listing 32.1.

Listing 32.1 33LIST01.TXT—MsgBox Constants Definitions

```
' MsgBox Arguments
vbOKOny = 0                  ' OK button only
vbOKCancel = 1               ' OK and Cancel buttons
vbAbortRetryIgnore = 2       ' Abort, Retry, and Ignore buttons
vbYesNoCancel = 3            ' Yes, No, and Cancel buttons
vbYesNo = 4                  ' Yes and No buttons
vbRetryCancel = 5            ' Retry and Cancel buttons

vbCritical = 16              ' Critical message
vbQuestion = 32              ' Warning query
vbExclamation = 48           ' Warning message
vbInformation = 64           ' Information message


vbApplicationModal = 0       ' Application Modal Message Box
vbDefbutton1 = 0             ' First button is default
vbDefbutton2 = 256           ' Second button is default
vbDefbutton3 = 512           ' Third button is default
vbSystemModal = 4096         ' System Modal

' MsgBox return values
vbOK = 1                     ' OK button pressed
vbCancel = 2                 ' Cancel button pressed
vbAbort = 3                  ' Abort button pressed
vbRetry = 4                  ' Retry button pressed
vbIgnore = 5                 ' Ignore button pressed
vbYES = 6                    ' Yes button pressed
vbNO = 7                     ' No button pressed
```

In your application, you will use both the `MsgBox` statement and function. Whenever the user cancels a function, you are going to ask the user, "Is it Okay to Save Data?" as shown in figure 32.7.

Figure 32.7
MsgBox statement showing Question.

When the user clicks on the OK button, you will display the message "Entry has been Saved" (see fig. 32.8). You display these messages by using the statement format of the MsgBox.

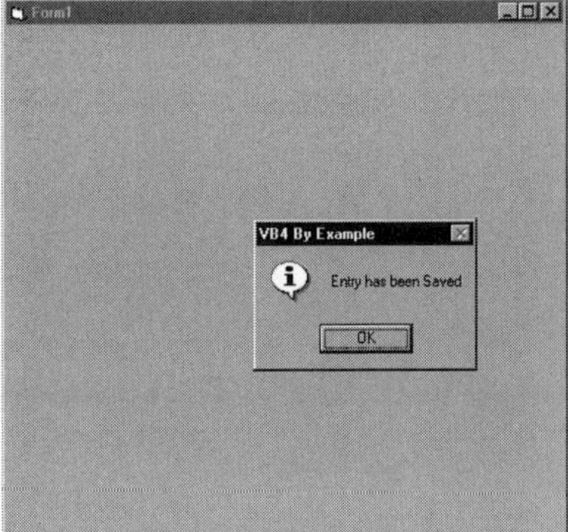

Figure 32.8
MsgBox statement showing save message.

Letting the User Decide the Next Step

The MsgBox can also be used as a function. When it is used as a function, more than one button can be displayed on the dialog box. The statement form of MsgBox can also display more than one button, but there is no way to detect which one was selected. A number will be returned by the MsgBox informing the program what button was clicked.

To let the user choose a course of action, you use the function format of the MsgBox. Whenever the user clicks on a delete button, you don't want to automatically delete the information. Instead, you should ask the user if he is sure about deleting it (see fig. 32.9). Depending on the question, you will check to see which button was clicked and then perform the required action.

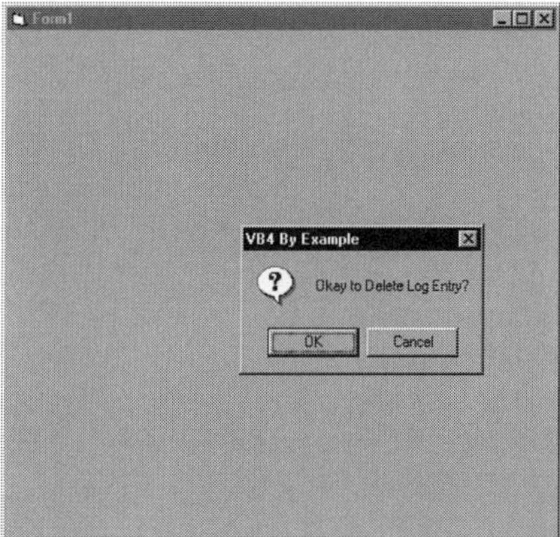

Figure 32.9

`MsgBox` function showing delete message.

This `MsgBox` requires you to add several lines of program logic in order for it to work properly. The code is placed in the procedure where you want to ask the question. The `MsgBox` function is used in conjunction with the `If` statement. If you want to display a message asking the user if it is okay to delete a record, you would need to code the following logic in your program:

```
ANS = MsgBox("Okay to Delete?", vbOKCancel + vbQuestion,
➥ "Checkbook System")
If ANS = vbOK THEN

    Call DeleteRecord

END IF
```

When the user clicks on the OK button of the message box, the program will call the `DeleteRecord` routine to delete the selected record.

Finally, if you need to ask the user for information, you will use the input box. The input box in figure 32.4 is displayed by the following Visual Basic program line:

```
ANSWER = InputBox$("Enter Starting Balance.",
➥"Account Balance", "0.00",,, "Check.HLP",
➥2500)
```

Let's break down this line by looking at the generic definition of the input box.

```
ANSWER = InputBox$(<prompt>, <title>, <default>, <xpos, ypos>,
➥ <Help, Context>)
```

The `<prompt>` is what will be displayed to the user in the Inputbox. It will tell the user what it is that you want entered. The heading of the input box is the `<title>` parameter. If the user clicks on the OK button without entering anything, you can specify what the `<default>` value will be. Finally, you can specify the position on the screen that the input box will appear. This is done by setting the `X` and `Y` position parameters in the function call. If `X` and `Y` parameters are not specified, placeholder commas are required, unless the `Helpfile` and `Context` arguments are not used either. You can also specify a Help file reference in the `InputBox` call, just like the `MsgBox` call.

In the coming chapters, you will be finishing the remaining forms from the Checkbook application that you have created. The following message boxes and input boxes will be needed after the forms are created. Now, to add these to your application, you are going to need several different messages for each of our forms. In addition, you are going to ask the user for the ending balance when they open the Balance Account form.

When the user closes the Checkbook Balance form, the application should check to see if the balance process is completed. If it is, the user is informed and the form is unloaded (see fig. 32.10).

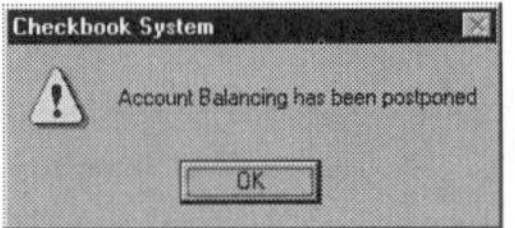

Figure 32.10

`MsgBox` informing user of completed function.

If the account is not balanced, then the user should be asked if he wants to postpone the balance process (see fig. 32.11).

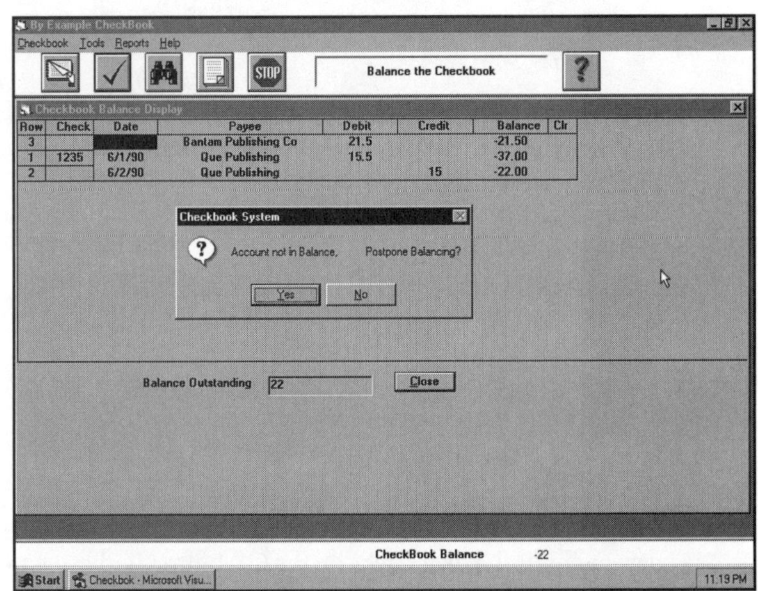

Figure 32.11

User being asked to postpone process.

If the user clicks the Yes button, then a message is displayed saying that the process is postponed and the form is unloaded. The code to perform this entire process is shown in Listing 32.2.

Listing 32.2 32LIST02.TXT—Message Box When Checkbook Out of Balance

```
If out_Balance <> 0 Then
    msg_ans = MsgBox("Account not in Balance," + Chr$(9) +
    ➥"Postpone Balancing?", vbYesNo + vbQuestion, APP.Title)
    If msg_ans = vbYes Then
        MsgBox "Account Balancing has been postponed",
        ➥ vbExclamation, APP.Title
        Unload Me
    End If
Else
    MsgBox "Account has been balanced", vbExclamation, APP.Title
    Unload Me
End If
```

You can see that there is very little code used to do all of the functions.

Using the `App` objects `Title` method lets you have a consistent title throughout the entire application.

The Line Entry form uses several message boxes in all three of its button routines. These routines ask the user if it is okay to continue or to cancel the current process. An example of the code for this form is shown in Listing 32.3.

Listing 32.3 32LIST03.TXT—btnCancel_Click () Routine

```
Private Sub btnCancel_Click()
msg_ans = MsgBox("Okay to Cancel?", vbYesNo + vbQuestion,
➥ APP.Title)
If msg_ans = vbYes Then
    Unload Me
End If
End Sub

Private Sub but_Continue_Click()
msg_ans = MsgBox("Save account entry before Closing?",
➥vbYesNoCancel + vbQuestion, APP.Title)
If msg_ans = vbCancel Then
    Exit Sub
ElseIf msg_ans = vbYes Then
    MsgBox "Entry Saved", vbExclamation, APP_Title
End If
Unload Me
End Sub
```

continues

Listing 32.3 Continued

```
Sub But_save_Click ()
msg_ans = MsgBox("Okay to save account entry?", vbOKCANCEL
➥+ vbquestion, app.title)
If msg_ans = vbok Then
    MsgBox "Entry Saved", vbexclamation, app.title
    Unload Me
End If
End Sub
```

Finally, whenever the user clicks the Account Balance button or the Account Balance menu item, he is prompted to enter the current account's ending balance (see fig. 32.12).

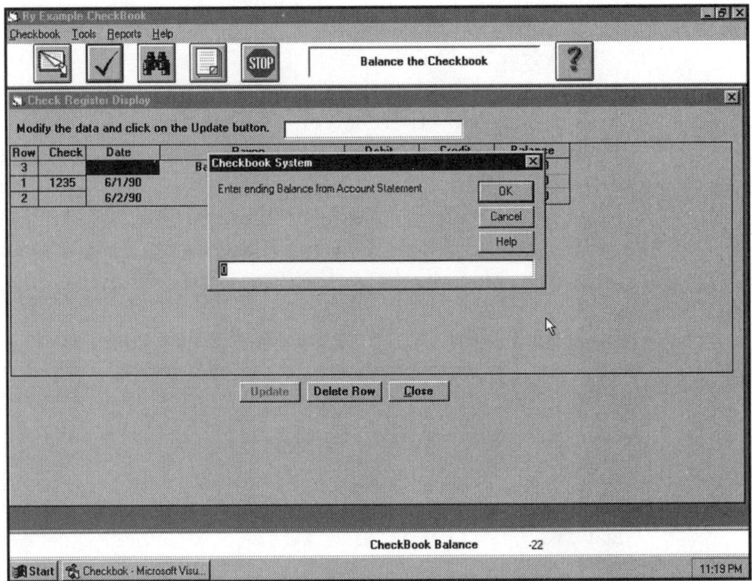

Figure 32.12 Input box asking for the ending account balance.

If the user clicks the Cancel button, the value that is returned is an empty string. But, if the user enters data then it is returned to the program. The logic for this more complex routine is shown in Listing 32.4.

Listing 32.4 32LIST04.TXT—btnBalance Click () Routine

```
Private Sub btnbalance_Click()
Dim input_str
input_str = InputBox("Enter ending Balance from Account
➥ Statement", APP.Title, "0",,, "Check.HLP", 2000)
If input_str = "" Then
    MsgBox "Account Balance Function Cancelled", vbExclamation,
     ➥ APP.Title
```

```
Else
    account_balance_amt = Val(input_str)
    If account_balance_amt > 0 Then
        chkbal.Show
    Else
        MsgBox "Ending Balance Amount must be greater than
        ➥ Zero!", vbExclamation, APP.Title
    End If
End If
End Sub
```

The addition of these message boxes and input boxes brings your application closer to finished product.

Scrolling Your Forms

We tend to think of scroll bars being used for a multi-line text box or window. However, they can be used to indicate the current position on a scale, to control the volume of sound or to show elapsed time. This allows the user to control a function simply by positioning the scroll bar where he wants it to be.

Scroll Bar controls differ from the built-in scroll bars used by Windows (see fig. 32.13).

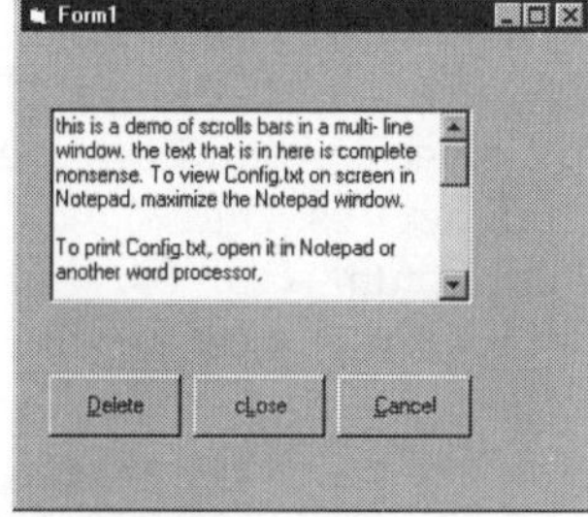

Figure 32.13
Built-in scroll bars in a multi-line text box.

These built-in scroll bars are controlled by the internal Windows logic. On the other hand, the scroll bar controls you can place on a form operate independently from the other controls on the form. Application code is used to control these scroll bars.

The Built-In Scroll Bars

Some of the Visual Basic objects that use built-in scroll bars are the Grid control, the Text Box control and the MDI form. Scroll bars will appear automatically on the objects only when needed. For example, on an MDI form, scroll bars will appear if part of a child form is moved past the border of the MDI form (see fig. 32.14).

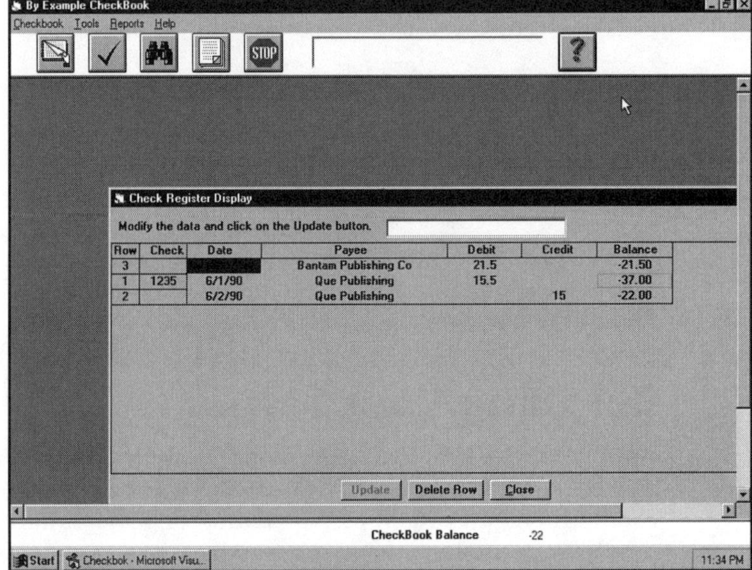

Figure 32.14

Scroll bars on a MDI form.

Using Scroll Bars For Input

Visual Basic comes with two types of scrolling controls. The first type are the scroll bars. As you have seen in Chapter 11, "The Scroll Bar Tools," these are used to move many different objects around on-screen. In addition, they can also be used for input and output devices. The second control is the Slider control. This control acts a lot like the horizontal scroll bar, but can only be used for input and output. It cannot be used to move objects around the screen (see fig. 32.15).

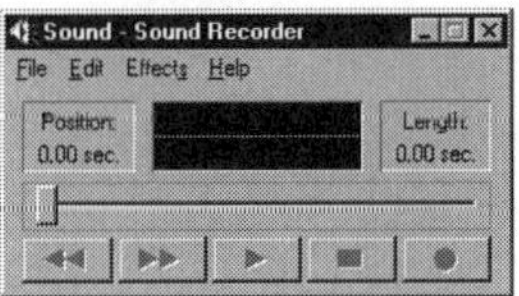

Figure 32.15

Slider showing elapsed time.

Figure 32.16 shows both types of scrolling controls. As you can see, they look different from each other as well as working differently.

One of the hardest things for a programmer to know is when not to use a particular function or control. Trying to force the use of a control just makes the control look out of place on the form. The Checkbook application that you are creating will use a scroll bar to control the grid you will add in the next chapter. But, let's investigate how to create a form that uses scroll bars for simple Data control.

When using Scroll Bar and Slider controls, the `Min` and `Max` properties are used to set the correct range of the control. When you click on the bar of the scroll bar or the

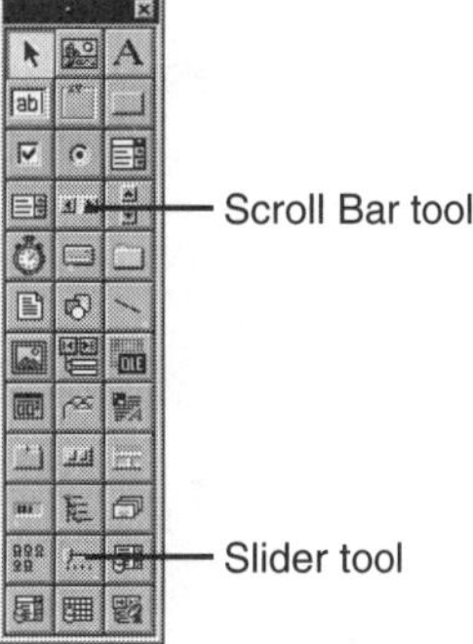

Figure 32.16
Scroll Bar and Slider tool buttons.

slider, the `Value` property increases or decreases by the amount set in the `Largechange` property. The `Smallchange` property controls the amount the scroll bar changes when the user clicks on the arrows at the ends of the scroll bar.

The `Largechange` and `Smallchange` properties are typically set at design time, but, you can change them while the application is running based on changes to the `Max` and `Min` values. However, even though changes to `Min` or `Max` may make it desirable to reset the `Largechange` and `SmallChange` properties, there is no direct link between the two.

Example

To work with these controls, start a new project in Visual Basic. On the empty form, place a horizontal scroll bar, a slider, and two labels on the form (see fig. 32.17).

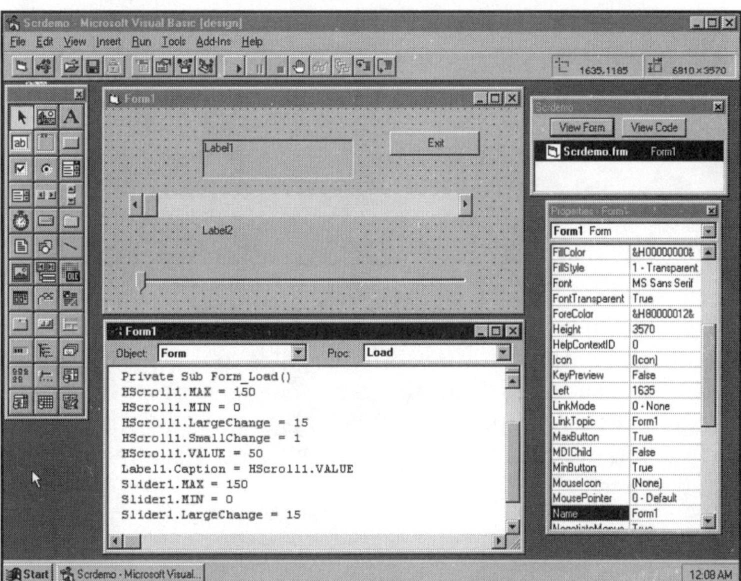

Figure 32.17
Form with Scroll Bar, Slider, and Label controls.

Also, place a command button on the form labeled Exit and put the the following line into the `Click` event for the button:

```
Unload Me
```

In the `Form Load` routine, you are going to set the scroll bar properties to the values shown below. In addition, change the name of `Label1` to `lblScrVal`.

```
hscroll1.Max = 150            'Maximum value of the scroll bar
hscroll1.Min = 0              'Minimum value of the scroll bar
hscroll1.LargeChange = 15     'Number that is added to the
                              'Value property when bar is clicked
hscroll1.SmallChange = 1      'Number that is added to the Value
                              'property when arrow is clicked
hscroll1.Value = 50           'Default number the bar starts at
lblscrval.Caption = hscroll1.Value    'Sets the Label to the
                                      'scroll bar value
```

This code will set the scroll bar and slider position and set the Label caption to the number in the scroll bar's `Value` property. Then in the scroll bar's `Change` event set the Label caption to the value of the scroll bar. In addition, set the slider value in the scroll bar change routine. Now, repeat the above code for the slider control to set its properties to the same values.

Run the application and click on the bar of the scroll bar to see what happens to its position. Then click on the arrows to see the difference in movement of the bar based on the large and small change values. Also click on the slider line or drag the slider pointer to see how it works (see fig. 32.18). It should be noted that `SmallChange` has no effect on the slider when used with the mouse, since it has no end buttons. However the arrow keys will work when the slider has the focus.

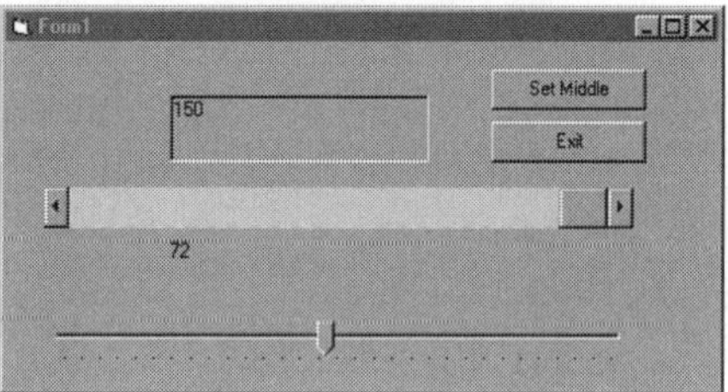

Figure 32.18
Form showing scroll bar and slider changes in the Label box.

On the scroll bars, the changes are greater when clicking the thumb than when clicking on the arrows. The `Max` value represents the highest number that the thumb can be and the `Min` value represents the lowest value that the thumb can be.

The `Value` property represents the current position of the control. Add another command button to the form. In the `Click` routine for this button add the following code:

```
hscroll1.Value = hscroll1.Max / 2
```

This statement sets the scroll bar value to the exact middle of the range. After moving the scroll bar around a few times, click this new button and the scroll bar will position itself to the middle of the bar (see fig. 32.19).

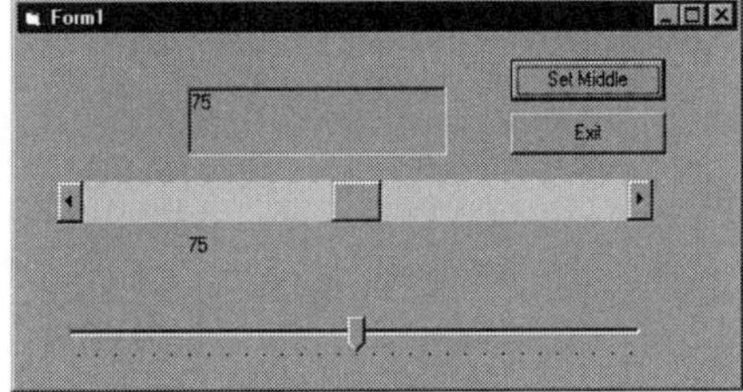

Figure 32.19
Form showing scroll bar set in the middle.

The vertical scroll bar works the exact same way as the horizontal scroll bar except that it moves up and down. You can see that the scroll bars can be used to input values.

Summary

Making use of message boxes can sometimes be the easiest part of an application's logic or the hardest part. This is due to the ease in which you can access the function.

As you've seen, message boxes appear in many different places in the application and for many different reasons. They can be used to inform and to question. In both cases, they help to control the processing flow of the application. The message boxes that you have placed in the application are not the only ones that you will need. As you add more program logic to the application , you will find that there are other messages and more information to display to the user.

Scroll bars and sliders can also be used in many different ways within an application. However, they can only be used in certain areas of the application. These controls are some you would like to use a great deal, however, there are very few ways to make real use them.

In the next chapter, you are going to add database access to the application. This will fill in a lot of the empty area in the application process. In addition, you will put the grid controls on the forms that will display the checkbook register. This control displays data in a standard spreadsheet format.

Review Questions

Answers to review questions are in Appendix B.

1. What are the two types of built-in dialog boxes?
2. How are scroll bar controls used?
3. How does a `MsgBox` statement differ from a `MsgBox` function?

4. How do you create a multiple-button message box?
5. What would cause a built-in scroll bar to appear?

6. What effect does changing the value property have on the scroll bar?
7. How does a message box display a long message?

Review Exercises

1. Display a message before the Checkbook application is closed.
2. Have the application ask the user to input her name when it starts executing.

3. Using the name input from Exercise 2, display a message that says "Hello" to the user and also displays the current date and time.
4. Think of a way that a scroll bar could be used for input in the Checkbook application.

CHAPTER 33

Adding Data and Grid Controls

Data controls have become one of the most important set of objects in Visual Basic. This is because they give us many built-in functions to access our database without having to write the code ourselves. After setting just a few properties of a Data control, any data-aware object will have access to the table specified in the Data control.

Once the Data control is on a form, you can have as many *data-aware* controls connected to that Data control as you need. A data-aware control is one that can be bound to a Data control that is on the form. This allows you to create a form that has objects bound to the Data control and can update the database table, and you do not have to write any code for the function.

You can also access your database by using program code to read and write data to the database. This method will allow a great deal of flexibility to your application process.

When you see a spreadsheet, what you are probably seeing is a grid control on a form. The grid allows you to display data in one of the most common formats used in business.

In this chapter, you will find out how to display data on a grid and how to change the format of the grid and the data in the `grdChkReg`. Also, you will find that Data controls and the associated data-aware controls are very good tools for displaying data to the user. In addition, you can mix the capabilities of non-bound controls, the Data control and programmed access to the database to create a tailored display of data in your application.

Working with Grids

When using grids in an application, you must decide whether to use a standard grid or a data-bound `grdChkReg`. By using the Data-Bound Grid, you can have very sophisticated processing without having to add large amounts of program code. However, at the time of the writing of this book, the Data-Bound Grid control in Visual Basic was not working correctly. Because of this, the examples in this chapter will still use the non-bound `grdChkReg`.

Be aware that much of the code that will be presented to you in this section on grids will become obsolete when the Data-Bound Grid is working properly.

The grid control displays the data in standard row/column format. The information is displayed in cells. A *cell* is a single location in the grid where a row and a column intersect.

You can set the contents of a cell in your application code. In addition, you will also have to set the grid's display layout by modifying the properties of the `grdChkReg`. Also, the data that you display in the grid can be formatted any way that you choose within the capabilities of the `grdChkReg`.

Unlike other controls, like the Text Box control, that allow you to display and modify data on a form, the Grid control does not allow you to edit the data that is displayed. To modify any data, you must add a text box that will display a selected cell's data. This will allow you to edit the data, and then by clicking a save button, move the data back into the cell (see fig. 33.1).

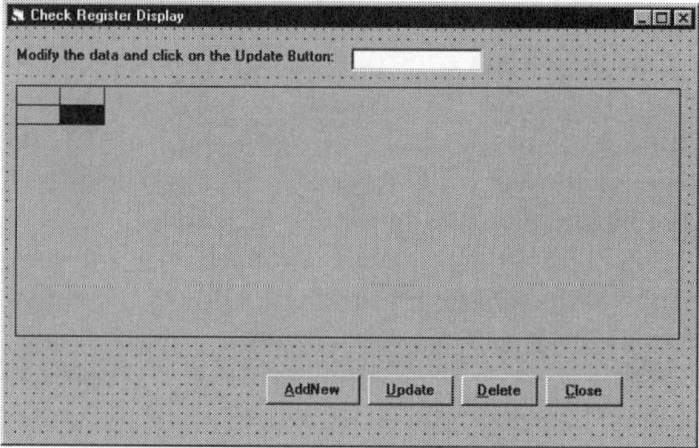

Figure 33.1

A text box used for editing of grid cell data.

Before you create the logic to modify the grid, you must first decide how the grid should look, how many rows and columns it will have and finally what method you will use to add data to the `grdChkReg`.

Setting Up a Grid Control

In deciding how many rows and columns the grid should have, you must understand how the grid control handles the data that is placed into it. By loading the grid with all the rows of data you can allow the grid to control the scrolling function. Or, you can load only the amount of data in the grid that can be displayed at one time.

At first, loading all the data might seem like the best way of processing. However, the more complex the data the harder it will be to load all of your data into the `grdChkReg`.

For small databases, loading all of the data is the best method. But, because of the limitation on the number of rows in a grid, if your database is large or will grow then the second method should be considered. A grid can contain a maximum of 2000 rows and 400 columns.

In creating the grid, you control exactly how you want the rows and columns to be displayed. You can have titles on the top or along the left side of the grid (see fig. 33.2).

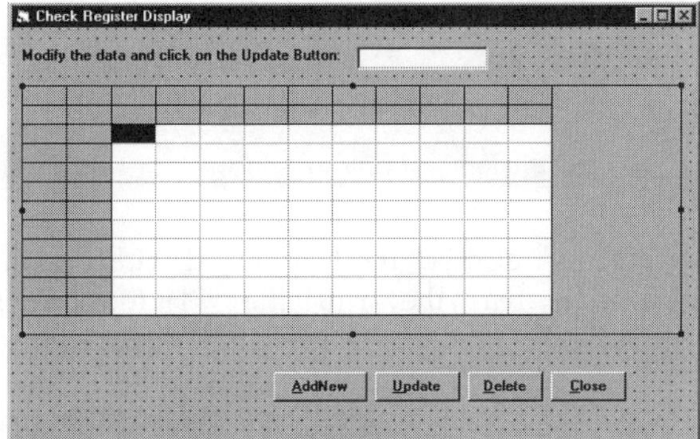

Figure 33.2

Fixed rows and columns on a grid.

These rows and columns are used to display headings for your data. These are commonly placed in a *fixed* row or column. Fixed means that the row or column will not move when you scroll the grid left/right or up/down. The color of a fixed row or column is gray and will differ from the non-fixed grid cells.

The other type of rows or columns that you can have on a grid are called *non-fixed*. A non-fixed row or column will move when the grid is scrolled in any direction. In addition, the non-fixed rows are the only ones that can be selected.

Your program can also change the contents and size of the grid using the grid's properties. These properties will let you set the color of the cells, the height and width of the cells, and whether the scroll bars will be automatically controlled by the grid (see fig. 33.3).

To change the width of a row or column you would make use of a Visual Basic function called `TextWidth`. This function will allow you to calculate the width of the data that will be placed into a particular column. The width of a column should be slightly larger than the largest string that will be placed in the column. The following statement would set the grid's second column to 10 times the width of a capital 'A' plus one-tenth more to allow for extra space:

```
GrdChkRegColWidth(1) = 1.1 * (TextWidth("A") * 10)
```

Check Register Display

Modify the data and click on the Update Button:

Row	Check	Date	Payee	Debit	Credit	Balance
18	1001	7/1/85	Que Publishing Inc	25.85	0.00	-25.85
33	1001	9/5/95 2:22:15 AM	Bantam Publishing Co	21.50	0.00	-47.35
34	1002	9/5/95 2:22:27 AM	Que Publishing Inc	15.50	0.00	-62.85
35		9/5/95 2:22:36	Bantam Publishing Co	0.00	15.00	-47.85

AddNew Update Delete Close

Figure 33.3

Grid showing scroll bars and different-sized columns.

You must also set the height and width of the grid itself so that it fills the appropriate area in the form. If the grid is too small, it will not look good on the form (see fig. 33.4).

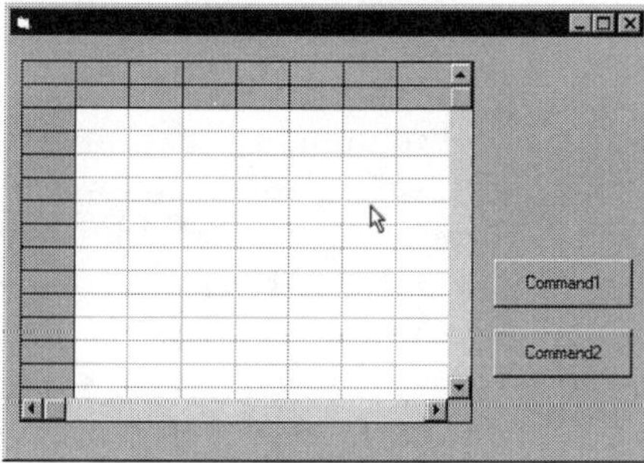

Figure 33.4

Form with a grid that is too small.

One method of setting the size of the grid is similar to the one you use to set the column width. You can set the width of the grid to the width of all the columns added together. If there are more columns than would fit on the form at one time, then this method is not recommended. The second method is to manually set the size of the grid at design time. For your checkbook application, you can use either of these methods. The third method is to have the grid size itself to the form's client area, after protecting the other controls on the form. The grid will always be the biggest size that can fit on the form, but it will never "go off the form." When the grid contains more rows or columns than can be displayed, the grid's scroll bars will make them accessible.

The height of the grid should be less than the total height of the form it is on. This will allow you to place other controls on the form that you might need (see fig. 33.5).

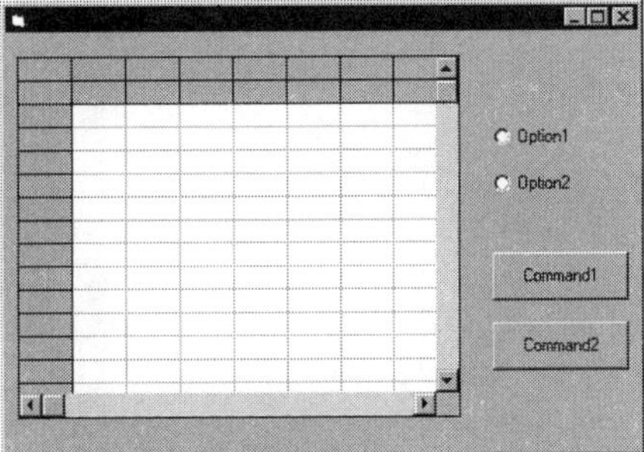

Figure 33.5
Form with a grid and other controls.

In the checkbook application, there will be seven columns displayed on the `grdChkReg`. This allows you to set the grid size at design time; however, you may find that the grid will have a large empty area (see fig. 33.6).

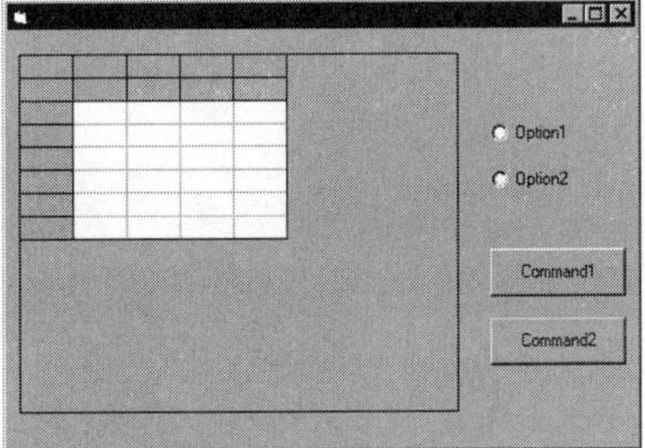

Figure 33.6
A grid that is larger than needed.

Example

Let's add the Check Register form to the project that was created in the previous chapters. Add a Form from the Insert menu and then add a Grid control to the form.

To add the grid to this form, click on the Grid button on the Visual Basic Toolbar (see fig. 33.7) and draw the grid on the form.

When you draw the grid, it does not have to cover the whole form because you will be setting the size in the code at run-time. Once the grid is on the form, set the width of the cells, the width of the grid itself and the height of the `grdChkReg`. Also, set the grid to the upper-left corner of the form. You do this by setting the `Top` and `Left` properties of the grid to 0 in the form's `Form Load` event.

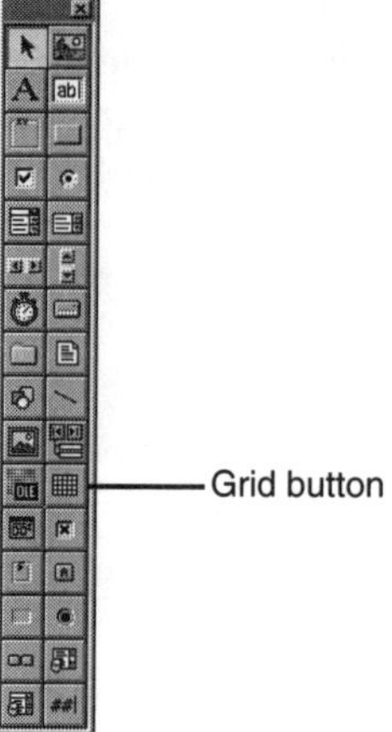

Figure 33.7
Grid button on the Toolbar.

In the `Load` event for the check register form, add the code in Listing 33.1.

Listing 33.1 33LIST01.TXT—Form Load Routine to Set Grid Sizes

```
Dim Tc As String * 1
chkreg.Width = CkBkMain.Width * 0.98
chkreg.Height = CkBkMain.Height * 0.75
chkreg.Top = 0
chkreg.Left = 0
grdChkReg.Width = chkreg.Width * 0.98
grdChkReg.Cols = 8
grdChkReg.Rows = 1
grdChkReg.Row = 0
grdChkReg.Col = 0
grdChkReg.Text = "Row"
grdChkReg.ColWidth(0) = 1.1 * (TextWidth("A") * 3)
grdChkReg.FixedAlignment(0) = 2
grdChkReg.Col = 1
grdChkReg.Text = "  Check"
grdChkReg.ColWidth(1) = 1.1 * (TextWidth("A") * 5)
grdChkReg.FixedAlignment(1) = 2
grdChkReg.Col = 2
grdChkReg.Text = "     Date"
grdChkReg.ColWidth(2) = 1.1 * (TextWidth("A") * 8)
grdChkReg.ColAlignment(2) = 2
grdChkReg.Col = 3
grdChkReg.Text = "                    Payee         "
grdChkReg.ColWidth(3) = 1.1 * (TextWidth("A") * 20)
grdChkReg.ColAlignment(3) = 2
grdChkReg.Col = 4
grdChkReg.Text = "     Debit"
grdChkReg.ColWidth(4) = 1.1 * (TextWidth("A") * 8)
grdChkReg.ColAlignment(4) = 2
```

```
grdChkReg.Col = 5
grdChkReg.Text = "      Credit"
grdChkReg.ColWidth(5) = 1.1 * (TextWidth("A") * 8)
grdChkReg.ColAlignment(5) = 2
grdChkReg.Col = 6
grdChkReg.Text = "       Balance"
grdChkReg.ColWidth(6) = 1.1 * (TextWidth("A") * 8)
grdChkReg.ColAlignment(6) = 2
grdChkReg.Col = 7
grdChkReg.Text = "       Cleared"
grdChkReg.ColWidth(7) = 1.1 * (TextWidth("A") * 8)
grdChkReg.ColAlignment(7) = 2
```

This code will set the size of the Check Register form, then position it on the MDI desktop. The grid will be initialized with six columns, 15 rows and headings in the first row of the `grdChkReg`. The headings are set by selecting the first row, which is the array element zero. Then for each column, set the text property to the appropriate heading.

To set fixed rows and columns, you can either change the values in the Properties property sheet to the number of rows and columns that you want fixed (see fig. 33.8) or use the Grid Control Properties property sheet to change these values (see fig. 33.9).

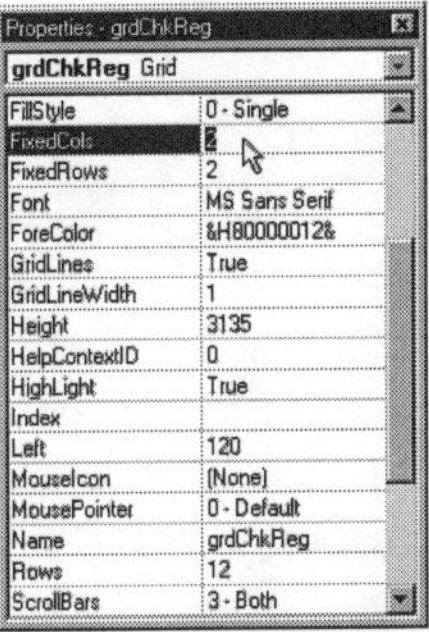

Figure 33.8

Fixed rows and columns properties.

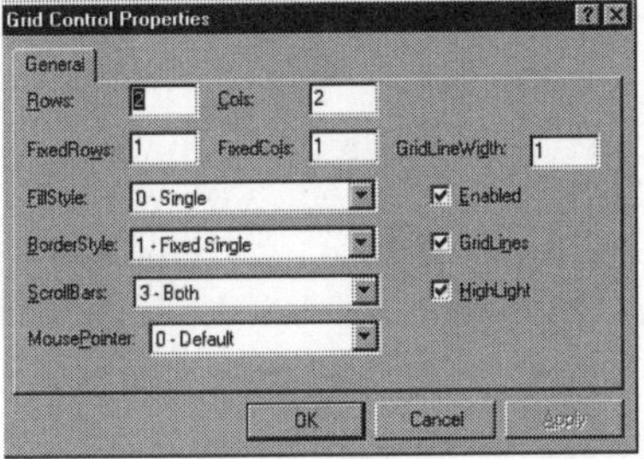

Figure 33.9

Grid Control Properties property sheet.

This can be reached via the `Custom` property in the Properties window, or from the Properties item on the context menu for the grid, which you activate by clicking the right button when pointing the mouse at the `grdChkReg`.

Now that you have created the grid on the Check Register form, data has to be placed in it. Once you have data in the grid cells, you will want to align the text so that all the information looks consistent (see fig. 33.10).

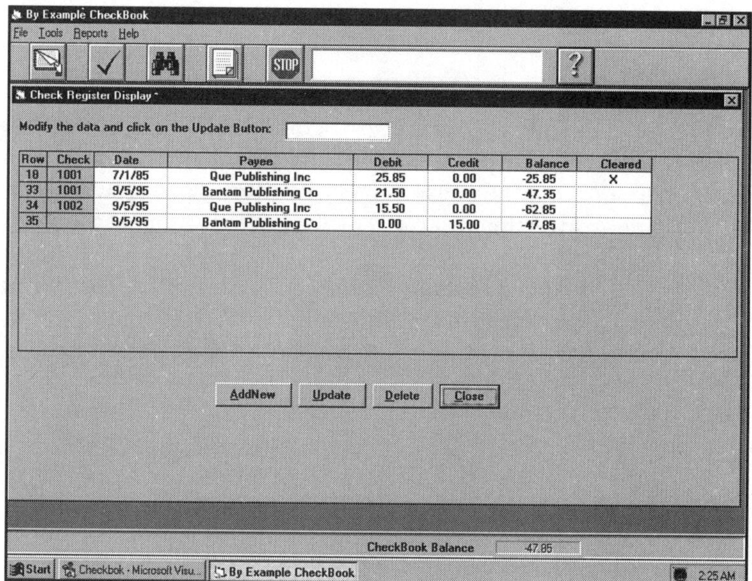

Figure 33.10
Grid with columns aligned.

You have the ability to control the alignment of text in the columns of a grid for both fixed and non-fixed columns. If you want to align the text in fixed cells, use the `FixedAlignment` property. For the non-fixed cells in a column, you would use the `ColAlignment` property.

```
'Set column to center the text
grdChkRegGrdChkRegColAlignment(1) = 2
```

This code will center the text in the specified column.

You can align text in a column either left justified, right justified or centered. When you have a column with both fixed and non-fixed cells, the `Colalignment` property affects only the non-fixed cells in that column, while the `FixedAlignment` property only affects the fixed cells in that column.

Loading a Grid with Data

Unless your database is too large for the grid to handle, the way to handle it is to load all the data into the grid at one time.

To load data into the grid, you need to have two program loops. One loop will control which row you are working with and the second loop will control the column that you are setting. In order to place data into a cell, you must set the `GrdChkRegRow` property to the row number that you want to work with. Then you set the `GrdChkRegCol` property to the column you want. Finally, set the `GrdChkRegText` property to the data item you want to place in the cell.

Example

The following code will loop through the database until all the rows are loaded into the `grdChkReg`. When there is no more data to load, the EOF (end of file) condition will be true. This will cause the program to exit this processing loop. Inside the loop, the six columns are being set for each row in the `grdChkReg`. Since the Row and Column count starts at zero, all the references to the rows and columns are one less than the actual number. The following code should be entered as the second part of the Form Load event.

```
Dim FileNum
FileNum = 1
Open "C:TESTDATA.DAT" for Input as FileNum
j = 1
'Read in a record of data
Do While Not EOF(FileNum)
    grdChkReg.Rows = j
    grdChkReg.Row = j-1
    Input FileNum, RecCol0, RecCol1, RecCol2, RecCol3,
    ➥ RecCol4, RecCol5
    grdChkReg.Col = 0
    grdChkReg.Text = RecCol0
    grdChkReg.Col = 1
    grdChkReg.Text = RecCol1
    grdChkReg.Col = 2
    grdChkReg.Text = RecCol2
    grdChkReg.Col = 3
    grdChkReg.Text = RecCol3
    j = j + 1
Loop
```

Another way to load data into a grid is to use the `AddItem` method at run-time. An example of the `AddItem` method follows:

```
GrdChkRegAddItem grid_text
```

This statement would load the data in item into the first cell in a new row. However, you can load the entire row in a single statement by using tab characters in the string. The tab character will cause the data after the tab to be placed in the next sequential column in the row. The index, if present, specifies the position the row will occupy in the `grdChkReg`. The above code segment can be re-done using the `Additem` method. An example of this follows:

```
Dim FileNum
Dim Tabchr as string * 1
Tabchr = chr$(9)
FileNum = 1
Open "C:TESTDATA.DAT" for Input as FileNum
 'Read in a record of data
Do While Not EOF(FileNum)
Input FileNum, RecCol0, RecCol1, RecCol2, RecCol3
    grdChkReg.AddItem RecCol0 & Tabchr & RecCol1 & Tabchr
      ➥ & RecCol2 & Tabchr & RecCol3
Loop
```

This code segment will perform the exact same function as the previous code segment except that there is less code involved. The `AddItem` method adds rows to the grid automatically as it is executed. You are allowing the Visual Basic language to perform the work for you, instead of creating the code yourself.

During the application's processing, you will have a need to delete data from a `grdChkReg`. When you have to delete a row from the grid, you can use the `RemoveItem` method to perform the function. The statement to remove the third row from a grid follows:

```
GrdChkRegRemoveItem 2
```

This statement will move all the rows following the deleted row up one row in the `grdChkReg`.

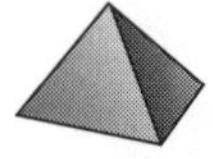

Tip: You cannot use either the `AddItem` or `RemoveItem` method on a fixed row.

You now have loaded your grid with data and can scroll through it. Now, to complete the grid processing functions, you have to be able to select a row to delete, or a cell to edit.

Editing Data in a Grid

To edit a cell or delete a row you have to select it. The Grid control allows you to select and highlight one or more cells. You can select a range of cells by clicking a cell and then drag the mouse to the ending cell (see fig. 33.11). However, you should only be able to delete a single row at a time.

If your grid has a fixed column and row, you can select the entire grid by clicking the cell where row(0) and column(0) intersect. In addition, you can select an entire row by clicking the cell in the fixed column for that row, or you can select an entire column by clicking the cell in the fixed row for that column.

When a cell or a range of cells is selected, you can highlight the selected cells to indicate that they have been selected. If the grid's `Highlight` property is `True` then selected cells will be highlighted.

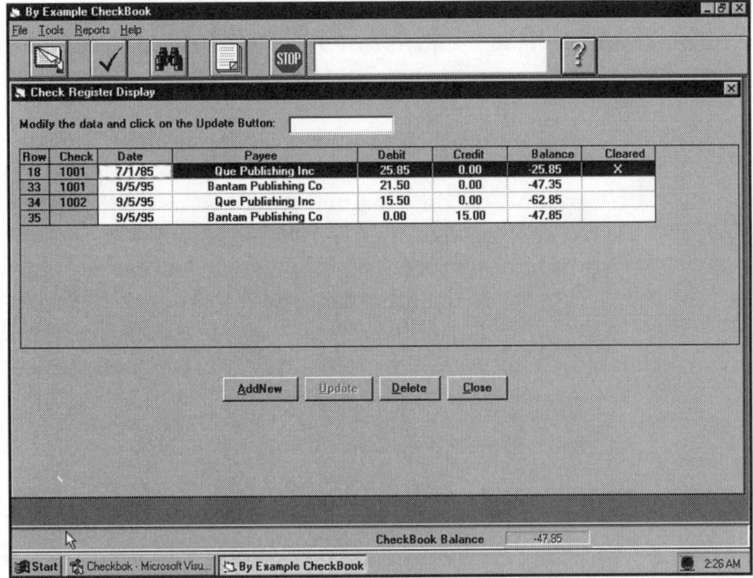

Figure 33.11
Grid with several cells selected.

Now that you can select any cell or range of cells in a grid at run-time, you can now execute code to delete a row or edit the data within a single cell.

Example

To delete a row from a grid, you need to have a command button on the form with the grid that will execute the code to remove the row when it is clicked. This code must verify that an entire row has been selected. An example of the code to do this is shown in Listing 33.2.

Listing 33.2 33LIST02.TXT—Code Segment to Check for Full Row Selected

```
If grdChkReg.SelStartRow = grdChkReg.SelEndRow Then
    If grdChkReg.SelStartCol = 1 And grdChkReg.SelEndCol = 7 Then
        If grdchkreg.rows = 2 then
           MsgBox "Cannot Delete last row", vbCritical, App.Title
        Else
          grdChkReg.RemoveItem grdChkReg.SelStartRow
        End If
    Else
        MsgBox "Cannot Delete a partial Row.", vbCritical, App.Title
    End If
Else
    MsgBox "Cannot Delete multiple Rows.", vbCritical, App.Title
End If
```

This code will verify that only a single row was selected before executing the `RemoveItem` statement, and, if a single row is not selected then it will display errors using `MsgBox` statements. To delete more than one row a loop would be needed to perform the process.

As you can see in the previous code segment, there are several properties that you can use to determine what row and column is selected by the user.

In order to edit data in a cell you must move the data into a text box, make any required changes and then move the data back to the cell.

This process requires several different routines within the program. By using the `DblClick` event of the grid, the code can move a single cell's data to a text box that is on the form. Then the user can edit the data in the text box and then update the cell by clicking another command button to move the modified data back into the `grdChkReg`. The code to perform these functions in the different routines is shown in Listing 33.3.

Listing 33.3 33LIST03.TXT—Several Event Routines

```
Sub btnupdate_Click ()
        grdChkReg.Text = txtInput.Text
        txtInput.Text = ""
        btnupdate.Enabled = False
End Sub

Sub GrdChkReg_Click ()
btnupdate.Enabled = False
End Sub

Sub GrdChkReg_DblClick ()
If grdChkReg.SelStartRow = grdChkReg.SelEndRow Then
    If grdChkReg.SelStartCol = grdChkReg.SelEndCol Then
        txtInput.Text = grdChkReg.Text
        btnupdate.Enabled = True
        btnupdate.SetFocus
    End If
End If
End Sub
```

The Update button on the form should only be enabled when there is data in the text box. Also, when the data in the text box is moved back to the grid, the contents text box should be erased.

The Grid control that is displayed in the Check Register (see fig. 33.12) can have the data modified, the rows deleted, and can have rows added when the Line Entry form is used.

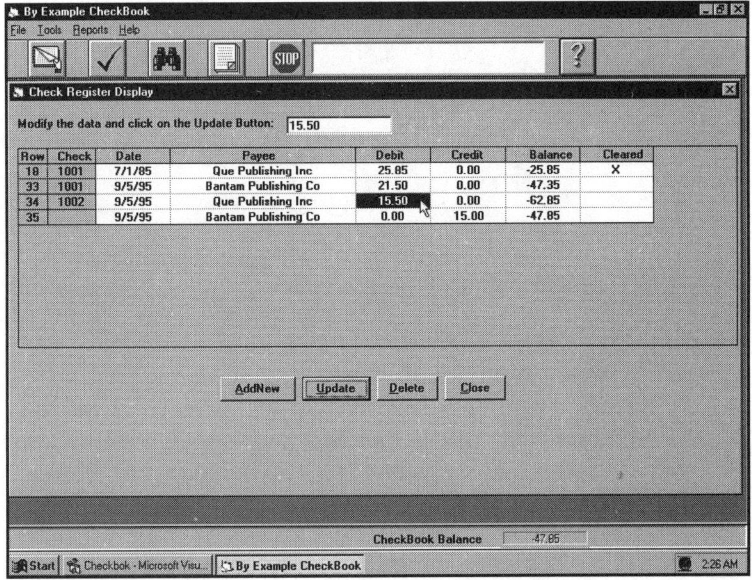

Figure 33.12
Completed check register form.

The Line Entry form will add data to the database and if the check register form is loaded it will add the data to the grid as well. To have the form add data to the grid, you would use an `AddItem` statement to add all of the data items in a single line of code as shown in Listing 33.4.

Listing 33.4 33LIST04.TXT—*Line Entry Save* Event Code

```
Sub Btnsave_Click ()
Dim chkdep As Integer
Dim grid_text As String
    Tc = Chr$(9)
    If txtChkNum.Text = "" Then
        grid_text = " " & Tc & mskDate.Text
    Else
        grid_text = txtChkNum.Text & Tc & mskDate.Text
    End If
    grid_text = grid_text & Tc & cboPayee.Text
    actkey.Caption = current_account
        memkey.Caption = ""
        If cboPayee.Text = "" Then
            MsgBox "No Payee Selected", vbCritical, App.Title
            Exit Sub
        End If
    If ent_check.Value = True Then
        enttyp.Caption = "C"
        chkdep = -1
        entchk.Caption = mskAmt.Text
```

```
        entdep.Caption = "0"
        grid_text = grid_text & Tc & mskAmt.Text & Tc & "0.00" & Tc
    ElseIf ent_deposit.Value = True Then
        enttyp.Caption = "D"
        chkdep = 1
        entchk.Caption = "0"
        entdep.Caption = mskAmt.Text
        grid_text = grid_text & Tc & "0.00" & Tc & mskAmt.Text & Tc
    End If
    MsgBox "Entry Saved", vbExclamation, App.Title
    mskAmt.Text = ""
    cboPayee.Text = ""
    lineitem.entry.Recordset.AddNew
```

The Account Balance form uses the same logic to load the grid as the Check Register form. In addition, you will need to move the Ending Balance number entered by the user to the Outstanding Balance Label on the Balance form.

When you double-click a row in the balance form, the code should place a capital X in the CLR column (see fig. 33.13).

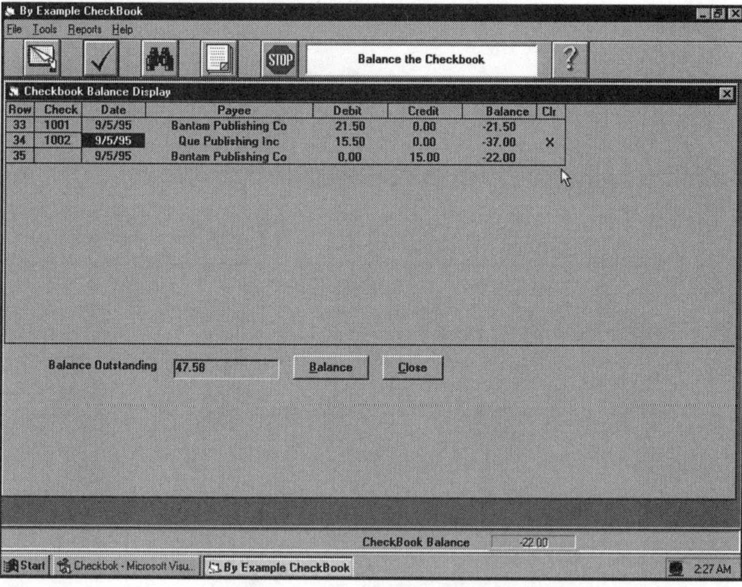

Figure 33.13

Account balance form with an X in the Clear column.

At the same time, you should subtract the credits from the outstanding balance and add the debits to the outstanding balance. In both the Check Register and Account Balance grids, you should only load the entries that have not been checked off.

Data Access Overview

To work with the information that you have stored in a database, you need to be able to access the database and retrieve the data as you need it. One method of access is to use the *data access objects* (DAO) provided with Visual Basic. This method enables you to manipulate the database directly. In addition, you can use the data-aware controls in Visual Basic to automate the database access. To use DAOs, you must have them included in the Reference Library list (see fig. 33.14) on the Tool menu list.

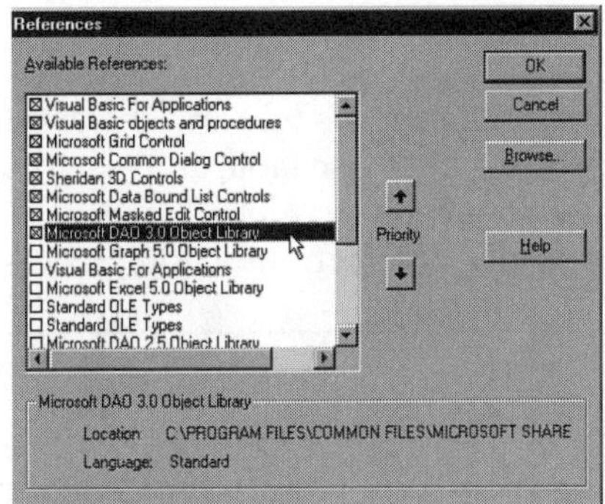

Figure 33.14
Reference selection form showing the DAO Object Library.

To make your application data-aware, you just add Data controls to your forms and specify the database that you want to access. Then you add data-aware controls such as a text box to your form and set the properties of the control to "bind" or attach the control to the Data control on the form. When you run your application, these "bound" controls will automatically display the current record's data from the database.

In the Professional Edition of Visual Basic you can use programmed data access, where you do not need Data controls on the form. You as the programmer will open the database tables, position the database to the record that you want and then read the data into program variables for access by the user.

Transaction Processing

When you have an application that is modifying data in a database, you must be able to enforce data integrity. To do this, you must be able to reverse the process if a problem occurs or the data fails to pass certain tests (for example, Check number already used).

Knowing how far back to *Undo* any changes in the database, requires you to understand the workings of a *Transaction*. A transaction is a logical set of changes made to a *recordset*. A recordset is created whenever a database table or query is opened. Using transactions allows you to verify the changes made to the data before saving them to the database.

For example, when you add an entry in your application, you will want to validate the data entered and make sure that the check number is correct. If either of these are incorrect, you do not want to add the information to the database. These changes can be something as small as modifying one field or as large as deleting several records at once.

When you start—or "begin"—a transaction, any changes you make to the data can be undone (or "rolled back"). When you have finished all of the processing and have decided that the work is complete, you can save (or "commit") the changes to the database.

If there are no transactions currently set, the transaction state of the database is *auto-commit*. This means that any changes to a recordset are made immediately to the underlying database table and is permanent.

Transactions function globally within a workspace. When you have more than one database open, the transaction processing will affect all open databases.

Note: You cannot roll-back one database without rolling back the pending transactions in all other databases as well.

Depending on the how complex the update function is, you will use transaction processing to reverse any changes that you do not want. To begin a transaction, you would use the command `BeginTrans`. Committing a transaction is done with a `CommitTrans` statement. To roll back any changes use `RollBack`. When you use only the default workspace, the transactions will span databases. Therefore, you do not have to associate these commands with a particular database.

However, if you open a single database several times or different databases, using more than one workspace, then you can have simultaneous transactions that are independant of one another. When using multiple workspaces, you must specify which workspace the transaction command applies to. An example of this is as follows:

```
MyWorkspace.CommitTrans
```

Caution: Any uncommitted transactions are rolled back automatically when the application ends.

When To Use Bound Controls

Bound controls can be used to display data from your database automatically. If there is no unique process that you want to perform with the data before displaying it, then you should use bound controls. However, if you want to process some of the data a certain way, you will have to use the Data Manipulation Language (DML).

Additionally, if you are displaying one record at a time, then bound controls should be considered as the method for manipulating the data. Bound controls usually display only the current row on the form at one time. The only way to have multiple records on the form is to use the Grid control to load multiple rows or the DBGrid control. When you place a Data control on a form, you can now automatically scroll through the records in the table that is connected to the Data control. Other bound controls that display multiple rows of data are the DBList and DBCombo controls, although only the DBGrid allows you to update the data.

In this section of the chapter, you will see how to add the processing that will allow your checkbook application to access your database. There are several forms that will display or manipulate data from the database. Some of these forms will use programmed access, while a few of them will use the data-aware controls. The simplest data-aware form in your application is the Account Selection form (see fig. 33.15).

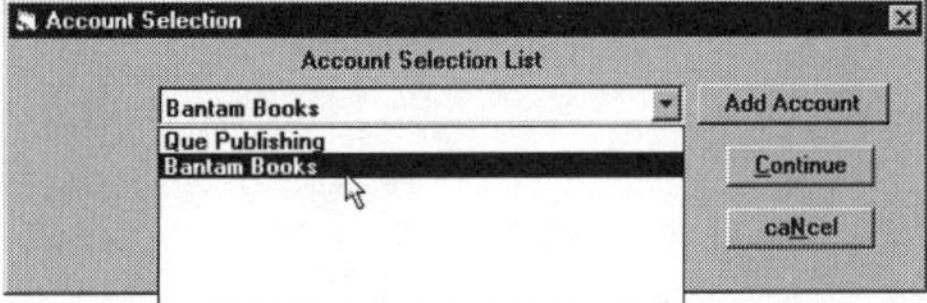

Figure 33.15
Account Selection form.

This form will always display the current account, if there is one. It will also let you add a new account to the application. And you can change the active account by scrolling through the account list by clicking the Data control arrows.

Example

Let's add this new form to the existing project that you have been working with. Create a new form and name it Acctsel. Then to put the Data control on the form, click the Data control button on the Visual Basic Toolbar.

Then draw the Data control on the form. Make the control wide enough to show the white box in between the arrow buttons (see fig. 33.16).

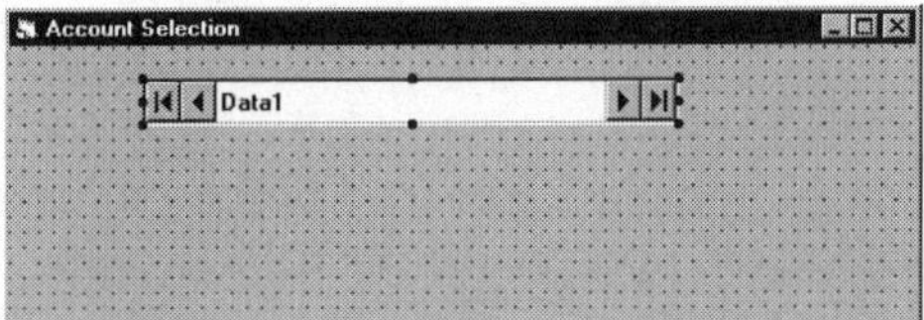

Figure 33.16
Account Selection form with the Data control.

This control has five parts to the visible control. The inner arrows allow you to move forward and backward through the table one record at a time. The outer arrows with the vertical lines will move you to the first or last record in the table. In between these arrows is the Data controls caption. You can display any information you want in it.

Once you have the Data control on the form, set the database name that the Data control will open in the properties list (see fig. 33.17).

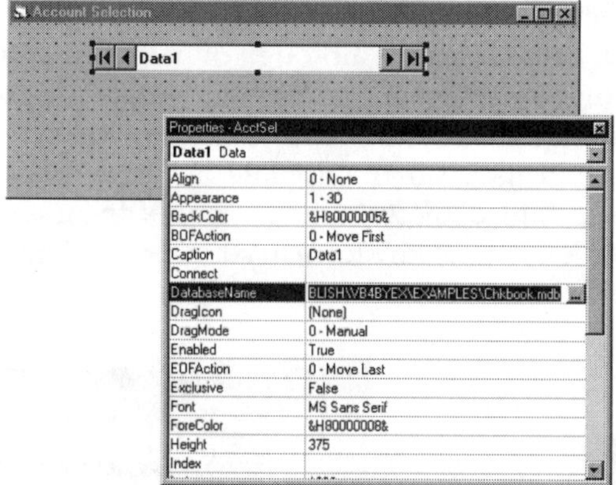

Figure 33.17
Data Control property box.

After specifying the database name, you need to set the table that this Data control will access. In the properties box, select the Account table when you click the `RecordSource` property to display the list of tables in the database that you can choose from (see fig. 33.18).

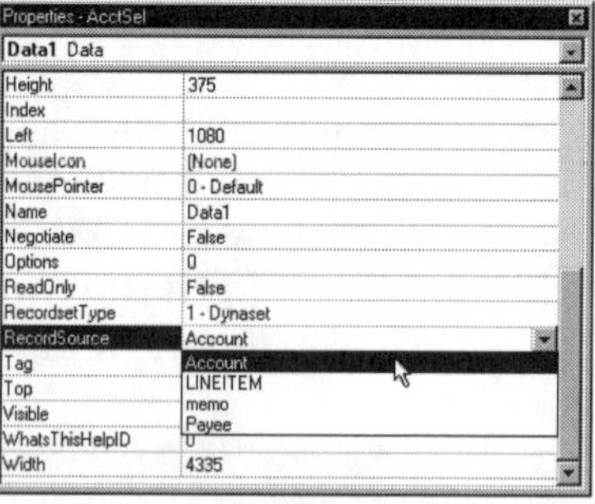

Figure 33.18
Data control `RecordSource` property selection list.

Since the underlying control of the database is SQL language, you can specify a SQL select statement as the recordsource for a Data control.

When the form is finished loading, the Data control will automatically open the database table or SQL query specified in the `RecordSource` property. Once open, you can access any field by referring to the *recordset* that is created. One way of accessing the Account Name would be as follows:

```
DataControl.Recordset("AccountName") = "This is a Test"
```

`DataControl` can be renamed any value you want. Use the properties form to change the name of the Data control. This statement will set the Account name of the current account to `"This is a Test"`.

In the application, you can have the Account Name displayed in the caption. To change the caption, you must know when the current record has changed.

When using Data controls, you have two very powerful events for manipulating the data. These methods are the `Reposition` event and the `Validate` event. These events are triggered whenever the database is accessed.

Whenever the current record changes, the `Reposition` routine is executed. In this routine you can check if there are any records in the table. If there are no records, then you can display a message to that effect in the Data control caption. If there are records, you can set the caption to the account name in the current record.

To check if there are any records, you would use the properties `EOF` (End of File) and `BOF` (Beginning of File). If both of them are `True` then there are no records in the table. An example of the code to set the caption to the account name is shown below. To use this code, place it in the data1 control `Reposition` sub-procedure.

```
If Not data1.Recordset.EOF And Not data1.Recordset.BOF and
➥Not NEWREC Then
    data1.Caption = data1.Recordset ("accountname")
    new_account = data1.Recordset("accountid")
Else
    data1.Caption = "No Account on File"
End If
```

The last process you can add is the `Validate` routine, which is triggered whenever the current row in the database is changed. This event allows you to check any changes made to the recordset before the new information is written to the database. There are two parameters in this routine that you can access.

If the `Save` parameter is `True`, then there have been changes made to data in the recordset. You can prevent the data from being saved by setting the `Save` parameter to `False`.

The `Action` parameter tells you what caused this event to be triggered. The value of the action parameter indicates which function was executed. By setting this parameter to zero, you can cancel any Data control action that triggered this event. These constants are defined in the VB Object Library included with Visual Basic (see fig. 33.19).

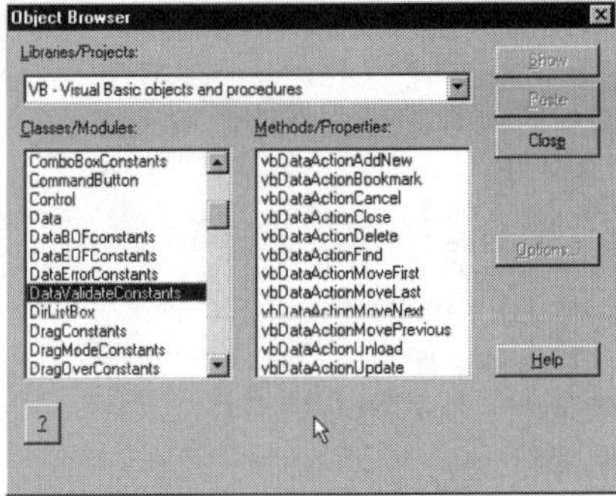

Figure 33.19

`DataAction` constants in VB Object list.

The values for the `DataAction` constants follow:

```
'Validate event Action arguments
vbDataActionCancel = 0
vbDataActionMoveFirst = 1
vbDataActionMovePrevious = 2
vbDataActionNMoveNext = 3
vbDataActionMoveLast = 4
vbDataActionAddNew = 5
vbDataActionUpdate = 6
vbDataActionDelete = 7
vbDataActionFind = 8
vbDataActionBookmark = 9
vbDataActionClose = 10
vbDataActionUnload = 11
```

Example

Let's change the form so that it is using the databound Dropdown ComboBox control. This control will allow the user to see all the accounts at once before selecting one of them from the list. First move the Data control to the lower left of the form. Now add the combo box by clicking on the data ComboBox button on the Toolbar.

Then draw the control on the form and set its `Style` property to `2 - Dropdown List`, while moving the command buttons to one side (see fig. 33.20).

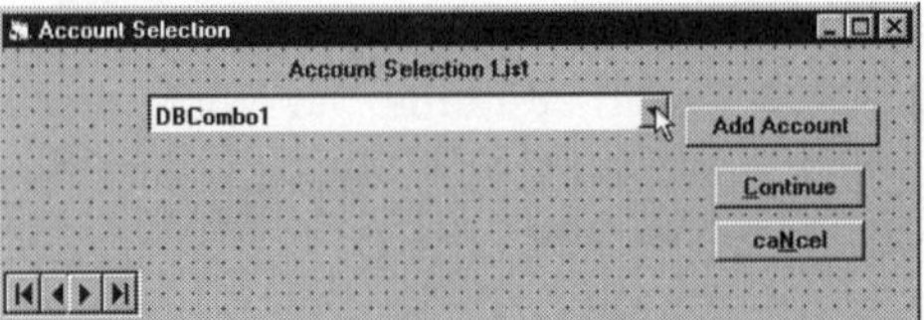

Figure 33.20

Account Selection form with a combo box.

Once this control is on the form, you no longer need to have the Data control visible. To hide the Data control, change the `Visible` property of the control to `False`.

Now, in the data ComboBox, set the `DataSource` property to the Data control on the form and set both the `BoundColumn` and `DataField` properties to the AccountName field in the database (see fig. 33.21).

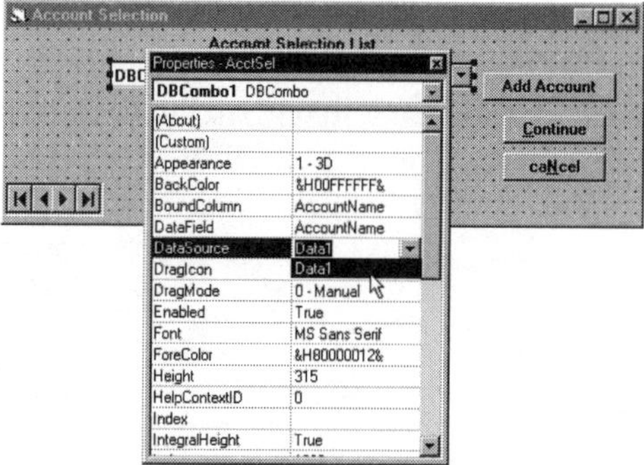

Figure 33.21
DataSource property of ComboBox.

After setting the datasource, you want to specify the column in the recordset that will be displayed when the combo box is opened. With this control you can bind the text box to one Data control while the list box is bound to another. In your application you will only bind the list portion of the control. The column that will be displayed should be the account name (see fig. 33.22).

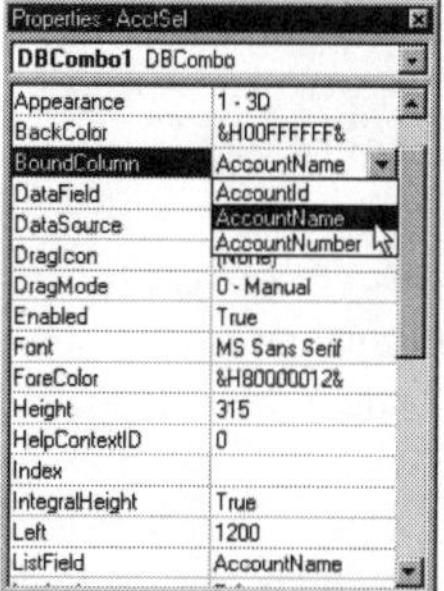

Figure 33.22
Combo box properties to set the List area on the control.

These additions to the form reduce the amount of code required. The `Reposition` routine from the Data control is no longer needed. That routine is replaced by one line of code in the combo box's `Click` routine. This line of code follows:

```
New_account = data1.recordset("accountid")
```

Now, re-execute the application to see how these changes improve the way you select an account. The final form shows the combo box but not the Data control (see fig. 33.23).

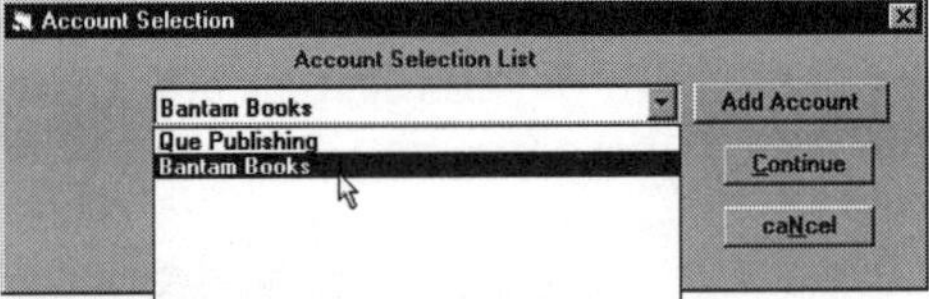

Figure 33.23
Completed Account Selection form.

The next form that you will make changes to is the Line Item Entry (see fig. 33.24). This form will allow you to add a new account entry to the database.

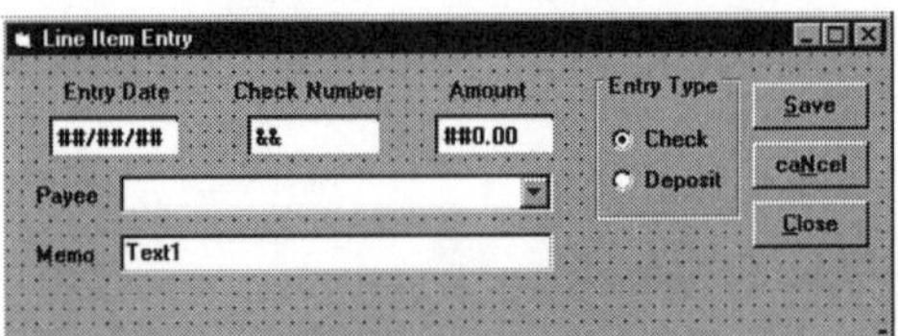

Figure 33.24
Line Item Entry form.

This form will use the `Load` command to load the entry form into memory. The reason for this is to execute an `AddNew` command for the Data control on the Line Item Entry form before the form is displayed to the user. Because a Data control cannot be accessed until the load routine is completed, the `AddNew` command would cause an error in that routine.

To add new data to the database, you must have a *blank* record to work with. Once you have the blank record, you can move the information into the fields in the record and then commit the changes. Because you would want to reverse any changes made if there was a problem, transaction processing should be used with this form.

You cannot access any of the database commands until after the form has completed the load process. This is because Visual Basic opens the database connected to a Data control only after the form is finished loading.

Caution: Do not attempt to execute any Data control methods before the form has finished loading.

When you want to use this form to add a new record, you must load the form using the `Load` command. After the form is loaded, you can execute the `AddNew` command to create a blank record to use. Once you have executed the `AddNew` command you can `Show` the form Modally. The routine to do this should look like the example shown below. To use this code, place it in both the `File_entry.Click` sub-procedure and the `Entry.Click` sub-procedures in the CKBKMain form.

```
If chkbal_loaded Then
    MsgBox "Entry cannot be added while Balance in process.",
```

```
    ➥ vbexclamation, app_title
Else
    BeginTrans
    Load lineitem
    lineitem!entry.Recordset.AddNew
    lineitem.Show modal
End If
```

After the form is displayed to the user, he will be able to enter the information for an account record. Even though you are using Data Bound controls, some of the text boxes will not be bound to the Data control. In addition, the combo box that will display the payee names will be loaded in a loop that will use programmed access. The memo field will also require programmed access to save the data.

The Continue button will ask if the record should be saved and if the user clicks on the Yes button, it will process the data and update the record. Also, if the check register form is displayed, it will add the record to the grid on the check register form.

During the update process, you must move the current account number into a non-visible label on the form that is bound to the `accountkey` field in the lineitem table. Another database field that you will have to set is the entry type field. This field is dependent on which of the two radio buttons is selected.

An example of the `Close` sub-procedure for the `Line Item Entry` form is shown in Listing 33.5.

Listing 33.5 33LIST05.TXT—Close Button Code in the Line Item Entry Form

```
Dim chkdep As Integer
Dim grid_text As String
no_save = False
msg_ans = MsgBox("Save account entry before Closing?",
➥ vbYesNoCancel + vbQuestion, App.Title)
If msg_ans = vbCancel Then
    Exit Sub
ElseIf msg_ans = vbYes Then    Tc = Chr$(9)
    If txtChkNum.Text = "" Then
        grid_text = " " & Tc & mskDate.Text
    Else
        grid_text = txtChkNum.Text & Tc & mskDate.Text
    End If
    grid_text = grid_text & Tc & cboPayee.Text
    actkey.Caption = current_account
        memkey.Caption = ""
        If cboPayee.Text = "" Then
            MsgBox "No Payee Selected", vbCritical, App.Title
            Exit Sub
        End If
    If ent_check.Value = True Then
```

```
        enttyp.Caption = "C"
        chkdep = -1
        entchk.Caption = mskAmt.Text
        entdep.Caption = "0"
        grid_text = grid_text & Tc & mskAmt.Text & Tc & "0.00" & Tc
    ElseIf ent_deposit.Value = True Then
        enttyp.Caption = "D"
        chkdep = 1
        entchk.Caption = "0"
        entdep.Caption = mskAmt.Text
        grid_text = grid_text & Tc & "0.00" & Tc & mskAmt.Text & Tc
    End If
    MsgBox "Entry Saved", vbExclamation, App.Title
    mskAmt.Text = ""
    cboPayee.Text = ""
    lineitem.entry.Recordset.AddNew
Else
    actkey.Caption = Str(current_account)
    itmkey.Caption = "9999"
    entry.Recordset.AddNew
End If
Unload Me
```

Finally, you should validate the data before adding it to the database. You would add the validation code in the Data controls validate routine. The entry date can be checked by using the Visual Basic `IsDate` function. If the date is invalid and an update was in progress, you should display a message (see fig. 33.25) telling the user to re-enter the date. The routine should also cancel the action by setting the `Action` parameter to zero.

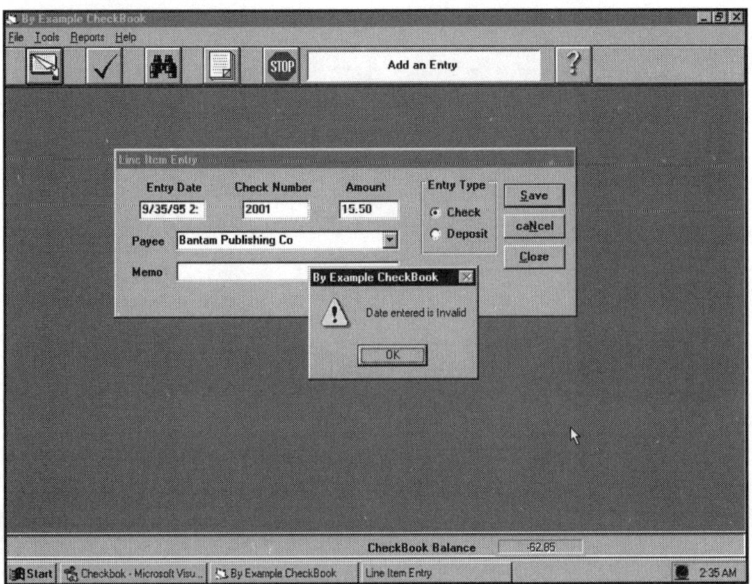

Figure 33.25
Invalid date message from the `Validate` routine.

When to Use Programmed Access

Even though using program code to access your database is more complex, this method will give you the most control of how your data is accessed, displayed and updated. In order to access your database, you must first open the database in the application code. The logical place to open the database is in the MDIforms `Load` routine. This allows you to create *dynasets* whenever you need them. A dynaset is a recordset created by programmed data access.

To open your database, use the following code:

```
Dim ChkDB as Database
DIM ChkSet as Recordset
Set ChkDb = OpenDatabase("ChkBook.MDB")
```

Once you have the database open you can create `Recordset` by executing the following:

```
Set ChkSet = ChkDB.OpenRecordset("Table", dbOpenDynaset)
```

This statement would open a type of recordset called `Dynaset`. When creating these dynasets, you can use SQL statements instead of a table name as the parameter to the `OpenRecordset` command. If you want to create a dynaset for the Check Register form that can only access entries for the current account and sort it by the date, you would code the following:

```
SQLSTR = "Select * from LineItem where AccountKey = "
➥ & Current_Account & " order by [entry date]"
Set ChkSet = ChkDB.OpenRecordset(SQLSTR, dbOpenDynaset)
```

This code sets a string variable to the SQL statement that specifies what you want to select. Then the `Set` statement creates the dynaset by executing the SQL statement against the open database. You must define the variables `ChkDB` and `ChkSet` as `Database` and `Dynaset`, respectively. These are special data types provided by Visual Basic to facilitate programmed data access.

Before starting on another form, let's finish the Line Item Entry form. To add the payee to the data record, we have to open that Payee table and find the correct payee record. Then, move the `payee` key into the `payeeid` field and close the dynaset. The code segment in Listing 33.6 shows one way of doing this function.

Listing 33.6 33LIST06.TXT—Program Code to Look for an Existing Payee

```
SQLSTR = "select * from payee where payeename = '" &
➥ ent_payee.Text & "'"
        Set payset = ChkDB.OpenRecordset(SQLSTR, dbOpenDynaset)
        If payset.NoMatch Then
            MsgBox "No Payee Selected", vbCritical, app_title
            Exit Sub
        End If
        paykey.Caption = Str(payset.recordset("payeeid"))
        payset.Close
```

The Check Register form will use programmed access to display the account entries in the `grdChkReg`. To add database access to the grid, you need to create a dynaset that will retrieve rows of data based on the account key in the row. Using the routine coded in the previous section of the chapter, change the grid load processing loop to access the open database and move the data from the dynaset to the `grdChkReg`.

Example

The following routine now creates a dynaset and loops through it, and moves any records that have not been cleared into the grid columns. If you try this segment of code you will notice that the payee is not being displayed. This is because the connection between the Payee table and the Lineitem table has not been created. The code in Listing 33.7 should be inserted into the `Form_Load` events for the Check register or Account Balance form, if either one is using a standard Grid control.

Listing 33.7 33LIST07.TXT—Grid-Loading Routine

```
' Processing loop to load data into the grid.
SQLSTR = "select * from LineItem where AccountKey = "
➥ & current_account & " order by [entry date]"
Set ChkSet = ChkDb.OpenRecordset(SQLSTR, dbOpenDynaset)
Set paySet = ChkDb.OpenRecordset("payee", dbOpenDynaset)
Tc = Chr$(9)
Prev_balance = 0
Do Until ChkSet.EOF
grdChkReg.Row = grdChkReg.Rows - 1
grdChkReg.Col = 6
Prev_balance = Val(grdChkReg.Text) + 0
grid_text = ""
If IsNull(ChkSet("chknum")) Then
    grid_text = ChkSet("itemkey") & Tc & " "
Else
    grid_text = ChkSet("itemkey") & Tc & ChkSet("chknum")
End If
grid_text = grid_text & Tc & ChkSet("Entry date")
paySet.FindFirst "payeeid = " & ChkSet("payeekey")
If paySet.NoMatch Then
    grid_text = grid_text & Tc & "No Payee Found"
Else
    grid_text = grid_text & Tc & paySet("payeename")
End If
If ChkSet("Entrytype") = "C" Then
    grid_text = grid_text & Tc & Format(ChkSet("amtpayed"),
     ➥ "#,##0.00") & Tc & "0.00"
    bal_amount = Prev_balance - ChkSet("amtpayed")
Else
    grid_text = grid_text & Tc & "0.00" & Tc &
     ➥ Format(ChkSet("amtdeposit"), "#,##0.00")
```

```
    bal_amount = Prev_balance + ChkSet("amtdeposit")
End If
grid_text = grid_text & Tc & Format(bal_amount, "#,##0.00")
➥ & Tc & ChkSet("clearrecv")
CkBkMain.lblBalance.Caption = Format(bal_amount, "#,##0.00")
grdChkReg.AddItem grid_text
ChkSet.MoveNext
grdChkReg.FixedRows = 1
grdChkReg.FixedCols = 2
Loop
ChkSet.Close
paySet.Close
```

You can connect the two tables by using `payeekey` in the lineitem record to position the Payee table to the correct record. Because you will be accessing the Payee table for every row you add to the grid, put the `OpenRecordset` statement in your code before the grid-loading code in the `Form_Load` routine.

To position the Payee table to the property record, you use the `Findfirst` method on the payee dynaset. An example of this statement is as follows:

```
payset.FindFirst "payeeid = " & chkset("payeekey")
```

This will position the table to the payee. However, you might have a situation where there is no payee on the table for an entry. To check for this condition, use the `NoMatch` property of the Dynaset. The code segment for this can look like the following:

```
    If Not payset.NoMatch Then
        grid_text = grid_text & Tc & "No Payee Found"
    Else
        grid_text = grid_text & Tc & payset("payeename")
    End If
```

The code segment for this should replace the If statement that was already inserted into the `Form_Load` routine. If there is no record for a payee, then a message is placed in the payee column, otherwise the payee name is placed in the column.

Note: If the `NoMatch` property is `True`, there is no record found. If the property is `False`, there is a record.

When the database access is added to the grid load event, the Check register will look like figure 33.26.

When you delete a grid row, you now must add the code to position the dynaset to the current record and delete it. To delete the record from the database, you use the dynaset's `Delete` method. Before you delete the row, you should now ask the user if it is okay (see fig. 33.27).

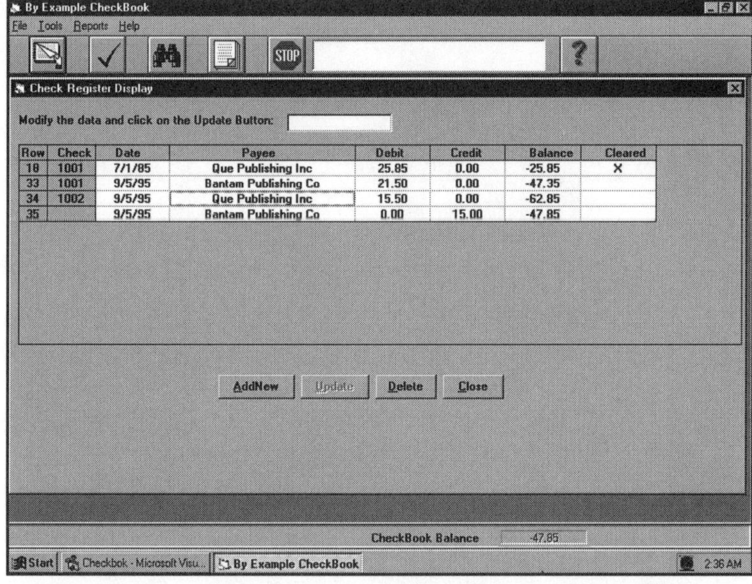

Figure 33.26

Check Register form showing database information.

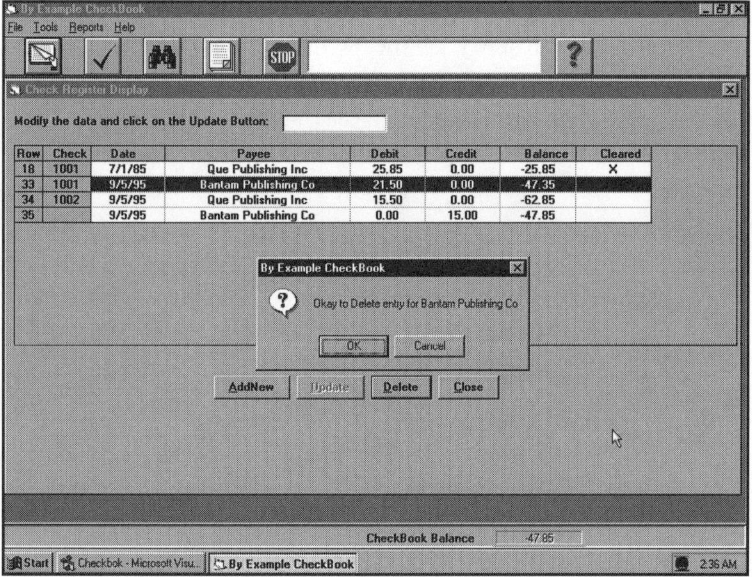

Figure 33.27

Message Box asking if it is okay to delete row.

This message should display the date and payee name to the user so the user can decide if she wants to delete it. If the user clicks the cancel button then display a message saying that the `Delete` function was canceled.

The last routine in the Check Register form that you have to modify for data access is the `Update` routine. When the `Update` routine is executed, you have to create a dynaset and position it to the current record. Then you have to determine which field is being updated and then move the new data into the field and update the record. One way of coding this routine is shown in Listing 33.8.

Listing 33.8 33LIST08.TXT—Grid Row Update Routine

```
Sub btnupdate_Click ()
grdChkReg.Text = Format(txtInput, "#,##0.00")
    saverow = grdChkReg.Row
    savecol = grdChkReg.Col
    SQLSTR = "Select * from LineItem where AccountKey = "
     ➥ & current_account & " order by [entry date]"
    Set ChkSet = ChkDb.OpenRecordset(SQLSTR, dbOpenDynaset)
    Set paySet = ChkDb.OpenRecordset("Payee", dbOpenDynaset)
    grdChkReg.Col = 0
    ChkSet.FindFirst "itemkey = " & grdChkReg.Text
    grdChkReg.Col = savecol
    ChkSet.Edit
    Select Case savecol
        Case 1
            ChkSet("chknum") = grdChkReg.Text
        Case 2
            ChkSet("entry date") = grdChkReg.Text
        Case 3
            paySet.FindFirst "payeeid = " & ChkSet("payeekey")
            If Not paySet.NoMatch Then
                paySet.Edit
                paySet("payeename") = grdChkReg.Text
                paySet.Update
            End If
            paySet.Close
        Case 4
            ChkSet("amtpayed") = grdChkReg.Text
            If ChkSet("amtpayed") > 0 Then
                ChkSet("entrytype") = "C"
                ChkSet("amtdeposit") = 0
                grdChkReg.Col = 5
                grdChkReg.Text = "0.00"
                grdChkReg.Col = savecol
            End If
        Case 5
            ChkSet("amtdeposit") = grdChkReg.Text
            If ChkSet("amtdeposit") > 0 Then
                ChkSet("entrytype") = "D"
                ChkSet("amtpayed") = 0
                grdChkReg.Col = 4
                grdChkReg.Text = "0.00"
                grdChkReg.Col = savecol
            End If
```

```
End Select
ChkSet.Update
ChkSet.Close
If grdChkReg.Col = 4 Or grdChkReg.Col = 5 Then
    bal_amount = Val(txtInput)
    If savecol = 4 Then
        bal_amount = bal_amount * -1
    End If
    If grdChkReg.Rows > 2 Then
        grdChkReg.Row = saverow - 1
        grdChkReg.Col = 6
        bal_amount = bal_amount + Val(grdChkReg.Text)
        grdChkReg.Row = saverow
        grdChkReg.Text = Format(bal_amount, "#,##0.00")
        For I = saverow + 1 To grdChkReg.Rows - 1
            grdChkReg.Row = I
            grdChkReg.Col = 4
            bal_amount = bal_amount - Val(grdChkReg.Text)
            grdChkReg.Col = 5
            bal_amount = bal_amount + Val(grdChkReg.Text)
            grdChkReg.Col = 6
            grdChkReg.Text = Format(bal_amount, "#,##0.00")
        Next I
    Else
        grdChkReg.Col = 6
        grdChkReg.Text = Format(bal_amount, "#,##0.00")
    End If
    CkBkMain.lblBalance.Caption = Format(bal_amount,
    ➥ "#,##0.00")
End If
txtInput.Text = ""
btnUpdate.Enabled = False
```

For both the `Delete` and `Update` routines, the balance column should be updated to reflect any changes made to the amount of the entry.

Finally, the Search form (see fig. 33.28) will use several of the Data control `Find` methods to locate the requested information. The user will enter the text for the program to search for. In addition, the user will select the field that you should search and finally the direction of the search.

This form will search for any of the fields that can be selected. In addition, if a find has already been done, you can perform a `FindNext` on the database. This allows the user to scroll the data, looking for particular records that match the entered text.

The routines that search the database use the `FindFirst` and the `FindNext` methods to scan the database records. The input to these methods is the condition portion of the `Where` condition of the `Select` statement.

This condition is set based on which field is selected to search for. If the data cannot be found, a message box is displayed telling the user that there is no data that matches the request (see fig. 33.29).

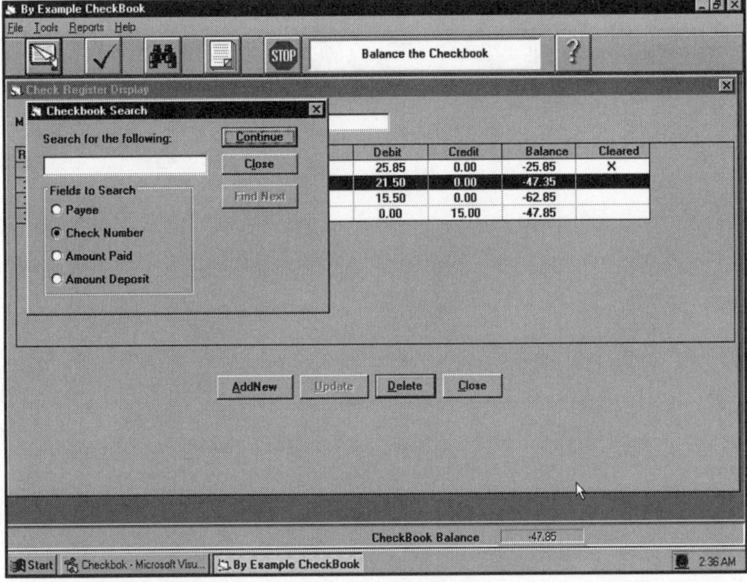

Figure 33.28

Account Search form.

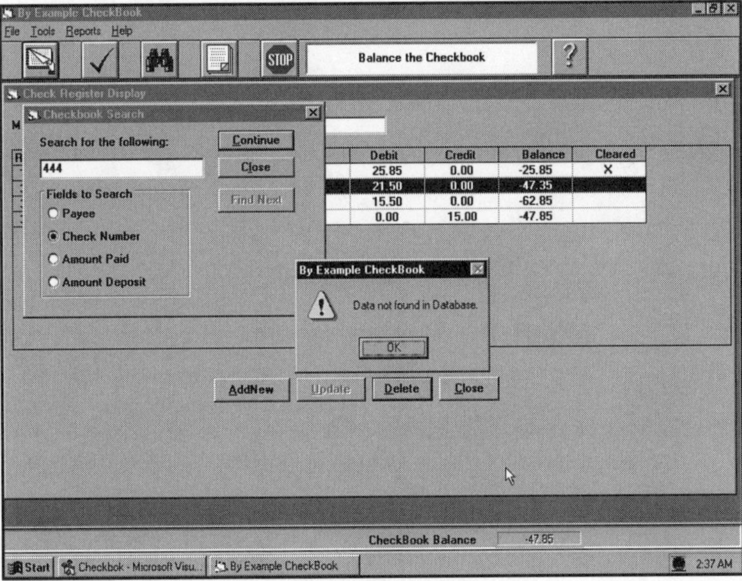

Figure 33.29

Message Box indicating that no data was found for search.

If the data is found, then the routine uses the record's `item` key to loop through the check register's grid looking for that record and then positions the grid to that record and highlights it (see fig. 33.30).

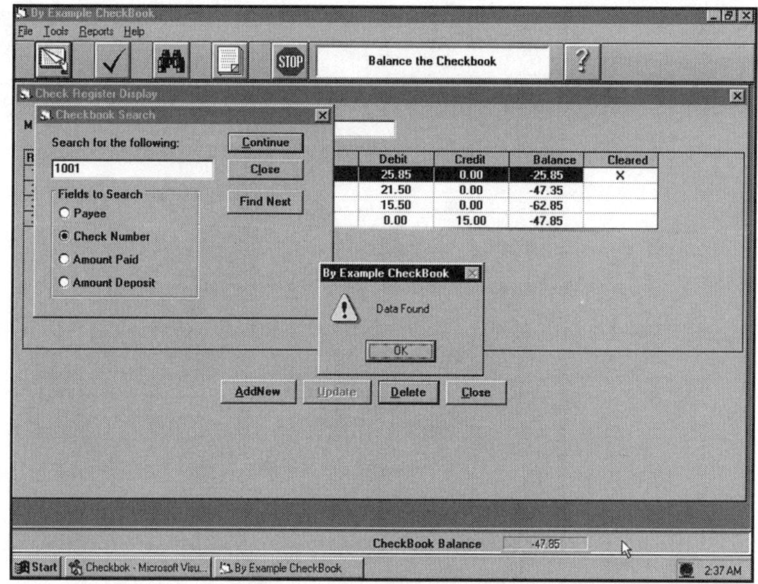

Figure 33.30
Check Register form with the found data highlighted.

The code segment that performs these tasks is shown in Listing 33.9.

Listing 33.9 33LIST09.TXT—Search Routine

```
If srchtxt.Text <> "" Then
    item_grid_data = srchtxt.Text
    If search_v1.Value Then
        paySet.FindFirst "payeename like '" & srchtxt.Text & "*'"
        ChkSet.FindFirst "payeekey = " & paySet("payeeid")
        If ChkSet.NoMatch Then GoTo notfound
        item_grid_line = ChkSet("itemkey")
    ElseIf search_v2.Value Then
        ChkSet.FindFirst "chknum = '" & srchtxt.Text & "'"
        If ChkSet.NoMatch Then GoTo notfound
        item_grid_line = ChkSet("itemkey")
    ElseIf search_v3.Value Then
        ChkSet.FindFirst "amtpayed = " & srchtxt.Text
        If ChkSet.NoMatch Then GoTo notfound
        item_grid_line = ChkSet("itemkey")
    ElseIf search_v4.Value Then
        ChkSet.FindFirst "amtdeposit = " & srchtxt.Text
        If ChkSet.NoMatch Then GoTo notfound
        item_grid_line = ChkSet("itemkey")
    End If
    For I = 1 To chkreg.grdChkReg.Rows - 1
        chkreg.grdChkReg.Row = I
        chkreg.grdChkReg.Col = 0
```

```
            If chkreg.grdChkReg.Text = item_grid_line Then
                Exit For
            End If
        Next I
        If chkreg.grdChkReg.Rows > 15 Then
            chkreg.grdChkReg.TopRow = I
        End If
        chkreg.grdChkReg.SelStartRow = I
        chkreg.grdChkReg.SelEndRow = I
        chkreg.grdChkReg.SelStartCol = 2
        chkreg.grdChkReg.SelEndCol = 6
        BtnNext.Enabled = True
        MsgBox "Data Found", vbExclamation, App.Title
    Else
        MsgBox "No text entered in Search Box", vbCritical, App.Title
    End If
    Exit Sub
    notfound:
        MsgBox "Data not found in Database.", vbExclamation, App.Title
```

You can see from this example that processing a database is not as easy as it seems. The need to open the database and position the table to the correct record is done by the programmer. If you forget to see if the `Find` actually found anything, your program can produce incorrect results.

Summary

Adding database access to your application is the most time-consuming phase of the creation process. Whenever you start working with multiple tables in a database, you have to make sure that the keys that you use to point to each table from another record is correct. Because the data access is automatic with the Data control, you might feel that there is nothing you have to watch for. As you can see, that is the furthest from the truth!

You must always check to see if a record was found when doing searches of the database. Also, if you are setting the key fields manually, then you have to verify that the key you picked is not a duplicate. By using the various Data control methods, you can create processing loops that allow for the loading of grids as well as the verification of data.

The Grid control is very useful when it comes to displaying data that is in a table format. By creating a loop to load the grid, you can set the information in any format that you want. In addition, because of the properties of the grid, you can manipulate the grid so that the user can scroll through the data. You have also seen how to allow updates to the fields in the `grdChkReg`.

In the next chapter, we are going to add error-handling to your application. Thus far, the application will not prevent any types of errors or incorrect data from being entered. You will see how to recover from certain errors and also which errors should not be recovered from.

Finally, we will discuss how to have the application perform at its best. This entails making global routines and changes to some of the code to make it more proficient.

Review Questions

Answers to questions appear in Appendix A.

1. How would you change the height of a row in a grid?
2. Why do you need to use loops to load data into a grid?
3. What is a transaction?

4. Can data displayed on a grid be modified by the user?
5. What routine would you use to set the clear column for an entry?
6. What does the `Reposition` routine do?

7. How do you delete a record from the database?
8. What methods can you use to position the database to a particular record?

Review Exercises

1. Place a grid on the Account Balance form and initialize it to look like the Check Register `grdChkReg`.
2. Create the code to place an X in the Clear column when the row is double-clicked.

3. Create a routine that would delete multiple rows from a `grdChkReg`.
4. Include code that will add the memo field to the entry record.

5. Add the logic to update the database when balancing the account.
6. Create a form that will print the account register to your printer.
7. Change the Check Balance form to use a data-bound `GrdChkReg`.

Error-Handling and Performance

If the world was perfect, the applications we create would not need any error-handling code at all. But, we live in an imperfect world where users make mistakes, files are deleted by accident, and disk drives become full. These types of problems and more cause what is called a *run-time* error. Run-time errors can be separated into two types. Those that are found and corrected during the testing process and those that must be handled while the application is executing. The first group can be forgotten after the testing and debugging is finished. However, the second group occurs during the normal processing of the application. To deal with these errors, error-handling routines need to be included in the application.

Because of the way Windows works, the size of an application affects its performance. As an application gets more complex, the size of the program increases. This causes the amount of memory they require and the speed at which they execute to become more of an issue to the programmer. You always want your application to run as fast and as efficiently as it can. This requires you to understand how the application is executed and what features of Visual Basic you can use to minimize memory or maximize the speed at which things happen. Performance can also be very subjective. If the user thinks there is a problem in the program, then there is a problem, even if one doesn't exist.

In this chapter, you are going to see how to anticipate some of the normal run-time errors that might occur. At the same time, you will see how to centralize these routines if possible. This keeps the error process uniform throughout the application. Also, you will learn some techniques that will help you tune your application to get good performance out of it.

Dealing with Errors

Unfortunately, no matter how good the testing is, there will always be errors that are not handled by the routines in the application. Because the coding of an error routine is not easy, fun or exciting, many programmers fall short in the anticipation of application errors. When this happens, Visual Basic often generates a run-time error that halts the application. At that point it is too late for the user to do anything that might have corrected the problem and resumed the application. If Visual Basic does not detect the error, the application might continue with unpredictable results.

Like anything else, error-handling requires a good design to do its job correctly. In a well designed application, errors should be handled by the application and not by Visual Basic. What this means is that the program should be able to *trap* or catch an error before Visual Basic ever 'sees' it.

Before starting to create error-handling routines, lets take a good look at the specific Visual Basic commands and objects that you can use. The Visual Basic command `On Error` gives you the ability of enabling and disabling error traps within the application as well as specifying the location of the error-handling routine within the procedure.

The `On Error` statement comes in three different flavors:

- `On Error GoTo` *`Line`*
- `On Error Resume Next`
- `On Error GoTo 0`

The first type enables the error-handling routine that begins at the *`Line`* (any line number or label). If an error occurs while this error routine is enabled, control jumps to the first line of code in the error-handling routine. This is the most common way of using the `On Error` statement.

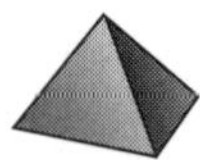

> **Tip:** The specified line number or label must be within the same procedure as the `On Error` statement.

If the second variation of the statement is used, control jumps to the statement immediately following the one where the error occurred. This lets you have simple, localized tests for those areas where errors are likely to happen. It is efficient, and easy to use. (You deal with the error where it happens, rather than decipher what happened and where it happened from a remote location in the code.)

The third and final form of the `On Error` statement will disable the error-handling routine in the current procedure.

Even though an error-handling routine has been enabled, it will only become active when it is processing an error. If an error occurs while an error-handling routine is active, the current procedure's error handler cannot process the error.

When this happens, control will be returned to the calling procedure. If that procedure's error handler is also active then control passes back through the previous calling procedures until an enabled but inactive error-handling routine is found. If no inactive routine is found then the program is terminated at the point of the error and an error message is displayed. The list of the active and pending procedures can be displayed by using the Calls list box (see fig. 34.1) from the Tools menu or the Calls button on the Toolbar.

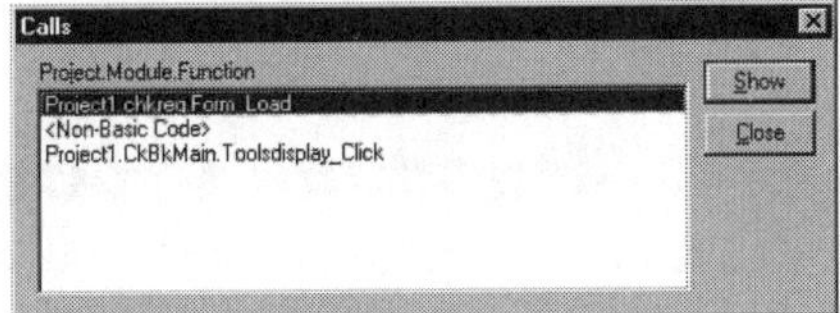

Figure 34.1
Calls list box showing the active and all pending procedures.

Once an error-handler is active, the only way to inactivate it is to execute a `Resume`, or by executing an `Exit` statement within the routine. The `Resume` statement, like the `On Error` statement, also comes in three flavors:

- `Resume` *`Line`*
- `Resume Next`
- `Resume [0]`

The first variation specifies the line number or label where execution will continue from. The second type of `Resume` statement causes execution to continue from the statement immediately following the one that caused the error. Finally, the third form re-executes the statement that caused the error.

> **Caution:** An error will occur if a `Resume` statement is used outside of an error-handling routine.

The final piece of the puzzle when processing errors is the `Err` object. When an error occurs, Visual Basic sets various properties of the `Err` object. These properties are used to determine the cause of the error. These properties are as follows:

- The error number
- The description of the error
- The source of the error
- The Help context value
- The Help file

The number and description of the error are fairly easy to understand. The source property returns the application or object name of where the error occurred. Finally, the Help file and `Help` context properties sets the Help file to display when Visual Basic displays an error message. You can use these properties to determine which error has occurred and how to process it. The `Help` properties can be used to display help information from the applications help file when using the `MsgBox` statement to display the error message.

Now that you have all of the parts needed to handle most errors that could occur, you are ready to create the error-handling routines for the application.

The Error-Handling Process

Whenever an error occurs, the question of what should be done, needs to be answered. Designing an error-handling process involves the following steps:

- Set or enable the error trap
- Create the error-handling routine
- Exit the error-handling routine

To see how the error-handling process works, let's add a new function to the application. In any good application, there is usually some way of backing up the data that the application uses.

Example

Insert a new menu item that will execute the backup routine. The following program segment is the initial backup code.

```
Sub BackitUp ()
FileCopy "c:\chkbook.mdb", "a:\chkbook.mdb"
End Sub
```

This routine looks pretty simple. When it is called, it will execute a `FileCopy` command to copy the database file to a disk in the A drive.

Looking closer at this routine, you can see that the routine doesn't check to see if there is a diskette in the drive or if the file it is copying exists. If there are no error-handling routines, Visual Basic will stop the program with a default error message (see fig. 34.2).

Once Visual Basic displays this message there is nothing the user can do to correct it. Some types of errors can be corrected by prompting the user (see fig. 34.3).

Other errors could be fixed by the program or possibly ignored. Depending on the severity of the error that was detected, you may decide that the program has to be stopped.

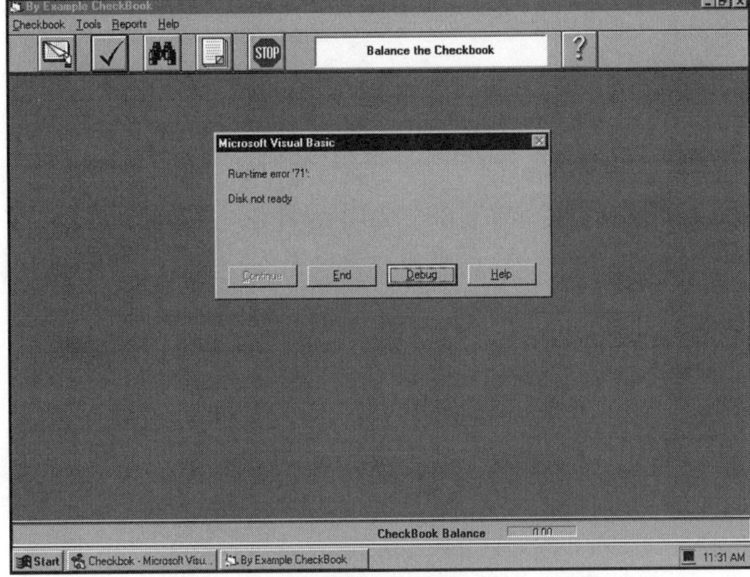

Figure 34.2

Error message displayed by Visual Basic.

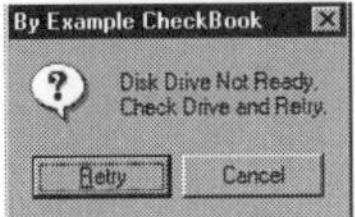

Figure 34.3

Error message asking the user to do something.

Setting the trap is as simple as coding the `On Error` command as shown below.

```
ON ERROR GOTO ErrHandle
```

This statement tells the application where to branch to if an error occurs. Now that this procedure can detect errors, you have to decide which errors you want to process. Any error that affects the data that this procedure processes or that can be corrected should be handled within the program.

By convention, an error-handling routine is placed at the end of a Procedure or Function. Placing an `Exit Sub` or `Exit Function` statement depending on context, before the error routine label, prevents the procedure from executing this code unless an error actually occurs.

When coding an error routine, you will normally use the `Number` property of the `Err` object in combination with an `IF/THEN/ELSE` or `SELECT CASE` statement to check the errors that will be processed. The backup routine is now checking for two standard disk-related errors.

Listing 34.1 34LIST01.TXT—Backup Routine

```
Sub BackitUp ()
On error goto ErrHandle
FileCopy "c:\chkbook.mdb", "a:\chkbook.mdb"
Exit Sub
ErrHandle:
    Select Case ERR.Number
        Case 61
            'Do something here
            Resume
        Case 71
            'Do something here
            Resume
        Case Else
            Msgbox "General Error #" & Err.Number & " has occurred.",
vbCritical, app.title
            'Ask the user what he wants to do when this happens
End Select
End Sub
```

Notice that if the error number is not found in the `Select` statement, a general error message is displayed (see fig. 34.4).

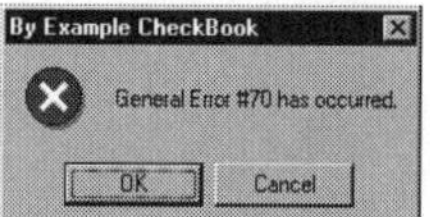

Figure 34.4
General error message displayed by program.

Once you have selected the error to process, you have to decide if it can be corrected. If the error can be corrected, then how do you want to do it? As an example, if there is no disk in the disk drive when the `FileCopy` statement is executed, then a error number 71 will be generated and detected. When this occurs, you want to notify the user that there is a problem with the disk drive (see fig. 34.5).

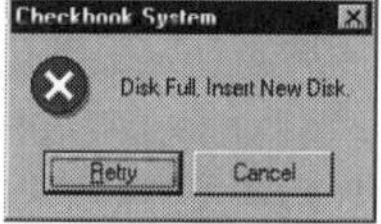

Figure 34.5
Error message that disk is full.

To do this, you just use a `MsgBox` function to inform the user and ask them if they want to continue. If they do, then the program will resume execution with the same statement that triggered the error. This will retry the statement. If the problem was corrected properly, the statement will execute. If they click the Cancel button, then the program is terminated with a message telling the user that the function has been canceled. The following is an example of this code segment:

```
Case 71
    If MsgBox("Disk Drive Not Ready!", vbQuestion + vbOkCancel,
app.title) = vbOk Then
        Resume
    Else
        MsgBox "Function Canceled!", vbExclamation, app.title
        Resume
Endif
```

To make it easier for you to maintain the application, declare constants for each of the error numbers that the program is checking for.

```
CONST ErrDiskNotReady = 71
```

By using the previous constant, the previous code segment becomes easier to understand.

```
Case ErrDiskNotReady
    If MsgBox("Disk Drive Not Ready!", vbQuestion + vbOkCancel, setmsg) =
vbOk Then
        Resume
    Else
        MsgBox "Function Canceled!", vbExclamation, app.title
        Resume
    Endif
```

Whenever you start adding error-handling routines to your code, you will quickly see that you are repeating some code over and over again. This will cause problems when you change the way a particular error is being handled. In addition, the more code you have in the application the larger it will get. This will eventually impact the performance of the application. You can prevent this by centralizing the actual error-checking code that can be called from the different error-handling routines in the application (see "Making the Program Perform Better" later in this chapter).

```
Sub BackitUp ()
On error goto ErrHandle
FileCopy "c:\chkbook.mdb", "a:\chkbook.mdb"
Exit Sub
ErrHandle:
    Error_Fixed = Error_Checker
    If Error_Fixed then
        Resume
    Else
        MsgBox "Function Canceled!", vbExclamation, app.title
        Resume
    Endif
End Sub
```

Moving the error-checking code into a function allows you to reduce the amount of code the program has and simplifies the code that determines if the program can continue.

You can see in the previous code that the error-checking routine is called and returns a value of `True` or `False` to signal if the error has been fixed. If the error was fixed then the program can continue.

The error-handling routine now looks like the code in Listing 34.2.

Listing 34.2 34LIST02.TXT—Error Checking Routine

```
Function Error_Checker ()
Const ErrDiskNotReady = 71
Const ErrDiskFull = 61
Const ErrFileNotFound = 53
Select Case ERR.NUMBER
    Case ErrFileNotFound
        if MsgBox("File Not Found.", vbRetryCancel + vbCritical,
app.title) = vbRetry then
            Error_Checker = True
        Else
            Error_Checker = False
        Endif
    Case ErrDiskFull
        if MsgBox("Disk full, Insert New Disk.", vbRetryCancel +
vbCritical, app.title) = vbRetry then
            Error_Checker = True
        Else
            Error_Checker = False
        Endif
        Case ErrDiskFull
            If MsgBox("Disk Drive Not Ready!", vbquestion +
vbretrycancel, app.title) = vbretry Then
                Error_Checker = True
            Else
                Error_Checker = False
            Endif
        Case Else
            Msgbox "General Error #" & Err.Number & " has occurred.",
vbCritical, app.title
            Error_Checker = False
    End Select
End Function
```

This routine will handle the errors that were selected to process and stop the program if an unexpected error is found.

You can use the `Raise` method to generate a particular error anywhere in the application code. This gives you the ability to test the error-handling routines that have been created. The syntax of the `Raise` method is as follows:

```
Err.Raise Number, Source, Description, Helpfile, Helpcontext
```

The parameters of the `Raise` method have the same definitions as the `Err` objects properties. With this method you can specify an error number, the description you want to use, the source of the error, and the help file and topic to display if the user presses the F1 key. Some of the errors that are handled in the application may never happen. To test these errors, you can use the `Raise` method to force these particular errors. This allows you to check all of the error-handling routines in the application.

In addition, the `Raise` method of the `Err` object can also be used to create custom errors for your own apps. (You may have conditions that can occur that you consider errors for the purpose of the logic in your program, but which are nevertheless "legal" in Visual Basic—you can create your own error numbers for them, and when they occur, you can "raise" them and deal with them as you see fit.)

All of the `Err` properties can be used to produce a meaningful error message (see fig. 34.6) from within the program.

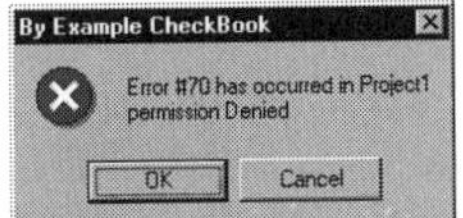

Figure 34.6
Error message using all of the `Err` properties.

The message in figure 34.6 is generated by the following segment of code:

```
Msg = "Error # " & str(Err.Number) & " has occurred in " & Err.Source &
chr(13) & Err.Description
MsgBox Msg, vbCritical, "Application Error", Err.Helpfile,
Err.Helpcontext
```

Handling Data-Access Errors

Data-access errors are more sensitive to the way they can be corrected. There are many more things to think of when working with a database. Because there are two ways of accessing your database, there are two ways of detecting data-access errors.

An error event is triggered for data-bound controls whenever a data-access error occurs and there is no Visual Basic code being executed. The `Error` event procedure has two parameters that can be used. The first one (`Dataerr`) has the error number that triggered the error event in it. The second parameter (`Response`) gives you the ability to inform Visual Basic whether you want the program to continue or terminate with an error message. The error event is triggered if a run-time error occurs when:

- a Data control button is clicked
- a Data control opens a database and loads a recordset after the form has been loaded

If you do not use the `Error` event procedure and a data error occurs, Visual Basic displays the error message and terminates the application.

Within this routine, you can check the error number in the variable `Dataerr` that is passed to the routine by Visual Basic. When you are using programmed data access, any errors that occur will be trapped using the `On Error` statement. That means you have to check the `Error` object as well as the `Err` object within an error-handling routine.

The real difference between the two types of error traps is that with the Data controls, the error trap or event is always enabled. So, if you place a minimum error routine within the event procedure, you will always process the error before Visual Basic does.

Whether you are using data controls or programmed access, the method for handling the error is slightly different then the normal types of errors. Because these errors are caused by some problem with the database, access data can be damaged if the error is handled incorrectly.

In handling data-access errors, you will make use of the transaction processing statements. The transaction processing commands allows you to control the final outcome of the data access process.

As you have seen in Chapter 33, transactions allow you to reverse a database function as shown in Listing 34.3.

Listing 34.3 34LIST03.TXT—Sample Code to Prompt User to Save Account Information

```
msg_ans = MsgBox("Save account entry before Closing?", vbYesNoCancel +
vbQuestion, App.title)
If msg_ans = vbCancel Then
    Exit Sub
ElseIf msg_ans = vbYes Then
    'Save data record process
    MsgBox "Entry Saved", vbExclamation, App.title
    MyWorkspace.CommitTrans
ElseIf msg_ans = vbNo then
    MyWorkspace.Rollback
End If
Unload Me
End Sub
```

As you can see from the previous code, if the user wants to save the data then a `CommitTrans` method is executed. Otherwise if the user says no, the changes are rolled back using the `Rollback` command.

Now that you have seen how to handle data-access errors, let's add the routine to handle a duplicate check number. When adding a line item to the Checkbook, if the user inputs a duplicate number, a duplicate key error (#??) will occur. If this happens, the `Error` event should change the number in the field and allow the program to try the add again. In the `Entry_Error` procedure insert the following code segment:

```
Sub Entry_Error (Dataerr as Integer, Response as Integer)
Select Case Dataerr
    Case vbDuplicateKey
        Entry.number = Entry.number + 1
        Response = vbDataErrContinue
    Case Else
        MyWorkspace.Rollback
        Response = vbDataErrDisplay
End Select

End Sub
```

If the duplicate-key error occurs, the routine will add 1 to the number and try adding the record again. If any other error occurs, a `Rollback` is executed, the message is displayed and the program is terminated.

However, there is a problem with the previous routine. What would happen if the number the code puts in the key is still a duplicate? You must put a limit on how many times the routine will attempt to fix this problem. Use a public variable as a counter and set it to zero when entering a data-access routine. Then every time the `Error` routine changes the key, it should add 1 to the `Counter` variable. If the `Counter` variable is greater than a specified number, do not try to fix it again.

Listing 34.4 34LIST04.TXT—Entry Error-Handling Subroutine

```
Sub Entry_Error (Dataerr as Integer, Response as Integer)
if counter > 5 then
        MyWorkspace.Rollback
        Response = vbDataErrDisplay
        End
EndIf
Select Case DataErr
    Case vbDuplicateKey
        Entry.number = Entry.number + 1
        Counter = Counter + 1
        Response = vbDataErrContinue
    Case Else
        MyWorkspace.Rollback
        Response = vbDataErrDisplay
End Select

End Sub
```

This routine assumes that the check number is a key field in the database. If it is not a key field, an error will not be triggered when a duplicate number is entered. In this case, you would have to create a programmed data-access routine that would search the database to see if there is a duplicate key.

Listing 34.5 34LIST05.TXT—Programmed Access to Check for Duplicate Keys

```
SQLSTR = "Select * from lineitem where chknum = " & ent_chknumber.text
Set Chkset = ChkDb.OpenRecordset(SQLSTR, dbOpenDynaset)
If NOT (Chkset.EOF and Chkset.BOF) then
    MsgBox "Check number already entered, Re-enter", vbCritical,
App.title
    Exit Sub
EndIf
Chkset.Close
```

The above routine uses SQL to check for duplicate check numbers; if there is one, the program exits the routine without adding the record.

Making the Program Perform Better

When someone talks about performance, most people think of cars. However, computer applications can also be tuned to perform better for the user. Because performance is a very subjective thing, there are many things you can do to the application that will make it run better or appear to run better.

As your application becomes more complex, the resources it will use as it executes will become more significant. Tuning or optimizing the application requires you to understand how the different functions, commands and data types affect the way your application performs.

One of the problems with tuning your application is that the changes you make may not always benefit you in the long run. Changes that you make to the application to improve its performance can cause the code to become more difficult to maintain, or change in the future. Sometimes a change can actually decrease the performance of the application.

What you will have to do is weigh what the final performance of the application will be against the changes you would have to make.

Changing the User's Impression

The first impression that your application gives a user is very important. This impression begins when the user starts the application. If the program takes a long time to display a form, it appears as if it is not working correctly. The larger and more complex your first form is, the slower it will load. If this form is using custom controls, they must be loaded at startup. In addition, if the first form has calls to procedures in other modules, these modules must also be loaded at startup time. All of these reasons cause the startup of the application to slow down.

Usually, when an application starts, the first thing that is displayed is a simple form (see fig. 34.7) displaying basic information about the application.

Figure 34.7
Startup form displayed when application is loading.

This startup form should have the minimum amount of code in it. This form should also load any other forms that will be needed. By using this form, it will appear as if your application is 'doing' something as it loads.

Example

Add the startup form to the application. Create a new form called '`CHKSTART`'. Set the form's `Maximize`, `Minimize`, and `Controlbox` properties to `False`. In addition, set the form's `BorderStyle` property to `1 - Single`. This prevents the user from re-sizing the form. Then place a label box on the form and make it the same size as the form (see fig.34.8).

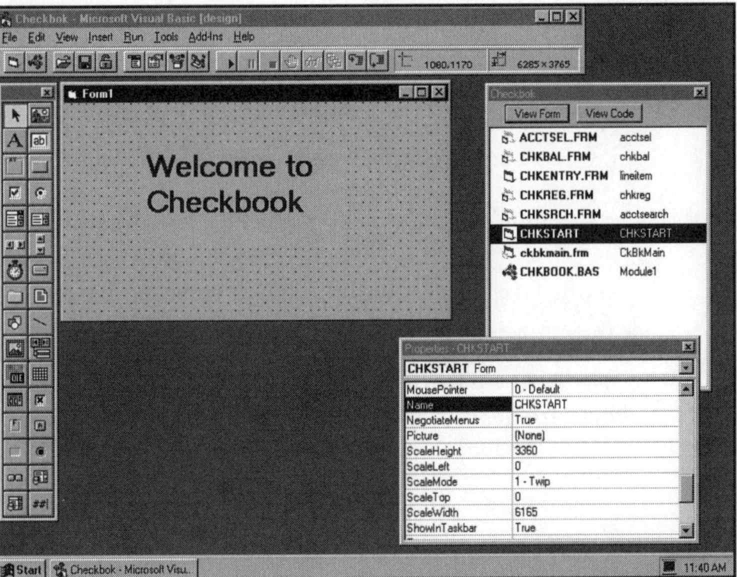

Figure 34.8
Startup form design.

Next, set the label caption to `Welcome to Checkbook`. Experiment with the font size, colors and style. Finally, change the form's title to `CheckBook Startup`.

When your application starts, it has to know what form to load first. To do this, choose Tools, Options, then click on the Project tab and set the Startup Form to **CHKSTART** (see fig. 34.9).

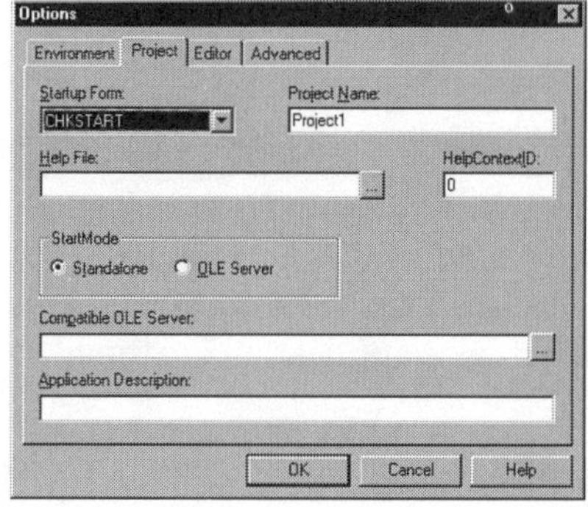

Figure 34.9
Visual Basic Project Options dialog box.

Now add a timer control (see fig. 34.10) to the startup form.

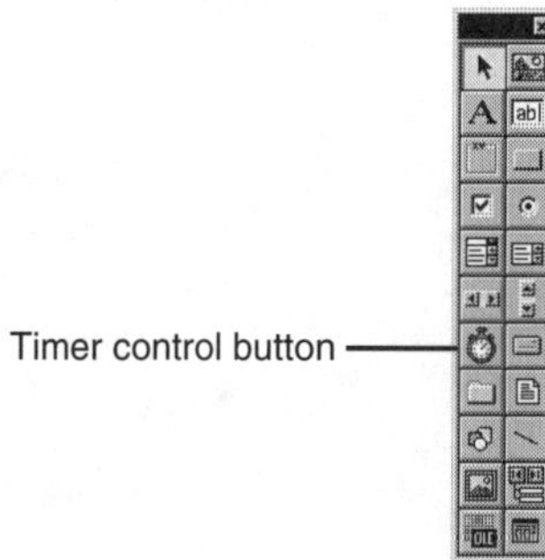

Figure 34.10
Timer control button on Toolbar.

In the `Timer` event routine, add the command to load the main checkbook form.

```
Load CkBkMain
```

The `Timer` control has a property called `Interval`. This allows you to specify how long to wait before executing the code in the `Timer` event routine. Set this value to 1000 milliseconds (see fig. 34.11).

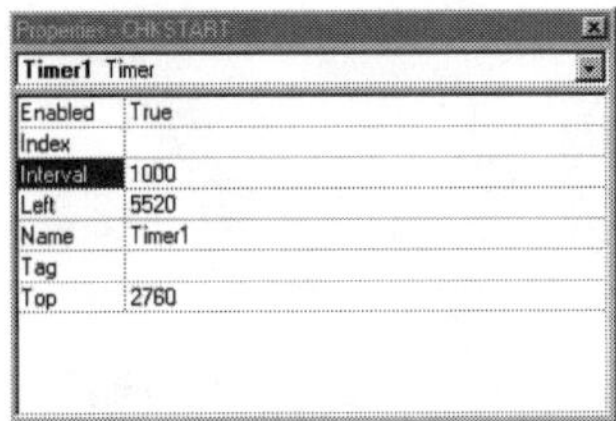

Figure 34.11
Timer control Interval property.

Finally, at the end of the CkBkMain Form_Load event, add the following code:

```
Unload ChkStart
CkBkMain.Show
```

This routine will unload the startup form after the main form is completely loaded. It will then Show (or display) the main form to the user.

Another reason an application appears to slow down is code that is processing large amounts of data without executing any commands that require calls to Visual Basic controls. This will cause the user to think that the computer has frozen or locked up. Windows cannot process any user input, such as mouseclicks, unless a Visual Basic control command or Windows call is executed.

You can prevent this impression by executing a DoEvents function during the data intensive processing. The DoEvents function will return control to Windows whenever it is executed. However, the DoEvents function should only be used in the 16-bit version of Visual Basic. With the 32-bit version of Visual Basic, using the Sleep API function is more appropriate for 'waiting' in code than using DoEvents. The declare for this function is as follows:

```
Declare Sub Sleep Lib "kernel32" Alias "Sleep" (ByVal dwMilliseconds As
➥Long)
```

To call the Sleep function, you could use code like the following:

```
Call Sleep (1000)
```

You can also use a form to display the status of a process (see fig. 34.12). By using a form to display the percent completion for a long-running routine, Windows will be able to process any user input. Many applications use a status form to display its progress. However, in Visual Basic 4, there is a new control called a Progress Bar, which gives you the same look as any Windows 95 progress bar function.

These are only a few of the ways to enhance the user's impression of your application.

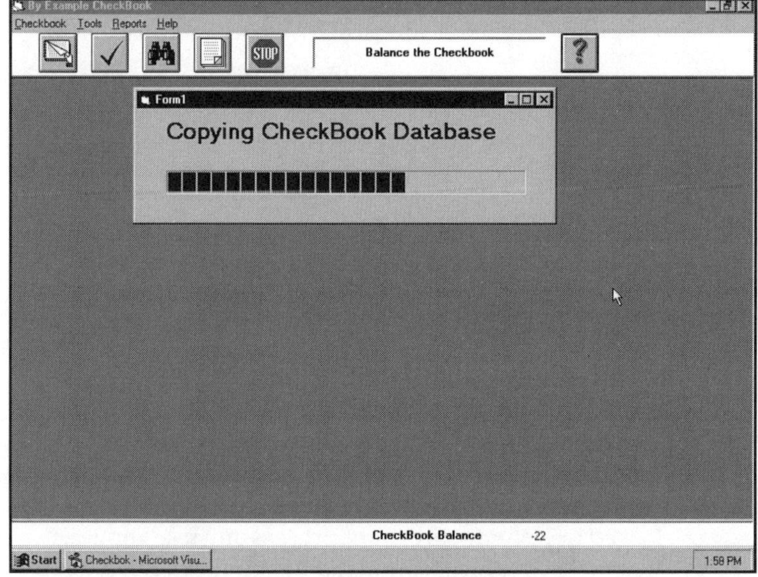

Figure 34.12
Status form showing Progress Bar control in use.

Other Thoughts on Enhancing Performance

All programmers (this author included) have their own list of "tricks" or techniques to enhance the speed of application code. But, you can improve your application speed more by using more efficient calculations and variable data types.

No matter how fast the computer gets (386, 486, Pentium), the mathematical functions are still done the exact same way. Each data type has its own drawback. Depending on what the calculation or process is, there is a data type that would best fit the situation.

The `Variant` data type is very useful when you are not sure what type of data you will be using . However, it is the slowest type for the computer to process. Each time your code references a `Variant` data type, the computer must check the data in the variable and create a temporary variable with the correct data type for the data. It then converts the data into this new variable and performs the calculation.

The entire process can be speeded up by just using a different data type, such as `Integer` or `Single` instead of `Variant`. These data types do not require any conversions to be done by the computer before the calculations are performed.

The `Integer` data type is the fastest data type and should be used for any calculations that do not require fractions or as the counter variable for any loop processing. In addition, you can define any variable that starts with a particular letter to be a given data type. An example of this follows:

```
DefInt X-Z
```

This tells Visual Basic that any variables that start with `X,Y` or `Z` are `Integer` variables. This `Def` declaration can be done with any of the Visual Basic data types.

Another thing that slows down the application is when you access object properties in your code. You can use values in variables faster than those same values in a property. For example, if you are coding a `For` loop where you are using a property from an object, you would make the routine run faster if you set a variable to the property's value outside the loop and then use the variable instead.

You can also use this same idea when checking return codes from Visual Basic functions. Whenever you access object properties or return values from functions, it requires internal program calls to related objects DLL.

Every time Visual Basic encounters a variable in your code, it needs to resolve the variable's value. If you are using variables for strings or numbers, then you should be using constants. Constants are resolved only once at compile time. In the Checkbook application, you are already using constants. An example of a constant that you are using is the constant for a disk-not-ready error.

```
Const ErrDiskNotReady = 71
```

Another way to optimize the performance in the application is to analyze the routines and/or segments of code that are used. If there are sections of code that are repeated within the program, they are prime candidates for becoming public routines that can be called from anywhere in the application. In the Checkbook application, the routine that calculates the balance column in the grid can be made into a public routine.

When the application is performing procedure calls, it always requires the program to do additional work. If you are calling a procedure in a loop, then it would slow down the program's process because of the branch to another module to execute the routine. You can speed up the routine by placing the procedure code in the loop instead of a subroutine.

However, if you add the same piece of code to several different areas in the program, it will increase the size of the program and impact the speed of the application. Not only will the performance be decreased, but you may not remember to update each copy of the code when you make changes.

Summary

The errors that can occur in the application, and how you handle them, is the last major obstacle you will have to overcome. As I stated earlier in this chapter, most programmers either do a fairly good job in coding error routines or they neglect to do it at all. Basically, it all depends on how good you want your application to appear to the user. If an error occurs, do you want the user to possibly lose hours of work or maybe important data?

By coding routines that handle any errors that might happen, you are making the application easier to use. The statements and objects provided by Visual Basic to process errors actually make it easy for you to create and maintain the error-handling routines. After inserting all of the code to check for errors, you will have an application that will not terminate unexpectedly.

Finally, you have seen how the performance of the application can be very subjective. And you have seen that making very minor changes in the way the application executes creates the impression of a fast-working application. Any time you make changes to increase the speed of an application, always re-test the application to make sure that the changes have not hurt the performance instead of helping it. You must also test for reliability after these changes. It's not uncommon to "break" working code when optimization is done later on.

The suggestions and techniques that you have seen in this chapter are by no means the only things you can do to the application to enhance performance. You might think that some of the suggestions for enhancing performance are too simple to help. However, the best changes you can make to an application are those that require more common sense than complex coding changes.

In the next chapter, you are going to learn how to debug your application. This will allow you to find any data-processing errors that would cause incorrect results or run-time errors that you do not want to occur in the application. You will also see how to use the Visual Basic Setupwiz application to create a copy of your application to distribute to other users.

Review Questions

1. What is an error trap?
2. What are the two types of run-time errors?
3. What is an `Err` object?
4. Why is using an `Integer` data type more efficient?

5. What does an `On Error` command do?
6. What types of errors can be fixed in order for the program to continue?
7. What can make an application appear slow?
8. How can you display the first form faster?

9. What are the different ways to continue after an error has occurred?
10. What segments of code in the application can be made into public sub-procedures?

Review Exercises

1. Define constants for the different errors that the program should check for.
2. Create a message box that will display the error number and the error description.

3. Create an error-handling routine to check for all of the errors you selected in the previous exercise.
4. Go through the application and find any variables that could be changed to constants. When doing this, always check the extensive list of built-in constants from Visual Basic.

5. Go back to the application and pick several routines where there should be error-handling code and insert it.
6. See if there are any segments of code that could be made into a sub-procedure and make the appropriate changes.

CHAPTER 35

Debugging and Distributing an Application

Whenever you create a new application or modify an existing one, there will usually be problems. The way that you remove these problems is by testing the application. When testing, the problems hopefully will show themselves. In this chapter, we will discuss the process by which you find these problems and the tools that Visual Basic gives you to do that.

Once you have finished creating a Visual Basic application, you may want to have other people use it. Visual Basic allows you to freely distribute an application to anyone who owns MS-Windows. We will see how to distribute the application and what Visual Basic files you need to include with your application.

Debugging Overview

What is debugging? Someone once said that testing is a never-ending process, or to put it in programmer's language, there is never just one more *bug*. What are bugs? How do we find them and fix them? In the 50's, when computers used hot vacuum tubes, it was simple. All you had to do was walk *into* the computer and remove the dead "bugs" that were preventing the computer's switches from working. Thus, the term *debugging* was born. These days it is not that simple.

But, what is testing and what is debugging? Testing is the process by which applications are run through a series of "test cases." It is during this process that an indication of an application error might be found. Debugging is a two-part process: the first part is the determination of the problem and its location in the program code; the second part is fixing it.

A bug means different things to different people. Bugs range from the mild (misspellings or alignment errors) to the serious (Windows terminates) to the deadly (lost information). To users of an application, a bug is anything that doesn't match the expected results. But, to a programmer, a bug is something that produces incorrect results or prevents the application from running. Now these two definitions sound the same, but, if we examine them more closely, we find that they are vastly different. The user's expected results might be something entirely different from what the programmer expected. The application runs just fine, but if the results are not what the user wants, that's a "bug." The programmer, on the other hand, defines a "bug" as any mistake in the technical execution of the application.

Finding the Problems

The programmer faces many problems in the debugging of an application. "How do I find the bugs in my application?" and "How can tell if my results are correct?" are among the problems that have to be answered. Careful planning before, during, and after the coding process will help you to reduce the time it takes to debug your application.

First, let's look at the effect the Windows environment has on the testing process. Because Visual Basic and Windows are interactive, the testing/debugging cycle is not as drawn out a process that it had been with older programming languages.

The reason that the testing process is not long and drawn out is that when an application has a bug in it, Visual Basic will stop execution of the application with an error message (see fig. 35.1) at that point. This error can usually be corrected and then execution can continue. This works well because you can really only fix one bug at a time. However, a single error can cascade into several others, which in turn cascade into even more reported bugs. If you fix the one root bug, you will have removed tons of phantom bugs.

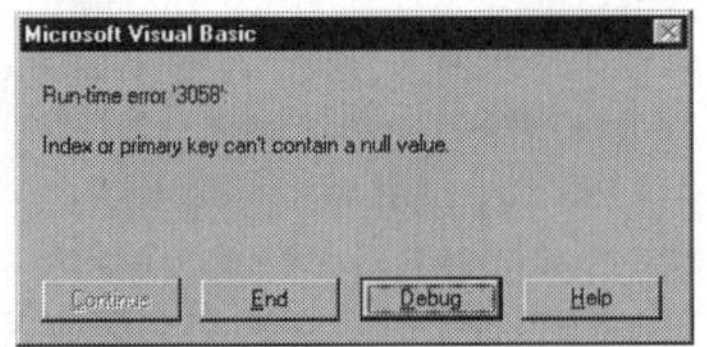

Figure 35.1
Error message displayed by Visual Basic.

Fixing the program problems

Although Visual Basic tells you where the error is, it does not fix it for you. Visual Basic provides several very good tools to help you test your application. With these tools you can look at how the application logic flows from one procedure to another. It also lets you look at how variables and property settings change as your program statements execute. These debugging tools allow you to see inside your application, and helps you to figure out what happened and why. In addition, you should keep your procedures short. No matter how good your code is, the larger the procedure the harder it will be to understand it.

Design problems

Design problems are probably the easiest ones to find. If you did your design properly, you should not see very many of these types of bugs. A design bug is where the application does not perform the functions required. Fixing these bugs might take a short time or a very long time, depending on how much of the design is wrong. If a large portion of the design is incorrect, you would have to go back to the beginning and re-evaluate the design, change it and then start the creation process again.

Program problems

A program bug will prevent the application from compiling or in some cases cause the application to stop running. These bugs can be as simple as a syntax error to very complex command statement problems. It can even mean that Windows will crash with a General Protection Fault(GPF). These must be fixed before we can continue. These bugs can be divided into *Compile* errors and *Run-Time* errors.

A compile error can result from misspelled keywords, omitting required punctuation, or as an example, by using an `IF` statement without the corresponding `End If` statement. Visual Basic will detect these types of errors when you compile or run your application. Another compile error is a *syntax* error. This is where you do not have all the required parameters for a given statement or have left out required punctuation. The Visual Basic editor will check each statement that you type in when you exit the line. If there is a problem (for example, missing close parenthesis) then the editor will display an error message. An example of a syntax error found by the editor is as follows:

```
Dateadd("d", 1, date()
```

In this statement, you can see that there is a missing close parenthesis.

Run-time errors occur when a statement attempts an operation that is impossible to carry out. Visual Basic detects these errors when running the application. A good example of a run-time error is an attempt to divide a number by zero.

```
AvgBal = TotalBal / NumEntry
```

If the variable `NumEntry` contains a zero, then the division would be an invalid operation. There is no way to determine the bug by looking at this statement, because the statement itself is valid. The application must be run before this type of error can be detected.

Another run-time error is even harder to locate. When you type in your variables, it is possible to misspell a variable. Because Visual Basic will dynamically define a variable for you, a misspelled one will undoubtedly be defined as a variable, unless it is a reserved word, or a sequence of characters that are illegal in a variable name. When this happens, calculations will not produce the expected results, because variables that you thought were being modified, are not.

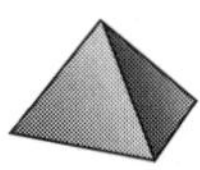

> **Tip:** To avoid this last type of error always use `OPTION EXPLICIT`. This will prevent Visual Basic from dynamically declaring variables.

Logic problems

Logic bugs happen when the application doesn't behave in an expected way. Your application can compile without any errors, run without any invalid operations, and still not produce the expected results. These logic bugs come in different varieties. Some happen all the time, while some can cause intermittent results.

> **Note:** Nothing is harder to find than a bug that doesn't happen all the time.

These bugs are usually found by checking the results that the application gives us against what the results are expected to be. This means that we have to perform the same functions by hand that the application will do, allowing us to check the answers.

A minor logic bug can be something along the lines of the application taking the wrong path through a particular section of code. While a major bug is one in which it becomes necessary to search through the entire application to locate the bug.

Debugging the Application

When debugging an application, there is no shortcut to finish the job. Also, there is no set way of going about the process that will work every time. Debugging will help you understand what's occurring while your application is running. The job that you have to do when debugging is to determine where something went wrong in your application. It might be that you forgot to initialize a variable, or maybe used the wrong formula.

Visual Basic gives you several very good tools for debugging your application. These tools include breakpoints, break expressions, watch expressions, single-stepping, and the ability to display what is in the variables and properties. In addition, you can set the next statement to execute and change the values of your variables.

The better you understand what your application is doing when it executes, the easier and faster you will be able to find any bugs. When running your application, it will stop at an error or when you hit the Ctrl+Break keys. This is called a *break*. When in break mode, variable and property settings can be viewed and analyzed to see the current state of your application. You can also make changes that will affect how your application runs.

The Visual Basic Run menu (see fig. 35.2) gives you control over many different tools for debugging the application. These tools will let you manipulate your entire application environment in order to find the problems in the code.

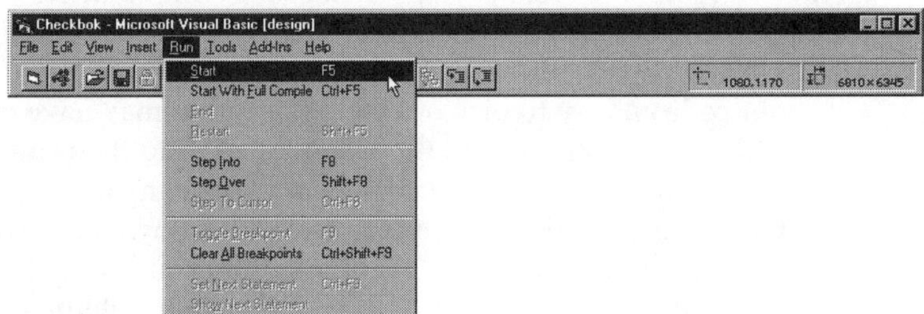

Figure 35.2
Visual Basic Run menu.

Using Breakpoints

It is possible to force your program to stop. There are two ways of doing this. The first is to code a STOP statement. This causes the program to stop and enter the Break mode. The problem with this method is that you must *add* the STOP statement into your code everywhere you want to stop the program. If you forget to take a STOP statement out, then when you run your program normally it will still stop.

An easier method for stopping your program is by setting dynamic stops or *breakpoints* in your code. You can set and remove breakpoints without having to change any of the program code. This prevents unwanted stops when running the application normally.

A breakpoint is set by selecting a specific line of code in the code windows for the form that you are working with. Once the line is selected, press **F9** or select the Toggle Breakpoint menu item from the Run menu. In addition, a breakpoint can be toggled by pressing a button on the toolbar. This has a picture of a white glove on it. When a breakpoint is set for a statement, it is displayed in a different color than the other lines of code (see fig 35.3).

Figure 35.3

A breakpoint is set on a line of code.

```
lineitem
Object: But_Continue          Proc: Click
        End If
        Debug.Print "Balance Amount = "; bal_amount
        CkBkMain!balance_box.Caption = bal_amount
        actkey.Caption = Str(current_account)
        SQLSTR = "select * from lineitem"
        Set ChkSet = ChkDb.OpenRecordset(SQLSTR, dbOpenDynaset)
        If ChkSet.EOF And ChkSet.BOF Then
            itmkey.Caption = "1"
        Else
            ChkSet.MoveLast
            itmkey.Caption = Str(ChkSet("itemkey") + 1)
        End If
        ChkSet.Close
        grid_text = grid_text & Format(bal_amount, "#,###.00")
'        SQLSTR = "select * from memo"
'        Set chkset = chkdb.CreateDynaset(SQLSTR)
'        chkset.AddNew
'        chkset("memo") = ent_note.Text
'        chkset("memoid") = Val(itmkey.Caption)
'        chkset.Update
        memkey.Caption = itmkey.Caption
```

To remove a breakpoint, just select the highlighted line and press the **F9** key again, click the Toggle Breakpoint menu item or click on the toggle toolbar button.

When your application produces incorrect results, you should browse through your code and try to pick out statements that may have caused the problem. You should set breakpoints on these statements and then run the application.

The application will stop at the first breakpoint that it encounters in the execution of the program. When the program stops, you will have control over the execution of the program processing. When stopped in break mode, Visual Basic uses a rectangular box (see fig. 35.4) to indicate what statement will execute next.

Figure 35.4

Code window showing next statement to execute.

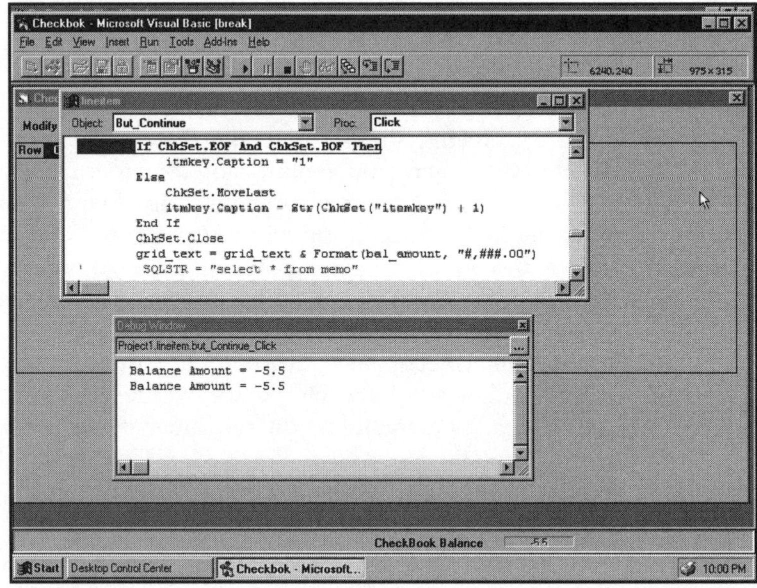

Single-Stepping is when one statement in the application is executed at a time. When you single-step or Step Into your program code, Visual Basic switches to run-time in order to execute the statement and then returns to the break mode.

Try setting some breakpoints in the code and run the application to see what happens. Once stopped, single-step several lines of code. As you single-step through your code, you will be able to follow the logic flow of your application even when there is a call to another procedure. The easiest way to single-step or Step Into the code is by using the F8 key. In addition, there is a button on the toolbar to perform the same function.

If you want to single-step through a procedure but not follow calls to other procedures, you should use the Step Over option in the Run menu or the button on the toolbar (see fig. 35.5).

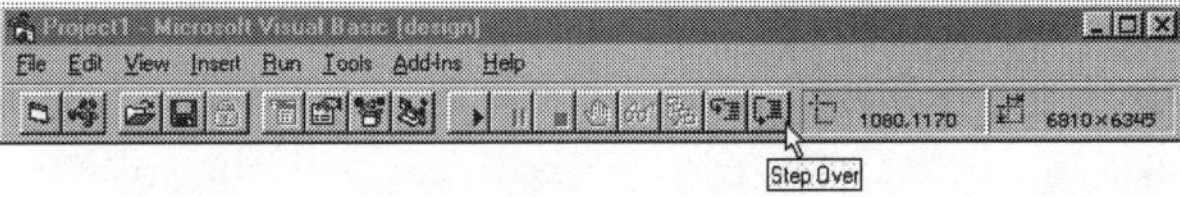

Figure 35.5
The Step Over button on the Visual Basic Toolbar.

If you want to execute a section of code and stop at the end of it, but do not want to set a breakpoint, then you can use the Step To Cursor option. To use this option place the cursor on the statement to stop at and then select the Step To option on the Run menu (see fig. 35.6) or press Ctrl+F8.

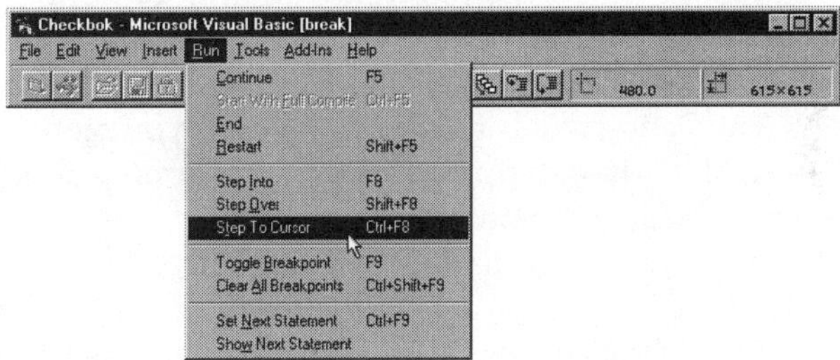

Figure 35.6
The Step To Cursor option on Visual Basic's Run menu.

Finally, when in Break mode, you can tell Visual Basic to change the statement to execute next, allowing you to change the flow of the program. This helps you to test different areas of your code in order to determine where the problem is.

Another useful tool that you have is the Calls properties sheet (see fig. 35.7). This is displayed by selecting the Calls option on the Tools menu, or by clicking the '...' button from the Debug windows. This displays all of the active procedure calls in the application.

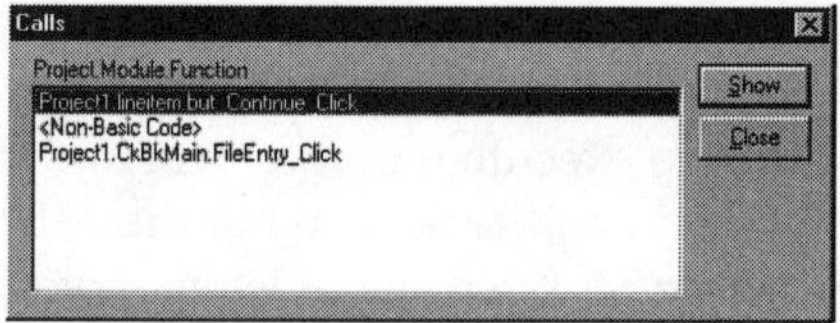

Figure 35.7
The Calls properties sheet.

An *active procedure call* is a procedure that was started by the application but has not completed yet. In addition, when you select a procedure in the list and then click the Show button, the debug window is displayed showing the statement in that procedure where the call took place. This helps you to trace the flow of the application backwards through the executed procedures to see what statements were performed.

If a problem occurs in a procedure that is called from several different places in the application, it is very hard to figure out what is actually happening. To solve this problem, set a breakpoint in the procedure and run the application. When the program stops in the procedure, check the calls list to see which procedures were called before getting to the one with the breakpoint.

The Debug Window

There are times when you will need to execute portions of your code in order to find the cause of a problem. In most cases, you will also have to analyze what is happening to the data as well. You might find that the problem is in a variable or a property with an invalid value in it. What you must do is find out how and why the value was changed.

The Debug window (see fig. 35.8) lets you monitor the values of expressions and variables while stepping through you application. This window will only appear when the application is stopped in break mode.

Also, it lets you change the values of your variables and properties while in the break mode to see how it will affect you application.

The Debug window is broken into two areas. The Watch area displays all current expressions defined in the Watch dialog box and the Immediate area lets you display information or change it by typing in any valid Visual Basic commands. The code is displayed in the Code properties sheet and shows the current section of code that was just executed. The line with the error is highlighted.

When you are testing your application, you will want to change the values of some variables, or test a particular procedure. You can even evaluate an expression to see what the answer is and how it would affect the application process. The immediate area can be used to accomplish this. You can print a variable or an expression in the immediate area by using the Visual Basic statement `PRINT` or the shorthand version `?` of the command (see fig. 35.9). This will display the result of an expression or the value of a variable.

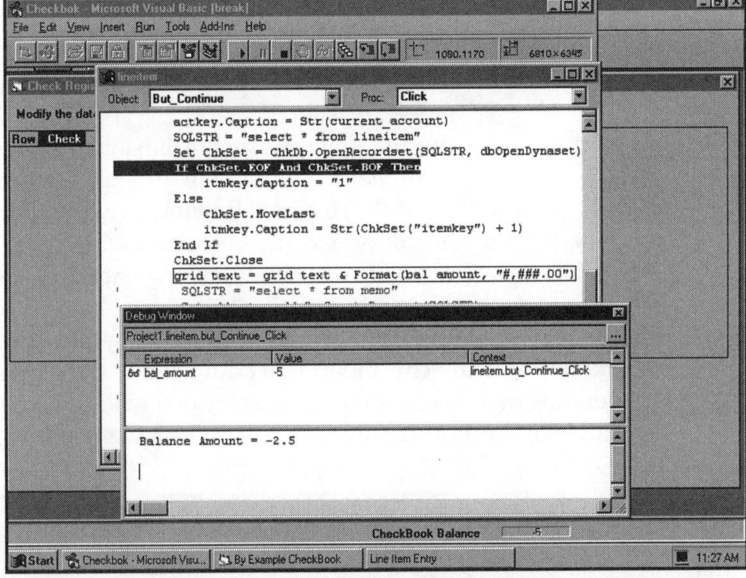

Figure 35.8

The Debug window showing Watch and Immediate areas.

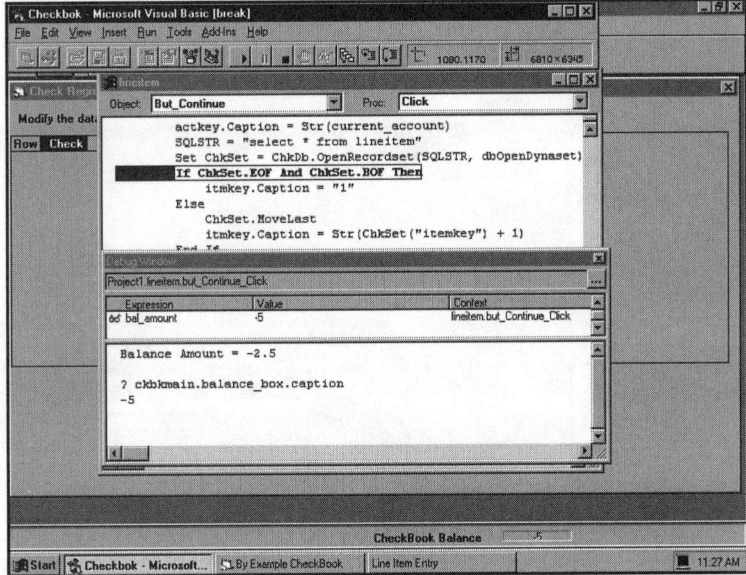

Figure 35.9

The Immediate area showing an expression being printed.

When in the Break mode, you can print any variable that is within the scope of the currently loaded form. In addition, you can print any of the current forms properties.

> **Note:** If you print a property from an unloaded form, that form will be automatically loaded by the Debug window.

In the Immediate area, you can execute the same statement over again by placing the cursor on that statement and pressing Enter. When you re-execute a statement, Visual Basic will print the results following any old output.

Finally, you can call or execute other procedures or functions from this area. Visual Basic will switch to run-time just long enough to execute the statement and then returns to Break mode. This can be very helpful in testing the effects of a procedure on a variable or property. By clicking the right mouse button, a pop-up menu will appear. This menu will allow you to perform several different options depending on where the mouse was located when clicked. Figure 35.10 shows one example of this pop-up menu when in the code window at a breakpoint.

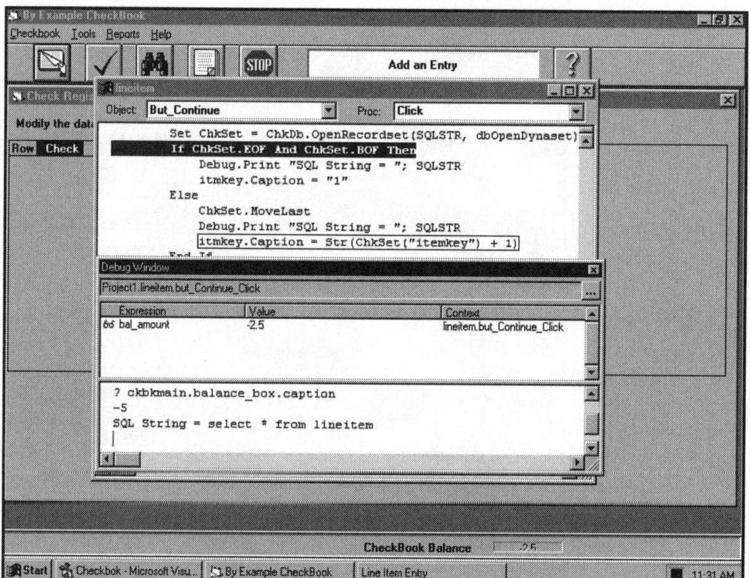

Figure 35.10
An Example of positional Pop-up Menu.

Using the *Debug* Object's Print Method

One of the oldest methods of debugging is to print the contents of variables after each calculation. The `Print` method enables you to do just that. The only change in this method is where the information is printed. The DEBUG object will direct the printed information to the Immediate area of the Debug window.

This method is very useful because you can place as many print statements as you like in you application. This way, you can run the application and see how the data changes without having to enter Break mode (see fig. 35.11).

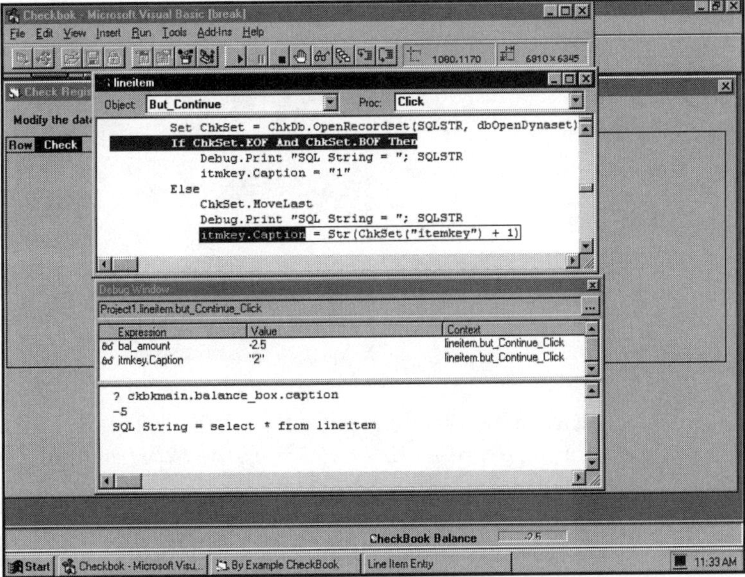

Figure 35.11
The Immediate area showing variables while application is running.

You can print as many variables as you want to. However, since the `Debug.Print` statement prints only the data, you will want to print a label with the data. An example of this follows:

```
Debug.Print "Account Balance = " ; Account_Balance
```

Using this technique will let you know what data you are looking at.

Working with the Watch Feature

During your debugging process continues, you may find that a bug occurs only when a variable has a certain value in it. Sometimes, problems cannot be traced to a single statement, so you will have to watch a variable or expression throughout an entire procedure.

The tool that Visual Basic gives you to monitor the variables and expressions is called a *Watch expression*. These expressions are displayed in the Watch window.

Watch expressions can be added at design time, before you run your application or while the application is in Break mode. This lets you add a watch expression as you decide you need them.

A Watch expression is added by using the Add Watch form (see fig. 35.12). You add a Watch expression by specifying the variable or expression you want to monitor.

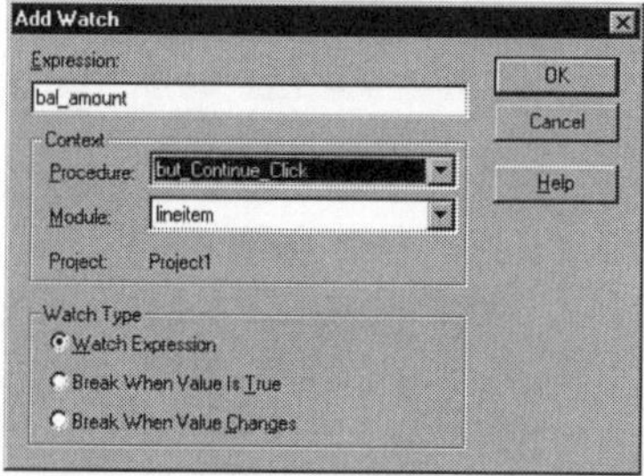

Figure 35.12

The Add Watch window.

You must then set the *context* of the Watch. This tells Visual Basic where it should monitor the expression. It can watch the expression in a single procedure, a form, a module, or the entire application.

The Watch type also lets you specify how you want Visual Basic to respond to the watch expression. It can just display the data in the expression as its value changes, break when its value is True, or break every time its value changes.

In addition, you can display the value of any variable or expression in the Instant Watch form (see fig. 35.13) by highlighting it and then selecting Instant Watch from the Tools menu or by pressing **Shift+F9**. In addition, by pointing the mouse at a variable and then clicking the right button, a pop-up menu will be displayed offering the same options.

Figure 35.13

The Instant Watch form showing the value of an expression.

If you then want to add this expression to the Watch expressions, click on the Add button on the form.

Finally, if you want to know the definition of an error number, execute the `Error` command in the immediate area with the error number in question. Visual Basic will display an error message box with the error description (see fig. 35.14).

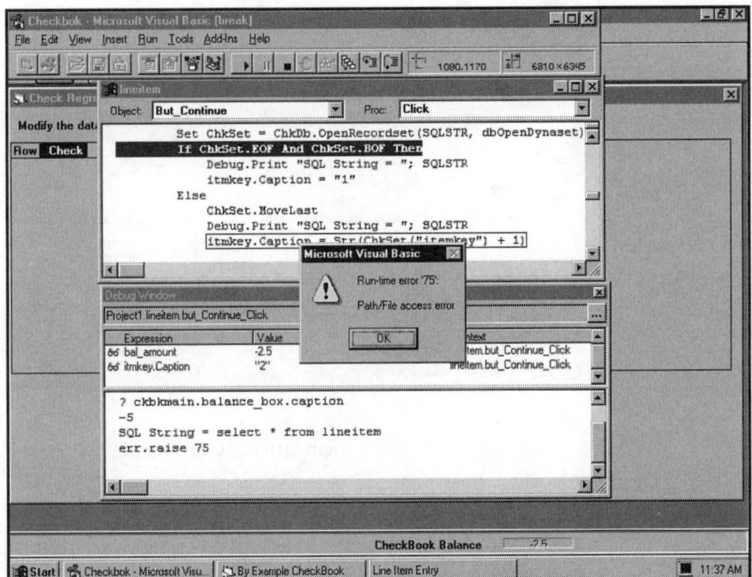

Figure 35.14

A message box displaying an error description.

Now that we have seen all of the debugging tools available to you in Visual Basic, let's work with them. In the application that you have been creating, there is a bug in the Check Register form. Run the application and see if you can spot the problem when you are deleting an entry from the Check Register.

If you haven't found the problem, don't worry. Using the debugging tools and a few hints, you will find the problem and fix it. First, the hint. When you delete an entry from the checkbook, the balance in the right column should be changed to reflect the deletion. If you have noticed the balance amount is still increasing even after deleting an entry. To find out what is happening, set a watch condition for `bal_amount` in the `But_Delete_Click` routine in the form `CHKREG`. In addition, set a breakpoint on the first statement in the routine that is setting `bal_amount`(see fig. 35.15).

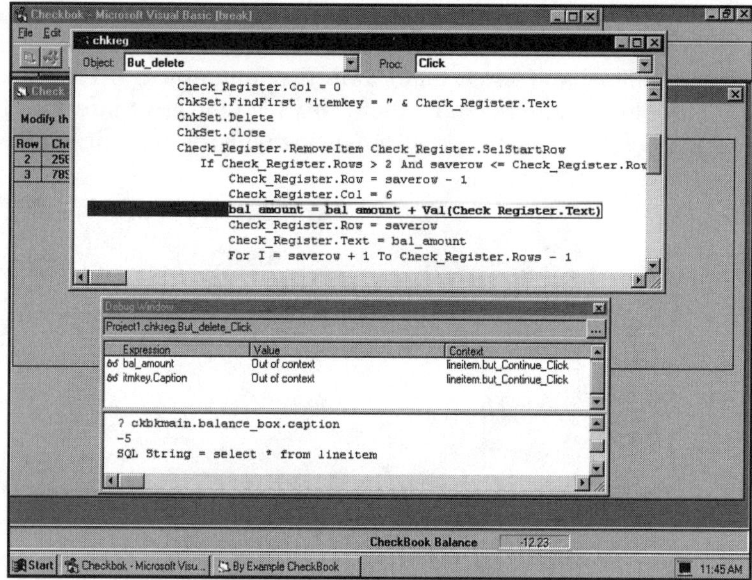

Figure 35.15

Setting a breakpoint on statement for `bal_amount`.

Now execute the application and try to delete an entry. You will be stopped at the breakpoint that you set (see fig. 35.16).

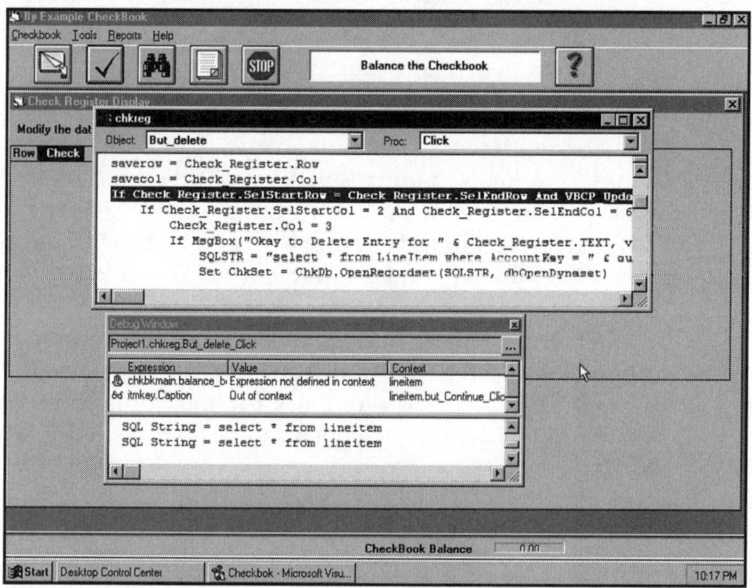

Figure 35.16

An application stopped at breakpoint.

Look at the watch window to see the value of `bal_amount`. Now single-step one statement, and check the value of `bal_amount`. You should notice that it has been doubled. Do you know why?

After the routine has removed the row that you wanted to delete, it starts the recalculation of the balance by getting the previous row's balance amount and then executing a processing loop to calculate the balance for each row that follows. It should be clear at this point what the problem is. Can you see that problem yet?

Well, the problem is that the routine is adding the balance from the previous row to the number that is already in `bal_amount`. This is a problem because `bal_amount` is a public variable and still has the total amount that was calculated when the Check Register form was loaded. To correct the problem, change the statement that sets the `bal_amount` from this:

```
bal_amount = bal_amount + Val(Check_Register.Text)
```

to the following to set the `bal_amount` to the correct balance before entering the processing loop:

```
bal_amount = Val(Check_Register.Text)
```

This will correct the problem of incorrect balances when deleting an entry.

Distributing the Application

Well, we have a working application. It may seem that we are done. However, the real work has just started. Now that the application is finished, we have to create the final copy of the working programs. This copy is called a *production copy* of the application. When you sell or give out your application you must include everything it needs to run.

Most MS-Windows applications perform this distribution by having a Setup program included on the diskette. This setup program will install your application on a user's computer. Visual Basic comes with a program that aids you in creating this setup program and the production diskettes that you need to distribute your application.

Finishing the Application

Your application is almost finished. One of the items you are still missing is the About box (see fig. 35.17), which is displayed from the Help menu.

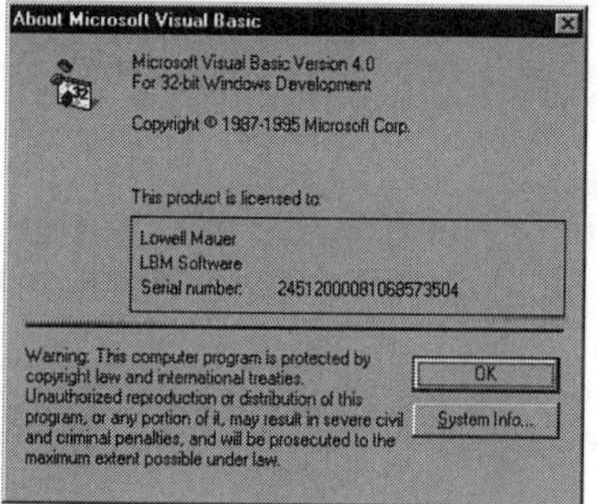

Figure 35.17
The About box from the Help menu.

The About box is a form created by you that usually displays the application's name and the person who wrote it. Select the About Visual Basic item from the Help menu to see what is says.

You can choose to add this forms to your application if you want. However, they are not needed for the application to be usable.

Using Application Setup Wizard

When creating a production set of diskettes for your application, there are several steps that you have to follow. You must do the following:

1. Create the application's executable file.
2. Decide which files go on which floppy disks.
3. Create a setup program.
4. Compress all the files needed for the application.
5. Copy the files to the floppy disks.

The Visual Basic Setup Wizard application will help you perform these steps based on the information that you provide while running it.

You start the Setup Wizard application by clicking on the Application Setup Wizard menu selection (see fig. 35.18) in the Visual Basic Windows group.

Figure 35.18

Setup Wizard Application Icon.

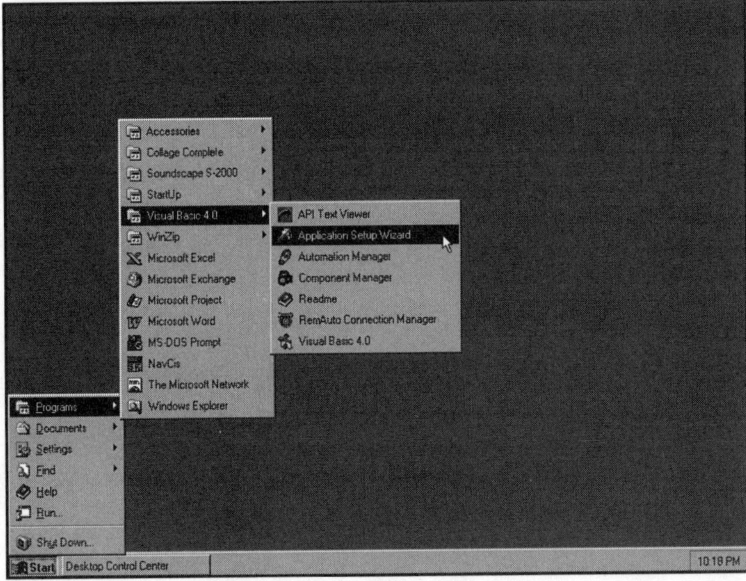

You will then be prompted to enter the path and file name for your project. VBP file (see fig. 35.19).

Figure 35.19

The Setup Wizard form showing the Project File Selection.

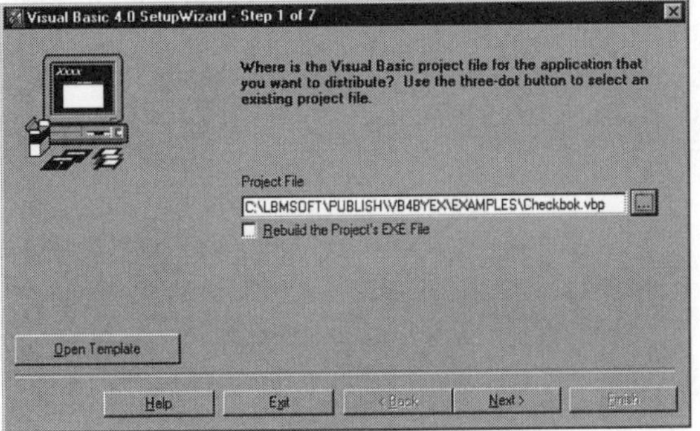

If you don't remember where your project is located, click on the '...' button to browse your files on the disk. Setup Wizard will automatically create your application's executable file if it does not exist. If it does, you can tell Setup Wizard to re-create it. Once you have selected the correct VBP file, click on the Next button to continue.

Setup Wizard will now search your Project file to determine which program files are needed by your application. However, this program is not perfect, so it will display a form asking you which ODBC or Data Access engine your application needs (see fig. 35.20).

Figure 35.20

Data Access selection in Setup Wizard.

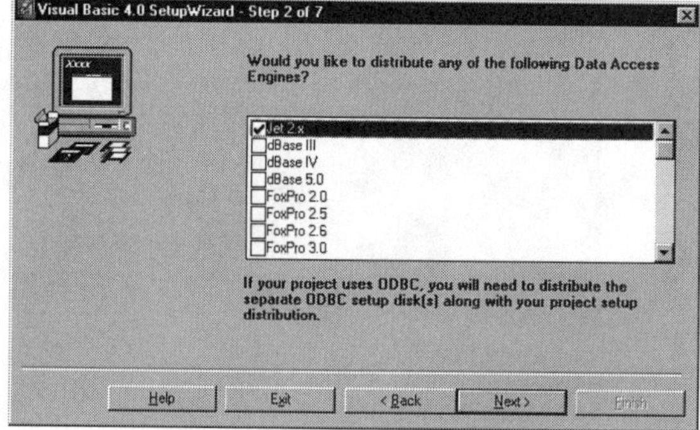

After selecting the features that are in your application, click on the Next button to continue.

The next form that is displayed asks you to select either the floppy drive or hard disk drive directory that you will use to create the diskette(s) or diskette (see fig. 35.21).

Figure 35.21

The disk-drive selection in Setup Wizard.

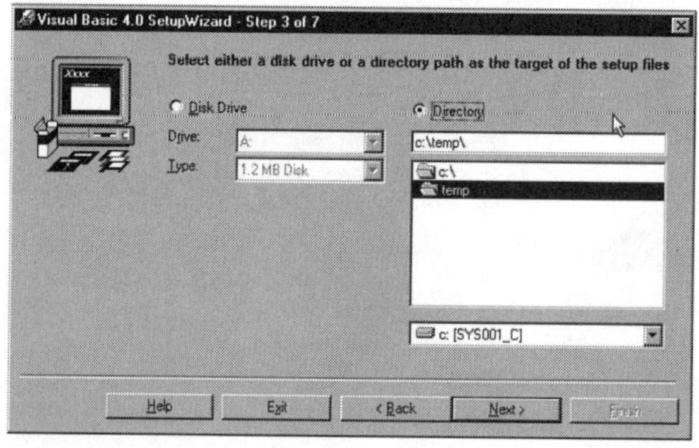

Setup Wizard will now prompt you for any OLE servers that you may need for the application(see fig. 35.22).

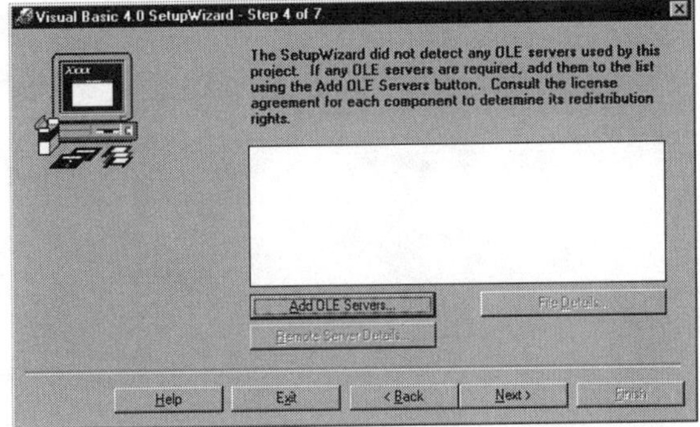

Figure 35.22
The OLE Server prompt in Setup Wizard.

You will now see a list of file dependencies the Setup Wizard found in the application (see fig. 35.23).

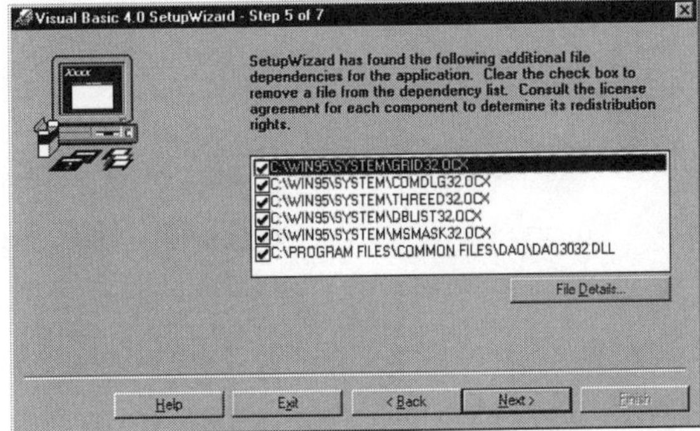

Figure 35.23
The file-dependent list in Setup Wizard.

Any files that you do not want to distribute or are not licensed to distribute should be removed from this list.

> **Caution:** The application may not operate properly unless the end user has these missing files and/or applications installed on his or her computer.

This lets Setup Wizard calculate which files will be copied to each disk. It will attempt to get as many files as can fit on each disk. Click the Next button again and Setup Wizard will display all the files it has determined are needed by your application (see fig. 35.24).

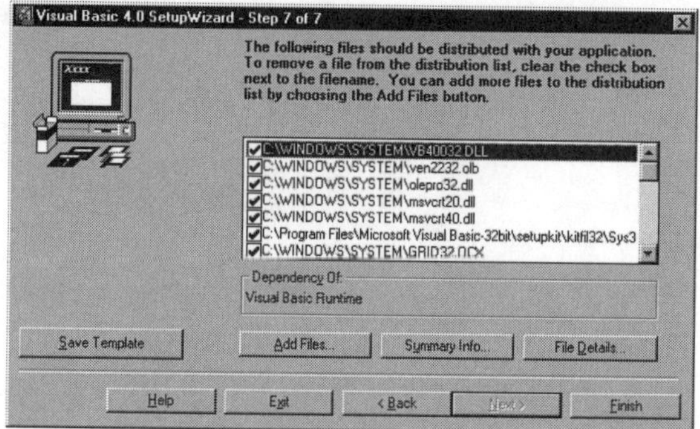

Figure 35.24
The list of all required files in Setupwiz.

At this point, you have the option to add any other files that your application needs.

> **Note:** Visual Basic does not recognize any files that are unique to your application. You must add these files to the list manually.

When you click the Next button again, Setupwiz will display several forms showing the status of the setup creation as it does the following:

- Compresses all the files needed by your application
- Creates the setup program
- Copies all compressed files to the diskettes or, to a directory

When the Setup Program is executed it will look like a standard Windows installation (see fig. 35.25).

The only time you would have to make changes to the setup project would be to add your own processing code to the program. Any form you add to the installation process must be created by you. Then you have to add the form to the Setup1 project and recreate the EXE file. The setup application actually consists of two programs, Setup and Setup1. Setup is created by Microsoft and is included with Visual Basic. This program calls Setup1, which is created by you and the Setup Wizard. Setup uses a file called SETUP.LST to know what files need to be copied onto the hard disk

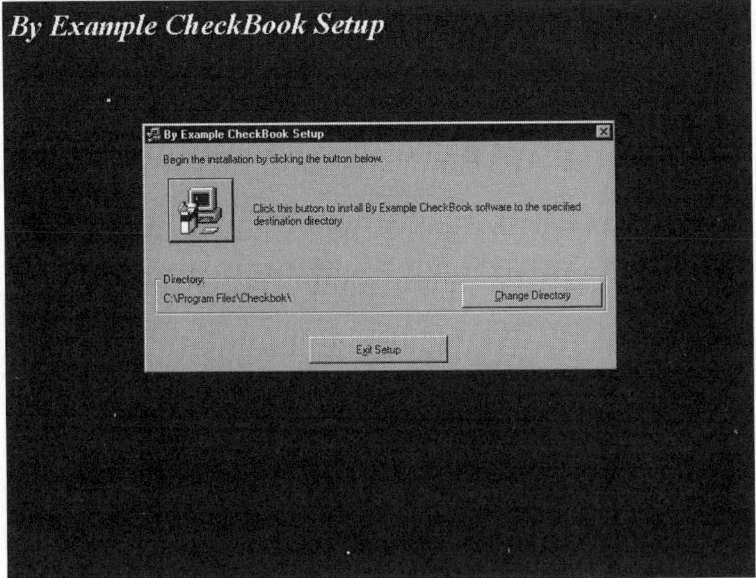

Figure 35.25
Running the Setup Application.

before installing your application. This file is also created by Setup Wizard.

To have the setup program display this form, you would first create the form and then modify the Setup1.VBP project that was created by the Setup Wizard. Insert a `FORM.SHOW` statement into the `form_load` routine of Setup1. You will see a comment, as shown below, that marks the exact location to add the command.

```
'
'This would be a good place to display an option dialog,
'allowing the user a chance to select installation options:
'samples, docs, help files, etc.
'Results of this dialog would be checked in the loop below
'
'ShowOptionsDialog (Function you could write with option
                    check boxes, etc.)
'
```

> **Note:** After making any modifications to the Setup1 code, remember to recompile the Setup1 application to commit these changes to the final Setup program. Also save the Setup Wizard Template to allow you to open it any time a change is needed.

You are now finished creating your application. Now, you should test the completed application diskettes. To do this, install your application on another computer and try it. If your application doesn't execute properly, you may have forgotten a file in the Setup Wizard files list.

Summary

Learning how to debug an application is a very personal procedure. No one person can really teach someone else how to debug a program. As you test your application and gain more knowledge of Visual Basic, you will begin to develop your own techniques for debugging. In addition, if you followed the program standards, the debugging process will probably be shorter than if you did not follow them.

This chapter can only describe the tools that Visual Basic gives you to help in the debugging process. Hopefully, it has given you some ideas on how to determine the problems in your application, and, by using the tools described, to locate and fix these problems.

When you are ready to distribute your application you will find that using Setupwiz is much easier then creating your own setup program. The Setupwiz application was created to alleviate most of the work in creating the application setup program.

Review Questions

1. What is a breakpoint?
2. How do you set a Watch expression?

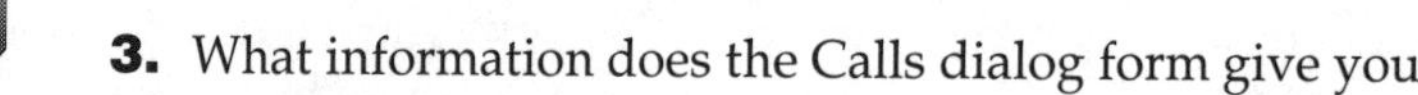

3. What information does the Calls dialog form give you?

4. What files are needed for you to distribute your application?

Review Exercises

1. Set several breakpoints in the application and see how the different forms are displayed.

2. Set a Watch expression on the `Balance` variable.
3. Change the value of the `Balance` variable during execution and see how the Watch expression changes.

4. Create the About box for your application and add it to the Help menu.
5. Use the `Debug.Print` object to display variable values in the Immediate area of the Debug window.

Answers to Review Questions

Here are the answers to each chapter's review questions.

Chapter 1

1. An object is a piece of software that has properties and a specific behavior. Objects also behave like data types, but are normally much more complex.
2. Code is the programming by which you instruct the computer to perform tasks. Visual Basic is a type of coding language.
3. An icon is a little picture that represents an application that has been minimized. It can also represent any folder or program on the Windows 95 desktop.
4. A custom control is a program component that has been written to enhance the power of Visual Basic. However, a custom control is not a built-in part of the language itself.
5. A **V**isual **B**asic e**X**tension (VBX) is a custom control that was written for Visual Basic versions 1,2 or 3. An **O**le **C**ontrol e**X**tension (OCX) is just like a VBX except that it is written for Visual Basic 4 and uses the new OLE technology and concepts to perform its custom tasks.
6. Properties are an object's variables and constants. By changing the value of the properties, you change the behavior of the object.

Chapter 2

1. A project is a collection of files that make up an organized effort to create a working program. The final result of a Visual Basic project is an executable application.
2. A VBP file is the text file that Visual Basic uses to know what to load.
3. The six windows are Form, Property, Control, Toolbox, Code, and Project windows.
4. The code windows display any code that you have written that will be executed whenever the event and non-event that the code is in occurs.
5. You can bring up the code windows by double-clicking on the object desired, clicking the code button on the project window, and by selecting the Code option from the View menu.
6. A module is a collection of subprograms and functions that are not associated with a specific form and can be called (executed) from anywhere in the application code (others are limited in scope).
7. The VBP file contains all of the file names that are associated with the project. As an example, the name of all of the modules, forms, and classes are contained in the VBP.

Chapter 3

1. An event is interaction between the user and the Windows environment that causes predefined event routines to execute. An example of an event is clicking the mouse on a command button.
2. An event-driven programming language is one that recognizes each different Windows event or action and allows you to specify what program action should be performed when the event happens.
3. An event procedure is a subprogram of code associated with a particular event and executes when its object has the focus and its event occurs.
4. Events can be triggered by things such as clicking either the left or right mouse button on an object or pressing the space bar when a command button has the focus. If the command button's default property is true, the Enter key will trigger an event, Defined hotkeys will trigger one, and an event can be triggered by the program code.
5. A state-change event is an event that occurs whenever something changes or is started within an application. An example is when a form is loaded for the first time a `Load` event occurs.
6. `Timer` events differ from any other event in that they are triggered by the ticking of the clock.

Chapter 4

1. A properties sheet is a window that displays available options or messages about an event that has just occurred.
2. The Control menu is the list of options that gives the user a way to manipulate the window as a whole, such as minimize or close.
3. The Windows Application Programming Interface (API) is a way of calling routines that are supplied by Windows and not Visual Basic.
4. The three components are: appearance of the screen, the values of variables in the program, and the contents of any files associated with the application.

Chapter 5

1. To track all of the files and settings for the application that you are creating.
2. Files can include the extensions FRM, BAS and CLS. These represent the Form, Basic and Class modules, respectively. They can also include OCX (and VBX in 16-bit VB4), as well as DLL references, RES, and Help file names.
3. A module file (*.BAS) contains code not associated with a particular event. These files can also include variable and type declarations.
4. An executable file is a compiled program that can be run outside the development environment of Visual Basic.
5. An executable file can be started in several ways. The first, and easiest, is to type in the name of the file at the DOS command line. Another way is to associate a Windows 95 shortcut with the program and double-click on the icon created by the shortcut.
6. The AUTO32LD.VBP project contains the default controls and properties that a new project will have. Modifying this project will affect any and all new projects started in Visual Basic.

Chapter 6

1. AUTO32LD.VBP.
2. By choosing File, Add File from the menu, or by pressing Ctrl+D.
3. In the ICONS subdirectory off of the subdirectory where you installed Visual Basic.

4. By creating an executable (EXE) file by choosing Make EXE File from the File menu.
5. An MDI form can contain other forms.
6. Custom controls are software devices created by developers for inclusion in Visual Basic. When you choose the Custom Control menu option, you access a property sheet that enables you to add and remove custom controls from the Toolbox. You can add them to a project by choosing Tools, References.
7. The procedure definition option allows you to place your cursor on the name of a function, and then Visual Basic will find the code associated with that function. The Last Position option will take you back to the last position of your cursor. By using these two options together, you can go to a function to see its code, and then return to where you started.

Chapter 7

1. A property is a characteristic of a control or form.
2. By modifying the values in the Property window.
3. The Maximize button is missing because the Visual Basic design team could see no advantage to a maximized Properties window.
4. They are the `Name`, `Caption` (or `Text` property), `BackColor`, `Width`, and `Height` properties.
5. One is to resize or move a control or form with the mouse. The second is to type in a new value in the Properties window. The third is to use a pull-down list of values in the Properties window to alter the value.
6. The background would have the `argyle.bmp` image in it.
7. True.

Chapter 8

1. False.
2. False.
3. By using the Object Browser.
4. An Object Library or a Type Library that can be added or removed from a project.

5. This is an unnecessary waste of resources and time. Projects, and EXE files created from them will load faster, and be smaller if you only include the files you really need.

Chapter 9

1. By changing the BackColor or Picture property in the Properties window
2. By changing the value(s) `Form.BackColor` or `Form.Picture`
3. A twip is a unit of measurement used to determine screen positions. A twip is equal to 1/1440 of an inch.
4. By removing the border from the form.
5. The Control menu allows the user to close, minimize, or maximize the window.
6. `LoadPicture()` is a function.

Chapter 10

1. A command button and a check box can respond to a `Click` event, while an option button can respond to a `Double-click` event. Option buttons can also be grouped and used in tandem with one another. A command button is a metaphor for a push button, whereas check boxes and option boxes are metaphors for their equivalents on paper forms.
2. A sub-procedure that is executed when an event, such as a mouse click, occurs.
3. They are patterned after the buttons and switches used in electrical devices.
4. By setting its `Visible` property to `False`.
5. Because all option buttons within a frame act together, and only one can be chosen at a time.
6. Visual Basic automatically sets the value of all option buttons except one to `False` when another one is selected. This doesn't clear the pictures from the screen, however. To clear all pictures from the form, the `Clear_Flags` sub-procedure is used.
7. To determine (or change) whether the picture can be seen.

Chapter 11

1. The `Change` event is triggered when the scroll bar is moved.
2. A thumb is the button that is moved within the scroll bar to display the position within the scrolling area.
3. The location of the scroll bar thumb is contained in the `Value` property.
4. The `Min` and `Max` properties of the scroll bar determine the range of values for a scroll bar.
5. The `Height` and `Width` properties work differently in the vertical and horizontal scroll bars.
6. The `Smallchange` property tells the scroll bar thumb how far to move when the up or down arrow on the scroll bar is clicked.
7. The `Largechange` property tells the scroll bar thumb how far to move when the mouse is clicked in the thumb bar area.
8. The thumb in a scroll bar can be moved by changing the number in the `Value` property. You can also use the four arrow keys and the Home, End, Page Up, and Page Down keys when a scroll bar has focus.
9. By setting the `Max` value to the lowest number and the `Min` value to the highest number in the range, the scroll bar values will be reversed from the normal direction when scrolling. (This will work only with scroll bars; it won't work with sliders.)

Chapter 12

1. A timer allows the user to attach a routine that must be executed based on time instead of a Windows event. An example of this is a clock display.
2. The Timer control uses a millisecond as its time measurement.
3. The counter variables were put in the declarations section to allow them to be accessed from anywhere within the application.
4. The `Tag` property is used to place any type of information about an object.

Chapter 13

1. A list box displays any information that is added to its List by using the `Additem` method.
2. A method is a subroutine associated with an object. Whereas a function is a subroutine written by the programmer, a method is a part of Visual Basic.

3. The difference between the three types of combo boxes is in how the data is displayed to the user and how the user can select from the presented list.
4. By setting the `MultiSelect` property to `2 - Extended`, the user can select multiple items from the list. `1-Simple` will also work.
5. Each item in the list is indexed and the selected property can be checked for each item to see if it was selected.
6. The text box will display the new drive's letter and volume name.
7. Click on the Directory List Box tool on the Toolbox and then draw the control on the form.

Chapter 14

1. The `Borderwidth` property determines the thickness of a line control.
2. The `Fillstyle` property determines the pattern of a shape.
3. Set the `Stretch` property to `True` and then resize the Image control.
4. Reducing the Timer controls interval will increase the speed in which the line will move.
5. In the `Timer` routine, add a `1` to the `Circle Width` property instead of subtracting `1` from it.
6. The `Image` tool can stretch an image in it and the Picture control cannot. Use a picture box control if you need any of the powerful graphics, the ability to print text, the DDE methods, the ability to serve as a container, or the ability to align to an MDI Form.
7. The `Drawmode` property is used to produce visual effects with `Shape` or `Line` controls or when drawing with the graphics methods

Chapter 15

1. OLE stands for **O**bject **L**inking and **E**mbedding.
2. The `Databasename` property tells Visual Basic which database is attached to a Data control.
3. The SQL query is the language that is used to request data from a relational database.
4. An OCX file is a custom control for Visual Basic.

5. The `Grid` tool is a custom control that is included with Visual Basic, but is not built in to Visual Basic.
6. An OLE container is a control that can have any OLE supported program placed within it.
7. Object linking "ties" your program to an external program. Embedding makes an external program seem to be part of your program.

Chapter 16

1. The Common Dialog control serves as a standard interface for general Windows functions, such as Save As.
2. The five common properties sheets are: Open, Save As, Color, Font, and Printer. There is also a call to the Help system.
3. This statement is True. You must place code into the routine that calls the Open properties sheet to process the file name that is returned.
4. The `Filter` property tells Windows which type of files to display in the window.
5. The `FilterIndex` property tells Windows which filter in the possible list to use as the default.
6. Flags are used to tell the Common Dialog control how to process the action. An example of what it controls is whether a path must exist when displaying files, or should the user be prompted when a file is about to be overwritten.
7. The Font common properties sheet must be told by the code what the properties are for the font. This is done by setting each of the separate properties by using the font properties of the text that you want to change.

Chapter 17

1. The `Click` event.
2. The name of the item is used to respond to the click event for that item. `MenuName_Click()` for example.
3. A hotkey is used to select an item from a menu that you can see. A shortcut key can be used to trigger an action from anywhere, regardless of whether or not the menu containing that option is visible.
4. By creating the option by using the Menu Editor.

5. A function can return a value and is not triggered by an event. An event procedure is a sub-procedure and cannot return a value.
6. Only the OK button would appear.
7. By indenting the menu selections for the cascading menu off of another menu choice during creation of the menu by using the Menu Editor.

Chapter 18

1. A variable is a named memory location used to store data.
2. Any Visual Basic data types as well as user-defined data types.
3. D, E, and F are valid names.
4. The keyword is DIM, for dimensioning a variable.
5. By using the `Option Explicit` statement in your program.
6. All procedures within that module can see the variable.
7. All procedures in the program can see the variable.
8. 2,4,6,8,10... Since the variable `Total` is declared as static, it retains its value, and every time it is called, it adds `2` to `Total`.
9. All variables can be affected. When two variables have the same name, a given procedure sees only the variable that has the scope nearest to the procedure. Local scope overrides both module and global scope. Module scope overrides only global scope.
10. A global variable can only be declared inside the code page of a project.

Chapter 19

1. The method name is `Print`.
2. The function is `MsgBox` function.
3. The function is the `InputBox` function.
4. The Debug window will never appear in a compiled program.
5. System modal refers to message boxes, input boxes, and forms. If one of these is system modal, then nothing else in the system can be selected or used until the window that is system modal is answered and/or dismissed for 16-bit VB applications.

6. The default choice would be English.
7. System modal means a window has focus and nothing in the system can be chosen until this window is answered. Application modal means that you can switch to another application in the system while an application modal window is shown, but you cannot continue working on that application until the window is dismissed in 16-bit VB applications.
8. The buttons available would be Abort, Retry, and Ignore. The icon would be a critical error X in a red circle, and the default button would be the Ignore button.

Chapter 20

1. The `/` operator is used for floating-point division.
2. The `^` operator is the exponentiation operator. It is used to raise one number to the power of another.
3. The `Mod` operator returns the remainder of an integer division operation.
4. Multiplication and floating-point division have the same precedence, and addition and subtraction also have the same precedence.
5. Exponentiation always get executed first.
6. The text in the message box will be `Result = 9`.
7. The text in the message box will be `Result = 30`.
8. They are evaluated in order from left to right.

Chapter 21

1. The `<>` operator is used to compare two values as being not equal.
2. The `<` operator is the less than operator.
3. Either `True` or `False` depending on if the value on the left is greater than or equal to the value on the right of the operator.
4. The `Or` operator.
5. The `Not` operator.
6. The `=` operator.

7. The value of `Result` would be:

a. `True`

b. `False`

c. `True`

d. `False`

Chapter 22

1. The `If-Then-Else` is used to conditionally execute code.

2. The `If` statement has several parts. They are: The `If` statement, the `Then` clause, the optional `ElseIf` statement, the `Optional Else` statement, and the `End If` statement.

3. The `End If` statement.

4. The `Else` statement generally contains default processing to be performed when all other conditions of the If statement were not met.

5. There is no limit to the number of cases a `Select-Case` statement can check.

6. Yes! There is no `CaseIf` statement. Change the `CaseIfs` to `Case`, and the code will perform as you would expect.

7. When you have to check one expression for a large number of possible choices.

8. `Each If`, or `ElseIf` can only check for one condition, but you can have as many `ElseIf` statements as you want. It is easier when dealing with a large number of conditions, however, to use the `Select-Case` statement.

Chapter 23

1. For most loops, to perform a repetitive task a given number of times.

2. The `Do` statement, either a `While` or `Until` statement, the condition needed to end the loop, an optional `Exit Do` statement (for exiting on error for example) and the `Loop` statement.

3. The very next line of code following the loop.

4. By encountering the `Exit Do` statement.

5. There is no limit.
6. 50 times.
7. A `Do-While` checks the condition at the top of the loop, and may never even execute the loop. A `Do-Until` loop checks the condition at the bottom of the loop and will always execute at least once.
8. One condition can be tested by the `Do` loop itself. There are no limits to how many other conditions can be checked inside of the loop using other conditional statements such as the `If-Then` and `Select-Case` statements.
9. A `Do-Until` loop will execute once. A `Do-While` loop may or may not execute at all, depending on the evaluation of the expression in the condition.

Chapter 24

1. To perform a repetitive task a certain number of times.
2. The `For` statement, the Start To End values that the loop will execute for, an optional Step value, An `Exit For` statement, and the `Next` statement.
3. The Step value and the `Exit For` statements are optional.
4. By encountering an `Exit For` statement.
5. There is no limit.
6. The loop will execute one time. The range states from one to some value. The loop will execute the first time with the value of one, then the loop will end since the step value exceeds the range of the loop.
7. A `Do-While` loop executes while a certain condition is true (or false), while a `For` loop executes a specific number of times.
8. A `For` loop does not test expressions, it executes a given number of times. You can test conditions inside a `For` loop using other conditional logic, such as the `If-Then` statement, the `Select-Case` statement or other loops.
9. A `For` loop will execute at least one time.

Chapter 25

1. Sub-procedures and functions.
2. The `Sub` statement, the sub-procedure name, any parameters, the body of the sub-procedure (consisting of the code to be executed inside the sub-procedure), and the `End Sub` statement.

3. The `Sub` statement, the sub-procedure name, any parameters, the optional return type, the body of the sub-procedure (consisting of the code to be executed inside the sub-procedure), and the `End Sub` statement.

4. By using the optional `Exit Sub` statement. By using the optional `Exit Function` statement.

5. There is no limit.

6. A function can return a value in its name, while a sub-procedure cannot.

7. You can use the sub-procedure name followed by the parameters, or you can enclose the parameters in parentheses and precede the sub-procedure name with the call statement as illustrated below.

```
Prompt_For_Input "Enter Your Name", "Name"
Call Prompt_For_Input("Enter Your Age", "Age")
```

8. Yes, *sub-procedure2* can call *sub-procedure3*. By using parameters that are passed by reference (ByRef), you could insure that *sub-procedure1* would know the return value of *sub-procedure3*.

Chapter 26

1. An array is a collection of variables of the same type with the same name, individually referenced by a subscript.

2. For the sake of simplicity and ease of use. You can access an array called `States` and move through the array with an index.

3. A range of an array is the upper and lower bounds of the subscript that can be accessed. If an array is declared as `MyArray(5)`, the range of the array would be 0 to 5.

4. A two-dimensional array is considered to consist of rows and columns of data, rather than just one row as in a single dimensional array.

5. The `For` statement is best suited for accessing an array.

6. Up to 60 arrays can be declared with one `Dim` statement. The type of arrays will all be variants unless you use an `As Type` clause or, a type declaration character.

7. A subscript out of range error.

8. `Lbound` and `Ubound`.

9. Arrays can be used for storing many different variables of the same type, and allowing easy access to these variables through the use of a subscript. Yes, you have an array that contains integers and strings provided the `Array` type is `Variant`.

Chapter 27

1. A user-defined type is a compound variable created by using other data types and/or other user-defined types. User-defined types are commonly called structures.
2. `Type` and `End Type`.
3. Structures can contain any type of variable.
4. Yes, you can create a structure that contains other structures. The only restriction is that the structure you are including must have already been defined.
5. You will receive a forward reference to a user-defined type error. In `UserType1`, you are trying to include the user defined type `UserType2`, which has not been defined yet. Switch the order of the two definitions and the code will work.
6. The absolute length of a string is the maximum number of characters a string can hold. You specify this within a structure by following the string declaration with `* Num`, where `Num` is the absolute length that you want to define for the string.
7. It would be easiest to use #2, an array of structures containing both the player and his/her average. This would make accessing the information within the array simpler and easier. You would only have to deal with one array, and not have to try to synchronize two arrays.
8. No, any data types can be used within a structure.
9. For random access to files you need to have an exact structure size for calculation of where in the file you need to read and write.

Chapter 28

1. A sequential-access file is a file that is opened and read from, or written to from beginning to end.
2. The only required parameters are the filename and the channel number.
3. Any number of files may be specified by their channel numbers. If you provide no specific channel number to close, all open files are closed.
4. Random access files can be read from and written to at any point in the file by using a known record size. A sequential-access file needs to be read to and written from the beginning to the end to insure data integrity.

5. A sequential file is being opened. The first record written out will be at the end of the file.
6. So they can navigate through the file record by record. Without knowing how large the record is, there is no way to insure data integrity.
7. Because with a random-access file you can jump right to the desired record by calculating the position of the record by using the record size and record number. To read in the 50th record from a sequential file, you would have to read in records 1 through 49 to get to the 50th record.
8. The formula is the record number times the size of the record. `RecordNum * RecordSize`.
9. So that you have a fixed size record, and that all records written have the exact same size to insure access will always be correct.

Chapter 29

1. An application is a program or set of programs that perform some useful task on a computer.
2. The major parts of an application can include: the database, the program, the user interface, and any reporting.
3. Psuedocode is a way of describing an application function in clear language.
4. A sequential file is read in a straight line, one record at a time, while relational files, or databases, can be read in any order.
5. SQL means **S**tructured **Q**uery **L**anguage. SQL is used to access any SQL-supported relational database.
6. Visual Basic uses the Data control on a form or the Data Access Objects in the program code.
7. The Data Manager is a program that comes with Visual Basic to maintain Access databases.
8. When you use programming standards, you make it easy on yourself or someone else to maintain and to enhance the application. This is because the standards make the program code easy to follow.

Chapter 30

1. The form is the frame or windows in which all other objects and controls related to an application are placed. It is the interface to the user.

2. You can add a control to the form by double-clicking the control's Toolbox button or by single-clicking it and drawing it on the form.
3. The principles of good forms design are as follows:
    a. Make all the forms consistent
    b. Use standards
    c. Keep command buttons in the same place if possible
    d. Use color
    e. Make a form easy to read
    f. Don't clutter the form
    g. Make data entry easy
4. An MDI (**M**ultiple-**D**ocument **I**nterface) form is a window that acts as the background of an application and is the container for forms that have their `MDIChild` property set to `True`.
5. A menu is a collection of options that are displayed as text selections in pull-down lists. A Toolbar is a group of options that are accessible by clicking a button.
6. Creating a Help file requires a rich-text-format-capable word processor and the Help compiler supplied with Visual Basic.

Chapter 31

1. An OLE object is any application that is OLE-compliant.
2. To add OLE Controls to the Toolbox, you would use the Tools, Custom Controls menu option.
3. Custom controls are usually written in C++.
4. Using Wordpad gave me standard word-processing capabilities to enter text and to format each word if necessary.

Chapter 32

1. The two types of built-in properties sheets are the message box and the input box.
2. Scroll bars are used in list boxes, combo boxes, grids, etc., to move other objects around the form, to scroll text in a text box, and to display values.

3. A `Msgbox` statement does not return a value denoting which button was clicked on the form. The `MsgBox` function does.

4. To create a multiple button on a `MsgBox`, just use the correct constant from the available list to set the value for the needed buttons. (for example, `vbOkCancel` puts two buttons on the `MsgBox`).

5. Moving a child form so that part of it is "outside" of the visible window would cause scroll bars to appear.

6. The `Value` property controls the position of the thumb on the scroll bar.

7. The `MsgBox` automatically wraps the long message so that it fits in the `MsgBox` text area.

Chapter 33

1. The height of a row in a grid is changed by modifying the `rowheight` property during the execution of the program, or the user can click on the border of a row and drag it to a new size.

2. Since the grid displays data a row at a time, like a database table. The loop will get a row of data and then insert it into the grid.

3. A transaction is a logical set of changes made to a recordset.

4. The non-bound grid does not allow direct modification of the cells. However, you can move the data into a text box, modify it and then move it back to the grid.

5. To set a column in the grid during the execution of the application, you would use the `Click` or `Doubleclick` events of the Grid control.

6. The `Reposition` event is called whenever the database recordset that is attached to a Data control is moved to another row.

7. Using the program access, you must use the `Delete` method of the Data control.

8. The methods to position the database are: `FindFirst`, `FindNext`, `FindPrev`, `FindLast`, `MoveLast`, `MoveFirst`, `MoveNext`, and `MoveLast`.

Chapter 34

1. An error trap is a term that describes the detection of an error during the execution of an application.

2. The first type is found and corrected during the testing process and the second type must be handled during the normal execution of the application.
3. The `Err` object contains information about an error that has just occurred.
4. An `Integer` data type does not require any conversions before a calculation is performed. An Integer is efficient because it avoids floating point overhead, and is limited to 2 bytes.
5. The `On Error` statement gives you the ability to control the error-handling process.
6. The errors that can be fixed during execution of the application are usually ones that are nondestructive. This means that the error has not caused any data problems. An example of a fixable error is `Disk Not Ready`.
7. When an application is loading, if users do not see anything happen for a few seconds, they can perceive it to be slow.
8. By using a start-up form to display a message to the user.
9. There are three ways to continue, `Resume Line`, `Resume Next`, and `Resume`.
10. Any segment of code in an application that is used in more than one place in the application is a good candidate to become a public sub-procedure.

Chapter 35

1. A breakpoint is a way of setting automatic stops within the program code to stop at a particular statement in order to debug a problem.
2. A `Watch` expression is set by using the Tools menu option `Add Watch` or by right-clicking on a variable and then selecting the `Add Watch` option or using `Quick Watch` by pressing F9 to check or `Add Watch` for current expression.
3. The `Calls` form displays all of the procedures that are active at that moment. It shows the call history so you can trace the branch of the call tree you are in, and how you got there.
4. There are many files that are needed to distribute your application. These include the Visual Basic run-time files and other system-related files.

Index

Symbols

A

B

C

D

E

F

G-H

I-J-K

L

N

O

P

Q-R

S

T

U-V

W-X-Y-Z

Tools

. Options

:C ___ Seperater

Complete and Return this Card for a *FREE* Computer Book Catalog

Thank you for purchasing this book! You have purchased a superior computer book written expressly for your needs. To continue to provide the kind of up-to-date, pertinent coverage you've come to expect from us, we need to hear from you. Please take a minute to complete and return this self-addressed, postage-paid form. In return, we'll send you a free catalog of all our computer books on topics ranging from word processing to programming and the internet.

ɅIr. ☐ Mrs. ☐ Ms. ☐ Dr. ☐

Ɉame (first) ☐☐☐☐☐☐☐☐☐☐☐ (M.I.) ☐ (last) ☐☐☐☐☐☐☐☐☐☐☐☐☐☐☐

ɅAddress ☐☐☐☐☐☐☐☐☐☐☐☐☐☐☐☐☐☐☐☐☐☐☐☐☐☐☐☐☐☐☐☐☐☐☐

☐☐☐☐☐☐☐☐☐☐☐☐☐☐☐☐☐☐☐☐☐☐☐☐☐☐☐☐☐☐☐☐☐☐☐

:ity ☐☐☐☐☐☐☐☐☐☐☐☐☐☐☐ State ☐☐ Zip ☐☐☐☐☐ ☐☐☐☐

hone ☐☐☐ ☐☐☐ ☐☐☐☐ Fax ☐☐☐ ☐☐☐ ☐☐☐☐

:ompany Name ☐☐☐☐☐☐☐☐☐☐☐☐☐☐☐☐☐☐☐☐☐☐☐☐☐☐☐☐☐☐☐☐☐

-mail address ☐☐☐☐☐☐☐☐☐☐☐☐☐☐☐☐☐☐☐☐☐☐☐☐☐☐☐☐☐☐☐☐☐

. Please check at least (3) influencing factors for purchasing this book.

ront or back cover information on book .... ☐
pecial approach to the content .... ☐
ompleteness of content .... ☐
uthor's reputation .... ☐
ublisher's reputation .... ☐
ook cover design or layout .... ☐
dex or table of contents of book .... ☐
ice of book .... ☐
pecial effects, graphics, illustrations .... ☐
ther (Please specify): ________________ ☐

How did you first learn about this book?

w in Macmillan Computer Publishing catalog .... ☐
commended by store personnel .... ☐
w the book on bookshelf at store .... ☐
commended by a friend .... ☐
ceived advertisement in the mail .... ☐
w an advertisement in: ________________ ☐
ad book review in: ________________ ☐
her (Please specify): ________________ ☐

How many computer books have you purchased in the last six months?

is book only .... ☐ 3 to 5 books .... ☐
ooks .... ☐ More than 5 .... ☐

4. Where did you purchase this book?

Bookstore .... ☐
Computer Store .... ☐
Consumer Electronics Store .... ☐
Department Store .... ☐
Office Club .... ☐
Warehouse Club .... ☐
Mail Order .... ☐
Direct from Publisher .... ☐
Internet site .... ☐
Other (Please specify): ________________ ☐

5. How long have you been using a computer?

☐ Less than 6 months ☐ 6 months to a year
☐ 1 to 3 years ☐ More than 3 years

6. What is your level of experience with personal computers and with the subject of this book?

	With PCs	With subject of book
New	☐	☐
Casual	☐	☐
Accomplished	☐	☐
Expert	☐	☐

Source Code ISBN: 0-7897-0000-x

7. Which of the following best describes your job title?

- Administrative Assistant ☐
- Coordinator ☐
- Manager/Supervisor ☐
- Director ☐
- Vice President ☐
- President/CEO/COO ☐
- Lawyer/Doctor/Medical Professional ☐
- Teacher/Educator/Trainer ☐
- Engineer/Technician ☐
- Consultant ☐
- Not employed/Student/Retired ☐
- Other (Please specify): ______________ ☐

8. Which of the following best describes the area of the company your job title falls under?

- Accounting ☐
- Engineering ☐
- Manufacturing ☐
- Operations ☐
- Marketing ☐
- Sales ☐
- Other (Please specify): ______________ ☐

9. What is your age?

- Under 20 ☐
- 21-29 ☐
- 30-39 ☐
- 40-49 ☐
- 50-59 ☐
- 60-over ☐

10. Are you:

- Male ☐
- Female ☐

11. Which computer publications do you read regularly? (Please list)

____

____

____

____

____

____

____

____

Comments: ______________________________

____

____

Fold here and scotch-tape to mail

NO POSTAGE NECESSARY IF MAILED IN THE UNITED STATES

BUSINESS REPLY MAIL

FIRST-CLASS MAIL PERMIT NO. 9918 INDIANAPOLIS IN

POSTAGE WILL BE PAID BY THE ADDRESSEE

ATTN MARKETING
MACMILLAN COMPUTER PUBLISHING
MACMILLAN PUBLISHING USA
201 W 103RD ST
INDIANAPOLIS IN 46209-9042